earch Press
Box 7113
versity Station
o, Utah
blishing arm of
Foundation for Ancient Research
Mormon Studies

 First edtition 1990
nd edtition 1996
ed in the United States of America

00 99 98 97 96 10 9 8 7 6 5 4 3 2 1

: 0-934893-23-3
volume set, ISBN: 0-934893-21-7)

Pre-Columbian Contact with the Americas across the Oceans

An Annotated Bibliography

John L. Sorenson
and Martin H. Raish

Second Edition, Revised

Volume 2
L–Z
and Index

Research Press
Provo, Utah

Annotations

L-001

AUTHOR: LaBarre, Weston
DATE: 1970
TITLE: Review of *Soma: Divine Mushroom of Immortality*, by R. Gordon Wasson
IN: American Anthropologist 72:368-373

Wasson [W-053] considered that since the Mexican teonanacatl mushroom and Eurasian agaric have been used for thousands of years, they were "autonomous" in origin. La Barre notes the occurrence in both hemispheres of such traits as the conical wigwam-tipi, bear ceremonialism, myth motifs such as Magic Flight and Orpheus, "the similarity of proto-Sinitic and proto-Athapaskan (and of the Eskimo and Altaic languages?)" [re: Shafer and Uhlenbeck?], trickster, Raven, bow and arrow, etc. He suggests "the possibility of cultural memory or now lost legends about, or substitute stimulus-diffusion of," narcotic mushroom use from Old to New World on the level of "Mesolithic horizons."

L-002B

AUTHORS: Lacombe, J.-P., and C. Chauchat
DATE: 1986
TITLE: Il y a 10.000 ans: l'Homme de Paijan (Pérou)
[Did Paijan Man (Peru) Live Ten Thousand Years Ago?]
IN: Archéologia 209:44-47 (Dijon)

The possibility of a European Late Paleolithic source reaching America.

L-003

AUTHOR: Lacy, Mary G.
DATE: 1911
TITLE: Pre-Columbian References to Maize in Persian Literature
IN: Science 33:968-970

Discussions of the history of maize in the first quarter of the 19th century (cites publications by Harshberger, Browne, and Bonafous) attached importance to an alleged mention of the word *rous*, supposed to be synonymous with *blé de Turquie*, a common name for maize. Use of the term *rous* was attributed in 1777-1778 to Mirkhond, a Persian historian of the 15th century, to describe a grain used in Russia. This seemed to indicate the pre-Columbian presence of maize in the Old World, but this was later discounted due to inability to locate Mirkhond's reference in his writings. Other orientalists, however, thought that the statement was from Khondemir, a grandson of Mirkhond who wrote contemporaneously with his grandfather. Lacy, at the U.S. Department of Agriculture, wishes to know if a copy of Khondemir's work is in the U.S. so that this point may be checked (a copy is in the British Museum). If the term does occur in

Khondemir, its significance would be almost equal to its use by Mirkhond as establishing the pre-discovery presence of maize in the Old World.

L-004

AUTHOR: Lafaye, Jacques
DATE: 1971
TITLE: Quetzalcoatl, à la lumiére de l'Edda Scandinave [Quetzalcoatl, in the Light of the Scandinavian Edda]
IN: Journal de la société des américanistes de Paris 60:305-308

Marked similarities in attributes of Quetzalcoatl with Nerthus and Njordr, deities of the Icelandic Eddas, deserve further study.

L-005

AUTHOR: Lafone y Quevedo, Samuel Alexander
DATE: 1901
TITLE: Supuesta derivación súmero-asiria de las lenguas Kechua y Aymara [Supposed Sumero-Assyrian Derivation of the Kechua and Aymara Languages]
IMPRINT: Coni: Buenos Aires [Reprinted from *Anales de la Sociedad científica Argentina* 51:123-134]

A minor piece in which he argues, mostly on logical rather than linguistic grounds, the untenability of Patrón's [P-039] claim that both Aymara and Kechua originated from an undifferentiated "Sumero-Assyrian."

L-006

AUTHOR: Laguesse, Janine
DATE: 1954
TITLE: Migration polynésienne moderne [Modern Polynesian Migration]
IN: Bulletin de la société d'études océaniennes 9:354-357

On several occasions in recent decades, Easter Islanders have sailed for Tahiti (2000 miles) in tiny craft without adequate food supplies or proper navigational equipment. Some have succeeded.

L-006B

AUTHOR: Laguna, Frederica de
DATE: 1947
TITLE: The Prehistory of Northern North America as Seen from the Yukon
IN: Society for American Archaeology, Memoirs [Supplement to *American Antiquity* 12/3, part 2]

Proposes a "circum-Pacific cultural drift" around the north rim between Asia and America.

L-007

AUTHOR: Laguna, Frederica de
DATE: 1949
TITLE: Review of *Archéologie du Pacifique-Nord* [Archaeology of the North Pacific], by André Leroi-Gourhan
IN: American Anthropologist 51:645-647

She admires his methodology but is sorry his data are so outdated. Mainly she is disappointed at his timidity in interpreting. He warns repeatedly that cultural similarities should not be taken as movement of peoples; the reviewer clearly is more willing to do so. "The author would rather take the safe, well trodden, pedestrian route away around by Bering Strait than launch a single native boat from the Aleutian or Kamchatkan shore as an experiment." His caution is a reaction against too-exuberant diffusionism, but it is paralyzing.

L-008

AUTHOR: Laguna, Frederica de
DATE: 1966

TITLE: Review of *Northwest Coast Indian Art,* by Bill Holm
IN: American Anthropologist 68:1054-1056

The reviewer feels that the author's uniquely perceptive [emic] analysis of elements of this art may now finally allow effective comparison of it with "the representational aspect of Old Bering Sea Eskimo and Shang Chinese art" as well as with "the purely nonrepresentational art of the Ainu, the contemporaries of our Indians across the North Pacific."

L-009

AUTHOR: Lahille, Fernand
DATE: 1926
TITLE: Matériaux pour servir à l'histoire des Oonas indigènes de la Terre du Feu [Historical Materials about the Onas, Natives of Tierra del Fuego]
IN: Revista del Museo de La Plata 29:339-361 (Buenos Aires)

Derives the Onas from Bactria, by way of the "Chans" of Indochina, but ultimately from Elam where they picked up Hebrew, Greek, Persian and Sanskrit elements.

L-010

AUTHOR: Lal, Chaman
DATE: 1940
TITLE: Hindu America. Revealing the Story of the Romance of the Surya Vanshi Hindus and Depicting the Imprints of Hindu Culture on the Two Americas
IMPRINT: New Book Co.: Bombay [Reprinted with the subtitle changed to *Depicting the Imprints of Hindu Culture on the Two Americas* (V. V. Research Institute: Hosiarpur, India, 1956)]

"My thesis is that the ancient civilisations (whether Aztecs, Maya or Inca) of the two Americas owe their origin to the Hindu culture of India." Consists mainly of short or long quotations from older Western researchers such as Hewitt, Mackenzie, Z. Nuttall, Verrill, etc. The Surya-Vanshi were "Children of the Sun," rulers of India who established kingdoms in Asia, Europe, and America. A sample only of beliefs and practices touched upon (and pictured): the four world ages, the Hindu Gurukula scheme of education, the panchayat system, the bazaar economy and guild system, the Soma Yagua sacrifice, worship of Indra, Ganesha (elephant), and other Hindu gods, various religious dances, child-birth customs, marriage customs, suttee, cremation, the Makara, ritual swinging and the volador (pole flying), and the Hindu system of priests. According to the Mahabharata, American rulers participated in the great battle of Kurukshetra and a prince (Arjun) married Alupi, the daughter of an American ruler. America was then known as Patala and was very rich in gold. Many of the parallels have been noted by others and some are very naive but are here given a unique spin. Appendix II is on Hindu ships, containing substantive information (e.g., description of sculptures depicting sizable ships, perhaps as early as the third century B.C., while a historian refers to five-masted ships, ships with built-in water-tight compartments like Chinese vessels, and use of the compass consisting of an iron fragment floating on oil).

L-010B

AUTHOR: Lal, Chaman
DATE: 1951
TITLE: Who Discovered America? Revealing the Pictorial Story of the Immortal Imprints of Ancient India on the Two Americas
IMPRINT: New Book Co.: Bombay

Includes snippets of statements from other sources [Ekholm, E-040, at length] pointing out cultural parallels between India and America, but this is mainly a set of comparative photographs or other illustrations partly overlapping in coverage with L-010A: Ganesha (long-nosed, elephant god) and his swastika, Siva, pyramidal structures, Naga snake, yogi, Olmec giant head as Buddha, makara, Hanuman monkey, conch shell, Charak-Puja (swinging penance rite), faces of Himalayan and other Indian persons compared with Mexican and Guatemalan persons, wheeled toys, cockfights, and many others of at least some interest, along with wholly trivial ones.

L-011

AUTHOR: Lal, Chaman
DATE: 1962
TITLE: Did Hindu Sailors Get There before Columbus?
IN: Asia Magazine 2/10:9-11

On a monument at Copan he saw Indra represented sitting on an elephant and three images of Hanuman, the monkey-faced god. Also, in Mexico he noticed the incarnation of Vishnu as a turtle. There must have been Indian visitors.

L-013

AUTHOR: Laming-Emperaire, Annette
DATE: 1964
TITLE: As Grandes Teorias sobre o Povoamento da América e o Ponto-de-vista de Arqueologia [The Major Theories on the Populating of America, from the Point of View of Archaeology]
IN: Origens do Homem Americano (Universidad de São Paulo: São Paulo), 429-448 [Probably a Spanish translation of the same, *El problema del poblamiento de América, in La Prehistoria* (Labor: Barcelona, 1972), 218-254]

See L-014.

L-014

AUTHOR: Laming-Emperaire, Annette
DATE: 1980
TITLE: Le problème des origines américaines: théories, hypothèses, documents [The Problem of American Origins: Theories, Hypotheses, Documents]
IMPRINT: Editions de la Maison des Sciences de l'Homme, Presses Universitaires de Lille: Lille

A small volume (147 pages) that necessarily covers lightly the huge topic it claims to address. An introduction includes half a dozen pages on "pseudo- scientific theories" (Hebrews and Egyptians in America, vanished continents, and extra-terrestrial visitors). A chapter on physical anthropology (including blood groups) recaps obvious literature.

Of special value is a summary (pages 37, 39-40) of F-120 which she considers to demonstrate convincingly that Ancylostoma duodenale, tinea imbricata, pierre noire, typhus murin, and other parasite-caused diseases were shared between Old World and pre-Columbian South American Indians.

A chapter on ethnological evidences of contacts concentrates on Heine-Geldern, Rivet, and Heyerdahl, then archaeological material is briefly treated (kulturkreis, Alcina Franch, Greenman). Data are interspersed with small critiques about method.

[The literature cited is disappointingly narrow; in particular English-language materials are missing, e.g., Kelley, Needham, Tolstoy, Kehoe, Edwards, and even *Man across the Sea* are not mentioned.]

L-015

AUTHOR: Landberg, Leif C. W.
DATE: 1965
TITLE: The Chumash Indians of Southern California
IMPRINT: Southwest Museum: Los Angeles

Pages 2-3: The outstanding technological feature of the Chumash (Hokan-speaking) Indian maritime climax development was the frameless plank canoe, which could go on the open sea. In association with the curved single-piece fishhook, this canoe points to Polynesian influence.

Page 5: As to its antiquity, Meighan has estimated that a fully maritime status for this culture can be detected as long as 4000 years ago.

Page 127: Such an early occurrence of the plank canoe "would just about preclude any possibilities of an Oceanic origin of the craft." An autocthonous development seems more probable.

Page 15: Photographs of a full-size plank canoe and a small steatite model found on the Channel Islands.

Page 128: Repeats Heizer's guess that the Oceanic-like fishhooks could have been brought to the area by a live fish. Such hooks were in use by about A.D. 100. Still these arguments do not preclude appeal to "boat-load" migration theories.

L-016

AUTHOR: Landberg, Leif C. W.
DATE: 1966
TITLE: Tuna Tagging and the Extra-oceanic Distribution of Curved Single-piece Shell Fishhooks in the Pacific
IN: American Antiquity 31:485-491

Examines the hypothesis that fish were possible transpacific carriers of the very similar shell fishhooks found in Oceania, Ecuador, Peru, northern Chile, and the Santa Barbara channel of California. A migration model for albacore suggests at least one possible route for the transport of shell fishhooks between Hawaii and the Santa Barbara region; yet there is no evidence that fish in fact did carry hooks across the ocean or even that they could do so.

The author also comments on Heyerdahl's view that the single-piece fishhook, together with the cosmogony of the southern California Chungichnish cult and the plank canoe, constituted a complex diffused from Polynesia [compare K-192, etc.] He argues that the unique features of the cult are not demonstrated to be pre-Spanish but rather [without citing evidence] that they might have derived from a wrecked Manila galleon that left a Spaniard or Micronesian sailor in southern California. But given the poor quality of the evidence, these items "cannot be relied on too heavily as evidence of pre-Columbian transpacific contacts." [Compare R-051.]

L-017

AUTHOR: Landberg, Leif C. W.
DATE: 1968
TITLE: Comments and Addenda on Tuna Tagging and Shell Fishhooks
IN: American Antiquity 33/1:98-100

Responds to criticism in R-051 by clarifying his position and offering supplementary material, still maintaining that tuna and other fish might have carried hooks to America. Now, however, he emphasizes even more the likelihood of independent invention, based on a report of an archaeological occurrence of a curved, single-piece shell fishhook "outside the Pacific Basin in Africa." This he takes as unquestionable evidence for at least one independent invention of this hook form.

L-018

AUTHOR: Landsberg, Marge E.
DATE: 1976a
TITLE: Materials for a Bibliography of Trans-linguistic Studies
IMPRINT: Indiana University Linguistics Club: Bloomington

To her it is patent that American languages connect to those of the Old World and that research should get on with investigating the matter [neither her observations nor bibliography are very useful to that end].

L-019

AUTHOR: Landsberg, Marge E.
DATE: 1976b
TITLE: Unde Origo?
IN: Epigraphic Society Occasional Publications 3/62:1-14

A reprinting of "the Amerind part" of L-018. The old, neat world of "Bloomfieldian etymological taxonomies of cognates" is now fatally flawed and is in process of being revolutionized in a form yet to be determined but which will "rewrite the whole of linguistic history."

Her 69 bibliographical items (e.g., Rivet, Mendoza, Leesberg, Uhlenbeck, Fell, Swadesh, Sherwin—all without annotation and including numerous errors) is vaguely indexed according to languages (including "African," "Asiatic," "Austric," "Mediterranean," Altaic, Eskimo, Uralic, Semitic, Chinese, and Egyptian).

L-023

AUTHOR: Landström, Björn
DATE: 1961
TITLE: The Ship: An Illustrated History
IMPRINT: Doubleday: Garden City, New York

Unusually complete drawings and helpful, though brief, text. Only a small section is on vessels outside the Mediterranean-European tradition. The first 135 pages cover through the 16th century.

L-024

AUTHOR: Landström, Björn
DATE: 1964
TITLE: Bold Voyages and Great Explorers: A History of Discovery and Exploration from the Expedition to the Land of Punt in 1493 B.C. to the Discovery of the Cape of Good Hope in 1488 A.D., in Words and Pictures
IMPRINT: Doubleday: Garden City, New York [Formerly published as *The Quest for India* (Vägen till Indien)]

Notable for unusually well-done artistic reconstructions, e.g., of Queen Hatshepsut's expedition boat landed at Punt and Scylax sailing down the Indus. Statements are not documented, and some assertions seem incautious, despite the author's acknowledged wide acquaintence with the literature.

L-025

AUTHOR: Landström, Björn
DATE: 1969
TITLE: Sailing Ships
IMPRINT: Doubleday: Garden City, New York

A concise, modified edition of L-023, with, for example, 18 meticulously illustrated pages on Egyptian ships. Only deals with the Mediterranean/Atlantic tradition of shipping.

L-026

AUTHOR: Landström, Björn
DATE: 1970
TITLE: Ships of the Pharaohs; 4000 Years of Egyptian Ship Building
IMPRINT: Doubleday: Garden City, New York

The best-informed and best-illustrated source on Egyptian ships, including papyrus boats.

L-027

AUTHOR: Landsverk, Ole Godfred
DATE: 1961
TITLE: The Kensington Runestone
IMPRINT: Church Press [i.e., privately printed]: Glendale, California

"A reappraisal of the circumstances under which the stone was discovered," insisting on its authenticity.

L-028

AUTHOR: Landsverk, Ole Godfred
DATE: 1967
TITLE: Norse Medieval Cryptography in American Runic Inscriptions
IN: American-Scandinavian Review 55/3:252-263

Reports what he considers cryptograms on many runic stones of Norse origin in Scandinavia, the Orkneys, Greenland, and North America. They are considered to refer to secret dates in the church calendar. A reading is offered on this basis for the Kingigtorssuaq runestone.

L-029

AUTHOR: Landsverk, Ole Godfred
DATE: 1969
TITLE: Ancient Norse Messages on American Stones
IMPRINT: Norseman Press: Glendale, California

Rune inscriptions in North American were encrypted, so clear interpretation can only be made when "the distortions that were introduced to fulfill the needs of the cryptography are first removed."

L-030

AUTHOR: Landsverk, Ole Godfred
DATE: 1970a
TITLE: Norsemen in Oklahoma
IN: Oklahoma Today 20/3:28-36

New evidence about the Norse comes from 10 runic inscriptions, five scattered widely over the eastern half of the U.S. and five in Oklahoma. They contain previously unsolved secret dates. Four dated ones are so similar in construction that they are most certainly the work of the same man (Massachusetts, A.D. 1009, Heavener, Poteau, and Tulsa, Oklahoma, A.D. 1012, 1017, and 1022) They would have reached Oklahoma via the Gulf of Mexico.

L-030B

AUTHOR: Landsverk, Ole Godfred
DATE: 1970b
TITLE: It Is Time to Shed the Blinders!
IN: NEARA [New England Antiquities Research Association] Journal 5:2-3

Two runic alphabets and the eight Heavener runes are related.

L-030C

AUTHOR: Landsverk, Ole Godfred
DATE: 1970c
TITLE: The Symbols of Mechanicsburg
IN: NEARA [New England Antiquities Research Association] Journal 5:38

Tabulation and comparison of the Pennsylvania "Phoenician" inscriptions of Strong.

L-031

AUTHOR: Landsverk, Ole Godfred
DATE: 1973a
TITLE: Spirit Pond Cryptography
IN: Man in the Northeast 6:67-75

A response to H-120 in which Haugen scoffed at Landsverk's claims of Norse cryptography in the runes. Landsverk recites his engineering and physics training. Only he and Mongé understand this "field of study." In a short response following, Haugen rudely dismisses him.

L-031B

AUTHOR: Landsverk, Ole Godfred
DATE: 1973b
TITLE: Cryptograms on the Spirit Pond Runestones: An Answer to Dr. Haugen
IN: NEARA [New England Antiquities Research Association] Journal 8:9-10

No different in substance than L-031.

L-032

AUTHOR: Landsverk, Ole Godfred
DATE: 1974a
TITLE: Runic Records of the Norsemen in America
IMPRINT: Erik J. Friis: n.p.

Continuation of his treatments of "Norse dated cryptography" at Spirit Pond and other sites with purported Norse finds. (Up to now, eighteen dated runic inscriptions have been discovered and solved, in Massachusetts, Oklahoma, New England, Illinois, and Minnesota [Kensington Stone].) These all contain secret dates from A.D. 1009 to 1362.

Seven dated inscriptions in New England provide a framework from which he purports to construct an outline of the activities of Henricus, bishop and papal legate to Greenland and Vinland, from A.D. 1112 to 1123. Among the "Norsemen" who sailed the North Atlantic were Celts, Anglo-Saxons, Danes, and Swedes.

Chapter 15 reports on "rune-inscribed bones" from Mandan and Arikara Indian sites.

L-032B

AUTHOR: Landsverk, Ole Godfred
DATE: 1974b
TITLE: The Vinland Map Is Authentic
IN: NEARA [New England Antiquities Research Association] Journal 9:58-59

Little more than vehement assertion.

L-032C

AUTHOR: Landsverk, Ole Godfred
DATE: 1975
TITLE: The Modena Map: 15th Century Evidence for Norse Landings in America
IN: NEARA [New England Antiquities Research Association] Journal 10:14-15

The map is dated A.D. 1424 on evidence from his runic cryptograms.

L-032D

AUTHOR: Landsverk, Ole Godfred
DATE: 1977a
TITLE: The Spirit Pond "Amulet": An Interpretation
IN: NEARA [New England Antiquities Research Association] Journal 12:16

A reading of characters as Norse. Few others agree with his view.

L-032E

AUTHOR: Landsverk, Ole Godfred
DATE: 1977b
TITLE: The Case of the Gran Tapes
IN: NEARA [New England Antiquities Research Association] Journal 12:35-37

A little material derived from oral history tapes made with some participants in the Kensington Stone affair he takes as not indicating fraud.

L-032F

AUTHOR: Landsverk, Ole Godfred
DATE: 1978
TITLE: Runic Inscriptions in the Western Hemisphere. Old Norse and Swedish Norwegian Alphabets
IN: NEARA [New England Antiquities Research Association] Journal 13:15-20

"The first attempt to undertake an overall survey of all runic inscriptions which have been discovered to date in North and South America." Distribution originated in Greenland, thence to central New England ("the heart of Vinland"), the Great Lakes, and on to West Virginia, Ohio, Minnesota, the Dakotas, Oklahoma, and Texas. Recently large numbers have been found in Paraguay and southern Brazil.

Mongé "made it clear that the misspellings, strange runic symbols and many other hitherto unexplained cryptographic features which had cast doubt on the (Kensington) inscription's authenticity were the result of forcing a massive dose of cryptography into a previously normal runic text." "An amazing 71 percent of the runes in the early 11th century cryptograms in the United States were taken from the ancient runic alphabet. But by 1000 A.D. ancient runes had not been in use for normal runic writing for two centuries. This did not, however, inhibit the knowledgeable puzzlemasters who were experts on runes and runic alphabets." There are also 20 non-cryptographic American inscriptions; they exhibit very little understanding of runes.

L-032G

AUTHOR: Landsverk, Ole Godfred
DATE: 1981a
TITLE: The Kensington Inscription
IN: NEARA [New England Antiquities Research Association] Journal 15:58-59

This is one of 18 cryptograms scattered over the eastern half of the U.S. which A. Mongé solved. The text is drawn and transliterated in this article. It consists of three parts, an acrostic cipher, a mesotic cipher, and a concealed date—24 April 1362.

L-032H

AUTHOR: Landsverk, Ole Godfred
DATE: 1981b
TITLE: The Tulsa Inscription
IN: NEARA [New England Antiquities Research Association] Journal 15:107-108

Why are runic inscriptions and Mediterranean alphabetic inscriptions often confused? By A.D. 200 "the ancient runic alphabet" was in at least limited use in Scandinavia, but it had been developed centuries earlier by Germanic tribes who borrowed symbols from Phoenician, Greek and Latin alphabets. That ancient alphabet had been abandoned for normal runic writing by A.D. 850, but the conservative Norse clergy continued its use. That is why it occurred in America, for priests or monks accompanied dangerous expeditions. Mongé solved a total of 67 runic cryptograms, six of which are in Oklahoma and are dated. Dates from 1012 to 1024 are given for each. "The puzzlemasters were clearly men of the Church."

L-034

AUTHOR: Lane, Frederico
DATE: 1958
TITLE: The Pellet-bow among South American Indians
IN: Miscellanea Paul Rivet, Octogenario Dicata, Universidad Nacional Autónoma de México, Publicaciones del Instituto de Historia 1/50, [Proceedings of the 31st International Congress of Americanists (São Paulo, 1954)], pages 257-266

Description from ethnographies of a device known in Oceania and Asia.

L-034B

AUTHOR: Lane Fox, A.
DATE: 1875
TITLE: On Early Modes of Navigation
IN: Journal of the Anthropological Institute 4:399-437

Detailed citation of ethnographic and historical materials on various forms of "primitive" vessels and their construction.

Pages 426-427: The "balzas" rafts of Ecuador are the perfection of raft navigation. The odd number of beams recalls New Guinea and India rafts. "They are called by the Indians of the Guayaquil jangadas, and by the Darien Indians puero." Those on the coast of Brazil "are also called jungadas." Professor [Thomas?] Wilson thinks it was by means of these vessels, driven off the coast of America westward, that the Polynesian and Malay islands were peopled.

L-034C

AUTHOR: Lane-Poole, R. H.
DATE: 1940
TITLE: Primitive Craft and Mediaeval Rigs in South America
IN: Mariner's Mirror 26:333-338

Three types are distinguished: canoes, sailing rafts of Brazil and Peru, and reed bundle craft of Lake Titicaca and the north Peruvian coast.

Page 334: Plan, cross-section, and sketch of a small jangada are given. He assumes that jangada is the Portuguese word for raft; "at least one Brazilian antiquary asserts that it was unknown before the arrival of the Portuguese; if so, it was probably introduced by them from the East Indies" [cf. Hornell 1926]. These rafts are used to fish 100 miles off the coast in high seas; they are often out for three days at a time. In 1922 one traveled from Recife to Rio de Janeiro and back, a combined distance of 2144 miles.

Page 337: "The balsa raft of Peru is a heavy edition of the jangada."

L-034D

AUTHOR: Läng, H.
DATE: 1976
TITLE: Indianer waren meine Freunde [Indians Were my Friends]
IMPRINT: Hallwag: Bern

The "white Mandan" Indians.

L-036

AUTHOR: Lang, John Dunsmore
DATE: 1876
TITLE: On the Origin and Migrations of the Polynesian Nation, Demonstrating Their Original Discovery and Progressive Settlement of the Continent of America
IN: Journal and Proceedings of the Royal Society of New South Wales 10:43-74

See L-037.

L-037

AUTHOR: Lang, John Dunsmore
DATE: 1877
TITLE: Origin and Migrations of the Polynesian Nation, Demonstrating Their Original Discovery and Progressive Settlement of the Continent of America, 2nd edition
IMPRINT: George Robertson: Sydney [1st edition *View of the Origin and Migrations of the Polynesian Nation, Demonstrating Their Ancient Discovery. . .* (Cochrane and M'Crone: London, 1834)]

Page 98: "The continent of America was first reached at a period of the highest antiquity in the history of mankind, somewhere near Copiapo, in Chile, by a handful of Polynesians, who had been caught in a sudden and violent gale of westerly wind off Easter Island, in the Southern Pacific, and had crossed the intervening tract of ocean to the American land; and . . . from these islanders and their descendants the whole Indo-American race of both continents is derived." Parallels used as evidence include such general features as pyramidal structures, terracing, colossal statues, human sacrifice, and tattooing.

L-038

AUTHOR: Langdon, Robert
DATE: 1975
TITLE: The Lost Caravel
IMPRINT: Pacific Publications: Sydney

Hypothesizes, then musters considerable detailed information in support of the idea, that a Spanish vessel wrecked in the Tuamotus in 1526, and that the survivors succeeded in introducing a significant range of biological, material, and symbolic elements into the native population and culture, and that these spread throughout much of Polynesia in subsequent centuries. They include some elements (e.g., red hair) considered by Heyerdahl as South American.

L-039

AUTHOR: Langdon, Robert
DATE: 1977
TITLE: Les indigènes de caractéristiques européennes dans Raroia et dans d'autres îles de Polynésie [The Indigenous People with European Characteristics on Raroia and Other Polynesian Islands]
IN: Bulletin de la société d'études océaniennes 200:15-22

Along the same lines as, but with other content than, L-040.

L-040

AUTHOR: Langdon, Robert
DATE: 1978
TITLE: The European-Looking People of Raroia and Other Polynesian Islands: A Reply to Bengt Danielsson
IN: Journal of the Polynesian Society 87:125-133

Detailed rejoinder to Danielsson's highly negative review of L-038. Danielsson makes a final brief response on page 265.

L-040B

AUTHOR: Langdon, Robert
DATE: 1982
TITLE: New World Cotton as a Clue to the Polynesian Past
IN: Oceanic Studies: Essays in Honour of Aarne A. Koskinen, edited by Jukka Siikala, Transactions of the Finnish Anthropological Society No. 11 (Helsinki), 179-192

An important contribution to questions about the New World history of cotton. Brings Polynesian linguistic data into play extensively as well as recapitulating some of the botanical literature in a novel way. Adduces several reasons for believing that a non-Polynesian people (he expects they were American Indians, ultimately from Ecuador) who cultivated cotton as a source of fiber reached the Tuamotus in ancient times and applied their word for cotton to the best fiber substitute they could find for it there (a shore plant, Triumfetta procumbens). Discusses why an American vessel is a better explanation for these facts than either a Polynesian visit to the mainland or natural drift. (Galapagos cotton is also discussed; Heyerdahl's archaeological finds there included a spindle whorl.) Those migrants in the Marquesas and Society Islands used the same name for the local fiber as was applied to pre-European cotton (which is apparently a variety of G. barbadense from Ecuador). Based on currents and winds the immediate source of the migrants appears to have been Easter Island, where there is also some evidence for the presence of cotton. No cotton grew west of the Societies until Europeans took it there.

Repeats his view that a non-Polynesian language element existed on Easter Island and two of the Tuamotus before the late arrival of Polynesian proper. Hypothesizes that cultivation of cotton was abandoned after the arrival of Polynesians from the west; they introduced the use of the bark of the paper mulberry tree for cloth. In turn they took over the sweet potato.

Page 184: Marquesans on Fatuhiva used the word for cotton (*vevai*) to refer also to the shrub Asclepias curassavica L. which is of American origin and "probably of aboriginal introduction in the Marquesas" (citing Brown 1935). On the nearby island of Hivaoa another term for cotton, *uruuru,* was involved in the native name there for the same shrub.

The presence of an American cotton, G. tomentosum, in Hawaii remains a separate problem entirely.

Page 185: One of the earliest visitors to the Marquesas (1767) reported not only the widespread presence of cotton but of the dye plant "indego" (indigo). [Compare J-078G.]

Page 182: [Re. the nature and success of "contact"] The explorer La Perouse on Easter Island had his gardener sow seeds of various European and American plants and gave the islanders pairs of hogs, goats and sheep, but no subsequent visitor saw any of the progeny of the animals nor edible produce from the sown seeds.

L-040C

AUTHOR: Langdon, Robert
DATE: 1983
TITLE: The Cultivated American Plants of Prehistoric Polynesia: A Review of the Historical Evidence
IN: Abstract in 15th Congress, Pacific Science Association: Program, Abstracts and Conference Information (University of Otago: Dunedin, New Zealand), 1:140

See L-040D.

L-040D

AUTHOR: Langdon, Robert
DATE: 1988
TITLE: Manioc, a Long Concealed Key to the Enigma of Easter Island
IN: The Geographical Journal 154:324-336

Manioc, an American food plant, is thought to have been introduced to the Pacific Islands only in the mid-nineteenth century. However, a recent book has revealed hitherto unknown evidence that manioc was reported on Easter Island in 1770 by a Spanish expedition. The term they used was *yuca,* a word borrowed into Peruvian Spanish from Quechua. Many of the documents in the new book (i.e., *Manuscritos y documentos españoles para la historia de la Isla de Pascua*) had not been published before. It reveals that when some of these documents were published for the Hakluyt Society early this century, the translation obscured the presence of manioc. The relation says that the Spaniards obtained from the natives "plátanos guineos, camotes y gallinas" (guinea plantains, sweet potatoes and hens, or fowls); the Hakluyt publication translated this as "plantains, chili peppers, sweet potatoes and fowls." This error lies behind Heyerdahl's claim that the chili pepper was known on Easter Island.

Other American plants are mentioned in later historical materials and conceivably could have been native cultigens, hence "scholars interested in the prehistory of eastern Polynesia must now seriously assess all possible ethnobotanical evidence for such contact, instead of sweeping it under the carpet as most have been apt to do in the past." Among the plants in question are: gourd, pineapple, 26-chromosome cotton, capsicum, soapberry, tomato, tobacco, the bullrush, and achira.

He sketches the history of scholarly thought from Cook's day on, which led to the assumption of Polynesian uniformity and a solely Asiatic origin and which lay behind the Hakluyt edition error. Incidentally, recent archaeology in northern Peru has revealed remains of capsicum, 26-chromosome cotton, gourd, and soapberry in middens dating to 1785 B.C., while later remains of sweet potato, manioc, and achira were also found. So now "the notion that that island [Easter] was the point of entry into eastern Polynesia for a sizeable array of American plants must be seriously considered along with all that that might imply."

L-041

AUTHORS: Langdon, Robert, and Darrell Tryon
DATE: 1983
TITLE: The Language of Easter Island: Its Development and Eastern Polynesian Relationships
IN: Institute for Polynesian Studies Monograph Series, No. 4 (Brigham Young University-Hawaii Campus: Laie)
[Summarized at length, *Kadath* 64 (1987): 46-49]

Examination of a wide range of linguistic data leads them to conclude that the language of historical Easter Island was formed from three sources: (1) East Futunan, the language of Wallis Island; (2) a Tahitic component; and (3) a non-Polynesian language present on Easter Island when Polynesians arrived. Some elements of the non-Polynesian material are visible not only on Easter Island but also in the Tuamotus and Marquesas. Archaeological and voyaging data are brought to bear on the linguistic treatment.

The Society Islands and the Marquesas, which have been suggested as sources for Polynesian settlement of Easter Island, are highly unlikely departure points due to sailing conditions. But Rapanui meets a wide range of criteria as the probable place from which the Polynesians left. Parties from Easter Island later went (north)westward to the Marquesas and the Tuamotus. Only plant evidence hinting of America suggests a source for the non-Polynesian language. Some 61 words are given that are said to occur nowhere else in Polynesia than Easter Island.

Pages 40-41. Previously proposed Proto-Polynesian reconstruction **kumala* (sweet potato) they consider without justification, for early European explorers did not record the sweet potato in Western Polynesia. Moreover, two early missionaries to Samoa stated that the sweet potato and its name were recent introductions; the plant was unknown on Niue until after 1900. In Tonga it has no place in traditional ceremonies, and there are no local names for it. Thus it is attested only in Eastern Polynesia and could have come from America fairly late in pre-European times.

L-042

AUTHOR: Langdon, S. H.
DATE: 1931
TITLE: Semitic, vol. 5 of Mythology of All Races, edited by Louis Herbert Gray, George Foot Moore, consulting editor
IMPRINT: Marshall Jones: Boston

Pages 93-94: Multiple heavens: Assyrians, three, 10th century; Sumerians three or seven heavens.

Page 159: The ziggurat at Borsippa had its seven stages colored, from the ground up: black, brown, red/rose, red, gold, white/gold, dark-blue/silver, each representing a planet. At Ur, of four stages, the bottom one was black and the top blue. [Mesoamerican parallels to use of colors on pyramid stages.]

L-043

AUTHOR: Langenberg, Inge
DATE: 1977
TITLE: Die Vinland-Fahrten: Die Entdeckungen Amerikas von Erik dem Roten bis Kolumbus (1000-1492)
[The Vinland Voyages: The Discovery of America from Erik the Red to Columbus (1000-1492)]
IMPRINT: Böhlau: Köln

Summary of the sources and issues in Norse-in-America studies, and a history of thought on the subject up to 1977. Appendix lists 155 authors and the locations they have assigned to Vinland, Markland, and Helluland.

L-047

AUTHOR: Langlois, Louis
DATE: 1928
TITLE: L'Amérique pré-colombienne et la conquête européenne
[Pre-Columbian America and the European Conquest]
IMPRINT: E. de Boccard: Paris

Pages 1-79: Lengthy discussion of the question of origins in which both Bering Strait and various transpacific migration views are accepted (e.g. Rivet, Mendes-Corrêa, Morice).

L-049

AUTHOR: Lanning, Edward P.
DATE: 1970

TITLE: South America as Source for Aspects of Polynesian Cultures
IN: Studies in Oceanic Culture History, edited by R. C. Green and M. Kelly, Pacific Anthropological Records 11, Department of Anthropology (Bernice P. Bishop Museum Press: Honolulu), 1:175-182

Intended as an even-handed consideration of the evidence, this work is restricted by the state of knowledge in the late 1960s, particularly concerning water craft. He concludes that the only possible sources for craft on the west coast of South America that could have reached Polynesia are Ecuador for the ocean-going raft and Chile for possible accidental canoes. Consideration of the published ceramic material from Heyerdahl et al. from the Galapagos leads him to the "apparent fact of prehistoric visits," the "Peruvian" pottery actually being, he suggests, made in extreme northern Peru but transmitted from Ecuador. While the bulk of Guayaquil and Polynesian artifact inventories and architectural styles seem foreign to each other, fishhooks, adzes, and sinkers (specified in detail) show similarities that could be due to contact, more likely by Polynesian visits to South America than the reverse. If remains of the sweet potato and (on Easter Island) the totora rush should be found archaeologically in Polynesia, we would at last have credible evidence.

L-050

AUTHOR: Lantis, Margaret
DATE: 1938
TITLE: The Alaskan Whale Cult and Its Affinities
IN: American Anthropologist 40:438-464

The distribution of 31 culture elements associated with this cult is given and comparisons are made. Features overlap each other forming a chain connecting whaling tribes in the whole area from Kamchatka (and the Ainu of Japan) to Hudson Bay and from Pt. Barrow to Washington.

L-051

AUTHOR: Lanyon-Orgill, P. A.
DATE: 1953
TITLE: Review of *American Indians in the Pacific,* by Thor Heyerdahl
IN: Journal of Austronesian Studies 1/1:152-155 (England)

Somewhat critical but in many ways appreciative of Heyerdahl's volume. The reviewer supposes "several waves of civilization" in the islands, of which those from British Columbia and Peru were only two.

The masonry of the pyramids of Mexico and Tonga has a common source, but claim the megalithic culture (citing Riesenfeld) widespread in the world was responsible. The sweet potato, bottle gourd, and 26-chromosome cotton were introduced into the Pacific islands from America, and perhaps the coconut and pineapple as well. The parallels Heyerdahl noted between the Polynesian islands and America were due to a people before the Polynesians were present.

L-051B

AUTHOR: Larco Hoyle, Rafael
DATE: 1943
TITLE: La escritura peruana sobre pallares [Peruvian Writing on Beans]
IN: Revista geográfica americana (Nov.) [As a separate under the same title in *Relaciones de la Sociedad Argentina de antropología*, 1944]

Hypothesizes that a series of signs drawn upon lima beans as represented on painted Mochica vessels constituted a writing system, although he is unable to explain how they could have formed a durable message. Reviews the chroniclers who reported use of a writing system without describing it adequately. [Compare J-030 and J-030B.]

L-052

AUTHOR: Larco Hoyle, Rafael
DATE: 1949

TITLE: A Culture Sequence for the North Coast of Peru
IN: The Andean Civilizations, volume 2 of Handbook of South American Indians, edited by Julian H. Steward, Smithsonian Institution, Bureau of American Ethnology Bulletin 143 (Washington D.C.), 149-175

Page 145: Reports an apparent true arch in Peru.

L-056 See L-057B.

L-057
AUTHOR: Larsen, Helge
DATE: 1968
TITLE: Near Ipiutak and Uwelen-Okvik
IN: Folk 10:81-90

Relates Near Ipiutak culture to Ipiutak, Norton, and other Eskimo cultures of Alaska, as well as to the Eskimo cemetery at Uelen on the Chukchi Peninsula. Roots of the Neo-Eskimo culture should be sought on islands of the northwest Pacific and the coast of northeast Asia and probably as far south as China, though it actually developed on the shores of Bering Strait.

L-057B
AUTHORS: Larsen, Helge, and Froelich Rainey
DATE: 1948
TITLE: Ipiutak and the Arctic Whale Hunting Culture
IMPRINT: American Museum of Natural History Anthropological Papers 42 (New York)

The Paleo-Eskimo basic culture of which their reported materials are a part dates c. A.D. 1-450. Elaborate ivory carving includes animal heads related to the Eurasiatic or Scytho-Siberian animal style. Ivory chain links are considered imitations of (Asiatic) metal chains. Iron-tipped engraving tools used nonmeteoric (presumably Asiatic) imported iron. They believe Ipiutak culture derived from the region of the Lower Ob and Yenesei rivers in the first millennium B.C.

L-058
AUTHOR: Larsen, Sofus
DATE: 1925a
TITLE: The Discovery of North America Twenty Years before Columbus
IMPRINT: Levin and Munksgaard: Copenhagen; and Hachette: London

The Portuguese king enlisted Scandinavian navigators in an attempt to find a northern passage to the Orient. Discussion of Pining and Pothorst, Scolvus and Corte-Real and their voyages between 1472 and 1476.

L-059
AUTHOR: Larsen, Sofus
DATE: 1925b
TITLE: Discovery of the North-American Mainland Twenty Years before Columbus
IN: Proceedings of the 21st International Congress of Americanists (Part 2, Gothenburg, Sweden, 1924), pages 285-293
[Danish version: "Nordamerikas Opdagelse 20 Aar for Columbus," *Geografisk Tidsskrift* 28 (1925): 88-110 (Copenhagen)]

He identifies Captains Pining and Pothorst, reported companions of the Pole (or Dane) Scolvus, as historical figures known to have visited Greenland in the 1470s. Larsen argues that they were sent by Portugal at the request of the king of Denmark to search for new lands in the western Atlantic and that Scolvus accompanied them.

L-062
AUTHOR: Larson, Laurence Marcellus
DATE: 1921
TITLE: The Kensington Rune Stone

IN: Wisconsin Magazine of History 4:382-391

Points out what he sees as flaws in data and logic in H-354 and H-355. Holand responds.

L-063

AUTHOR: Larson, Laurence Marcellus
DATE: 1922
TITLE: Did John Scolvus Visit Labrador and New-Foundland in or about 1476?
IN: Scandinavian Studies and Notes 7:81-89 (Society for the Advancement of Scandinavian Study, Menasha, Wisconsin)

A thorough examination of the literature on John Scolvus from the first mention in 1859 by Kunstmann. There is reason to believe that a voyage was sent out by the Portuguese 20 years before Columbus and that it reached northeastern North America; Pining, Scolvus, and Cortereal were aboard.

L-064

AUTHOR: Larson, Laurence Marcellus
DATE: 1923
TITLE: The Viking Voyages
IN: American Scandinavian Review 11:531-547

An undocumented but intelligent composite recapitulation of the sagas. Nansen's revisionist comparison of the sagas to the tales of the Fortunate Isles made few converts, as obviously the sagas describe an actual, not-very-ideal land. The enthusiasm for grapes is understandable as wine was scarce throughout the north lands, usually not even being available for the mass. Greenland and Iceland, meanwhile, grew no real grain crops, hence the mistake about wild grass being "grain" (citations show that 17th century explorers said the same thing about the area).

L-065

AUTHOR: Larson, Laurence Marcellus
DATE: 1936
TITLE: The Kensington Rune Stone
IN: Minnesota History 17:20-37

With the publication of Holand's book on the stone, many who were previously skeptical decided for the monument's authenticity. He seemed to have met all the objections that had been raised. But Holand's proofs offered are often speculative, not based on scholarship and not fully convincing. Additional objections are raised here. He concludes the Kensington Stone is a fraud. [See H-360 for Holand's response.]

L-066

AUTHOR: Larson, Robert
DATE: 1966
TITLE: Was America the Wonderful Land of Fusang?
IN: American Heritage 17/3:106-109

Answer:"It seems quite likely." His map has Hwui Shan, in A.D. 458, reaching the Acapulco area.

L-067

AUTHORS: Lastres, Juan B., and Fernando Cabieses
DATE: 1960
TITLE: La trepanación del cráneo en al antiguo Perú [Cranial Trepanation in Ancient Peru]
IMPRINT: Universidad Nacional Mayor de San Marcos: Lima

Comprehensive comparative review of trepanation around the world,

emphasizing its development in the medical practice of pre-Columbian Peru, its distribution and frequency, and the surgical instruments and techniques employed. Contains 177 figures, 633 bibliographic entries, and a glossary of Quechua medical terms. [See also W-237 missed by them.]

L-068

AUTHOR: Latcham, Ricardo E.

DATE: 1904

TITLE: Notes on Some Ancient Chilian Skulls and Other Remains

IN: Journal of the Anthropological Institute of Great Britain and Ireland 7:234-254

These materials from Chile, he says, favor the view of the polygenesis of South American Indians.

L-069

AUTHOR: Latcham, Ricardo E.

DATE: 1909

TITLE: Antropología chilena [Chilean Anthropology]

IN: Trabajos, 4ª Congreso científico americano (Santiago, December 1908-January 1909), 14:24-84

See L-068.

L-069B

AUTHOR: Latcham, Ricardo E.

DATE: 1922

TITLE: Los animales domésticos de la America pre-Colombiana [The Domestic Animals of Pre-Columbian America]

IN: Museo de Etnología e Antropología Publicación 3, 1:1-199 (Santiago, Chile)

Page 175: Chickens (at least three kinds) of the Chilean Indians were different from those brought by Europeans. The former were definitely present before the conquest and are still represented among the fowls of the Araucanians. They lay blue and olive green eggs, are tailless, and wear tufts of feathers in the form of a ball at the sides of their heads [as do fowls in China that lay blue eggs].

L-070

AUTHOR: Latcham, Ricardo E.

DATE: 1927

TITLE: Las relaciones prehistóricas entre América y la Oceánia [Prehistoric Relations between America and Oceania]

IN: La Información 16/122: 545ff.

A summary of arguments on the question of Oceanic-American relationships.

L-071

AUTHOR: Latcham, Ricardo E.

DATE: 1929

TITLE: Figuras que parecen geroglifos en la alfarería protonazca [Figures That Seem to Be Hieroglyphs on Proto-Nazca Pottery]

IN: Boletín del Museo Nacional de Chile 12:93-101 (Santiago)

Some Peruvian painted signs look like writing.

L-072

AUTHOR: Latcham, Ricardo E.

DATE: 1936

TITLE: La agricultura precolombina en Chile y los países vecinos [Pre-Columbian Agriculture in Chile and Neighboring Countries]

IMPRINT: Ediciones de la Universidad de Chile: Santiago

Planting in moist beds below ground level [as in Polynesia].

L-073

AUTHOR: Lathrap, Donald W.

DATE: 1961

TITLE: Review of *Excavaciones arqueológicas en San Pablo: informe preliminar* [Archaeological Excavations in San Pablo:

Preliminary Report], by Carlos Zevallos Menendez and Olaf Holm

IN: American Antiquity 26/3:452

"The degree to which bearers of Valdivia culture practiced deep-sea fishing and were thus truly sea-faring people is of great importance to our ultimate understanding of the origins and extent of influence of this unique culture." If deep-sea fishing was done, that should go a long way in answering the origin question. "Sometime in the near future detailed comparisons should be made between the shell fishhooks of Valdivia culture and those of various other areas around the Pacific Ocean, as there are close formal similarities not only to those of Coastal Peru and Chile, but also to those of California and Oceania."

L-074

AUTHOR: Lathrap, Donald W.

DATE: 1967

TITLE: Review of *Early Formative Period of Coastal Ecuador*, by B. J. Meggers, C. Evans, and E. Estrada

IN: American Anthropologist 69:96-98

He is, expectably, unwilling to accept an overseas origin for Valdivia ceramics, for he sees the tropical forest where he worked as the developmental zone for South American civilizations.

L-075

AUTHOR: Lathrap, Donald W.

DATE: 1973a

TITLE: Summary or Model Building: How Does One Achieve a Meaningful Overview of a Continent's Prehistory? Review of *An Introduction to American Archeology*, vol. 2 of *South America*, by Gordon R. Willey

IN: American Anthropologist 75:1755-1767

Pages 1760-1763: Objects to Willey's acceptance of a Japan-Valdivia connection.

L-076

AUTHOR: Lathrap, Donald W.

DATE: 1973b

TITLE: The Antiquity and Importance of Long Distance Trade Relationships in the Moist Tropics of Pre-Columbian South America

IN: World Archaeology 5:170-186

A jointed wooden doll from Ancón, Peru, dated to ca. 1200 B.C. is described. [Compare later jointed figurines of Guatemala and Mexico?]

L-077B

AUTHOR: Lathrap, Donald W.

DATE: 1977

TITLE: Our Father the Cayman, Our Mother the Gourd: Spinden Revisited, or a Unitary Model for the Emergence of Agriculture in the New World

IN: The Origins of Agriculture, edited by Charles A. Reed (Aldine: Chicago), 713-751

Proposes that West African fishermen were lost and carried to sea to Brazil by 16,000 years ago. They brought with them the gourd (Lagenaria), watercraft, fishing techniques including poisons, cotton, and two-toned log signalling. From northern South America where various plants were domesticated [compare S-057] features of the resulting complex spread throughout tropical America.

L-078

AUTHOR: Latocha, Hartwig

DATE: 1982

TITLE: Die Rolle des Hundes bei südamerikanischen Indianern [The Role of the Dog among South American Indians]

IMPRINT: Klaus Renner: Munich

In the course of an exhaustive treatment of "indigenous canicuculture" the author in Chapter G treats a widely dispersed mythic theme of a dog who has sexual relations with a woman. Based on the literature cited, he supposes this represents a northern Asiatic feature diffused into North and South America.

L-080

AUTHOR: Laufer, Berthold
DATE: 1906
TITLE: The Bird-chariot in China and Europe
IN: Anthropological Papers Written in Honor of Franz Boas and Presented to him on the 25th Anniversary of his Doctorate, edited by Berthold Laufer (Stechert: New York), 410-424
[Reprinted *Kleinere Schriften (of Laufer),* edited by H. Walravens (Steiner: Wiesbaden, 1976), 1/2:944ff.]

Wheeled miniature cultic vehicles. [For comparison to Mesoamerica.]

L-081

AUTHOR: Laufer, Berthold
DATE: 1907a
TITLE: The Introduction of Maize into Eastern Asia
IN: Proceedings of the 15th International Congress of Americanists (Quebec, 1906), 1:223-257

Maize reached China c. 1540, not by the sea coast but overland from Tibet. By 1560-1570 it had reached eastern China. It probably reached India via the Portuguese.

L-082

AUTHOR: Laufer, Berthold
DATE: 1907b
TITLE: Note on the Introduction of the Ground-Nut into China
IN: Proceedings of the 15th International Congress of Americanists (Quebec, 1906), 1:259-262

The evidence seems to show that the peanut reached China from the Malay archipelago or Philippines via Chinese sailors or the traders of Fukien. The earliest date is 1573. [Contrast C-163.]

L-083

AUTHOR: Laufer, Berthold
DATE: 1913
TITLE: Notes on Turquois [*sic*] in the East
IN: Field Museum of Natural History, Publication 169, Anthropological Series 13/1 (Chicago)

Page 62: Color symbolism is an ancient and conspicuous feature of Chinese rites and was originally associated with the four quarters and cosmic deities. At a later time it was affiliated also with the five elements. Nuttall [N-118] compared the Chinese system to those found in North America and Mexico and held them to be fundamentally similar. "The whole problem, of course, is not historical but purely psychological." Thus at the Temple of Heaven all was blue, at the Temple of the Sun, red, and at the Temple of the Moon, moonlight white.

L-084

AUTHOR: Laufer, Berthold
DATE: 1919
TITLE: Coca and Betel Chewing: A Query
IN: American Anthropologist 21:335-336

Wissler's book, *The American Indian*, called attention to the striking coincidence between coca-chewing with lime and betel-nut consumption in Melanesia and southeastern asia. "The analogy is so manifest and complete that the assumption of an historical connection becomes inevitable." But was it pre-Columbian? A book by Steffen in 1883 claimed that lime use with coca was post-Spanish. Is this so? he asks. [See the following page for a negative reply, M-229.]

L-085

AUTHOR: Laufer, Berthold
DATE: 1921
TITLE: Review of *Africa and the Discovery of America,* by Leo Wiener
IN: Literary Review, February 1

Expectably negative.

L-086

AUTHOR: Laufer, Berthold
DATE: 1929
TITLE: The American Plant Migration
IN: Scientific Monthly 28:230-251 [Reprinted Field Museum of Natural History Publication 418 (Chicago, 1938)]

Establishes "conclusively" that the sweet potato reached Oceania after European discovery.

L-087

AUTHOR: Laufer, Berthold
DATE: 1931a
TITLE: Columbus and Cathay: The Meaning of America to the Orientalist
IN: Journal of the American Oriental Society 51:87-103

After asserting that any influence from East Asia to America would have come "overland" through northeastern Asia across Bering Strait, he then mentions and even discusses a number of parallels (e.g., scapulimancy, pachisi, ball games, bear ceremonials, Magic Flute motif), even in South America. He allows that a good deal more serious study of such parallels should go on but with no expectation that his view would change.

L-088

AUTHOR: Laufer, Berthold
DATE: 1931b
TITLE: Tobacco in New Guinea: An Epilogue
IN: American Anthropologist 33:138-140

He had written about the spread of American tobacco into Asia, Europe, and Africa, but Melanesia and Australia are different. He supports L-194. There are native tobaccos in New Guinea, he is assured, and the method of smoking them there is unique and likely very old. [Compare M-229 and others.]

L-089

AUTHOR: Laufer, Berthold
DATE: 1946
TITLE: Jade: A Study in Chinese Archaeology and Religion, 2nd edition
IMPRINT: P. D. & Ione Perkins, in co-operation with The Westwood Press and W. M. Hawley: South Pasadena, California [Originally published Field Museum of Natural History: Chicago, 1912]

Pages 20-21: Mention of possible stone mirrors from China with Peruvian stone mirrors as a potential comparison.

Pages 50-53: Among the stone implements of Shantung he illustrates in Plate XIII a grooved diorite axe, the only known example of this type from China and "a type very widely spread in North America." (Citations to an illustration and study of distribution) Also reports examples from India, a shell-mound on Sakhalin, Ainu shell-mounds, and the Chukchi area, with citations.

"Nobody competent to judge will deny at present that there have been mutual historical influences between Asia and America revealed by numerous indications, steadily growing as our knowledge advances." He believes in an indigenous North-Pacific culture-area going on "for ages" through which ideas have "poured in from Asia into America, and from America into Asia." The grooved stone axe may be autochthonous to North America, then it reached Asia. America may have borrowed stone weights (Lower Columbia Valley, citing Harlan I. Smith, *American Anthropologist* (1906): 305) from Asia; their shapes and peculiar handles agree with Chinese bronze weights of the Ts'in dynasty (B.C. 246-207).

Page 327: Van Aalst (Chinese Music, 48) remarks that the use of sonorous stone to make musical instruments may be peculiar to China, however such instruments are recorded for Peru and Ecuador (citations) [also perhaps California].

L-090

AUTHOR: Laughlin, William S.
DATE: 1948
TITLE: Japanese Glass Fishing-net Floats
IN: American Anthropologist 50:575

These artifacts are found in vast numbers where the Japanese current deposits them on the Aleutians, the Northwest Coast and Hawaii. Studying their distribution would permit determining the length of time involved in circumpacific drift, which could have put Asiatic objects ashore in America as a basis for stimulus diffusion.

L-091

AUTHOR: Laureani Ciccarelli, Camila
DATE: 1982
TITLE: Los ahu de la Isla de Pascua [The ahus of Easter Island]
IN: Aisthesis 14 (Julio): 87-100 (Instituto de Estética, Pontífica Universidad Católica: Santiago, Chile)

Postulates that the Vinapú ahu was built in the 14th century by the *hanau eepe* (fat people) of Quechua origin. This minority dominated the *hanau momoko* (thin people), who were native Polynesians. The latter destroyed the rulers in the 17th century and discontinued building and using the imposed ceremonial centers and apparatus, continuing, however, use of the old, ancestral, simple ahu.

L-091B

AUTHOR: Laureani Ciccarelli, Camila
DATE: 1985
TITLE: Los moai de Isla de Pascua [The Moai of Easter Island]
IN: Aisthesis 18:55-75 (Instituto de Estética, Pontífica Universidad Católica: Santiago, Chile)

Recognizes strong similarities between early monuments pictured by Heyerdahl and company on Easter Island and Andean monuments. Attributing this to coincidence is no more plausible than callingl on extraterrestrial visitors.

L-093

AUTHOR: Lauridsen, P.
DATE: 1979
TITLE: Bibliographia Groenlandica, eller Fortegnelse paa Vaerker, Afhandlinger og danske Manuskripter, der handle om Grønland indtil Aaret 1880 include. [Greenlandic Bibliography]
IMPRINT: Rosenkilde og Bagger: Copenhagen [Reprint of C. G. F. Pfaff's *Bibliographia Groenlandica* of 1890]

Pages 127-137: 131 titles are listed in chronological order concerning voyages to Vinland and Greenland itself, starting with the 1846 edition of Adam of Bremen.

L-094

AUTHOR: Lavachery, Henri
DATE: 1936
TITLE: Easter Island, Polynesia
IN: Antiquity 10:54-60

He had been an expeditionary on Easter Island in 1934 and here reports in very general terms. The people probably came from the Gambiers and found a barren island in the 12th-13th centuries. There is no evidence for the existence of two cultures, hence present inhabitants must be descendants of the builders of the monuments.

L-095

AUTHOR: Lavachery, Henri
DATE: 1937
TITLE: Easter Island, Polynesia
IN: Annual Report of the Board of Regents of the Smithsonian Institution . . . [for] 1936, pages 391-396

Asserts that cultural features found on Easter Island are of Polynesian origin.

L-096

AUTHOR: Lavachery, Henri
DATE: 1965
TITLE: Thor Heyerdahl et le Pacifique [Thor Heyerdahl and the Pacific]
IN: Journal de la société des océanistes 21:151-159

Defends Heyerdahl in part.

L-097

AUTHOR: Laviosa Zambotti, Pia
DATE: 1947
TITLE: Origini e diffusione della civiltà [The Origin and Diffusion of Civilization]
IN: Publicazioni 1, Istituto de Ricerche Preistoriche e Archeologiche, Socíetà Archeologica Comense (Dott. Carlo Marzorati: Milan)
[French translation, *Les origines et la diffusion de la civilisation: introduction à l'histoire universelle* (Payot: Paris, 1950); German translation, *Ursprung und Ausbreitung der Kultur,* foreword by P. Bosch-Gimpera, (Verlag für Kunst und Wissenschaft: Baden-Baden, 1950); Spanish translation, *Origen y diffusión de la civilización, Ediciones* (Omega: Barcelona, 1958)]

[German edition] Pages 321-351: Heading—"The Farming Cultures in South India, Indo-China, Indonesia, Melanesia, and America," and pages 404-420, heading—"State Culture in America." Melanesian "neo-matriarchal horticulture" was carried to the Amazon basin. Polynesians reached South America and were very much related to the Haida. Voyages also reached the Atlantic side, and the high civilizations of the Mediterranean and Near East affected the state-cultures of America.

L-098

AUTHOR: Law, R. G.
DATE: 1970
TITLE: The Introduction of Kumara into New Zealand
IN: Archaeology and Physical Anthropology in Oceania 5:114-127

Information from archaeology and on early climate is slim, but tentatively he proposes that the sweet potato could have been introduced by the earliest settlers of New Zealand around A.D. 800. This depends in part on whether Polynesians were the bearers of the plant from South America or whether South Americans introduced the plant; either are plausible. It could have been prior to the date indicated.

L-099

AUTHOR: Lawrence, Harold G. [Kofi Wangara]
DATE: 1962
TITLE: African Explorers of the New World
IN: The Crisis 69:321-332

A paean to African achievements leads to a routine review of the older ideas and evidences for the New World presence of blacks before Columbus (i.e., Olmec "negroid" stone heads).

L-100

AUTHOR: Lawrence, Harold G. [Kofi Wangara]
DATE: 1987
TITLE: Mandinga Voyages across the Atlantic
IN: African Presence in Early America, edited by Ivan van Sertima (n.p.: n.p.), 202-247 ["Incorporating Journal of African Civilizations," Dec. 1986, vol. 8, no. 2. "All inquiries should be addressed to Transaction Books, Rutgers—the State University, New Brunswick, New Jersey"]

A good deal of circumstantial historical and ethnological information is rehearsed to support the thesis that "the Mandinga made several voyages to the Americas where they carried on the gold and cloth trade. A number of settlements established by them were renamed after places in their original African homeland. These settlements were bases from which this trade was extended throughout the Americas. Some of the Mandinga merchants mixed in with the local populations and passed on to them some aspects of African culture."

L-101

AUTHORS: Layrisse, Miguel, Zulay Layrisse, and Johannes Wilbert
DATE: 1963
TITLE: Blood Group Antigen Studies of Four Chibchan Tribes
IN: American Anthropologist 65:36-55

Methodology. Cultural, physical anthropological and linguistic data are examined for four Chibchan-speaking groups in Venezuela. The conclusion is that Chibchan-speaking tribes do not form a homogeneous genetic group, and that more intensive studies, including those of blood groups, are needed to clarify the confused situation. Chibchan speakers may have occupied the territory of the Tunebo and Warrau relatively recently, with linguistic acculturation obscuring earlier diversity. [This suggests the need for caution in reading language distribution in terms of population history.]

L-102

AUTHORS: Layrisse, Miguel, and Johannes Wilbert
DATE: 1960
TITLE: El antigeno del sistema sanguineo diego [The Antigen of the Diego Blood System]
IMPRINT: La Fundación Creole y la Fundación Eugenio Mendoza, Editorial Sucre: Caracas

Summarizes results of serological studies broadly and especially on the Diego factor as they apply to the interpretation of the racial or ethnic status of American Indians. Hypotheses are cited or constructed to manage the significant degree of differentiation in serology among Amerinds, but the authors admit that many readers will find them inadequate. Discussion of Heyerdahl's position in light of blood data shows that not only ABO but lesser-known data support or accommodate his views.

L-103

AUTHORS: Layrisse, Miguel, and Johannes Wilbert
DATE: 1961
TITLE: Absence of the Diego Antigen, a Genetic Characteristic of Early Immigrants to South America
IN: Science 134/3485:1077-1078

The absence of the Diego gene in Waica Indians, and its very low frequencies in Warrau and Yaruro Indians, suggest that it represents a genetic characteristic of Marginal American Indians. Since Marginal Indians are considered to be early comers to the New World, the authors suggest that Diego-negative populations were the first to arrive and to extend throughout South America, while the Diego-positive tribes came later. At the least, the dichotomy shows genetic diversity.

L-103B

AUTHOR: Leary, Daniel J.

DATE: 1987

TITLE: Mystery Hill: The North Salem Stone Ruins, 1641-1680, Part I

IN: NEARA [New England Antiquities Research Association] Journal 22/1, 2

Raises questions from historical sources about the status of this controversial site prior to the time when J. Pattee, the person often supposed to have built it, moved there.

L-103C

AUTHOR: Leary, Daniel J.

DATE: 1989

TITLE: North Salem Stone Ruins, A Historical Essay, Part II, The Pattee Story, 1644-1850

IN: NEARA [New England Antiquities Research Association] Journal 23:49-54

A critique of the assumptions and "findings" of Goodwin, Hencken, and others about the Mystery Hill site at North Salem, Massachusetts, in relation to J. Pattee. Critique is followed by a history of the Pattee family that goes beyond previous treatments. The history raises questions about commonly-held assumptions concerning "Pattee's Caves." But Leary is inclined to consider them of colonial era age (not due to earlier visitors from Europe), with J. Pattee responsible for only some aspects of their visible condition.

L-104

AUTHOR: Lebzelter, Viktor

DATE: 1925

TITLE: Ein Onaschädel aus Feuerland; zur Frage des Vorkommens eines australoiden Rassenelementes in Süd-Amerika [An Ona Skull from Tierra del Fuego; on the Question of the Presence of an Australoid Racial Element in South America]

IN: Proceedings of the 21st International Congress of Americanists (Part 2, Gothenburg, Sweden, 1924), 422-434

Willing enough to see a linkage, he points out australoid elements in (measurements on) this cranium, then finally notes that physical anthropology cannot settle the question of connections; ethnological and linguistic evidence too must also be considered.

L-105

AUTHOR: Lechler, George [Jörg?]

DATE: 1939 [a?]

TITLE: The Viking Finds from Beardmore, Ontario

IN: Art Quarterly 2:128-133

Reports basic information on the Beardmore find including a quote from a letter from C. T. Currelly, director of the Royal Ontario Museum, on the events of the discovery. There can be no doubt that this was a burial and that it represents a complete outfit of a Viking warrior from Greenland. The sword is compared in detail with Viking swords. Explains how ice patterns in Davis Strait would lead inevitably to discovery of the entrance to Hudson Bay, and a map implies that the same expedition reached both Kensington and Beardmore by that approach before returning via James Bay. In a footnote he credits H-358 with largely reestablishing the credibility of the Kensington Stone "in which a great number of scientists have concurred." The only possible objections now are runological and linguistic but Prof. Lindroth feels those remaining objections are not credible.

L-106

AUTHOR: Lechler, Jörg [George?]

DATE: 1939 [b?]

TITLE: Die Entdecker Amerikas vor Columbus

[The Discoverers of America before Columbus]
IMPRINT: C. Kabitzch: Leipzig

Pages 51-57: Discusses the Kensington Stone critically in terms of the opinions of previous commentators. No one has yet examined it truly impartially; all have either wished to disprove it or prove it. The principal arguments against the authenticity of the stone so far presented are not important.

L-107
AUTHOR: Leclerq, Jules
DATE: 1924
TITLE: Le découverte de l'Amérique par les Islandais
[The Discovery of America by Icelanders]
IN: Proceedings of the 21st International Congress of Americanists (Part 1, The Hague, 1924), 418-422

Insubstantial. Yes, the Norse ("Icelanders") reached New England, but only Columbus' discovery had historical effect.

L-108
AUTHOR: Lecocq, Marie
DATE: 1902
TITLE: Notes pour un vocabulaire comparée des langues américaines et raccords aux langues de l'Ancien Monde
[Notes for a Comparative Vocabulary of American Languages and Links with Old World Languages]
IN: Proceedings of the 12th International Congress of Americanists (Paris, 1900), pages 299-304

In very random fashion certain words in various New World languages are compared with Finno-Ugric words.

L-109
AUTHOR: Ledergerber C., Paulina
DATE: 1982
TITLE: El origen de más de un cuarto de siglo de investigaciones sobre la cultura Valdivia
[The Origin of More Than a Quarter Century of Investigations of the Valdivia Culture]
IN: Boletín de la Academia Nacional de Historia 65/139-140:25-44 (Quito)

An appraisal of the effects of the transpacific origin thesis on subsequent archaeological investigations in Ecuador and a review of principal objections to the thesis.

L-110
AUTHOR: Lee, Robert E.
DATE: 1982
TITLE: L'Anse aux Meadows—Can There Really Be No Doubt?
IN: Anthropological Journal of Canada 20/4:18-32

Yes, there can be doubt that it is Vinland. He is skeptical of the interpretive methodology used by the Ingstads.

L-111
AUTHOR: Lee, Thomas E.
DATE: 1965
TITLE: Review of *The Wine Dark Sea,* by Henriette Mertz
IN: Anthropological Journal of Canada 3/1:28
[Reprinted in *New World Antiquity* 12/1, 2:20-21]

"I think that it will be hard, even for defenders of the 'Hands Off America' principle, to refute some of the points she makes." Whether we agree with her thesis or not (that Homer's Odyssey tells of travel to North America), we are reminded of a growing body of opinion and evidence concerning the arrival of other than

Amerinds to the New World very long before the Norse or Columbus. Her most significant contribution is to show "the relative ease with which such crossings" might have been made.

L-112

AUTHOR: Lee, Thomas E.
DATE: 1967
TITLE: Ancient European Settlement Revealed at Payne Lake, Ungava, 1965
IN: Travaux Divers 16:28-116 (Centre d'études nordiques, Université Laval: Québec)

See L-115.

L-113

AUTHOR: Lee, Thomas E.
DATE: 1968a
TITLE: A Summary of Norse Evidence at Ungava, 1968
IN: Anthropological Journal of Canada 6/4:17-21
[Reprinted in *NEARA Journal* 4/2:55-57]

Presents thirty-seven points of data he believes establishes these Ungava remains as being Norse rather than Eskimo.

L-114

AUTHOR: Lee, Thomas E.
DATE: 1968b
TITLE: The Question of Indian Origins, Again
IN: Anthropological Journal of Canada 6/4:22-32

Page 23: "The astonishingly diverse people whom we have conveniently lumped together under the term Indian. . . ." Because of lack of pertinent archaeological material in Alaska on the anticipated scale, entry via the Bering Strait increasingly seems doubtful as an explanation for Indian origin(s). Trans- Atlantic routes (indications in Spaulding, Gjessing, Griffin) should not be arbitrarily ruled out. "If we argue that there is no evidence for sustained trans-Atlantic contacts, let us also apply this test to the 8,000 mile route across Bering."

L-115

AUTHOR: Lee, Thomas E.
DATE: 1968c
TITLE: Archaeological Discoveries, Payne Bay Region, Ungava, 1966
IMPRINT: Centre d'études nordiques, Université Laval: Québec

The presence of a European-type village is indicated on the south shore of Payne Lake. Stone beacons up the Arnaud estuary and northward are attributed to the Norse, and house ruins on Pamiok Island are Norse longhouses, reoccupied by Dorset peoples; these are considerably earlier than those at Payne Lake. Many stone-vaulted tombs are near. The remains represent sizable colonies of at least two periods, with the earlier period perhaps representing the Kingdom of Skuggifjord of the sagas.

L-116

AUTHOR: Lee, Thomas E.
DATE: 1970
TITLE: The Ungava Norse: A Reply to Birgitta Wallace
IN: Anthropological Journal of Canada 8/1:21-23
[Preprinted *NEARA Journal* (1969) 4:59-60]

Other archaeologists find no "European settlement" traces in Ungava as claimed by Lee. He defends himself.

L-118

AUTHOR: Lee, Thomas E.
DATE: 1973
TITLE: The Norse Presence in Arctic Ungava

IN: American-Scandinavian Review 61:242-257

Well illustrated popular presentation of his investigations on the Ungava Peninsula which revealed large stone structures that appear Norse. Timber for the huge longhouse ruins had to be brought from a minimum 150 miles to the south, so only people with ships could have built these, not Dorset folk. Also an ancient iron ax of Norse type was found, and the architectural styles match those of Iceland and Greenland in A.D. 1100-1200. Vikings were not the kind of men to be satisfied sitting in Greenland for 500 years without exploring their surroundings this far away. What is remarkable is that there are any records preserved, not that there are so few.

L-119B

AUTHOR: Lee, Thomas E.
DATE: 1975
TITLE: Pre-Columbian European Traces in Ungava Peninsula
IN: NEARA [New England Antiquities Research Association] Journal 10:50-51

See L-118.

L-119C

AUTHOR: Lee, Thomas E.
DATE: 1976a
TITLE: The Norse in Ungava
IN: NEARA [New England Antiquities Research Association] Journal 11:5

See L-118.

L-120

AUTHOR: Lee, Thomas E.
DATE: 1976b
TITLE: Et tu, Hanno?
IN: Anthropological Journal of Canada 14/2:40

Concerns the inscription from Sherbrooke, eastern Canada, associated with Lee. He speaks of an unnamed Harvard professor [obviously Barry Fell] who said he could immediately read the inscription (it concerned Hanno, he said), since it was "Libyan." Lee concluded that the reading he proposed was an imposture. Prof. George Sotiroff showed Lee pictures of identical characters which are known from Bulgaria to Mongolia.

L-120B

AUTHOR: Lee, Thomas E.
DATE: 1976c
TITLE: Review of *Northern Mists,* by Carl Sauer
IN: NEARA [New England Antiquities Research Association] Journal 11:4

Sympathetic with Sauer's view that non-Viking, pre-Columbian voyagers crossed the North Atlantic.

L-120C

AUTHOR: Lee, Thomas E.
DATE: 1979
TITLE: Who Is This Man?
IN: Anthropological Journal of Canada 17/2:44-48

What appears to be a Norse sculpture picked up in Ungava is shown and briefly discussed.

L-121

AUTHOR: Leesberg, Arnold C. M.
DATE: 1903
TITLE: Comparative Philology; A Comparison between Semitic and American Languages
IMPRINT: Brill: Leiden

A lawyer and amateur philologist constructs a table of 900 English terms with equivalents in "Semitics" (which includes some 1200 terms, mainly Hebrew, with some Aramaic and Arabic), Aymara, Kichua [Quechua], Chiapanec (and

Mangue), Maya, Taino and Carib, and "Chukchee and North America." He tried other comparisons which failed to reveal parallels: Nahuatl, Chibcha, and "the Isthmian languages." Mentions a score of writers who have argued for a Semitic connection of American Indian languages. Parallels are found for about half the list for Aymara, a fourth for Kichua and a fifth for Maya. Moreover, many roots are found that show variant meanings which are the same in Hebrew as in Aymara and Kichua. He believes Maya, Aymara and Kichua all sprang from a single language and that that language showed a greater resemblance with the Semitic than with any other linguistic family ("in remote antiquity").

L-127

AUTHOR: Lehmann, Henri
DATE: 1964
TITLE: Maisons de céramique, Nayarit, Mexique
[Ceramic Model Houses from Nayarit, Mexico]
IN: Objets et mondes 4:107-118

After illustrating and discussing examples, he notes similarities to model houses of Ecuador, China, and New Guinea. Among Ecuadorean (Esmeraldas) examples (citing Estrada and Meggers on the Bahia complex) are some that are like specimens from Asia and modern Oceania. Between those of Oceania and Nayarit there are also similarities, pointing to details on a New Guinea house. There is no doubt about the analogies, but exactly what areas influenced others would require more detailed study.

L-128

AUTHOR: Lehmann, Walter H.
DATE: 1907
TITLE: Essai d'une monographie bibliographique sur l'île de Pâques
[Attempt at a Bibliographic Monograph on Easter Island]
IN: Anthropos 2:141-151, 257-268

Page 149: Mentions, without a citation, "the tradition of an immigration coming from the Galapagos Islands" but says it has very little guarantee of authenticity. [Bibliographic additions are in S-139.]

L-129

AUTHOR: Lehmann, Walter H.
DATE: 1909
TITLE: Methods and Results in Mexican Research
IMPRINT: n.p.: Paris
[In German in *Archiv für Anthropologie* (1907) 6:113-168]

Pages 42ff.: Criticizes the somatologists who have claimed to connect American Indians with the Old World, by any route or means. These theories are too vague to be disproved or corroborated. If Indian ancestors were already in America in late glacial times, there is no point trying to look to alternative connections. No reliable evidence of a connection in language between the continents has been brought forward.

L-131

AUTHOR: Lehmann, Walter H.
DATE: 1930
TITLE: Die Frage völkerkundlicher Beziehungen zwischen der Südsee und Amerika
[The Question of Ethnological Relations between the South Sea and America]
IN: Orientalische Literaturzeitung 33/5:322-339

A critical collation of Indian traditions about ships, perhaps from Oceania, reaching the coasts of America. Also includes data referring to negroid characteristics in American Indians (Lower California, Panama, Guaikeri of Venezuela, San Agustin in Colombia, coastal Peru, lowland Bolivia, and in the Olmec area) which he attributes to Melanesian admixture.

L-134

AUTHOR: Lehmann-Nitsche, Robert

DATE: 1899a

TITLE: ¿Lepra precolombiana? Ensayo crítico [Pre-Columbian Leprosy? Critical Essay]

IN: Revista del Museo de La Plata 9:337-371 (Buenos Aires)

He reprises the hypotheses of Virchow that certain figurines appear to show the pre-Columbian presence of leprosy in Peru, and the view of Ashmead (supported by Polakowsky and Carrasquilla) that there is no such acceptable evidence. This author concludes that leprosy was almost certainly not involved but probably syphilis was the cause of the lesions observed.

L-135

AUTHOR: Lehmann-Nitsche, Robert

DATE: 1899b

TITLE: Präcolumbianische Lepra und die verstümmelten peruanischen Thon-Figuren des La Plata-Museums vor dem ersten wissenschaftlichen lateinisch-amerikanischen Kongresse zu Buenos-Aires; die angebliche Krankheit llaga und briefliche Nachrichten von Hrn. Carasquilla [Pre-Columbian Leprosy and the Silent Figurines of the La Plata Museum, for the First Latin-American Scientific Congress in Buenos Aires; the Supposed Disease "llaga" and a Brief Notice from Sr. Carasquilla]

IN: Verhandlungen der Berliner Gesellschaft für Anthropologie, Ethnologie und Urgeschichte 31:81-89

See L-134.

L-137

AUTHOR: Lehmann-Nitsche, Robert

DATE: 1904

TITLE: Patología en la alfarería peruana [Pathology (Shown) on Peruvian Pottery]

IN: Revista del Museo de La Plata 11:29-35 (Buenos Aires)

See L-134.

L-138

AUTHOR: Lehmann-Nitsche, Robert

DATE: 1906

TITLE: Märchen der argentinischen Indianer [Tales of the Argentinian Indians]

IN: Zeitschrift für Volkskunde 2:156-164

He gives texts of six Araucanian tales with parallels in European folklore: story of a tiger and a man, of the old witch, the fox and the frog (compares the hare and the hedgehog), the dog and the rat, old woman and her husband, and the donkey, pig, cat, and cock. How much of these tales is really of European origin (by post-discovery borrowing) is still to be determined.

L-140

AUTHOR: Lehmann-Nitsche, Robert

DATE: 1908

TITLE: Patagonische Gesang und Musikbogen [Patagonian Songs and Musical Bows]

IN: Anthropos 3:916-940

Describes a musical bow [considered by some absent in pre-Columbian times].

L-141

AUTHOR: Lehmann-Nitsche, Robert

DATE: 1909-1910a

TITLE: Clavas cefalomorfas de piedra procedentes de Chile y Argentina

[Fish-shaped Stone Clubs from Chile and Argentina]
IN: Revista del Museo de La Plata 16:150-170 (Buenos Aires)

Identifies clubs of the type Imbelloni denominates "mere" and notes their similarity to those of Polynesia.

L-142
AUTHOR: Lehmann-Nitsche, Robert
DATE: 1909-1910b
TITLE: Hachas y placas de ceremonia de la Patagonia
[Ceremonial Axes and Plaques from Patagonia]
IN: Revista del Museo de La Plata 16:204-240 (Buenos Aires)

See L-141.

L-143
AUTHOR: Lehmann-Nitsche, Robert
DATE: 1920
TITLE: Ursprung und Verbreitung von Lasso und Wurfkugeln
[Origin and Dissemination of the Lasso and Throwing Stones (Bolas?)]
IN: Zeitschrift des deutschen wissenschaftlichen Vereins zur Kultur- und Landeskunde argentiniens, pages 81-82

In Argentina. [Both have been proposed as features diffused from the Old World.]

L-144
AUTHOR: Lehmann-Nitsche, Robert
DATE: 1921
TITLE: Mitología sudamericana IV: Las constelaciones del Orión y de las Pléyades y su pretendida identidad de interpretación en las esferas Eurasiática y Sudamericana
[South American Mythology IV: The Constellations of Orion and the Pleiades and Their Pretended Similarity of Interpretation in the Eurasiatic and South American Spheres]
IN: Revista del Museo de La Plata 26/4:17-69 (Buenos Aires)

South American peoples lacked any names of constellations recalling Eurasia, nor did they have the zodiac, yet he is sure that the Mexican calendar was of Asiatic origin.

L-145
AUTHOR: Lehmann-Nitsche, Robert
DATE: 1937
TITLE: Steinerne Vogelkopfkeulen aus Chile und dem argentinischen Andengebiete (Melanesisches in Südamerika I)
[Stone Clubs in the Shape of Bird Heads, from the Argentine Andes (Melanesians in South America I)]
IN: Zeitschrift für Ethnologie 69:220-233

Reviews literature on Polynesian club forms found in South America. Interprets them as clubs in the shape of birds heads used in dance and maps their distribution.

L-146
AUTHORS: Lehner, Ernest, and Johanna Lehner
DATE: 1966
TITLE: How They Saw the New World
IMPRINT: Tudor: New York

Includes a section on "pre-Columbian maps," meaning 15th-century ones.

L-147
AUTHOR: Leicht, Hermann
DATE: 1960
TITLE: Pre-Inca Art and Culture
IMPRINT: Orion: New York
[Also as *Arte y cultura preincaicos;*

un milenio de imperio (Chimú, Aguilar: Madrid, 1963)]

Pages 211-212 (1963 edition): Supposes that the rafts of Tupac Yupanqui reached only the islands 20 or 65 kilometers off the coast of Peru.

L-148

AUTHOR: Leigh, Howard
DATE: 1958
TITLE: Zapotec Glyphs
IN: Boletín de estudios oaxaqueños 2:4-6
[Same information in briefer form in, "Further Discussion of Oaxaca Archaeology: A Reply to Mr. Paddock," *Boletín de estudios oaxaqueños* 8:3-4]

Notes a "pyramid glyph" found in Oaxaca in Monte Alban I (500-100 B.C.) which means "mountain," while the same glyph in Mesopotamia means "celestial mountain" and in Egypt "primeval mound"; he does not offer any explanation for the parallel.

L-149

AUTHOR: Leigh, Howard
DATE: 1966
TITLE: The Evolution of Zapotec Glyph C
IN: Ancient Oaxaca, edited by John Paddock (Stanford University Press: Stanford, California), 265-269

The vase overflowing with water is an element in the symbolism of astro- calendrical religion. Cites A-005 on the Old World which also notes that "such ideas are as likely to turn up in the New World as not." At Monte Alban, Old World symbols mentioned by Ackerman include the twin brothers, the S glyph, Milky Way felines, mountain glyph, inverted mountain glyph, Greek key and cross, Maltese cross, half the gamma cross, the net of the sky god, the tomoye (Japanese name for a three-lobed form found also at Teotihuacan), fish, stick through a circle, tree, the flowing vase (streams representing the Milky Way), together with Cipactli (cayman), Earth Monster or Sky Monster.

L-150

AUTHOR: Leip, Hans
DATE: 1957
TITLE: River in the Sea: Story of the Gulf Stream
IMPRINT: Jarrolds: London
[Also Putnam's: New York, 1958]

Sees Saint Brendan fitting the Toltec tradition of the arrival and departure of a foreign visitor. The name Tula he links with Norse Thule.

L-151

AUTHOR: Leland, Charles Godfrey
DATE: 1875
TITLE: Fusang, or the Discovery of America by Chinese Buddhist Priests in the Fifth Century
IMPRINT: J. W. Bouton: New York
[Reprinted Curzon Press: London, 1973]

One of the most influential treatments on Fu-sang. Asserts that the Dakota language is directly related to Asia.

L-152

AUTHOR: Leland, Charles Godfrey
DATE: 1884a
TITLE: The Edda among the Algonquin Indians
IN: Atlantic Monthly 54:222-234

An impact of the Vikings, he claims.

L-153

AUTHOR: Leland, Charles Godfrey
DATE: 1884b
TITLE: The Algonquin Legends of New England
IMPRINT: Houghton: Boston

Certain myths of the Algonquins are similar to those of the Norse. For example, the Ojibway legend figure Manobozho "closely corresponds" with Egyptian Typhon and Scandinavian Midgard. [Compare G-030 and T-086.]

L-154

AUTHOR: Leland, Charles Godfrey
DATE: 1887
TITLE: The Mythology, Legends, and Folk-lore of the Algonkins
IN: Transactions of the Royal Society of Literature 14/1:68-91

See L-152 and L-153.

L-156B

AUTHOR: Lenik, Edward J.
DATE: 1973
TITLE: The "Norse Wall" Stone at Provincetown, Massachusetts
IN: NEARA [New England Antiquities Research Association] Journal 8:37-38

Very briefly describes a site on Cape Cod which is claimed locally to have been a Norse landing site because the stones used in a wall "were evidently from some foreign country as none are to be found on the Cape, nor in any place in this country" [*sic*]. The editor comments that a Norse origin seems highly unlikely but that it is possible that it marks the landing spot of other trans-atlantic voyagers from much earlier.

L-156C

AUTHOR: Lenik, Edward J.
DATE: 1974
TITLE: The Riddle of the Prehistoric Walls of Ramapo, New York
IN: NEARA [New England Antiquities Research Association] Journal 9:42-4
[A longer version appeared in 1975 as "The Riddle of the Prehistoric Walls, Ramapo, New York," *New York State Archaeological Association Bulletin* 63:1-14]

This mountainous area has rock walls and cairns, here reported from the field and after extensive historical research. It is simply not possible to say whether they were prehistoric. Possibly they were constructed by farmers in recent centuries, but that is only one conjecture.

L-158

AUTHOR: Lenik, Edward J.
DATE: 1975b
TITLE: Excavations at Spirit Pond
IN: Man in the Northeast 9:54-60

Excavations at this Maine site find no evidence of the Norse, only of Amerindians.

L-158B

AUTHOR: Lenik, Edward J.
DATE: 1977
TITLE: Ancient Inscriptions in Western Connecticut
IN: NEARA [New England Antiquities Research Association] Journal 11/3:34-38

An 1809 travel book had reported a "Hebrew inscription." Several years of research and search located a 1789 manuscript reference to this inscription which resulted in locating it. Four Hebrew names are indeed present, but the old source indicates that it was probably made around 1760. Another inscription was found (illustrated) some distance away but what it might signify is not apparent. Apparently it was in place about 150 years ago.

L-158C

AUTHOR: Lenik, Edward J.
DATE: 1978
TITLE: Riddles on Rocks: Non-aboriginal Petroglyphs in Maine

IN: NEARA [New England Antiquities Research Association] Journal 12/4:76-79

He has come across four petroglyph sites (illustrated) that appear not to be of Indian origin. They were clearly executed by European-Americans.

L-158D

AUTHOR: Lenik, Edward J.
DATE: 1978-1979
TITLE: Iron in Prehistoric North America: Its Procurement and Use
IN: New Hampshire Archaeologist 20:49-61

Treats the iron minerals obtained by native peoples of mainly eastern North America. They utilized meteoric iron, hematite, limonite, and magnetite for pigments and certain artifacts. Cites reference to iron specimens in some old standard sources—Moorehead, Shetrone, Jennings, and Ford. These are assumed to be of meteoric iron [actually few analyses have been done]. These included accumulations of red ochre (iron oxide) in the shape of artifacts, although these were dismissed in the reports as a ceremonial formation of red-ochre powder into the shape of an artifact. [In light of N-017B and N-017C, museum specimens or iron artifacts deserve systematic testing for meteoric or terrestrial origin.]

L-158E

AUTHORS: Lenik, Edward J, Clyde Keeler, and Howard LaHurreau
DATE: 1976
TITLE: A Lenni Lenape's Mide Stone
IN: NEARA [New England Antiquities Research Association] Journal 11:2-3

An inscribed oval river pebble from New Jersey considered to have been part of a shaman's apparatus.

L-163

AUTHOR: Léon Borja de Szaszdi, Dora
DATE: 1964
TITLE: Prehistoria de la costa ecuatoriana [Prehistory of the Ecuadorian Coast]
IN: Anuario de estudios americanos 21:381-436 (Sevilla)

Pages 395-396: From the Esmeraldas river to the island of Puna was the only part of Ecuador where the large wooden balsa was used in pre-Columbian times, because the appropriate trees grew solely there. Only in colonial times were these balsas used south of that section. Furthermore, pre-Spanish sails were used only on rafts built between Esmeraldas and Tumbez.

L-165

AUTHOR: León Portilla, Miguel
DATE: 1963
TITLE: Aztec Thought and Culture: A Study of the Ancient Nahuatl Mind
IMPRINT: University of Oklahoma Press: Norman

Quotes E. Seler: "These four distinct prehistoric or precosmic ages of the Mexicans, each one oriented toward a different direction of the heavens, are astonishingly related to the four elements, water, earth, wind, and fire, known to classical antiquity, and which even now constitute the way that the civilized peoples of East Asia look upon nature." [See also L-166.]

L-166

AUTHOR: León Portilla, Miguel
DATE: 1971
TITLE: Pre-hispanic Literature
IN: Archaeology of Northern Mesoamerica, part 1, edited by Gordon F. Ekholm and Ignacio Bernal, vol. 10 of Handbook of Middle American Indians (University of Texas Press: Austin), 452-458

On Nahuatl poetic forms [for which there are Near Eastern parallels].

Page 455: As an example of Nahuatl epic poetry, he gives a passage from the Codex Matritense, obtained by Sahagun from informants, which recounts how their ancestors came to the land by ships from across the sea and settled, later moving southward to Guatemala. [See also S-358.]

L-167

AUTHOR: Leonard, Phillip M., and William R. McGlone
DATE: 1988
TITLE: The Anubis Caves: Transcriptions and Interpretations
IN: NEARA [New England Antiquities Research Association] Journal 22/3-4:46-50

A critique of transcriptions and readings by others of inscriptions in the Anubis rock shelters of western Oklahoma. Fell and others have worked from faulty transcriptions; on the scene itself, visible elements of the inscription(s) are notably different from what has been published. The authors point out corrections and suggest astronomical and mythological connections which they believe continue to indicate a Celtic origin for the epigraphic remains. On page 53 Gloria Farley, one of those criticized, responds briefly.

L-167B

AUTHORS: Leonard, Phillip M., and William H. McGlone
DATE: 1988a
TITLE: Anubis Caves: Transcriptions and Interpretations, Western Oklahoma. Old World Libyan and Ogam Script
IN: NEARA [New England Antiquities Research Association] Journal 22:46-50

Propose an astronomical interpretation for one of the inscriptions, after noting that previous interpretations, by Fell, Farley and Washburn, had all been flawed by inaccurate transcription of the markings.

L-167C

AUTHORS: Leonard, Phillip M., and William H. McGlone
DATE: 1988b
TITLE: An Epigraphic Hoax on Trial in New Mexico
IN: Epigraphic Society Occasional Papers 17:206-219

Present evidence, later used in a court trial for fraud, which demonstrates why certain engraved stones in Hebrew writing were misinterpreted and ultimately proved fraudulent.

L-168B

AUTHOR: Lepper, Bradley T.
DATE: 1991
TITLE: "Holy Stones" of Newark, Ohio, Not So Holy after All
IN: Skeptical Inquirer 15:117-119

Insists on the inauthenticity of the stones.

L-169

AUTHOR: LePlongeon, Augustus
DATE: 1881
TITLE: Vestiges of the Mayas; or, Facts Tending to Prove That Communications and Intimate Relations Must Have Existed in Very Remote Times, between the Inhabitants of Mayab and Those of Asia and Africa
IMPRINT: J. Polhemus [i.e., privately printed]: New York

Isis, Osiris, Chaacmol, etc., between Egypt and the Maya area as in L-171.

L-170

AUTHOR: LePlongeon, Augustus
DATE: 1886

TITLE: Sacred Mysteries among the Mayas and the Quiche 11,500 Years Ago
IMPRINT: Robert Macoy: New York

See L-171, which is an elaboration of this item.

L-171

AUTHOR: LePlongeon, Augustus
DATE: 1896
TITLE: Queen Moo and the Egyptian Sphinx
IMPRINT: Privately printed: New York

"Abundant proofs of the intimate communications of the ancient Mayas with the civilized nations of Asia, Africa, and Europe are to be found among the remains of their ruined cities. Their peculiar architecture, embodying their cosmogonic and religious notions, is easily recognized in the ancient architectural monuments of India, Chaldea, Egypt, and Greece; in the great pyramid of Ghizeh, in the famed Parthenon of Athens."

The American continent was visited by Carthaginians a few years before Plato wrote about Atlantis, hence the idea. The Egyptian account of Isis and Osiris corresponds exactly to that of Queen Moo and her brother-husband Prince Coh, whose charred heart was found by the author preserved in a stone urn in his mausoleum at Chichen Itza. Queen Moo fled the wrath of her brother in Yucatan and, failing to find refuge in the remnants of the Land of Mu (Azores), she at last reached the Maya colonies established years earlier on the banks of the Nile, where the people called her Isis and proclaimed her their queen.

Comparative cultural evidence is mustered in support of the idea of interhemispheric communication. For example: (based on his interpretation of the monuments) both Mayan and Egyptian women tied their dresses around their waists and uncovered their breasts when a friend died; quite similar winged sun disks are shown from Egypt and from Ocosingo, Mexico. Pages 204-206: LePlongeon prints a letter he had sent to arch-critic Daniel Brinton "which contains an invitation to a scientific duel!"

L-172

AUTHOR: LePlongeon, Augustus
DATE: 1914
TITLE: The Origin of the Egyptians
IN: The Word Magazine 17:9-20, 70-83, 161-176, 196-209, 273-281, 345-360; 18:47-60, 67-84, 181-190, 224-228 (Theosophical Publishing Company)

An attempt to show that the Maya founded Egyptian civilization.

L-173

AUTHOR: Leroi-Gourhan, André
DATE: 1946
TITLE: Archéologie du Pacifique-Nord; matériaux pour l'étude des relations entre les peuples riverains d'Asie et d'Amérique
[The Archaeology of the North Pacific; Material for the Study of Relations between the Riverine Peoples of Asia and America]
IN: Université de Paris, Institut d'Ethnologie, Travaux et Mémoires 47
[For a review, see L-007]

An extensive survey of ethnological and archaeological materials around the North Pacific. On the basis of loose criteria of similarity, he finds many types of shared artifacts throughout the zone, leading him to conclude that there was a (pre-European) "North Pacific civilization" sharing basic ideas in the same manner we speak of "European civilization." This cultural entity stretched at least from Japan to California. Numerous maps of artifact distributions are shown, extending to southeast Asia on the one hand and northern South America on the other.

L-174

AUTHOR: Leser, Paul
DATE: 1977
TITLE: Fritz Graebner—eine Würdigung. Zum 100. Geburtstag am 4. März 1977
[Fritz Graebner—An Appreciation. For his 100th Birthday, 4 March 1977]
IN: Anthropos 72:1-55

Although frequently considered a diffusionist, Graebner repeatedly stated that his work was not directed toward a theory of diffusion, nor did he consider himself an exponent of the Kulturkreislehre, a term to which he consistently objected. His goal was to work out a genetic classification of culture using the same comparative methods as historical linguists, historians, and biologists.

L-177

AUTHOR: Lessa, William A.
DATE: 1961
TITLE: Tales from Ulithi Atoll: A Comparative Study in Oceanic Folklore
IN: University of California Folklore Studies 13 (Berkeley)

Page 445: On trickster tales, although some (e.g., Kelley in his dissertation) "would connect them with the American Indian coyote tales, I am not willing to go that far."

A section on the Post-hole Murder tale does not note the Guatemalan occurrence on which Stewart has written [S-452 and S-453].

L-177B

AUTHOR: Lesser, W. Hunter
DATE: 1989
TITLE: How Science Works—and How It Doesn't
IN: West Virginia Archaeologist 41/1:20-22

Denunciation of Fell's reading of West Virginia inscriptions, calling it pseudoscience.

L-178

AUTHOR: Lesson, A.
DATE: 1880-1884
TITLE: Les Polynésiens: leur origine, leurs migrations, leur langue, 4 vols.
[The Polynesians: Their Origin, Migrations, and Language]
IMPRINT: Ernest Leroux: Paris

Opposes claims that Polynesia had been peopled from America.

L-179

AUTHOR: Lethbridge, Thomas Charles
DATE: 1950
TITLE: Herdsmen and Hermits: Celtic Seafarers in the Northern Seas
IMPRINT: Bowes and Bowes: Cambridge

He believes that inhabitants of the Greenland western settlement moved to America and were absorbed; those of the eastern settlement later may have done so also. The Kensington Stone may be genuine.

L-180

AUTHOR: Lethbridge, Thomas Charles
DATE: 1952
TITLE: Boats and Boatmen
IMPRINT: Thames and Hudson: London

An experienced sailor and writer describes various forms and rigs, with some unusual historical views on the development of boats. He includes a good deal on human aspects of sailing, the oculus, sea gods, boat burials, and such incidental topics. Ships with objects of Roman manufacture sailed as far as Iceland.

L-181

AUTHOR: Leuthner, Margaret Barry
DATE: 1988

TITLE: Crusade to Vinland: The Kensington Runestone
IMPRINT: Explorer [i.e., privately printed]: Alexandria, Minnesota

Those who came with Paul Knutson in 1354 were not Vikings but archers and bowmen and knights wearing the Crusader's red cross who had vowed to preserve Christianity. The stone's broken grammar was deliberate, "to clue us to codes and ciphers and acrostics that reveal the whole story." They spoke Norse, Swedish, Latin, English, and French. The text is in Swedish but was written by Greenlanders who spoke English as a second language.

L-181B

AUTHOR: Levin, M. G., translated and edited by H. N. Michael
DATE: 1963
TITLE: Ethnic Origins of the Peoples of Northeastern Asia
IN: Anthropology of the North, Translations from the Russian Series No. 3 (Arctic Institute of North America: Toronto)

Page 318: Many have attempted to identify "Americanoid" physical traits in eastern and northern Asia. Were these to point to chronologically and geographically isolated units, the effort would be interesting, but most such treatments, especially ten Kate's, fail by being only impressionistic or statistical without focus.

L-181C

AUTHORS: Levin, M. G., and D. A. Sergeyev
DATE: 1964
TITLE: The Penetration of Iron into the Arctic
IN: The Archaeology and Geomorphology of Northern Asia: Selected Works, edited by Henry N. Michael, Anthropology of the North, Translations from the Russian Sources 5 (Arctic Institute of North America, Toronot), 319-326

Trade in metals was established from northern Asia into arctic North America before European contact.

L-182

AUTHOR: Lévi-Strauss, Claude
DATE: 1943
TITLE: The Art of the North West Coast at the American Museum of Natural History
IN: Gazette des beaux-arts, 6th series, 24:175-182 (New York)

See L-184.

L-183

AUTHOR: Lévi-Strauss, Claude
DATE: 1958
TITLE: Anthropologie structurale [Structural Anthropology]
IMPRINT: Plon: Paris

Pages 269-294: Notes similarities in art between the Northwest Coast and early China.

L-184

AUTHOR: Lévi-Strauss, Claude
DATE: 1963
TITLE: Split Representation in the Art of Asia and America
IN: Structural Anthropology (Basic Books, New York), 245-268 [Originally "Le dédoublement de la représentation dans les arts de l'Asie et de l'Amérique," *Renaissance* 2-3 (1944-1945): 168-186 (The École Libre des Hautes Études: New York); reprinted in his *Anthropologie structurale* (Plon: Paris, 1958), 269-294]

Pages 247-248: "The negative attitude of [the diffusionists'] cautious opponents is no more satisfactory than the fabulous pretensions which the latter merely reject. Comparative studies of primitive art have probably been jeopardized by the zeal of investigators of cultural contacts and borrowings. But let us state in no uncertain terms that these studies have been jeopardized even more by intellectual pharisees who prefer to deny obvious relationships because science does not yet provide an adequate method for their interpretation." [We have here a Gallic Gladwin!] "We reserve the right" to compare American Indian art with that of China or New Zealand even if it has been proved a thousand times over that the Maori could not have brought their weapons and ornaments to the Pacific Coast. Cultural contact doubtless constitutes the one hypothesis which most easily accounts for complex similarities that chance cannot explain. But if historians maintain that contact is impossible, this does not prove that the similarities are illusory, but only that one must look elsewhere for the explanation. "The fruitfulness of the diffusionist approach derives precisely from its systematic exploration of the possibilities of history."

Page 258: But even if the most ambitious reconstructions of the diffusionist school were to be confirmed, we should still be faced with an essential problem which has nothing to do with history: why should a cultural trait that has been borrowed or diffused through a long history remain intact? Stability is no less mysterious than change.

He musters materials from the Northwest Coast, China, Siberia, New Zealand, India, and Persia about split representations, citing approvingly Hentze and L. Adam. He also compares split representation in Caduveo (Brazil) and Maori art. Some of the Maori-Northwest Coast parallels which have been cited by others strike him as sometimes specious but at other times more valid.

Page 263: A Shang bronze shown by Hentze looks as though it could be the reduction of a carved pole, as slate reductions were derived from British Columbia totem poles.

Page 267: A Chaldean-originated way to represent an animal (head in front view and body in profile) may relate to Northwest Coast art, perhaps owing to a connection such as may be suggested by the art theme of the "whirl of animals" of the Eurasian steppes and in certain areas of America, especially at Moundville. However, it is also possible that the beast with two bodies derives independently in Asia and America out of the technique of split representation which failed to survive in Near Eastern sites but did in China and the Pacific.

L-185

AUTHOR:	Lévi-Strauss, Claude
DATE:	1968
TITLE:	Religions comparées des peuples sans écriture [Comparative Religions of Non-literate Peoples]
IN:	Problémes et méthodes d'histoire des religions: mélanges publiés par la section des sciences religieuses à l'occasion du centenaire de l'École Pratique des Hautes Études (Presses universitaires de France: Paris) 1-7 [Translated as "Comparative Religions of Nonliterate Peoples," in his *Structural Anthropology*, volume 2 (Basic Books: New York, 1976), 60-67]

From 1951-1953 he analyzed the pantheons of the Pueblo tribes, which fit the typologies of groups elsewhere. He established the pre-Columbian character of a mediator (a phallic god consecrated to ashes and refuse, master of wild animals, fog, dew, and precious garments, occurring from Mexico to Canada), which had generally been held to be a recent importation. This figure presents, even in detail, in spite of systematic inversion of all the terms (which excludes borrowing), a regular correspondence to a character reduced to a minor role on the European and Asiatic scene, i.e., Cinderella.

L-186

AUTHOR: Lévi-Strauss, Claude
DATE: 1970
TITLE: Les champignons dans la culture [Mushrooms in Culture]
IN: L'Homme 10/1:5-16 [Reprinted as "Mushrooms in Culture: Apropos of a Book by R. G. Wasson," in *Structural Anthropology* (Basic Books: New York, 1976), 2:222-237]

This review of W-055 adds more ethnographic material on mushroom use and associations throughout much of North America and eastern South America. In northern Eurasia, as in those parts of America, mushrooms are connected with the dead, are thought spawned from celestial or meteorological events, and are associated with animal excrement; but psychotropic uses are limited largely to Mexico.

L-187

AUTHOR: Lévi-Strauss, Claude
DATE: 1971
TITLE: Comment meurent les mythes [How Myths Die]
IN: Science et conscience de la société: mélanges en l'honneur de Raymond Aron, volume 1 (Calmann-Lévy: Paris), 131-143 [Reprinted 1974 as "How Myths Die," *New Literary History* 5:269-281. Also with the same English title, in his *Structural Anthropology* (Basic Books: New York, 1976), 2:256-268]

Methodological. Uses a myth extant among Northwest Coast and Plateau groups to show how dissemination of a text through space may disintegrate the narrative formula. [Could help explain changes in diffused folklore or even calendrical materials.]

L-188

AUTHOR: Lévi-Strauss, Claude
DATE: 1975
TITLE: La voie des masques, 2 volumes (constituting Part 1 only) [The Way of the Masks]
IMPRINT: Editions d'art Albert Skira: Geneve [Reissued in one volume, with the addition of Part 2, Librairie Plon: Paris, 1979. Both parts published in English as *The Way of the Masks* (University of Washington Press: Seattle, 1982)]

Page 127: Points out "some curious analogies" between the mythology of earthquakes in ancient Japan and in the American Northwest, which might seem far-fetched if prehistoric finds made in the latter region were not singularly reminiscent of others from northern Japan. Also some Chinese tombs (late Chou) have yielded sculpted wooden effigies that look strikingly like the Salish Swaihwé mask (Chinese example illustrated).

L-189

AUTHOR: Lévi-Strauss, Claude
DATE: 1983
TITLE: Le regard éloigné [The View from Afar]
IMPRINT: Librairie Plon: Paris [English Basic Books: New York, 1985]

Page 191 (of the English edition): We have seen that the affinities between the Greek and the North American myths extend to their very metaphors. This would confirm—were confirmation necessary—that even in a case that defies geographic or historical connection, the repertoire from which mythical thinking draws its themes and motifs has limited resources.

Pages 192-200: A paper (chapter) titled "Pythagoras in America," compares beliefs about the place of beans in notions about the relation of living and dead which are not only

Pythagorean but widespread in America. No explanation can be offered at this time for the parallels.

L-190

AUTHOR: Lévi-Strauss, Claude
DATE: 1984
TITLE: Paroles données [(My) Words Delivered]
IMPRINT: Librairie Plon: Paris [Reprinted as *Anthropology and Myth* in the USA, but in England as *Anthropology and Myth: Lectures 1951-1982*, both Basil Blackwell: Oxford and New York, 1987]

A number of the pieces make comparisons involving Amerindian myths and those of the Old World, which might be a result of diffusion in some cases.

Page 106: He weighs arguments for and against diffusion in the case of tales of the Grail or equivalent.

L-191

AUTHORS: Levison, Michael, R. Gerard Ward, and John W. Webb
DATE: 1973
TITLE: The Settlement of Polynesia: A Computer Simulation
IMPRINT: Australian National University Press: Canberra; and University of Minnesota Press: Minneapolis

In reference to Sharp's thesis, computer simulation of 100,000 voyages indicates only a minute chance that the extremities of Polynesia could have been settled by accidental drifts. The stretch of sea separating the Solomon Islands and New Hebrides from Polynesia particularly "presents a formidable barrier to eastward drifts." It is highly unlikely that men entered the Polynesian triangle from anywhere due to accidental drift voyages. However over a third of voyages originated from Ecuador landed on Polynesian islands, usually within three months of starting.

L-191B

AUTHOR: Levtzion, Nehemia, and J. F. P. Hopkins
DATE: 1981
TITLE: Corpus of Early Arabic Sources for West African History
IMPRINT: Cambridge University Press: Cambridge

Includes the account of the voyage of the king of Mali, Abu Bakr, as presented by Van Sertima.

L-192

AUTHOR: Levy-Bing [no first name used]
DATE: 1875
TITLE: L'inscription de Grave-Creek [The Grave-Creek Inscription]
IN: Proceedings of the 1st International Congress of Americanists (Nancy, 1875), 1:215-230

The inscription is in Phoenician or Canaanite.

L-193

AUTHOR: Lewis, Albert B.
DATE: 1924
TITLE: Use of Tobacco in New Guinea and Neighboring Regions
IN: Field Museum of Natural History Anthropology Leaflet 1 (Chicago)

See L-194.

L-194

AUTHOR: Lewis, Albert B.
DATE: 1931
TITLE: Tobacco in New Guinea
IN: American Anthropologist 33:134-138

He has claimed the pre-European presence of tobacco in New Guinea, while others suppose it came from America via the Spanish. He argues again for independent domestication and use of it on the island.

L-195

AUTHOR: Lewis, Archibald R.
DATE: 1958
TITLE: The Northern Seas: Shipping and Commerce in Northern Europe, A.D. 300-1100
IMPRINT: Princeton University Press: Princeton

In the preface he states that he considers that the seas "are not barriers now and were not in the Middle Ages. Rather they were highways which connected, influenced and tended to unify the lands whose shores they touched." Emphasizes the lack of relevant information. But past opinion by historians highly critical of tradition, such as in the Irish legend and Norse sagas, he suggests has been too sweeping and too uncritical. Little concrete is said in this work of voyaging to America, only the usual acknowledgement of Vinland, but the socioeconomic context of voyaging in the medieval years is laid out clearly and quite a bit is provided on nautical capabilities in that era.

L-196

AUTHOR: Lewis, David H.
DATE: 1964
TITLE: Polynesian Navigational Methods
IN: Journal of the Polynesian Society 73:364-374

Discussion of the technical feasibility of long-distance Polynesian voyages— "whether it was possible, with the navigational and geographical knowledge known or believed to have been possessed by the early Polynesians, for them to have made 'deliberate' voyages at all."

The map on page 368 displays "island blocks" of central Polynesia, formed by drawing a circle of 30 mile radius round each island, on the assumption that to come that close would have permitted sighting and landfall. The article ends contra Sharp, saying that conscious expeditions of discovery "can hardly be doubted."

L-197

AUTHOR: Lewis, David H.
DATE: 1966
TITLE: Stars of the Sea Road
IN: Journal of the Polynesian Society 75:85-94

He attempted in 1965 to sail a modern catamaran from Tahiti to New Zealand via Raiatea and Rarotonga by using the Polynesian navigation system exclusively. A European navigator rode in one hull, checking Lewis' course and calculations which he made in the other hull. Except for one error in the Cook Islands, Lewis' Polynesian navigating was reasonably accurate and enabled him to achieve his ultimate objective.

L-201

AUTHOR: Lewis, David H.
DATE: 1972
TITLE: We, the Navigators: The Ancient Art of Landfinding in the Pacific
IMPRINT: Australian National University Press: Canberra

An exposition of elements of the traditional knowledge of navigation and the sea as learned from his Marshall Island informants. A section discusses reasons for voyaging, which seem somewhat trivial to modern Western observers.

Pages 253-254: Oceanic vessels deserve the name ship, for "canoe" misrepresents them to the mind of European readers. Some were longer than Captain Cook's ship. Yet despite those large ones, throughout Oceania "the preferred size of vessel for deep sea voyaging seems to have been in the 50-75 foot range." These middle-sized craft had proved least liable to accident during stormy weather. Adequate provisions for a crew of dozens could be carried. Given good winds, a range of 3000-4500 miles is not unreasonable. He feels voyages to Easter Island could not have been intentional, for returns could not have been planned. No mention is made of voyaging to America.

L-201B

AUTHOR: Lewis, David H.
DATE: 1976
TITLE: Ice Bird: The First Single-Handed Voyage to Antarctica
IMPRINT: W. W. Norton: New York

In a 32-foot steel sloop he sailed 10,000 miles from Sydney to the American base in Antarctica then later on to South Africa, capsizing three times and suffering extreme hardships.

L-202

AUTHOR: Lewis, David H.
DATE: 1977
TITLE: Mau Piailug's Navigation of Hokule'a from Hawaii to Tahiti
IN: East-West Center Culture Learning Institute, Topics in Culture Learning 5:1-23

The voyage of the Hokule'a double canoe from Hawaii to Tahiti in 1976 was a test of the ability of the Micronesian navigator Mau Piailug to expand his knowledge applicable in the Caroline Islands to another area of the Pacific. The success of the voyage entirely supports the point. This article recounts the pattern of training Piailug underwent from age six and the avenues of information he and other "Indo-Pacific" navigators control now and controlled in the past.

L-204

AUTHOR: Lewis, David H.
DATE: 1978
TITLE: The Voyaging Stars: Secrets of the Pacific Island Navigators
IMPRINT: Collins: Sydney and London

Recounts his quest to find a navigator with traditional Micronesian skills in order to learn from him. The final part describes application of those skills in the voyage of the Hokule'a from Hawaii to Tahiti.

L-205

AUTHOR: Lewis, Gilbert N.
DATE: 1947
TITLE: Beginning of Civilization in America
IN: American Anthropologist 49:1-24

The author, a well-known chemist, argues that logic and the statistics against independent inventions combine with diffusionist evidence to favor the view that a Parent American Culture (in Peru) developed very early, then seeded the Old World neolithic via transpacific commerce that ceased not later than 3000 B.C.

L-205B

AUTHOR: Lewthwaite, Gordon R.
DATE: 1966
TITLE: Tupaia's Map: The Horizons of a Polynesian Geographer
IN: Yearbook of the Association of Pacific Coast Geographers 28:41-53

Tupaia, a Tahitian navigator quizzed by the first European explorers of eastern Polynesia, revealed knowledge of distant islands and how to get to them. Did he know about them as a result of voyages by him and his colleagues? Varied maps produced by European cartographers using his information have confused the question of what was actually in his head, but evidently he did have knowledge of groups from the Marquesas to western Polynesia.

L-206

AUTHOR: Lewthwaite, Gordon R.
DATE: 1967
TITLE: Geographical Knowledge of Pacific Peoples
IN: The Pacific Basin: A History of Its Geographical Exploration, edited by H. R. Friis, American Geographical Society Collection Special Publication 38 (New York), 57-86

[Reviewed by Andrew Sharp, *Journal of the Polynesian Society* 76 (1967): 516, with rejoinder from Lewthwaite, and reply from Sharp, in 77 (1968): 300-306]

Various hints and evidences leave still unresolved the question of deliberate two-way voyaging within Polynesia, but it seems possible. Trips between eastern Polynesian islands and South America also seem possible. Despite confusion, "the virtually unanimous agreement [is] that Polynesians and American Indians had in fact been in contact."

L-206B

AUTHOR: Lewthwaite, Gordon R.
DATE: 1970
TITLE: The Puzzle of Tupaia's Map
IN: New Zealand Geographer 26:1-19

A slightly shortened version of L-205B.

L-207

AUTHOR: Li Chi
DATE: 1956
TITLE: Diverse Backgrounds of the Decorative Art of the Yin Dynasty
IN: Proceedings of the Fourth Far Eastern Prehistory, and of the Anthropology Division of the Eighth Pacific Science, Congresses Combined (Quezón City, Philippines, 1953), 1/1:179-194

Northwest Coast art parallels with early China.

L-208

AUTHOR: Li Chi
DATE: 1957
TITLE: The Beginnings of Chinese Civilization
IMPRINT: University of Washington Press: Seattle

Pages 29-32: Suggests a relationship between art of early China and the Northwest Coast.

L-209

AUTHOR: Li Hui-lin
DATE: 1961
TITLE: Mu-lan-p'i: A Case for Pre-Columbian Transatlantic Travel by Arab Ships
IN: Harvard Journal of Asiatic Studies 23:114-126

Same as H-482; author's name varies.

L-211

AUTHOR: Liapunova, R. G.
DATE: 1987
TITLE: Raven in the Folklore and Mythology of the Aleuts
IN: Soviet Anthropology and Archaeology 26/1:3-20 [Translated from "Voron v vol'klore i mifologii aleutov," *Fol'klor i etnografiia*, edited by B. N. Putilov (Nauka: Leningrad, 1984), 23-34]

Retraces scholarship on the two-continental distribution of the Raven cycle, including the Russian-language studies, but without settling much except that the cycle is old.

L-212

AUTHOR: Liestol, Aslak
DATE: 1968
TITLE: Cryptograms in Runic Carvings; A Critical Analysis
IN: Bulletin of Minnesota History 41:34-42

A critique of Mongé and Landsverk on runic cryptograms. Many details significant to their argument do not appear on the original inscriptions but only on the reproductions they have used. Points out many calculational, logical, and linguistic errors in their treatment. They have no evident qualifications in crucial areas necessary for such a study, and their book does not contain a single valid contribution.

L-214

AUTHOR: Lighthall, W. D.
DATE: 1933
TITLE: The Origin of the Maya Civilization: Can China Contribute to Its Solution?
IN: Transactions of the Royal Society of Canada 2/27:47-55

"Today . . . the Pacific is more and more admitted to be a source" of American civilization. Summarizes main lines of the diffusionist argument for transpacific influences as an introduction to the paper by Kiang Kang-hu [K-074]. Mentions that Barbeau saw similarities of Northwest Coast music to Chinese [compare B-047].

L-214B

AUTHOR: Liller, William
DATE: 1990
TITLE: Anciens observatoires célestes à l'Ile de Pâques [Ancient Celestial Observatories on Easter Island]
IN: Kadath: Chroniques des civilisations disparues 73:4-11 (Brussels)

An astronomer reports on archaeoastronomical discoveries on the island by Ferdon, himself, and others. The ahu Huri a Urenga gives "irrefutable evidence of having been specifically planned as a solar observatory like Stonehenge, the Caracol of the Mayas, and the Sun Temple of the Andes." No specific diffusionary hypothesis is offered.

L-215

AUTHOR: Lindblom, Gerhard
DATE: 1927
TITLE: The Use of Stilts Especially in Africa and America
IMPRINT: Smärre Meddelanden 3 (Riksmuseets Etnografiska Avdelning: Stockholm)

Joint occurrence of stilts and masks indicates to him a predominantly ritualistic significance for stilts. This is true of both Africa and pre-Columbian Yucatan among other places. Distribution in Europe and Asia is also given. He considers the hypothesis tempting that American and Oceanian stilts go back to a common origin.

L-216

AUTHOR: Lindblom, Gerhard
DATE: 1928
TITLE: Further Notes on the Use of Stilts
IMPRINT: Smärre Meddelanden 6 (Riksmuseets Etnografiska Avdelning: Stockholm)

Additional ethnographic cases are noted. See L-215.

L-217

AUTHOR: Lindblom, Gerhard
DATE: 1939
TITLE: Der Lasso in Africa: Einige ethnographischkulturgeschichtliche Notizen [The Lasso in Africa: Some Ethnographic/Culture Historical Notes]
IN: Kultur und Rasse, Festschrift Otto Reche, edited by Michael Hesch and Günther Spannaus (J. F. Lehmanns Verlag: Munich), 386-393

Includes data on the lasso in America and Oceania.

L-218

AUTHOR: Lindblom, Gerhard
DATE: 1940
TITLE: Thread-crosses Particularly in South America and Africa
IN: Ethnos 5:89-111

Illustrates and discusses museum pieces of "straw crowns" or "thread crosses" or specimens in the literature representing much of the world. Their significance is not clear, aside from being "ornaments" but seems originally to have involved fertility magic and protective magic. In South America the Brazilian instances he supposes originated in (diffused from) the Andean high cultures. Oceania and Southeast Asia derive from Indochina, Tibet, and Mongolia. He makes no statement about a connection between those two continental areas, nor Africa, but ends by posing the question whether the device sprang from a single origin point. He admits he has no definite answer but grants that the distribution suggests the affirmative. [Compare F-161.]

L-219

AUTHOR: Lindblom, Gerhard
DATE: 1942
TITLE: Vessels with Star-shaped Lids
IN: Ethnos 1:55

Compares containers with star-shaped lids from South America and China.

L-220

AUTHOR: Lindblom, Gerhard
DATE: 1949
TITLE: The One-leg Resting Position (Nilotenstellung) in Africa and Elsewhere
IMPRINT: Smärre Meddelanden 22 (Riksmuseets Etnografiska Avdelning: Stockholm)

Including South America.

L-221

AUTHOR: Lindemann, Hannes, edited by Jozefa Stuart
DATE: 1957a
TITLE: Alone at Sea
IMPRINT: Random House: New York [In German, *Allein über den Ozean; ein Arzt*, Einbaum und Faltboot, (H. Scheffler: Frankfurt, 1957). A skeletal version of the second part in English, *Life* 43/4:92-108. Reprinted in *Great Voyages in Small Boats: Solo Transatlantic*, John deGraff (Clinton Corners: New York, 1982)]

Sails a Liberian dugout canoe from the Canaries to the Antilles alone, then repeats the course in a folding boat of rubberized canvas. Both were fraught with difficulty, but more mental than physical. Regarding non-sailors' view of "dangers," he and sailing friends agree, "It takes a damn fool to sink a boat on the high seas."

L-223

AUTHOR: Lindemann, Hannes
DATE: 1961
TITLE: Ein Mann, ein Boot, zwei Kontinente; zum dritten Mal auf grosser Fahrt [A Man, a Boat, Two Continents; for the Third Time on a Great Voyage]
IMPRINT: Delius: Klasing

Yet again from Africa to the West Indies alone. [See L-221.]

L-224

AUTHOR: Linderman, Frank B.
DATE: 1931
TITLE: Old Man Coyote (Crow)
IMPRINT: John Day: New York

All the Indian tribes of the northwestern plains have legends of blue-eyed and bearded makers of stone arrow points and medicine wheels. [Implies Vikings.]

L-225B

AUTHOR: Lindsay, Charles
DATE: 1977
TITLE: Was l'Anse aux Meadows a Norse Outpost?

IN: Canadian Geographical Journal 94/1:36-43 (Ottawa)

A neutral Canadian archaeologist neatly describes the site and the claims made for it. While physically it is "not unlike" the saga description for Leif's place, the similarities are not sufficient to permit a positive identification. That Leif was here is "not proven," although surely some Norse were here sometime.

L-226

AUTHOR: Ling Man-Li (Mary)
DATE: 1960
TITLE: Bark-cloth in Taiwan and the Circum-Pacific Area
IN: Bulletin of the Institute of Ethnology, Academia Sinica 9:355-360 (Taipei) [Reprinted in *Bark-cloth, Impressed Pottery and the Inventions of Paper and Printing*, edited by Ling Shun-Shêng, Monograph 3, Institute of Ethnology (Academia Sinica: Nankang, Taiwan, 1963)]

English summary of a preceding article in Chinese.

After presenting data gathered from a survivor of the Ami tribe who recalled bark-cloth manufacture, the author makes comparisons. Among various aboriginal Formosan dialects "tap" or "kap" is a common prefix to terms related to cloth; compare Polynesian "tapa" for bark cloth. Bark-cloth was made from Madagascar and East Africa to Sakhalin and Korea on the north and in Middle and South America. According to the documents, ancient Taiwan's inhabitants had a highly developed method of making bark-cloth, including parallel-groove beaters, felting, stamping, and the use of stencil and designed tablets, resembling the products of Polynesia and Indonesia. [Compare T-106.]

L-227

AUTHOR: Ling Man-li (Mary)
DATE: 1961
TITLE: Musical Instruments of the Ami Tribe
IN: Bulletin of the Institute of Ethnology, Academia Sinica 11:217-220 (Taipei)

English summary of a preceding article in Chinese.

Classifies and describes four categories of instruments used among this aboriginal Formosan group. Four instruments—the nose flute, musical bow, mouth harp, and wooden drum—are found throughout the Pacific area. The aboriginal bronze bells have parallels in round bronze bells with spiral designs from Laos. "There are round bronze bells in the shape of human face found in existence in South America" (citing I-109). Local bronze [*sic*] dog's teeth anklets of Hawaii are instruments of the same type but merely of different materials (citing R-127). In addition, the method of the Ami in fastening the jingle bells or rattles completely resembles that practiced by the Indian tribes of South America.

L-228

AUTHOR: Ling Shun-Shêng
DATE: 1956a
TITLE: Formosan Sea-going Raft and Its Origin in Ancient China
IN: Bulletin of the Institute of Ethnology, Academia Sinica 1:25-54 (Taipei)

Translation of a preceding article in Chinese.

New proposals and evidence about transpacific voyaging and diffusion in recent years should have persuaded anyone that such influence passed from Asia to the New World. Continuing opponents are not well informed, especially about the ability to cross the ocean.

The first part of this study is based on field work in five port areas on Taiwan done in 1955-1956. Raft users are fishermen, who also use their rafts for commerce. They speak a South Fukien dialect and their ancestors came to Taiwan about 300 years ago. He does not discuss river-lake rafts, which are fairly casual. In 1955 almost 14,000 raft boats were in use in Formosa. Those for coastal travel are paddled only; those for sea use have sails. A full description is given of the manufacture of the sea-going bamboo raft and all its appurtenances (including vertical center boards for stabilizing, as well as a helming paddle), and techniques of sailing. (Each craft usually uses a two-man crew and may have a bamboo platform for quarters.) [On Vietnamese rafts, generally of the same form as the Formosan ones, see C-249.]

He also briefly surveys the literature on rafts off Peru. "The author has studied the terminology for rafts in China and is greatly surprised at the similarity of the facts he meets here with what he learned about the same subject for America and Oceania." He notes use of the Korean term *palson* for fishing rafts, similar to balsa. Basically he supposes that the major terms for rafts as well as boats in Oceania and Peru originated from the large vocabulary of Chinese terms for vessels. As early as the 5th century B.C. in coastal China raft communication was ordinary, by the 1st century B.C. rafts were out on the open sea, and he gives citations in Chinese records on some sort of raft use dating perhaps as early as the 33rd century B.C.

L-229

AUTHOR: Ling Shun-Shêng
DATE: 1956b
TITLE: Human Figures with Protruding Tongue Found in the T'aitung Prefecture, Formosa, and Their Affinities Found in Other Pacific Areas [Summary]
IN: Bulletin of the Institute of Ethnology, Academia Sinica 2:150-152 (Taipei)

English summary of a preceding article in Chinese.

A carved human figure with protruding tongue was recently discovered in the Puyuma tribe of aborigines on Formosa, where such figures are believed to represent ancestors. Similar figures (illustrated) are known from Maori, New Zealand and the Haida Indians of British Columbia. Also shown is a Mexican earth goddess with a protruding tongue ("after Wingert," but without citation).

L-230

AUTHOR: Ling Shun-Shêng
DATE: 1956c
TITLE: Patu Found in Taiwan and Other East Asiatic Regions and Its Parallels in Oceania and America
IN: Department of Archaeology and Anthropology, Bulletin 71 (Taipei, Taiwan), 82-104

The writer shows that the patu form of club of Oceania and America also occurs in Taiwan and mainland Asia and suggests possible routes of diffusion.

L-231

AUTHOR: Ling Shun-Shêng
DATE: 1957
TITLE: Dog Sacrifice in Ancient China and the Pacific Area
IN: Bulletin of the Institute of Ethnology, Academia Sinica 3:37-40 (Taipei)

English summary of an article in Chinese that precedes.

Dog sacrifice is archaeologically old in China and is also found in Southeast Asia (including Malaysia and Assam), Northeast Asia (Tungus, Chukchee, Koryak), and among the Eskimo, Haida, Iowa and Sac, Iroquois, Maya, and rarely in South America, as well as Polynesia (with a few traces in Melanesia). In China and the circumpacific area dogs were sacrificed to heaven, earth, sun, moon, stars, mountains, rivers, wind, rain, ancestors, etc., by burning, dismembering, burying, stabbing, beheading, drowning, and gutting.

He does not believe that the "striking similarities of the dog-sacrifice complexes" mentioned can be explained as accidental or superficial parallels. Notably the Iroquois White Dog Sacrifice was (1) offered to Heaven at New Year, (2) had to be entirely white, then was elaborately ornamented, (3) was burnt and the ashes cast away. These identical features were ancient Chinese.

L-232

AUTHOR: Ling Shun-Shêng
DATE: 1957b
TITLE: Kava-drinking in China and East Asia
IN: Bulletin of the Institute of Ethnology, Academia Sinica 4:25-30 (Taipei)

English summary of a preceding article in Chinese. See L-233.

L-233

AUTHOR: Ling Shun-Shêng
DATE: 1958a
TITLE: A Comparative Study of Kava-drinking in the Pacific Regions [Summary]
IN: Bulletin of the Institute of Ethnology, Academia Sinica 5:77-86 (Taipei)

English summary of a preceding article written in Chjinese.

In the previous issue (L-232) the author described kava-drinking (="wine-making and wine-chewing") in China, Formosa, Sakhalin, Japan, the Ryukyus, and Cambodia. Here he describes and sketches the distribution of kava-drinking in the Pacific region. He follows Cooper on preparation of these beverages by mastication of starchy seeds in Central and South America. Gives names for kava drink in many languages, classifying them into three groups, two of which are represented in America. Most of the names are related to words for chewing. Describes who makes the drink and what paraphernalia are involved.

Origin legends are given for Asia and Oceania, but he could find none for America. This is a single cultural complex. More of these elements are shared between East Asia and Central and South America than between any other regions. For example, chenopodium or pigweed was the first source of wine in South America (citing J-408, page 263), while chenopodium remains the raw material to make wine in Formosa. In 1643 H. Brouwer suggested that Polynesian kava-drinking originated in Chile. Moerenhout, Friederici, and Brown have stressed the affiliation of kava with South American chicha. Handy (1929) [compare H-063] considered the Polynesian kava ceremony to be adapted from Buddhist ceremonial tea drinking, while Piddington (1939) thought it resembled the soma rite of Vedic religion. Chinese wine-chewing is documented 3000 years ago, hence the author takes North China as its origin point, from which it spread eastward [and southward].

L-234

AUTHOR: Ling Shun-Shêng
DATE: 1958b
TITLE: Ancestor Temple and Earth Altar among the Formosan Aborigines
IN: Bulletin of the Institute of Ethnology, Academia Sinica 6:47-57 (Taipei)

English summary of a preceding article in Chinese.

Points out resemblances between Formosan ancestral temples and earth altars and those of Polynesia. Some ancestral images engraved on wooden or stone posts appear to be related to totem poles on the Northwest Coast of North America, and some seem related to human statues on Easter Island and at Tiahuanaco, Bolivia. The earth altar, stepped pyramid platform, stone pillars (menhir-like) and ceremonial altar (dolmen-like) testify to the presence in Formosa even today of what Heine-Geldern called "an earlier megalithic culture" in Southeast Asia. There is a strong possibility that this megalithic culture came from the Chinese mainland rather than Southeast Asia. Relates the temple and altar complex/cult ultimately to Mesopotamia, citing Quaritch Wales (1953).

L-237

AUTHOR: Ling Shun-Shêng
DATE: 1960
TITLE: Certain Jade and Stone Weapons of Ancient China and Their Affinities in the Pacific
IN: Bulletin of the Institute of Ethnology, Academia Sinica 10:27-40 (Taipei)

Translation of a preceding article in Chinese.

Illustrates and discusses a series of weapons (or "sceptres") widespread in and around the Pacific which he demonstrates originated in China. They include the patu club of New Zealand and eastern Polynesia (as well as Melanesia and Indonesia). Examples are illustrated from "the state of Washington" (no citation) and Argentina (citing I-054).

L-238

AUTHOR: Ling Shun-Shêng
DATE: 1961
TITLE: Bark-cloth Culture and the Invention of Paper-making in Ancient China
IN: Bulletin of the Institute of Ethnology, Academia Sinica 11:29-50 (Taipei)

Slightly abridged version of a paper written in Chinese which precedes. The abridgement was presented at the Tenth Pacific Science Congress, 1961, Honolulu.

Long before the beginning of our era, Chinese were using bark cloth (and also a silk paper) not only for clothing but to write on. The invention of true paper dating to A.D. 105 came out of the bark cloth foundation. Of course Maya and Mexican peoples used bark cloth as a writing or painting base (Dresden Codex illustrated). Also cites Steward [S-448] to the effect that probably bark cloth was the ancestor of the paper used by aboriginal Mexicans. And bark-cloth design block printing probably was ancestral to Chinese printing.

L-239

AUTHOR: Ling Shun-Shêng
DATE: 1962
TITLE: Stone Bark-cloth Beaters in South China, Southeast Asia, and Central America
IN: Bulletin of the Institute of Ethnology, Academia Sinica 13:195-212 (Taipei)

Bark-cloth culture spread from its East and South Asian source and finally reached Central and South America.

L-240

AUTHOR: Ling Shun-Shêng, editor
DATE: 1963a
TITLE: Bark-cloth, Impressed Pottery, and the Inventions of Paper and Printing
IMPRINT: Institute of Ethnology Monograph 3 (Academia Sinica: Nankang, Taiwan)

See L-238.

L-241

AUTHOR: Ling Shun-Shêng
DATE: 1963b
TITLE: The Sacred Enclosures and Stepped Pyramidal Platforms of Peiping
IN: Bulletin of the Institute of

Ethnology, Academia Sinica 16:1-82 (Taipei)

See L-244.

L-242

AUTHOR: Ling Shun-Shêng
DATE: 1964a
TITLE: The Origin of the Shê in Ancient China
IN: Bulletin of the Institute of Ethnology, Academia Sinica 17:36-44 (Taipei)

English summary of a preceding article in Chinese.

Holy sacrificial sites—*shê*—were used in China for millennia. Elements included an earthen pyramid, or at least a stela, a tree or a dense wood. He connects the complex with "menhirs and dolmens" of eastern China and monoliths and stone pyramids of Southeast Asia. It may have stemmed from the ziggurat of Mesopotamia, or it may go back to an early neolithic origin. Analogues are found in Polynesia, Melanesia and the Americas.

L-243

AUTHOR: Ling Shun-Shêng
DATE: 1964b
TITLE: The Sacred Places of the Chin and Han Periods
IN: Bulletin of the Institute of Ethnology, Academia Sinica 18:113-135 (Taipei)

Seven-page English abridgement of an article written in Chinese. Several traditional types of religious structures are discussed from the historical literature. Their apparently varied names turn out to be pronounced essentially identically and to derive from the name of the Mesopotamia *ziggurat*. The culture of the ziggurat was introduced into China in prehistorical ages at different times and places resulting in the differing pronunciations but with core meaning or functions shared. [In L-248 he carries this form to America.]

L-244

AUTHOR: Ling Shun-Shêng
DATE: 1965
TITLE: A Comparative Study of the Ancient Chinese Feng-Shan and the Ziggurats of Mesopotamia
IN: Bulletin of the Institute of Ethnology, Academia Sinica 19:39-51 (Taipei)

A long summary in English of an article written in Chinese which it follows. He believes that cultural interflow between Mesopotamia and China dates far back and continued long: beginning the 27th century B.C., then in the 10th century B.C., 5th century B.C., and 3rd-2nd centuries B.C. He describes several types of Chinese structures used for sacrifices and as tombs or royal mausoleums and compares them with Mesopotamian platforms. [In L-248 he carries these to America.]

L-246

AUTHOR: Ling Shun-Shêng
DATE: 1967
TITLE: The Pyramids of Egypt and the Royal Tombs of Ancient China
IN: Bulletin of the Institute of Ethnology, Academia Sinica 24:187-215 (Taipei)

From a two-page English summary with many illustrations. Follows the evolution of the Egyptian pyramids (after Edwards). It developed originally from the 'mound,' through the 'tan' (ziggurat), then to its final form. Chinese royal tombs went through the same stages. Such tombs are common in China; for example in Chi An county, Antung province, where the ancient capital of Korea was located, no less than 10,000 ancient tombs remain today and all are pyramidal structures of seven layers. The earth tombs are mostly built with a square base. [In L-248 he carries the form to America.]

L-247

AUTHOR: Ling Shun-Shêng

DATE: 1968a

TITLE: Outrigger Canoes in Ancient China and the Indo-Pacific Oceans

IN: Bulletin of the Institute of Ethnology, Academia Sinica 26 (Taipei)

See L-249.

L-248

AUTHOR: Ling Shun-Shêng

DATE: 1968b

TITLE: The Mound Cultures of East China and of South-eastern North America

IMPRINT: Monograph 15, Institute of Ethnology (Academia Sinica: Taipei, Taiwan)

(From the 11-page English summary). A competent summary of the literature on burial and temple mounds in the Eastern United States and similar structures in China is followed by loose comparisons. Many similarities persuade him that the American (including Mexican and Peruvian) structures derive, several millennia removed, from the Chinese. "We should understand that the route by land through Siberia and Alaska had not been the only way for travel and traffic between Asia and America during the old days. Thus, we should first study the rafts, outriggers, double canoes, and deck canoes of the coastal areas of East China, for since times immemorial, such vessels had been used for travels along the coast and voyages over the ocean. Therefore, instead of obstructing the traffic and travel, the Pacific Ocean had, in fact, served as a thoroughfare between Asia and America during ancient times."

L-249

AUTHOR: Ling Shun-Shêng

DATE: 1969

TITLE: The Double Canoe and Decked Canoe in Ancient China and Oceania

IN: Bulletin of the Institute of Ethnology, Academia Sinica 28 (Taipei)

(English summary) A continuation of L-247. There were anciently four types of watercraft for sea travel in the Pacific and Indian Oceans: the raft, the outrigger canoe, the double canoe, and the deck canoe. With their help Austronesian people emigrated throughout the islands as far as the coast of Africa and to South America. It may be induced that the rafts possibly originated in China, traditionally from the 33rd century B.C. In the 27th century the raft was converted into a boat. A postscript describes the Yi and Yueh (Austronesian) peoples of south China who were heavily oriented to boats.

L-250

AUTHOR: Ling Shun-Shêng [English translation here uses: Shun-Sheng Ling]

DATE: 1970

TITLE: A Study of the Raft, Outrigger Canoe, Double Canoe, and Decked Canoe of Ancient China, the Pacific Ocean and the Indian Ocean

IMPRINT: Monograph 16, Institute of Ethnology (Academia Sinica: Taipei)
[Portions published earlier in *Bulletin of the Institute of Ethnology, Academia Sinica*, 1 (1956), 26 (1968), and 28 (1969)]

Following an Introduction, this work incorporates as chapters various previous publications.

Introduction: He studied with Paul Rivet in Paris in 1927 and was heavily influenced. To date 21 specimens of Oceanic patu-patu or mere stone clubs have been discovered in North and South America; these are similar to the kuei or hu (jade tablet or sceptre) of China.

Chapter 1: "A Comparative Study of the Watercraft of Ancient China and South America." There have been contacts by water since very early days; the sequence of appearance of vessels was rafts, outrigger canoes, double-deck canoes, and junks. "These watercraft had . . . connected the Old World, the New World and Oceania together as one big area." Mentions increasing concern by Chinese scholars with the question, notably monographs (only in Chinese) by Ta Chien-san, Fa Hsien's Discovery of America, published March 1969, and Wei Chu-hsien, Discovery of America by Chinese, in October 1969 [see W-075].

Chapter 2 (abridgement): "Formosan Sea-going Raft and its Origin in Ancient China." All seven types of watercraft mentioned by Edwards [E-016] as present on the Pacific coast of South America are manifested in Chinese materials, and three other Chinese types were known in the Pacific Ocean as well (outrigger, double canoe, and deck canoe). "Although we dare not say that all South American watercraft were originated from ancient China, yet the distinct similarities between the watercraft of the aboriginal people of South America and the sea-going vessels of ancient China really deserve much of our attention." Characteristics and distribution of the first seven are treated. (Illustrated.)

Chapter 3 (complete translation): Construction and operation of Formosan sea-going rafts is followed by comparison of the rafts of Peru and Formosa ("derived from a common origin") and then names of vessels ("the term balsa in South America and vaka and paepae in Oceania originated very probably from China"). A final section is on the origin of the raft in China and its use as a seafaring vessel in the pre-Christian era. (Illustrated.)

Chapter 4 (summary): "Outrigger Canoes in Ancient China and the Indo-Pacific Ocean." The outrigger canoes of China anciently were probably the same as the outrigger canoes sailing over today's Indian and Pacific Oceans. (Illustrated.)

Chapter 5 (summary): "The Double Canoes of Ancient China and the Pacific Area." Compares documents about Chinese double canoes with what is known from Oceania on that form. (Illustrated.)

Chapter 6 (summary): "The Deck Canoes of Ancient China and the Oceanian Area." All forms and styles of decked canoes. (Illustrated.)

Chapter 7 (summary): "The Origin of the Junk and Sampan." Includes a chronological sequence of the stages of development of Chinese watercraft, based on records in ancient Chinese writings, from 33rd-century B.C. rafts to the Lou Chuan fleet of deck canoes of 113 B.C.

Chapter 8 (summary): "The Yi and Yueh People." Infers that the Yi and Mo people originally resided in the coastal areas of ancient China and after inventing watercraft gradually moved to various Pacific islands. In the early days the raft of the Yi people was called *vaka* and that of the Yueh was *paepae*. These later became the general names in use in Oceania for boats.

L-251

AUTHOR: Linné, Sigvald
DATE: 1938a
TITLE: American Roof-apex of Clay
IN: Ethnos 3:18-32

A parallel with Oceania cited by Rivet.

L-252

AUTHOR: Linné, Sigvald
DATE: 1938b
TITLE: Zapotecan Antiquities and the Paulson Collection in the Ethnographical Museum of Sweden
IMPRINT: Bokförlags Aktiebolaget Thule: Stockholm

Page 74: Reports a Mesoamerican process of coating copper or silver objects with gold using a chemical process involving mercury, known also in the Old World.

L-254

AUTHOR: Linné, Sigvald
DATE: 1951
TITLE: A Wheeled Toy from Guerrero, Mexico
IN: Ethnos 16:141-152

Objects to Ekholm's comparison of Mesoamerican wheeled toys to a bronze elephant on a wheeled platform from India. "They are actually no more related to the Mexican dogs than the toy horses on wheeled platforms which are still a lively part of European nurseries. For similarity to imply anything more than just similarity, stronger proofs are necessary." But "no proofs can fully convince a person who does not believe." Suggests some reasons why Mesoamerican wheels never were put to practical use.

L-255

AUTHOR: Linton, Ralph
DATE: 1923
TITLE: The Material Culture of the Marquesas Islands
IN: Memoirs 8/5 (Bernice P. Bishop Museum: Honolulu)

Stiltwalking in Polynesia. [Compare L-215.]

L-256

AUTHOR: Linton, Ralph
DATE: 1926
TITLE: Ethnology of Polynesia and Micronesia
IN: Department of Anthropology Guide, Part 6 (Field Museum of Natural History: Chicago)

Opposes the idea that Peruvians had seagoing rafts.

L-257

AUTHOR: Linton, Ralph
DATE: 1936a
TITLE: The Study of Man: An Introduction
IMPRINT: Appleton-Century: New York

Pages 324-346: "Diffusion." "There is probably no culture today which owes more than 10 percent of its total elements to inventions made by members of its own society." This section includes his much-quoted paragraphs on "100 percent American," poking fun at those who chauvinistically denigrate diffusion. The discussion is perhaps the most cogent statement of the understanding among American anthropologists of the diffusion process as of the 1930s, although it does not address directly the issue of transoceanic diffusion.

Page 379: He notes the uncertainty of ethnological and linguistic reconstructions of agricultural history. Based only on ethnology, that is, ignoring historical data to the contrary, he satirically "finds" that corn can be claimed to have been developed in northern French Equatorial Africa shortly after the establishment of neolithic culture there.

L-258

AUTHOR: Linton, Ralph
DATE: 1936b
TITLE: Error in Anthropology
IN: The Story of Human Error, edited by Joseph Jastrow (D. Appleton-Century: New York and London), 292-321

Pages 310-311 and 317-319: Diffusionists such as Smith and Perry and the Kulturkreis school are held up as examples.

L-260

AUTHOR: Linton, Ralph
DATE: 1944
TITLE: North American Cooking Pots
IN: American Antiquity 9:369-380

All northern North America pottery vessels have only one apparent function, boiling food. The "Woodland" shape pot is found also throughout far northern Eurasia, while the "flower pot" shape finds close parallels in Kamchatka and northern Japan. Resemblances in paste, decoration, and surface finish are so close and numerous that "many of these Old World pots would be accepted unhesitatingly as American Woodland." This pot probably was diffused into North America [implies via Bering Strait].

L-261

AUTHOR: Linton, Ralph
DATE: 1948
TITLE: Review of *Men out of Asia,* by Harold S. Gladwin
IN: American Antiquity 13:331-332

Parallels between the hemispheres offered as evidence of contact are often overrated. For example, the lost wax technique shows many significant differences. Gladwin will find no serious opposition to his theory of Polynesian contacts from any anthropologists who are familiar with the evidence, but there was only "a little two-way traffic." Gladwin's strongest point is that we have no explanation for the rapid rise of high civilizations in America. We should not ignore this problem.

L-262

AUTHOR: Linton, Ralph
DATE: 1954
TITLE: Review of *American Indians in the Pacific,* by Thor Heyerdahl
IN: American Anthropologist 56:122-124

Heyerdahl adduces about all possible material in support of his views and little against them. Another book half the size of this one would be required to deal with his evidence adequately. The most important objection is linguistic, but discussion of technology is one-sided. "It is hard to believe that Peruvian migrants would have failed to introduce the arts of loom weaving and pottery" into Polynesia. He also is loose in comparing stone sculptures, "but it is worth noting that the use of irregularly cut and fitted blocks, characteristic of Andean masonry, is limited to Easter Island."

While the author has not proved his thesis, Linton grants "that a careful and impartial review of the evidence for trans-Pacific contacts during pre-Columbian times is in order." "There may have been two-way traffic." The resemblances between Northwest Coast and Polynesian technology also seem to require explanation; convergence will not serve. Castaways may be involved.

L-263

AUTHOR: Lisker, Rubén
DATE: 1966
TITLE: El origen de los grupos humanos en América: serología y hematología en general de los Ameríndios y sus posibles relaciones trans-pacíficas [The Origin of the Human Groups in America: Serology and Hematology in General of the Amerindians and Their Possible Trans-Pacific Relations]
IN: Proceedings of the 36th International Congress of Americanists (Barcelona and Seville, 1964), 1:43-51

Notes a need for integrated analysis of all the known polymorphic systems, in order to attempt any statements as to origins and relationships of New World populations. "The Amerindians possess more recent ancestors in common with the Polynesians than with any other racial group," citing Mourant.

L-263B

AUTHOR: Lisón Tolosana, Carmelo
DATE: 1971
TITLE: Difusión y evolución: estado de la cuestión en antropología [Diffusion and Evolution: State of the Question in Anthropology]
IN: Anuario de estudios atlánticos 17:67-94 (Madrid/Las Palmas)

Sees both positions part of the general question of "social or cultural change" with some emphasis on neo-evolutionism. On pages 84-85 is an ambitious outline of the potential elements to be considered as part of the problem of cultural contact. Types of contact situations, psychological-cultural mechanisms, operating processes, and results are subdivided in a thoughtful way. For example, under results (of contact) his list includes resistance, new formulation, acceptance, assimilation, incorporation, integration/congruence, adaptation, persistence, and rejection.

L-266

AUTHOR: Lister, Robert H.
DATE: 1941
TITLE: Cerro Oztuma, Guerrero
IN: El México Antiguo 5 (7-10, Junio): 209-219

Describes this Aztec fortified site and lists two reasons why the true arch visible there may be considered Spanish, and three reasons for an Aztec origin. Rebuts H-203 which considers it surely Spanish.

L-267

AUTHORS: Littauer, M. A., and J. H. Crouwel
DATE: 1979
TITLE: Wheeled Vehicles and Ridden Animals in the Ancient Near East
IMPRINT: Brill: Leiden

An outstanding discussion of the development of wheeled vehicles, of concern in relation both to the lack of practical vehicles in America and the occurrence there of wheeled cult vehicles. A number of inobvious points emerge, all of which suggest reasons why practical vehicles went unused in much of the Old World for a long time even after the basic idea was known: suitable harnessing for single draft horses did not develop until the Han Chinese in the third century B.C.; there was "surprising delay" (unexplained) in the use of horses for mounted riders; lack of a horse shoe apparently seriously hindered use of the animals until it was invented; only quite late did suitable articulation of the front axle with chassis develop which would allow effective turning of a four-wheeled vehicle.

Throughout, substantial information is given about cult uses, both of models and of actual vehicles used to carry a corpse to the grave and sometimes to be interred with it. [Compare C-248.]

L-268

AUTHOR: Little, George A.
DATE: 1946
TITLE: Brendan the Navigator
IMPRINT: M. H. Gill: Dublin

Another attempt to identify Brendan's lands in America. Good material on the Irish curragh boat.

L-269

AUTHOR: Little Turtle
DATE: 1985
TITLE: The Fell Trilogy: Synopses and Commentary
IN: NEARA [New England Antiquities Research Association] Journal 19/4:79-95

Presents a total of 40 points to represent the key data and results in Barry Fell's three books [F-037, F-049, F-052]. The author follows with a generally skeptical commentary from his "Native American" point of view. At the end he cites four books "which conflict with Fell's hypothesis." Immediately following (pages 85-90) is J. Louis Bauer, "Index to Barry Fell's Books."

L-270

AUTHOR: Livingstone, Frank B.
DATE: 1969
TITLE: An Analysis of the ABO Blood Group Clines in Europe

IN: American Journal of Physical Anthropology 31:1-10

Supports the idea that ABO groupings are adaptive to environmental conditions [thus not simply usable as evidence of historical relationships].

L-270B

AUTHOR: Livingstone, Frank B.
DATE: 1991
TITLE: On the Origin of Syphilis: An Alternative Hypothesis
IN: Current Anthropology 32:587-590

There is a relative paucity of evidence of treponematosis in Europe prior to the post-Columbian epidemic, although the view that the epidemic evolved from an already present non-venereal ancestor has some adherents. There is a comparable position that it was only in the 16th century that syphilis was recognized as a distinctive disease separate from leprosy. Baker and Armelagos argue that the origin of the outbreak of syphilis in Europe in the 16th century was due to an organism imported from the New World. They further argue that the treponemes were ubiquitous in human populations in both hemispheres but changed in different habitats. Most of the new evidence they present, and particularly that from the New World, implies that adaptation to a venereal mode of transmission has occurred many times in the last 10,000 years, but from an epidemiological standpoint this does not make much sense. The evidence of pathologies on bones could have been caused by other organisms. Epidemics of diseases no longer present but which had pathologies similar to modern treponemes no doubt occurred in the past. Syphilis in Europe was a recent evolution. Its ancestor may have come from the New World, but the tropical regions of the Old World seem a more likely source. While the outbreak of syphilis in Europe coincided with the discovery of America, but at that same time there was also increased contact with tropical Africa—far more contact with Africa—and consequently much more opportunity for a nonvenereal treponeme from Africa to make this adaptation. So the author thinks that syphilis is one of the world's newest diseases and that marked post-Columbian increase in its occurrence in the Americas is evidence of a virulent strain brought from the Old World (i.e., Africa) at the time of Columbus.

L-270C

AUTHOR: Lizardi Ramos, César
DATE: 1957
TITLE: Extraña escultura negroide en unas grutas de Yucatán [A Strange Negroid Sculpture in Some Caves in Yucatan]
IN: Katunob 5/1:22-23 (Greeley, Colorado) [Reprinted from the Mexican newspaper *Excelsior*, March 3, 1965]

Inside Loltun Cave in 1964 a stone statue of an individual with a coarse, negroid physiognomy was found.

L-271B

AUTHOR: Lloyd-Russell, Vincent
DATE: 1938
TITLE: The Serpent as the Prime Symbol of Immortality, Has Its Origin in the Semitic-Sumerian Culture
IMPRINT: Unpublished; Ph. D. dissertation, University of Southern California

Quite good scholarship for the time. Throughout the Near East essentially the same civilization prevailed, at least in regard to cult. This Semitic-Sumerian influence ("snake love") was similar and continuous as shown in the Persian or Elamite sources, through the Zend-Avesta into Vedic texts, and on into China, Tibet, North Borneo, and Ceylon. "The same fundamental features characterize the snake worship in all these culture patterns . . . ," being concerned with immortality, procreation, knowledge and custody of the Waters of Life. Did it reach America also? Yes. He questions whether the orthodox view of exclusively Bering Strait settlement of America holds up. At least the evidence regarding transoceanic contact has not been carefully examined.

Regardless of the route, he claims to demonstrate that "the serpent cult maintains itself across the Pacific in a manner indicating continuity of the source-tradition which at least must go back to an early period." "This serpent cult took possession not only of the Great Mexican cultural pattern but swept over the entire North America area and reveals the same basic ideas in the concept of immortality, procreation, cunning, phallic elements, and custody of the sources of knowledge." "There may be those who would deny the value of any single one of these features but it would certainly be ignoring all evidences to deny the entire complex when it appears continuously." "A generic unity of the human mind, will not, unaided, be able to explain identical symbolic interpretations, nor [will] any theories founded on a Freudian or other thesis, satisfy the demands." Does not discuss the route of this transfer, but one must notice "the persistence of the snake-worship in the island settlements of the Pacific" (even on snakeless Tonga).

The serpent cult of the Inca area would embrace Ecuador, Peru, and Bolivia and the contiguous portions of Colombia, Argentina, and Chile. But archaic patterns also appear scattered over wide areas along the Amazon, the Guianas, the Gran Chaco and Tierra del Fuego." Early Chimu pottery designs "remind one forcibly of Egyptian motifs. Men are disguised as birds and birds as men, in a fashion reminiscent of the representation of the soul of Osiris." "The fanged God with serpents bears a more than close, almost an identical, resemblance with the ancient Babylonian seals" (illustrated). "In another vase of this (Chimu) period, the serpent god is surrounded by sun rays in the manner we have already noted in Cambodia." Further, the Weeping God "is a phallic serpent which is generally associated with signs representing water, as we find it among figures on Chinese neolithic ceramics and in the Codex Cortesianus and among the Zuni." Other parallels are noted.

L-273

AUTHOR: Loayza, Francisco A.
DATE: 1926
TITLE: Manko Kapa, el fundador del imperio de los Incas, fue japonés [Manko Kapa, the Founder of the Empire of the Incas, Was Japanese]
IMPRINT: n. p.: Belem, Brazil

See L-274.

L-274

AUTHOR: Loayza, Francisco A.
DATE: 1948
TITLE: Chinos llegaron antes que Colón; tesis arqueológica, transcendental, sustentada por 150 de los más famosos autores, antiguos y modernos [Chinese Arrived before Columbus; an Archaeological, Transcendental Thesis, Sustained by 150 of the Most Famous Authors, Ancient and Modern]
IMPRINT: D. Miranda: Lima

Pages 37ff.: The divinatory Tai-ki emblem known in China and Japan appears on Peruvian ceramics and at Copan on a stela.

Pages 42-43: Fr. Antonio de la Calancha in 1638 reported finding in 1602 a *huaca* (ruin) at Trujillo, Peru, with a painted wall showing armed horsemen with swords and lances, taken by Loayza to have depicted Chinese. Squier in 1877 reported another Peruvian ruin with stone statues representing similar armed men.

Pages 44-45: Prof. William Niven, as reported in cited newspapers in Mexico, 1921, and in *Journal de la société des americanistes de Paris* 10 (1913): 303, found slabs at Teotihuacan containing Chinese characters (illustrated) which were easily read by the secretary of the Chinese legation, as well as a tomb and statue said to be wholly Chinese in design. The "Mongol type" skeleton in the tomb was said to have borne a necklace of green jade.

Pages 45-48: Sir H. Wheeler, engineer, in 1923 found within an earth mound at Teotihuacan a jade medallion with Chinese letters on one side and a putatively Chinese scene engraved on the other. [Carter, among others, has reproduced this item, shown by Loayza on page 46.]

Pages 49-65: Recognizes that many fake metal objects with Chinese characters on them have been made and passed in Peru, but they are easily distinguished from two silver "idols" from Trujillo illustrated and described here. The first is that, found in 1865, owned by Conde Guaqui, which was presented first at the 1879 ICA in Brussels. The other also came from Trujillo, found in 1872, here illustrated on page 54. Motifs and characters are clearly Chinese. [Compare W-075, pages 19-20.]

Pages 56-59: A bowl discovered by Dr. Olaechea is shown, which seems to have on it "perfect Chinese ideograms."

Pages 67-69: A pre-Incaic mummy is shown, on the headdress of which are four Chinese characters, illustrated.

Pages 70-94: Other Chinese finds from Peru are discussed and shown.

Page 95ff.: Chinese arrived before the Inca era; the latter proscribed the use of writing, according to Montesinos.

Pages 104-154: Gives well over 100 Peruvian toponyms with Chinese equivalents. The name "Peru" comes from Chinese.

Page 155ff.: Customs, beliefs, and material objects further link Peru with China. Shared folktales are given.

Page 160ff.: The custom of placing a piece of silver in the mouth of a corpse; shown are sketches of "Chinese coins" found in the mouths of Inca mummies.

Page 169ff.: The quipu was invented in China over 5000 years ago; stone musical instruments (gongs) were also shared. Jade. Balance scales. An odd method of slaughtering animals. Dragons. Messages sent by relays of fire signals.

Page 191ff.: Stone guardian figures at entrances, "the dogs of Fo"; superstitions about eclipses, maleficent influence of the fox, criminals made eunuchs/guards, system of cruel punishments, sacrifices and offerings, the festival of virility, and the building of great defensive walls many miles long.

Large bibliography on Fu-sang.

L-275

AUTHOR: Loberg, Leif
DATE: 1962
TITLE: Nørrone Amerikaferders utstrekning [The Extent of the Travels of the Norse Discoverers of America]
IN: Historisk Tidsskrift 41:233-252

Describes lands beyond Greenland explored by the Norse according to the sagas, placing these no farther than Newfoundland, extending from southern Baffin Island to Grand Miquelon. In the 13th and 14th centuries other expeditions seem to have reached Jones Sound, Kane Basin, and Robeson Channel. Discusses the confusion about the latitude observations.

L-276

AUTHOR: Lobscheid, William
DATE: 1864
TITLE: Grammar of the Chinese Language [in two parts]
IMPRINT: n.p.: Hong Kong [Reprinted 1904, 2 vols. in 1, at the office of the "Daily Press": Hong Kong]

The introduction cites many parallels between the civilizations of Mexico and China.

L-277

AUTHOR: Lobscheid, William
DATE: 1872

TITLE: Evidence of the Affinity of the Polynesians and American Indians with the Chinese and Other Races of Asia, Derived from the Languages, Legends and History of Those Races
IMPRINT: De Souza: Hong Kong

See L-276.

L-278
AUTHOR: Locke, L. Leland
DATE: 1912
TITLE: The Ancient Quipu, a Peruvian Knot Record
IN: American Anthropologist 14:325-332

Cites several sources on China documenting that knot records are said to have preceded the knowledge of writing, but he makes no statement relating Chinese to Peruvian knotted records. Overall considers the quipu poor evidence for transoceanic diffusion since it seems to occur "in all lands."

L-279
AUTHOR: Locke, L. Leland
DATE: 1923
TITLE: The Ancient Quipu or Peruvian Knot Record
IMPRINT: American Museum of Natural History: New York

Surveys and synthesizes the highly varied literature from the time of European discovery up to the work of modern ethnographers. Sources cited mention quipu-like devices in China, Egypt, Oregon, Mexico, Polynesia, etc.

L-282
AUTHOR: Lodge, Henry Cabot
DATE: 1874
TITLE: Gravier's Découverte de l'Amérique [Gravier's "Discovery of America"]
IN: North American Review 119:166-182

A devastating critical review of the arguments by a Norse enthusiast [G-197] who favored seeing widespread Norse influence in the western hemisphere.

L-283
AUTHOR: Loeb, Edwin M.
DATE: 1923
TITLE: Blood Sacrifice Complex
IN: Memoir 30, American Anthropological Association (Menasha, Wisconsin) [Reprinted Kraus: New York, 1964]

Blood-letting, circumcision, scarification, tattooing distributions, including Mesoamerica and Eurasia.

L-286
AUTHOR: Loeb, Edwin M.
DATE: 1958
TITLE: The Twin Cult in the Old and the New World
IN: Miscellanea Paul Rivet, Octogenario Dicata, Universidad Nacional Autónoma de México, Publicaciones del Instituto de Historia 1/50, [Proceedings of the 31st International Congress of Americanists (São Paulo, 1954), 1:150-174]

An essay in description and comparison rather than a diffusionist study, still he notes the presence of divine kingship in Peru along with beliefs and customs involving cross-gender twins, both of which may have come across the Pacific.

L-287
AUTHOR: Loewenstein, (Prince) John
DATE: 1958
TITLE: The "Eskimo Ulu" in the Malayan Neolithic
IN: Man 58:37-41

Semi-lunar or quasi-rectangular stone blades pierced with holes come from Malaya, the Neolithic of East Asia, and Indian and Eskimo settlements of the New World. The ultimate origin must be in the Lake Baikal Neolithic.

L-288

AUTHOR: Loewenstein, (Prince) John
DATE: 1959
TITLE: Who Settled First in Polynesia? A New Theory
IN: The Listener 61:711-713 (London)

An inadequately-researched and weakly argued view that Peruvians on rafts probably reached eastern Polynesia, but only after settlers from the west already inhabited there.

L-289

AUTHOR: Loewenstein, (Prince) John
DATE: 1961
TITLE: Rainbow and Serpent
IN: Anthropos 56:31-40

Studies the distribution of the concept that the rainbow represents the body of a great snake. On pages 35-37 cites occurrences in tropical South America. The idea could not have reached there via "the thinly dotted island groups of Polynesia, quite apart from the fact that land snakes do not occur east of Samoa." But the mixture of the notion with Christian and other beliefs in the South American instances indicate that it was introduced by Negroes brought by the slave trade.

L-289B

AUTHOR: Loewenthal, John
DATE: 1919
TITLE: Ein altmexikanisches Gottesurteil [An Ancient Mexican Divine Judgement]
IN: Zeitschrift für vergleichenden Rechtswissenschaft 37

A certain snake ordeal in Mexico had a close parallel in India: the snake was supposed to bite without fail the guilty person.

L-291

AUTHOR: Loewenthal, John
DATE: 1923
TITLE: Isländische Rechtssymbole in Alt-America [Icelandic Legal Symbols in Ancient America]
IN: Zeitschrift für vergleichende Rechtswissenschaft 40:362-370

Legal and other symbols are claimed found among Indians of northeastern North America as a result of Icelandic communication.

L-292

AUTHOR: Loewenthal, John
DATE: 1926
TITLE: Spuren der Isländerfahrten in Nova Scotia [Traces in Nova Scotia of Voyages by the Icelanders]
IN: Mitteilungen der anthropologischen gesellschaft in Wien 56:66-77

Norse influence is seen behind eastern Algonkin motifs such as the wind bird.

L-292B

AUTHOR: Loewenthal, John
DATE: 1929
TITLE: Alteuropäisch-altozeanische Parallelen [Parallels between Ancient Europe and Ancient Oceania]
IN: Mitteilungen der Anthropologischen Gesellschaft in Wien 58:1-8

Methodological. Compares the two areas on several traits: tattooing, fish poisoning, catching fish with a noose, use of sail boat, bull-roarer, outrigger, men's house, and others. [Inasmuch as parallels can be adduced between these two distant areas, they will be considered, by many, to represent clear cases of convergence. Similar convergence, instead of diffusion, could in that case explain parallels of the same order between, say, Oceania and America.]

L-294

AUTHOR: Loffler, L. G.
DATE: 1955
TITLE: Das zeremoniells Ballspiel im Raum Hinterindiens [The Ceremonial Ball Game in Southeast Asia]
IN: Paideuma 6/2:86-91

Comparisons between the Thai/Miao sacred ballgame and that of Mesoamerica leads him to suggest a direct connection.

L-295

AUTHOR: Logan, F. Donald
DATE: 1983
TITLE: The Vikings in History
IMPRINT: Hutchinson: London

Chapter 4, "The Vikings and the New World," is rather better researched than most popularizing books (the author is a historian, but not of this period and area). It handles Brendan, the Viking Map, Kensington, Beardmore, and of course L'Anse aux Meadows in addition to the usual sagas/Vinland material. He considers Fell's readings of inscriptions "intriguing" though yet to be established, but the Parahyba and Bat Creek inscriptions are clever forgeries, because "scholars are now virtually unanimous" to that effect. On the Ingstad site, he hedges a bit about the vegetation, but, as nearly always, he relies on "the scholars" to settle his issues. Still he does not rule out the possibility of Lee's having found Viking material at Ungava Bay nor even that Irish remains could someday be found in North America.

L-296

AUTHORS: Lomax, Alan, and Edsin E. Erickson
DATE: 1968
TITLE: The World Song Style Map
IN: Folk Song Style and Culture, edited by Alan Lomax, American Association for the Advancement of Science Publication 88 (Washington) 75-110

This chapter of the overall report of the Cantometrics Project gives the results of regression analysis of a sample of about 40 songs from each of 56 culture areas in the world coded on 37 style elements. (These are used to define dominant regional cantometric styles, defined as "the framework that the performers and the audiences in a culture agree is suitable for making music.") "Homogeneity mapping" or degree of sharing of style features was computed to demonstrate linkages among the 56 regions and nine areas which they form.

Page 84: South America is linked with North America (other than Plains and Pueblo) and also with Arctic Asia, Proto-Malay, and New Guinea. The authors note that this soft-voiced, subdued, feminine-sounding, polyphonic style of South America and Tribal Oceania [i.e., Proto-Malay and New Guinea] "seems to be an ancient and specialized trans-Pacific model found along the paths that connect the cultures of the Andes with the civilizations of Mexico."

Page 85: The only significant links for North America beyond that continent are with Eastern Brazil and the Mato Grosso (not, incidentally, with Arctic Asia).

Page 87-88: The overall Insular Pacific area is homogeneous with but two areas: Northwest Coast and Eastern Brazil. But Oceania shares notable features specifically with the Old European style, including some which were "almost surely present before contact with European explorers in the eighteenth century." But at the level of specific regions, rather than the overall Oceanic area, seven of the Amerindian areas fall into the top third of the Proto-Malay similarity wave, whereas only one Amerindian area lies in the same range for Western Polynesia. Hence the similarity between the hemispheres here appears comparatively old or basic and not mediated primarily through Polynesia.

Page 92: Africa and the New World have no significant links.

Page 101: "The Australian pattern specifically places that area squarely in both Amerindia and Old High Culture (central Eurasia)." The specific regions with which Australia shows homogeneity are Patagonia and six of the North American regions, but not Arctic Asia.

Page 106: Arctic Asia maps homogeneously with eight American regions, from Eastern Woodland through Mexico and the Caribbean to Eastern Brazil (but not Andes).

L-297

AUTHOR: Lommel, Andreas
DATE: 1962
TITLE: Motiv und Variation in der Kunst des zirkumpazifischen Raumes [Motif and Variation in the Art of the Circum-Pacific Area]
IMPRINT: Staatliches Museum für Völkerkunde: München

The hocker and other motifs are illustrated in Asia, Oceania and America.

L-297B

AUTHOR: Lommel, Andreas
DATE: 1964
TITLE: Zur Deutung von Felsbildern [Toward the Interpretation of Rock Art]
IN: Festschrift für Ad. E. Jensen, edited by Eike Haberland, Meinhard Schuster, and Helmut Straube (Klaus Renner: Munich), 1:353-364

Pages 360-361: An "X-ray" style of representing animals skeletally appears in scattered locations in Eurasia (from Magdalenian on) and Australasia as well as in Alaska, the Southwest and elsewhere in North America, and in Panama, all summarized on the map on page 361.

L-300

AUTHOR: Long, Richard C. E.
DATE: 1948
TITLE: Some Remarks on Maya Arithmetic
IN: Notes on Middle American Archaeology and Ethnology 90:219-223, (Division of Historical Research, Carnegie Institution of Washington: Washington, D.C.)

He agrees with Charles C. Fulton that the Maya system of positional notation is likely to be overstressed, and that it was in the main "rather a sorry thing." Doubtless at first the zero symbol was inserted on the usual Maya principle of filling up blank spaces and without any conception of the potentialities of a positional system. Incidentally, the Peruvian quipu had a decimal notation with a blank space or position equivalent to zero.

In the Old World the Sumerians and Chinese used positional notation, but "it is not clear how far the principle was grasped in either of these cases." [The inclarity of the significance of positional notation in both Old World and New World cases calls into question the significance of the diffusionist argument that both hemispheres "had the concept of zero."]

L-302

AUTHOR: Longacre, Robert E.
DATE: 1961
TITLE: Swadesh's Macro-Mixtecan Hypothesis
IN: International Journal of American Linquistics 21/1:9-29

Methodological and substantive critique of this type of reconstruction [and thus of historical links or their lack, inferred from lexicostatistics].

L-302B

AUTHOR: Longman, Byron

DATE: 1977

TITLE: Who Really Discovered the New World?

IN: The World's Last Mysteries (The Reader's Digest Association, Inc.: Pleasantville, New York), 50-61 [Volume first published 1976 as *Les derniers mystères du monde*]

A generally skeptical popular treatment of possible Phoenician, Norse, and Chinese discoverers reaching America. Includes images of sculptured heads that appear Semitic, African and Asiatic. A section asking "Was Quetzalcoatl a Viking?" depends on Mahieu.

L-302C

AUTHOR: Looser, Gualterio

DATE: 1938

TITLE: Las balsas de cueros de lobos de la costa de Chile [Seal-skin Rafts from the Coast of Chile]

IN: Revista chilena de historia natural 42:232-266 (Santiago)

Describes the form and uses of small rafts sustained by inflated seal-skins. [See L-303.]

L-303

AUTHOR: Looser, Gualterio

DATE: 1960

TITLE: Las balsas de cueros de lobo inflados de la costa de Chile: adiciones [Seal-skin Rafts from the Coast of Chile: Additions]

IN: Revista universitaría 44/45:247-273 (Santiago, Chile)

Adds information gained since 1938 from documents (excerpted at length in an appendix), archaeology, and other colleagues. An archaeological specimen assures that this type of balsa was pre-Columbian. This craft is almost identical to a kind known in China. He grants that there may have been occasional landfalls by Old World vessels but considers American cultures essentially independent. The China-Chile parallel in this case is a convergence. Critical of Ibarra Grasso for uncritical enthusiasm for diffusion. He does not believe the South Pacific was ever a route of importance for primitive peoples. Relies heavily on Merrill's negative judgement about lack of plant relations with the Old World.

L-304

AUTHOR: Lopatin, Ivan A.

DATE: 1940

TITLE: The Extinct and Near-extinct Tribes of Northeastern Asia as Compared with the American Indian

IN: American Antiquity 5/3:202-208

"Old Siberian" tribes (e.g., the Ostyaks and Samoyeds), now nearly extinct, are remnants of a population which was crowded Bering-ward and changed or exterminated first by "New Siberians" (Turks, Mongols) and then by Russians. Those ancestors of the American Indians were already physically and linguistically heterogenous while in Asia.

L-305

AUTHOR: Lopatin, Ivan A.

DATE: 1960

TITLE: Origin of the Native American Steam Bath

IN: American Anthropologist 62:977-993

Prior to the Russian colonization of Siberia, the Scandinavian area and nearby northwestern Russia and Iceland shared the water vapor or sauna bath with no one else in the Old World; apparently the idea developed there in "the Stone Age." However, most of North America, Middle America (with substantial archaeological time depth), and parts of South America also had the practice. He supposes that it was introduced to America by early immigrants from Europe via Iceland. [This directly contradicts the Old World distribution given by Driver and Massey, who are in error, he avers.] In a concluding footnote, he acknowledges that critics have suggested that the South American cases were post-European. He effectively counters that idea.

The distribution of the steam bath in America clearly indicates its northern origin. If the Atlantic Ocean did not intervene, we could state that there is a continuity with northwestern Europe. "If the Norsemen in the 10th century were able to cross the Atlantic Ocean without perhaps the use of the sail, why could their predecessors not have done the same thing from five to ten thousand years earlier?"

L-306

AUTHOR: López, Vicente Fidél
DATE: 1871
TITLE: Les races aryennes du Pérou: leur langue; leur religion; leur histoire [Aryan Races of Peru: Their Language, Their Religion, Their History]
IMPRINT: Librairie A. Franck: Paris; and Chez l'Auteur: Montevideo

Tries to demonstrate that Quechua is an Aryan language and that the ancient Peruvians were descendants of the Greeks or their progenitors, the Pelasgians, who migrated to America where they founded the Incan empire. By the same methods, he supposes it would be possible to demonstrate the Aryan or Semitic origin of all the American languages.

L-307

AUTHOR: López, Vicente Fidél
DATE: 1875
TITLE: Le Quichua est une langue aryenne agglutinante [Quichua Is an Agglutinative Aryan Language]
IN: Proceedings of the 1st International Congress of Americanists (Nancy, 1875), 2:10-12

Non-substantive. See L-306.

L-307B

AUTHOR: Lopez Austin, Alfredo
DATE: 1972
TITLE: El mal aire en el México prehispánico [The "Bad Air" (Complex) in Prehispanic Mexico]
IN: Religión de Mesoamerica, Sociedad Mexicana de Antropología, XII Mesa Rodonda, (México, 1972), 399-406

This theory of disease is shown by reference to the writings of Torquemada, Sahagun, and other chroniclers as well as ethnography to have been prehispanic and to fit completely into the world view of the peoples of central Mexico. [Compare M-387B; the complex has often been assumed to be a Spanish import from the Mediterranean world.]

L-307C

AUTHOR: Lopez Austin, Alfredo
DATE: 1988
TITLE: The Human Body and Ideology: Concepts of the Ancient Nahuas. 2 vols.
IMPRINT: University of Utah Press: Salt Lake City

Vol. I: 270-276: Hot-cold classification and "aires" theory of disease had been developed "independently" in central Mexico and overlaps the Spanish system.

L-310

AUTHOR: López Valdés, Pablo
DATE: 1966
TITLE: La rueda en Mesoamérica [The Wheel in Mesoamerica]
IN: Cuadernos americanos 145/25:137-144 (México)

Reviews Old World and Mesoamerican "wheeled toys." Contexts show that these were ceremonial objects. Elaboration of the complex is shown by the fact that there are three distinct methods for mounting the axles or wheels. Thinks that in Mesoamerica this wheel use has the characteristics of a cultural borrowing rather than an invention.

L-312

AUTHOR: Lorena, Antonio
DATE: 1932
TITLE: Influencia de polinesios y asiáticos en América [Influence of Polynesians and Asiatics on America]
IN: Revista universitaría 9/32:35-48 (Cuzco)

Physical anthropological considerations of presumed contacts.

L-314

AUTHOR: Lothrop, Samuel K.
DATE: 1932
TITLE: Aboriginal Navigation off the West Coast of South America
IN: Journal of the Royal Anthropological Institute of Great Britain and Ireland 62:229-256

On the basis of types of vessels used on the coast of South America, he demonstrates the presence of sails on native craft before European conquest, while rejecting the likelihood of the arrival of Polynesian vessels or their influence. Emphasizes the difficulty of ocean crossing.

L-317

AUTHOR: Lothrop, Samuel K.
DATE: 1948
TITLE: Random Thoughts on "Men Out of Asia"
IN: American Anthropologist 50:568-571

A general argument against Gladwin, strongly critical but weak at times. Lothrop does not think discovery of metals was culturally difficult. "If the house (containing an attractive nugget) burned in a high wind, you would automatically learn that metal could be melted." [Just so!]

L-319

AUTHOR: Lou Wing-Sou, Dennis [Liu Tun-Li]
DATE: 1956
TITLE: Similarities of Rain Worshipping of the Ancient Yuehs in South China and Certain American Indian Tribes
IMPRINT: Unpublished; M.A. thesis, Texas Christian University

This typewritten thesis gives the author's name as "Dennis Wing-sou Lou" which appears to have been his preferred identification while in America as a student. For other names used later by the author, see L-320 and L-326.

"The first effort to establish the possibilities of a[n] early cultural contact between the ancient Yuehs of South China and the American Indian." Much of his material on the Yueh comes from friends and acquaintances living in Formosa and Hong Kong. Emphasizes the difficulty of working with existing Chinese records due to ethnic name changes and obscure references. The American sources he uses are standard but very limited.

The area of the Yueh, south of the Yangtze River, included Hainan Island, Indo-China and the Malay area, but their center was in Szechuan, Yunnan, Kwangtung and Kwangsi provinces—"the South." It was co-occupied by a "Negroid," "Blackish dwarf group." He speculates that they might be related to the Negrito Sakai of the Malay peninsula, while a "Negrito element" was also found in legends all over Formosa. The Yueh were experts on maneuvering boats but did not have knowledge of horses, carts, arrows or bows, for example. The Yueh appear related to the makers of Neolithic pottery in the South China area. The cultural significance of the dragon and serpent are next emphasized. Most of the characteristics of the Mesoamerican serpent are found in the dragon or serpent of the Yueh. Criticizes G. E. Smith's hypothesis that the Mayan Chac derives from Indra and that Babylonian influence on India is behind the origin of the dragon concept; the Chinese dragon pre-dates any such influences. The frog or toad motif in China is compared with American Indian beliefs.

Page 102, 105: "It is very possible that the cultural similarities which the American Indian had with the Yuehs were introduced traits from Asia." Those contacts may have been made by boat by the Yuehs. They built ships up to 100, or perhaps 200, feet in length during the Han period. But other contacts may have occurred around the North Pacific also.

L-320

AUTHOR: Lou Wing-Sou, Dennis [Liu Tun-Li] [also listed as Liu Tzu-Chien; see L-258]
DATE: 1957
TITLE: Rain Worship among the Ancient Chinese and the Nahua and Maya Indians
IN: Bulletin of the Institute of Ethnology, Academia Sinica 4:31-108 (Taipei)

English with a Chinese summary. Essentially the same as L-319.

L-321

AUTHOR: Lou Wing-Sou, Dennis [Liu Tun-Li]
DATE: 1966
TITLE: Meso-American "Mushroom-stones" and Chinese Ancestor Tablets
IN: Proceedings of the 36th International Congress of Americanists (Barcelona and Seville, 1964), 1:91

Summary only. Mesoamerican so-called mushroom stones are derived from ancestral remembrance objects in the form of a phallus that first showed up in the Shang period in China but over time evolved to the form of a gravestone.

L-323

AUTHOR: Lou Wing-Sou, Dennis [Liu Tun-Li]
DATE: 1968
TITLE: Chinese Inscriptions Found in Pre-Columbian Objects
IN: Proceedings of the 37th International Congress of Americanists (Mar del Plata, Argentina, 1966), 4:179-182

Describes one pot from Colima, Mexico, with an apparent Chinese character on it, and a Nazca pot and a Peruvian "idol," both of which have Chinese characters. [On the latter see P-044 and L-274.] Feels that the evidence that these may be authentic is sufficiently strong and interesting that Americanists should locate and examine them for authenticity.

L-325

AUTHOR: Lou Wing-Sou, Dennis [Liu Tun-Li]
DATE: 1970
TITLE: Chinese Cultural Influences in Pre-Columbian America
IN: Chu Hai Hsüeh Pao 3:200ff. (Hong Kong)

Discusses similarity of mushroom-shaped stones found in Mesoamerica, Japan and mainland Asia, concluding that these are not so much testimony to the use of hallucinogenic fungi as images of a phallic nature related to honoring the ancestors.

L-326

AUTHOR: Lou Wing-Sou, Dennis [Liu Tun-Li]
DATE: 1971
TITLE: Introduction
IN: The Discovery of Chinese Inscriptions in America, by Wei Chu-Hsein, vol. 1: China and America: A Study of Ancient

Communication between the Two Lands (privately printed: Hong Kong), 7-13

A carefully-phrased statement putting Wei's contribution into historical context of the diffusion controversy. He is unsatisfied by the independent inventionist viewpoint and asks how and why the American high civilizations arose when and where they did and why their neighbors did not become civilized equally.

In 1954 Lou found at least half a dozen strikingly similar cultural complexes linking ancient Chinese and the American Indians (see especially L-319 and L-320). He discusses mushroom stones briefly and suggests linkage to similar phallic-shaped objects of Shang dynasty date identifiable as ancestor tablets (also found in Japan and Indonesia). He also summarizes data on the Chinese Nine Gods, like those of the Maya. Comments are added on some Chinese characters discovered in the New World and discussed later by Wei. He sees two general periods of influence on America: 1000 B.C. to the Christian era and from then to about the 10th century, the latter dominated by influence from India, Southeast Asia, Indonesia, or Polynesia. Voyaging technology is also discussed.

L-328

AUTHOR: Loukotka, Cestmir
DATE: 1948
TITLE: Sobre la clasificación de las lenguas indígenas de América del Sur [Concerning the Classification of the Native Languages of South America]
IN: Proceedings of the 26th International Congress of Americanists (Seville, 1935), 1:409-415

Page 414: Notes claims that Polynesian languages are related to Quechua, but he considers the matter unsettled. However, he claims to have found "vestiges" of Australian languages in Alakaluf, Puelche, and Araucano-Mapuche of extreme southern South America, though not in Yamana or Yaghan, in support of Rivet's claim of Australian words in the Chon group.

L-329

AUTHOR: Louvot, Ferdinand
DATE: 1882
TITLE: Des voyages réels ou prétendus des juifs, avant Christophe Colomb [On Real or Purported Voyages by Jews, before Christopher Columbus]
IN: Proceedings of the 4th International Congress of Americanists (Madrid, 1881), 1:179-190

Surveys the literature on this topic from the previous three centuries. The resemblances appealed to there, in customs, language, and physical traits, are insufficient to justify a belief that Jews reached America before Columbus.

L-330

AUTHOR: Löve, Áskell
DATE: 1954a
TITLE: Locating Vineland the Good
IMPRINT: Huitième congrès international de botanique, Paris, Rapports et communications parvenus avant le Congrès aux Sections 21 à 27, pages 168-170

On the basis of his interpretation of the plants mentioned in the Norse sagas, he locates Vineland around Cape Cod.

L-331

AUTHOR: Löve, Áskell
DATE: 1954b
TITLE: The Plants of Wineland the Good
IN: Icelandic Canadian 10/2:15-22

An Icelander in Canada as a botany professor looks at the distribution of possible plants described by the Norse sagas with regard to Wineland. Wild rice is the only possible self-sown grain. Vin had to be Vitis Labrasca, a grape not unlike that of northern Europe, the only acceptable one of five North American possibilities. The combined distribution of these plants limits the landing area to near the coast between Maine and Long Island.

L-332

AUTHOR: Lovén, Sven
DATE: 1924
TITLE: Über die Wurzlen der Tainischen Kultur I: Materielle Kultur [On the Roots of Taino Culture I: Material Culture]
IMPRINT: Elanders Boktryckeri Aktiebolag: Göteborg, Sweden

Page 400: Following P. Martyr he notes that turtles are caught in the West Indies by the use of sucking fish, the same as around the Indian Ocean. [See G-245B.]

L-333

AUTHOR: Lowe, Gareth W.
DATE: 1965
TITLE: Desarrollo y función del incensario en Izapa [Development and Function of the Incense Burner at Izapa]
IN: Estudios de cultura maya 5:53-64

Censer bowls were set upon horns projecting up from the edge of incense burners. [Compare M-195.]

L-335

AUTHORS: Lowe, Gareth W., Thomas A. Lee, Jr., and Eduardo Martinez Espinosa
DATE: 1982
TITLE: Izapa: An Introduction to the Ruins and Monuments
IMPRINT: Paper 31, New World Archaeological Foundation, Brigham Young University: Provo, Utah

Pages 271-273: Uses the Canaanite high place and associated symbolism as "understandable parallels" to compare in an unspecified way with temple platforms, sacred precincts, trees, and beliefs about procreation and ancestors at Izapa and elsewhere in Mesoamerica.

L-336

AUTHOR: Löwenthal, John [probably the same author as L-289B to L-292B]
DATE: 1922
TITLE: Das altmexikanische Ritual "tlacacaliliztli" und seine Parallelen in den Vegetationskulten der alten Welt [The Ancient Mexican Ritual "tlacacaliliztli" and Its Parallels to Vegetation Worship in the Old World]
IN: Mitteilungen der Anthropologischen Gesellschaft in Wien 52:1-22

Gives lengthy examples of rituals in the Old World related to Mexico, and other areas of North America involving arrow-sacrifice, the Orpheus theme, the Euridice theme, Attis, Tammuz, etc. He supposes that the vegetation revival cult came into America at the same time as agriculture [implying direct contact].

L-338

AUTHOR: Lowie, Robert H.
DATE: 1908
TITLE: The Test-Theme in North American Mythology
IN: Journal of American Folk-Lore 21:98-148

He examines psychic unity and diffusionist explanations for mythic similarities, then reviews at length an intermediate theory, by Ehrenreich [E-029 and E-030]. Lowie then compares Ehrenreich's solar myth theory and a new rival theory in which the characters are human, against a specific body of data: trial-theme stories in North America. Apart from theory, Lowie presents a valuable resume of North American test-theme tales proper as well as hero tales.

Pages 144-146: "In order to indicate the form assumed by the trial-theme outside of North America, I append a few stories from other geographical areas." These are from the Chukchee, Yukaghir, Koryak, Japan, Mongolia, Finland, Germany, and Samoa.

L-339

AUTHOR: Lowie, Robert H.
DATE: 1912
TITLE: On the Principle of Convergence in Ethnology
IN: Journal of American Folk-Lore 25:24-42

Discusses and critiques Graebner's and Ehrenreich's ("convergent evolution") methodology and theory. In general he faults facile classification by anyone, but comes down hardest on the diffusionists. While "Dr. Graebner's ambitious attempt to trace historical connections between remote areas cannot be dismissed wholesale" on the basis of this critique, neither can independent invention be ruled out.

L-340

AUTHOR: Lowie, Robert H.
DATE: 1917a
TITLE: Review of *Oceania,* by Roland B. Dixon, volume 9 of *The Mythology of All Races*
IN: American Anthropologist 19:86-88

"He might well have gone somewhat farther in the treatment of American parallels. For the benefit of his colleagues it would have been a highly desirable thing to present a systematic enumeration of such similarities, together with their provenience, and to discuss somewhat less summarily than he has done the conclusions that can legitimately be drawn therefrom." [Dixon in D-134 takes umbrage at the review.]

L-341

AUTHOR: Lowie, Robert H.
DATE: 1917b
TITLE: Edward B. Tylor
IN: American Anthropologist 19:262-268

A necrology which credits Tylor's fine critical judgement and his emphasis on cultural borrowing.

Page 265: In Tylor's introduction to the English translation of Ratzel's *History of Mankind,* he goes much farther down the diffusionist road than modern American ethnologists are inclined to follow, while another chapter of the same book "pre-figures in principle the recent hypothesis of a cultural connection between aboriginal America and the Old World," although he was not always consistent.

L-342

AUTHOR: Lowie, Robert H.
DATE: 1918
TITLE: Review of *Oceania,* by Roland B. Dixon, volume 9 of*The Mythology of All Races*
IN: New Republic 13/166:288-289 (New York)

Briefly critical of Dixon's culture contact and migration ideas. [See L-340 and D-134.]

L-343

AUTHOR: Lowie, Robert H.
DATE: 1924a
TITLE: The Origin and Spread of Culture
IN: American Mercury 1:463-465

Assertions with little data about how multiple inventions are expectable vs. the diffusionists' claim of unique or limited inventive ability.

L-344

AUTHOR: Lowie, Robert H.
DATE: 1924b
TITLE: Review of *The Children of the Sun,* by W. J. Perry
IN: American Anthropologist 26:86-90

Perry is ignorant of both ethnological theory and ethnographic fact. "I have rarely encountered a more parochially dogmatic work." After detailed consideration of objections to data and reasoning, the reviewer concludes, the work "represents nothing more than the well-meant but futile efforts of the proverbial iconoclast."

L-345

AUTHOR: Lowie, Robert H.

DATE: 1925

TITLE: On the Historical Connection between Certain Old World and New World Beliefs

IN: Proceedings of the 21st International Congress of Americanists (Part 2, Gothenburg, Sweden, 1924), pages 546-549

New World, then worldwide, distributions of the intrusion and soul-loss theories of disease are used to display in a paradigmatic way how ethnologists of the 1920s dealt with "some of the most basic questions of our science—the convertibility of geographical distribution data into a chronological sequence and the interpretation of observed similarities." He believes that intrusion theory was a Paleolithic notion. Independent invention of soul-loss theory in South America is possible but an unattractive explanation. Will have none of "Perry's strange notion" of an Egyptian origin of these beliefs.

L-346

AUTHOR: Lowie, Robert H.

DATE: 1926

TITLE: Zur Verbreitung der Flutsagen [On the Distribution of the Flood Myth]

IN: Anthropos 21:615-616

North American Earth Diver myths probably are genetically connected to Asiatic ones.

L-347

AUTHOR: Lowie, Robert H.

DATE: 1929

TITLE: Review of *Pots and Pans, the History of Ceramics,* by H. S. Harrison

IN: American Anthropologist 31:504-506

Lowie says he himself "has steadily tended to attach greater weight to the diffusionist argument wherever technological considerations enter." He positively dissents from a statement by Dixon [D-140] about sun-dried clay virtually inviting the discovery of pottery making, observing, rather, that after reading Linne on the techniques of South American ceramics, he has come to regard the invention of ceramics as little short of miraculous. He is quite willing to believe it was invented only once. "If earthenware is so obvious a thing, why was it never produced by the Magdalenians?"

On similar grounds, he cannot accept multiple invention of the bow, favored by Tozzer. And on the subject of domestic beasts, he is obliged to take a view even more extreme than Elliot Smith's, which seems to consider the domestication of animals a very simple thing compared to, say, totemism. Indeed the *concept* [emphasis in original] of a domestic beast may be simple, but "a chasm yawns between a species *conceived* [emphasis in original] as breeding freely under human control and one that actually is brought to the point of so breeding." Da Vinci conceived flying, but it took centuries to make it a reality. "Those who glibly assume that mechanical inventions, domestication of animals, and so forth, may have recurred an indefinite number of times in the history of culture may profitably occupy their leisure moments trying to manufacture earthenware vessels from local clays," etc. [Compare L-317.]

L-348

AUTHOR: Lowie, Robert H.

DATE: 1933

TITLE: Queries

IN: American Anthropologist 35:288-296

A challenge to lazy logic among his contemporaries. How can Boas, for example, attack Elliot Smith for depending on long continued stability (of Egyptian elements), while holding precisely the same view regarding Northwest Coast and Paleo-Siberian mythologies? And why is diffusion always supposed to go from higher culture level to lower when we know that the reverse sometimes happened historically?

L-349

AUTHOR: Lowie, Robert H.
DATE: 1934
TITLE: Religious Ideas and Practices of the Eurasiatic and North American Areas
IN: *Essays Presented to C. G. Seligman,* edited by E. E. Evans-Pritchard, et al. (Kegan Paul, Trench, Trubner: London), 113-143

Parallels in religious expressions among Lapps and Naskapi include rock drawings, shamanism and the bear cult, among others.

L-350

AUTHOR: Lowie, Robert H.
DATE: 1937
TITLE: The History of Ethnological Theory
IMPRINT: Farrar and Rinehart: New York

A highly-opinionated critique of positions and personalities involving the British and German diffusionist schools and discussions thereof. He, not surprisingly, considers the Germans' scholarship "incomparably superior" to the British, although it too was flawed. Lowie's sketch of this matter is not illuminating.

L-351

AUTHOR: Lowie, Robert H.
DATE: 1940
TITLE: American Culture History
IN: American Anthropologist 42:409-428

Page 409: "Kidder is . . . keenly aware of our old archaeological scandal—our inability to confront the Elliot Smith school with anything but faith" so long as there are no antecedent American stages for the high cultures.

Page 411: "It is only very recently that an archaeologist has dared express the belief the Eastern Woodland Ceramics may have an Asiatic and, mirabile dictu, a pre-agricultural, source."

L-352

AUTHOR: Lowie, Robert H.
DATE: 1944
TITLE: Franz Boas (1858-1942)
IN: Journal of American Folklore 57:59-69

This necrology includes a discussion of Boas' treatment of diffusion. After due praise, Lowie is in part critical. Boas neglected form in his writings, often writing obscurely and inconsistently. Furthermore, he neglected to smooth out patent contradictions in his thinking. Early on he had mentioned spirit possession among Northwestern Indians; in later papers he repeatedly emphasized the exclusively Old World distribution of the trait. Also, he reproached British diffusionists with ignoring the fact of the instability of culture, yet he argued from the similarity of Paleo-Asiatic and American myths for extremely ancient contact. And he never clearly handled the age-area problem but left it muddled.

L-353

AUTHOR: Lowie, Robert H.
DATE: 1948
TITLE: Primitive Religion
IMPRINT: Liveright: New York

Pages 356-357: In the light of new cases from South America, he revises his earlier view that soul-loss illness theory was a relatively late intrusion from Asia.

L-354

AUTHOR: Lowie, Robert H.
DATE: 1951
TITLE: Some Problems of Geographical Distribution
IN: Südseestudien: Gedenkschrift zur Erinnerung an Felix Speisen (Museum für Völkerkunde und Schweizerischen Museum für Volkskunde: Basel), 11-26

Brief discussion, with well chosen examples, of the question of transpacific influences on pre-Columbian American Indian cultures.

Page 13: After citing Tylor on patolli and American games, he observes, "The concatenation of details puts the parallels far outside any probability [of independent invention] on which reasonable men could count." Further, while we do not know by what route this feature spread to America, "it is at least equally obscure by what psychological channels two unrelated populations would develop the same complex game."

L-355

AUTHOR: Lubensky, Earl H.
DATE: 1984
TITLE: Emil Orcitirix Forrer 1894-. Biography
IMPRINT: Unpublished; copy in the possession of John L. Sorenson

Compare S-549, for which this Lubensky paper constituted a key source. Beginning on page 18, Lubensky recounts Forrer's encounter with a Latin source which convinced him that America was known anciently to the Mediterranean peoples. He claimed to have deciphered the Mayan hieroglyphic texts and said that America had been discovered at least 12 times (based on Norse, Irish, and Greco-Roman sources). Among the prehistoric movements he identified were the "Oyster-eaters" of 7-4000 B.C., the "Immortalists" around 2700 B.C. (based on a religious concept originated by pharaoh Sesochris in Egypt) which spread worldwide, and the "Megalithics" who were manifest from Stonehenge to Russia and India and on to Easter Island and San Agustin, Colombia. He also saw relations between the languages of the Nahuas and Indo-European. But his three prime "discoveries" were those reported in the Silenus story (involving Tartessus), that in the story of Pytheas of Massilia, and the tale told by Plutarch about a strange foreigner from Carthage whom Forrer dubbed Ultramarinus. Lubensky recaps these three on pages 21-28. (One of the Olmec giant stone heads is shown, being denominated by Forrer as King Theron of the Tartessians.) In all of this, he seems little aware of, let alone influenced by, other diffusionists.

L-356

AUTHOR: Lubensky, Earl H.
DATE: 1991
TITLE: Valdivia Figurines
IN: The New World Figurine Project, vol. 1, edited by Terry Stocker (Research Press: Provo, Utah), 21-36

Page 33: The ability of ancient peoples to travel the seven seas and overland, to pass ideas and technology to others, and to learn from one another, probably has been greatly underrated.

Diffusion should be considered an important force of cultural change, with what could be called "dependent invention" modifying and building upon what is learned from others. "Independent invention" also must have been a significant, though much rarer, factor in the history of man, reflecting possibly the "psychic unity of man" and involving occasional outbursts of human genius that brought about scientific revolutions and new paradigms for others to follow.

Meggers' arguments . . . for "transpacific influence" on the Valdivian culture, as distinct from "transpacific origin . . ." should be considered potentially valid, although there is no clear archaeological evidence yet for the mechanism of transpacific contact in either direction.

L-357

AUTHOR: Luca de Tena, T.
DATE: 1966
TITLE: The Influence of Literature on Cartography and the Vinland Map
IN: Geographical Journal 132:515-518

Discusses the influence of legends on medieval cartography. He completely discounts inclusion of Vinland on this claimed fifteenth-century map as evidence of actual Norse voyages to North America.

L-358

AUTHOR: Lucas, Frederick W.
DATE: 1898
TITLE: The Annals of the Voyages of the Brothers Nicolo and Antonio Zeno in the North Atlantic about the End of the Fourteenth Century and the Claim Founded Thereon to a Venetian Discovery of America: A Criticism and an Indictment
IMPRINT: H. Stevens: London

Terms the account "one of the most ingenious, most successful, and most enduring literary impostures which has ever gulled a confiding public."

L-359

AUTHOR: Lucas, Jack A.
DATE: 1978
TITLE: The Significance of Diffusion in German and Austrian Historical Ethnology
IN: Diffusion and Migration: Their Roles in Cultural Development, edited by P. G. Duke, et al. (University of Calgary Archaeological Association: Calgary), 30-44

Aims to clarify and correct misapprehensions about precisely what German-speaking anthropologists thought about and did with the idea of diffusion. Notes that German lacks a clear term to translate English "diffusion." Distribution and the quality of equivalence were central concerns. Process was not, for it could not be reconstructed, and, in fact, the historical aspect of diffusion will often have to remain open for lack of adequate knowledge.

Cases are used to demonstrate the differences in emphases, concepts and analytic procedures utilized by Graebner, Leser, and Heine-Geldern. Additional discussion relates Schmidt, Frobenius, Koppers, and others to the various currents only broadly labelled by the over-simplified term *kulturkreislehre.*

L-361

AUTHOR: Luce, J. V.
DATE: 1971
TITLE: Ancient Explorers
IN: The Quest for America, edited by Geoffrey Ashe (Praeger: New York; Pall Mall: London), 53-95

A careful treatment of ships and traditions of long-distance sailing, mainly into the Atlantic, by Egyptians and others. "There can be no doubt that Phoenicians, Carthaginians, Greeks and Romans all had ships capable of making an Atlantic crossing. . . . But there is no evidence that an Atlantic crossing was ever achieved, or even attempted, by any ancient captain."

Pages 90-91: Recaps the story told by Pomponius Mela and Pliny of the reputed arrival on the coast of Germany of dark-skinned shipwrecked sailors whom all the sources somehow link to "India." Also summarizes the better documented incident of an apparently American Indian vessel off the coast of the British Isles in 1508 as reported by Cardinal Bembo.

L-363

AUTHOR: Lumpkin, Beatrice
DATE: 1987
TITLE: Pyramids—America and African: A Comparison
IN: African Presence in Early America, edited by Ivan van Sertima, (n.p.:n.p.), 169-187 ["Incorporating Journal of African Civilizations, Dec. 1986, vol. 8, no. 2." "All inquiries should be addressed to Transaction Books, Rutgers—the State University, New Brunswick, New Jersey"]

Rather general parallels, such as the presence of walls around the pyramid precinct and "astronomical orientation," are considered "evidence for an early, significant, African presence in Mesoamerica."

L-364B

AUTHOR: Lunde, Paul
DATE: 1992
TITLE: The Middle East and the Age of Discovery
IN: ARAMCO World 43/3 (May-June): whole issue

A series of articles by an Arabist and historian concentrating on Arab sources of knowledge of geography and voyages as both a prelude to Columbus and a result of his discovery. He was familiar with at least some Arabic learning in the form of maps and accounts of earlier travels along the African coast and into the eastern Atlantic.

The earliest stamp seals from the Canary Islands ("the first stepping stone toward the New World") date to the second millennium B.C. Central American seals have very similar patterns. Al-Idrisi's account tells of explorers before A.D. 1147 who reached islands, probably the Azores, where the local king told them his father had sent ships westward for a month-long voyage but found "nothing of use." A voyage by men of Cordoba, prior to A.D. 942, sailed west and returned with "rich booty." Piri Reis' map depended, for the Caribbean area, on a map drawn by Columbus.

Pages 50-55: Questionable Origins: In a discussion of the bringing to Europe, Asia, and Africa of the earliest American plants after Columbus' discovery, he discusses evidence in art for the pre-Columbian Old World presence of the (American) pineapple (Assyria, Pompeii, Egypt) and the annona, concluding that probably some other plants were represented. But two plants that definitely were shared between the two hemispheres were the coconut and sugar cane (found by the Portuguese on coastal Brazil). The purported turkeys on the Bayeux Tapestry, which he has examined, do not look like turkeys to him; in any case there are recent questions about its purported A.D. 1100 date. Information from Jeffreys on early maize in Africa is reprised, along with statements plausibly indicating that maize may have been in Cordoba before Columbus' return and was surprisingly familiar to da Vinci by ca. 1500-1505. These combine with attributions by early European herbalist writers to point to a Middle eastern source for early maize. Unlike marginally important food plants which may be adopted quite quickly, new grains require a revolution in deeply lodged customs, making the widespread presence of maize plantings in China very early in the 16th century unlikely to be explainable by Portuguese introduction.

L-365

AUTHOR: Lundman, Bertil
DATE: 1954-1955
TITLE: The Montanoid Race Elements
IN: International Anthropological and Linguistic Review 2/1-2:87ff.

Tibet was the homeland of the Amerindians.

L-366

AUTHOR: Lundman, Bertil
DATE: 1959

TITLE: Eine Neuere Arbeiten über die vorkolumbische Rassengeschichte Amerikas
[A New Work on Pre-Columbian Racial History of the Americas]
IN: Ethnos 24:58-63

A brief review of the ultra migrationist approach to New World racial anthropology by the "Argentine School" (Imbelloni, Canals Frau, Menghin), and its critics' views in North America. The author sides with neither group and stresses that scientific analysis and synthesis will ultimately clarify the racial anthropology of the pre-Columbian New World.

L-366B

AUTHOR: Luo Rongqu [Lo Jung-ch'ü]
DATE: 1962
TITLE: Lun suo wei Chung kuo jen fa hsien Mei chou de wen t'i
[On the Problem of the Supposed Discovery of America by the Chinese]
IN: Pei ching ta hsüeh hsüeh pao, no. 4 (Beijing)

Based on reconsideration of the Chinese historical sources and recent scholarship on them, he places Fu-Sang and its culture, which, after all, is portrayed as not very different from that of China, somewhere in northeast Asia, not in America.

L-367

AUTHOR: Luo Rongqu [Lo Jung-ch'ü]
DATE: 1983
TITLE: Legends, Stone Anchors, and the "Chinese Columbus" Theory
IN: China Reconstructs 32/4:8-9

Doubtful that claimed Chinese anchors off California were such.

L-367B

AUTHOR: Luo Rongqu (Lo Jung-ch'ü)
DATE: 1983
TITLE: Fu sang kuo ts'ai hsiang yü Mei chou di fahsien
[The Fu-Sang Hypothesis and the Discovery of America]
IN: Li shih yen chiu [Historical Investigations] 2:42-59 (Beijing)

See L-366B.

L-368

AUTHOR: Luomala, Katharine
DATE: 1940
TITLE: Oceanic, American Indian, and African Myths of Snaring the Sun
IN: Bernice P. Bishop Museum Bulletin 168 (Honolulu)

Pages 22-23: The North American distribution is northern Woodland, northern Plains, and Mackenzie Valley. But the sun-snaring myth among the Yurok of California, isolated from the other areas, cannot be explained satisfactorily. Apparently it is not due to European influence. She knows of no evidence to link this occurrence to Asia.

Page 24: Occurrences in Polynesia are almost totally in eastern Polynesia.

Pages 42-43: Paiutes (citing Lowie, *Shoshonean Tales,* 1924) say that Coyote hurled a magic stone or fire drill or shot the sun with arrows so that it exploded and started a great fire on earth, a "coincidence" recalling a Gilbert Islands account which has diffusionary links with Polynesia. Introduction of the sun-snaring motif by Europeans in Polynesia is unlikely.

Pages 47-48: A Brazilian (Karaya) and a Hawaiian variant both have the element that the sun's leg is broken intentionally to make it slow down. Paul Ehrenreich [E-027] considered the similarities striking but explained it in terms of psychic unity. Luomala is impressed with the possibility of diffusion but would want other evidence of cultural contact. She suggests post-European use of Oceanic slaves as a possible explanation.

Page 52-53: Pre-European contact between North America [nothing said here of the Yurok] and Polynesia has little to recommend it, although she hints she would consider new evidence if offered.

L-370

AUTHOR: Luomala, Katharine
DATE: 1964
TITLE: Motif A 728: Sun Caught in Snare and Certain Related Motifs
IN: Fabula 6:213-252

A continuation of L-368. Mentions Old-New World parallels given by Barton and Skeat and Blagden [S-270B]. Another shared motif is Hero fights with sun and breaks its legs, from Hawaii, the Marquesas, and the Karaya of Brazil. People in India and North America enjoy adding incidents about the sun's imprisonment to the account of how a hero had snared and hidden it. But her monograph had already shown that the sun-snaring motif is present on every major continent and in the Pacific, which suggests its great antiquity "and compatability with human fantasy."

L-372

AUTHOR: Luria, Ben Zion
DATE: 1981
TITLE: "And a Fountain Shall Come Forth from the House of the Lord"
IN: Dor le Dor 10:48-58 (World Bible Society, Jerusalem)

Water was prophetically expected to emerge from the underground sea beneath the Israelite temple. [Compare P-245 regarding the Cholula pyramid.]

L-374

AUTHOR: Luxton, Eleanor Georgina, editor
DATE: 1971
TITLE: Tilikum: Luxton's Pacific Crossing, Being the Journal of Norman Kenny Luxton, Mate of the Tilikum, May 20, 1901, Victoria, B.C. to October 18, 1901, Suva, Fiji
IMPRINT: Gray's Publishing: Sidney, British Columbia

A "Siwash Indian" dugout canoe of red cedar with a keel of 28 feet and over a hundred years old was somewhat modified in British Columbia by Luxton and J. C. Voss, the latter an experienced seaman who had been around Cape Horn several times. Their 10,000 mile voyage via Penrhyn and Manihiki to Fiji, though difficult, succeeded because of the cautious, experienced seamanship of Voss and their superb vessel.

Because of illness, Luxton left the vessel in Suva, but Voss went on, with various others, to Australia, New Zealand, South Africa, Brazil, the Azores, and London, as reported in Voss' book [V-080].

One of the plates shows a large Samoan double-hulled working vessel photographed by the author at Apia in 1901.

L-375

AUTHOR: Luyties, Otto
DATE: 1922
TITLE: Egyptian Visits to America: Some Curious Evidence Discovered
IMPRINT: Privately printed: New York

Only 26 pages long. Egypt and Yucatan were in close communication long before our era, from several indications about 3000 B.C., and established an American colony. The language of the modern Maya Indians includes several hundred recognizable Egyptian words. The hieroglyphic alphabet of the ancient Mayas (of Bishop Landa) contains at least twelve letters expressing the same sound for the same thought as the Egyptian. There are identities in several letters. It is even possible to read a few words of the Mayan hieroglyphics by spelling them out directly in Egyptian. Egyptian voyaging ability could have reached America. The Maya Itzamna was a child of a divinity named Hunabku. Egyptians originally worshipped a rain-god represented as a plumed serpent and call the child of Ha-nebu. Certain features of Mayan statues he sees as Egyptian. The four sky bearers (bacabs) had Egyptian equivalents. A table gives 42 similarities in words. Another displays "Agreement of Alphabets (Signs)." Four other hypotheses are mentioned also as possible explanations for similarities (e.g., Atlantis, or an intermediate nation as common source).

L-377

AUTHOR: Lynch, Thomas F.
DATE: 1974
TITLE: Andean South America
IN: American Antiquity 39:383-386

Page 383: Notes wheel-made pottery and the use of "rotary tools" as discovered by Grieder. [Compare G-221.]

M-001

AUTHOR: Macalister, R. A. Stewart
DATE: 1912
TITLE: The Excavation of Gezer
IMPRINT: J. Murray: London

Pages 105-107: "High place" with aligned standing stelae or masseboth. [Compare S-238, for example, re. Guatemala.]

M-001B

AUTHOR: Mac Cana, Proinsias
DATE: 1989
TITLE: The Voyage of St. Brendan: Literary and Historical Origins
IN: Atlantic Visions (Proceedings of the First International Conference of the Society of Saint Brendan, September 1985, Dublin and Kerry), edited by John de Courcy Ireland and David C. Sheehy (Boole Press, Dún Laoghaire, Co.: Dublin, Ireland), 3-16

Literary analysis shows the Navigatio Brendani to be one of a genre of Old Irish voyage tales in which many mythical elements are incorporated. The present version was probably written down in its present form around the ninth century. Given the genre elements it contains, it is impossible to construct a clear chronological sequence of the Irish and Latin voyages which may lie behind the tales.

M-002

AUTHOR: MacCord, Howard A.
DATE: 1960
TITLE: Cultural Sequence in Hokkaido, Japan
IN: Proceedings of the United States National Museum 112:481-503 (Paper 3443)

From the preceramic (pre-2000 B.C.) period on Hokkaido comes one type of stemmed arrowpoint identical to many found in America, and Japanese archeologists refer to it as the "American Indian type." It is more common on Sakhalin and less common on Honshu. Distribution suggests a common origin, probably in northeastern Siberia, for those in America and Japan.

M-003

AUTHOR: MacCulloch, J. A.
DATE: 1951
TITLE: Incense
IN: Encyclopedia of Religion and Ethics, edited by James Hastings (Scribner's: New York), 7:201-205

Pages 201-203: Serpent-incense association in Mexico and the Near East.

Pages 202ff.: In both Mesoamerica and the Near East, incense was used in ritual to induce rain. Smoke symbolized prayer ascending to the heavens. In Egypt, the soul of the deceased was thought to ascend to the heavens via incense smoke. [For Mesoamerica, see B-031, 2:799.]

Page 203: Near East required use of "sacred fire" for incense. [Compare T-139.]

M-003B

AUTHOR: MacDermott, Anthony
DATE: 1944
TITLE: St. Brandan the Navigator
IN: Mariner's Mirror 30:73-80

An undocumented admiration sketch of his life: "Perhaps the greatest navigator of all time." He is considered to have arrived on "some part of the American continent."

M-006

AUTHOR: Macgowan, Kenneth
DATE: 1950
TITLE: Early Man in the New World
IMPRINT: Macmillan: New York

Pages 26-27: On the difficulty of establishing a final isolationist position. For example, Dixon changed his mind on the sweet potato, and Nordenskiöld "three times . . . cites facts that contradict his thesis" of no contact, each time offering "a kind of self-conscious apology."

Pages 163ff.: Précis of Dixon, Hooton, Mendes-Corrêa, Rivet, Imbelloni, and at greater length, Gladwin.

Pages 175ff.: "Did the Indian invent or borrow his culture?" noting panpipes, similar fishhooks, patolli, etc. On the whole he is open-minded about the evidences as showing need for careful research on possible direct contacts, though he is presently skeptical.

Page 176: The vertical loom used in Egypt and in Nuclear America had the same 11 working parts.

M-007

AUTHORS: Macgowan, Kenneth, and Joseph A. Hester, Jr.
DATE: 1962
TITLE: Early Man in the New World, revised edition
IMPRINT: Doubleday/Anchor: Garden City

Discuss transpacific contacts, pointing out some parallels. They remain open to further evidence while not making much of what is known.

M-008

AUTHOR: Mackenzie, Donald A.
DATE: 1924
TITLE: Myths of Pre-Columbian America
IMPRINT: Gresham: London

[The author had previously written other volumes in this series, "Myth and Legend in Literature and Art," on Teutons, Egypt, India, Babylonia and Assyria, Pre-Hellenic Europe, China, and Japan.]

Pages iii-x: Rejects psychic unity as an explanation for the fact that many myths, deities, beliefs, etc., common to the Old World are found in the New, or at least he puts the onus of proof on the isolationists.

Page viii: "Throughout this volume many links are traced between the Old and New Worlds, but none is more remarkable than that afforded by the American story of yappan, which so closely resembles, in all its essential features, a characteristic Hindu myth found in the Mabá-bhárata. With that piece of evidence alone, a good circumstantial case is made for the transference to pre-Columbian America of Hindu modes of thought, Hindu myths and deities, and Hindu religious practices, coloured somewhat by influences to which they had been subjected on the way between India and America and after being localized in the New World."

The rest of book treats snake-worship; ascetics engaged in penitential exercises and begging for alms with bowls in hands; elephant-like figures and ornamentation thereof; Quetzalcoatl as Buddha with associated symbols; Tlaloc lore/Chinese and Japanese Dragon lore/Naga lore of India; goddess of jade or jadeite, water and herbs (Mexican goddess' herb is the same as that of Isis).

Parallel beliefs about gold in Asia, America, Europe; jewels offered to deities; "fighting-chance combat"; religious "merit" in wealth; jewels buried with the dead; swastika-gold association. Gold-sun and silver-moon associations; jewels as "tutelary spirits"; connection between metals and social classes or castes. Bird and serpent myths including conflict between the two animals; the water-confining serpent; horned serpent; serpent/lizard/fish/elephant/toad- dragons; island-pool beneath a tree as dragon's home; oracle bird on the tree. Winged disc symbol; disc on temple door lintels; symbolism of portals; world ages; color and metal symbolism connected to world ages; colors associated with directions; Babylonian time calculation system in Mesoamerica; gold discs and crosses; symbolism of colored garments; blue symbolism; ten-year cycle; color of internal organs.

Phoenicians, Semites, Norse, Madoc, Brendan, white bearded men; Gaelic numerals in Darien. [While the author allows for Norse discovery and a "possibility" that others crossed the Atlantic, he looks rather to the Pacific.] Mummification, surgery, plate armor, sacred pillar and fish goddess, head flattening.

He reports a case of a Huron woman sold from tribe to tribe until reaching Tartary. The "blood bag" myth; routes across the Pacific; Polynesian and American boats; pearl and shell beliefs; earthly paradise and the well of life and the plant of life. Water burials and the (bird-shaped) ship of death. Cremation, grave fires; fire/sun beliefs, fire baptism; widow's ordeal and widow strangling; head-burning, erect burials, platform burials.

Milk pot and water pot, pot of plenty; earth mother; churning of the ocean; twins spring from foam; underworld; milk-yielding trees, river of milk; fish-god links. Virgin-mother goddess, her connection with water and precious stones; symbolism of shells, jade and herbs; "jewel water" as life blood, green stones as funerary amulets; deluge legends; "lady of the lake" baptism; lustration by fire; fire/butterfly/soul connection; mugwort (Artemisia) beliefs.

Gardens and trees of life, western paradises; love-inspiring flowers; yappan temptation myth; sin eater; confession and absolution; grand-mother deity, snake mother; flight from Hades; first parents pot-born; Xolotl and Bes; goddess of snake skirt and snake mountain; Tlaloc, Nagas and the dragon; deer and deer god; bad and good rain; thunder/axe connection.

White missionaries and white gods. Legends of seafarers reaching America; feathered-serpent/dragon. Mirror phenomena; spider's web myth, oracular humming-bird; skull oracles; human sacrifices. Motives for migrations.

M-009

AUTHOR: Mackenzie, Donald A.
DATE: 1926
TITLE: The Migration of Symbols and Their Relation to Beliefs and Customs
IMPRINT: Kegan Paul: London

Many myth and symbol parallels between the hemispheres, often detailed, are pointed out such as Mexican-Hindu, Mayan-Polynesian, Mexican-Egyptian. [Compare M-008.]

M-012

AUTHOR: MacLeod, William Christie
DATE: 1925
TITLE: Certain Mortuary Aspects of Northwest Coast Culture
IN: American Anthropologist 27:122-148

Mummification, practiced by Aleut and southern Eskimo only in northwestern North America, is similar in detail to that among the Ainu. He supposes diffusion took place, probably early in the 18th century.

M-013

AUTHOR: MacLeod, William Christie
DATE: 1928

TITLE: Priests, Temples, and the Practice of Mummification in Southeastern North America
IN: Proceedings of the 22nd International Congress of Americanists (Rome, 1926), 2:207-230

Mummification could have arisen locally, by specialization of shamans without outside influence.

M-014

AUTHOR: MacLeod, William Christie
DATE: 1930
TITLE: The Distribution of Secondary Cremation and the Drinking of Ashes
IN: American Anthropologist 32:576-577

Mentions instances of the drinking of ashes after secondary cremation in the Old and New Worlds.

M-016

AUTHOR: MacLeod, William Christie
DATE: 1934
TITLE: The Nature, Origin, and Linkages of the Rite of Hookswinging, with Special Reference to North America
IN: Anthropos 29:1-39

Pages 20-21: Ritual fire-walking, incensing, dry-earth painted altars, prayer sticks, stilt dancing, ceremonial fools, stone-of-combat sacrifice, finger sacrifice, and the gazing dance with whistling are cultural features with American and Asian/Oceanian distributions discussed (some mapped). They deserve further study in terms of contacts. "Certainly we cannot refrain from seeing a probable relationship of stilt rituals in the Central Provinces of India (where alone in India such are noted) and among the Maya."

Pages 29-30: The peculiar practice of weeping as a form of greeting persons returning home or arriving for a visit is distributed in a solid area from the Chaco into Tupian Brazil, with a possibility that it existed on the coast of Yucatan, then also from the Texas coast up the Mississippi valley and among Plains tribes. This form of greeting in the Old World is restricted to Melanesia, Australia, and New Zealand.

The complete hookswinging rite which he describes occurs only in northern North America (where it was received from Central America) and Dravidian India. He grants that convergent development of the two independently might be possible, but he does not think that this happened. He considers that the elaborated hookswinging rites in the two areas are survivals of a single origination, probably in India. The fire-walk and pole-climb are rites that he tentatively considers to belong to the same kulturkreis as hookswinging.

M-017

AUTHOR: MacLeod, William Christie
DATE: 1928a
TITLE: The American Indian Frontier
IMPRINT: Knopf: New York

Chapter 1, "Origin of the Indian," includes notions like these: there is little doubt that different Mongolian types came into America at different times; Eskimo language is related to Turkish (Sauvageot, Thalbitzer); Eskimos are as much Indian as any others; Navajo is related to Chinese (Sapir); it is eminently probable that Asians reached America through Polynesia (Rivet).

Pages 10-11: Lengthy lists of traits that came from Asia by various routes including Bering Strait, Aleutians, drifts from Japan and China, and perhaps Polynesia (e.g. Earth Diver, sweat bath, plank house, Mongolian arrow release, rod armor, Japanese type head-rest; see the lists). A Polynesian feather-work article among the Tlingit might be due to Cook's voyaging (Hall); a Tlingit mask with eyes made of Chinese coins may be from the Russian trade era (Bolles); a bronze bell-handle of Hindu origin found on the coast of British Columbia may come from the time of Spanish galleons (Boas).

Page 12: Eskimo snow-house may be an imitation of dome building by Scandinavians in Greenland; bannerstones were probably imitations of an axe form of Northwestern Europe; Eskimo ball game may be from the Norse (Hovgaard and Thalbitzer); a specialized adze-like gouge (Hough) and the Great Dipper as a Great Bear could have a Norse source.

Page 13: Circumstantial evidence of contact from Polynesia to the Aztecs and Incas is too overwhelming to ignore. African elements (Wiener) undoubtedly passed across the Pacific [*sic*] to the Mayans and Aztecs. Traits to America through Polynesia: blow gun, certain musical instruments, certain club types, balsa, double canoe, parasol, litter, official staff, mirrors, fans, censing, cremation, central type mummification, cross, baptism, confession, "jumping over" as a religious practice, bull-roarer, boomerang, bola, bronze, bark cloth, river Styx and Charon theme in mortuary lore, loom, zodiac, agriculture and pottery, mound or pyramid building, hook-swinging rite, lime with masticated herbs, tripod incense burners and other pottery, negative painting, mosaic feather work, a unique type of perforated ornamental axe, possibly the Venus calendar, possibly the style of figure on the Tuxtla Statuette of the Maya, pottery stamps, men's house, cities of refuge, fish poisoning, widow servitude and suttee, lip plug and nostril perforation, lost-wax casting, as well as quipu, notched stick, and tally records, (page 562) wood sewing, (page 563) divining crystal, (scale) balance, zero concept, ta-ki and yin-yang symbols, swastika, worm-toothache idea, and toe-string sandals.

Page 14: How Malays reached Madagascar is a greater mystery than how Polynesians reached America.

Pages 56ff.: Norse and other North Atlantic possibilities, briefly.

Appendix 11, pages 561-563: His observations on methodology. His derivations of native American culture include considerable amounts of his own research, some published. Diffusionists have too much of a case to be ignored; "convergencists" have done a service in being critical of diffusionists, but go much too far. He does not relish the methods of Smith, Perry, or Wiener, but is flattered if categorized with Rivet, Graebner, etc.

M-018

AUTHOR:	MacLeod, William Christie
DATE:	1928b
TITLE:	"Jumping Over" from West Africa to South America
IN:	American Anthropologist 30:107-111

The ceremonial custom of "jumping over" or "stepping over" an object, place or person is found in Africa and America. Here he reports such practices for Kutchin, Kwakiutl, Hupa, Ojibwa, Delaware, Arawak, etc. It is, of course, common in Europe. This may be another "paleolithic" concept.

M-019

AUTHOR:	MacLeod, William Christie
DATE:	1929
TITLE:	On the Southeast Asiatic Origins of American Culture
IN:	American Anthropologist 31:554-560

A rejoinder to Dixon [D-140] whom he considers to seriously downplay Southeast Asian-American diffusion. He likes Graebnerian theory but finds little good in Smith/Perry. Dixon neglects the localization of the parallels in question, the volume of parallels, and the complexity of the traits considered. And finally he believes that the argument that the species of animals and plants involved in some parallel practices between hemispheres differ is largely meaningless. "What are species anyway?" What difference does it really make whether cotton species differ if dyeing, weaving, the loom, etc., used in treating the cotton, were similar?

Traits he says Dixon ignored or underplayed: balsa, quipu, zero, toe string sandals, mosaic featherwork, paddle and anvil pottery making, cotton cultivation, elements of myth, divining crystal, the cross in various forms, vestal virgins guarding sacred fire, cremation, mummification, tripod pottery, baptism, and absolution of sins through confession.

M-020

AUTHOR: MacLeod, William Christie
DATE: 1931
TITLE: Hook-swinging in the Old World and in America: A Problem in Cultural Integration and Disintegration
IN: Anthropos 26:551-561

Among other matters, compares the Mexican volador ritual with Hindu hook swinging, although in the latter the participants are fastened at the shoulders rather than the feet. [H-180 reports an old description and illustration from India in which participants are attached by ropes tied to their feet, as in the volador rite.]

M-021B

AUTHOR: MacLeod, William Christie
DATE: 1934
TITLE: The Nature, Origin, and Linkages of the Rite of Hookswinging: with Special Reference to North America
IN: Anthropos 29:1-38

Largely a restatement of M-016.

M-022

AUTHOR: MacNabb, J. W.
DATE: 1967
TITLE: Sweet Potatoes and Settlement in the Pacific
IN: Journal of the Polynesian Society 76:219-221

Polynesian contact with South America which resulted in transfer of the sweet potato to the islands must have occurred before maize became an important crop on the mainland, i.e., pre-750 B.C. Surely the Polynesians would have carried with them such an important food. The contact of the carriers must have been of at least some months' duration, since they learned the name, *kumara,* exactly, as well as knowledge of storage methods. Given the early date this idea calls for, only western Polynesians could have made the South American voyage, although their return may not have been completed all the way to the west.

M-023

AUTHOR: MacNeish, Richard S.
DATE: 1964
TITLE: The Peopling of the New World as Seen from Northwest America
IN: Proceedings of the 35th International Congress of Americanists (Mexico, 1962), 1:121-132

A rambling guess ("surmise," "speculations") that all but ignores the literature on northeast Asia and chronology there. Of the Arctic Small Tool tradition between about 2500 B.C. and 1500 B.C., he says its western groups "were receiving a steady flow of items from Asia (perhaps via southwest Alaska), such as pottery, bifurcated-base antler arrows, semi-subterranean house types, antler spoons, combs," etc. Some were readapted locally and some "(such as pottery)," diffused through the culture and were perhaps integrated into another tradition (such as the Eastern Woodland?).

M-024

AUTHORS: MacNeish, Richard S., and C. Earle Smith
DATE: 1964
TITLE: Antiquity of American Polyploid Cotton
IN: Science 173:675-676

Tehuacan Valley cotton finds are so early that the idea of importation by human voyaging is unacceptable.

M-025

AUTHORS: MacNeish, Richard S., Annette Nelken-Terner, and Irmgard W. Johnson
DATE: 1967
TITLE: The Prehistory of the Tehuacan Valley, Volume 2: Nonceramic Artifacts
IMPRINT: University of Texas Press: Austin

Page 85: Consider one type of bark beater here remarkably similar to some in Java and Celebes and find it "extremely difficult" to believe in their independent invention. [Compare C-152 and T-106.]

M-026

AUTHOR: MacRitchie, David
DATE: 1912a
TITLE: A Tribe of White Eskimos
IN: Nature 90:133

V. Stefansson had reported discovering 13 tribes of white Eskimos around Coronation Gulf and Victoria Island. He concluded that they were descended from a Viking colony.

In 1658 an account (De Poincy, *Histoire naturelle et morale des Iles Antilles de l'Amerique, Rotterdam*, chapter 18) was given of a captain of Flushing who had found on Davis Straits in 1656 both short olive-skinned people and taller, fairer people. Perhaps the latter were descended from Norse colonists and moved westward to Victoria Land in the following centuries.

M-027

AUTHOR: MacRitchie, David
DATE: 1912b
TITLE: The Kayak in North-Western Europe
IN: Journal of the Royal Anthropological Institute of Great Britain and Ireland 42:493-510

Details on Eskimo kayaks which had landed in Europe.

M-028

AUTHOR: Madier de Montjau, Edouard
DATE: 1875
TITLE: La tradition de l'homme blanc [The Tradition of the White Man]
IN: Proceedings of the 1st International Congress of Americanists (Nancy, 1875), 1:384-386

Believes that certain native traditions lend credence to the arrival of shipwrecked Europeans on the Atlantic coasts of America in the pre-Columbian era.

M-029

AUTHOR: Madiera, Percy C., Jr.
DATE: 1933
TITLE: A Discussion of Trans-Pacific Influences on the Material Traits of Certain of the Higher Pre-Columbian American Cultures
IMPRINT: Unpublished; M.A. thesis, University of Pensylvania

"It is, of course, the writer's conclusion . . . that here in America certain primitive peoples, notably the Mayas, by their own unaided efforts developed out of a Neolithic stage of living a remarkable culture." "Elementary traits which have Old World parallels represent survivals in the New of those traits brought overland by Asiatics many thousands of years ago. These . . . included nearly all the parallels between Melanesian and South American peoples with perhaps the blow gun, the pan pipes and a few other traits as separate independent inventions in these two areas of almost identical environment."

No migrations have come into America in the last eight or ten thousand years. A few features, such as the sinew-backed bow, the Raven and Magic Flight myths and others might have diffused in afterward. Polynesians were not in position to make contact until a few hundred years before European discovery; a few incidental voyages might have been made by them. The Chinese did not become a maritime people much before the third century A.D., so they could not have affected seriously the already developed civilizations of the Maya and Peruvians. The same applies to south-east Asia.

Andean parallels briefly discussed illustrate the treatment: tie dyeing, advanced weaving, planked boats, metallurgy, gauze, quipu, irrigation, mummification, and belief in solar dynasties.

"As far as the writer knows, no system remotely resembling the Maya calendar has ever been reported from the Old World." "There are some extraordinary parallels between the architecture of the Khmers . . . and that of the Mayas," but the former occurred later. The New World zodiac might at first be thought similar to that of the Old, however such astronomical knowledge is not the result of an invention or discovery but purely the result of personal observation.

[A remarkable exhibit of the dogmatism produced by anthropogical training in American schools in the two decades before World War II.]

M-029B

AUTHOR: Maeth Ch., Russell
DATE: 1990
TITLE: Nuevos estudios sobre el problema de Fu-Sang [New Studies on the Problem of Fu-Sang]
IN: Estudios de Asia y Africa 25:461-488

Following Luo Rongqu's (Lo Jung-ch'ü's) analysis of the relevant Chinese sources on Fu-Sang, he finds no basis for supposing any connection with America.

M-035

AUTHOR: Magnusson, Magnus
DATE: 1973
TITLE: Viking Expansion Westwards
IMPRINT: H. Z. Walck: New York; and Bodley Head: London

A popular, well-illustrated account of Viking activity including Vinland. Excellent illustrations of ships.

Chapter 8, "Vinland: North America Discovered." Not very substantive, but note (page 143) that he believes that the Beardmore objects have been "discredited" by mere voiced suspicions of hoax, not by serious study, for the objects themselves are unquestionably of the 11th century. He also allows that Lee's Ungava structures are puzzlingly indeterminate, even though L'Anse aux Meadows is the big find (yet it cannot possibly have been the Vinland of the sagas for lack of grapes).

M-036

AUTHOR: Magnusson, Magnus
DATE: 1980
TITLE: The Ultimate Outpost
IN: Scandinavian Review 68/1:6-29

An excerpt from *Vikings!* (Bodley Head and BBC Publications: London, 1979). This is his own free synthesis—virtual historical fiction—of the events behind the Vinland sagas. His opinion is that Vinland can never be located with any precision on the evidence of the sagas, which are literature, not history. Vinland is not so much a place as a concept.

M-038

AUTHOR: Mahan, Joseph B, Jr.
DATE: 1971
TITLE: The Bat Creek Stone
IN: Tennessee Archaeologist 27/2:38-44

Reprises basic information on the discovery of the stone. He earlier concluded that the characters are not related to the Cherokee script but that the inscription as published ought to be turned upside-down, whereupon it became evident that the characters are Old Hebrew. He quotes correspondence from Cyrus Gordon whom he solicited to initiate the restudy [see G-163]. An early Christian era dating seemed likely. The metal artifacts dug up with the stone are illustrated.

M-039

AUTHOR: Mahan, Joseph B, Jr.
DATE: 1977
TITLE: They Actually WERE Indians
IN: Oklahoma Today, Autumn

After spending five months researching in Pakistan and India, he has solid evidence to show that in addition to cultural diffusion, there were actual migrations from there to America. It includes the names of the peoples. Members of certain tribes living now in Oklahoma are direct descendants of those who built the Indus Valley cities 5000 years ago. These included "Mediterranean," "Dravidian," and "Alpine" type peoples. It is apparent from studying nineteenth-century portraits of American Indian leaders that there were many parallels between their costumes, jewelry, and personal adornment, and those of historical peoples of India. Also an enormous body of written material in our libraries and archives accumulated since colonial times, but ignored by researchers, documents numerous finds of coins, metal and glass objects, and alphabetic inscriptions indicating extensive, long-time contacts between the Americas and Western Europe, the Mediterranean and the Near East. Most of this material has been found in cultivating fields or digging wells on the sites of prehistoric Indian towns.

He has positively identified two groups: the Yuchi, whose relatives in India were the Yueh-Chih, from whom came the Kusbana dynasty of kings in northern India in the first and second centuries of our era. Of eight names by which the Yuchi knew themselves, six are found in association with the Yueh-Chih. The other identified group is the Tama. The names of at least six of the Dravidian speaking peoples who were part of the Mohenjo-daro population are identical to the names of tribes or towns living together, along with the Yuchi, in the Southeast when DeSoto arrived in 1539.

M-040

AUTHOR: Mahan, Joseph B, Jr.
DATE: 1983
TITLE: The Secret: America in World History before Columbus
IMPRINT: Privately printed: Columbus, Georgia

The Yuchi Indians of the Southeastern United States were the same people known as the Yueh-chih in China and comprised the governing element of an elaborate socio-religious organization based on a religion acclaiming the union of earth and sky. This same organization was a league or alliance among the original Mediterraneans, Semites, Aryans, and people of the Indus Valley. Indus valley inhabitants traded by sea with Sumer, Egypt, southern Africa and Tiahuanaco. They are identified with Quetzalcoatl, Viracocha and Kontiki. Sumerians were in Georgia in the 21st century B.C., and transoceanic commerce and colonization continued long after.

Page 31: Ritual use of chickens was reported by Southeastern Indians from the earliest period of European reporting.

Pages 46-49, 62-63: Iron objects have been found in burial mounds.

Pages 49-57: Bat Creek finds and coins.

Page 106: Rattles made of coconut shells were very ancient according to the Yuchi [coconut is conventionally claimed to be a Spanish import].

Pages 114-119: Yuchi symbols resemble letters in Mediterranean scripts.

Pages 124ff.: The Cherokee alphabet is related to writing in India.

Pages 188-191: Suggests worldwide travel and colonization by Indus Valley people.

M-040B

AUTHOR: Mahan, Joseph B.
DATE: 1989
TITLE: There Was a "Great Ireland"

IN: NEARA [New England Antiquities Research Association] Journal 24/1-2:23-26

Summary of claims of proponents of the notion, especially Goodwin and Mallery.

M-040C

AUTHOR: Mahan, Joseph B.
DATE: 1992
TITLE: North American Sun Kings: Keepers of the Flame
IMPRINT: ISAC Press: Columbus, Georgia

See M-040. "Traces the line of American sun kings from the 20th century backward to Mississippian period and ultimate relationship to Egyptian forebears."

M-041

AUTHORS: Mahan, Joseph B., and D. Braithwaite
DATE: 1975
TITLE: Discovery of Ancient Coins in the United States
IN: Anthropological Journal of Canada 13/2:15-18

Reports from historical sources over a dozen European or Near Eastern coins found since 1803 in the Southeastern United States under unexplained circumstances.

M-041B

AUTHOR: Mahieu, Jacques de
DATE: 1970
TITLE: El origen étnico de los "Indios blancos" Guayakis del Paraguay [The Ethnic Origin of "White Indians," the Guayakis of Paraguay]
IMPRINT: Instituto de la Ciéncia del Hombre: Buenos Aires

See M-042.

M-042

AUTHOR: Mahieu, Jacques de
DATE: 1971
TITLE: Le grand voyage du Dieu-Soleil [The Great Voyage of the Sun-God]
IMPRINT: Edition spéciale: n.p. [German edition, *Des Sonnengottes grosse Reise: die Wikinger in Mexiko und Peru 967-1532* (Grabert: Tübingen, 1972); Spanish edition, *El gran viaje del Dios-Sol: los Vikingos en México y en el Perú (967-1532)* (Hachette: Buenos Aires, 1976)]

While allowing probable transpacific contacts, his thesis here is that Irish and Norse voyagers travelled not only to northeastern North America but also to Mexico, then Venezuela, Ecuador, Peru, and Brazil (via Tiahuanaco, which was "a Norse settlement," from which some went on to Easter Island), all approximately between A.D. 950-1250. They were responsible for the traditions of Quetzalcoatl, Bochica and Huirakocha. They left in their course evidences of Christianity, Scandinavian languages, runic writing and material culture (e.g., the Mexican *temascal* or sauna), and their descendants account for blond/white Indians found in South America, notably the Guayakis.

M-042B

AUTHOR: Mahieu, Jacques de
DATE: 1972
TITLE: Les inscriptions runiques précolombiennes du Paraguay [The Pre-Columbian Runic Inscriptions of Paraguay]
IMPRINT: Instituto de la Ciéncia del Hombre: Buenos Aires

See M-053.

M-043

AUTHOR: Mahieu, Jacques de
DATE: 1973

TITLE: Des Sonnengottes Todeskampf: die Wikinger in Paraguay
[The Sun God's Death Agony: The Vikings in Paraguay]

IMPRINT: Grabert: Tübingen
[French edition, *L'agonie du Dieu-Soleil; les Vikings en Amérique du Sud* (R. Laffont: Paris, 1974); Spanish edition, *La Agonía del Dios-Sol: los Vikingos en el Paraguay* (Hachette: Buenos Aires, 1977)]

Parallels M-042 emphasizing runic inscriptions from Paraguay.

M-044

AUTHOR: Mahieu, Jacques de

DATE: 1975a

TITLE: Des Sonnengottes heilige Steinen: die Wikinger in Brasilien
[The Holy Stones of the Sun God: The Vikings in Brazil]

IMPRINT: Grabert: Tübingen

Parallels M-042 and M-043 but with emphasis on Brazil.

M-044B

AUTHOR: Mahieu, Jacques de

DATE: 1975b

TITLE: Les inscriptions runiques du Paraguay
[The Runic Inscriptions of Paraguay]

IN: Kadath: Chroniques des civilisations disparues 15:10-15 (Brussels)

See M-053 and M-043. A general, brief presentation of his claims about white gods and the "white Indians" of Paraguay. A few illustrations (not very distinct photos and three drawings) are presented of "runic" material.

M-044C

AUTHOR: Mahieu, Jacques de

DATE: 1975c

TITLE: Les inscriptions runiques du Paraguay
[The Runic Inscriptions of Paraguay]

IN: Anthropological Journal of Canada 13/4:28-30

Pictures, describes, documents in the literature, "normalizes," and translates an inscription at Cerro Guazú.

M-045

AUTHOR: Mahieu, Jacques de

DATE: 1977

TITLE: Drakkars sur l'Amazone. Les Vikings de l'Amérique précolombienne
[Drakkars (i.e., Viking Ships) on the Amazon. The Vikings of Pre-Columbian America]

IMPRINT: Copernic: Paris
[Spanish edition, *Drakkares en el Amazonas: Los Vikingos en el Brasil* (Hachette: Buenos Aires, 1978)]

More of M-044.

M-046

AUTHOR: Mahieu, Jacques de

DATE: 1978a

TITLE: La geografía secreta de América antes de Colón
[The Secret Geography of America before Columbus]

IMPRINT: Hachette: Buenos Aires

See M-046B.

M-046B

AUTHOR: Mahieu, Jacques de

DATE: 1978b

TITLE: Protocartographie de l'Amérique [Early Cartography of America]
IN: Kadath: Chroniques des civilisations disparues 30:35-38 (Brussels)

Following Mallery, Hapgood, and others, he claims that certain early maps show that Europeans had knowledge of South American and Antarctic coasts not known or knowable in the early Age of Discovery. The knowledge must have come from much earlier explorers including Vikings whose maps were passed down to the 15th and 16th centuries. This knowledge was known to Columbus and enabled his voyage.

M-046C
AUTHOR: Mahieu, Jacques de
DATE: 1978c
TITLE: Un estoc viking dans la Cordillèr des Andes? [Was There Viking Stock in the Andean Cordillera?]
IN: Kadath: Chroniques des civilisations disparues 30:33-34 (Brussels) [A book with the same title and publication year came from Grabert: Tübingen]

Materials on which are "runoid" inscriptions in the Argentine Andes call for consideration by specialists. He reviews various arguments for possible Viking presence in the area. [See M-042, M-049, etc.]

M-046D
AUTHOR: Mahieu, Jacques de
DATE: 1978d
TITLE: Der Weisse König von Ipir. Die Wikinger in Amambay [The White King of Ipir. The Vikings in Amambay]
IMPRINT: Grabert: Tübingen

See M-042, M-046C, and M-049B.

M-047
AUTHOR: Mahieu, Jacques de
DATE: 1979a
TITLE: L'imposture de Christophe Colomb [The Deception of Christopher Columbus]
IMPRINT: Copernic: Paris

Columbus's "imposture" was in claiming a new discovery when he knew from Viking information of the existence of America.

M-048
AUTHOR: Mahieu, Jacques de
DATE: 1979b
TITLE: El rey vikingo del Paraguay [The Viking King of Paraguay]
IMPRINT: Hachette: Argentina

Just another phrasing of Viking-rulers-were-there. See M-043, M-046D, etc.

M-049
AUTHOR: Mahieu, Jacques de
DATE: 1979c
TITLE: Die Templer in Amerika, oder das Silber der Kathedralen [The Knight Templars in America, or the Silver of the Cathedrals]
IMPRINT: Grabert: Tübingen [French edition, *Les templiers en Amérique* (R. Laffont: Paris, 1981)]

Christian Normans were in Brazil and the Andean area from the 11th century on, where their exploitation of the silver mines of Potosí, Bolivia, furnished the capital to construct the French Gothic cathedrals of the 12th and 13th centuries.

M-049B
AUTHOR: Mahieu, Jacques de
DATE: 1981
TITLE: Das Wikingerreich von Tiahuanacu [The Viking King of Tiahuanaco]

IMPRINT: Grabert: Tübingen

See M-042.

M-050

AUTHOR: Mahieu, Jacques de
DATE: 1982a
TITLE: Die Erben Trojas. Auf der Spuren der Megalithiken in Südamerika [The Heritage of Troy. On the Trail of the Megalith Builders in South America]
IMPRINT: Grabert: Tübingen

Reprises the materials of the Wagners [W-004] and adds to it—Trojan designs, "Cro-Magnon Man" skulls, etc.

M-050B

AUTHOR: Mahieu, Jacques de
DATE: 1982b
TITLE: L'horloge astronomique d'El Mollar en Argentine [The Astronomical Clock of El Mollar, Argentina]
IN: Kadath: Chroniques des civilisations disparues 47:11-15 (Brussels)

A megalithic arrangement in northern Argentina is argued to have archaeoastronomical significance and to function as a kind of "clock." Diffusion from the Old World is implied but hardly discussed.

M-050C

AUTHOR: Mahieu, Jacques de
DATE: 1982c
TITLE: Santiago del Estero: les héritiers de Troie [Santiago del Estero: The Heirs of Troy]
IN: Kadath: Chroniques des civilisations disparues 47:11-15 (Brussels)

A précis of M-050.

M-050D

AUTHOR: Mahieu, Jacques de
DATE: 1983a
TITLE: Voici les momies blondes du Pérou [Behold the Blond Mummies of Peru]
IN: Kadath: Chroniques des civilisations disparues 51:23-31 (Brussels)

Synthesizes materials from Trotter, Heyerdahl, and others to argue that in Paracas and other archaeological cultures there have been found mummies with blond-to-chestnut hair that was not, contrary to assertions, merely decolored accidentally after burial but is of a cross-section and form (wavy) that compares with that of Nordics and Cro-Magnons. Blood types confirm such an element in the mummies as at least a part of their ancestry. It would not be surprising to find such in post-Viking age mummies, but these must be otherwise accounted for because they occur earlier. Also, at Chichen Itza murals show yellow-haired white-skinned people being attacked by darker warriors.

M-050E

AUTHOR: Mahieu, Jacques de
DATE: 1983b
TITLE: L'Etrangère de Chancay [The Stranger of Chancay]
IN: Kadath: Chroniques des civilisations disparues 53:44 (Brussels)

A supposed white person of European origin in Peruvian art.

M-050F

AUTHOR: Mahieu, Jacques de
DATE: 1984
TITLE: Les "pygmées" d'Amérique et d'ailleurs [The "Pygmies" of America and Elsewhere]
IN: Kadath: Chroniques des civilisations disparues 56:15-22 (Brussels)

His review of the literature, such as Comas, persuades him there were such here.

M-051

AUTHOR: Mahieu, Jacques de
DATE: 1985a
TITLE: Die Flucht der Trojaner. Wie ihre Hochkultur Afrika und die Kanarische Inseln nach Amerika gelangte
[The Flight of the Trojans. How Their High Culture Reached America via Africa and the Canary Islands]
IMPRINT: Grabert: Tubingen

A take-off on the Wagners' work and interpretations of remains at Santiago del Estero, Argentina [compare M-050 and W-004].

M-051B

AUTHOR: Mahieu, Jacques de
DATE: 1985b
TITLE: De Cro-Magnon en Amérique
[Of Cro-Magnons in America]
IN: Kadath: Chroniques des civilisations disparues 59:29-31 (Brussels)

See M-050D and M-052.

M-052

AUTHOR: Mahieu, Jacques de
DATE: 1988a
TITLE: La langue, l'écriture et les runes
[Language, Writing, and the Runes]
IN: Kadath: Chroniques des civilisations disparues 68:3-10 (Brussels)

Cro-Magnons bore Indo-European languages and spread from the area of France to Libya and Egypt and eastward as well. These "hyper-boreans" reached the Canaries, Mexico, and South America 2200 years before the Vikings. A table with commentary shows comparative characters from Portugal (Alvão), from classic runic, and from "Numidic" characters adjacent to inscriptions from Spain, predynastic Egypt, and Glozel. These were used to form the type of runic writing called futhark.

M-053

AUTHOR: Mahieu, Jacques de
DATE: 1988b
TITLE: Corpus des inscriptions runiques d'Amérique du Sud
[Corpus of Runic Inscriptions of South America]
IN: Kadath: Chroniques des civilisations disparues 68:11-42 (Brussels)

He includes separate sections on "The Hyperborean Inscriptions of Argentina," "The Alphabetical Inscriptions of Brazil," "The Alphabetical Inscriptions of Paraguay," and "The Alphabetical Inscriptions of Argentina."

His figure 4, on the first page, shows a "runic inscription" from the Canaries, following Berthelot, alongside [substantially different] characters from a statuette from La Venta, Mexico, said taken from P. Drucker's report.

Many illustrations of inscriptions accompany the article, from San Agustin, Argentina, Sherbrooke (Quebec), Brazil, etc. The material on South American inscriptions is far more substantive and comprehensive than anything previously published. For each of the scores of items cited, he offers a drawing of the characters, his own "normalization" to runic, a transliteration, and a translation.

M-053B

AUTHOR: Mahieu, Jacques de
DATE: 1989
TITLE: La momie de Ramsès II et sa nicotine
[Ramses II's Mummy and Its Nicotine]
IN: Kadath: Chroniques des civilisations disparues 71:8-12 (Brussels)

Blond hair indicates racial affinity with Berbers, who are of Cro-Magnon origin. In the dynastic era there were three racial elements together in Egypt—Proto-Bushmen, Cro-Magnon men, and Proto-Arab Semites. Claims that tobacco was found in the most inaccessible parts of the abdomen. What was tobacco, a New World plant, doing in Egypt in Ramses' mummy? A postscript comments negatively on Bucaille's strictures [Mahieu's remarks refer to the French-language volume on the mummy by Bucaille, which was published in 1987; see now B-423B, in English, published 1990].

M-055B

AUTHORS: Mainfort, Robert C., Jr., and Mary L. Kwas
DATE: 1991
TITLE: The Bat Creek Stone: Judeans in Tennessee?
IN: Tennessee Anthropologist 16:1-19

McCulloch's and Gordon's claim that the inscription on the stone is Hebrew is invalid. The stone was inscribed in historic Cherokee script, not Hebrew. The nineteenth-century excavation, although under Smithsonian auspices, was carried out by a man with "problems" including drinking; hence his report, which indicates that the mound yielding the inscribed stone was prehistoric, is unreliable. Gordon is called a "rogue scholar" and McCulloch a "cult archaeologist."

M-056

AUTHOR: Major, Richard Henry, editor
DATE: 1873
TITLE: The Voyages of the Venetian Brothers Nicolo & Antonio Zeno to the Northern Seas in the XIVth Century, Comprising the Latest Known Accounts of the Lost Colony of Greenland
IMPRINT: Hakluyt Society, 1st series, vol. 50 (London)
[Reprinted Burt Franklin: New York, n.d.]

An impartial analysis of the Zeno claim, concluding that Antonio may have reached North America. [Unusually cool scholarship for this period.]

M-058

AUTHOR: Makemson, Maude W.
DATE: 1941
TITLE: The Morning Star Rises: An Account of Polynesian Astronomy
IMPRINT: Yale University Press: New Haven

Early Polynesian navigation was based on legends and mythic concepts of the universe. Includes a detailed account of the practice of Polynesian navigation and myths about the sun, moon, stars, and planets. Several Amerindian groups adopted the Pleiades as one of their ancestors, also true in parts of Oceania.

M-059

AUTHOR: Mallery, Arlington H.
DATE: 1951
TITLE: Lost America: The Story of Iron-Age Civilization Prior to Columbus
IMPRINT: The Overlook Company: Washington; and Clark, Irwin: Toronto

Foreword by Matthew W. Stirling.

Celts preceded the Norse and Danes in settling northeastern North America, but the Black Death reached Vinland in the 14th century with the few Norse survivors then being absorbed by aboriginals whom they had formerly dominated. Out of this mixture the Iroquois emerged. Cultural as well as biological comparisons are used to support this claim.

Iron-smelting furnaces have been found by him inside two ancient Ohio mounds, demonstrating that Europeans with knowledge of this technology lived there. At least 17 locations in

Newfoundland have yielded prehistoric Scandinavian stone and iron tools. Newport Tower is of Celtic date. In the centuries of Viking ascendancy, the Arctic was far warmer and northern waters more easily navigable than today.

M-060

AUTHOR: Mallery, Arlington H.
DATE: 1958
TITLE: The Pre-Columbian Discovery of America: A Reply to W. S. Godfrey
IN: American Anthropologist 60:141-152

Godfrey [G-129] claimed to summarize the evidence pro and con about Vikings in America, but he omitted evidence of ancient maps and navigation charts which were preserved in Iceland and Scandinavia. The author here describes or mentions "a series of more than 35 maps . . . which have been preserved for thousands of years in various parts of the Old World" and which represent accurately parts of eastern North America. [He cites W-037.]

There are some 60 sagas in which mention is made of explorations of the coast of North America. Newfoundland was Vinland, as confirmed by sites described by him elsewhere. He also discusses the iron smelting furnaces of Ohio, similar to those of Sweden, as well as Newport Tower, which he examined as an engineer, concluding that it had to be at least 300 years old by 1675. The linear unit used in the tower was not the English foot but a Scandinavian one used in constructing Christian churches; Newport Tower was the first Christian church in America.

M-061

AUTHORS: Mallery, Arlington H., and Mary Roberts Harrison
DATE: 1979
TITLE: The Rediscovery of Lost America
IMPRINT: Dutton: New York; and Clarke, Irwin: Toronto
[Revised edition of M-059]

The argument is in three parts. First, they report his excavations in Ohio mounds which he believes reveal pre-European settlement iron-smelting furnaces (duplicated in Europe in the Hallstatt era). Second, the settlement of Iceland, Greenland, and Vinland by the Norse along routes according to his interpretation of landfalls mentioned in the sagas. Settlers on the mainland in time fled up the St. Lawrence from enemy Irish-Celt inhabitants already present; the refugees carried out mining activity in the Lake Superior area and Ohio. Third, the Piri Reis map shows knowledge of the earth and navigation ability unknown in Columbus' day. Because the map shows the true ground outline of Antarctica and Greenland as three islands, the knowledge must have come from millennia ago when the oceans and climate were different. The pre-Columbian American iron producers maintained intercontinental trade until travel across the ocean was blocked by advance of the polar ice cap in the mini-ice age of the Middle Ages. They also list loan words between North America and Europe and compare Scandinavian and Iroquoian pottery.

M-062

AUTHOR: Mallery, Garrick
DATE: 1889
TITLE: Israelite and Indian; A Parallel in Planes of Culture
IMPRINT: D. Appleton: New York
[Reprinted from *Popular Science Monthly* 36 (1889): 52-76, 193-213. Summarized by H. W. Henshaw, "Israelite and Indian," *Journal of American Folk-Lore* 3 (1890): 74-76]

The author cites many North American Indian customs as practically identical with those of ancient Israelites, adding many new examples to the long lists from Adair and others. His interpretation of these parallels is that they merely indicate that in their "mental construction" the "races of the world" are akin, and given "the same plane of culture" and similar environmental conditions the results are everywhere similar. In addition to more general parallels, such as notions of pollution, purification and taboo, more specific ones are noted, such as sacrifice (e.g., the Iroquois feast of the white dog saw them load the creature with the sins of the people symbolized by strings of wampum, whereupon all was burned), the feast of the new moon, circumcision, and totemism.

M-063

AUTHOR: Mallery, Garrick
DATE: 1893
TITLE: Picture-Writing of the American Indians
IN: Tenth Annual Report of the Bureau of Ethnology to the Secretary of the Smithsonian Institution for 1888-1889
[Reprinted Dover Publications: New York, 1972]

Page 772: A possible outside influence for some designs is allowed, from Japanese or Chinese vessels driven onto the west coast.

M-064

AUTHOR: Malmström, Vincent H.
DATE: 1976a
TITLE: Izapa: Cultural Hearth of the Olmecs?
IN: Proceedings of the Association of American Geographers 8:32-35

A basalt boulder at Izapa, Chiapas, was carved in the form of a turtle in such a manner that the magnetic lines of force were concentrated in the turtle's head. No other monument there is magnetic. Since people of the area were apparently sea travellers, with connections at least to Ecuador, he supposes that Izapans would have observed great migrations of Ridley turtles between Baja California and Ecuador or the black turtle homing via magnetism, of which they and contemporary Olmecs were apparently aware. Mentions the possibility that Shang Chinese influences as per Meggers might have been involved at Izapa.

M-065

AUTHOR: Malmström, Vincent H.
DATE: 1976b
TITLE: Knowledge of Magnetism in Pre-Columbian Meso-America
IN: Nature 259:390

See M-064.

M-066

AUTHOR: Malmström, Vincent H.
DATE: 1981
TITLE: Architecture, Astronomy, and Calendrics in Pre-Columbian Mesoamerica
IN: Archaeoastronomy in the Americas, edited by Ray A. Williamson, Anthropological Papers 22 (Ballena Press: Los Altos, California), 249-261

While tracing the history of the Mesoamerican calendar from internal data, he holds open the possibility of transoceanic diffusion from Asia as a source for some features of the calendar.

M-067

AUTHOR: Malone, Joseph L.
DATE: 1973
TITLE: Review of *The Indo-European and Semitic Languages: An Exploration of Structural Similarities Related to Accent, Chiefly in Greek, Sanskrit, and Hebrew*, by Saul Levin
IN: Language 49:204-209

The reviewer makes the important distinction between "similarism," as in the work of Levin, and "cognatism," the dominant theory of historical linguistics. What Levin points out as resemblances between Indo-European and Semitic are indeed real and multifarious, but the reason, according to Malone, is typological (convergence because of limitations of the linguistic medium), not historical. To test this, he examined a grammar and lexicon of Maidu, a California Indian language with which he had not been familiar. [Callaghan and Miller in C-004 did this same thing with English and Macro-Mixtecan.] Malone was able to jot down various resemblances to Hebrew off the top of his head. Since "similarities" indeed appear between these clearly unrelated languages, he concludes that "similarism is not viable as a theory of historical linguistics." [Obviously, much of the language comparison heretofore done across the oceans proceeds on the basis of similarism, not cognatism.]

M-067B

AUTHOR: Manaila, Alexandru V.
DATE: 1978-1979
TITLE: Mystery Hill. Local Historical Development or Part of a Worldwide Culture?
IN: NEARA [New England Antiquities Research Association] Journal 12-14:62; 2-5, 26-28, 50-54; 2-4

In five parts. Part I: Evolution and History of Dacian People. Subsequent installments treat other supposed contacts with Europe.

M-068

AUTHOR: Mangelsdorf, Paul C.
DATE: 1950
TITLE: The Mystery of Corn
IN: Scientific American 183 (1 July): 20-29

Includes comments on what he considers the essentially nil possibility of pre-Columbian occurrence of maize in Asia.

M-068B

AUTHOR: Mangelsdorf, Paul C.
DATE: 1953
TITLE: Review of *Agricultural Origins and Dispersals,* by C. Sauer
IN: American Antiquity 19:87-90

Negative in regard to Sauer's diffusionist leanings.

M-070

AUTHOR: Mangelsdorf, Paul C.
DATE: 1974
TITLE: Corn: Its Origin, Evolution, and Improvement
IMPRINT: Harvard University Press: Cambridge

Pages 201-206: Discusses evidence for pre-Columbian occurrence of maize in Asia; it does not convince him. Lists botanists who have argued for an Asian origin of maize.

M-071

AUTHORS: Mangelsdorf, Paul C., Richard S. MacNeish, and Walter Galinat
DATE: 1964
TITLE: Domestication of Corn
IN: Science 143:538-545

Summary of data on the Mesoamerican domestication of corn, from which they conclude that any idea that this crop was indigenous to Asia, based on art, its popularity in 16th century China, and the claim that ancient kernels were found in Assam, cannot hold.

M-072

AUTHORS: Mangelsdorf, Paul C., and Douglas L. Oliver
DATE: 1951a
TITLE: Whence Came Maize to Asia?
IN: Science 165:263-264

See M-073.

M-073

AUTHORS: Mangelsdorf, Paul C., and Douglas L. Oliver

DATE: 1951b
TITLE: Whence Came Maize to Asia?
IN: Harvard University Botanical Museum Leaflets 14/10:263-291

An intended refutation of Stonor and Anderson [S-488], based upon four main facts which they say those authors misinterpret: maize in Assam is not unique but is comparable to maize still found in America; there is no record of maize in Asia before 1492; the distribution of the plant in Asia is explained best by supposing a recent introduction; and resemblances between sorghum and maize from Assam and from Bat Cave are superficial and not significant.

M-074

AUTHORS: Mangelsdorf, Paul C., and R. G. Reeves
DATE: 1945
TITLE: The Origin of Maize: Present Status of the Problem
IN: American Anthropologist 47:235-243

They assert that the American, non-Asiatic origin of maize is established,.

M-075

AUTHORS: Mangelsdorf, Paul C., and R. G. Reeves
DATE: 1954
TITLE: New Evidence on the Origin and Ancestry of Maize
IN: American Antiquity 20:409-410

Fossil pollen of wild maize from a core drilled in the subsoil beneath Mexico City establishes the plant as present by 60,000 years ago, hence not originated in Asia.

M-076

AUTHORS: Mangelsdorf, Paul C., and R. G. Reeves
DATE: 1959
TITLE: The Origin of Corn
IN: Harvard University, Botanical Museum Leaflets 18:329-440

See M-071.

M-077

AUTHOR: Manter, H. W.
DATE: 1967
TITLE: Some Aspects of the Geographical Distribution of Parasites
IN: Journal of Parasitology 53:1-9

Hookworm might have been brought with Jomon/Valdivia voyagers, if Meggers/Evans' belief based on early Ecuador material is sound. [Compare F-120 and F-121.]

M-078

AUTHOR: Marble, Samuel D.
DATE: 1980
TITLE: Before Columbus: The New History of Celtic, Egyptian, Phoenician, Viking, Black African, and Asian Contacts and Impacts in the Americas before 1492
IMPRINT: A. S. Barnes: New York; and Thomas Yoseloff: London

An uncritical potpourri of Celtic visitors, medieval Christian teachers, Phoenicians, Egyptians, the Micmac, Vikings, Mandans, etc.

M-079

AUTHOR: Marchal, Henri
DATE: 1934
TITLE: Rapprochements entre l'art Khmer, et les civilisations polynésiennes et précolombiennes [Similarities between Khmer Art and Pre-Columbian Polynesian Civilizations]
IN: Journal de la société des américanistes de Paris 26:213-222

Gives undetailed parallels in art and architecture (e.g., the naga serpent and stone mosaic facades) between the Khmer and Polynesians, Chichen Itza, Palenque, etc.

M-080

AUTHOR: Marco Dorta, Enrique
DATE: 1971
TITLE: Viajes accidentales a América [Accidental Voyages to America]
IN: Anuario de estudios atlánticos 17:561-572 (Madrid)

Recounts stories from the Canaries and the Antilles about the ease and speed of sailing from one to the other. Example: in 1789 a round-trip was made from Cadíz to Cartagena to Havana to Cadíz in only 72 days, while Acosta reported his own passage from the Canaries to the West Indies in only 15 days. Summarizes sources that show Greeks, Romans, Phoenicians and others reached the eastern Atlantic islands. The Roman figurine head found by García Payón in Mexico assures us that at least some vessel crossed, probably disabled and unable to return.

M-084

AUTHOR: Marcos, Jorge G.
DATE: 1986
TITLE: Breve prehistoria del Ecuador [Brief Prehistory of Ecuador]
IN: Arqueología de la costa ecuatoriana: Nuevos enfoques (Biblioteca ecuatoriana de arqueología 1), edited by Jorge G. Marcos (ESPOL [Escuela Politécnica del Litoral, Centro de Estudios Arqueológicos y Antropológicos] y Corporación Editora Nacional: Guayaquíl), 25-50

Thoroughly up-to-date survey of coastal Ecuadorian archaeology. The Meggers/Evans/Estrada hypothesis is viewed as problematic but in any case discomforting to nationalist-minded archaeologists as well as evolutionists. The role of recent finds in complicating the picture of a Jomon incursion is presented. Emphasis goes to the place of the Spondylus cult and its influence through sea trade reaching as far as the Gulf of California and lasting for thousands of years.

M-089

AUTHOR: Marcou, Philippe B.
DATE: 1924
TITLE: Utilité des comparaisons entre les langues indigènes d'Amérique et les langues Indo-Européenes [The Utility of Comparisons between Native American Languages and Indo-European Languages]
IN: Proceedings of the 21st International Congress of Americanists (Part 1, The Hague, 1924), part 320-322

He thinks he sees some similarities between "primitive Indo-European" and some languages of Mexico and the Caribbean, but the examples given are trivial.

M-090

AUTHOR: Marcus, Geoffrey Jules
DATE: 1980
TITLE: Conquest of the North Atlantic
IMPRINT: Boydell: Ipswich [Also as *The Conquest of the North Atlantic* (Oxford University Press: New York, 1981)]

Specifically refutes M-416 and its pessimism about the maritime capability of medieval times. Offers here perhaps the most carefully done and comprehensive general history of Irish, Norse, English, and Hanse voyaging and navigation. Informed by a sailor's point of view, he gently scoffs at a good deal of academic comment on nautical matters as misinformed. He separately treats navigation, ship technology, geographic knowledge, and legends, concluding that the small boats of northwestern Europe could and probably did cross the ocean. The Irish reached the Faeroes A.D. 700 then Iceland, so there is no reason to deny them the possibility of continuing to North America. Includes a discussion of possible voyages by Bristol sailors across the North Atlantic in the 1480s.

Page 165: "It can no longer be accepted as an absolute certainty that Columbus was the first to arrive in American waters in the age of the great discoveries."

But the only boats capable of sailing in the North Atlantic during the Bronze Age were of skin. Their first literary mention is around 500 B.C.

A short section on Vinland, Newport Tower, Beardmore, and the Kensington Stone relies on received opinion only. The Vinland Map is nautical nonsense.

M-093

AUTHORS: Marcus, Joyce, Kent V. Flannery, and Ronald Spores
DATE: 1983
TITLE: The Cultural Legacy of the Oaxacan Preceramic
IN: The Cloud People: Divergent Evolution of the Zapotec and Mixtec Civilizations, edited by Kent V. Flannery and Joyce Marcus (Academic Press: New York), 36-39

Pages 38-39: The concept of color-related world quarters is so widespread among Amerindians as well as in Asia (citing Nowotny) as to suggest that it may have been part of the cultural baggage of the first immigrants to cross the Bering Straits. Wide distribution of the concept suggests great time depth rather than diffusion. Related concepts, such as world trees, could easily have been adaptations from the original notions.

M-094

AUTHOR: Marcy, Georges
DATE: 1962
TITLE: Notas sobre algunos topónimos y nombres antiguos de tribus bereberes en las Islas Canarias [Notes on Some Toponyms and Ancient Names of the Berber Tribes in the Canary Islands]
IN: Annuarios de estudios atlánticos 8:239-289 (Madrid)

The Romans, around the beginning of our era, visited the Canary archipelago.

M-095

AUTHOR: Marett, Robert Ranulph
DATE: 1932
TITLE: The Diffusion of Culture
IN: The Frazer Lectures 1922-1932, edited by W. R. Dawson (Macmillan: London), 172-189

Defends Tylor and Frazer against Elliot Smith's onslaught and puts Smith in his place, as it were. Diffusion is fine, to be sure, but it cannot take over all study of culture as Smith would have it, nor can the Egyptians be granted the only creative minds. While he finds the man charming personally, his harsh and dogmatic statements in print are without basis in fact and harmful to scholarship.

M-097

AUTHOR: Markham, Clements R.
DATE: 1893
TITLE: Pytheas, the Discoverer of Britain
IN: Geographical Journal 1:504-524

In about the third century B.C., Pytheas' ship, in which he reportedly reached the British Isles and Ultima Thule, was larger and more seaworthy than those of Columbus.

M-098

AUTHOR: Markham, Clements R., translator and editor
DATE: 1907
TITLE: Introduction
IN: History of the Incas by Pedro Sarmiento de Gamboa; and The Execution of the Inca Tupac Amaru, by Captain Baltasar de Ocampo (Hakluyt Society: Cambridge)

Pages ix-xxii: Accepts that the expedition by raft under Tupac Yupanqui which was reported by Sarmiento reached the Galapagos Islands.

M-099

AUTHOR: Markham, Clements R.
DATE: 1912
TITLE: The Incas of Peru, 2nd edition
IMPRINT: John Murray: London

Pages 29-38, 127, 138: Various Incan traits (e.g., use of fermented beverage, quipu) also appear in Oceanic cultures. He draws no conclusion as to their origin, merely indicating that Peruvian tradition derived the megalithic people from the south in remote antiquity.

M-101

AUTHOR: Márquez Miranda, Fernando
DATE: 1923
TITLE: Existencia de tierras habitadas al oeste de las Columnas de Hercules; noticias tradicionales en la antiguedad [Existence of Inhabited Lands to the West of the Columns of Hercules; Traditional and Ancient Notices]
IN: Humanidades 5:443-485 (La Plata, Argentina)

A prolix survey of Diodorus, the Atlantis claims, etc., concluding that there was no Atlantis and that the notion has no relevance to any Americanist concern. Then does the same for Fusang.

M-104

AUTHOR: Márquez Miranda, Fernando
DATE: 1939
TITLE: Los "tokis" (a propósito de un nuevo "toki" de Patagonia) ["Tokis" (Apropos of a New "Toki" from Patagonia)]
IN: Notas del Museo de La Plata (Antropología) 4:17-45

Stone clubs of Polynesian form in South America are discussed. [See I-054.]

M-105

AUTHOR: Márquez Miranda, Fernando
DATE: 1940
TITLE: Los aborígenes de América del Sur [The Aborigines of South America]
IN: Historia de América, edited by Ricardo Levene (Buenos Aires), 2:3-22

Pages 3-22: Lagoa Santa and Oceanic physical anthropological parallels are discussed in this section on fossil men.

M-106

AUTHOR: Márquez Miranda, Fernando
DATE: 1962
TITLE: Dos rutas de exploración de relaciones traspacíficas y trasandinas con respecto al noroeste Argentino [Two Routes of Exploration for Transpacific and Trans-Andean Relations with Respect to Northwest Argentina]
IN: Jornadas Internacionales de Arqueología y Etnografía: Segunda Mesa Redonda International de Arqueología y Etnografía, "La Arqueología y Etnografía Argentina y sus Correlaciones Continentales y Extracontinentales," 2:72-89, Comisión Nacional Ejecutiva, 150o. Aniversario de la Revolución de Mayo, Buenos Aires

He links in a vague "working hypothesis" the occurrence of the hair style of Hopi women with a similar form on Japanese warriors and Ainu men, as well as on figurines in Catamarca, Argentina, as shown. The Valdivia-Jomon similarity in pottery must be linked to this shared hair feature, as also probably Coe's observations about balsa travel between Mesoamerica and Ecuador. The Hopi and Zuñi he considers the northernmost outliers of an early Andean stratum.

M-107

AUTHOR: Marschall, Wolfgang
DATE: 1966
TITLE: Die Panpfeife im circumpazifischen Raum
[The Panpipe in the Circumpacific Area]
IN: Dresden Staatlichen Museum für Völkerkunde, Abhandlungen und Berichte 25:127-151

An extensive review of the ethnographic and archaeological literature. The panpipe spread from the Peru area to other areas of the New World. Its source was China. Large bibliography and illustrations.

M-108

AUTHOR: Marschall, Wolfgang
DATE: 1972a
TITLE: Review of *La representación de América en mapas romanos de tiempos de Cristo* [The Representation of America on Roman Maps of the Time of Christ], by Dick Edgar Ibarra Grasso
IN: Zeitschrift für Ethnologie 97:304-306

He agrees with the author's basic view that the early maps discussed show unexpected knowledge on the part of Old World navigators of the coasts of America.

M-109

AUTHOR: Marschall, Wolfgang
DATE: 1972b
TITLE: Transpazifische Kulturbeziehungen: Studien zu ihrer Geschichte
[Transpacific Cultural Relations: Historical Studies]
IMPRINT: Klaus Renner: Munich
[Spanish edition, *Influencias Asiáticas en las Culturas de la América Antigua: Estudios de su Historia* (Ediciones Euroamericanas Klaus Theile: México, 1979).
Reviewed 1973, *Man* 8:115-116]

Part 1 reviews the historiography of Old and New World parallels, with a critical evaluation of methodology in recent studies. Part 2 contains detailed comparisons of four trait complexes (blowgun; house models and death cult; figurines on wheels; weaving and dyeing techniques) in order to verify and expand previously published research. Part 3 deals with processes of cultural transmission, possibilities of navigation and nautical technology, and theoretical considerations. Written from a diffusionist viewpoint, the author nevertheless withholds final judgement on the problem of transpacific contacts.

Page 61 (Spanish edition): Notes that while the amount of cultural parallels between Indonesia and Madagascar, including language, is extremely large, not a single object attributable to Indonesia has been located yet in Madagascar.

Pages 49-67: A detailed summary, logical analysis, and devastating critique of three recent anti-diffusionist pieces, by Caso [C-121], Rowe [R-193], and Phillips [P-159].

Pages 75-110: First he critically reviews earlier studies of the blowgun, e.g., by Riley, Nordenskiöld, and Yde, pointing out serious deficiencies in their use of data then available as well as in their logic. Detailed information is next provided on distribution of this device in 75 locations in Southeast Asia and Madagascar. After more methodologically relevant discussion, he concludes that congruent forms, general distribution, and cultural hiatuses speak in favor of historical relations between Southeast Asian and American blowguns. Name comparisons are also given.

Pages 111-126: The focus of this discussion is "house models and the cult of the dead," but the materials go beyond, leading to this list of similarities grouped in time and space which seem to relate South China and West Mexico: clay house models, clay figurines of the inhabitants of these houses occupied with daily activities, straight rooflines with rising ends, structures with one or several stories with outside stairways, representations of animals (dogs and birds) in the house models, rhomboid designs on walls and ceilings, representations of persons on the shoulders of others, representation of acrobatic games, supposed shamanistic action, use of the models as offerings (in tombs), and gongs. He interprets all this as a cult of the dead diffused from China.

Pages 127-134: A brief but reasonably comprehensive consideration of "wheeled animal figurines," which he thinks likely came from Asiatic prototypes; jointed figurines could have arrived together with wheeled animals, except that the early date (ca. 1000 B.C.) proposed for the former by Borhegyi and others could point to a separate transmission. [That early date was erroneous; in the 1990s the date appears to be no earlier than ca. 500 B.C.]

Pages 135-143: Techniques of weaving and dyeing. Surveys information on the origin of weaving, technology of looms, batik [not proven present in America, he maintains, erroneously], ikat and plangi varieties of reserve dyeing, and myths associated with weaving. He feels the evidence justifies favoring an Asiatic (Chinese and Southeast Asian) origin for Andean and Mexican techniques.

Pages 147-156: A brief survey of some literature on nautical capabilities in East Asia by which transpacific influences could have reached America in the times indicated by the comparative cultural evidence.

M-109B

AUTHOR: Marsh, R. O.
DATE: 1925
TITLE: Blond Indians of the Darien Jungle
IN: The World's Work 49/5:483-497

The "True Cuna" in the mountains of eastern Panama are "as white as ourselves" and "may be descendants of early Norwegians." "The white Indians have always dominated the other Indians intellectually and have created all the real civilizations that flourished in prehistoric times in Mexico, Central America, Peru and Brazil." Their language is "wholly unrelated to any American Indian dialect, with a grammar similar to ancient Sanscrit." Photographs. Claims that they are not albinos.

M-110

AUTHOR: Marshall, Yvonne
DATE: 1985
TITLE: Who Made the Lapita Pots? A Case Study in Gender Archaeology
IN: Journal of the Polynesian Society 94:205-233

Methodology. Suggests that loss of pottery-making resulted from changing social roles, particularly due to decrease in trade. [The notion could be applied to other situations where a (diffused) cultural item was lost due to ill fit.]

M-111

AUTHOR: Marstrand, Vilhelm
DATE: 1949
TITLE: The Runic Inscription on No Man's Land
IN: New England Quarterly 22:85-92

Shows that the runes on this small New England island were probably carved in 1913. [Compare H-362.]

M-115

AUTHOR: Marszewski, Tomasz
DATE: 1960
TITLE: Remarques sur l'état des recherches concernant les contacts entre les peuples de l'Asie et de l'Amérique précolombienne
[Remarks on the State of Research Concerning Contacts between the Peoples of Asia and Pre-Columbian America]
IN: Folia Orientalia 2:117-204 (Krakow, Poland)

A discussion of arguments in favor of and against Asian influence in the New World.

M-115B

AUTHOR: Marszewski, Tomasz
DATE: 1961
TITLE: Remarques sur l'état des recherches concernant lec contacts entre les peuples de l'Asie et de l'Amérique précolombienne [Remarks on the Status of Research Concerning Contacts between the Peoples of Asia and Pre-Columbian America]
IN: Folia Orientalia 2:192-205 (Krakow, Poland)

Based on plant linkages between the two areas, which he considers clear and definite.

M-116

AUTHOR: Marszewski, Tomasz
DATE: 1963
TITLE: The Age of Maize Cultivation in Asia (A Review of Hypotheses and New Ethnographical, Linguistic and Historical Data)
IN: Folia Orientalia 4:243-295 (Krakow, Poland)

A very careful review of the evidence relating to all the hypotheses for the presence of maize in south Asia and possible connections to America. To this point in time he concludes that there is much in favor of accepting the pre-Columbian cultivation of this crop in Southeast Asia, and in any case the possibility cannot be excluded.

M-117

AUTHOR: Marszewski, Tomasz
DATE: 1968
TITLE: The Age of Maize Cultivation in Asia (Further Investigations)
IN: Folia Orientalia 10:91-192 (Krakow, Poland)

Surveys natural science data relating to the history of the introduction of maize to Asia, including the recently discovered and identified first find of alleged sub-fossil maize pollen in Asia. Archaeobotanical, linguistic, and iconographic data are also given.

M-118

AUTHOR: Marszewski, Tomasz
DATE: 1975
TITLE: The Problem of the Introduction of "Primitive" Maize into South-east Asia, Part I
IN: Folia Orientalia 16:237-260 (Krakow, Poland)

Hypothesizes that "primitive" forms of maize were introduced into Southeast Asia from the northern part of South America or the southern part of Central America at an unspecified pre-Columbian time. This could have been done by Cham or other sailors from the Vietnam area who returned home from a voyage to America.

M-119

AUTHOR: Marszewski, Tomasz
DATE: 1978
TITLE: The Problem of the Introduction of "Primitive" Maize into South-east Asia, Part II
IN: Folia Orientalia 19:127-163 (Krakow, Poland)

A more detailed examination of data relating to the hypothesis of M-118. Z. mays appears in 13th-century literature in China. "Persian" type races of maize, now spottily cultivated in South and North-West China, in the 16th century were widely cultivated, as attested by written sources [see C-217C] and were probably introduced into China from the west, beyond its southwestern frontiers (i.e., from Tibet or Burma) before the earliest Portuguese or Spanish voyages to east Asia.

Pages 135-136: Based on the palaeobotanical data from Kashmir [see V-061, V-062], which is subject to diverse possible difficulties in interpretation of the evidence, "it seems, that at least some primitive forms of maize might have been grown in that region," perhaps, but far from surely, beginning in the 13th-14th century.

Page 137: "Vivid discussion, creating many controversies," has ensued from studies of the forms of maize from South China and the Himalayan zone along with similar forms from other regions of East and South Asia. "One should remark, however, that among the agriculturalists and botanists who have studied them in detail in respect to their morphology, genetics, physiology, and distribution, almost all (are) inclined to admit their pre-Columbian occurrence in some at least of the above mentioned regions."

M-120

AUTHOR: Marszewski, Tomasz
DATE: 1987a
TITLE: Some Implications of the Comparative Studies of the Vernacular Names of Maize and other Cultigens from South-East Asia, Parts 1 and 2
IN: Sprawozdania z Posiedzen Komisji Naukowych, Polska Akademia Nauk, Oddzial w Krakowie 28/1-2, styczen-grudzien: 101-102, 103-105 (Warsaw)

Part 1 is an abstract in English of a lecture given in 1984. Vernacular names for maize in India, obtained in his 1960 field work, are examined in relation to possible connections with America.

Part 2, also an abstract in English, distinguishes three series of cultigen names. The first he supposes was comprised of Austronesian maize names from southern Vietnam and Indonesia (one of those, *kötor, tôr,* from the Jarai people, he had previously compared with certain names from Peru and Bolivia—e.g., *turu, tara* in Uru and *turu* in Colombian Atanquez). [Compare J-091B.] Now additional, complicating data are given.

M-121B

AUTHOR: Marszewski, Tomasz
DATE: 1987b
TITLE: Badania nad dawnoscia uprawy kukurydzy no polnocno-wschodnich kresah indii [Investigations on History of Maize Cultivation in Northeastern Borderlands of India]
IN: Na egzotycznych szlakach. O polskich badaniach etnograficznych w Afryce, Ameryce i Azji w dobie powojenej, edited by Leszek Dziegiel, Archiwum Etnograficzne [Polish Ethnographical Field-Studies in Africa, America and Asia during the Post-war Period, Ethnographic Archives] 33:193-203 [Polskie Towarzystwo Ludoznawcze=Polish Ethnological Society, Warsaw]

(From English summary) The author's interest in the history of maize cultivation in Asia is to shed new light on pre-Columbian relationships between the Old and New World. He recounts his experience in field work and library research. "Information gathered seems to support the assumption of an early [i.e. pre-Columbian] transfer of maize across the Pacific, from America to Asia or the opposite way." A corroborating datum is that among Mizo tribes and in Bhutan maize cultivation precedes in time rice cultivation, maize playing the more important role in local religious rituals and ceremonies. The direction of spread of maize cultivation, from Burma and Tibet, excludes its introduction from former coastal Portuguese colonies.

M-121C

AUTHOR: Marszewski, Tomasz
DATE: 1988
TITLE: Asiatic Parallels to Some Cultural and Linguistic Elements of the Pre-Columbian Mexico as Seen by Professor Tadeusz Milewski

IN: Sprawozdania z Posiedzen Komisji Naukowych, Polska Akademia Nauk, Oddzial w Krakowie 30/1-2, styczen-grudzien: 37-39 (Warsaw)

A summary of the contents of a number of Milewski's publications, and thus the development of his thought and valuable data, from 1957 through 1966. [See M-340B through M-342C.]

[In a personal communication to Sorenson in 1992, Marszewski mentions two other relevant publications which a determined investigator of plant contacts may be able to locate whereas we have been unable to do so. One is a paper by "Prof. P. K. Gode in a local commemorative volume edited in Poona on the history of maize in India." The second is an article by "Prof. B. I. Kuznetsov in a local Buryat popular magazine on the Tibetan reception of an ancient Persian map of the world, briefly remarking the references to tobacco in the old Tibetan literature."]

M-126

AUTHOR: Martí, Samuel
DATE: 1970
TITLE: Mudra: manos simbólicas en Asia y América
[Mudra: Symbolic Hands in Asia and America]
IN: Cuadernos americanos 69/2:146-165

Certain Mesoamerican gestures (mudras) were derived from India. A selection from M-127.

M-127

AUTHOR: Martí, Samuel
DATE: 1971a
TITLE: Mudra: manos simbólicas en Asia y América
[Mudra: Symbolic Hands in Asia and America]
IMPRINT: Litexa: México

Reviews the significance of symbolic hand movements (mudras) in Hindu religion and points out parallels in Mexican and Maya iconography, quoting numerous lengthy passages from the documents. Includes 55 line drawings of hands in the Codex Dresden and 30 photographs, none of which are specifically referred to in the text. Data merit further analysis.

M-128

AUTHOR: Martí, Samuel
DATE: 1971b
TITLE: ¿Los Olmecas vinieron del Indo?
[Did the Olmecs Come from India?]
IN: Cuadernos americanos 75/2:115-122

Cites extensive passages from various sources on the cultures of the Indus Valley to suggest an Asian origin of Olmec civilization, but the argument is fragmentary. Included in M-127.

M-130

AUTHOR: Martín Mínguez, Bernardino
DATE: 1883
TITLE: [untitled]
IN: Proceedings of the 4th International Congress of Americanists (Madrid, 1881), 1:299-302

Historical parallelism between America and the Old World. Egyptians and Greeks inhabited America.

M-131

AUTHOR: Martineau, LaVan
DATE: 1973
TITLE: The Rocks Begin to Speak
IMPRINT: KC Publications: Las Vegas, Nevada

He surveys and interprets the meanings of a series of repeated American Indian rock art symbols.

Pages 147-158: "World Comparisons." Especially in his chart 6 on page 152, he shows similarities in signs among (North American)

"Indian," Sumerian, Egyptian, Chinese, and Aztec art corpuses. The meanings he considers largely obvious and either due to convergence or to a common origin very anciently, probably in Asia.

M-134

AUTHOR: Martínez del Río, Pablo
DATE: 1934
TITLE: Les chasses "chacu" au Méxique et les ruines de Zacatepec [The "Chacu" (Mode of Hunting) in Mexico and the Ruins of Zacatepec]
IN: Journal de la société des americanistes de Paris 26:293-300

A particular type of hunt was known in both the Old and New Worlds.

M-135

AUTHOR: Martínez del Río, Pablo
DATE: 1940
TITLE: Los Melanesios y los Polynesios en América [Melanesians and Polynesians in America]
IN: Revista de estudios universitarios 1/3:341-362 (Universidad Nacional Autónoma de México)

See M-136.

M-136

AUTHOR: Martínez del Río, Pablo
DATE: 1936
TITLE: Los origines americanos [American Origins]
IMPRINT: Porrua: México [Second edition, A. V. Chavez: México, 1943; third edition, Porrua: México, 1952]

Pages 276ff.: Elements in common between Oceania and America: two-headed eagle, fishhooks, quilted and plate armor, pellet-shooting bow, musical bow, bow reinforced with animal tendons, adobes, cotton, a certain type of hoe, architectural elements, wooden headrests, folding fans, wooden seats, boomerang, bannerstones, balsa rafts, inserted labial decoration, bull-roarer, bracelets of shell or turtle-shell, sweet potato, polychrome fabric belts, divining crystals, houses on stilts, earth-covered houses, tree houses, plank houses, beehive-shaped huts, the cross, trophy heads, shells as money, murex shell, shell offerings, shell trumpets, bark beaters, bark canoes, blowguns, calendar, star-shaped lids on a calabash container, masked dances and dances of the huaupua type, winged disk, dragon as a decorative motif, double canoes, plank canoes, mirrors to make fire, stone statues, figurines with coffee-bean eyes, platform burials, shields, panpipes, fortresses, unfeathered arrow, a type of gouge, vertical oar holder, hammocks, sling, adze, grooved axe, polished petal-shaped axehead, leaf raincoat, dental incrustations, Chinese or Japanese or Buddha type idols, censers, quipus, knuckle dusters, a type of lance, lacquer, litters, lances or darts with a Roman point, star-shaped annular stone club heads, Oceanic type clubs [patu, mere?], masks, megaliths, Northwest Coast type mantle, skin mantles of Tierra del Fuego type, massage, meander design, compound comb, bamboo and bone awls, eye design painted on boats, poncho, pyramids, game (parchisi), hanging bridges, carved posts, penis sheath, paper, coconut, stones carved in the shape of a human, string made of human hair, pillars, pearl ornaments, palisades, sand painting, perforated and handled stones, beads in the form of a rosary, roman balance, crutch-shaped oar, double oars, parasols, swastika, elephant trunk as decorative motif, tepee, tripod vessels, signal drums, cylindrical membrane drums, ikat dyeing, agricultural terraces, turbans, certain textiles, the toki club, the wake, tetrapodal wooden vessels, and stilts.

Items he considers diffused between Old and New Worlds include: agriculture, religious fasting, absolution of sin by confession, burning of undergrowth for fields initiated by chief, baptism, ceramics, basketry, women consecrated to a religious life having their hair cut, the four "elements," circumcision, couvade, cultural heroes, cremation, chacu hunting, duck hunting by hiding the hunter's head in a calabash, use of the remora to capture turtles, creation myth, crossing the legs, division of rule between two chiefs, use of bamboo water containers, cranial deformation, phallic cult, flagellation of the young to strengthen them, certain forms of tribal government, walking on live coals, new fire ceremony, threads suspended from branches [?], hepatoscopy, irrigation, belief that the stones have spirits, cunita game, lustrations on the head of the deceased, labyrinth, lime used in mastication of coca and tobacco, metallurgy, mummification, mastication of grain to ferment beverages, finger mutilation, dyeing teeth, belief in migration of the soul after death, feathers for decoration, woodworking, belief in the petrification of human beings, potlatch, fishing using cone-shaped baskets, painting the hand shape on rocks, fish poisoning, suspension ritual (volador), ear perforation, certain procedures in making nets, suttee, greeting with tears, sun cult, serpent cult, prestidigitation games, human sacrifice, tattooing, a manner of attaching sandals to the feet, sanctuaries, weaving, trepanation, tetrarchy, certain taboos, totemism, traction using dogs, certain cosmogonic myths, flood tradition, funerary urns of certain forms, crossing streams by means of ropes and baskets, stories of divine twins and origin of the people by incestuous union, the Euridice myth, Magic Flight motif, tale of dwarfs and giants, seclusion of young women, groups of virgins having a religious character, and various ways to transport bundles.

Page 339: Citing G. and J. Soustelle (Folklore chilien: Paris, n.d.), he reports an Araucanian rite used while felling a tree to make a canoe which uses a Maori magical invocation. [Compare I-056.]

M-137

AUTHOR: Martínez del Río, Pablo
DATE: 1946
TITLE: II. México, Egipto y Mesopotamia
IN: México prehispánico: culturas, deidades, monumentos; antologia de Esta Semana/This Week, 1935-1946, edited by Jorge A. Vivó (Editorial Emma Hurtado: Mexico), 39-59 [Part reprinted from *Por la ventana de la prehistoria,* by the author, (Polis: México, 1939), 95-124. Part reprinted from *Abside* 1/7:3-22, 1937 (México)]

A popular-level explanation of his views in three sections: comparative study and material culture; art and literature, and politics and religion. Comparison of cultural features between areas is not easy. Much has been written comparing Egyptian pyramids and Mesoamerican temple platforms, but Mesopotamian temple mounds are the more appropriate comparison. No Mesoamerican platforms were used for tombs as were Egyptian pyramids. But there are no specific evidences that New World civilizations originated from the Old. (The Northwest Coast, and perhaps the Santa Barbara area of California show what may be Asian or Oceanic features.) His comparison focuses on whether Old World centers were "more advanced" than the American civilizations. They were, but we needn't apologize for "ours" because in mental matters they did themselves proud too, despite lack of material complexity, e.g. metals, domestic animals, etc.

M-139

AUTHOR: Martínez Gracida, Manuel
DATE: 1910
TITLE: Estatua China
[Chinese Statue]
IN: Boletín de la Sociedad Mexicana de Geografía y Estadística, 5ª época, 7:553-559

Describes a statue or figurine showing a patently Chinese man in typical Chinese clothing. It was found in 1875 in a mound near Huehuetlan, Distrito de Teotitlan del Camino, Mexico. Community leaders and workers involved in digging the mound are named. Tomb contained human bones and several pieces of rough ceramic composing a patojo vessel, two "cinerary" urns, and three small ollas; inside one of the latter was the bronze statue. Also stone beads and curious decorations of ancient Indian type. Was it pre-Columbian? He thinks not. It would need some Chinese artifacts or structures to justify that. Spanish ships travelled from the Orient and that must be how this item arrived here, although it is a mystery how it then would have reached this Oaxaca site.

Mentions two other cases of apparent early remains which he considers actually post-Columbian: (1) the Crypt of Xoxo, found in 1885, which had on a slab four large black "letters" (implies European style) which he says shows that some Indians had learned to write after the Conquest but while still using the tomb; (2) the Crypt of the Eagle Knights in the Zimatlan district, found in 1893, containing human bones and a "ring of calamine" (a mineral of zinc oxide and ferrous oxide) together with a collar of gold beads and a bracelet with gilded copper heads representing Eagle Knights. The calamine must mean that it dated after the Spanish arrival. Also mentions in a note "the inscriptions of the state of Sonora, which, if they come to be identified as Chinese, would verify the arrival of the Buddhist priest Hoei-Chin." But the Indians are not Asiatic at all; they are sui generis, nothing but American, for geologists assure us that they date back as far as 250,000 years.

M-140

AUTHOR: Martínez-Hidalgo, José María
DATE: 1966
TITLE: Columbus' Ships
IMPRINT: Barre Publishers: Barre, Massachusetts

Dimensions and other characteristics of each. The smallest was only about 60 feet long.

M-143

AUTHORS: Marx, Jenifer, and Robert R. Marx
DATE: 1979
TITLE: The Phoenician Candidate: Transoceanic Explorations of the First Maritime Traders
IN: Oceans 12/4:16-20

A general recapitulation of suppositions regarding Phoenicians' reaching the New World, but contains no new information. Includes mention of a planned project to reconstruct a Phoenician ship replica and then sail it from Israel to Brazil to Yucatan and back to Tyre. "A Swiss ethnologist, Dr. Ludwig Schwennhagen, reported finding a Phoenician settlement, now named Sete Cicades, in the jungles of Brazil. Until archaeologists have completed their excavations and studies of the site, Brazilian authorities will neither deny nor confirm the controversial find."

M-144

AUTHOR: Marx, Robert R.
DATE: 1973a
TITLE: Who Really Discovered America?
IN: Argosy 376/4 (April)

Claims to have discovered frescoes near Chichen Itza of "horses . . . some mounted with riders." [Horse bones were found in unmistakably pre-Columbian stratigraphic contexts during the Carnegie excavations at Mayapan, near Chichen Itza. See H. E. D. Pollock and C. E. Ray, *Notes on Vertebrate Animal Remains from Mayapan*, Carnegie Institution of Washington, Department of Archaeology, Current Reports 41 (August 1957), 663-656; and C. E. Ray, "Pre-Columbian Horses from Yucatan," *Journal of Mammalogy* 38 (1957): 278.]

M-145

AUTHOR: Marx, Robert R.
DATE: 1973b
TITLE: Who Really Discovered the New World?

IN: Oceans 6/6:18-27

A general sketch of the diffusionist controversy. Ocean-crossing vessels existed long ago, and in any case modern sailors have shown that even small vessels were potentially viable on the ocean. Includes discussion of Valdivia, Parahyba, Bat Creek, and Roman objects.

E. D. Merrill accepted the depiction of a pineapple in a mural at Pompeii as proof of contact between the two hemispheres [?]. A "Greco-Roman torso of Venus" was found in the 1880s near Veracruz, but the date of the context is uncertain; it might be post-Columbian. "Dozens of classical Greco-Roman oil lamps were recently uncovered in northern Peru in pre-Inca tombs." García Payón discovered "a large hoard of Roman jewelry in six graves near Mexico City." Heine-Geldern and Prof. Boehringer have identified them as Roman and dating from 150 B.C. "Scientific dating of the bones and other material found in association with the jewelry indicates that the burials took place no later than 100 B.C." [Several of these assertions are not justified on the basis of García Payón's publications.]

A rock on the beach near York, Maine, known since the days of the first settlers in the region, bears a Latin inscription. Nearby a Roman coin was found dated A.D. 237. In the last century a ceramic jar containing several hundred Roman coins, dating from the reign of Augustus down to A.D. 350 and covering every intervening period, was found on a beach in Venezuela. Study of the coins in this hoard, now at the Smithsonian, shows that it was not the misplaced collection of a modern collector but probably a Roman sailor's ready cash perhaps washed ashore in a shipwreck. Two years ago a farmer in Missouri unearthed metal items and bronze drinking cup which is identical to several found at Pompeii. Tests of the metals indicate they were formed by "the direct process used in the days of the Roman Empire."

Page 21: There is a photograph of a "bronze ax head," said to be "at least 1000 years old" from Cozumel, Mexico. "Chemical analysis indicates manufacture in the eastern Mediterranean region."

M-146

AUTHOR: Marx, Robert R.
DATE: 1984
TITLE: Romans in Rio?
IN: Oceans 17/4:18-21

Page 18: An amphora of Roman appearance taken from the bay at Rio de Janeiro is shown.

Page 19: In 1972 a shipwreck was found off the Caribbean coast of Honduras with a cargo of Punic (Carthaginian or Phoenician) amphorae, but this was only noted in the press. The discoverers sent photos to the Honduran government and sought expert help, but nothing happened. Honduran government officials recently told Marx that they wanted no examination of the wreck— "an affront to Columbus's discovery of America."

According to various scholars in Brazil, the Parahyba stone was destroyed soon after its discovery in the last century in order to ensure Cabral's place in history as the discoverer of Brazil.

A young diver in 1976 found evidence of a Roman shipwreck near Rio. He sold one retrieved amphora to a tourist; the government seized the other two. Angry, he would not show the site to anyone thereafter, until Marx persuaded him some years later. Some further investigation was done, but Marx feels that what was able to be done without a major effort, for which permission could not be obtained, has not yet demonstrated the presence of ship remains.

Dozens of classical oil lamps were found in excavated pre-Inca tombs in northern Peru. García Payón in 1961 uncovered a large hoard of jewelry in six graves near Mexico City which were pronounced Roman. [His 1961 article does not mention any such finds, though it is possible that the item was published at a different time than the figurine discovery.]

M-146B

AUTHOR: Marx, Robert R., and Jenifer Marx
DATE: 1992
TITLE: In Quest of the Great White Gods: Contact between the Old and New World from the Dawn of History
IMPRINT: Crown: New York

A set of adventurer's sketches laced with diffusionist data and ideas. Chapter 1 surveys legends, including the Vikings and Brendan, and the positions of Fell and Gordon.

Pages 36-43: Early and "primitive" boats, including unique data.

Page 49: In the Royal Academy of History in Madrid he found a document by a Spanish bishop who visited Yucatan around 1550 and saw at Mani unique buildings like some he had seen in the Holy Land, bearing stone roofs "held in place by iron rods." Local elders reported a tradition that a band of white men had once come there "from a place called Carthage."

Page 88: Opposite, a plate shows a "bronze axe-head of eastern Mediterranean origin" found among ruins on Cozumel Island. In the state of Quintana Roo in a small room within a ruin inside a mound (which he and a companion once chanced upon but could not later relocate) he observed frescos showing Greek or Roman galleys manned by men with beards and light reddish hair, with shields, spears and long swords. On an unnumbered plate following page 88 is a photograph of the author at Tulum in front of a "carving of a bull" (looks to be partly-destroyed, of modelled stucco, and rather like a Cretan bull). Another plate displays Hindu figurines "found in Guatemala." A plate following page 216 shows a stone lintel in place in remnants of a "16th century church" at Thosuch [Tihosuco], Yucatan, which bears a lengthy, clear "Phoenician" inscription. [See J-092.]

Chapter 12 gives details of the story of the discovery of Roman amphorae near Rio de Janeiro as related in M-146.

M-147

AUTHOR: Mason, George C., Jr.
DATE: 1879
TITLE: The Old Stone Mill at Newport: Construction versus Theory
IN: Magazine of American History 3:541-549

He began with the belief then common that the Newport Tower was of Norse construction, but certain peculiarities in design which he found in his 1878 architectural investigation at the site forces him now to believe that it was built in the last quarter of the 17th century and that Governor Benedict Arnold was probably the designer.

M-148

AUTHOR: Mason, J. Alden
DATE: 1951
TITLE: On Two Chinese Figurines Found in Mesoamerica
IN: Homenaje al Doctor Alfonso Caso, edited by Juan Comas, et al. (Imprenta Nuevo Mundo: México), 271-276

After considering small Chinese stone figures found in collections or on the surface, he offers the explanation that they were brought and lost by Chinese laborers in modern times, while allowing that the question is still open whether they might be ancient in America.

M-149

AUTHOR: Mason, J. Alden
DATE: 1968
TITLE: The Ancient Civilizations of Peru, revised edition
IMPRINT: Penguin: Harmondsworth, England

Pages 21-24: No theory of transatlantic migration—or even of influence—has ever received any consideration from scientists of repute; it is supported by no credible evidence. But "evidences of trans-Pacific contacts are strong enough to be convincing to many good anthropologists." "There are many curious and close resemblances in cultural elements between several regions in mainland America and Polynesia, Melanesia, and south-eastern Asia that are difficult to account for on other grounds than historical contact."

Voyages over a long period seem called for, although the effect of any introductions on "the general American cultural pattern" was relatively unimportant. Some American traits may have been carried to Polynesia, Malaya, or southeastern Asia. Mentions cotton and other crops, patu clubs, panpipes ("astonishing similarities" to "early China"), betel-coca, bark cloth, tie-dyeing, sweet potato, lost-wax casting. Seems to accept a Jomon-Valdivia connection.

M-150

AUTHOR: Mason, Otis Tuftin
DATE: 1886
TITLE: Resemblances in Arts Widely Separated
IN: American Naturalist 20:246-251

Page 249: "Those arts that involve the fewest causes, the shortest concentrations of causes, have the greatest chance of arising independently; while those that involve the greatest number of complicated and connected causes give the strongest evidence of absolute identity of origin."

M-151

AUTHOR: Mason, Otis Tuftin
DATE: 1895
TITLE: Similarities in Culture
IN: American Anthropologist 7:101-117

Malay and Polynesian influence in Central America.

M-152

AUTHOR: Mason, Otis Tuftin
DATE: 1896
TITLE: Migration and the Food Quest: A Study in the Peopling of America
IN: Annual Report of the Board of Regents of the Smithsonian Institution . . . [for] 1894, pages 523-539

Two routes peopled the New World: the Bering Strait and island-hopping around the rim of the north Pacific.

M-153

AUTHOR: Mason, Otis Tuftin
DATE: 1897
TITLE: Geographical Distribution of the Musical Bow
IN: American Anthropologist (o.s.) 10:377

Describes specimens in U. S. National Museum from Africa, Oceania, Brazil, California, and New Mexico but concludes none were pre-Columbian.

M-154

AUTHOR: Mason, Otis Tuftin
DATE: 1898
TITLE: Alaskan and Hawaiian Hammers Compared
IN: American Anthropologist (o.s.) 11:382

Poi pounders from the islands and mainland "pestles" or rather hammers are "strikingly indicative of the same authorship." Historic period Russian trade with both areas may explain the fact.

M-155

AUTHOR: Mason, Otis Tuftin
DATE: 1901a
TITLE: A Primitive Frame for Weaving Narrow Fabrics
IN: Report of the United States National Museum for the year ending June 30, 1899, Part 2, Number 2, pages 485-510

The heddle frame was known among Pueblos, Algonquians, Finns, Germans, Italians and New Englanders. Its home, he believes was in Europe or southwestern Asia, and it was a post-Columbian import to American Indians.

M-156

AUTHOR: Mason, Otis Tuftin
DATE: 1901b
TITLE: Pointed Bark Canoes of the Kutenai and the Amur
IN: Report of the United States National Museum for the year ending June 30, 1899, Part 2, Number 4, pages 523-537

This unique American form of vessel, among Salishan tribes and the Gilyak, Goldi, Tungus and Yakut of northeast Asia, is pointed at both ends below the water line. This distribution "gives rise to interesting speculations."

M-157

AUTHOR: Mason, Otis Tuftin
DATE: 1901c
TITLE: The Technic [*sic*]of Aboriginal American Basketry
IN: American Anthropologist 3:109-128

Concerning the grass-coil foundation type basketry seen among the Hopi, he notes great similarity to a style of basketry found in Egypt and northern Africa. He suggests that the Hopi may have received it by acculturation since they were early in contact with Spaniards and African slaves.

M-157B

AUTHOR: Mason, Otis Tuftin
DATE: 1902
TITLE: Aboriginal American Basketry: Studies in a Textile Art without Machinery
IN: Report of the United States National Museum for 1902, pages 171-548

Page 257: "Fuegian coiled basketry bears striking resemblance to Asiatic types in the Pacific."

Page 420: The basketry double hat of the Northwest Coast is very similar to hats of China, a fact he explains as due to direct introduction from the Orient by ships of the royal Spanish fleet which used to stop regularly at Vancouver in the course of returning from Manila. Another basketry hat form, which he terms "Trunks," was brought by Hudson Bay Co. people by way of Hawaii.

M-158

AUTHOR: Massed[e?]glia, Luigi
DATE: 1927
TITLE: Il mais e la vita rurale italiana [Maize and Rural Italian Life]
IMPRINT: Piacenza, Italy

He believes that maize was in Italy in pre-Columbian times.

M-159

AUTHOR: Massip, Salvador
DATE: 1918
TITLE: The Discovery of America by the Chinese
IN: Inter-America 1:267-275 [Reprinted from *Revista Bimestre Cubana*]

A routine treatment of the question of Fu-Sang in America (Northwest Coast, Mexico, Central America).

M-160

AUTHOR: Massip, Salvador
DATE: 1919
TITLE: Descubrimiento de América por los Chinos [The Discovery of America by the Chinese]
IN: Revista americana, 94-109 (Rio de Janeiro)

First third is on Chinese voyaging contacts with Roman and Byzantine civilizations.

Pages 97-107: Chinese vessels had the capability to voyage intentionally via Kamchatka and the Aleutians to North America. Fu-Sang was located there. Includes Spanish translations of portions of the Fu-Sang material and surveys the literature (de Guignes, Buache, Klaproth, Vining).

M-161

AUTHOR: Massip, Salvador
DATE: 1921
TITLE: Un viaje precolombino de los Chinos a la América del Norte [A Pre-Columbian Journey of the Chinese to North America]
IN: II Congreso de Historia y Geografía Hispano-Americanas (Seville, 1921), 331-348

See M-159.

M-162

AUTHOR: Mastáche de Escobar, Alba Guadalupe
DATE: 1972-1973
TITLE: Dos fragmentos de tejido decorados con la técnica de plangi [Two Fabric Fragments Decorated in the Plangi Technique]
IN: Anales, Instituto Nacional de Antropología e Historia 4:251-262 (México)

First evidence of prehispanic plangi-dyed textiles in Mesoamerica.

M-163

AUTHOR: Masters, Frederik J.
DATE: 1894
TITLE: Did a Chinaman Discover America?
IN: Bulletin, Geographical Society of California 2 (May): 59-76

"The Chinese scholar cannot study the Indian dialects of the Pacific Coast without being struck with their affinity to Chinese." Mentions various features of technology, architecture, and customs supporting his point. Wolcott Brooks, "a celebrated Oriental scholar," even claimed that the orientals were native to America then migrated to Asia. Wrecked vessels are instanced. The Fusang tradition is summarized; with tongue in cheek he suggests that the exaggerations and anomalies in the Hwei Sham account might have been due to an enterprising [newspaper] reporter, "as reckless of truth as the interviewer of our day."

M-165

AUTHOR: Matheny, Ray T.
DATE: 1963
TITLE: Ancient Chinese-American Contacts? Review of a Series of Articles in the Bulletin of the Institute of Ethnology, Academia Sinica
IN: Progress in Archaeology: An Anthology, edited by Ross T. Christensen, Special Publication No. 4 ([Brigham Young] University Archaeological Society: Provo, Utah), 75-79

Summarizes articles by Ling Shun-Shêng and Dennis Wing-Sou Lou.

M-166

AUTHOR: Matheny, Ray T.
DATE: 1978
TITLE: An Analysis of the Padilla Gold Plates
IN: Brigham Young University Studies 19/1:21-40

A set of inscribed gold sheets, purportedly found in a tomb in Mexico, is examined and found on many technological grounds to be modern.

M-167

AUTHOR: Mathiassen, Therkel
DATE: 1927
TITLE: Archaeology of the Central Eskimos
IMPRINT: Report of the Fifth Thule Expedition 1921-24, vol. 4 (Gyldendalske Boghandel: Copenhagen)

The "Tunnit" (Tunit, Tornit) people referred to in Eskimo legend and supposed by some to be descended from the Norse, cannot be such but were Eskimo. Nor are ground slate implements derived from prototypes of European metal techniques, as Solberg supposed.

M-168

AUTHOR: Mathiassen, Therkel
DATE: 1928
TITLE: Norse Ruins in Labrador?
IN: American Anthropologist 30:569-579 [Same (?) as "Nørdboruiner i Labrador," *Geografisk Tidsskrift* 31 (1928): 75-86]

No reliable evidence exists.

M-169

AUTHOR: Matiegka, Heinrich
DATE: 1910
TITLE: Über Parallelen oder Beziehungen zwischen der nordamerikan- ischen und der mitteleuropäischen steinzeitlichen Keramik [On Parallels or Relationships between North American and Middle European Stone Age Ceramics]
IN: Proceedings of the 16th International Congress of Americanists (Vienna, 1908), 1:111-120

Compares seven types of pottery. He tends to favor communication rather than convergence, although the case is not settled. A few supporting data are also supplied.

M-170

AUTHOR: Matienzo, Augustín
DATE: 1895
TITLE: Estudio filológico de los idiomas de los antiguos Ingas del Perú [Philological Study of the Languages of the Ancient Incas of Peru]
IMPRINT: Europea: Buenos Aires

Relates Quechua with Sanskrit.

M-171

AUTHOR: Matos Mendieta, R.
DATE: 1966
TITLE: Un nuevo libro y una nueva teoria sobre archaeología andina [A New Book and a New Theory on Andean Archaeology]
IN: Boletin de la Sociedad Geográfica de Lima 85:82-88

Accepts the transoceanic origin of Valdivia.

M-172

AUTHOR: Matos Moctezuma, Eduardo
DATE: 1987
TITLE: Ideas acerca del origen del hombre americano (1570-1916) [Ideas Concerning the Origin of American Man (1570-1916)]
IMPRINT: Secretaría de Educación Pública: México

A compilation of short pieces by 11 authors on the topic, ranging from Fathers Durán and Sahagún through Manuel Gamio. Two are of interest: Alfredo Chavero, pages 61-76 from his *México a través de los siglos* (1887), here pages 127-156; and Nicolás León, pages 17-41 from *Historia general de México* (1902), here pages 169-188.

Chavero: America was formerly connected by land to Asia across the Pacific, via New Guinea, New Caledonia, the Marquesas and California, and also between southern South America and

New Zealand and Australia. Only by these land connections can we explain the existence of men of certain races in different places. Migration via Bering Strait, Carthaginian voyages and Jewish presence, as well as Chinese Fu-sang voyaging, are absurd hypotheses.

The Otomí of Mexico are "autocthonous," but the black race was present widely in America even earlier, when the continents were still connected. Those early peoples account for the petroglyphs, and the Otomis spoke a monosyllabic (very primitive) language.

There were later contacts, however. A Chinese-type idol was found in 1867 in a sepulchre at Ichcaquixtla, Puebla. In fact Padre Nágera [Nájera 1835] maintained that the Otomí language was closely related to Chinese. Furthermore the Nahuas and Basques are probably related, both likely remnants of Atlantis.

León: Uses much the same kind of argument, although he is geologically more modern. He emphasizes a Negro substratum, based on the then-known Olmec giant head at Hueyapan. Polynesians seem also to have arrived. He gives a highly racist sketch of the cultural characteristics of the Otomí as at about the Tasmanian level, and their monosyllabic language and gross physiognomy so like the Chinese both show they came from the north, for Otomían is so closely related to Athabascan that they are mutually comprehensible.

M-173

AUTHORS: Matson, G. Albin, H. Eldon Sutton, Raul Etcheverry B., Jane Swanson, and Abner Robinson
DATE: 1967
TITLE: In Chile, with Inferences Concerning Genetic Connections between Polynesia and America, part 4 of Distribution of Hereditary Blood Groups among Indians in South America
IN: American Journal of Physical Anthropology, 27:157-193

The closest fit of Chilean blood features is with Polynesia.

M-175

AUTHOR: Matthews, Washington
DATE: 1902
TITLE: Myths of Gestation and Parturition
IN: American Anthropologist 4:737-742

Discusses the origin of a myth widely distributed on the American continent and islands of the Pacific with traces in the eastern world. The human race is represented as having originated within the earth, emerging via a hole in the ground, ascending via a tree, vine or reed, and a deluge is associated with the emergence. His interpretation: this is based on the womb, birth canal, umbilical cord, etc.

M-176

AUTHOR: Maude, H. E.
DATE: 1981
TITLE: Slavers in Paradise: The Peruvian Labour Trade in Polynesia, 1862-1864
IMPRINT: Australian National University and University of the South Pacific: Canberra and Suva

Occurrence of Polynesian artifacts in Peru could conceivably be explained as a result of the kidnapping and transportation of 3634 Polynesians to work as impressed laborers in Peru in the 1860s, as documented in this book.

M-177

AUTHOR: Maudslay, Alfred P.
DATE: 1889-1902
TITLE: Biologia Centrali-Americana; or, Contributions to the Knowledge of the Fauna and Flora of Mexico and Central America
IMPRINT: Porter and Dulau: London

Part 10 on House E at Palenque notes presence of figures holding double- headed serpent bars very similar to those found in early Chinese art.

M-177B

AUTHOR: Maudslay, Alfred P.
DATE: 1912
TITLE: Some American Problems
IN: Journal of the [Royal] Anthropological Institute 24:9-22

In his presidential address to the Institute he touches upon the question of Old World influence on the New. There were none of consequence, he supposes, based on two points—lack of shared crops and time depth of the distinctive art styles.

M-178

AUTHOR: Mauny, Raymond
DATE: 1954
TITLE: Cerne, l'île de Herne, et la question des navigation antiques sur la côte ouest-africaine [Cerne, the Isle of Herne, and the Question of Ancient Navigation to the West-African Coast]
IN: IV Conférence Internationale des Africanistes de l'Ouest 2:73-80

Carthaginian vessels were probably incapable of sailing south of the Sahara coast [hence could not have crossed, intentionally, to America].

M-179

AUTHOR: Mauny, Raymond
DATE: 1960
TITLE: Les navigations médiévales sur les côtes sahariennes antérieures à la découverte portugaise (1434) [Medieval Navigations along the Saharan Coasts before the Portuguese Discovery (1434)]
IMPRINT: Centre des études historiques ultra-marines: Lisbon

In discussing late medieval nautical capabilities he doubts that the purported Malian fleet reached America.

M-181

AUTHOR: Mauny, Raymond
DATE: 1971
TITLE: Hypothéses concernant les relations précolombiennes entre l'Afrique et l'Amerique [Hypotheses about Pre-Columbian Contacts between Africa and America]
IN: Anuario de estudios atlánticos 17:369-389 (Madrid)

Gives his version of the pros and cons of each hypothesis. Based in considerable part on assurances from archaeological colleagues in Mexico, he believes it improbable, though not impossible, that vessels were blown to Mesoamerica. Even less likely would be any contact from America to the Old World across the Atlantic. Regarding RA II, that vessel would not have been in condition to have continued the voyage from its Barbados landfall to Yucatan. A young French couple tried to sail on the same route on a raft ("jangada") of cedar but had to be rescued no great distance at sea.

M-182

AUTHOR: Mauss, Marcel
DATE: 1920
TITLE: L'extension du potlach en Mélanésie [The Distribution of the Potlatch into Melanesia]
IN: L'Anthropologie 30:396-397

Finds all the essential features of British Columbian potlatch reproduced in Melanesia.

M-183

AUTHOR: Mauss, Marcel
DATE: 1925
TITLE: The Gift
IMPRINT: Norton: New York

Pages 45-46: The potlatch was shared by the Northwest Coast, the island world of the Pacific, parts of mainland Southeast Asia, and ancient India.

M-184

AUTHOR: Mavor, James W., Jr., and Byron E. Dix
DATE: 1987
TITLE: Manitou; Stone Structures Reveal New England's Native Civilization
IMPRINT: Lindisfarne Press: Great Barrington, Massachusetts

See M-184B.

M-184B

AUTHORS: Mavor, James W., Jr., and Byron E. Dix
DATE: 1989a
TITLE: Manitou: The Sacred Landscape of New England's Native Civilization
IMPRINT: Inner Traditions International: Rochester, Vermont

Cairns, caves, petroglyphs, walls, and other stone objects in relation to solar phenomena. They consider how these alignments were used by Native Americans to fit into their world of supernatural force worshipped under the name Manitou. Alignments of stones in New England are not merely piles collected by European settlers clearing their fields, but pre-Columbian Indians could and did construct such intentionally, for ritual reasons. Indian alignments did not depend upon any transatlantic voyagers.

M-184C

AUTHORS: Mavor, James W., Jr., and Byron E. Dix
DATE: 1989b
TITLE: An Icelandic Horizon Calendar, Key to Vinland
IN: Atlantic Visions (Proceedings of the First International Conference of the Society of Saint Brendan, September 1985, Dublin and Kerry), edited by John de Courcy Ireland and David C. Sheehy (Boole Press, Dún Laoghaire, Co.: Dublin, Ireland), 143-154

They delineate the Old Icelandic calendar as described in the sagas/eddas. They also used maps, photographs, and astronomical information applicable to the Icelandic home of Snorri Sturluson who described the solar calendar in the 13th century. This information is then related conjecturally to Leif's statements about calendar in Vinland.

M-184D

AUTHORS: Mavor, James W., Jr., and the spirit of Byron E. Dix [*sic*]
DATE: 1995
TITLE: Earth, Stones, and Sky: Universality and Continuity in American Cosmology
IN: NEARA [New England Antiquities Research Association] Journal 24/3-4:91-105

A partial recreation by Mavor of a joint lecture by him and the late Dix at the ABC conference in 1992. Huge numbers of stone features in New England are similar to those in the Maritime Archaic tradition of the North Atlantic and also share many features westward in North America. Some of these ("mound groups") they believe were built as markers for places of shamanic ritual, including the vision quest. They were locations of important events, including astronomical sightings to mark important dates. Particularly described is the array of stone mounds and stone rows on Pratt Hill near Upton, Massachusetts, where they have excavated, "which has every appearance of being both Native American and European in origin." A narrow, darkened chamber built of stones permits a significant view of equinoctial sunrise. They adduce evidence, in part from conversations with Native Americans in Massachusetts, in support of the view that some sighting structures are still in use and were even built as late as a century ago. Not just solar and lunar but also stellar phenomena were observed.

M-185

AUTHOR: May, Herbert Gordon
DATE: 1935
TITLE: Material Remains of the Megiddo Cult
IMPRINT: Oriental Institute Publication 26 (University of Chicago: Chicago)

[Mesoamerican parallels exist to:]

Page 12: Limestone altars associated with fertility cult. Incense burner stands [resembling Guatemalan examples].

Page 13: Horned altars are limited to the Levant, except one from Nineveh. Doubtful prototypes are from Asia Minor and Egypt. Aegean Middle Minoan II possibly.

Pages 15-16: Sphinxes are related to the mother goddess and have a Palestinian distribution.

Pages 23, 18: Gazelle association with the fertility cult. [Compare deer in Mesoamerica?]

Pages 23-24: Wheeled vehicles and wheeled animal figurines were without doubt votive objects as used in earlier Mesopotamia. Old Testament documentation is given of such practice in relation to sun worship that was part of the syncretistic cult of the Hebrews at c. 600 B.C.

Page 25: Legs of certain ceramic figurines suggest movable limbs. [Compare E-050. These would not be toys but mother goddess representations. Compare B-277.]

M-186

AUTHOR: Mayer, A. B.
DATE: 1904
TITLE: Alte Südseegegenstände in Amerika [Old South Sea Objects in America]
IN: Globus 86:202-3

From a German museum, he gives notes on a "Samoan club" from Peru and a mask from Atacama of Oceanian origin, which probably reached the mainland in post-Columbian times.

M-188

AUTHOR: Mayntzhusen, F. C.
DATE: 1924
TITLE: Los pigmeos en leyendas de los Guaranies [Pygmies in the Legends of the Guarani]
IN: Proceedings of the 20th International Congress of Americanists (Rio de Janeiro, 1922), 1:207-209

Title self explanatory.

M-189

AUTHOR: McAllister, J. Gilbert
DATE: 1933
TITLE: Archaeology of Oahu
IMPRINT: Bernice P. Bishop Museum Bulletin 104 (Honolulu)

A major irrigation ditch of earth and stone. [Compare Meso- or South America? Linton reported irrigation ditching in the Marquesas. See S-357, page 45.]

M-190

AUTHOR: McBryde, Felix Webster
DATE: 1945
TITLE: Cultural and Historical Geography of Southwest Guatemala
IN: Institute of Social Anthropology, Publication No. 4 (Smithsonian Institution: Washington, D.C.)

Page 36: "Bananas are mentioned in the *Cakchiquel Annals* (Brinton, 1885, p. 107), and some varieties seem to have grown in America prior to the Conquest." The varieties introduced from the Old World became the most desirable ones.

Page 137: Notes that Cucurbita ficifolia, said by Standley and Calderon

to be a native of the Old World, was in native [implied pre-Columbian] use in Guatemala. [Also found at Huaca Prieta; see Whitaker and Bird 1949.]

Page 138: Zhitenev, in Bukasov 1930, disagrees with Spinden and Sapper in their thinking that the marimba may not be "a recent instrument of African origin," but rather pre-Columbian. Luffa aegyptica, a cucurbit of Old World origin but widely naturalized in America, was possibly used in pre-Columbian times by Indians.

Pages 145-146: Palm wine, made from the trunk of the coyol palm, apparently dates from pre-Columbian times in Guatemala. [Contra Bruman who concluded that this practice in West Mexico originated with the Manila galleon trade; see B-416.]

Page 147: The swordbean, frijol haba, Canavalia ensiformis has 24 American species and only 13 from the Old World. Archaeology seems to confirm it as old in Peru. Found in Oaxaca, Chiapas, and Guatemala, and it may be, it is implied, pre-Columbian in Middle America.

M-191B

AUTHOR: McCartney, Allen P.
DATE: 1988
TITLE: Late Prehistoric Metal Use in the New World Arctic
IN: The Late Prehistoric Development of Alaska's Native People, edited by Robert D. Shaw, Roger K. Harritt, and Don E. Dumond, Alaska Anthropological Association Monograph Series 4, pages 57-79

See M-192. He believes that the use of metal "was so common that Alaskan Neo-eskimos developed an epi-metallurgical technology about 1,500-2,000 years prior to direct Russian contact." The metal was obtained by trade, direct or indirect, with northeast Asiatic peoples.

M-192

AUTHORS: McCartney, Allen P., and D. J. Mack
DATE: 1973
TITLE: Iron Utilization by Thule Eskimos of Central Canada
IN: American Antiquity 38:328-339

Specimens of meteoric and terrestrial iron are surveyed. Terrestrial iron was used for over two millennia in the western Arctic, suggesting that it was more significant in the Eskimo tool kit than has been thought and implying a very long distance trade network, presumably involving northern Asia. In the eastern Arctic as far west as the western Hudson Bay coast, iron supposed of Norse Greenlandic origin was in use at least 400 years before any non-Norse European contact; it appears to have travelled by a route as long as 1400 miles.

M-194

AUTHOR: McCown, C. C.
DATE: 1947
TITLE: Tell en-Nasbeh, vol. 1: Archaeological and Historical Results
IMPRINT: The Palestine Institute of the Pacific School of Religion: Berkeley; and American Schools of Oriental Research: New Haven

Pages 236-242: Incense burner stands with ceramic horns atop [comparable to horned censer stands from Mesoamerica] were normally covered with a white wash. [Compare B-275.]

Pages 244-245: Small pottery wheels and boxes were quite clearly from model chariots (also at Gerar and Megiddo), dating in this case to Middle-Late Iron. If they were cult objects, as is plausible, they would have been connected with sun worship.

M-195

AUTHOR: McCown, C. C.
DATE: 1950

TITLE: Hebrew High Places and Cult Remains
IN: Journal of Biblical Literature 69:205-219

Incense burning stands of limestone include cylindrical as well as cubical horned forms. [See B-275.]

Censer bowls were usually set upon horns projecting up from the edge of incense altars. [Compare L-333.]

M-196

AUTHOR: McCown, Theodore D.
DATE: 1952
TITLE: Ancient Man in South America
IN: Indian Tribes of Aboriginal America; Selected Papers of the 29th International Congress of Americanists (New York, 1949), edited by Sol Tax (University of Chicago Press: Chicago), 374-379

In a survey of cranial material, he observes that the so-called Australian, Tasmanian, and New Guinea crania, from Punín or elsewhere on the continent, are not outside the norms for American Indians and cannot serve as independent evidence for the arrival of Old World peoples from across the ocean.

M-196B

AUTHOR: McCrone, Walter C.
DATE: 1976
TITLE: Authenticity of Medieval Document Tested by Small Particle Analysis
IN: Analytical Chemistry 48/8:676A-679A

See M-196C.

M-196C

AUTHOR: McCrone, Walter C.
DATE: 1988
TITLE: The Vinland Map
IN: Analytical Chemistry 48:1009-1018

Rebuts C-001A and M-204B. New tests on the ink on the map show that it contains a product only available since 1917, hence the document must be a fake.

M-197

AUTHOR: McCulloch, J. Huston
DATE: 1988
TITLE: The Bat Creek Inscription: Cherokee or Hebrew?
IN: Tennessee Anthropologist 13/2:79-123

A detailed review of the circumstances attending discovery of the Bat Creek inscription in eastern Tennessee in 1889 by a Smithsonian Institution investigator and the controversial literature stemming therefrom. On evidence presented here, he concludes that the inscription is indisputably pre-Columbian, not historic Cherokee as some (most recently McKusick) have asserted. Moreover, comparisons of the characters with those of archaic Hebrew, the Cherokee syllabary, and English show substantially closest similarity to the Hebrew.

The "copper" bracelets associated with the stone are also reported in detail; they are actually of brass and have parallels in the Mediterranean world only during the first and second centuries of the Christian era, supporting the reading of the inscription as Hebrew of that period. The Bar Kokhba coins found in the area are also surveyed, as is the possibility of forgery.

Reviewed by Curtiss Hoffman, *Massachusetts Archaeological Society Newsletter,* Fall 1988, which ends: "Altogether, the Bat Creek inscription, in its context, is the strongest evidence yet produced for pre-Columbian contact across the Atlantic."

M-197B

AUTHOR: McCulloch, J. Huston
DATE: 1989
TITLE: The Newark Hebrew Stones: Wyrick's Letter to Joseph Henry
IN: Midwestern Epigraphic Journal 6:5-10

The letter says that two of the five stones from Newark were fabricated by Nicoll.

M-197C

AUTHOR: McCulloch, J. Huston
DATE: 1990
TITLE: The Newark, Ohio, Inscribed Head—a New Translation
IN: Epigraphic Society Occasional Publications 19:75-79

Three of the Newark pieces, including this head, are inscribed in a peculiar square Hebrew script. Two of the five stones from the area are patent fakes, planted to discredit the original discovery. The fifth stone, the "Johnson-Bradner Stone," was discovered in 1867 deep in the same mound as the first two. The account of the finding of the Inscribed Head (the third stone "found") is examined. On the basis of a careful new transcription by McCulloch, he reads the inscription on it as "J - H - Nicol," written in Hebrew characters. This was the name of a man who was present at the dig, but the account of the find leaves uncertain how Nicol could have succeeded in planting it while present with other, apparently innocent persons. The fourth ("Cooper") stone was found the following day in loose dirt at this same mound. Similarity of the characters make Nicol the probable source of this fourth stone also. But "there is . . . no reason to dismiss out of hand the possibility that the" first two and fifth stones in the Newark set "are genuine ancient Hebrew artifacts" because two have been found fraudulent.

M-197D

AUTHOR: McCulloch, J. Huston
DATE: 1992
TITLE: Annotated Transcription of the Ohio Decalogue Stone
IN: Epigraphic Society Occasional Publications 21:56-71

A fully detailed transcription of the Newark "Ohio Decalogue" stone with discussion and notes on differences in letters, figure represented ("Moses"), and text from the Masoretic and other relevant versions of Exodus 20 and anomalies from standard Hebrew. Treats historically those persons who have transcribed or translated the stone before. Summarizes the theory that Wyrick faked the inscription and points out cogent reasons why this could not be. Cites sources not listed in this bibliography. With Alrutz [A-094] this is one of the fundamental pieces for any further study of this inscribed stone.

M-197E

AUTHOR: McCulloch, J. Huston
DATE: 1993
TITLE: Did Judean Refugees Escape to Tennessee
IN: Biblical Archaeology Review, July/August, pages 47-53 [Rebutted by Bible scholar P. Kyle McCarter, Jr., "Let's Be Serious about the Bat Creek Stone," pages 54-55 in the same issue. McCulloch replies to McCarter in the following November/December issue, pages 14-16, followed by a letter from Robert Stieglitz [see S-467 to S-469] in support of Huston; then McCarter responds to both. Mainfort and Kwas [see M-055B] add their comments on pages 18 and 76]

See M-197.

M-197F

AUTHOR: McCulloch, J. Huston
DATE: 1993
TITLE: The Bat Creek Stone: A Reply to Mainfort and Kwas
IN: Tennessee Anthropologist 18 (Spring): 1-26

A detailed rebuttal of three issues about the ancient authenticity of the Bat Creek stone raised in M-055B.

M-199

AUTHOR: McElrath, Clifford
DATE: 1966
TITLE: The Last Tomolo
IN: Noticias 12/4:1-4

Possibly the last of the plank canoes made by Indians on the Santa Barbara Channel was used on Santa Cruz Island in the 1870s. This author says that the design "was possibly influenced by the Aleuts" [accompanying the Russians in 18th century California?].

M-201

AUTHORS: McEwan, G. F., and B. Dickson
DATE: 1978
TITLE: Valdivia, Jomon Fishermen, and the Nature of the North Pacific: Some Nautical Problems with Meggers, Evans and Estrada's (1965) Transoceanic Contact Thesis
IN: American Antiquity 43:362-365

Maintain that a drift vessel would take 19 months minimum with no chance for survivors. [Compare M-252 and N-023.]

M-202

AUTHOR: McGhee, Robert
DATE: 1982a
TITLE: Norsemen and Eskimos in Arctic Canada
IN: Vikings in the West, edited by E. Guralnick (Archaeological Institute of America: Chicago), 38-52

See M-204.

M-203

AUTHOR: McGhee, Robert
DATE: 1982b
TITLE: Possible Norse-Eskimo Contacts in the Eastern Arctic
IN: Early European Settlement and Exploration in Arctic Canada, edited by G. M. Story (St. John's Memorial University of Newfoundland: St. John's), 31-40

See M-204.

M-204

AUTHOR: McGhee, Robert
DATE: 1984
TITLE: Contact between Native North Americans and the Medieval Norse: A Review of the Evidence
IN: American Antiquity 49:4-26

Historical and archaeological evidence of Norse activities in eastern North America early in the second millennium A.D. is reviewed, together with archaeological evidence relating to aboriginal occupations of those regions at the time when the Norse might have visited. The Norse probably contacted Indian populations in southern Labrador and Newfoundland, Dorset Palaeoeskimos in northern Labrador, and Thule Eskimos in Greenland and perhaps in the eastern Canadian Arctic. Speculation on the nature of relationships between the Norse and those groups is presented; it is concluded that occasional contacts involving both trade and plundering probably occurred over a period of several centuries.

There is no evidence to indicate that these contacts had any major influence on aboriginal North American populations. Despite a review of claims of Norse sites, objects, and influences, particularly in Lee's writings, the author concludes, tentatively, that "we know of no North American archaeological site where direct contact with the Norse can be demonstrated." Yet finds in native sites probably to be attributed to the Norse suggest that contacts must have occurred more frequently than recorded in the Norse historical accounts. No indication of European-originated disease is evident at native sites. Little evidence of contact might, in fact, be expected, since the cultural level of the Norse who came was barely, if at all, superior to that of the natives.

M-204B

AUTHOR: McGhee, Robert
DATE: 1987a
TITLE: The Vinland Map: Hoax or History?
IN: The Beaver (April-May): 37-44

Points out that when the three parts of this medieval document (the map, the volumes of Tartar Relations, and the Speculum Historiale) which had been separated were brought together and lined up, the holes of worms that ate through the pages were in alignment. He takes this as evidence of authenticity. Maintains that the ink test purporting to show use of a modern ink was indeterminate.

M-204C

AUTHOR: McGhee, Robert
DATE: 1987b
TITLE: Norsemen and Eskimos in Arctic Canada
IN: Vikings in the West, edited by Eleanor Guralnick (University of Chicago Press: Chicago), 38-52

Who were the Skraelings? Eskimo. Summarizes the aboriginal culture sequence for northeastern North America. The Maine penny was minted several decades after the last Norse voyage recorded in the sagas so it must have been from one of the later sporadic trips and traded or carried southward in Indian hands. Recounts Norse objects found in legitimate archaeological contexts, as far west as the west coast of Hudson Bay. Eskimos had substantial amounts of iron, some meteoric but "some of the iron and perhaps the techniques of cold working iron may have originated in the Norse colonies." All finds date before the end of the Norse Greenland colonies. There is "wide distribution of smelted iron, bronze, and copper in Canadian arctic Eskimo sites." Metal was a valued commodity; perhaps ivory was traded for it. A bronze bar, part of a folding balance, was found in a site 2000 kms. northwest of the Norse colonies, suggesting that a Norse trader might have penetrated there. Recaps T. Lee's Ungava Peninsula sites but considers them Dorset (Eskimo). At least a Norse presence is not proven.

M-204D

AUTHORS: McGhee, Robert, and James Tuck
DATE: 1977
TITLE: Did the Medieval Irish Visit Newfoundland?
IN: Canadian Geographical Journal 95:66-73

Possibly, they think, noting the presence of a lichen-covered stone on which is ogham-like writing about 10 miles from L'Anse aux Meadows, Newfoundland. The Hvritmannaland of the Norse saga might have been an Irish settlement (there was "an Irish component" in Iceland and Greenland and some in Norse sailing groups may have been familiar with the ogham alphabet).

M-205

AUTHOR: McGinty, Brian
DATE: 1980
TITLE: China Crossing
IN: Westways 72 (August) (San Francisco)

Claims that large stones found off the coast of California were anchors from Chinese ships.

M-205B

AUTHOR: McGinty, Brian
DATE: 1983
TITLE: Mystery of the Eastern Connection. Did Ancient Oriental Mariners Sail to our West Coast?
IN: American West 20:57-62

See M-205.

M-206

AUTHORS: McGlone, William R., and Phillip M. Leonard
DATE: 1986
TITLE: Ancient Celtic America
IMPRINT: Panorama West Books: Fresno, California

A study of petroglyph sites in North America, making a case for the presence of messages in the Ogam script.

M-206B

AUTHORS: McGlone, William R., Ted Barker, and Phillip M. Leonard
DATE: 1994
TITLE: Petroglyphs of Southeast Colorado and the Oklahoma Panhandle
IMPRINT: Mithras: Kamas, Utah

Heavily illustrated, many petroglyphs of the area in color and black and white photographs and also drawings. Describes characteristics of Indian (three styles), historic, and enigmatic petroglyphs. Makes a provisional attempt to date these either by style or by direct chemical dating. Includes many inscriptions, such as those at Anubis Cave, that have archaeoastronomical significance. The discussion and illustrations together constitute a straightforward guide to the petroglyphs of southeastern Colorado useful to scholar or amateur.

Page 17: Many sites have geometric signs which are classified as "Pecked Abstract" style. "These signs show a remarkable correspondence to letters of the North Arabian alphabets, Thamudic, and Safaitic. Scholars of Arabic have tried to read them without success, but think they may be writing and have encouraged further study of their possible connection to the Old World. These signs have been dated from 1900 to 2300 years old, the time of the use of the Thamudic and Safaitic alphabets in Arabia." On page 27 are sketches of "North Arabian script [which] was used in the Old World about the time of Christ." "They are not North Arabian writing directly transferred to Colorado, since scholars are unable to read them in the same way they are read in the Old World."

Page 65: Some sets of parallel lines may be Ogam writing. "We believe it is probable that a somewhat earlier version of Ogam, dated possibly as early as 1000 B.C., is found in a limited portion of southeast Colorado." "Few scholars accept the Ogam identification or the implication of pre-Columbian Old World visitation suggested by this interpretation."

M-206C

AUTHORS: McGlone, William R., Phillip M. Leonard, and James L. Guthrie
DATE: 1990
TITLE: The Case of the Voweled Ogam: Epigraphic Fraudulence in Kentucky
IN: Myth Makers: Epigraphic Illusion in America, edited by James P. Whittall, Jr., Early Sites Research Society Epigraphic Series No. 1 (Rowley, Massachusetts), 15-31

A report of technical investigations on purported ancient inscriptions in Kentucky which were found to be manifest modern fakes.

M-206D

AUTHORS: McGlone, William R., Phillip M. Leonard, James L. Guthrie, Rollin W. Gillespie, and James P. Whittall, Jr.
DATE: 1993
TITLE: Ancient American Inscriptions: Plow Marks or History?

IMPRINT: Early Sites Research Society: Rowley, Massachusetts

A sweeping, indispensable discussion of issues involved in the identification, evaluation, and translation of Ogam-like and other North American inscriptions. They critique their own past work as well as all other treatments of this topic, pro and con. Fell's transcriptions and interpretations are particularly criticized. This volume supersedes M-206.

M-206E

AUTHORS: McGlone, William R., Phillip M. Leonard, James L. Guthrie, James P. Whittall, Jr., and Rollin W. Gillespie
DATE: 1993
TITLE: A Brief Report on SCRIPT 89
IN: The Eclectic Epigrapher, edited by Donald L. Cyr (Stonehenge Viewpoint: Santa Barbara, California), 68-71

Annalistic impressions of events at a pivotal field symposium in southeastern Colorado over September equinox 1989 where both proponents and opponents of the idea that European writing appears in rock inscriptions in that area were present [see C-455]. Those attending, including skeptics, were impressed that certain inscribed features that appear to be readable in West European terms are placed in relation to solar phenomena. This item and accompanying articles in Cyr's volume provide commentaries on what different observers felt took place at the symposium.

M-206F

AUTHORS: McGlone, William R., Phillip M. Leonard, and Rollin W. Gillespie
DATE: 1989
TITLE: The Ogam Corridor of Southeast Colorado
IN: Rock Art of the Western Canyons, Memoir No. 3 (Colorado Archaeological Society and Denver Museum of Natural History: Boulder, Colorado), 157-170

Chiefly a selection of material from M-206 referring to a zone between the Arkansas and Cimarron Rivers where many inscriptions are found which they consider Ogam.

M-208

AUTHOR: McGovern, Thomas H.
DATE: 1980
TITLE: The Vinland Adventure: A North Atlantic Perspective
IN: North American Archaeologist 2:285-308

The negative evidence is overwhelming that the Viking settlement in North America was unsuccessful. Considers why: distance from market and capital/supplies base in Scandinavia, for Greenland was weak itself; vulnerability to Skraeling raids; general Atlantic economic and nautical tendencies, especially waning prosperity. The chances for successful colonization were never good.

M-209

AUTHOR: McGovern, Thomas H.
DATE: 1987
TITLE: Review of *The Vikings and America*, by Erik Wahlgren
IN: Arctic, Journal of the Arctic Institute of North America 40/2:161

"Most of the available archaeological and paleoecological work is either ignored or badly misused, and the book contains a regrettable number of glaring errors of fact and interpretation." Following is a response from Wahlgren who tries to put the best face he can on the review but is not very successful.

M-210B

AUTHOR: McGrail, Seán
DATE: 1981
TITLE: Rafts, Boats and Ships

IMPRINT: HMSO: London

Pages 16-25: Summarizes the evidence for types of water-transport in use in later prehistoric (late first millennium B.C.) northern and western Europe. The earliest evidence for indigenous sail in northern and western Europe is from the first century B.C. Subsequent pages include information on early historical (Roman period) shipping.

M-210C

AUTHOR: McGrail, Seán
DATE: 1989
TITLE: Pilotage and Navigation in the Times of St. Brendan
IN: Atlantic Visions (Proceedings of the First International Conference of the Society of Saint Brendan, September 1985, Dublin and Kerry), edited by John de Courcy Ireland and David C. Sheehy (Boole, Dún Laoghaire, Co.: Dublin, Ireland), 25-35

Not until the 12th century did non-instrumental pilotage and navigational techniques begin to be replaced by quantitative methods in the seas off northwest Europe. There is little artifactual or documentary evidence for methods. Archaeological and documentary evidence suggest that the main problems of pilotage and non-instrumental navigation were solved to an acceptable degree of accuracy in the seas between France and Britain and elsewhere well before the sixth century A.D. Possible methods are described. Brendan and his contemporaries in the sixth century A.D. thus would have had to have used techniques inherited from their predecessors, which would not have been unfamiliar eight centuries later, or even fourteen centuries later in some parts of the world (e.g., in Polynesia).

M-211

AUTHOR: McGrath, Patrick
DATE: 1979
TITLE: Bristol and America, 1480-1631
IN: The Westward Enterprise: English Activities in Ireland, the Atlantic and America, 1480-1650, edited by K. R. Andrews (Wayne State University Press: Detroit), 81-102

Finding no financial records of voyages by Bristol sailors across the North Atlantic in the 1480s as claimed by some, the author concludes that no more than one isolated expedition was made. There is no evidence that they attempted permanent settlement or affected Indian life.

M-211B

AUTHORS: McGraw, Alva, Bennett E. Kelley, and Clyde E. Keeler
DATE: 1973
TITLE: Bog Iron in Pre-Columbian Graves?
IN: NEARA [New England Antiquities Research Association] Journal 8:75-78

Recaps the literature on iron found in Ohio archaeological sites. It is established that meteoric iron occurred, but also now bog iron fragments and rust appear (based on chemical analyses), so "Moundbuilders" apparently had access to both types of iron. The bog iron could be from Viking activities.

M-212

AUTHORS: McGregor, J. C., and W. L. Wadlow
DATE: 1951
TITLE: A Trephined Indian Skull from Illinois?
IN: American Anthropologist 53:148-151

They consider a skull from Illinois unquestionably intentionally trephined while alive and that the operation was similar in all respects to that practiced in Peru. This was the only sure case known from North America as of 1951.

M-212B

AUTHOR: McKelvie, B. A.
DATE: 1955
TITLE: Pageant of B. C.
IMPRINT: Thomas Nelson: Toronto

Cites several Chinese artifacts discovered in British Columbia that he had previously reported in newspapers as evidence that Chinese had reached the area before European discovery.

M-214

AUTHOR: McKern, William C.
DATE: 1937
TITLE: An Hypothesis for the Asiatic Origin of the Woodland Pattern
IN: American Antiquity 3:138-143

While knowledge of the distribution and characteristics of North American pottery is still incomplete, what is known suggests the possibility of at least one Indian ceramic ware ("Woodland-like") independent of maize distribution but extending from central North America northwestward into eastern Asia, or vice versa.

M-215

AUTHOR: McKusick, Marshall B.
DATE: 1960
TITLE: Aboriginal Canoes in the West Indies
IN: Yale University Publications in Anthropology, no. 63 (Yale University Press: New Haven)

A short paper summarizes the early historical sources on Caribbean, including Mayan, canoes or ships. He is convinced that sails were used in pre-Columbian days off Yucatan and Central America but not in the Antilles.

M-216

AUTHOR: McKusick, Marshall B.
DATE: 1970
TITLE: The Davenport Conspiracy
IMPRINT: State Archaeologist Report 1 (University of Iowa: Iowa City)

Gives evidence that the Davenport stone of the 19th century was bogus, intended to embarrass a certain minister, rather than being an artifact produced by pre-Columbian European visitors.

M-217

AUTHOR: McKusick, Marshall B.
DATE: 1979a
TITLE: A Cryptogram in the Phoenician Inscription from Brazil
IN: Biblical Archaeology Review 5/4:50-54

Gordon has erred four times in decipherment: Kensington Stone, Vinland Map, Spirit Pond rune stone, and Parahyba. All have been dismissed by experts despite his insistent readings and justification of their authenticity. McKusick is convinced that there never was a Parahyba stone but only Neto's false handwritten version.

M-218

AUTHOR: McKusick, Marshall B.
DATE: 1979b
TITLE: Canaanites in America: A New Scripture in Stone?
IN: Biblical Archaeologist 42:137-140

Supports the anti-diffusionist critique of Goddard and Fitzhugh [G-119] here telling why six purported evidences for Phoenician explorations in America—New England Ogam, Davenport, Grave Creek, Bat Creek, Metcalf, Paraiba—should be considered "poor substitutes for reality."

M-219

AUTHOR: McKusick, Marshall B.
DATE: 1979c
TITLE: North American Periphery of Antique Vermont
IN: Antiquity 53:121-123

He is exasperated that orthodox archaeologists have failed to stand up and be counted against the heretics (Fell, Trento, Chandler, Cohane, Gordon, Sertima, et al.) who challenge conventional views without satisfactory evidence.

M-219B

AUTHOR: McKusick, Marshall B.
DATE: 1979d
TITLE: Some Historical Implications of the Norse Penny from Maine
IN: Norwegian Numismatic Journal 3:20-23

See M-223.

M-219C

AUTHOR: McKusick, Marshall B.
DATE: 1981a
TITLE: The Davenport Conspiracy: A Hoax Unraveled
IN: Early Man 1:9-12

"It is perfectly clear that the so-called [by Fell] American Rosetta Stone [i.e., the Davenport Stone] is a forgery." It was part of a broader group of hoaxes and forgeries pepetrated in the Davenport area during the 1870s. Settlers from New England planned to put an aggressive German-speaking clergyman in his place by salting his dig with fraudulent pieces which they made. They later denied anything, but individuals at one point in time confessed participation. Fell's books are of a type popular nowadays "that contain little archaeology and much speculation."

M-220

AUTHOR: McKusick, Marshall B.
DATE: 1980
TITLE: Ungava Bay Discoveries Reconsidered
IN: Anthropological Journal of Canada 18/3:2-8

T. Lee's view of Norse structures here will not do.

M-220B

AUTHOR: McKusick, Marshall B.
DATE: 1981b
TITLE: Deciphering Ancient America: Barry Fell's Claims of Ancient New World Settlers Fall before Scholarly Analysis
IN: The Skeptical Inquirer (Spring): 44-50

A short denunciation addressed to those already skeptical about Fell. Fell does not know the languages behind the scripts; linguists have found no grammar or vocabulary in America to coincide with his claims. Rather persistent in claiming "plow marks" as inscription grist for Fell's mill.

M-221

AUTHOR: McKusick, Marshall B.
DATE: 1981
TITLE: Review of *Saga America*, by Barry Fell
IN: Archaeology 34/1:62-66

Extremely negative. "That such a book . . . could be perpetrated upon a naive reading public as authentic prehistory represents a scandal deserving censure of the issuing press and author alike."

M-221B

AUTHOR: McKusick, Marshall B.
DATE: 1991
TITLE: The Davenport Conspiracy Revisited
IMPRINT: Iowa State University: Ames

A revision and extension of M-216.

M-222

AUTHORS: McKusick, Marshall B., and Eric Wahlgren

DATE: 1980a
TITLE: Vikings in America: Fact and Fiction
IN: Early Man 2/4:7-11

In absolute language ("clumsy frauds," "refuse to accept the facts," "evidence is conclusive"), they insist that most of the claimed Viking finds are hoaxes or misidentifications.

M-223

AUTHORS: McKusick, Marshall B., and Erik Wahlgren
DATE: 1980b
TITLE: The Norse Penny Mystery
IN: Archaeology of Eastern North America 8:1-10

A coin found in an Indian site in Maine is evidently legitimately Norse, but it must have reached this Indian site via trade.

M-223B

AUTHORS: McKusick, Marshall B., and Eric Wahlgren
DATE: 1980c
TI TLE: Does Cryptogrammic Analysis Reveal Pre-Columbian Voyages to America?
IN: Biblical Archaeology Review 6/2:55-56, 58

They vehemently disbelieve Gordon's arguments in G-172.

M-224

AUTHOR: McLean, Mervyn
DATE: 1979
TITLE: Towards the Differentiation of Music Areas in Oceania
IN: Anthropos 74:717-736

Some 38 traits from 44 areas are compared in an attempt along lines marked out by Driver to define musical areas. Any study attempting to evaluate possible diffusion of music instruments and other features between Asia, Oceania, and the Americas should consult this study, for example, in regard to the musical bow, panpipes, and slit drums.

M-225B

AUTHOR: McMahan, Basil B.
DATE: 1965
TITLE: The Mystery of the Old Stone Fort
IMPRINT: Tennessee Book Co.: Nashville

Notes speculations by local observers about these ruins in Tennessee, including attribution to Vikings, Madoc (Welsh), Spanish buccaneers, the Yuchi Indians, and "Mound Builders." Charles H. Faulkner *(The Old Stone Fort: Exploring an Archaeological Mystery* [University of Tennessee Studies in Anthropology: Knoxville, 1968]) demonstrated that the enclosure was apparently constructed by Hopewellian Middle Woodland Indians in the early centuries A.D.

M-226

AUTHOR: McManis, Douglas R.
DATE: 1969
TITLE: The Traditions of Vinland
IN: Annals of the Association of American Geographers 55:797-814

Groups arguments and interpretations about Vinland into schools or traditions and identifies recurring issues: the character and interpretation of acceptable evidence, route, identities of sites, vegetation, natives' identity, and relations of the Norse voyages to later voyages to the New World.

M-227

AUTHOR: McNeill, William H.
DATE: 1963
TITLE: The Rise of the West: A History of the Human Community
IMPRINT: University of Chicago Press: Chicago

In a world-scope history notable for not being Europe-centered, the author is rather willing to allow for transpacific influences on pre-Columbian America.

M-228B

AUTHOR: McNeill, William H.
DATE: 1988
TITLE: Diffusion in History
IN: The Transfer and Transformation of Ideas and Material Culture, edited by Peter J. Hugill and D. Bruce Dickson (Texas A & M University Press: College Station, Texas), 75-90

A short history of transportation as affecting the possibility of diffusion. Because its sources are not up-to-date, the conclusions of this paper are very conservative, emphasizing the relative lateness and untrustworthiness of ancient shipping (e.g., Polynesians crossed the Pacific to Easter Island beginning about A.D. 600, while safe rough-weather shipping by the Chinese waited until A.D. 1000). Still, occasional drift voyages of unusual length must have occurred from the time sailors began to cross the seas at all. If one could stay afloat long enough, America would be reached, though the effect on culture might be slight from such contacts.

When Europeans expanded throughout the world, they became persuaded that the world with which they had (recently) been familiar—Europe and the Near East—had always been the center of historical progress, thus they doubted that anything as important as gunpowder or printing had come from China, unless historically documented. [He implies that this viewpoint also predisposes anthropologists to doubt that borrowing—"diffusion"—occurred in the absence of documentary "proof."] Actually borrowing is always accompanied by a measure of invention because the conditions in the source area can never be duplicated exactly.

M-228C

AUTHOR: McPherson, H. R.
DATE: 1973
TITLE: More about the Seip Mound and the Seip Mound Coin
IN: NEARA [New England Antiquities Research Association] Journal 8:34

See K-030C.

M-229

AUTHOR: Mead, C. W.
DATE: 1919
TITLE: Coca and Betel Chewing: A Reply
IN: American Anthropologist 21:337

Response to Laufer (1919) [L-084]. The finding of many lime-gourds and representations on pottery of men taking lime with coca proves that the use of lime antedated the advent of Europeans in Peru.

M-230

AUTHOR: Mead, Sidney M.
DATE: 1975
TITLE: The Origins of Maori Art: Polynesian or Chinese?
IN: Oceania 45:173-211

Polynesian, of course. If resemblances in the arts of the Northwest Coast of America, China, and New Zealand are to be explained, historical explanation is not the answer. "We need to pasture the old nags and ride out on fresh horses," something like a Lévi-Straussian stallion which will orient our studies to trying to discover "how art systems work."

M-231

AUTHOR: Mead, Sidney M.
DATE: 1976
TITLE: Review of *Comparatively Speaking: Studies in Pacific Material Culture 1921-1972*, by Henry Devenish Skinner
IN: Journal of the Polynesian Society 85:426-429

Page 428: He quarrels with diffusion-minded Skinner about the transmissible nature of specific art forms and motifs. Do apparent resemblences in the form of objects or motifs justify assuming that a form has one and only one meaning? Why would people from another culture want to import an art motif, and why would the inventor want to "trade" it to far-off lands? Still, Skinner has clearly demonstrated that forms do resemble one another to a remarkable degree, and only diffusionists have offered an adequate explanation. There must be other explanations, but he has no suggestion.

M-231B

AUTHOR: Meade, Joaquín
DATE: 1942
TITLE: La Huasteca: época antigua
IMPRINT: Publicaciones Históricas: México

Believes that the civilizer group that arrived at Pánuco, according to Mexican tradition, was Irish.

M-232

AUTHOR: Means, Philip Ainsworth
DATE: 1916
TITLE: Some Objections to Mr. Elliot Smith's Theory
IN: Science 44:533-534

Points out objections to the theory—no wheel in America, lack of adequate ships, and insufficient time to allow for a wave of culture to cover so much territory—but he also mentions the large amount of seemingly corroborative evidence mustered.

M-233

AUTHOR: Means, Philip Ainsworth
DATE: 1931
TITLE: Ancient Civilizations of the Andes
IMPRINT: Scribner's: New York

Lack of advanced seafaring techniques on the coast of South America does much to refute the claim of Oceanic origin of South American peoples.

M-234

AUTHOR: Means, Phillip Ainsworth
DATE: 1942a
TITLE: Pre-Spanish Navigation off the Andean Coast
IN: American Neptune 2/2:115-119

Documents the use of sails on pre-Spanish watercraft [contrary to the later views of Rydén and Suggs].

M-235

AUTHOR: Means, Phillip Ainsworth
DATE: 1942b
TITLE: The Newport Tower
IMPRINT: Holt: New York

He is a believer in pre-English construction and he accepts the authenticity of the Kensington Stone. Vinland was between Cape Cod and the Hudson.

M-236

AUTHOR: Medellín Zenil, Alfonso
DATE: 1960
TITLE: Monolitos inéditos olmecas [Unknown Olmec Monoliths]
IN: La palabra y el hombre 16:75-97 [Revista de la Universidad Veracruzana, Xalapa]

From Stirling's observation that an Olmec stone head at San Lorenzo had a spot of purple color on it, Medellín infers that the head had once all been painted. [S-198 then supposes that the purple constitutes evidence for early murex shellfish dye.]

M-238

AUTHOR: Medina, Alberto
DATE: 1984
TITLE: Embarcaciones chilenas precolombinas: la dalca de Chiloé [Pre-Columbian Chilean Boats: The Dalca of Chiloe]

IN: Revista chilena de antropología 4:121-138 (Santiago)

Based upon ethnohistoric sources from the 16th through 19th centuries. Compares the dalca with the Luiseño canoe from California.

M-239

AUTHOR: Medvedov, Daniel

DATE: 1982

TITLE: Anatomía maya: el lenguaje simbólico de la mano [abstract only] [Maya Anatomy: The Symbolic Language of the Hand]

IN: Abstracts of Papers, 44th International Congress of Americanists (Manchester, 1982), page 207, School of Geography, Manchester University: Manchester, England

Mudras, Hindu gestures, Maya gestures. [Compare M-127.]

M-240

AUTHOR: Meggers, Betty J.

DATE: 1963a

TITLE: Review of *Reports of the Norwegian Archaeological Expedition to Easter Island and the East Pacific*, vol. 1: Archaeology of Easter Island, edited by Thor Heyerdahl and Edwin N. Ferdon, Jr.

IN: American Journal of Archaeology 67:330-331

Less extensively and intensively critical of this volume than Golson, she accepts the purported stratigraphy and believes the claimed dates for contact with Ecuador and Peru (A.D. 400 and 1100) "appear reasonable." Yet it strikes her as peculiar that the comparisons cited are chiefly with Tiahuanaco, which only affected the coast ca. A.D. 1000. They should consider that just as their work found new materials on Easter Island, further archaeology elsewhere in Polynesia could show that what they find analogous to the mainland may actually be in Polynesia somewhere, undiscovered. Still it is "impossible to dispute their evidence that contact took place between Easter Island and the South American mainland."

M-241

AUTHOR: Meggers, Betty J.

DATE: 1963b

TITLE: Cultural Development in Latin America: An Interpretative Overview

IN: Aboriginal Cultural Development in Latin America: An Interpretative Review, edited by Betty J. Meggers and Clifford Evans, Smithsonian Miscellaneous Collections 146/1, (Smithsonian Institution: Washington, D.C.), 131-148

Summary of a symposium reviewing current knowledge of the archaeology of Latin America. The great importance of diffusion between the several centers of New World cultures is emphasized, and various comments on the probability of transpacific relationships are included.

M-242

AUTHOR: Meggers, Betty J.

DATE: 1964

TITLE: North and South American Cultural Connections and Convergences

IN: Prehistoric Man in the New World, edited by Jesse D. Jennings and Edward Norbeck (published for Rice University by the University of Chicago Press: Chicago), 511-526

See M-247.

M-243

AUTHOR: Meggers, Betty J.

DATE: 1966a

TITLE: Ecuador

IMPRINT: Praeger: New York

Summary of well-known material on similarities of Jomon and Valdivia ceramics, Mesoamerican contacts beginning in Machalilla, and later.

M-244

AUTHOR: Meggers, Betty J.
DATE: 1966b
TITLE: Transpacific Origin of Valdivia Phase Pottery on Coastal Ecuador
IN: Proceedings of the 36th International Congress of Americanists (Barcelona and Sevilla, 1964), 1:63-67

See M-254.

M-245

AUTHOR: Meggers, Betty J.
DATE: 1971
TITLE: Contacts from Asia
IN: The Quest for America, edited by Geoffrey Ashe (Praeger: New York; and Pall Mall: London), 239-259

A quick sweep through Jomon-Valdivia, the Bahia complex, Chinese-Olmec connections, Southeast Asian art, etc.

M-246

AUTHOR: Meggers, Betty J.
DATE: 1975a
TITLE: The Transpacific Origin of Mesoamerican Civilization: A Preliminary Review of the Evidence and Its Theoretical Implications
IN: American Anthropologist 77:1-27 [Reprinted 1977 as "El origen transoceánico de la civilización Mesoamericana: un informe preliminar de las evidencias y sus implicaciones teóricas," *Hombre y cultura* Revista del Centro de Investigaciones Antropológicas de la Universidad Nacional, Panama 3/2:21-68]

The rise of the Olmec may have been provoked (or enhanced) by input from Shang China.

Pages 11-14: Jade artifacts found in buried offerings at La Venta are similar in form and size to jade yan kuei ritual objects which evolved from celts in China.

M-247

AUTHOR: Meggers, Betty J.
DATE: 1975b
TITLE: Conexiones y convergencias culturales entre Norte América y América del Sur [Cultural Connections and Convergences between North and South America]
IN: Anales de la Universidad de Cuenca 31/1-2:112-127 (Ecuador)

Considers various possible explanations, including diffusion and multilinear evolution, to account for what, in some cases, are almost identical artifacts of indigenous peoples in North and South America. Methodological exercise.

M-248

AUTHOR: Meggers, Betty J.
DATE: 1976
TITLE: Yes If by Land, No If by Sea: The Double Standard in Interpreting Cultural Similarities
IN: American Anthropologist 78:637-639

American archaeologists are willing to accept diffusion if a purely landbound route can be established within the hemisphere, such as from Mesoamerica to the Southwest; but they cannot abide sea-travel as a mode of communication. Such reasoning is completely inconsistent on their part.

M-249

AUTHOR: Meggers, Betty J.
DATE: 1979

TITLE: Prehistoric America: An Ecological Perspective, 2nd edition
IMPRINT: Aldine: New York
[First edition, 1972]

Aside from a brief description and defense of the Jomon-Valdivia pottery connection, the only discussion of transoceanic diffusion is on pages 174-177 where a general treatment of the issues is given. Emphasis is on the need for ecological situations to be receptive to continuance of any cultural element that may be diffused, otherwise no trace of the fact of diffusion is likely to be preserved. At certain times and places the possibility of diffusion "taking" are far higher than at others. Transpacific contacts probably affected American Indian cultures significantly.

M-250

AUTHOR: Meggers, Betty J.
DATE: 1980
TITLE: Did Japanese Fishermen Really Reach Ecuador 5,000 Years Ago?
IN: Early Man 2/4:15-19 (Evanston, Illinois)

Yes, it appears so, if one accepts that complicated inventions are not made independently.

M-251

AUTHOR: Meggers, Betty J.
DATE: 1985
TITLE: El significado de la difusión como factor de evolución
[The Significance of Diffusion as a Factor of Evolution]
IN: Revista Chungará 14:81-90 (Arica, Chile)

See M-253.

M-252

AUTHOR: Meggers, Betty J.
DATE: 1987
TITLE: El origen transpacífico de la cerámica Valdivia; una revaluación
[The Transpacific Origin of Valdivia Ceramics; a Re-evaluation]
IN: Boletín del Museo Chileño de Arte Precolombino 2:9-31 (Santiago)

An important, comprehensive restatement of her position deriving Valdivia ceramics from those of the Jomon period in Japan, utilizing new data and arguments on Ecuadorian stratigraphy and chronology, Jomon museum material, documented voyaging, etc. Specifically rebuts a series of critics.

M-253

AUTHOR: Meggers, Betty J.
DATE: 1989
TITLE: The Significance of Diffusion as a Factor in Evolution
IN: Reprint Proceedings, Circum-Pacific Prehistory Conference, Seattle, August 1-6, 1989, part VIII: Prehistoric Trans-Pacific Contacts (Washington State University Press: Pullman), articles separately paginated

Abstract only printed. The absence of a theoretical framework makes the significance of similarities in cultural traits and complexes as evidence of contact impossible to assess objectively. Neither rules for differentiating diffusion from independent invention nor details of form and content satisfy the demands of anti-diffusionists for "proof." Recognizing that the principal advantage of culturally determined behavior is its potential capacity for transmittal, we see diffusion becoming a probable explanation for the occurrence of many widespread cultural traits.

M-253B

AUTHOR: Meggers, Betty J.
DATE: 1992
TITLE: Jomon-Valdivia Similarities: Convergence or Contact?

IN: NEARA [New England Antiquities Research Association] Journal 27:22-32

A précis of M-252.

M-254

AUTHORS: Meggers, Betty J., and Clifford Evans
DATE: 1966
TITLE: A Trans-Pacific Contact in 3000 B.C.
IN: Scientific American 214/1:28-35

Popular account of M-256 claiming that the early Valdivia culture pottery of coastal Ecuador is the result of accidental drifting of Middle Jomon Period fishermen from Japan.

M-256

AUTHORS: Meggers, Betty J., Clifford Evans, and Emilio Estrada
DATE: 1965
TITLE: Early Formative Period of Coastal Ecuador; The Valdivia and Machalilla Phases
IMPRINT: Smithsonian Contributions to Anthropology 1 (Smithsonian Institution: Washington, D.C.) [Reviewed by Thomas C. Patterson in *Archaeology* 20 (1967): 236]

Detailed description of the excavations and artifacts from the Early Formative period in the Guayas Basin of coastal Ecuador, done from 1957-1961. Valdivia culture has one of the earliest series of C-14 dates in the New World for ceramic-using peoples (5150-4120 B.P. for Period A). Extensive discussion of dating, origins, and affiliations of Valdivia Culture as being derived from transpacific contact from Kyushu Japan in the Middle Jomon Period. Demonstrates coexistence of Machalilla with Periods C and D of Valdivia.

M-257

AUTHOR: Meier, Robert
DATE: 1969
TITLE: Review of *Cranial and Postcranial Skeletal Remains from Easter Island*, by Rupert I. Murrill
IN: American Anthropologist 71:360-361

Murrill construes the skeletal material, which had been seen as divided into earlier vs. later populations, as indicating one continuous Polynesian population that may have come from the Marquesas. Meier critiques the data and believes that no specimens come from the period A.D. 400-1100, thus neither the single racial (Polynesian) origin theory nor multiple origin theories appear amenable to testing from the biological standpoint with extant data.

M-261

AUTHOR: Meinhold, Peter
DATE: 1954
TITLE: Die Anfänge des Amerikanischen Geschichtsbewusstseins [The Beginning of American Historical Awareness]
IN: Saeculum 5:65-86

An unusual scholarly discussion, apparently by a non-believer, which considers the Book of Mormon account historically noteworthy.

M-262

AUTHOR: Mejía Xesspe, M. Toribio
DATE: 1942
TITLE: Acueductos y caminos antiguos de la hoya del Río Grande de Nasca [Ancient Aqueducts and Roads in the Valley of the Rio Grande de Nazca]
IN: Proceedings of the 27th International Congress of Americanists (Part 2, Lima, 1939), 1:559-569

Discusses chain wells or qanat water systems, some of which he believes may be prehispanic.

M-264

AUTHOR: Meldgaard, Jorgen

DATE: 1961

TITLE: Om de gamle nørdboer og deres skaebne; betragtninger over Helge Ingstads bog *Landet under polarstjernen*
[On the Old Norsemen and Their Fate; Comments on Helge Ingstad's Book *Landet under Polarstjernen*]

IN: Grønland 3:93-102 (Copenhagen)

Argues against H. Ingstad's belief that the Norse of West Greenland emigrated to continental North America.

M-265

AUTHOR: Meletinsky, Elizar M.

DATE: 1980

TITLE: The Epic of the Raven among the Paleoasiatics: Relations between Northern Asia and Northwest America in Folklore

IN: Diogenes 110:98-133
[Also in *Cultures of the Bering Sea Region: Papers from an International Symposium,* edited by Henry N. Michael and James W. VanStone (International Research and Exchanges Board (IREX): Washington, 1983), 227-248]

In America the Raven epic covers Alaska. Navahos and Apaches, Southwest Athabascans, show only traces of Raven material. Typologically Raven compares with Coyote at greater distances in North America, as civilizing hero or trickster. An "Eskaleutian ethnic zone" over the last several thousand years has been "the principal channel of transmission of the myths of the Raven from Asia toward America," but the Eskaleuts pay less attention to Raven than people beyond them in either direction.

M-266

AUTHOR: Melgar, José M.

DATE: 1871

TITLE: Estudio sobre la antigüedad y el origen de la cabeza colosal de tipo etiópico que existe en Hueyapám del canton de Los Tuxtlas
[Study on the Antiquity and the Origin of the Colossal Head of Ethiopian Type that Exists in Hueyapan in the Los Tuxtlas Canton]

IN: Boletín de la Sociedad de Geografía y Estadística, 2ª época, 3:104-109 (México)

At Palenque the symbols, particularly the tau sign, strongly suggest an Egyptian origin. Further, two idols found south of Mexico City display the symbol of the cosmogonic egg (creation) and the bursting forth of an egg, symbols not found in Aztec mythology but belonging to Indian, Egyptian, Greek, Persian, and Japanese cosmogonies. He refers to Hindu writings to sustain his view that colonists came from there to Mexico. He also provides a list of 14 words for which he claims Hebrew and Chiapanec parallels in sound and meaning.

First report of a giant Olmec head, which he considers "Ethiopean" in appearance.

M-267

AUTHOR: Melgarejo Vivanco, José Luis

DATE: 1959

TITLE: Navegación prehispánica en América
[Prehispanic Navigation in America]

IN: La palabra y el hombre 3:151-162 (Jalapa, México)

Rounds up but barely analyzes about every reference he can find to any form of vessel and navigation in Mesoamerica, with a bit of Titicaca and the Antilles thrown in. Intended, and serves, as baseline information awaiting further study.

M-267B

AUTHOR: Melgarejo Vivanco, José Luis
DATE: 1988
TITLE: Un opinante veracruzano acerca del origen del hombre y la cultura en América
[A Veracruzan Opinion Concerning the Origin of Man and Culture in America]
IN: Orígenes del hombre americano (seminario), compiled by Alba González Jácome (Secretaría de Educación Pública: México), 237-243

Offers unorthodox opinions about possible transoceanic settlers, with more hints than a corpus of evidence behind the proposals. Alcina Franch and Santiago Genovés on possible Atlantic crossings in the second millennium B.C. tentatively connectible with the archaeological Olmecs. Also physical and cultural Semites could have arrived in central Veracruz around 1500 B.C. In this same general period could be placed the culturally foreign influence at Valdivia, Ecuador, which some consider of Japanese origin, although Alfonso Medellín Zenil (the author's mentor, to whom this paper is dedicated) after careful examination of Japanese ceramics considered there to be no basis for that idea. We don't have the slightest idea of where they came from, but the Toltecs arrived via the Pacific Ocean to Huatulco, Oaxaca. The historical Olmecs are evidenced on the Lienzo de Jucutácato, Michoacán. They are shown with dark skin, curly hair, platyrrhine nose, prognathism, spherical cranial deformation, and the presence of dwarfs that recall pygmies. Other cultural and linguistic features are mentioned which he considers suggestive of an African influence. Further, Late Classic masks discovered at Arroyo Pesquero, Veracruz, positively recall Japan. A few other "curiosities" are also mentioned that call for investigation and an open mind, such as the parallel between Greek theos and Náhuatl téotl, both meaning God, whose Mexican hieroglyphic is a greek cross, seen already in the Preclassic at Viejón, Veracruz. Also worthy of investigation is the question of why the katun calendar round "had its first initiation in the third year of the Era, when Jewish historians mark the birth of Christ."

M-267C

AUTHOR: Mellen Blanco, Francisco
DATE: 1986
TITLE: Manuscritos y documentos españoles para la historia de la Isla de Pascua
[Spanish Manuscripts and Documents for the History of Easter Island]
IMPRINT: Centro de estudios de obras publicos y urbanismo: Madrid

Includes documents reporting the presence of manioc on the island, a matter previously obscured by only a faulty English translation being widely available.

M-267D

AUTHOR: Melnitsky, Benjamin
DATE: 1952
TITLE: Who Thought of It First?
IN: Natural History 61/2:63-67

"Dramatic coincidences of history have occurred when two or more persons invented the same thing at the same time." Stellar discovery [not an invention] and some utilitarian inventions are mentioned but they show only that duplication can come "from a fertile field where they have actually long been germinating," [hence the argument here is not relevant to the question of truly independent invention.]

M-269

AUTHOR: Mena, Ramón
DATE: 1923
TITLE: Arqueología comparada. México y el Brasil
[Comparative Archaeology. Mexico and Brazil]
IN: Boletín del Museo Nacional de México 2:92-95

Evidence of relations between the New World and the Old are Mongol characters on a vessel from the Island of Marajó (Brazil), Chinese characters on a cameo found in Mexico, a cylinder [seal?] similar to those of the "Chaldeans," and a Chaldean-like crown on Mexican statues.

M-271

AUTHOR: Mena, Ramón
DATE: 1938
TITLE: Signos orientales en los monumentos mayas
[Oriental Signs on Maya Monuments]
IMPRINT: Tipográfica Yucateca: Mérida

Locates on Maya monuments "signs" which he takes to be Egyptian (hieroglyphic, demotic, coptic), Babylonian, Greek, Chaldean, etc., often one mark being followed by another of a completely "different system," or divergent signs appear simultaneously in an artistic scene. [See also A-098, B-017B, and M-271 and M-272.]

M-272

AUTHORS: Mena, Ramón, and Yeeshing L. Tao
DATE: 1921
TITLE: Vasos chinos de Azcapotzalco
[Chinese Vases of Azcapotzalco]
IN: Prehistorische chinesische Funde in Mexiko, by Friedrich Koch-Wawra, Deutsch-mexicanische Rundschau December, 1921, reprinted in Mexican Review. Summary by René Le Conte in Journal de la société des américanistes de Paris 14 (1922): 230-231

Ceramic vessels considered to show writing which is read as Chinese by Tao. [See also M-271.]

M-273

AUTHOR: Mendelsohn, Simon
DATE: 1951
TITLE: Evolution of the Cremation Cult
IN: Ciba Symposia 11/8:1318-1332

Says he follows leading scholarship in attributing the origin of cremation to the Aryans in northern Europe. Cremation in the Roman, Persian, and Indian worlds is described. It was also practiced as far east as Laos and the Chukchee of Siberia. "Certain anthropologists are convinced that countless ages ago the aborigines of the western hemisphere were subjected to the influences of cultural diffusion that could only have been transplanted as the result of vast migrations of heliolithic peoples from eastern and western Asia." Cremation being sporadically present in the Pacific Islands provides indication that the custom might have been transmitted to America by that route. Western North America and Mexico are places where cremation was common.

M-274

AUTHOR: Mendes-Corrêa, A. A.
DATE: 1925
TITLE: Significado genealogico do "Australopithecus" e do cráneo de tabgha e o arco antropolético indico
[The Genealogical Significance of "Australopithecus," of the Tabgha Cranium and of the Anthropoletic Arc Index]
IN: Trabalhos de Sociedad Portuguesa de Antropologia e Etnologia 2/3 (Porto, Portugal)

Australia to southern South America connection is claimed.

M-275

AUTHOR: Mendes-Corrêa, A. A.
DATE: 1928
TITLE: Nouvelle hypothèses sur le peuplement primitif de l'Amérique du Sud
[A New Hypothesis on the Ancient Peopling of South America]
IMPRINT: Proceedings of the 22nd International Congress of Americanists (Rome, 1926),

1:97-118
[Reprinted in *Annais de Faculdade de Sciencias do Porto* 15:5-31 (Portugal)]

Involves Wegener's hypothesis of the movements of the continents to support his view that South America at one time had a virtual land connection with Australia via Antarctica, and that man from Australia and Tasmania reached South America by this route, which was broken only by a few straits and small islands.

M-277

AUTHOR: Mendieta Alatorre, Angeles
DATE: 1970
TITLE: La serpiente: diós protector
[The Serpent: Protector God]
IN: Humanitas 11:735-742 (Tucumán, Argentina)

Brief summary of ethnographic and archaeological research on the serpent as symbol, myth, and migratory expression of ancient Indo [India]-American cultures.

M-278

AUTHOR: Mendoza, Edelmiro A.
DATE: 1959
TITLE: Origen del hombre americano
[Origin of Amērican Man]
IMPRINT: Librería Perlado: Buenos Aires

A little bauble that bows to Chinese, Phoenicians, etc., while disastrously ill-informed.

M-279

AUTHOR: Mendoza, Gumesindo
DATE: 1877a
TITLE: Estudio comparativo entre el Sánscrito y el Náhuatl
[Comparative Study between Sanskrit and Nahuatl]
IN: Anales del Museo Nacional, 1ª época, 1:75-84 (México)

Lists comparative vocabulary as indicated, with occasional references to Greek and Latin words. Many of the comparisons are strained; some are striking. Seeks to prove that Nahuatl was Aryan, descended from Sanskrit.

M-280

AUTHOR: Mendoza, Gumesindo
DATE: 1877b
TITLE: Trabajo comparativo entre el Sánscrito, el Náhuatl, Griego y Latín
[Comparative Work among Sanskrit, Nahuatl, Greek and Latin]
IN: Anales del Museo Nacional, 1ª época, 1:286-288 (México)

The third part of a series beginning with M-279. Refers to the middle piece but gives no reference.

M-282

AUTHOR: Mendoza, Vicente T.
DATE: 1962
TITLE: El plano o mundo inferior, Mictlán, Xibalbá, Nith y Hel
[The Lower Plane or World: Mictlan, Xibalba, Nith, and Hell]
IN: Estudios de cultura náhuatl 3:75-99

Discussion of various concepts associated with the underworld of the deceased in pre-Hispanic Mesoamerica, with special attention to the beliefs of the Nahua speakers of central Mexico, the Quiché of highland Guatemala, and the Tarascan speakers of Michoacán based on documentary and native pictorial sources. Comparison is made between these Mesoamerican concepts and those of pre-Christian northern Europe.

M-286

AUTHOR: Menghin, Oswald F. A.
DATE: 1952
TITLE: Kontiki wissenschaftliche gesehen
[Kon Tiki Viewed Scientifically]

IN: Südamerika 2/6:1237ff. (Buenos Aires)

Strongly critical of Heyerdahl's theory.

M-287

AUTHOR: Menghin, Oswald F. A.
DATE: 1957
TITLE: Das Protolithikum in Amerika [The Protolithic in America]
IN: Acta praehistórica 1:5-40 (Buenos Aires)

Even though most American scientists do not believe that the Lower Paleolithic period (as known in Europe) also occurred in the New World, he feels the evidence proves man was in the New World longer than the now currently accepted 25,000 years or so. Reviews the old literature as well as some of the more recent theories, such as Carter's and Ibarra Grasso's, in support of the point. The European background of the author has obviously colored (i.e., liberalized) his view of New World archaeology.

In German with a short Spanish abstract.

M-288

AUTHOR: Menghin, Oswald F. A.
DATE: 1960
TITLE: Urgeschichte der Kanuindianer des südlichsten Amerika [Ancient History of the Canoe-using Indians of Southernmost America]
IN: Festschrift für Lothar F. Zotz; Steinzeitfragen der Alten und Neuen Welt, edited by Gisela Freund (L. Röhrscheid: Bonn), 343-375 [Spanish edition 1971, Anales de arqueología y etnología 26:5-42, (Mendoza, Argentina), technically revised by Juan Schobinger and with an introduction and appendix by Amalia Sanguinetti de Bórmida]

Pages 13-14: The Neolithic could only have reached America by way of the Pacific Ocean. Those who defend independent invention to explain the abundant parallels with Asia simply have not examined the facts sufficiently. Immigrants arrived by boat by approximately 2000 B.C.

M-289

AUTHOR: Menghin, Oswald F. A.
DATE: 1962
TITLE: Relaciones traspacíficas de la cultura araucana [Transpacific Relations of Araucanian Culture]
IN: Jornadas internacionales de Arqueología y Etnología: Segunda Mesa Redonda Internacional de Arqueología y Etnografía, vol. 2: Continentales y extracontinentales, (Nov./Dic. 1960), pages 90-98, Comisión Nacional Ejecutiva, 150o. Aniversario de la Revolución de Mayo, Buenos Aires

Discusses methodological problems in attempts to explain several types of stone clubs found in Chile which Imbelloni considers to have come from Oceania. He sees only a very general relationship in them to ideas "common to all the primitive agricultural cultures of South Asia, Oceania and South America." The matter cannot be settled until more data are at hand.

M-289B

AUTHOR: Menghin, Oswald F. A.
DATE: 1964
TITLE: Origen y desarrollo racial de la especie humana, 2a. edición [Origin and Racial Development of the Human Species, 2d edition]
IMPRINT: Nova: Buenos Aires

Includes the intrusion of Old World races to America.

M-290

AUTHOR: Menghin, Oswald F. A.
DATE: 1967
TITLE: Relaciones transpacíficas de América precolombina [Transpacific Relations of Pre-Columbian America]
IN: Runa 10/1-2:83-97

Oceanic migrations took place from 3000 B.C. to A.D. 1000, in three phases. The first was "neolithic" and is seen in ethnographic survivals in the Amazon area. The second stemmed from disturbances in the Black Sea area c. 800 B.C. that resulted in incursions into the western Chou area in China, thence to southern China and Indochina, yielding Dongson. That culture then became the vehicle for the spread of "many surprising similarities" between the Caucasus and eastern Europe (as well as China) on the one hand and Peru and Mexico on the other. The third movement was of Hindu cultural influences across the Pacific to Mesoamerica (e.g., the parasol).

M-291

AUTHOR: Mercer, John
DATE: 1980
TITLE: The Canary Islanders; Their Prehistory, Conquest and Survival
IMPRINT: Rex Collings: London

An anthropological study of the prehistoric islanders and of conditions today. [They are seen by some diffusionists as intermediaries for transatlantic diffusion.]

M-292

AUTHOR: Mercer, Samuel Alfred Brown
DATE: 1951
TITLE: The Pyramid Texts
IMPRINT: Longmans, Green: London

Vol. 4 page 214: In discussing the "sons of Horus," he notes that each deceased pharaoh was considered the father of the four sons of Horus. They were gods of the canopic jars involved in mummification and are called in the Pyramid Texts the four spirits, four royal intimates, etc. They were also supporters of the sky; as such they have "a parallel in the Bacabs of Mayan mythology, who supported the sky standing one at each corner of the world, and jars containing their effigies held entrails of the dead similar to the Egyptian Canopic jars."

M-293

AUTHOR: Merle, Rene
DATE: 1925
TITLE: La decouverte de l'Amerique . . . par les Oceaniens [The Discovery of America . . . by the Oceanians]
IN: La Nature 2654:106-109 (Paris)

Gives a general rundown on the history of argumentation about the possible presence of Oceanians in America. In December of the previous year M. Meillet presented to the Académie des Inscriptions et Belles-Lettres an oral communication (never published?) on "Mélano-Polynésiens et Australiens en Amérique" in which he claimed that Rivet's hypothesis is now a certainty. Merle here lists the "Mélanéso-Polynésien" and "Hoka(n)" and "Australien" and "Tson" words which Rivet had previously published. He considers Rivet's presentations a "remarkable concordance of anthropology, ethnography and linguistics."

M-294

AUTHOR: Merriam, Alan P.
DATE: 1964
TITLE: The Anthropology of Music
IMPRINT: Northwestern University Press: Evanston, Illinois

Pages 286ff.: He emphasizes the degree to which music comparison entered into the formation of kulturkreis theory. The first move in that direction was by Ratzel who drew attention to similarities between West African and Melanesian bows, and Frobenius carried this further. In his

Geist und Werden der Musikinstrumente (1929) Curt Sachs used kulturkreis theory to lay out a world history of instruments in the form of 23 strata. While those scholars' formulations are no longer tenable, the facts they cited, including those involving America, remain to be managed currently.

M-295

AUTHOR: Merrien, Jean [Rene Marie de la Poix de Freminville]
DATE: 1954
TITLE: Lonely Voyagers
IMPRINT: Putnam: New York [Translation of *Les navigateurs solitaires*]

Pages 25-96: Dramatically recounts in sequence most of the successful small-boat attempts to cross the Atlantic, in both directions. Joins many other sailor-authors in emphasizing that the ocean is not that hard to manage for a competent sailor in a good (or even not-so-good) small boat, subject to luck.

M-296

AUTHOR: Merrill, Elmer Drew
DATE: 1920
TITLE: Comments on Cook's Theory as to the American Origin and Prehistoric Polynesian Distribution of Certain Economic Plants, Especially Hibiscus tiliaceus Linnaeus
IN: Philippine Journal of Science 17:377-384

No American cultigens were known in pre-European Polynesia.

M-297

AUTHOR: Merrill, Elmer Drew
DATE: 1930a
TITLE: The Improbability of Pre-Columbian Eurasian-American Contacts in the Light of the Origin and Distribution of Cultivated Plants
IN: Journal of the New York Botanical Garden 31:209-212

No cultigens were shared.

M-298

AUTHOR: Merrill, Elmer Drew
DATE: 1930b
TITLE: Tobacco in New Guinea
IN: American Anthropologist 32:101-105

He claims that all tobacco in New Guinea resulted from post-European introduction, via Malaysia. [Compare L-194 who maintained that tobacco and its use were indigenous to New Guinea. In that case it could be argued that tobacco was introduced to the island in pre-Columbian times from America. See also L-088]

M-299

AUTHOR: Merrill, Elmer Drew
DATE: 1931a
TITLE: The Phytogeography of Cultivated Plants in Relation to Assumed Pre-Columbian Eurasian-American Contacts
IN: American Anthropologist 33:375-382 [Summary in *Social Science Abstracts* 4 (1932): 101]

An article much cited by opponents of diffusionism. The author categorically states that no plants were shared between the hemispheres [a position from which he progressively retreated].

M-300

AUTHOR: Merrill, Elmer Drew
DATE: 1931b
TITLE: Crops Raised by the Indians
IN: Science 74 (1918): 12-14

Focus on the Vikings. Surveys 400 writers and provides a good survey of and assessment of Rafn and Storm, which he considers key pieces.

Sees no solution yet to the question of placement and presence of the Norse.

M-300B

AUTHOR: Merrill, Elmer Drew
DATE: 1934
TITLE: The Problem of Economic Plants in Relation to Man in Pre-Columbian America
IN: Fifth Pacific Science Congress Proceedings, pages 759-767

The same argument and basic content as in M-301, M-302 and M-303.

M-301

AUTHOR: Merrill, Elmer Drew
DATE: 1936
TITLE: Plants and Civilization
IN: Scientific Monthly 43:430-439

The same essential content as M-302 and M-303. M-301 appeared also in the Harvard Tercentenary Publication entitled "Independence, Convergence, and Borrowing," (Cambridge, 1937) pages 33-43.

M-302

AUTHOR: Merrill, Elmer Drew
DATE: 1937
TITLE: Domesticated Plants in Relation to the Diffusion of Culture
IN: Early Man, edited by George Grant MacCurdy (Lippincott: Philadelphia), 277-284

Lack of cultigens shared with the Old World before European discovery is conclusive evidence that American agriculture and cultures were "autocthonous."

M-303

AUTHOR: Merrill, Elmer Drew
DATE: 1938
TITLE: Domesticated Plants in Relation to the Diffusion of Culture
IN: Botanical Review 4:1-20

He says M-302 was a short version of this paper.

M-304

AUTHOR: Merrill, Elmer Drew
DATE: 1939
TITLE: Man's Influence on the Vegetation of Polynesia, with Special References to Introduced Species
IN: Proceedings of the Sixth Pacific Science Congress of the Pacific Science Association, 4:629-639

Following Buck, he assumes Polynesia was settled beginning in the fifth century A.D., from the west. These ancestors of the present Polynesians replaced a somewhat more primitive, nonagricultural race who had occupied some of the islands not more than a few hundred years earlier. The Polynesians brought with them from Malaysia the cultivated plants known in the area later. During the period of exploration they certainly reached the west coast of America but failed to establish themselves there permanently, yet they did introduce back into Polynesia the sweet potato, which they spread from Hawaii to New Zealand in the 13th and 14th centuries. It may be assumed that at the same time they may have introduced a very few weeds of American origin. But most of the American weeds (the subject of this article) reached Polynesia after the advent of European explorers. He dismisses Cook's claims about cultigen sharing with the New World as disproven.

Page 631: He summarizes Seemann's view of the weeds of Fiji (Flora Vitiensis, 1865) that many New World weeds in Fiji were evidence of a bridge of some kind to there. Merrill points out that the nature of the weeds demands that humans be the agents for any such movements, then proceeds to argue that such human activity could not have been prehistoric, given the ethnological history.

M-305
AUTHOR: Merrill, Elmer Drew
DATE: 1945
TITLE: Plant Life of the Pacific World
IMPRINT: Macmillan: New York

Pages 225-226: Repeats the message of M-301.

M-306
AUTHOR: Merrill, Elmer Drew
DATE: 1946
TITLE: Further Notes on Tobacco in New Guinea
IN: American Anthropologist 48:22-30

See M-298.

M-307
AUTHOR: Merrill, Elmer Drew
DATE: 1950
TITLE: Observations on Cultivated Plants with Reference to Certain American Problems
IN: Ceiba 1/1:2-36 (Tegucigalpa, Honduras)

The cultivated gourd, as well as the sweet potato, was shared by South America and Polynesia, and the former occurrence may have been due to human transmission.

M-308
AUTHOR: Merrill, Elmer Drew
DATE: 1954
TITLE: The Botany of Cook's Voyages and Its Unexpected Significance in Relation to Anthropology, Biogeography and History
IMPRINT: Chronica Botanica 14/5-6:165-385

We now have incontrovertible evidence that man was responsible for the presence of the cultivated gourd in both hemispheres. It is "most certain" that Polynesians introduced the coconut to the west coast of America not long before the Spaniards arrived. One or more plantain varieties may have been carried by the Polynesians to South America, where they reached the Amazon basin. He gives reasons for thinking more than one form of Gossypium was present in the Society Islands soon after European contact and refers to "numerous hybrids between New World and Old World cotton species" which might well have reached Tahiti through the agency of man "before the long voyages of the Polynesians had ceased."

Also admits the possibility that African castaways may have reached the American east coast.

The sweet potato must have been transmitted consciously and with much care, in fact in soil, to remain viable on a voyage to Polynesia from South America.

M-309
AUTHOR: Merrill, William Stetson
DATE: 1928
TITLE: The Catholic Contribution to the History of the Norse Discovery of America
IN: Catholic Historical Review 13:589-619

Surveys the contributions of Catholic scholars to the Vinland question, contra charges of bias toward Columbus' claims.

M-311
AUTHOR: Mertz, Henriette
DATE: 1957
TITLE: The Nephtali: One Lost Tribe
IMPRINT: Privately printed: Chicago

Re-examines the "lost tribes of Israel" and argues that members of the Mandan tribe of North America may have descended in part from one of the Israelite tribes.

M-312
AUTHOR: Mertz, Henriette
DATE: [c. 1958]

TITLE: Pale Ink: Two Ancient Records of Chinese Exploration in America
IMPRINT: Privately printed: Chicago [2nd edition, revised, 1972, Swallow Press: Chicago. Reprinted 1972, 1975, as Gods from the Far East: How the Chinese Discovered America (Ballantine: New York)]

Identifies the geography of the Shan Hai Ching record, ca. eighth century B.C. onwards, with real geographical features of southwest and central North America.

M-313
AUTHOR: Mertz, Henriette
DATE: 1965
TITLE: The Wine Dark Sea: Homer's Heroic Epic of the North Atlantic
IMPRINT: Privately printed: Chicago

The Odyssey of Homer not only traversed the Mediterranean but crossed the Atlantic to the West Indies, then via the Gulf Stream to Nova Scotia and on to the Azores, back to Florida, and then home.

M-314
AUTHOR: Mertz, Henriette
DATE: 1969a
TITLE: The Echenique Plaque
IN: Proceedings of the 38th International Congress of Americanists (Stuttgart-Munich, 1968), 1:479-483

This famous artifact from Cuzco, first studied by Markham and now in the Museum of the American Indian in New York, she proposes as "an ancient mariner's compass of winds in the Mediterranean."

M-315
AUTHOR: Mertz, Henriette
DATE: 1969b
TITLE: Carved Statue at Tiwanaku
IN: Proceedings of the 38th International Congress of Americanists (Stuttgart-Munich, 1968), 1:485-489

States that the Greek myth of Apollonius and the land Colchis mentioned therein, assumed until now to be mythical, in fact can be located at Tiwanaku, where the Spaniards chased out the tribe of Colchiquens.

M-317
AUTHOR: Mertz, Henriette
DATE: 1977
TITLE: Greek Place Names in South America
IN: Epigraphic Society Occasional Publications 4/83:1-6

Names are listed which are "interwoven with Greek mythology" and which "appeared on maps prior to World War II." She suggests that these are related to Mycenaean-age exploring ships. [It is historically obvious that most, if not all, the names were conferred on settlements by modern inhabitants with classical leanings.]

M-318
AUTHOR: Mertz, Henriette
DATE: 1981
TITLE: An Inscribed Tablet from Newberry, Michigan
IN: Epigraphic Society Occasional Publications 9/217:127-131

See M-319.

M-319
AUTHOR: Mertz, Henriette
DATE: 1986
TITLE: The Mystic Symbol: Mark of the Michigan Mound Builders
IMPRINT: Global Books: Gaithersburg, Maryland

From the 1870s up through 1920, slate, copper, and clay tablets were reportedly dug up from mounds in Michigan by farmers and others. On them were characters in cuneiform, Egyptian hieroglyphics, Greek, and Phoenician. Mertz argues that these tablets were authentic and could have been inscribed by fourth-century Christians who came to North America from the Mediterranean to escape persecution. [See T-002 and F-055F.]

M-319B

AUTHOR: Messer, Ellen
DATE: 1987
TITLE: The Hot and Cold in Mesoamerican Indigenous and Hispanicized Thought
IN: Social Science and Medicine 25:339-346

"Hot-cold" binary classification of disease was already in Amerindian thought before Europeans arrived, especially as suggested by the fact that groups isolated and only recently contacted share the conceptual scheme. [It has usually been claimed that this system in the New World was wholly of Iberian origin.]

M-322

AUTHOR: Métraux, Alfred
DATE: 1925
TITLE: Sur un mode américain du rite de balancement [On an American Style Balancing Rite]
IN: Proceedings of the 21st International Congress of Americanists (Part 2, Gothenburg, Sweden, 1924), pages 596-606

A curious festival in commemoration of the dead which has a parallel in ancient Greece.

M-324

AUTHOR: Métraux, Alfred
DATE: 1936
TITLE: Numerals from Easter Island
IN: Man 36/254:190-191

Denies that an unexplained, non-Polynesian set of numerals was used on Easter Island. [Compare R-166.]

M-326

AUTHOR: Métraux, Alfred
DATE: 1940
TITLE: Ethnology of Easter Island
IMPRINT: Bernice P. Bishop Museum Bulletin 160 (Honolulu)

Page 416: Considers cultural parallels adduced between Easter Island and Peru to be "fanciful or naive." Regarding A-037, which reported two Easter Island spearheads found in an Indian grave in Chile, he says the specimens are undoubtedly from Easter Island, however, "for sixty years Chile has been flooded with artifacts brought from the Easter Island by the crew" of the regular ship service.

M-328

AUTHOR: Métraux, Alfred
DATE: 1951a
TITLE: L'origine des indiens d'Amérique [The Origin of the American Indians]
IN: Conférences du Palais de la Découverte [Paris], pages 13-23

A vague and general summary of Bering Strait sources, dolichocephals preceded brachycephals, etc., but carefully hedged about. A polite bow to Rivet, maybe a few Polynesians arrived, if we knew more, etc.

M-329

AUTHOR: Métraux, Alfred
DATE: 1951b
TITLE: Le voyage du Kon-Tiki et l'origine des Polynésiens [The Voyage of the Kon-Tiki and the Origin of the Polynesians]

IN: Revue de Paris (Juillet): 119-129

See M-331.

M-331

AUTHOR: Métraux, Alfred
DATE: 1957
TITLE: Easter Island: A Stone Age Civilization of the Pacific
IMPRINT: Oxford University Press: New York

Pages 221-229: Critical of Heyerdahl. The parallel in stoneworking is the best evidence for a South American connection.

M-332

AUTHOR: Meyer, Adolf B.
DATE: 1888
TITLE: The Nephrite Question
IN: American Anthropologist 1:231-242

He notes the opinion of Prof. H. Fischer of Freiburg and other savants in Europe and America that American nephrite and jadeite objects originated in Asia whence they were carried to Europe then by chance to America, or, alternatively, directly from Asia to America. Meyer shows on a mineralogical basis why this view is untenable. The American pieces were uniquely American.

M-333

AUTHOR: Meyer, Adolf B.
DATE: 1889
TITLE: Masken von Neu-Guinea und den Bismarck Archipel [Masks from New Guinea and the Bismarck Archipelago]
IMPRINT: Stengel und Markert: Dresden

A New Ireland mask was found on the Atacama coast of South America.

M-334

AUTHOR: Meyer, Adolf B.
DATE: 1904
TITLE: Alte Südseegegenstände in Südamerika [Ancient South Sea Objects in South America]
IN: Globus 86:202-206

Certain clubs used in Polynesia and Melanesia are very much like those used in Peru and among the Tlingit. Also mentions particular Oceanic artifacts of other sorts found in South America.

M-335

AUTHORS: Meyer, Adolf B., and P. Richter
DATE: 1902 [1903?]
TITLE: Ethnographische Miszellen 2 [Ethnological Miscellanea 2]
IMPRINT: Abhandlungen und Berichte des königlichen zoologischen und anthropologisch-ethnographischen Museum zu Dresden 10/6 (Berlin)

Pages 30ff.: Distribution of the ikat technique of dyeing.

M-336

AUTHOR: Meyer, David F.
DATE: [1988]
TITLE: The Posthumous Hoax of James Norman Hall
IMPRINT: Unpublished; ms. copy in possession of John L. Sorenson

Paper read at meetings of the Deseret Language and Linguistics Society, Provo, Utah, 1988.

Regarding H-034 and V-056, he analyzes the list of "non-Polynesian" words purportedly collected by Hall on one of the Tuamotus in 1923 and which have close Tupí (South America) parallels. He first shows that no island with the purported name is known. Based partly on biographical research on Hall, he then shows with high probability that the whole thing was a hoax. On phonological grounds the words would have been impossible for Tuamotuan informants to have produced. Instead, it is evident that they were taken from K. Oberg's 1953 Smithsonian monograph on the Mato Grosso. Meyer concludes that Hall, apparently with the help of Oberg or someone inside the Smithsonian, got access to Oberg's manuscript before it was published (for Hall died two years before the publication appeared) and intended to expose the imposture later in order to embarrass Heyerdahl, whose views he strongly opposed.

M-337 See L-181B.

M-339
AUTHOR: Michelis, E. de
DATE: 1903
TITLE: L'origine degli indo-europei [The Origin of Indo-Europeans]
IMPRINT: Fratelli Boeca: Turin

Page 258: Greek *potamos,* river, is compared with various North American rivers named Potomac.

M-339B
AUTHOR: Michlovic, Michael G.
DATE: 1990
TITLE: Folk Archaeology in Anthropological Perspective
IN: Current Anthropology 31:103-107

A condescending picture of diffusionists as a folk whose quaint notions and persistence could furnish interesting grist for the mills of sociocultural anthropologists.

M-340
AUTHOR: Milewski, Tadeusz
DATE: 1955
TITLE: La comparaison des systèmes phonologiques des langues caucasiennes et américaines [The Comparison of Phonological Systems of the Caucasian and American Languages]
IN: Lingua Posnaniensis 5:136-165 (Posnan, Poland)

Draws parallels between Caucasus and American Indian languages, in particular comparing the phoneme systems of Rutul and Lutuami, Georgian and Kechua, Arci and Coeur d'Alene, Ubyx and Coos. He believes the similarities go back to an old Central Asian speech grouping.

M-340B
AUTHOR: Milewski, Tadeusz
DATE: 1957
TITLE: Elementy panteistyczne religii Azeków [Pantheistic Elements in the Aztec Religion]
IN: Roczniki Filozoficzne Towarzystwa Naukowego KUL V/1

At the beginning of his studies of Mesoamerican civilization, mainly on the Aztecs, he finds the cultural parallels between that area and the Old World consisted of only broad typological similarities. He still takes that position, but now proposes juxtaposing Aztec religion specifically with the religious systems of Egypt, Mesopotamia, Syria, Asia Minor, Greece and India in the second millennium B.C., which he considers to be particularly parallel, although not having any genetic relationship. Points out particular resemblances between Aztec, and the Vedic religions.

M-340C
AUTHOR: Milewski, Tadeusz
DATE: 1959
TITLE: La comparaison des systèmes anthroponymiques aztèques et indo-européens [Comparison of Aztec and Indo-European (proper) names]
IN: Onomastica 5/1:119-175 (Krakow, Poland)

He analyzes semantically and otherwise 214 Aztec proper names, mainly denoting deities, kings, governors, high priests, eminent warriors, etc. Many compare with Sanskrit names. For example Aztec *Ome-tecoh-tli,* The Lord of the

Two (worlds), with Sanskrit *Trai-lokya-raja,* The Lord of the Three Worlds, and *Chalchiuh-nene-tzin,* Having the Bosom of Emeralds, with *Ratna-garbha,* Having the Bosom of Pearls. In addition to names, prepositions, numerals, verbs, and various compounds also show more or less correspondence. The parallels are mainly related to gods, deified animals, items of luxury, religious attitude, and gender or social rank. Only Sanskrit among Indo-European languages shows such correspondences. He does not exclude the effects of sporadic transpacific contacts.

M-341B

AUTHOR: Milewski, Tadeusz
DATE: 1960
TITLE: Similarities between the Asiatic and American Indian Languages
IN: International Journal of American Linguistics 26:265-274

He further compares Aztec names with Sanskrit (see M-340C) and concludes that in some cases contacts are not attested and resemblances could arise independently (by convergence). But where relationships have been proven, the parallels show some impulses from different regions of Asia and Oceania having reached the west coast of America, impacting the original local cultures. Most such impacts relate to religious life. Aztec references to the snake he suggests show connections with Buddhism. Some names may have been adapted at intermediate locations between Asia and America. At least two eras of contact may be suggested, one before 1000 B.C. and the other in the last 15 centuries.

M-342

AUTHOR: Milewski, Tadeusz
DATE: 1961a
TITLE: IAzykovye sviazi Azii i Ameriki: avtoreferat dvukh rabot [Linguistic Connections of Asia and America: An Abstract of Two Works]
IN: Soobshcheniia pol'skikh orientalistov [Reports of Polish Orientalists], pages 74-90 (Moscow)

See M-340, M-340B, and M-341B.

M-342B

AUTHOR: Milewski, Tadeusz
DATE: 1961b
TITLE: Nowe poglady na geneze kultury srodkowoamerykanskiej [A New Viewpoint on the Origin of the Mesoamerican Culture]
IMPRINT: Oriental Commission of the Polish Academy of Science (Kraków section) (Kraków, Poland[?])

Continues interpreting name parallels as due both to convergence and to contacts. He adds to the names in M-341B names of Zapotec rulers, Cozijo-eza and Cozijo-pi, juxtaposing them with certain Indian names [see M-342C].

M-342C

AUTHOR: Milewski, Tadeusz
DATE: 1966
TITLE: Pochodzenie ludnosci Ameryki przedkolumbijskiej w odbiciu jezykowym [The Origin of the Peoples of Pre-Columbian America in the Light of Language]
IN: Etnografia Polska 10

Continuing his analysis from M-342B, he points out Sanskrit counterparts, *Vayu-datta* and *Vayu-ka,* for Zapotec *Cozijo-eza* and *Cozijo-pi.* He also argues for both a semantic and phonetic link between Aztec *teotl* and Sanskrit *devah.* Since *teotl* does not appear elsewhere in the Uto-Aztecan family, he is inclined to see it as a loan word. The period for penetration of Sanskrit materials must have been long; he assumes that the Zapotecs and Teotihuacanos might have been the first to adapt these patterns, which later were imitated by the Toltecs and Aztecs. He relates the Sanskrit situation to a list of cultural parallels which archaeologists and ethnologists have suggested may be due to transpacific contacts. Special attention goes to Paul Kirchoff's hypotheses about the calendar. Also he discusses the allegation of Polish mineralogist Jan Kinle that Burmese jadeite was introduced into Mesoamerica; there is a possibility that utilization of this mineral may be attested in Sahagun's Book 9 for a people living on the Pacific coast at the Isthmus of Tehuantepec.

M-343

AUTHORS: Milewski, Tadeusz, Jan Kinle, and Tomasz Marszewski
DATE: 1968
TITLE: Methodological Notes on the Investigations of Linguistic and Cultural Contacts between Asia and America in Pre-Columbian Era [*sic*]
IN: Folia Orientalia 10:297-298 (Krakow, Poland)

Cautions regarding possibilities for convergences while convinced that language similarites make direct contacts highly probable.

M-345

AUTHORS: Miller, Madeleine S., and J. Lane Miller
DATE: 1944
TITLE: Encyclopedia of Bible Life
IMPRINT: Harper: New York [Revised edition, 1955]

Page 187: Both quilted textile and metal leaf armor were used in the Near East [as in Mesoamerica].

M-345B

AUTHORS: Miller, Orlo
DATE: 1976
TITLE: The Day-spring: The Story of the Unknown Apostle to the Americas
IMPRINT: McClelland and Stewart: Toronto

A popular but not wholly uninformed treatment of the Quetzalcoatl tradition (including Bochica and Naymlap from South America). Supposes communication from the Old World around the second century A.D.

Page 164: Jewish influence.

Page 169: "It is entirely possible that Quetzalcoatl was a relative of Jesus of Nazareth." Other contacts are possible.

M-346

AUTHOR: Mills, J. V. [J. R.?]
DATE: 1951
TITLE: Notes on Early Chinese Voyages
IN: Journal of the Royal Asiatic Society, pages 3-25

A broad and valuable synthesis on the topic.

Pages 4-6: The Chinese reached the coast at the mouth of the Yangtze probably about 1200 B.C. By Confucian times (ca. 500 B.C.) navigation was highly developed in the area of that mouth, and the following century saw a great extension of navigation in what is now Shantung. Navigation on the high seas is first spoken of in the fourth century B.C.; in 219 B.C. they reached Japan and into the Indian Ocean to Madras in the first century B.C. From the beginning of the Christian era, there existed Javanese, Khmer, Cham, and Chinese navies which fought each other. From the seventh century on there was energetic expansion, sharing in navigation developments with Arab traders.

Page 9: By Sung times (960-1127) vessels carried up to 600 people. The mariner's compass was first used at the end of the eleventh century, but it was of little significance due to reliance on older methods.

M-347

AUTHOR: Mills, J. R. [J. V.?]
DATE: 1960
TITLE: The Largest Chinese Junk and Its Displacement

IN: Mariner's Mirror 46:147-148

A short note lists the largest known ships, with key bibliography. The largest craft was 600 feet long but was not sea-going. The largest at sea were those in the fleet under Cheng Ho, who crossed the Indian Ocean during the 15th century; his largest were 440 feet long and 180 broad, though some find objections to accepting this literally. Ibn Battuta (c. 1343) wrote that Chinese ships had four decks, twelve sails, and a complement of 1000 men. Needham judges that the Chinese built sea-going ships 300 feet long.

M-347B

AUTHOR: Milner, George R.

DATE: 1992

TITLE: Disease and Sociopolitical Systems in Late Prehistoric Illinois

IN: Disease and Demography in the Americas, edited by John W. Verano and Douglas H. Ubelaker (Smithsonian Institution Press: Washington, D.C.), 103-116

Hitherto undocumented and often unsuspected variations in late prehistoric social and demographic landscapes complicate interpretations of the consequences of Native American contacts with Europeans. Were novel pathogens regularly transmitted among populations distributed across large portions of the Americas? The data now show that diverse and discontinuous social, demographic, biotic, and physical landscapes existed which make it unlikely that infectious diseases, once introduced, resulted in pandemics. Some demographic declines that have been blamed on new disease may well have included, for example, warfare itself, and the effects of warfare which interfered with routine food acquisition resulting in nutritional inadequacy that affected resistance to existing pathogens. Contrary to romantic portrayals of North America as a disease-free paradise, some prehistoric populations experienced a considerable disease load, and existing poor levels of health would have affected responses to novel pathogens. [Drastic demographic declines due to supposedly new Old World pathogens may thus have been less consequential than usually presumed, which tends to undermine the anti-diffusionist notion of the complete prior separation of the two hemispheres.]

M-347C

AUTHOR: Milton, Charles

DATE: 1971

TITLE: The Mechanicsburg Stones

IN: NEARA [New England Antiquities Research Association] Journal 6:51-53

Includes a geological report by Robert E. Stone on these inscribed objects from Pennsylvania.

M-348

AUTHOR: Miner, Horace

DATE: 1939

TITLE: Parallelism in Alkaloid-alkali Quids

IN: American Anthropologist 41:617-619

Chewing of areca nut, tobacco, coca, and pituri with lime in Melanesia, Malaysia, southern India, Australia, and America would be chemically functionless without accompanying lime (alkali) to release the desired alkaloid. He claims that this relationship somehow increases the likelihood that the use of lime was independently invented, not diffused.

M-348B

AUTHOR: Minnaert, Paul

DATE: 1933

TITLE: Le pseudo-totémisme au Pérou et en Polynésie [Pseudo-totemism in Peru and Polynesia]

IN: Bulletin de la sociéte de americanistes de la Belgique (mars): 3-34

It is probable that anciently a Polynesian or pre-Polynesian influence was exercised on the Andean region. He carefully surveys the limited sources on totemic-like beliefs and practices that accord with that view. For one example, (pages 23-26) there is the very curious idea which relates a totem to the stellar world (examples specified).

M-348C

AUTHOR: Minnaert, Paul
DATE: 1933
TITLE: Le culte des pierres à l'île de Flores et au Pérou
IN: Bulletin de la société des américanistes de belgique (March): 35-40

It is well established that the Andean region from Tiahuanaco to San Augustín, Colombia, in "primitive epochs," was home to a megalithic civilization tied to a lunar cult. In an essay he published in August 1930 in this journal, he tried to establish a parallel between the cult of stones in Peru and similar practices on the island of Soemba, near Java. He believes the similarities evidence a close relationship between the two religions. Heine-Geldern (in *Anthropos*, 1928) showed that the megaliths of that area were linked to burial commemorations. Now Arndt (also in *Anthropos,* 1929-1930) reported on the religion of the Nadas of the island of Flores in relation to megaliths. That is his point of comparison in this article. The name of the moon is "stone." Stones as protectors of fields and houses are found among the Nagas of India and in New Caledonia, New Zealand, Soemba, Peru, etc. Points out various other beliefs shared between the Flores moon/stone cult and Peru.

M-349

AUTHOR: Minnaert, Paul
DATE: 1951
TITLE: Polynésiens et Andéens [Polynesians and Andean Peoples]
IN: Journal de la société des americanistes de Belgique (March): 3-28

Probably isolated expeditions of Polynesians arrived on the coasts of Peru or Ecuador, and, under favorable conditions, could have founded new settlements or at least have brought new cultural features to the original population. Evidences: traditions of the arrival in Peru of invading groups, religious practices and beliefs such as Kon-Tiki, elements of social organization, customs, and architecture.

M-350

AUTHOR: Minnesota Historical Society
DATE: 1918
TITLE: Report of the Committee on the Kensington Rune Stone
IN: Minnesota Historical Society Collections 15:221-286

A lukewarm endorsement of the authenticity of the inscription on the stone as Norse, a conclusion heavily influenced by Holand's involvement and advocacy.

M-351

AUTHOR: Minnich, Helen Benton
DATE: 1963
TITLE: Japanese Costume and the Makers of Its Elegant Tradition
IMPRINT: Tuttle: Rutland, Vermont

Japanese purple dye was from a vegetable source, not shellfish.

M-352

AUTHOR: Minnis, Joan B.
DATE: 1985
TITLE: [letter]
IN: Smithsonian 15/11:18, 20

Two men crossed the Atlantic from Brooklyn, New York, to the Scilly Islands off Great Britain in 1896 in 55 days in a rowboat to win a prize.

M-353
AUTHOR: Miracle, Marvin P.
DATE: 1963
TITLE: Interpretation of Evidence on the Introduction of Maize into West Africa
IN: Africa 33:132-135

He is reluctant to give full credence to arguments of J-048 because the evidence remains circumstantial and even equivocal.

M-354
AUTHOR: Miracle, Marvin P.
DATE: 1965
TITLE: Introduction and Spread of Maize in Africa
IN: Journal of African History 6:39-45

The common assertion that the Portuguese brought maize to tropical Africa from the New World cannot be documented. They may have been the first, but not the only ones, to introduce maize, for we find it appearing at more than one point and more than one time in Africa. Arab traders may also have brought it.

M-355
AUTHOR: Miracle, Marvin P.
DATE: 1966
TITLE: Maize in Tropical Africa
IMPRINT: University of Wisconsin Press: Madison

Pages 87-89: Miracle presents what he considers conclusive evidence for Portuguese or other post-Columbian introduction of maize to Africa.

Page 89: The only archeological evidence on the (pre-Columbian) introduction of maize to western Africa is pottery with an imprint resembling an ear of maize, found at Ifé, Nigeria, which is thought by some to have been manufactured in A.D. 1100, a date estimated from the depth at which it was found. This is certainly contrary to the hypothesis of Portuguese introduction, but it has not been definitely established that the date of manufacture is pre-Columbian. [See G-159.]

M-356
AUTHOR: Miranda Rivera, Porfiro
DATE: 1958
TITLE: Quipus y jeroglíficos [Quipus and Hieroglyphics]
IN: Zeitschrift für Ethnologie 83/1:118-132

Describes a system of symbolic writing that he claims predates the quipu and was not invented by Spanish missionaries. Makes comparison to works of Posnansky and Ibarra Grasso on systems of symbolic writing used by Indians today in the Andean area.

M-357
AUTHOR: Mitchell, J. Leslie
DATE: 1931
TITLE: Inka and Pre-Inka
IN: Antiquity 5:172-174

Notes and allows three theories of South American settlement: via the Bering Strait, from Europe via Greenland, and out of Oceania.

Reports documentary evidence for a true masonry arch on an ancient site near Lima, of wheel-like disks at Tiahuanaco, and possible writing symbols from Sahhuayacu, and thinks these deserve investigation as possible evidence for an intrusive complex. "Extra-American influences from the Pacific seaboard" can no longer be denied. The main arguments against transpacific diffusion have been overthrown (e.g., the Polynesians were acquainted with rice but abandoned it in favor of the breadfruit which was in turn supplanted in America by maize). The earliest Peruvian epoch that he recognizes has the most Oceanic evidence: e.g., mummification, coastal supremacy in textiles and ceramics, pyramid building with temples.

M-361

AUTHOR: Mitra, Sarat Chandra
DATE: 1929
TITLE: On the Cosmological Myth of the Birhors and Its Santali and American Indian Parallels
IN: Journal of the Anthropological Society of Bombay 14:468-478

A myth of creation by diving beneath the water, etc., is found among the Birhors and Santals (Dravidian groups) and among the Orang Dusuns of Borneo, the Ahoms of Assam, in California and among Huron and Algonkin Indians. These similarities are due to the psychic unity of peoples. [No consideration of why psychic unity failed to produce the myth in other peoples.]

M-364

AUTHOR: Mjelde, M. M.
DATE: 1927
TITLE: Eykstarstadr-Problemet og Vinlandsreisene [The Eykstarstadr Problem and the Vinland Voyages]
IN: Historisk Tidsskrift 6/5:259-281 (Oslo) [with English summary]

Based on siting information in the sagas, he suggested a new theory for Leif's location based on the reported sun observations. Naess, trying to prove Mjelde correct, calculated that Leif's winter Budir could not have been farther north than 37 degrees, hence it was somewhere on Chesapeake Bay.

M-366

AUTHOR: Mochon, Marion Johnson
DATE: 1976
TITLE: The Nature of Theory and Its Validation: Transpacific Origins
IN: American Anthropologist 78:106-110

A little lecture-cum-critique on M-246. In a following note, Meggers says the critic has missed most points and added nothing.

M-367

AUTHOR: Moeller, Klara von
DATE: 1937
TITLE: Die Österinsel und Peru [Easter Island and Peru]
IN: Zeitschrift für Ethnologie 69:7-22

Entirely on artistic motifs and other parallels between Easter Island and Peru.

M-368

AUTHOR: Moffat, Charles R.
DATE: 1980
TITLE: On the Diffusion vs Independent Invention Controversy: Reconsideration of Premises
IN: Journal of the Steward Anthropological Society 12:323-352 (Urbana, Illinois)

An obviously student-written paper gives a general discussion of the inventionist/diffusionist controversy cast in history-of-the-discipline form, but serious omissions (e.g., *Man across the Sea*) render it of little value. It ends up pessimistic about any resolution of the basic issue and without value in pursuing it.

M-370

AUTHOR: Molinari, Diego Luis
DATE: 1964
TITLE: Descubrimiento y conquista de América de Erik el Rojo a Hernán Cortés [Discovery and Conquest of America from Eric the Red to Hernando Cortez]
IMPRINT: Editorial Universitaria de Buenos Aires: Buenos Aires

Despite the title, this says nothing substantive about Norse nor any other voyaging to America prior to Columbus. In the first two chapters are routine summaries of the state of astronomical and geographical knowledge in western Europe from the 11th to the 15th centuries.

M-373

AUTHOR: Moller, Fredrik Andreas
DATE: 1956
TITLE: The Origin of the Indians and America's First Inhabitants Discovered
IMPRINT: n.p.: Pasco, Washington

Translated from Norwegian and edited by Olga Moller Lidahl, 1955. A Christian pastor concludes that American Indians are all descended from Edomites, the descendants of Esau (="red skin") who came to America in a fleet prepared by King Solomon and were ruled by him at a distance for a time.

M-374

AUTHOR: Moltke, Erik
DATE: 1950
TITLE: The Kensington Stone
IN: Antiquity 24:87-93

Cites many details of runic history and circumstances surrounding the stone which he considers to rule out totally its authenticity, as a large number of the best runologists have always maintained.

M-375

AUTHOR: Moltke, Erik
DATE: 1951
TITLE: The Kensington Stone
IN: Antiquity 25:87-93

A refutation of H-027 by an unbeliever.

M-376

AUTHOR: Moltke, Erik
DATE: 1953
TITLE: The Ghost of the Kensington Stone
IN: Scandinavian Studies 25:1-14

An exorcism. Jansson has recently demonstrated that the stone is a modern fraud, Holand's philological qualifications were dealt severe blows, and Thalbitzer's statements were thoroughly discounted. Musters other authorities. One of Holand's sins is lack of "professonal schooling." "Well, and that is the end of it, an inscription condemned from the beginning by every competent runologist, defended by none, an inscription suspect in every detail." That it has lived so long is "because it has never before been subjected to a penetrating scholarly analysis."

M-378B

AUTHORS: Moncreiffe, Iain
DATE: 1982
TITLE: The Highland Clans, revised edition
IMPRINT: Clarkson N. Potter: New York [First published 1967, Barrie & Rockcliff]

Pages 94-95. The Gunn coat-of-arms is illustrated, and the appended comment includes this statement: "Startlingly enough, the earliest surviving example of the Gunn chiefs' coat-of-arms appears to have been punch-marked by a mediaeval armourer-smith on a rock in Massachusetts in or about 1395 (see Sinclair)." "The effigy at Westford in Massachusetts may therefore possibly mark the grave of a Gunn companion-of-arms of Henry Sinclair, Jarl of Orkney, on his celebrated voyage of exploration in the far West."

Page 220: Sketches information about Henry Sinclair, Jarl of Orkney, who sailed west in 1395 "to seek new lands reported in the far West across the Atlantic Ocean, and he wintered there after he had made a successful landfall, in order to continue his explorations." His course had brought him to Nova Scotia and then he "may have stayed awhile in Massachusetts." He sent A. Zeno home with the main fleet before winter set in. The coat-of-arms at Westford, "if it is not a clever hoax by some truly learned heraldic scholar, . . . would seem to have been punch-marked by a mediaeval lord's armourer-smith to mark the grave of a companion-in-arms." Quotes at length from Charles Boland's description [B-257] of the discovery of this stone. The heraldic identification was made eventually by Moncreiffe himself, being then "Unicorn Pursuivant" [the official expert on heraldry], at the instance of the curator of the museum at Cambridge to whom a drawing of the scene had been sent by F. Glynn. "There is of course, nothing remarkable in the idea of the Jarl of Orkney, premier noble of Norway, sailing to America in the fourteenth century; for the Norsemen had certainly been crossing the Atlantic since at least four centuries before, and the great Scandinavian houses were all interrelated."

M-378C

AUTHOR: Mongé, Alf
DATE: 1974
TITLE: Dr. Haugen's "Non-existent Cryptography"
IN: NEARA [New England Antiquities Research Association] Journal 9:69

A defense against Haugen's scoffing that encrypted runic messages are a figment of modern interpreters' minds.

M-379

AUTHORS: Mongé, Alf, and Ole G. Landsverk
DATE: 1967
TITLE: Norse Medieval Cryptography in Runic Carvings
IMPRINT: Norseman Press: Glendale, California

A military cryptographer and Norse partisan, Mongé has discovered a number of cryptograms in runic inscriptions, most recently on the Kensington Stone. Chapter 20 reports a project being undertaken to test metallurgically certain artifacts found in North America which have been claimed to be of Norse origin.

M-381

AUTHOR: Montandon, George
DATE: 1933
TITLE: La race, les races [Race, Races]
IMPRINT: Payot: Paris

Melanesians could have arrived in America, as seems indicated on biological grounds, as slaves of the Malay-Polynesians. In any case the Polynesians are racially complex and could include Melanesian elements.

M-385

AUTHOR: Montell, Gösta
DATE: 1925
TITLE: Le vrai poncho, un élément post-colombien [The True Poncho, a Post-Columbian Element]
IN: Journal de la société des americanistes de Paris 18:173-183

See M-386.

M-386

AUTHOR: Montell, Gösta
DATE: 1929
TITLE: Dress and Ornaments in Ancient Peru: Archaeological and Historical Studies
IMPRINT: Elanders Boktryckeri Aktiebolag: Göteborg

Pages 237-244: Historical and ethnological data show that the poncho did not originate in South America until post-Columbian times under stimulus of use of the horse, a Spanish import. [Others have considered it a pre-Columbian parallel with Polynesia.]

M-387

AUTHOR: Montell, Gösta
DATE: 1937
TITLE: Distilling in Mongolia

IN: Ethnos 2:321-332

Page 328: Similarity is noted between Mongolian and Huichol (Mexico) distilling apparatus. [See B-416.]

M-387B

AUTHOR: Montoya Briones, José de Jesús
DATE: 1975
TITLE: El complejo de los aires en la cosmología de los Nahuas en la Sierra de Puebla
[The "los aires" Complex in the Cosmology of the Nahuas of the Sierra de Puebla (Mexico)]
IN: Boletín INAH [Instituto Nacional de Antropología e Historia] (época 2a.) 13 (Abr.-Jun.): 53-58

The parallelisms between Old and New Worlds in respect to practices and beliefs of this complex, which is used to explain, diagnose and treat illnesses, are abundant, so much so that it poses a problem that is hard to resolve to account for them. His fieldwork reported here convinces him that this is definitely a pre-Columbian complex, in which he agrees with Redfield, Villa Rojas, Soustelle, and Lopez Austin. [Others maintain, because of the parallelisms with the Mediterranean world, that these concepts were imported by the Spaniards.]

M-390

AUTHOR: Mookerji, Radhakumud
DATE: 1912
TITLE: Indian Shipping: A History of the Sea-borne Trade and Maritime Activity of the Indians from the Earliest Times
IMPRINT: Longmans, Green: Bombay, Calcutta, and London
[2nd edition, Kitab Mahal: Allahabad, 1962]

A comprehensive survey of shipping of all periods. Statements and allusions in early documents are supplemented by art and coin representations. According to these sources, sea-going vessels capable of carrying hundreds of people were in use well before the Christian era. For example, a Sanskrit manuscript has a treatise on ships which are one-, two-, three- or four-masted.

M-391B

AUTHOR: Mooney, James
DATE: 1900
TITLE: Myths of the Cherokee
IN: Annual Report, Bureau of American Ethnology, Smithsonian Institution, Part 1 (Washington, D.C.), 3-548

Pages 22-23: Informants are quoted witnessing the presence of "a dim but persistent tradition of a strange white race preceding the Cherokee." Their forts extended down the Tennessee River out of the Appalachian mountains.

M-392

AUTHOR: Moorehead, Warren K.
DATE: 1917
TITLE: Stone Ornaments Used by Indians in the United States and Canada, Being a Description of Certain Charm Stones, Gorgets, Tubes, Bird Stones and Problematical Forms
IMPRINT: Andover Press: Andover, Massachusetts

Pages 367-377: Quotes extensively from G-175 about the bannerstone. Holmes supposes the form derived from the European double axe introduced to North America by the Norse. Gordon, with Moorehead agreeing, maintains that examples are too early for that and provides an alternative, indigenous explanation.

M-392B

AUTHOR: Moorwood, John
DATE: 1989
TITLE: Archaic Navigational Instruments
IN: Atlantic Visions (Proceedings of the First International Conference of the

Society of Saint Brendan, September 1985, Dublin and Kerry), edited by John de Courcy Ireland and David C. Sheehy (Boole Press, Dún Laoghaire, Co.: Dublin, Ireland), 199-209

"All known navigational instruments which could have been available to St. Brendan are reviewed and described." Discusses what he says is his discovery that Christian crosses and an object in the shape of the Egyptian ankh sign served as sun compasses and latitude-finders. Mainly undocumented.

M-394

AUTHOR: Morales Belda, Francisco
DATE: 1970
TITLE: La marina de Al-Andalus [The Navy of Al-Andalus]
IMPRINT: Ediciones Ariel: Barcelona

From the 9th to the 14th centuries a number of Arab expeditions went out into the Atlantic. Some of their vessels had a length as great as 25 meters and a beam of 5.6 meters.

M-395

AUTHOR: Morales Padrón, Francisco
DATE: 1971
TITLE: Los descubrimientos en los siglos XIV y XV y los archipiélagos atlánticos [The Discoveries in the 14th and 15th Centuries and the Atlantic Archipelagoes]
IN: Anuario de estudios atlánticos 17:429-465 (Madrid)

For at least 40 years beginning 1342 Mallorcan expeditions traversed the seas of West Africa and the Canaries. In 1352 missionaries were landed in the Canaries ("Fortunate Islands") and the inhabitants learned Christianity. [At least accidental passages to America were thus possible at that time.]

M-396

AUTHOR: Morales Padrón, Francisco
DATE: 1981
TITLE: Historia del descubrimiento y conquista de América [History of the Discovery and Conquest of America]
IMPRINT: Editora Nacional: Madrid

Pages 51-61: On Portuguese voyaging in the Atlantic in the 15th century, with the discovery and settling of Madeira in 1419 and the Azores in 1427.

M-397

AUTHOR: Moran, Hugh A.
DATE: 1952
TITLE: The Alphabet and the Ancient Calendar Signs: Astrological Elements in the Origin of the Alphabet
IMPRINT: Pacific Books: Palo Alto

See M-398.

M-398

AUTHORS: Moran, Hugh A., and David H. Kelley
DATE: 1969
TITLE: The Alphabet and the Ancient Calendar Signs, 2nd edition
IMPRINT: Daily Press: Palo Alto

A revision and expansion of M-397 which is considered the "first edition." Moran argues that the letters of the alphabet are derived from the astrological signs that portrayed the 28 to 30 lunar houses (the lunar zodiac being older than the solar zodiac). These signs are found widely in Eurasian civilizations and also in America.

Kelley adds Part Two: "American Parallels," based upon his 1960 article on calendar animals and deities, which concentrated on the Aztec and Maya day names in relation to India, China, western Asia, and Polynesia. He argues that the Mesoamerican calendar derived from India around the second century B.C. Includes an extended critique of K-100.

M-398B

AUTHOR: Morehouse, George E.
DATE: 1985
TITLE: The Los Lunas Inscriptions: A Geological Study
IN: Epigraphic Society Ocassional Publications 13 (August): 44-53

Observations justifying the possible antiquity of the inscription. In the same issue, pages 35-43, Fell writes on Ancient Punctuation and the Los Lunas Text. Three additional articles on this incription are found in *ESOP* 10. None of these additional four is listed separately in this bibliography.

M-399

AUTHOR: Moreno, Francisco P.
DATE: 1901
TITLE: Notes on the Anthropogeography of Argentina
IN: Geographical Journal 18:576-589

Polynesian and American populations represent a "union" of types. He notes "Papuan skulls" from South America, Maori stone implement at Cuzco and in Argentina, Marquesan carved wood clubs from the ruins near Trujillo and elsewhere in Peru and from Quillota, Chile, as well as Colombia and Ecuador, etc.

M-400

AUTHOR: Moreno Rodríguez, Eduardo
DATE: 1936
TITLE: Correos precolombinos y rápidas disquisiciones demonstrativas de que América se pobló por el Pacífico [Pre-Columbian Mails and Rapid Communications Demonstrating That America was Populated by Way of the Pacific]
IN: Sociedad geográfica nacional, Boletín 76:83-99 (Madrid)

Bernal's note: "Fenicios [Phoenicians], etc."

M-400B

AUTHOR: Morera de Guijarro, Juan Ignacio
DATE: 1978
TITLE: Le dieu civilisateur de mesoamerique [The Civilizing God of Mesoamerica]
IN: Kadath: Chroniques des civilisations disparues, no. 26:33-39 (Brussels)

Contrary to speculations or hypotheses by some writers, he finds Quetzalcoatl to have been an indigenous person, not a being arrived from the Old World. [Compare C-007B.]

M-401B

AUTHOR: Morgan, Arthur E.
DATE: 1946
TITLE: Nowhere Was Somewhere
IMPRINT: University of North Carolina Press: Chapel Hill

Pages 191-198: Portuguese voyaging to West Africa and into the Atlantic.

M-402

AUTHOR: Morgan, Jacques de
DATE: 1920
TITLE: Notes d'archéologie préhistorique, 1: Une hache de type américain au Caucase [Prehistoric Archaeological Notes, 1: An American Style Axe in the Caucasus]
IN: L'Anthropologie 30:497-502

An axe or mining tool of diorite found in the salt mines of Culpa, the Caucasus, and which is in the museum at Tiflis, is the same (form) as an implement used by Indians of Arizona and New Mexico.

M-404

AUTHOR: Morgenstern, Julian
DATE: 1963
TITLE: The Fire upon the Altar
IMPRINT: Quadrangle Books: Chicago

Explication of Israelite ritual as he reads it from the biblical text and comparative Near Eastern sources. Among points of interest [for comparison with Mesoamerica]: distinction between holy and profane fire; censing for atonement and cleansing; fire and (sun) glory representing the power and cleansing force of Yahweh; equinoctial (New Year's day) rays of the morning sun entering the sanctuary through doors opened only one day of the year, with light ("the glory of the Lord") animatedly moving across the floor as the sun rises; shrine dedications at New Year; extinguishing of old fires at night and lighting of "new fire" on New Year's day; the king's crucial participation in these rites; sun's exit from the underworld on the east of the temple associated with resurrection of the dead.

M-405

AUTHOR: Moriarty, G. Andrews
DATE: 1946
TITLE: Newport's Old Stone Mill
IN: New England Quarterly 19:111-113

Reply to P-200. Moriarty argues that a 1632 reference in a colonial paper to a stone tower cannot refer to an existing structure and in any case not to the Newport Tower. Also, if a Norse colony existed for centuries at Newport, it is remarkable that it left behind no trace except the tower.

M-407

AUTHOR: Morice, Adrien-Gabriel
DATE: 1895
TITLE: Notes Archaeological, Industrial, and Sociological on the Western Dénés, with an Ethnographical Sketch of the Same
IN: Transactions of the Canadian Institute 4:1-222

Compares ceremonial dress of the Carrier Indians with that of Assyrians and Jews.

M-408

AUTHOR: Morice, Adrien-Gabriel
DATE: 1899
TITLE: The Use and Abuse of Philology; Review of *The Dénés of America Identified with the Tungus of Asia*, by John Campbell
IN: Transactions of the Canadian Institute 6:84-100

Severe criticism of the methodology and results of the "comparative philology" employed by John Campbell in his efforts to connect American Indian and Asiatic languages.

M-409

AUTHOR: Morice, Adrien-Gabriel
DATE: 1914
TITLE: Northwestern Dénés and Northeastern Asiatics
IN: Transactions of the Canadian Institute 10:131-193

See M-410.

M-410

AUTHOR: Morice, Adrien-Gabriel
DATE: 1916
TITLE: Essai sur l'origine des Dénés de l'Amérique du Nord [Essay on the Origin of the Denes of North America]
IMPRINT: n.p.: Saint Boniface, Manitoba

An elaborate comparison of the Déné, whom he knew as a missionary, with northern Asiatic peoples, in order to demonstrate the Asiatic origin of the former. A laborious compilation of similarities results in his tracing their ultimate origin to the Israelite Ten Tribes. (The Déné are said to have a tradition of living in a land abounding in snakes and monkeys.) The Carrier language of British Columbia is said to be a composite of Chinese, Ural-Altaic, and Semitic. [Compare M-412.]

M-411

AUTHOR: Morice, Adrien-Gabriel
DATE: 1921
TITLE: Smoking and Tobacco among the Northern Dénés
IN: American Anthropologist 23:482-488

In support of Dixon's critique of Wiener, this author further attacks Wiener's discussion of some tobacco names.

M-412

AUTHOR: Morice, Adrien-Gabriel
DATE: 1922
TITLE: Prejudice or Linguistic Short-coming?
IN: American Anthropologist 24:385-390

A slashing response to a review the previous year by Roland B. Dixon of the author's "Essai sur l'origine des Dénés de l'Amérique du Nord." He accuses the reviewer, and documents his charges, that his book had been miscast as kook literature by an "office scientist," "professor though he be," who perhaps has never seen a Déné. (Morice was a missionary for 40 years among them.) In volume 25, page 109, Dixon responds, briefly and icily, which the impassioned Morice in turn blasts on pages 425-427.

M-414

AUTHOR: Morison, Samuel Eliot
DATE: 1940
TITLE: Portuguese Voyages to America in the Fifteenth Century
IMPRINT: Harvard University Press: Cambridge

An appendix lists chronologically Portuguese and other voyages to or towards America between 1447 and 1500.

M-415B

AUTHOR: Morison, Samuel Eliot
DATE: 1965
TITLE: The Oxford History of the American People
IMPRINT: Oxford University Press: Oxford

Pages 18-19: He has no doubt that "Irishmen discovered and settled Iceland when it was empty of human life, and that Norsemen expelled them about A.D. 850." He supposes that they reached North America and settled there, although they never returned and "left no trace."

M-416

AUTHOR: Morison, Samuel Eliot
DATE: 1971
TITLE: The European Discovery of America: the Northern Voyages, A.D. 500-1600
IMPRINT: Oxford University Press: New York

The first four chapters are on voyages (none to America) and knowledge from (European) antiquity, St. Brendan (a hilariously irreverant version parodies the original) and the Irish, the Norsemen and Vinland, as well as "Flyaway Islands and False Voyages, 1100-1492." Chapter 8 is on the French maritime background from 1453. In his magisterial assurance, Morison does not bother to document his statements, but the bibliographical discussion and notes at the end of each chapter are quite good.

M-417

AUTHOR: Morley, Sylvanus G.
DATE: 1920
TITLE: The Inscriptions at Copan

IMPRINT: Carnegie Institution of Washington: Washington, D.C.

Says the notion that an Asiatic elephant is represented on Stela B is "an extravagant hypothesis" of no value.

M-418

AUTHOR: Morley, Sylvanus G.
DATE: 1927
TITLE: Maya Civilization 100% American
IN: The Forum 78:226-236

A rhetorically baroque version of the "rise of Maya civilization." There is "no vestige, no infinitesimal trace of Old World influence . . . to detract from the genius of our [*sic*] native American mind." The supposed "Asiatic jade"—this "Banquo's ghost of American archaeology"—has been laid to rest by petrographic analysis. The claimed elephant trunks on Mayan monuments "have been identified under . . . the more critical comparative methods of modern research as the bills of parrots or macaws!" "There is no room for foreign origins here." [Morley's title and much of his phraseology remarkably reflect the popular xenophobia, nationalism, and isolationism, as well as the language, of the 1920s which resulted in legislation excluding orientals and other "foreigners" from immigrating to the U.S.]

M-419

AUTHOR: Morley, Sylvanus G.
DATE: 1946
TITLE: The Ancient Maya
IMPRINT: Stanford University Press: Stanford, California
[Third edition, revised by G. W. Brainerd (Stanford University Press: Stanford, 1956)]

First edition, page 113, plate 88b: Litter carries important personages, Classic date.

Third edition, page 206: Heads of important people were preserved for adoration by descendants.

M-420

AUTHOR: Morote Best, Efraín
DATE: 1958
TITLE: La huída mágica, estudio de un cuento popular en el Perú [The Magic Flight, a Study of a Popular Story in Peru]
IN: Miscellanea Paul Rivet, Octogenario Dicata, Universidad Nacional Autónoma de México, Publicaciones del Instituto de Historia 1/50 [Proceedings of the 31st International Congress of Americanists (São Paulo, 1954)], 1:797-848

Pages 798-799: Kroeber excluded South America from his distribution of the Magic Flight tale. This paper rebuts that by showing widespread, thus ancient, he maintains, distribution among Peruvian Indian groups.

Page 798: He gives the six diffusion routes of the tale from its supposed origin in central Europe. Kroeber has no doubt that the tale had a single origin, despite variants. His world map is reproduced on page 803 with the author's Peruvian cases inserted. Routes into the Americas are left unclear, particularly to South America.

M-420B

AUTHOR: Morrell, Virginia
DATE: 1990
TITLE: Research News: Confusion in Earliest America
IN: Science 248 (April 27): 439-441

Reports on a conference held March 1990 on the Greenberg proposal for New World language classification and settlement. "An emerging consensus that the Americas were inhabited earlier than has been thought has undone a neat synthesis of linguistic, dental, and archeological evidence." Greenberg's picture was attacked not only by the archaeologists (Monte Verde and Meadowcroft are firmly dated too early for his position) but by linguists (Campbell and others) who claim his work is "shoddy." (In a sidebar his impressive credentials are recapped.) Rebecca Cann, a geneticist from the University of Hawaii, argued that there must have been more than three migrations. A mitochondrial DNA study had indicated in 1983 that all the American Indians were descended from one lineage. "But we now know that there were at least 11 major lineages, possibly more. To accumulate that kind of genetic diversity, there either had to be more migrations or bigger migrating groups." Her report was based in part on recent research by S. Paabo of the University of California at Berkeley which uses "the polymerase chain reaction on a much more varied population sample than the one used in the earlier studies and came up with a much greater number of genetic lineages."

M-421

AUTHOR: Morrill, Sibley S.
DATE: 1968
TITLE: Pre-Columbian Indians Used the Wheel
IN: Indian Historian 1/4:18-21

Quotes Charnay, who had discovered the first Mesoamerican wheeled "toys," that the historian Juarros, writing of a battle of Guatemalans against Alvarado, tells of the native use of "war-engines" or carts moving on "rodadellos" [rollers] to different parts of the battlefield to supply armament. Charnay considered these to have been wheeled carts. [See J-130B.]

M-421B

AUTHOR: Morrison, David A.
DATE: 1987
TITLE: Thule and Historic Copper Use in the Copper Inuit Area
IN: American Antiquity 52/1:3-12

[Some of the implement forms shown are similar to European copper artifacts.]

M-421C

AUTHOR: Morrison, Kristi
DATE: 1995
TITLE: [Truths No Longer Hidden, 5]
IN: Introducing The Institute for the Study of American Cultures and The ISAC Press (The ISAC Press, Institute for the Study of American Cultures, Inc.: Columbus, Georgia), 4

Cited as proof of the following description is a video available from ISAC in which Paul Shaffranke and Horatio [*sic*] demonstrate the deciphering of tablets from a cache, in Burrows Cave, that are written in Latin in the Etruscan alphabet. "Historical documents and religious art inscribed on stones recovered from an undisclosed site in southern Illinois record details of a colony of refugees from Ptolemaic Egypt, including a Jewish contingent, from Rome and the Kingdom of Mauretania. They were secretly sent to America in ships provided by the Mauretanian king, Juba II, and his wife and co-monarch, Cleopatra Selene, daughter of Cleopatra and Marc Antony. Included among the refugees were the queen's two brothers, who disappeared from Rome—and recorded history—in A.D. 17, Alexander Helios and Ptolemy Philadelphus. Helios seems to have been the 'sun king,' ruling the group fleeing to America. It is recorded on the stones that he is the 'representative and descendant of the Ptolemies of Egypt,' and that he is the 'possessor of the Ptolemaic kings.' "

M-425

AUTHOR: Morse, Dan
DATE: 1967
TITLE: Tuberculosis
IN: Diseases in Antiquity: A Survey of the Diseases, Injuries and Surgery of Early Populations, compiled and edited by Don Brothwell and A. T. Sandison (Charles C. Thomas: Springfield, Illinois), 249-271

Page 250: In a section on Prehistoric Tuberculosis in America, he notes that tuberculosis would be unlikely to have been brought to America via small hunting groups across the Arctic. "Another possible source of introduction," the only other channel mentioned, is via the Vikings, but this he considers unlikely.

His survey of the literature shows 15 apparent cases of the disease in the Americas, but he is not well pleased with the quality of much of this evidence. He concludes by supposing that tuberculosis was probably a post-Columbian introduction, but the Vikings conceivably could have brought it.

M-426

AUTHOR: Morse, Edward S.
DATE: 1898
TITLE: Was Middle America Peopled from Asia?
IN: Popular Science Monthly 54/1:1-15

A cautious treatment of America as the site of Fu-sang. Cites a few striking parallels in support, then argues at length that since roofing tiles, the plow, tea, chopsticks, etc., are nowhere found in the New World, Chinese contact could not have taken place.

M-428

AUTHOR: Mortier, Florent
DATE: 1930
TITLE: L'expansion chinoise: le pays de Fou-Sang est-il l'Amérique? [Chinese Expansion: Is The Country of Fu-sang America?]
IN: Bulletin de la société des américanistes de Belgique (Décembre): 22-23

The answer is "no."

M-428B

AUTHOR: Mortillet, A. de
DATE: 1913
TITLE: L'age du bronze en Chine [The Chinese Bronze Age]
IN: Revue anthropologique 23:397-415

Notes an axe head from a tomb in Argentina which shares interesting details with Chinese metal axe heads.

M-429

AUTHOR: Morton, Henry A.
DATE: 1975
TITLE: The Wind Commands: Sailors and Sailing Ships in the Pacific
IMPRINT: University of British Columbia: Vancouver; and Wesleyan University Press: Middletown, Connecticut

Filled with details on indigenous Pacific watercraft (rafts, floats, skin boats, canoes, proas, junks), European-built ships in the Pacific, maintenance and movement (navigation, routes, superstitions, materials, repairs, worms, rigging, anchors, etc.), health and diet, and shipboard culture (command, mutinies, drinking, women, music, the clash of cultures). Documentation is exemplary. Illustrations are noteworthy, not only drawings made especially for the book but old photographs of the Tillikum, the Joseph Conrad, the Spray, and many other actual vessels and models. The author says little of diffusion as shown by vessels, but he seems open to the possiblity that Northwest Coast and some western Pacific boats could be related.

M-432

AUTHOR: Moseley, Michael Edward
DATE: 1969
TITLE: Assessing the Archaeological Significance of Mahames
IN: American Antiquity 34:485-487

South American mahames or sunken garden plots were a supplement to canal irrigation. [Polynesian parallel.]

M-433

AUTHOR: Moseley, Michael Edward
DATE: 1975

TITLE: The Maritime Foundations of Andean Civilization
IMPRINT: Cummings: Menlo Park

Page 76: Trepanation, without metal tools, is evident at the site named Asia in the "Cotton Preceramic" stage, between 2500-1500 B.C. This is the earliest example of this practice in coastal Peru.

M-434

AUTHOR: Moser, Christopher L.
DATE: 1977
TITLE: The Wheel Problem in Ancient Mesoamerica
IN: Katunob 10/1:59-63 (Greeley, Colorado)

He examines a number of hypotheses which can be offered to explain why practical wheeled vehicles seem not to have been used in Mesoamerica, although the concept of a wheeled vehicle (in miniature) was well known. Two he finds most persuasive and deserving of further study: socio-economics (abundance of human porters/slaves/captives put vehicles at a cost-effectiveness disadvantage), and failure to solve basic mechanical problems (no effective lubricants available, lack of braking systems, wheel wear, road maintenance).

M-435

AUTHOR: Mossi, Miguel Angel
DATE: 1926 [1889]
TITLE: Diccionario analítico sintético universal
[A Universal Analytic and Synthetic Dictionary]
IMPRINT: Universidad Nacional de Tucumán: Tucumán, Argentina
[Written in 1889, published posthumously]

Quechua is related to Hebrew.

M-438

AUTHORS: Mountjoy, Joseph B., and John P. Smith
DATE: 1985
TITLE: An Archaeological Patolli from Tomatlán, Jalisco, Mexico
IN: Contributions to the Archaeology and Ethnohistory of Greater Mesoamerica, edited by William J. Folan (Southern Illinois University Press: Carbondale and Edwardsville), 240-262

A study of a recently discovered stone upon which is pecked a design strongly resembling the pattern of some presumed patolli designs from other Mesoamerican sites. Discusses the distribution and chronology of such designs and thus of the patolli game, extending back at least into Classic times.

M-440

AUTHOR: Moura Pessoa, Marialice
DATE: 1950
TITLE: O mito do diluvio nas Americas: Estudo analitico e bibliografico
[The Flood Myth of the Americas: An Analytic and Bibliographic Study]
IN: Revista do Museo Paulista 4:7-48 (São Paulo)
[From her 1948 M.A. thesis at Columbia University]

Comprehensive presentation of the distribution of flood motifs in the New World [for comparison with Old World instances as a check on claimed diffusion]. Text is in Portuguese and English.

M-441

AUTHOR: Mourant, A. E.
DATE: 1954
TITLE: The Distribution of Human Blood Groups

IMPRINT: C. C. Thomas: Springfield, Illinois; and Blackwell Scientific Publications: London

Pages 144-147: The origin of the Polynesians. Previous discussions of genetic data in relation to Heyerdahl's proposals have been incomplete. He reports that "observations on the ABO, MNS and Rh blood group systems are . . . all consistent with the theory of Heyerdahl. The results of tests for the other blood group systems in America are not sufficiently uniform to allow detailed comparisons with the Polynesians." Also, "it may be said that a large part of the genetic constitution of the Polynesians can be accounted for on the basis of an American, and especially a north-west American origin, but there must have been a considerable amount of mixing with other peoples. . . ." And, "Even if the hypothesis of migrations from America to Polynesia should prove untenable, there would still be a strong suggestion that Polynesians and North American Indians had in the not very distant past received many genes from a common pool."

M-442

AUTHOR: Mourant, A. E.

DATE: 1962

TITLE: Blood Groups in the Pacific Area

IN: Proceedings of the 8th Congress of the International Society of Blood Transfusion (Tokyo 1960), pages 149-153

How blood group data relate to possible contact between Polynesians and American Indians. The writer now believes that the blood-group evidence does not support Heyerdahl's thesis.

M-443

AUTHORS: Mourant, A. E., Ada C. Kopec, and Kazimiera Domaniewska-Sobczak

DATE: 1976

TITLE: The Distribution of the Human Blood Groups and Other Polymorphisms, Second edition

IMPRINT: Oxford University Press: London

This is a second edition of M-441.

Page 117: There is a strong case to be made for limited cultural contact having occurred, no doubt with some inflow of genes, across the mid-Pacific, and it is not impossible even that some persons entered America before 1492 across the mid-Atlantic, but we must look almost solely to eastern Siberia for the source of most American Indian genes.

Page 120: The Miskito and Subtiaba of Nicaragua show the V antigen; the results should be carefully confirmed, and if so would suggest a relationship, "obviously very remote, to the Ainu of Japan." A number of tribes in South America, especially in the Andean area, which apart from their blood groups appear to be of pure Amerindian descent, possess A and B genes, and it has been suggested that these are derived from immigrants who came in across the mid-Pacific; it seems doubtful that this explanation would account for the findings. Most workers appear to accept the view that all A and B genes in these populations are of post-Columbian introduction.

Page 122: A few tribes, especially in Surinam, French Guiana, and Venezuela have been found to possess transferrin variants, and where close identification has been achieved, the type has proved to relate these peoples to those of eastern Asia.

Page 137: New data on the distribution of a certain transferrin allele shows it present in Finns and other Finno-Ugric speakers, various Siberian groups, and in Amerinds of Middle America. These variants may provide an important clue to the interrelations of the circumpolar peoples, and to the relationship of those of the Old World to the American Indians.

M-444

AUTHOR: Mowat, Farley

DATE: 1965

TITLE: Westviking: The Ancient Norse in Greenland and North America

IMPRINT: Little, Brown: Boston; McClelland and Stewart: Canada; and Secker and Warburg: London

Synthesis by a well-informed non-specialist. He tries to reconcile conflicting data and interpretations, arriving at a route and probable Vinland not much different from Ingstad's. Believes that J. Scolvuss, the Dane, reached the mainland in 1476. Includes a substantial section on Viking navigation.

M-445

AUTHOR: Mowat, Farley
DATE: 1966
TITLE: Vinland Map, a Commentary
IN: Canadian Cartographer 3/1:6-13

Identifies geographic locations of the main features on the map, postulating that the "Island ov Vinland" was based on charts made and used by ancient Norse.

M-446

AUTHOR: Moziño, José Mariano [translated and edited by Iris Higbie Wilson]
DATE: 1970
TITLE: Notícias de Nutka [Nootka Notices]; an Account of Nootka Sound in 1792
IMPRINT: University of Washington Press: Seattle; and McClelland and Stewart: Toronto

Page 64: Note by Wilson: the Northwest Coast had iron when discovered by Captain Cook. P. Drucker suggests that it came around the northern rim of the Pacific.

M-447

AUTHOR: Mudrak, O. A.
DATE: 1984
TITLE: K voprosu o vnesnix sv'az'ax èskimosskix jazykov [On the External Relationships of Eskimo Languages]
IN: Linguisticeskaja rekonstrukcija i drevnejsaja istorija Vostoka. Tezisy i doklady konferencii, Cast' I (Nauka: Moscow), 64-70

Eskimo and Aleut belong to the Nostratic language grouping of north Eurasia.

M-449

AUTHOR: Muffett, David J. M.
DATE: 1987
TITLE: Leo Wiener—A Plea for Re-examination
IN: African Presence in Early America, edited by Ivan van Sertima (n.p.: n.p.), 188-196 ["Incorporating Journal of African Civilizations, Dec. 1986, vol. 8, no. 2." "All inquiries should be addressed to Transaction Books, Rutgers—the State University, New Brunswick, New Jersey"]

Because several cited reviewers were positive about Wiener's scholarship and conclusions (that Africa had a strong influence on ancient America) when the three volumes first came out, Muffett feels that his work should be newly appreciated. [Anthropologists and linguists were generally appalled by it.]

Pages 197-201 reprint "the first [laudatory] review of Leo Wiener," in the *Journal of Negro History*, 1920.

M-453

AUTHOR: Mukerji, Dhirendra Nath
DATE: 1936
TITLE: A Correlation of the Maya and Hindu Calendars
IN: Indian Culture 2/4:685-692

A study of this subject was made at the request of Dr. B. Datta. She presents "the astronomical verification that the epoch of the Mayan and Hindu calendars are identically the same." Six dates in the Dresden Codex were converted to

Julian equivalents by applying the Kali Yuga equation of 588466. The results show Mars/Mercury/Venus/Jupiter/Saturn phenomena of interest for five of those dates, something Thompson could not discover by his equation. Many other sets of comparative data are also given, mostly from Copan. Hindu astral symbolism applies nicely to some of these.

M-454

AUTHOR: Müller, Florencia
DATE: 1978
TITLE: La cerámica del centro ceremonial de Teotihuacán
[Ceramics from the Ceremonial Center of Teotihuacan]
IMPRINT: Instituto Nacional de Antropología e Historia: México

Wheeled miniatures date to almost the beginning of the Christian era.

M-455

AUTHOR: Müller, Gertrude
DATE: 1936
TITLE: Einige interessante Einzelheiten aus der medico-historischen Ausstellung in Wien
[Some Interesting Particulars from the Medical-Historical Exhibit in Vienna]
IN: Anthropos 31:242-243

Page 243: Occurrence of the venesection bow in Polynesia and America.

M-456

AUTHOR: Muller, H. P. N.
DATE: 1904
TITLE: The Mitla Ruins and the Mexican Natives
IN: Handbuch, Nederlandisch Anthropologisch Verhandlung 1:14-25 (The Hague)

The author is impressed by "strong Japanese and Egyptian (physical) types" in northern and central Mexico, and also by resemblance of figures in drawings and sculptures of natives in all Mexico to Buddha ornaments in southern and eastern Asia.

M-457

AUTHOR: Muller, Jon
DATE: 1968
TITLE: A Comment on Ford's Review of Early Formative Period of Coastal Ecuador
IN: American Antiquity 33:254-255

He is not impressed by Ford's comments [F-130] which strongly support the Jomon-Valdivia pottery connection proposed by Evans, Meggers and Estrada. "Given the incredible diversity of early Japanese ceramics . . . it would be surprising were it not possible to find *sherds* which closely resemble nearly any sherds from any place in the world. . ." [*sic*].

M-460

AUTHOR: Müller, Werner
DATE: 1958
TITLE: Stufenpyramiden in Mexiko und Kambodsche
[Stepped Pyramids in Mexico and Cambodia]
IN: Paideuma 6/8:473-489

Comparison of layout and architectural form of the Cambodian stepped pyramid and the world view behind it are made with Mesoamerica, and a direct historical connection is indicated.

M-461

AUTHOR: Müller, Werner
DATE: 1962, 1973, 1979
TITLE: Raum und Zeit in Sprachen und Kalendern Nordamerikas und Alteuropas
[Space and Time in the Languages

	and Calendars of North America and Old Europe]
IN:	Anthropos 57:568-590; 68:156-180; 74:443-464

See M-463.

M-463

AUTHOR:	Müller, Werner
DATE:	1982
TITLE:	Die Neue oder die Alte Welt? [The New or the Old World?]
IMPRINT:	Dietrich Reimer: Berlin [One-page English summary on page 207]

The author, who has published on Algonquian ethnology since 1930, proposes that the North Sea region from Ireland to Scandinavia served as a bridgehead across which very ancient North American cultural forms, some of which have survived to the present, reached Europe. The New World was the source of the Late Paleolithic developments in Europe.

Treats evidences from architecture, calendars, New Year ritual relating to death and rebirth, myth of giant supporting the earth, origin myths, and Eskimo language relations to proto-Indo-European.

M-464

AUTHOR:	Müller-Karpe, Hermann
DATE:	1982a
TITLE:	Zur Seefahrt im 3. und 2. Jahrtausend v. Chr. [On Sea Travel in the Second and Third Millennia B.C.]
IN:	Zur geschichtlichen Bedeutung der frühen Seefahrt, edited by Hermann Müller-Karpe, (Kolloquien zur Allgemeinen und Vergleichenden Archäologie, Band 2) (C. H. Beck: München), 1-20

A thoroughly up-to-date discussion of current knowledge on nautical basics for the indicated period in the Mediterranean, northwestern Europe, and the Indian Ocean.

M-465

AUTHOR:	Müller-Karpe, Hermann
DATE:	1982b
TITLE:	Zur Seefahrt in der griechisch-römischen Antike [On Sea Travel in Greek-Roman Antiquity]
IN:	Zur geschichtlichen Bedeutung der frühen Seefahrt, edited by Hermann Müller-Karpe, (Kolloquien zur Allgemeinen und Vergleichenden Archäologie, Band 2) (C. H. Beck: München), 45-50

Brief summary of current information, citing previous major works.

M-467

AUTHOR:	Mulloy, William
DATE:	1975a
TITLE:	A Solstice Oriented ahu on Easter Island
IN:	Archaeology and Physical Anthropology in Oceania 10/1:1-39

The earliest ahu on the island that is solar oriented has a C-14-based date of around A.D. 1200. An Andean source is possible but not capable of clear demonstration. He discusses literature by archaeologists and anthropologists on such Andean knowledge and practice [but archaeoastronomical literature as such is not considered]. Little suggests a Polynesian source for the idea of solstice orientation, if it was not invented locally.

M-468

AUTHOR:	Mulloy, William
DATE:	1975b
TITLE:	Double Canoes on Easter Island?
IN:	Archaeology and Physical Anthropology in Oceania 10/3:181-184

A petroglyph seems to show a double canoe, though with odd appearance. A review of evidence about Easter Island vessels suggests a slight possibility that a double canoe might have been known there.

M-469

AUTHORS: Mulloy, William, and Gonzalo Figueroa
DATE: 1978
TITLE: The A Kivi-Vai Teka Complex and Its Relationship to Easter Island Architectural Prehistory
IMPRINT: Asian and Pacific Archaeological Series No. 8 (Social Sciences Research Institute, University of Hawaii: Honolulu)

They doubt the soundness of Golson's reasons for reversing the order of construction of Vinapu ahus 1 and 2, but they agree that the order should indeed be reversed. An implication is that Easter Island's archaeological sequence manifests continuity from beginning to end, not two distinct cultural phases as Heyerdahl would have.

M-470

AUTHOR: Mumelin, Ragnar
DATE: 1937
TITLE: The Wandering Spirit
IMPRINT: Macmillan: London

Why, when, where, and how men have wandered.

M-471

AUTHOR: Munch, Guido
DATE: 1982
TITLE: El paraiso entre los indígenas del sur de Veracruz
[Paradise among the Natives of Southern Veracruz]
IN: Abstracts of Papers, 44th International Congress of Americanists (Manchester, 1982), (School of Geography, Manchester University: Manchester, England), 283

Themes addressed include: the black dog and black chickens *(gallinas),* the serpent of fire, river of blood, food and utensils for the dead one. One's relatives and friends help one resolve the seven mysteries, whereupon resurrection comes. [Compare J-089 regarding pre-Columbian use of chickens in ritual.]

M-472

AUTHOR: Mundkur, Balaji
DATE: 1976
TITLE: The Cult of the Serpent in the Americas: Its Asian Background
IN: Current Anthropology 17:429-455

The same general lines of argumentation as in M-473, a variant of "psychic unity," with divergent comments by others.

M-473

AUTHOR: Mundkur, Balaji
DATE: 1978
TITLE: On The Alleged Diffusion of Hindu Divine Symbols into Pre-Columbian Mesoamerica: A Critique
IN: Current Anthropology 19:541-583

He argues that diffusionist claims for a Mesoamerican connection are based on misguided treatment of the Indian sources, since these sources show a great deal of variability, rather than the cultural specifics cited by the proponents of diffusionism. Comments from other scholars (with a wide range of knowledge, and its lack) are appended, some of which point to the author's straw-man argumentation, reliance on doubtful concepts, and inadequate knowledge of the New World material, while others welcome and support his views.

Page 571: Michael Coe points out serious errors and weaknesses in Mundkur's handling of the Mesoamerican materials and argues for a some transpacific connection, noting, "I hold that some Asian-Mesoamerican correspondences will turn out to be homologies and not just analogies."

M-474

AUTHOR: Mundkur, Balaji
DATE: 1980
TITLE: On Pre-Columbian Maize in India and Elephantine Deities in Mesoamerica
IN: Current Anthropology 21:676-679

Brief, facile argument that pre-Columbian maize could not have been known in Asia nor elephants to Mesoamericans. The cobs of corn claimed by Jett and others [see J-095] in Indian sculptural art are stylized pomegranates or whatever.

M-475

AUTHOR: Mundkur, Balaji
DATE: 1984
TITLE: The Bicephalous "Animal Style" in Northern Eurasian Religious Art and Its Western Hemispheric Analogues
IN: Current Anthropology 25:451-482

He rejects any diffusionist explanation. Includes comments by Stephen C. Jett and other scholars.

M-477

AUTHOR: Munizaga, Juan R.
DATE: 1963
TITLE: Estudio de un rasgo de variación discontinua en las poblaciones americanas [Study of a Trait of Discontinuous Variation in the American Population]
IMPRINT: Centro de Estudios Antropológicas, Universidad de Chile: Santiago

Gruber's Canal is taken as a phenotypic character of discrete variation; this is a study of its form and presence or absence in 5,082 skulls representing 67 series grouped in 18 geographical zones. The geographical gradient shows highest frequency in the central zones of the New World (Florida to Peru) and a near absence in Asia (U'ga and Buriat Mongol), and the extreme north and south: Alaska (Point Hope and Wales), and Tierra del Fuego (Ona and Alacaluf).

M-484B

AUTHOR: Murphy, John J., Jr.
DATE: 1979
TITLE: Trento's Lost America—A Critique
IN: NEARA [New England Antiquities Research Association] Journal 13:78

A review of T-147.

M-485

AUTHOR: Murrill, Rupert I.
DATE: 1965
TITLE: Cranial and Postcranial Skeletal Remains from Easter Island
IN: Reports of the Norwegian Archaeological Expedition to Easter Island and the East Pacific, vol. 2, Miscellaneous Papers, edited by Thor Heyerdahl and Edwin N. Ferdon, Jr., Monographs of the School of American Research and the Museum of New Mexico, and the Kon-Tiki Museum, No. 24, Part 2, (Rand McNally: Chicago), 225-324

See M-486.

M-486

AUTHOR: Murrill, Rupert I.
DATE: 1968
TITLE: Cranial and Postcranial Skeletal Remains from Easter Island
IMPRINT: University of Minnesota Press: Minneapolis

A slightly revised version of M-485.

Murrill delivers an osteologist's view of the Long-ear/Short-ear legend and critically assesses physical evidence for Heyerdahl's theory of an eastern origin for the populating of Polynesia. He concludes that the sample (25 males, 8 females, and one calvarium of a child from three documented archaeological sites with C-14 dates) is a homogeneous one displaying continuity from what Heyerdahl considered distinct "Middle" to "Late" periods. All is representative of a Polynesian people who may have come from the Marquesas Islands.

Pages 77-79: A superior critique of the use of ABO frequencies for historical interpretation purposes. A "pure" sample is elusive, and most studies in Oceania have failed on that test as well as from failing to consider small group drift, the possibility of natural selective factors at play, etc.

M-486B

AUTHOR: Museum of Primitive Art
DATE: 1964
TITLE: A Maya Sculpture in Wood
IMPRINT: Museum of Primitive Art: New York

Illustrates and discusses a remarkably well-preserved wooden figure of the Classic era, a human male kneeling "in a posture of adoration," which was acquired by the Museum "through commercial channels."

Page 9: The elaborate handlebar mustache "raises difficult problems . . . for although beards were often depicted in Mesoamerican art, representations of mustaches are not common," and no other is as luxuriant as this one. "It raises the often argued question as to whether the Mongoloid American Indian could have had sufficient facial hair to grow a heavy beard—or a mustache such as this—and as to who might have been the model for this figure. There is no easy solution to this problem."

N-001

AUTHOR: Nachtigall, Horst von
DATE: 1958
TITLE: Die amerikanischen Megalithkulturen: Vorstudien zu einer Untersuchung [The American Megalith Cultures: A Preliminary Study towards an Investigation]
IMPRINT: Dietrich Reimer: Berlin [Reviewed by Gerardo Reichel-Dolmatoff, *American Anthropologist* 61 (1959): 151-152; reviewed by Udo Oberem, *Zeitschrift für Ethnologie* 85 (1960): 164-165]

Supposes transpacific influences on Mesoamerican culture but fails to document the position.

N-002

AUTHOR: Nachtigall, Horst von
DATE: 1960
TITLE: Zur Entstehung der amerikanischen Hochkulturen [On the Origin of American Advanced Cultures]
IN: Paideuma 7:151-162

The analysis of cultural parallels between America and East and Southeast Asia fails to show complete cultures implanted in the New World but only certain elements, indicating sporadic contacts. The megalithic culture originated in Mesopotamia and is older there and in surrounding areas of the Old World, hence that must be the source of the megalithic elements in America. Beginning about the eighth century B.C. we see startling parallels in art motifs between South America and China. Culture contacts with Asia continued until the 12th century A.D., i.e. between Cambodia and the Maya area. Megalithic influence is particularly evident on America from the first century B.C., coming from a source in the Deccan of India.

N-003

AUTHOR: Nadaillac, Jean Francois Albert du Pouget, Marquis de
DATE: 1899
TITLE: Pre-Historic America

IMPRINT: Putnam's: New York [Translation of *L'Amerique préhistorique* (Masson: Paris, 1883)]

A very popular work and influential with the American public. He cautiously allows possible Old World connections other than via Bering Strait.

Pages 327-328: A statue from Palenque he feels resembles some Egyptian statues and has a head-dress a little like that of Assyrians. Hieroglyphics there show "a very distinct resemblance" to some of Egypt.

Page 336: Supposed elephant trunks may turn out to be an indication of the Asiatic origin of the civilization.

Page 342: He refers to two Aymara vases in the museum at La Paz on which are representations of an elephant carrying a palanquin.

Pages 356-357: Charnay at Tula found porcelain and part of "a glass bottle iridescent like ancient Roman glass." Of these he is skeptical, however, since Charnay allowed that iron he found there dated from the Spanish period, so why not the porcelain and glass?

Page 522: Physical characteristics of some Indians suggest Melanesian origin; he considers this probable. But overall the results of research in America "testify to the orderly reign of evolution here as in the Old World."

N-006

AUTHOR: Nakao, Sasuke, and Jonathan Sauer

DATE: 1957

TITLE: Grain Amaranths

IN: Scientific Results of the Japanese Expedition to Nepal Himalaya, 1952-1953, edited by Hitoshi Kihara, vol. 2, Land and Crops of Nepal Himalaya (Fauna and Flora Research Society: Kyoto), 141-146

Reports the presence of two species of amaranth in the Himalayas. "If we postulate that both species were carried to Asia by Europeans, it appears that we must also postulate not only that certain culture traits associated with the plants were reinvented independently in Asia but also that the same rare mutant form with pale seeds was developed there independently." "An alternative possibility remains, namely that at least one species, A. leucocarpus, was introduced to Asia as a crop in pre-Columbian times."

N-007

AUTHOR: Nansen, Fridtjof

DATE: 1911

TITLE: In Northern Mists: Arctic Exploration in Early Times, 2 vols.

IMPRINT: William Heinemann: London [Translated from Danish. German translation, Nebelheim; Entdeckung und Erforschung der nördlichen Länder und Meere: Leipzig, 1911]

Vol. 1, pages 233-258: Norse shipbuilding and navigation.

Pages 312-384: Wineland the Good, the Fortunate Isles, and the Discovery of America. Accounts often taken as literal and descriptive about "Wineland" are in considerable part a reworking of Irish and older, classical Mediterranean myths of legends about the fortunate isles of the west, related to the Brendan material.

Vol. 2, pages 1-65: Continuation of the discussion on Wineland, Fortunate Isles and the discovery of America. Extended treatment of the sources leads him to conclude that the idea of grapes or "wine" in the discovered western land is part of the mythology, not descriptive fact.

Pages 38-41: Presents evidence that the game of lacrosse, widely played in northeastern North America, originated from the Norse game knattleikr known from the sagas.

Page 103: Believes that early Norse in Greenland were not exterminated by Eskimos but were absorbed by them through intermarriage.

N-007B

AUTHOR: Naroll, Raoul
DATE: 1961
TITLE: Two Solutions to Galton's Problem
IN: Philosophy of Science 28/1:15-39 [Reprinted *Readings in Cross-cultural Methodology,* edited by Frank W. Moore, Human Relations Area Files (New Haven, Connecticut), 217-241]

A classic methodological problem is addressed—how can one distinguish statistically between independently occurring and historically-produced (that is, diffused) similarities on the basis of geographical distributions?

N-007C

AUTHORS: Naroll, Raoul, and Roy G. D'Andrade
DATE: 1963
TITLE: Two Further Solutions to Galton's Problem
IN: American Anthropologist 65:1053-1067

See N-007B.

N-008

AUTHOR: Naudou, Jean
DATE: 1962
TITLE: A propos d'un éventuel emprunt de l'art Maya aux arts de l'Inde extérieure [About a Possible Borrowing of Mayan Art in the Arts of Greater India]
IN: Proceedings of the 34th International Congress of Americanists (Vienna, 1960), pages 340-347

The lotus panels from Chichen Itza are compared in some detail with those of India and Southeast Asia. The complex of various elements that occurs in both places is considered to be proof of relationship, although the exact place of origin in Asia is uncertain.

N-009

AUTHOR: Naumann, W.
DATE: 1940a
TITLE: Bark Cloth in the Reports of the First Explorers of the South Seas
IN: Ciba Review 23:1175-1179

American-Polynesian and other Oceanic parallels.

N-011

AUTHOR: Navarrete, Carlos
DATE: 1978
TITLE: Un Reconocimiento de la Sierra Madre de Chiapas. Apuntes de un Diario de Campo [A Reconnaissance in the Sierra Madre of Chiapas. Notes from a Field Diary]
IMPRINT: Universidad Nacional Autónoma de México, Centro de Estudios Mayas, Cuadernos 13

A stamp seal found in the Sierra Madre above the Soconusco displays non-pictorial characters [which look like they could be alphabetic writing]. [Compare D-062.]

N-012

AUTHOR: Naville, René
DATE: 1966
TITLE: Une écriture andine [An Andean Writing System]
IN: Bulletin der schweizerischen Amerikanisten-Gesellschaft 20:43-38 (Geneva)

A number of the chroniclers reported that pre-Spanish writing existed in South America. Bertoni reported a system among the Guaraní. Ibarra Grasso found a script in use in Bolivia. The question remains whether the latter writing was pre- or post-Columbian. An introduction by

Spanish missionaries has been claimed, but some of the symbols seem to have a more remote origin, and the fact that the writing was in boustrophedon supports the idea.

N-015

AUTHOR: Needham, Joseph
DATE: 1959
TITLE: An Archaeological Study-tour in China, 1958
IN: Antiquity 33:113-119

Page 116: Chinese documents mention pottery drain pipes as early as Han. Some have now been discovered. [Also in Mexico; see S-079.]

N-016

AUTHORS: Needham, Joseph, and Lu Gwei-Djen
DATE: 1985
TITLE: Trans-Pacific Echoes and Resonances; Listening Once Again
IMPRINT: World Scientific: Singapore and Philadelphia

One of the most important single sources having to do with transoceanic diffusion. Supplements the material in their *Science and Civilisation in China,* volume 4, supporting the idea of China-America contacts in pre-Columbian times. The authors feel that while nothing can diminish the originality of the Amerindian civilizations, a multitude of culture-traits do point to influences from, and contacts with, the Old World.

Extensive data are presented under the headings of: recording and writing; artistic elements; religion, myth and folklore; natural philosophy, cosmology and calendrical astronomy; technology; and ethno-botany, ethno-zoology and ethno-helminthology. They also treat theoretical considerations and provide a 21-page bibliography, the most salient entries of which have been incorporated into this bibliography.

Page 4: A major period of intentional Chinese voyaging into the Pacific was third century B.C. to second century A.D., and also the first half of the 15th century A.D. South Chinese-Vietnamese sailing rafts with center boards were quite capable of making landfall on the American continent.

Page 5: Doubt the evidential value of stone anchors found off the California coast; they are probably recent. [Compare P-167 and F-212.]

Page 6: Believe Asians reached America on various occasions by sea, but none are likely to have gone back.

Page 8: Chinese and Aztec/Mayan jade uses (an amulet painted red is placed in the mouth of the dead) are reviewed. Sacrifice of attendants in the tomb at Palenque and elsewhere "invite comparison" with Shang tombs.

Pages 7-15: "Collocative" trait complexes are required for convincing evidence of contact. Excellent methodological discussion.

Pages 9ff.: The patolli-pachisi game is discussed as a good example of a collocative complex. Pachisi is equivalent to the Iranian nard and Arabic tab games.

Page 13: Argue that the onus of proof lies on those claiming independent development, not the reverse. And experience shows that the further one goes back in history, the more unlikely independent invention was.

Page 24: Cite an unpublished study by G. J. Tee, "Evidence for the Chinese Origin of the Jaguar Motif in Chavin Art," in which Tee shows for an early Chavin carving of the jaguar and earlier or contemporary Chou bronze castings of tigers the following: similar posture, teeth bared, ears pointing forward, elongation of the foot-pads, semi-regular patterns on the bodies, rings around the tails, which curve like a fern frond, and both have hollow backs. Overall they share intricate detail in representing fantastic felines but little realism or naturalism.

Pages 27-28: They had noted in *Science and Civilisation in China* (Vol. 4, Part 1) in 1971 the parallelism between Aztec teponaztli drums or wooden gongs and the mu yü of Chinese and

Japanese temples. They also looked at panpipe parallels and observed that the richness of ancient Chinese orchestras in percussion instruments (raspers and rattles) recalled Mexico.

Page 29: They support K-048 noting that in the nine lords of the night of Mesoamerica, which were associated with nine layers of the heavens, there is strong resonance with the Chinese conception of nine levels or spheres which occurs in documents of the fourth century B.C. Also, long-handled incensarios of Cholula are extremely reminiscent of those seen on the Thang frescoes at Tunhuang.

Page 30: They also note similarity between divinatory aspects of the Mexican ball-game and the use of a board game by the Chinese in which representations of heavenly bodies were moved to determine the balance of Yin and Yang forces in the universe. Every Sinologist visiting Mexico is amazed that the Aztecs had the idea that there is a rabbit in the moon since this notion is so characteristically Chinese [also Indian, see J-008]. The Mexican rabbit was associated with the gods of pulque and of drug plants, as also with sex, procreation, and licentiousness. In the Chinese idea of the palace of the Lady of the Moon, the rabbit perpetually pounded the drugs of the elixir of immortality.

Pages 31-32: Some ideas associated with alchemy (amulets painted red with cinnabar and use of metallic mercury in tombs) appear in Mesoamerica, although no general wish for "material prolongevity" or immortality, one of the key motivations for Old World alchemy, was apparently present.

Page 40: The balanced shoulder-pole or coolie-yoke, obviously related to the principle of the equal-armed balance and the steelyard, is characteristic of East Asia and appears in Mesoamerica and South America.

Page 41: The cult "bird-chariot," long reported from China and the Western Bronze Age, cannot dogmatically be said not to have been invented twice. Twenty or more Mesoamerican representations show a central column with a non-continuous driving belt twined round it, recalling the churning of the sea of milk in Indian and Khmer [as well as European] lore and art.

Page 45: The suspension bridge is Andean [Mayan] and west Chinese also but was not used in Western Europe until the 18th century.

Page 46: Among hydraulic features, the earth-fill inside the stone revetments of the early Tehuacan Valley dam was separated into compartments internally by dry-wall structures, resembling shear-walls in Chinese arch bridges. Qanats are Chinese as well as Middle Eastern (and American).

Pages 48-49: The essential features of sailing rafts of Asia and South America are so close that "we would not hesitate to say that we believe the American sailing-rafts to be the direct descendants of the Southeast Asian types through an influence mediated by actual trans-Pacific voyages over many centuries, voluntary or involuntary."

Page 50: The Jomon-Valdivia ceramic comparisons combine with other data to indicate that "influential voyages of some kind [date from] the beginning of the [third] millennium onwards" via the North Pacific, even though it is possible that the decorative techniques could have been devised independently. They then cite four more complicated vessel forms from Mexico for which Asian resemblances are notable. Meanwhile the cutting of star-shaped lids from calabashes or bottle-gourds they are inclined to believe was invented but once, in Asia on chronological grounds.

Page 52: Bark cloth and paper complexes are old in Asia and the comparison with America is pointed. So too with purple mollusc dye; the number of steps involved in its production and use convince them that this is a collocative complex for which an Old World link seems indubitable. Nahua people folded their codices concertina-style just as the Chinese had done long before.

Page 54: Kava/chicha/ "chewed wine" of Asia—"we doubt whether saccharification by ptyalin is a process . . . invented more than once." And if some urge that pre-mastication of food for infants by mothers is extremely widespread, why should chewing roots or grains to produce psychotropic consequences not be equally so?

Page 56: "The traditional distillation methods of Mexico were East Asian and not Hellenistic," utilizing a convex, cooled still-head into either a central cup (Mongolian type) or a spoon-shaped collector with a side-tube (Chinese type). The Huichol use the Mongolian still, while Tarascans, Zapotecs, and Cora use the Chinese type. The two-bodied vessels, with bifid and trifid tubes, from Colima since the second millennium B.C., could have been used for Mongolian distilling, although there is argument whether any of the ethnographic practices mentioned pre-dated Spanish influence.

Page 57: Use of night soil as fertilizer is not at all characteristic of the western Old World but unites Mexico with China.

Page 58: The American practice of soldering microscopic metal beads onto decorated objects with copper oxide, copper carbonate and organic binder was reminiscent of Etruscan practice. Lost wax. Alloying. Gilding (all the known forms). Surface enrichment. All these were characteristic of the Old World and all are described here.

Page 59: Cites Cyril Stanley Smith (personal communication), eminent historian of metallurgy, that bronze-working could only have been invented once in the world (contra Nordenskiöld) and spread in all directions, although we do not know where that point was. They count metal money as a parallel, based on the use of small copper axe-blades, beginning in the northern Andes.

Page 60: Ethnobotanical evidence for transoceanic voyaging is now restrained as against two decades ago.

Page 62: Regarding cotton, finding of wild tetraploids in Yucatan, Ecuador, and the Galapagos probably means that they existed there before cultivation, so man may have had nothing to do with its reaching the New World and being domesticated there [but contrast S-246].

Page 63: The presence and uses of amaranth grain and greens on both sides of the Pacific leads one to wonder now whether it was native on both, hence independently put to use. [See N-006.]

N-017

AUTHORS: Needham, Joseph, Wang Ling and Lu Gwei-Djen
DATE: 1971
TITLE: Science and Civilisation in China, vol. 4: Physics and Physical Technology, part III: Civil Engineering and Nautics
IMPRINT: Cambridge University Press: Cambridge

Chapter 29 (more than 300 pages) deals with nautics: construction of junks and sampans, history of Chinese ships, etc., including a section on China and pre- Columbian America.

Page 73: Notes the ancient and widespread view that the heavens were round but the earth square. [The Maya view was that the earth was a cube.]

Pages 540ff.: "Palpable similarities between many features of the high Central American civilisations and those of East and South-east Asia." Among them: predominance of horizontal line in architecture, omnipresent sky-dragon motifs, amphisbaenas (reptilians with heads at both ends), split-face designs resembling the thao-thieh, (Aztec) teponaztli drums like Chinese muyü, tripod pottery reminiscent of li forms, terra-cotta figures and groups, and paintings, so similar to those of Chhu and Han. Also dresses made of feathers, double permutation system of calendars, ideographic script, symbolic correlations (color, animals, compass-points, etc.), and cosmological legend.

They also mention games (patolli), divination (including scapulimancy), computing devices, art forms, etc. The jade complex, including red ochre rubbed on. All combine "to give an overwhelming impression of cultural influences exerted upon the Amerindian cultures by those of Asia."

"A mountain of evidence is accumulating that between the 7th century [B.C.] and the 16th [century A.D.], i.e., throughout the pre-Columbian ages, occasional visits of Asian people to the Americas took place, bringing with them a multitude of culture traits, art motifs and material objects (especially plants), as well as ideas and knowledge of different kinds."

Page 544: "When a technique has a long history in one culture prior to its appearance in another, I feel that the onus of proof lies on the adherents of independence."

Other items mentioned: rabbit-in-moon notion, opening and closing of the gap in the rims of sky and earth, twin divinities, knotted cord tabulating, squared spiral motif in art. Also maize and cotton, hookworm infestations, metallurgy (bronze, lost-wax), paper, a Chou "totem pole" evocative of the Northwest Coast, Great Walls, roads, music (notched flute, nailed drums, sonorous stones, pan-pipes), folklore motifs, divinatory games (ball game, "star chess"), agricultural practices (use of night-soil, agricultural terracing), hanging bridge, perhaps dress, armor (slat, rod and plate), etc. Throughout they mention in notes additional treatments of some of these points in earlier volumes of this series.

Pages 548-554: Discussion of materials in Chinese and Japanese literature about exploratory journeys to the east and lands found there. Mention is made of several possibilities, and perhaps many, from Chou through Han.

[See R-151 for an abridged version of this material.]

N-017B

AUTHOR: Neiburger, E. J.
DATE: 1987
TITLE: Did Midwest Pre-Columbian Indians Cast Metal? . . . A New Look
IN: Central States Archaeological Journal 34:60-74

Early archaeologists believed that artifacts from the Old Copper Complex of Minnesota were cast metal; some supposed that this technology originated in Europe. Current thought denies the presence of technology to melt and cast copper in that area and for that time period. Most of the known 20,000+ artifacts appear to be hammered from float copper, yet a new xeroradiographic study of a random sample of Wisconsin artifacts demonstrates the presence of casting characteristics for many specimens. Additional bibliography is given.

N-017C

AUTHOR: Neiburger, E. J.
DATE: 1991
TITLE: Melted Copper from the Archaic Midwest (1000 B.C.)
IN: North American Archaeologist 12:351-360

A large lump of hammered copper from a site in Michigan, here discussed technically, provides firm evidence for casting. It is unlikely that the melting could have occurred without deliberate planning. It is also unlikely that this particular specimen is a fake or product of later manufacture. Lack of other evidence of metallurgy at the site could be due to a pattern known in Old World cultures where special metal manufacturing processes were kept secret thus keeping the supply of a particular product to a minimum. [See also B-101C.]

N-018

AUTHOR: Neill, Wilfred T.
DATE: 1954

TITLE: Coracles or Skin Boats of the Southeastern Indians
IN: Florida Anthropologist 7/4:119-126

The historical literature reveals that the coracle was little-used in the U.S. southeast area. There is some reason to believe it was not aboriginal there at all but a British introduction (that is, of the colonial era).

N-018B

AUTHOR: Neill, Wilfred T.
DATE: 1956
TITLE: Sailing Vessels of the Florida Seminole
IN: Florida Anthropologist 9:76-86

Vague indications of use of sailing vessels off Florida and in Caribbean waters are brought forward. Most of the information is from the historic period. The dugout, coracle or skin boat, catamaran, and raft are also discussed.

N-019

AUTHORS: Nei, Masatoshi, and Arun K. Roychoudhury
DATE: 1982
TITLE: Genetic Relationship and Evolution of Human Races
IN: Evolutionary Biology, vol. 14, edited by Max K. Hecht, Bruce Wallace, and Ghillean T. Prance (Plenum: New York), 1-59

Their primary racial division in the New World is between North and South American Indians, rather than seeing hemispheric unity.

N-019B

AUTHOR: Nelin, Gustavo
DATE: 1990
TITLE: La Saga de Votan [The Saga of Votan]
IMPRINT: Privately published: Cuernavaca, México

The tenth-century Quetzalcoatl figure was a christianized Norseman, one Ari Marson, an exile from Iceland in A.D. 982; Tula=T(h)ule and the Norse called their vessels "flying serpents."

N-020

AUTHOR: Nelson, Fred W., Jr.
DATE: 1970
TITLE: The Colossal Stone Heads of the Southern Gulf-Coast Region of Mexico
IN: Transoceanic Crossings to Ancient America, edited by Ross T. Christensen (Society for Early Historic Archaeology: Provo, Utah), 10-16

Critical historical, archaeological and physical anthropological discussion of the Olmec stone heads as evidence for "Negroid" characteristics and African contacts with Mesoamerica. His conclusion is that the heads are not reliable evidence for that claim.

N-021

AUTHOR: Nelson, Jame Gordon
DATE: 1959
TITLE: The Geography of the Balsa: A Case Study in the Geography of Primitive Watercraft
IMPRINT: Unpublished; Ph.D. dissertation, Johns Hopkins University

Chapters 1 and 2 discuss at lenth the advantages and disadvantages of geographic study of primitive watercraft as a way to learn about early human movements by water and thus the development of culture in various parts of the world. The issues of independent invention and diffusion are discussed usefully in specific relation to watercraft in chapter 1. In chapter 2 the causes and significance of loss and persistence of such craft are treated with valuable cases discussed (watercraft seem to be particularly persistent cultural products). In the rest of the document, one craft, the Peruvian log balsa, is then taken as a test case of the principles laid out.

Actually there are two distinct forms of Peruvian log balsa, the large freighter and the shaped balsa. Parallels to the large freighter occur only in central and southern Asia but these seem distinct (independent) in their development from the Peruvian model. The shaped balsa is distributed in the Mediterranean and Red Seas, Southern Arabia, South India, Ceylon, Melanesia, and Polynesia. Lack of evidence, particularly on chronology, prevents a definite decision about origin, but he feels this type of raft to be a diffused concept (reasons given). The original invention was perhaps in India; at least it was not in Southeast Asia as has often been speculated. The study all but eliminates any possibility that the balsa could have reached the Americas via the Bering Strait route.

Pages 80-83: Various drift voyages are reprised from the literature (particularly Best [1954]).

While the literature on this topic has expanded greatly since this dissertation was completed in 1959, it remains a major source which deserves careful mining in any attempt to synthesize the history of the balsa.

N-022

AUTHOR: Nelson, Jame Gordon
DATE: 1961
TITLE: The Geography of the Balsa
IN: American Neptune 21:157-195

Supposes an Old World origin for rafts, including those of South America, which, like those of Asia, exhibit tapered form and odd-log construction, on sailing and nonsailing rafts alike.

N-023

AUTHOR: Nelson, Jame Gordon
DATE: 1962
TITLE: Drift Voyages between Asia and the Americas
IN: Canadian Geographer 6:54-59

He considers whether Brooks' sample of Japanese drifts in the nineteenth century might have been affected by the government policy of isolation (he would expect an unusual number of escapes as a result) but concludes there is no basis for such a supposition. There could have been drifts for centuries or even a millennium. He does not assume that those aboard would be slain. Historical cases of the greeting of European explorers indicate that treatment was varied. Some drifters might have formed isolated settlements, other have been absorbed. Hence drifts might explain certain parallels (mentioned).

N-024

AUTHOR: Nelson, James Gordon
DATE: 1963
TITLE: Drift Voyages in the Pacific
IN: American Neptune 23:113-130

See N-023.

N-024B

AUTHOR: Nelson, James Gordon
DATE: 1972
TITLE: Review of *Man across the Sea*
IN: Association of American Geographers, Annals 62/3:706-708

Two aspects of the papers in the volume are of particular interest to him: evidences for transpacific voyages and contacts, and processes involved in any consequent culture change. His treatment of selected papers in the volume follows a format of on-the-one-hand-but-then-on-the-other. "I am one of those who believe that the evidence for early voyaging and for cultural and biological resemblances indicates that some contact and diffusion of ideas took place between the Old and the New Worlds in pre-Columbian times." In regard to the problem of process, he cites two distinct cases of shipwrecks—an English physician in Fiji and Portuguese in east Africa—in both of which survivors had little effect but rather were themselves heavily indigenized.

N-025

AUTHOR: Nelson, N. C.
DATE: 1918
TITLE: Review of *Primitive Man,* by G. Elliot Smith
IN: American Anthropologist 20:437-446

Negative about the book's methodology and substance, in a gentlemanly way. Regarding possible communication from southwestern Asia to Middle America and Peru, the land route is so long that Smith would have to consider "direct oversea communication," "and [while] it is a very enticing hypothesis," it can safely be eliminated on present evidence. Nelson is prepared to explain widely separated cultural similarities more or less evenly between psychic unity and diffusion.

N-028B

AUTHOR: Ness, Donald
DATE: 1970
TITLE: The Hawley Stone: Newest Discovery of a Possibly Pre-Columbian Inscription
IN: NEARA [New England Antiquities Research Association] Journal 5:88

A large photograph and a small explanation: an inscribed stone was found last year in a stream bed in northeast Pennsylvania. The deeply inscribed characters faintly resemble runes. They do not seem to relate to any known script.

N-029

AUTHOR: Nettl, Bruno
DATE: 1953
TITLE: American Indian Music North of Mexico: Its Styles and Areas
IMPRINT: Unpublished; Ph.D. dissertation, Indiana University [University Microfiloms International Order No. 0005873. This 239-page dissertation was published in 51 pages in *Journal of American Folklore Memoirs* 45 (1954)]

He compares all North American areas with Asiatic and European areas. Primary musical influence on North America was from the northern part of Asia and from Middle America.

N-030

AUTHOR: Nettl, Bruno
DATE: 1958
TITLE: Transposition as a Composition Technique in Folk and Primitive Music
IN: Ethnomusicology 2:56-65

He postulates a broad belt of "transposing cultures" which use transposition as a composition technique. This belt stretches from Western Europe across north Asia into North America. "It is possible that transposition as a specific technique originated at one point, perhaps in Central Asia, and became diffused in all directions." Yet the notion of transposition is so simple and so widely encountered that multiple origin "also seems likely."

N-031

AUTHOR: Nettl, Bruno
DATE: 1964
TITLE: Theory and Method in Ethnomusicology
IMPRINT: Free Press of Glencoe: New York

Page 253: In a 1956 work he attempted to divide the world into three large ethnomusicological areas on racial grounds. The Americas and the Far East made up one area for him, "although it is evident that the cultural influences of Asia on America may be responsible for the similarities between Far Eastern and American Indian music, rather than any biologically inherited style preference."

N-031B

AUTHOR: Netto, Ladislau

DATE: 1885

TITLE: Lettre à Monsieur Renan à propos de l'inscription Phénicienne apocryphe soumise en 1872 à l'Institut historique, géographique et ethnographique du Brésil [Letter to Monsieur Renan Concerning the Apocryphal Phoenician Inscription Sent in 1872 to the Institut Historique, Géographique et Ethnographique of Brazil]

IMPRINT: Lombaerta: Rio de Janeiro

The Parahaiba inscription discussed by the primary source on the affair.

N-032

AUTHOR: Neudorfer, Giovanna

DATE: 1979

TITLE: Vermont's Stone Chambers: Their Myths and Their History

IN: Vermont History 47:79-147

Detailed refutation of the claims by Barry Fell and associates of the presence in New England of remains of pre-Columbian European visitors. [Appreciatively reviewed by John R. Cole, *Archaeoastronomy* 4/4 (1981): 46-47.]

N-033

AUTHOR: Neudorfer, Giovanna

DATE: 1980

TITLE: Vermont's Stone Chambers: An Inquiry into Their Past

IMPRINT: Vermont Historical Society: Montpelier

There is no reliable evidence that these structures were pre-Columbian although so claimed by Fell and others.

N-034

AUTHOR: Neugebauer, Otto

DATE: 1951

TITLE: The Exact Sciences in Antiquity

IMPRINT: Ejnar Munksgaard: Copenhagen [Reprinted Princeton University Press: Princeton, 1952]

Pages 18, 140-146: Place value notation was the most striking feature of the Babylonian system and all later Old World expressions of it came from Babylonia. The zero concept was in Babylonia possibly as early as 700 B.C., quite probably by 500 B.C.

N-034B

AUTHOR: Neumann, Georg K.

DATE: 1940

TITLE: Evidence for the Antiquity of Scalping from Central Illinois

IN: American Antiquity 5:287-289

[Scalping has Old World parallels, hence its chronology could relate to a diffusionist claim.]

N-034C

AUTHOR: Neumann, Georg K.

DATE: 1952

TITLE: Archaeology and Race in the American Indians

IN: Archaeology and Eastern United States, edited by James B. Griffin (University of Chicago Press: Chicago), 13-34

On the basis of metric and morphological data he constructs eight physical types in North America, four of them in the east. [Impinges on the question of the uniformity or heterogeneity of "the American Indian."]

N-035

AUTHOR: Neumann, Karl Friedrich

DATE: 1841

TITLE: Ost-Asien und West-Amerika nach chinesischen Quellen aus dem fünften, sechsten und siebienten Jahrhunderte
[East Asia and Western America According to Chinese Sources of the Fifth, Sixth, and Seventh Centuries]
IN: Zeitschrift für allgemeine Erdkunde 16:305-330 (Berlin)
[Reprinted 1850, "California and Mexico in the Fifth Century, from Chinese Sources," *The Knickerbocker* 36:301-320. Translated in Leland (1875), pages 1-46; and in Vining (1885), pages 78-103

Gives a translation of one of the Chinese documents reporting Fu-sang, noting that the Chinese character "ma," meaning horse, could mean other animals, and its use in the Fu-sang account could refer to an American animal, not a literal horse.

N-038

AUTHOR: Nevermann, Hans
DATE: 1938
TITLE: Die indo-ozeanische Weberei
[Indo-Oceanic Weaving]
IN: Mitteilungen 30 (Museum für Völkerkunde: Hamburg)

Pages 325-339: On distributional data, he argues that phenomena associated with weaving arrived in America from the Old World in two currents, one across the Atlantic and later across the Pacific from Southeast Asia. In addition to mechanical aspects of the comparison, he notes the relationship between sexuality and weaving as shown in myths and related deity attributes.

N-040

AUTHOR: Nevermann, Hans
DATE: 1965
TITLE: Die polynesische Hochkultur
[Polynesian Civilization]
IN: Saeculum Weltgeschichte, edited by Herbert Franke, et al., Band 1: Ursprung und Frühkulturen, Primäre Zentren der Hochkultur, Weltgeschichtliche Berührungszonen (Herder, Freiburg), 355-378

A capable resume of Polynesian culture and history including significant discussion of voyaging capabilities.

Pages 377-378: Cultural contacts between Polynesia and America. [See also K-053.]

N-041

AUTHOR: Newell, W. W.
DATE: 1900
TITLE: The Bear in Hellenic Astral Mythology
IN: Journal of American Folk-Lore 13:147-149

He happily follows H-018 in suggesting that American Indian and Greek parallels in relation to the Bear constellation can be handled without resorting to diffusion. [Compare G-084.]

N-042

AUTHOR: Newman, John B.
DATE: 1952
TITLE: Origin of the Red Man
IMPRINT: John C. Wells: New York

From the Phoenicians.

N-043

AUTHOR: Newman, Marshall T.
DATE: 1935
TITLE: The Sequence of Indian Physical Types in South America
IN: Smithsonian Institution Miscellaneous Collections 94/11:69-97

Since Imbelloni's racial classification for South America built upon the most important previous work and is the most recent, it is the focus of

Newman's discussion. He finds that "the impressionistic ultra-migrationist approach of Imbelloni as well as the more empirical method of this (Newman's) paper have failed to delineate demonstrable sequences of racial types in South America" due to totally inadequate data, including limited archaeology. Imbelloni may be on weak ground calling upon an Old World schema to explain New World events.

N-044

AUTHOR: Newman, Marshall T.
DATE: 1950
TITLE: The Blond Mandan: A Critical Review of an Old Problem
IN: Southwestern Journal of Anthropology 6:255-272

Reprises sources and popular views from 1720 on of the Mandans as unusually white-skinned, light-haired, and bearded. Early white admixture in the gene pool and lack of candid studies of the unmixed population make study of the question difficult today. Catlin at first held the view of Welsh (Madoc) admixture, but later backed off somewhat. Maximilian in 1832 saw the Mandan as largely like other Indians, despite a minority with odd hair. Other western Indians showed similarly lightish skins, lighter than some Spaniards or Frenchmen.

After discussing the considerable variability in hair, skin color, and other features among American Indians, the author doubts that a small party of Scandinavians or Welsh, centuries earlier, could have had significant genetic effect on the Mandans or others. The supposedly atypical characteristics of the Mandans are more plausibly explained by variability, augmented by 18th and 19th century white admixture, than by problematic pre-Columbian European mixing.

N-045

AUTHOR: Newman, Marshall T,
DATE: 1951
TITLE: The Sequence of Indian Physical Types in South America
IN: Papers on the Physical Anthropology of the American Indian, edited by William S. Laughlin (Viking Fund: New York), 69-94

Critically reviews the classifications of von Eickstedt and Imbelloni. Shows that these schemes fail to take into account culture areas and horizons. Moreover, the available data they utilized are wholly inadequate for their purpose.

N-047

AUTHOR: Newman, Marshall T.
DATE: 1976
TITLE: Aboriginal New World Epidemiology and Medical Care, and the Impact of Old World Disease Imports
IN: American Journal of Physical Anthropology 45:667-672

A sketchy epidemiological profile of the "precontact" New World population and effects of diseases considered to have been introduced during European conquest—smallpox, yellow fever, malaria, etc. Cites T. D. Stewart that aboriginal Americans were relatively disease-free because of the Bering Strait cold-screen that eliminated many pathogens, and due to paucity of domestic animals. Evidence indicates that pre-contact Americans had their own strains of treponemic and many other diseases. He considers the presence of tuberculosis and typhus questionable (although the Aztecs had a name for the latter). Virtually all crowd-type disease, such as smallpox, measles, and malaria, appear absent from the New World. New diseases may not have depleted the population as much as is commonly believed. [Weak on coverage of the literature.]

N-049

AUTHOR: Neyret, Jean Marie
DATE: 1976
TITLE: Pirogues océaniennes, 2nd edition [Oceanian Canoes]

IMPRINT: Association des amis des musées de la marine: Paris
[Originally a lengthy series of articles in *Triton,* a "journal" within the journal *Neptunia*, during the 1960s]

An unparalleled atlas and gallery of detailed drawings of canoes and rafts and their appurtenances throughout Australia, New Guinea, and Melanesia (vol. 1) and Polynesia, Micronesia, Indonesia, the Indian Ocean and its periphery, early Europe, and the Americas (vol. 2) resulting from 45 years of research and residence in Oceania. Not seriously historical nor analytical in this treatment. He is comfortable with Heyerdahl's voyage and ideas and hints acceptance of the possibilities of transpacific crossings.

N-050

AUTHOR: Niblack, Albert P.
DATE: 1890
TITLE: The Coast Indians of Southern Alaska and Northern British Columbia
IN: Report of the United States National Museum for the Year Ending June 30, 1888, Part 3, Number 1, pages 225-386

Includes a list and discussion of similarities between Haida and Maori, including jasper adzes, skull boxes, and the protruding tongue motif on ancestor funeral posts. "The cloaks of shredded inner bark in the National Museum from New Zealand and the Queen Charlotte Islands are so much alike, that it takes a close inspection to distinguish them."

N-051

AUTHOR: Nibley, Hugh
DATE: 1951
TITLE: The Hierocentric State
IN: Western Political Quarterly 4:226-253

Features of the Eurasian "hierocentric state" complex based on ancient history [most of which are found in the New World as well]: New Year assembly and renewal dramatization, emphasis on the four quarters of the world including censing to those four quarters, concept of omphalus or navel of the world (especially a pyramid, ziggurat, or mountain as marker of such a spot), new fire ceremony, dragon as protector of water sources, color-direction symbolism, and games and competitions at the New Year assembly.

Page 235: At the Mesopotamian hieratic center, four streams were considered to flow out to water the four regions of the earth. [Compare V-011.]

N-052

AUTHOR: Nichols, Dale
DATE: 1969
TITLE: The Pyramid Text of the Ancient Maya
IMPRINT: Mazdan Press [i.e., privately printed]: Antigua, Guatemala

A brochure. A numerological and mystical treatment of dimensions of Mayan buildings, Pythagorean notions, the Pentagram, and the Golden Rectangle. The Popol Vuh parallels the Egyptian Book of the Dead. Central America was the last stand and refuge of the Phoenicians after the Punic Wars.

N-053

AUTHOR: Nichols, Dale
DATE: [c. 1971]
TITLE: Magnificent Mystery, Tikal
IMPRINT: Mazdan Press [i.e., privately printed]: Antigua, Guatemala

Another brochure. American Indians came some 20,000 years ago via Bering Strait and did little until bearded white men came from the East—Asia Minor and the Mediterranean—in the 6th century B.C. Phoenician ships brought them (human sacrifice is Phoenician) and Pythagorean "mathemagics" was used to try to convert the native hunters to numerology, i.e., to civilization.

Mediterranean type faces were suddenly replaced at A.D. 200 by Indian faces. They erected (phallic) temples which followed geometrical forms.

N-054

AUTHOR: Nichols, Dale
DATE: 1973
TITLE: The Mayan Mystery
IMPRINT: Mazdan Press [i.e., privately printed]: Antigua, Guatemala

Who were the bearded white men referred to in the books of the Maya? The sources say that they came from the east, were warriors, were interested in precious goods, and were connected with cocoa. "East is Africa. The third largest producer of cocoa in our times is Ghana. Did seafaring 'warriors' bring potted cocoa plants from this African area?"

A first Kukulcan, who may have been Pythagoras himself, was among the earliest immigrants (by sea), c. 500 B.C. (South America was first discovered—thus Parahyba—in 531 B.C.) A second Kukulcan arrived later who understood (cabbalistic) Hebrew and Pythagorean ("cult of Venus") numerology and took advantage of Postclassic political and cultural confusion to teach his system. A numerological scheme is illustrated in dimensions on his profile drawings of Mesoamerican temples.

N-056B

AUTHOR: Nicklin, Keith
DATE: 1971
TITLE: Stability and Innovation in Pottery Manufacture
IN: World Archaeology 3/1:13-48

Extensive discussion on the acceptance, loss (cases given), and value of the potter's wheel versus hand methods. It is unclear that the wheel is superior to direct hand manufacture, so one need not be surprised at its absence in a particular area.

N-057

AUTHOR: Nicolaison, W. F. H.
DATE: 1979
TITLE: Celtic Place Names in America B.C.
IN: Vermont History 47:148-160

A substantial linguistic attack on the accuracy of Fell's suppositions about the presence of Celtic language in North America.

N-058

AUTHOR: Nicolle, Charles
DATE: 1932
TITLE: Un argument médical en faveur de l'opinion de Paul Rivet sur l'origine océanienne de certaines tribus indiennes du Nouveau Monde [A Medical Argument in Favor of the Opinion of Paul Rivet on the Oceanic Origin of Certain Indian Tribes of the New World]
IN: Journal de la société des américanistes de Paris 24:225-229

The typhus of Mexico and Guatemala differed from Eurasian typhus but was the same as that of Oceania, Australia, and east and north Asia.

N-060

AUTHOR: Nielsen, Richard
DATE: 1986a
TITLE: The Arabic Numbering System on the Kensington Rune Stone
IN: Epigraphic Society Occasional Publications 15:47-61

[Part 1?] The inscription contains unusual forms for numbers and dates on the stone which, nevertheless, had considerable precedent in the runic record. One number is an Arabic 10.

N-060B

AUTHOR: Nielsen, Richard
DATE: 1986b

TITLE: An Old Norse Translation of the Heavener Runes
IN: Epigraphic Society Occasional Publications 15:133-141

Reports an extensive literature on the Heavener, Oklahoma, Runestone, the substance of which is such that no translation has been possible. When certain variations in "the common Old Germanic runes called the FUTHARK alphabet" are noted, a transliteration is easy. Explains errors in previous transliterations. He gives the reading, "Glom's Valley" and suggests this may have been a boundary marker. The date is more or less A.D. 800 based on letter forms. Certain features in rune history which he notes leads him to support Gordon's handling of the Spirit Pond Runestones as probably correct.

N-061

AUTHOR: Nielsen, Richard
DATE: 1987a
TITLE: The Kensington Runestone, Part 2: Aberrant Letters. New Evidence from Greenland, Iceland and Scandinavia
IN: Epigraphic Society Occasional Publications 16:51-83
[In N-062 the author refers to "The Aberrant Letters on the Kensington Runestone," *ESOP* 16, 1987, but apparently he is referring to this item, title for which is taken from the publication itself]

In this and N-060, the author brings forward extensive evidence that what critics have called "aberrant" features in this text are not so. They were in fact found in the old south Norwegian province and dialect of Bohuslän at least by A.D. 1200. The scholarship exhibited by previous investigators, who seem to have been unaware of important aspects of the language history of Scandinavia, was faulty, he asserts.

N-062

AUTHOR: Nielsen, Richard
DATE: 1987b
TITLE: New Linguistic and Runic Evidence Which Supports Hall's Thesis That the Kensington Runestone Is Genuine
IN: 14th LACUS Forum (Toronto, 4-8 August 1987) (Linguistic Association of Canada and the United States: Lake Bluff, Illinois), 378-395

Surveys the literature, pro and con, on the question of the fit of the Kensington Stone's language to medieval vs. modern Norwegian. He demonstrates that the claimed modern anomalies are actually representative of the Bohuslän dialect [see N-061]. The result of his work, he says, is that "all arguments raised by other linguistic and runic investigators . . . which have been used to dispute the authenticity of the stone have been removed, and shown to be without foundation."

N-062B

AUTHOR: Nielsen, Richard
DATE: 1988
TITLE: The Kensington Runestone: Linguistic Evidence for Its Authenticity
IN: Epigraphic Society Occasional Publications 17:124-178

See N-061. Apparently "Part 2."

N-062C

AUTHOR: Nielsen, Richard
DATE: 1989
TITLE: The Kensington Runestone. Part 3: Linguistic Evidence for Its Authenticity
IN: Epigraphic Society Occasional Publications 18:110-132

See N-061.

N-063

AUTHOR: Nielsen, Yngvar
DATE: 1905
TITLE: Nordmaend og Skraelinger i Vinland [Norsemen and Skraelings in Vinland]
IN: Historisk Tidsskrift 3/4:248-293

Compares lacrosse and the Norse game of knattleikr. [See H-250 and N-007.]

N-065

AUTHOR: Niemeyer F., Hans
DATE: 1965-1966
TITLE: Una balsa de cueros de lobo de la valeta de Chañaral de Aceitunas, Provincia de Atacama, Chile [A Raft of Sea Lion Skins from Chañaral de Aceitunas, Atacama Province, Chile]
IN: Revista universitaría 50-51/2:257-269 (Universidad Católica de Chile)

Describes a float or "raft" made of inflated sea lion skins which was still in use in 1965. Discusses the origin of the device and its archaeological manifestations.

N-066

AUTHOR: Nies, James B.
DATE: 1914
TITLE: The Boomerang in Ancient Babylonia
IN: American Anthropologist 16:26-32

At least three objects seem to require a common source; the argument from psychic unity is not applicable. One is the cosmic step-pyramid of Egypt, Asia, and America, the same in appearance and purpose. Another is the swastika or sun symbol, in Europe, Asia, and America. And the third is the boomerang of ancient Egypt and modern Australia.

N-066B

AUTHOR: Nilsestuen, Rolf M.
DATE: 1994
TITLE: The Kensington Runestone Vindicated
IN: University Press of America: Lanham, Maryland, and London

Linguist Robert A. Hall, Jr., writes in the foreword: "Nilsestuen summarizes the evidence covering the period from 1898 until the present, thus sparing interested persons the time and trouble of assembling references from distant libraries. He defends the authenticity of the Runestone, and the integrity of Hjalmar Holand and Olof Ohman, with an impassioned but well-reasoned analysis of the information now available." "All objections to the language and symbols have been proven invalid, as have Wahlgren's irresponsible charges against the evidence regarding the discovery."

The author notes that Hall has in preparation a volume entitled *The Kensington Runestone, Critical Edition.*

Gives a highly detailed, devastating critique of all specifics in Wahlgren's Smithsonian and its people in putting down the stone, putting them in a very dark light. Includes information on halberds and other "Norse artifacts," mooring holes, the Mandans and other categories of "evidence."

This is an essential book on the subject by a careful scientist which is soundly argued and highly documented, although indeed "impassioned" in its denunciation of "scientific arrogance."

N-067

AUTHOR: Nilsson, M. P.
DATE: 1920
TITLE: Primitive Time Reckoning
IN: Acta Societatis Humanorum et Litterarum Lundensis (Lund, Sweden)

Page 274ff.: Pleiades-based calendrics in both Old and New Worlds.

N-069

AUTHOR: Nimtz, Michael John
DATE: 1968
TITLE: Problems of Trans-Pacific Contact with Regard to Central and South America
IMPRINT: Unpublished; M.S. thesis, University of Wisconsin

Beginning, with but slight acquaintance with the material but with the feeling that it was both possible and probable that transpacific contacts had occurred, the author ends up concluding the reverse. Chapters are on botanical, cultural and navigational evidence. [The sources used are entirely conventional.]

N-070

AUTHOR: Nishimura, Shinji
DATE: 1925
TITLE: Ancient Rafts of Japan
IMPRINT: Waseda University Press: Waseda

Rafts, not boats, were in use from early in Japanese prehistory, and American rafts are derivative from Asiatic sailing rafts via the islands of the mid-Pacific.

N-070B

AUTHOR: Nishimura, Shinji
DATE: 1934
TITLE: The Hisago-Buné or Calabash Boat
IMPRINT: The Society of Naval Architects [Waseda University]: Tokyo

Sixteen years ago he published *The Hisago-Buné or Gourd-Ship* as volume 2 of his serial publication, *A Study of Ancient Ships of Japan*. This is a second edition, much expanded, forming still (but now revised) Section I, Part I of the series. After summarizing Japanese and Korean myths or legends about calabashes and botanical and linguistic studies on the same, he documents their use anciently to support sailing vessels. Survivals of the ancient culture exist in the South Sea islands and in America where much pottery is in the form of calabashes. "It is undeniable that in the forgotten remote antiquity the utilization of calabashes and the art of making vessels into calabash[-supported]-form were introduced from the Old World to the two American Continents where they still survive" (page 66). There are many evidences of links between Japan and the South Sea region anciently (gourd names are given that seem to show such). Not wooden rafts but calabash-supported rafts he considers the oldest in the Japanese nautical tradition. It was a product brought from South China by the Wai people of Indo-Chinese stock in the pre-historic period. The ancient Japanese appear to have made rather daring voyages very frequently to and from South China or Korea on (these) frail craft (page 70).

[Reviewed 1935 in *American Anthropologist* 37:352, as "a mixture of the most rigorous historical research and of pan-diffusionistic conclusions" reminiscent of Elliot Smith, whom Nishimura indeed acknowledges.]

N-071

AUTHOR: Nishimura, Shinji
DATE: 1936
TITLE: A Study of Ancient Ships of Japan, vol. 2, part 1: Floats
IMPRINT: Society of Naval Architects, Waseda University: Tokyo

He discusses calabash, deerskin, and clay floats in early Japan. The material on calabash boats had been published separately [reviewed in *American Anthropologist* (1935) 37:352].

N-072

AUTHOR: Nishiyama, Ichizo
DATE: 1963
TITLE: The Origin of the Sweet Potato Plant
IN: Plants and the Migrations of Pacific Peoples, A Symposium Held at the

Tenth Pacific Sciences Congress (Honolulu, 1961), edited by Jacques Barrau (Bernice P. Bishop Museum Press: Honolulu), 119-128

Three homes have been proposed for the sweet potato: America, Asia, and Africa. This cytological study finds it probable that the place of origin was tropical America.

N-073

AUTHOR: Nitkin, Nathaniel
DATE: 1976
TITLE: Viking New England
IN: New England Galaxy 17/4:40-45

Recounts Viking settlement in Newfoundland around A.D. 1000 and Viking explorations in Maine and Massachusetts, judging by runestones in those areas as well as Indian use of Icelandic numerals and of sails similar to those of the Vikings.

N-074

AUTHOR: Nitsche, Roland
DATE: 1953
TITLE: Uralte Wege, ewige Fahrt: Handel entdeckt die Welt
[Ancient Paths, Eternal Travels: Trade Discovers the World]
IMPRINT: Alexander Duncker: München

Recounts some drift voyages in various parts of the Pacific. These seem not random but related to winds and currents, hence quasi-predictable. Generally they proceed from east to west, but periods of westerlies contrary to the trade winds are known which last for weeks and could have provided means for eastward sailing.

N-076

AUTHOR: Nocentini, L.
DATE: 1894
TITLE: La scoperta dell'America attribuita ai Cinesi
[The Discovery of America Attributed to the Chinese]
IN: Primo Congresso Geografico Italiano (Genova, 1892), 2:312-323

Identifies Japan, not America, as Fu-sang.

N-079

AUTHOR: Noguera, Eduardo
DATE: 1976
TITLE: El asiento en el Mundo Antiguo y en el época prehispánica
[The Seat in the Old World and in the Prehispanic Epoch]
IN: Anales de antropología 13:77-86 (México)

On the use of seats as symbols of authority in Old and New World cultures.

N-080

AUTHOR: Noice, H. H.
DATE: 1922
TITLE: Further Discussion of the "Blond" Eskimo
IN: American Anthropologist 24:228-232

An old Arctic hand maintains that Jenness glossed over real European-like biological characteristics which were to be seen among the Copper Eskimo, implying a Norse source.

N-082

AUTHOR: Nooteboom, C.
DATE: 1952
TITLE: Trois problèmes d'éthnologie maritime
[Three Problems of Maritime Ethnology]
IMPRINT: Museum voor Landen Volkenkunde en Maritiem Museum "Prinz Hendrick": Rotterdam

He includes discussion of the origins and diffusion of sail types in east Asia. The views of some American and European diffusionists are briefly restated. The conclusion drawn is that water-borne diffusion is not likely to result in a concentric pattern on the map but a linear one.

N-083

AUTHOR: Norbeck, Edward
DATE: 1952
TITLE: Review of *American Indians in the Pacific,* by Thor Heyerdahl
IN: American Antiquity 19:92-94

Strongly critical though not particularly well informed.

N-084

AUTHOR: Norbeck, Edward
DATE: 1955
TITLE: Trans-Pacific Similarities in Folklore: A Research Lead
IN: Papers of the Kroeber Anthropological Society 12:62-69

His own field work in tandem with personal communications from G. Reichel-Dolmatoff and Sol Tax draws attention to "trans-Pacific similarities or coincidences in folklore motifs which seem to suggest an interpretation other than independent development" in mountain Luzon and inner Formosa and in Colombia and Guatemala. Notable is a tale in which a man visits then escapes from a strange land/underworld where the inhabitants eat only the vapor of food and lacked anuses. He speculates that American Indians who might have been carried to the Philippines by the Spaniards [no evidence for such an event is mentioned] could have carried this tale but admits that it is hard to see how it would then occur among the mountain tribes, far from the Spanish plantations. For the Formosa tale he has no explanation at all. [He does not so much as hint that pre-Spanish contact might be involved. Compare S-453.]

N-090

AUTHOR: Nordenskiöld, Erland
DATE: 1912
TITLE: Une contribution à la connaissance de l'Anthropogéographie de l'Amérique
[Contribution to the Knowledge of Anthropogeography of America]
IN: Journal de la société des americanistes de Paris 9:19-26

He agrees with Graebner in seeing a single kulturkreis circle encompassing Oceania and South America.

N-090B

AUTHOR: Nordenskiöld, Erland
DATE: 1919
TITLE: An Ethno-geographical Analysis of the Material Culture of Two Indian Tribes in the Gran Chaco, vol. 1 of Comparative Ethnographical Studies
IMPRINT: Pehrssons: Göteborg

Distribution of various features known from Oceania: the pellet bow, cylindrical drum with skin membrane, musical bow, etc.

N-090C

AUTHOR: Nordenskiöld, Erland
DATE: 1920
TITLE: The Changes in the Material Culture of Two Indian Tribes under the Influence of New Surroundings, vol. 2 of Comparative Ethnographical Studies
IMPRINT: Pehrssons: Göteborg

Map 3 shows the distribution of the hammock in South America, which compares with Melanesian use, as well as the pellet bow, pan pipes and other features found in Oceania.

N-092

AUTHOR: Nordenskiöld, Erland
DATE: 1921a

TITLE: The Copper and Bronze Ages in South America, vol. 4 of Comparative Ethnographical Studies
IMPRINT: Pehrssons: Göteborg [Reprinted AMS: New York, 1979]

Assumes independent New World development of metallurgy.

N-093
AUTHOR: Nordenskiöld, Erland
DATE: 1921b
TITLE: Emploi de la balance romaine en Amérique du Sud avant la conquête [Usage of the Roman Balance Scale in South America before the Conquest]
IN: Journal de la société des américanistes de Paris 13:169-171

Describes balance scales apparently used at the time of the conquest in Venezuela, Ecuador, and Peru (and probably Colombia) according to early historical reports. The closest he comes to acknowledging the possibility of a diffusionary explanation is his statement that it is "remarkable" that the device was known in the New as well as in the Old World.

N-094
AUTHOR: Nordenskiöld, Erland
DATE: 1922a
TITLE: Deductions Suggested by the Geographical Distribution of Some Post-Columbian Words Used by Indians of South America, vol. 5 of Comparative Ethnographical Studies
IMPRINT: Pehrssons: Göteborg [Reprinted AMS: New York, 1979]

Some consideration of the issue of transpacific influences, which he doubts.

N-095
AUTHOR: Nordenskiöld, Erland
DATE: 1922b
TITLE: La moustiquaire est-elle indigène en Amérique du Sud? [Mosquito Netting, Is It Indigenous to South America?]
IN: Journal de la société des américanistes de Paris 14:119-126

Mosquito netting was a post-Columbian feature brought by Europeans. Also mentions other things for which he finds some authority or other to support the idea that Europeans brought them (including the gourd, Lagenaria).

N-096
AUTHOR: Nordenskiöld, Erland
DATE: 1924
TITLE: The Ethnography of South-America Seen from Mojos in Bolivia, vol. 3 of Comparative Ethnographical Studies
IMPRINT: Pehrssons: Göteborg [Reprinted AMS: New York, 1979]

Includes discussion on and distribution in tropical America of the Asiatic style coolie yoke, the pellet bow, cylindrical drums with skin membrane, the musical bow, bark cloth and stone beaters, the penis sheath, poison blow guns, and other Oceanic features.

N-098
AUTHOR: Nordenskiöld, Erland
DATE: 1926
TITLE: Miroirs convexes et concaves en Amérique [Convex and Concave Mirrors in America]
IN: Journal de la société des americanistes de Paris 18:103-110

American polished stone mirrors [which also occur in eastern Polynesia and China].

N-099
AUTHOR: Nordenskiöld, Erland, editor
DATE: 1928-1930

TITLE: Picture-Writings and Other Documents, by Néle, Paramount Chief of the Cuna Indians, and Ruben Pérez Kantule, his Secretary, vol. 7 of Comparative Ethnographical Studies
IMPRINT: Pehrssons: Göteborg [Reprinted AMS: New York, 1979]

See his introduction, pages 13-22. He believes that apparent similarities between signs used on Easter Island and among the Cuna of Panama are due to the fact that both represent posture-language rather than being arbitrary signs. Reports finding hieroglyphics drawn in red paint in a tomb in Peru.

N-100

AUTHOR: Nordenskiöld, Erland
DATE: 1929
TITLE: The American Indian as an Inventor
IN: Journal of the Royal Anthropological Institute of Great Britain and Ireland 59:273-309

A large number of technological features are discussed. Largely on distributional grounds the author considers these to be local inventions even when he points out Old World parallels. He warns that the subject is complicated but seems to mean this as a warning only to diffusionists.

N-101

AUTHOR: Nordenskiöld, Erland
DATE: 1930
TITLE: Modifications in Indian Culture through Inventions and Loans, vol. 8 of Comparative Ethnographical Studies
IMPRINT: Pehrssons: Göteborg [Reprinted AMS: New York, 1989]

His argument, as in others of his publications, is that parallels with the Old World are evidence of the inventive capacity of American Indians. Among many other discussions of features known in both hemispheres, in appendices he treats bee-keeping, quipus, bridges, gongs, carrying pole, pincers (tweezers), sugar- mill, pump-drill, and whistling arrows and darts.

Page 14: The Indians manufacture bark cloth, but since a similar process is known in Oceania, "it cannot definitely be asserted that in this case the Indians have made an entirely independent discovery. Similarity between the implements used within and outside America in the preparation of bark cloth even speaks against such a supposition."

N-103

AUTHOR: Nordenskiöld, Erland
DATE: 1933
TITLE: The Origin of the Indian Civilization in South America
IN: Comparative Ethnographical Studies, vol. 9, edited by Erland Nordenskiöld (Pehrssons: Göteborg), 1-75 (plus appendices) [Reprinted in *The American Aborigines: Their Origin and Antiquity. A Collection of Papers by Ten Authors, Assembled and Edited by Diamond Jenness. Published for Presentation at the Fifth Pacific Science Congress* (Canada, 1933) (University of Toronto Press: Toronto), 249-311. On page 249 an editorial note says that although the late Baron Nordenskiöld himself published this paper as cited, it had been written for the Jenness volume and was republished there because "its omission would create an awkward gap in the plan for the book." Reprinted 1938-39 in *Revista chilena de historia y geografía* 84:232-263; 85:280-318. Reprinted 1946, *Origen de las civilizaciones indígenas en la América del Sud* (Editorial Bajel: Buenos Aires). Reprinted Russell and Russell: New York, 1972; reprinted AMS: New York, 1979]

A main concern in this paper is not the announced title but rather to establish "that these (South American) peoples have made quite a number of discoveries and inventions that were unknown in the Old World." Yet after we identify the local inventions or discoveries, "there remain a good many which in America are known only from certain parts of South America . . . and at the same time from the Old World." We must consider the possibility that these were imported into South America directly from across the oceans.

Page 261: "Of communication in the pre-Columbian era between South America and the Old World in the east there is not a trace of probability."

Table II, pages 262-263, lists forty-nine "Oceanic culture-elements in South America" most of which he discusses. He credits most of these to Rivet, Friederici, Graebner, and Schmidt. These may have derived from the crew of a shipwreck or from actual immigration from directly across the ocean at a remote date, or from independent invention. But we find few, if any, Oceanian culture elements in North America that do not also occur in South America. Also Melanesian-Indian parallels are much more important in the list than Polynesian-Indian ones. It is "obvious," however, that no actual movements of a regular character can have taken place between South America and Oceania since very far back in time.

Page 269: Noting the similarity of artifacts made from dried gourds in South America and Oceania, he refers to the plant as the principal proof of pre-Columbian communication between Oceania and America.

Page 286: True embalming with preservative oils was done by ancient fishermen of Africa, which he takes as evidence of independent development.

Pages 275ff.: Discusses the high civilizations of America in relation to Asia. He has acknowledged and described what he considers "a great number of noteworthy parallels" with the Old World, yet on various grounds he concludes that most of these were independent inventions, in particular because no cultivated plant is shared between the hemispheres.

Page 278: "When we know that in all probability the Indians have independently achieved inventions as difficult as that of bronze, we must also find it highly probable that they have independently invented all the metal tools and metal ornaments that they were using in pre-Columbian times." [Of course, this stands the argument of associations usually presented by diffusionists completely on its head.] Thus, "the high civilizations in America developed independently of any Asiatic influence directly from across the ocean."

Examples of parallels between the civilized areas of the two hemispheres which he cites or discusses: parasols used by chiefs, T-shaped axes, duck-hunting with a calabash, catching turtles using sucking fish, fishing with cormorants, coolie yoke, quilted armor, ikat and batik, negative painting, beam scale, steelyard, weights that are multiples of a unit, rope conveyor over a river, animal-skin rafts, mirrors, lacquer, tooth-filling decoration, litter, tipoy, adobe, true embalming, and games of hazard with a counting board.

N-106

AUTHORS: Norman, Daniel, and W. W. A. Johnson

DATE: 1941

TITLE: Note on a Spectroscopic Study of Central American and Asiatic Jades

IN: Journal of the Optical Society of America 31/1:85-86

They claim a striking resemblance on mineralogical grounds between a Chinese nephrite object and Mesoamerican pieces. [However F-142 questions the adequacy of their determination.]

N-107

AUTHOR: Norman, V. Garth

DATE: 1976

TITLE: Izapa Sculpture, Part 2: Text

IMPRINT: Paper 30, New World Archaeological Foundation Brigham Young University: Provo, Utah

Possible or actual Old World parallels:

Page 68: Maya Early Classic burials, as at Chama, have a jadeite bead in the mouth of the corpse. Rands (1965) suggests a sacred association of jadeite with water, and here with life and green-blue color. Jade is also represented as leaves or fruit of sacred trees. Parallels are cited to Babylonian tree of life fruit and the Chinese sign of immortality.

Page 77: Discussion of horned incense burners, uses and symbolism associated with rain, clouds, and fish.

Page 78: In a larger sense, the conjunction of incensing, rain, and sacrifice likely extends to water-as-life and the extension of man's life beyond the grave, as "in ancient Near Eastern 'water of life' symbolism and elsewhere."

Pages 105-106: Suggests the beetle at Izapa is a sky deity related to fertility, but also to death. [Compare Egypt?]

Pages 110-111: Mesoamerican traditions and myths say souls of the dead become stars, while children come from star heaven.

Page 123-124: Sedan chair to carry Maya dignitaries, see Stela 21.

Page 142: He interprets bee and butterfly as representing metamorphosis from a pupa, with a sense of resurrection.

Page 143: Star, Quetzalcoatl, and Xolotl are associated with the bee, butterfly, or firefly, and the insects may represent the souls of the dead.

Pages 147-148: Cites Thompson (1950) regarding the quincunx and death symbols indicating dawn/ sunrise. Quincunx also as Mexican and Mayan Venus-morning star/sun/day.

Page 154: Stela 67 shows a figure (rain god?—page 157) in a boat holding in each hand sceptre-like objects quite resembling the Egyptian ankh sign, which means life and prosperity, here perhaps rendering the "life" meaning of the Ik symbol.

Page 158: The theme of heavenly origin and destiny for the human soul aligned with the rain cycle and seen as central in Izapan iconography by the author, "may [through boat scenes] be adapted on Stelae 22 and 67 to express a transoceanic origin of ancestors" related to Guatemalan and Mexican myths.

Page 172: Stela 5 (dated c. second century B.C.) includes a fringed parasol, "a Maya and Old World emblem of royalty."

Pages 219-220: Relation of female Mesoamerican goddesses with death- childbirth, procreation, tree, and so on, offers "a striking resemblance" to Egyptian mythology where the goddess Nut pours a libation from the holy tree for the benefit of the dead who are led west to the underworld/night by the dog or dog star.

Page 288: El Jobo Stela 1 shows a priestly deity with two right hands, typical of some Egyptian art, and also found on two Izapa stelae.

N-109

AUTHOR: Northern, Rebecca T.

DATE: 1968

TITLE: The Birdman Bead

IN: Américas 20/3:14-20

Compares a birdman on a bead or spindle whorl from Puna Island, Ecuador, probably of Manteño culture, with birdman motifs on Easter Island as well as Peru's Mochica culture.

N-109B

AUTHOR: Norton, Presley
DATE: 1987
TITLE: El señorio de Salangone y la liga de mercaderes: el cartel spondylus-balsa [The Dominion of Salangone and the Merchants' League: The Spondylus-Balsa Cartel]
IN: Arquelolgía y etnohistoria del sur de Colombia y norte del Ecuador, (Miscelanea Antropológica Ecuatoriana Monográfico 6), compilers José Alcina Franch and Segundo Moreno Yánez, Banco Central del Ecuador (Boletín de los Museos del Banco Central del Ecuador 6), and Ediciones Abya-Yala: Cayambe, Ecuador (Simpósio del 45o Congreso Internacional de Americanistas, 1985, Bogatá)

Reviews recent archaeological findings combine with historical records to show that a "cartel" in the distribution of the valued spondylus shell was held by merchants on the north-central coast and nearby islands of Salango and La Plata, whose role recalls that fulfilled by the Phoenicians in the Mediterranean or the Hanseatic League of mercantile ports [no intimation of contact intended]. Balsa wood is only found on this coast (to as far north as Tumaco, Colombia); balsa rafts were used by the time of Valdivia 3 2500 B.C. when La Plata was first occupied. Only two species of spondylus were valued and traded in the New World before the arrival of the Europeans (S. princeps and S. calcifer). A specimen from Huaca Prieta shows raft trade from Ecuador even in the Peruvian pre-ceramic, probably starting locally by 3000 B.C. Large numbers of the shells were traded to the Teotihuacan area. The literature on balsa rafts from the early Spaniards is reprised. Recaps the Heyerdahl group's finds of archaeological materials on Galapagos. He has examined the sherd collections at the settlement on the islands together with the published material and concludes that while a large part of the Galapagos material could have been made in the 16th century and left by European ships [as claimed by Suggs], many fragments are definitively earlier, even of the Bahia culture (ca. A.D. 1-600). There is no question that balsas from the Ecuadorian coast visited the archipelago at least since 2000 years ago. Based on what Dampier and Baleato saw centuries ago we know there were balsas, with sail, of many different types and sizes designed for different functions. We lack concrete archaeological proof of the age of sails but the presence of Valdivia 3 material on La Plata island is a strong argument that they date to at lest 2500 B.C. [This valuable article is marred by the absence of a bibliography to identify the numerous citations.]

N-114

AUTHOR: Nowotny, Karl A.
DATE: 1969
TITLE: Beiträge zur Geschichte des Weltbildes: Farben und Weltrichtungen [Contributions to the History of World View: Colors and the Perception of the World]
IMPRINT: Wiener Beiträge zur Kulturgeschichte und Linguistik 17, Ferdinand Berger: Vienna

Compares Asian and American distribution of colors in relation to directions and related concepts. [Compare B-084.]

N-116

AUTHOR: Nuttall, Zelia
DATE: 1900
TITLE: The Meaning of the Ancient Mexican Calendar Stone [abstract]
IN: Proceedings of the American Association for the Advancement of Science 49:320

She believes that "a single, primitive cosmical scheme and plan of government prevailed through ancient America," identical to "the primitive Old World scheme."

N-118

AUTHOR: Nuttall, Zelia
DATE: 1901
TITLE: The Fundamental Principles of Old and New World Civilization
IMPRINT: Archaeological and Ethnological Papers of the Peabody Museum, vol. 2 (Harvard University: Cambridge, Massachusetts)

She proposes the origin in America of the swastika from observation of the sweep of Ursa Major around Polaris. She also argues at length that all parts of the world retain portions of a "Great Plan" in accordance with which lands and population were divided, and government and religion were arranged. In particular she regards it as possible that followers of Themistius, a contemporary of Constantine, were driven from their own land by Christian persecutors to become established in the New World empire of Temistitlan, the land of Temis, later Mexico, which at Spanish arrival was still an epitome of the Themistian philosophy. Another parallel: orders of eagle and tiger knights, known in the Old World as well as Mexico.

N-119

AUTHOR: Nuttall, Zelia
DATE: 1906a
TITLE: Some Unsolved Problems in Mexican Archaeology
IN: American Anthropologist 8:133-149

The author believes that Montezuma's account of his ancestry given to Cortez in 1520 is not to be interpreted as a solar myth but as "a plain historical tradition handed down from his forefathers." He, of all Mexicans, would have known of the traditions, which had his ancestors originating in a land over the sea, as remote as Spain.

In the calendar system of Mexico she finds Greek elements. She supposes that "foreign colonists" were the origin of "incongruous" elements in ancient Mexican civilization.

Page 146: L. von Schroeder attempted to prove that the five elements (earth, fire, water, air, and ether) were known in India as far back as the 7th century B.C. and reached Greece from there.

The Aztecs had four of the elements (not ether). Motion (ollin) was a fundamental underlying principle of the calendar and cosmic view of both Greek and Aztec civilization. Other common denominators include tetraktos or tetrarchical government, odd and even numbers in a cyclical system, pyramids, and all-embracing deities. If such parallels were found anywhere else in the world, we would postulate a connection to Greece.

N-120

AUTHOR: Nuttall, Zelia
DATE: 1906b
TITLE: The Earliest Historical Relations between Mexico and Japan
IN: University of California Publications in American Archaeology and Ethnology 4/1:46-47

Early Spanish explorers apparently carried Japanese raincoats to Mexico.

N-121

AUTHOR: Nuttall, Zelia
DATE: 1909
TITLE: A Curious Survival in Mexico of the Use of the Purpura Shellfish for Dyeing
IN: Putnam Anniversary Volume, edited by Franz Boas (Stechert: New York), 368-384
[Spanish translation, *Sociedad Mexicana de Geografía y Estadística, Boletín* 5/4:347-350, 381-392]

A thorough rundown on earlier reports of the preparation and use of purpura dye in Mesoamerica, Central America, and Peru, together with her own observations from Tehuantepec. Various species of molluscs were used in the Old World as well as in the New. She connects co-occurring cultural features into a potential complex which could have been brought by, perhaps, a single shipload of Mediterranean voyagers: (1) the purple dye industry and skill in weaving [to which may also be added accompanying beliefs and practices unknown to Nuttall but later reported in G-077 and elsewhere]; (2) the use of pearls and conch-shell trumpets; (3) mining, working, and trafficking in copper, silver, and gold; (4) the tetrarchical form of government; (5) the conception of "Four Elements"; (6) the cyclical form of calendar. Those who believe these were developed independently in the New World must face the fact that the natives unanimously disclaim invention but rather assign introduction of these features to strangers of superior culture from distant and unknown parts. Moreover, those who know the enervating climate of the area will not question that an immigrant source is more likely than local invention under such conditions. But the problem remains baffling whether there was contact or none.

N-122

AUTHOR: Nuttall, Zelia
DATE: 1920
TITLE: Comments on *Handbook of Aboriginal American Antiquities,* by William H. Holmes
IN: American Anthropologist 22:301-303

She takes Holmes to task for "surprising statements" about the archaeology of Mexico and Central America. Contrary to what her earlier diffusionist stance would lead one to expect, here she does not like Holmes' noting analogy between Southeast Asiatic pyramids and Mesoamerican ones, nor does the author's "whiskered men in Yucatan" please her—she wants him to prove that these are not mere ceremonial masks. Neither does she allow Charnay's discovery of a wheeled toy; it could not be pre-Columbian.

N-124

AUTHOR: Nykl, A. R.
DATE: 1926
TITLE: The Quinary-Vigesimal System of Counting in Europe, Asia, and America
IN: Language 2:165-173

The distribution of this system can be explained by an origin in Sumer or in "the original home of the Palaeo-Asiatic peoples" followed by spread via Bering Strait to some parts of North America. Some contacts between Mexico and the west of Europe are possible but not evidenced.

O-001

AUTHOR: Obayashi, Taryo
DATE: 1959
TITLE: Divination from Entrails among the Ancient Inca and Its Relation to Practices in Southeast Asia
IN: Proceedings of the 33rd International Congress of Americanists (San José, Costa Rica, 1958), 1:327-332

Chronicle accounts describe divination from animal sacrifice and study of entrails in Peru as in Asia. Archaeology in Peru shows llama sacrifice began as early as the Chavin Period. The author believes that this practice came across the Pacific from south China in the Late Chou Period, not through Dongson influence later.

O-002

AUTHOR: Obayashi, Taryo
DATE: 1960
TITLE: On the Origin of the "Inau" Cult-sticks of the Ainu
IN: Japanese Journal of Ethnology 24:1-30 (Tokyo)

These little sticks with long, curled pendant shavings relate to the concept of mediation between man and god. Myths of the origin of the *inau* suggest connection with northern Asia, and related cult-sticks occur in northern Eurasia, but apparently prior to the development of pastoral cultures in Central Asia. "The cult sticks found in North America also belong to the cultural heritage of the hunters who crossed into North America."

O-003

AUTHOR: Oberem, Udo, and Roswith Hartmann
DATE: 1982
TITLE: Zur Seefahrt in den Hochkulturen Alt-Amerikas [On Sea Travel in Ancient American Civilizations]
IN: Zur geschichtlichen Bedeutung der frühen Seefahrt, edited by Hermann Müller-Karpe, (Kolloquien zur Allgemeinen und Vergleichenden Archäologie, Band 2), (C. H. Beck: Munich), 121-157

A valuable roundup of the subject, like others in this volume not adding anything new, yet soundly updating the reader. Oberem treats Mesoamerica and Hartmann Andean South America (ending with a quote from Doran on the unquestionable feasibility of raft crossings of the Pacific).

O-006

AUTHOR: O'Brien, Patricia J.
DATE: 1968
TITLE: Doctrinaire Diffusionism and Acts of Faith
IN: American Antiquity 33:386-387

A letter masquerading as an article, aimed at Jett and Carter [J-079] as well as F-131. Says that until unequivocal evidence in support of unorthodox diffusionist claims can be found, it is impossible to test them conclusively as hypotheses [which is what J-079 had said, urging that such claims not be discarded until tested].

O-007

AUTHOR: O'Brien, Patricia J.
DATE: 1972
TITLE: The Sweet Potato: Its Origin and Dispersal
IN: American Anthropologist 74:342-365

The sweet-potato originated in northwestern South America, and its domestication is associated with tropical forest agricultural villages ca. 2500 B.C. The Spanish introduced it to Europe and from there it spread to China, Japan, Malaysia, and the Moluccas. The Portuguese carried it to India, Indonesia, and Africa. Reexamination of the literature suggests new theories to the author. She believes that there was a pre-Magellan accidental introduction of the sweet potato into the Samoa area by about A.D. 1 (birds carrying seed or fortuitous casting of a vessel). From there it spread throughout the rest of the Pacific. The author, however, does not believe that the similarity between Andean and Polynesian terms for sweet potato ("kumara") indicates pre-Hispanic contact.

O-007B

AUTHOR: Ó Caoimh, Tomas
DATE: 1989
TITLE: St. Brendan Sources: St. Brendan and Early Irish Hagiography
IN: Atlantic Visions (Proceedings of the First International Conference of the Society of Saint Brendan, September 1985, Dublin and Kerry), edited by John de Courcy Ireland and David C. Sheehy (Boole Press, Dún Laoghaire, Co.: Dublin, Ireland), 17-24

"The Irish [of tradition] think of their history mythologically; and so too, of their geography." This is our guiding light when dealing with the St. Brendan literature. Myth and reality constantly interpenetrate each other, symbol is all-important; a legend which seems fantastic may reflect a historical event or possibly a twist in the destiny of some sept or dynastic group. After all the analysis we can perform, the material often cannot give us definite information about the person, time, or place. What we can glean from the literature concerning Brendan may point to particular events, real characters, or accurate historical information, but to settle on definite dates or personalities in a definite order is a very risky business. The voyage was possible and place names associated with Brendan are to be found, but we cannot say whether the Navigatio and related material are an actual record. In short this is hagiography, which is not the same as history. Lists the seven different treatments of the life of Brendan available today and comments briefly on their special characteristics.

O-008

AUTHOR: Ochoa, Lorenzo
DATE: 1979
TITLE: Historia prehispánica de la Huaxteca [Prehispanic History of the Huasteca]
IMPRINT: Instituto de Investigaciones Antropológicas, Serie Antropológica 26 (Universidad Nacional Autónoma de México: México)

Pages 112-118: On canoes and shipping along the Gulf Coast from the Maya area to the Huasteca. Still today, in certain places in the Huasteca, traditions exist paralleling Sahagun's, to the effect that ancestors arrived by sea navigating in "turtle shells." Piña Chan thought that the Sahagun tradition referred to the Late Formative. This author thinks of the local Late Classic, perhaps originating in the Maya area. He considers regular voyaging for commercial ends likely. Colonial sources refer to the dexterity of canoe-users on the Huastecan coast.

O-009

AUTHOR: O'Donaghue, Denis
DATE: 1893
TITLE: Brendaniana
IMPRINT: Brown and Nolan: Dublin

A non-scholarly attempt to identify the islands reached by Brendan, which he believes included Mexico.

O-010

AUTHOR: Oetteking, Bruno
DATE: 1932
TITLE: Morphologie und menschliches Altertum in Amerika [Morphology and Human Antiquity in America]
IN: Anthropos 27:899-903

Despite physical differences produced by immigration of various population elements at different times, overall Amerindians show certain uniformities. Interhemispheric parallels in culture he finds can hardly be by coincidence.

O-011

AUTHOR: Oetteking, Bruno
DATE: 1934
TITLE: Anthropomorphologische Beziehungen zwischen der Osterinsel und Amerika [Anthropomorphological Relationships between Easter Island and America]
IN: [Eugen Fischer Festband] Zeitschrift für Morphologie und Anthropologie 34:303-313

Compares an Easter Island cranium with others from San Nicolas Island (California), Satan Canyon (Texas), and the Ona, finding great similarities.

O-012

AUTHOR: Ogburn, W. F.
DATE: 1938
TITLE: Social Change
IMPRINT: Viking: New York

Pages 90-102: Ogburn and Thomas have compiled a list, given here, of almost 150 apparent parallel or simultaneous inventions. [Compare C-158 and R-013.]

O-013

AUTHOR: Oiticica, José
DATE: 1934
TITLE: Do método no estudo das línguas sudamericanas [On Method in the Study of South American Languages]
IN: Proceedings of the 24th International Congress of Americanists (Hamburg, 1930), 272-297

In the course of giving methodological advice on systematic instead of impressionistic language comparisons (Dempwolff on Oceanic languages being an example of the former, Vignaud of the latter), he mentions the following items of literature without giving adequate bibliographical data on them [while also mentioning items already included in this bibliography, such as L-306 and B-149]:

Brasseur de Bourbourg claimed in his *Gramática* the affiliation of Quiché and Flemish, and Charencey of Quiché with Basque.

Coute de Magalhïes claimed analogies between Tupí and Greek.

Viscount Porto Seguro published a book on the Turanian origin of Tupí-Carib and also compared Tupí with Egyptian and Coptic.

Father Degenettes in his 1904 letter on the Caiapós in the *Revista do Instituto Histórico*, declared himself convinced of the identity of many Tupí roots with Sanscrit but gave no evidence.

Júlio Platzmann in his book *Americanisch-asiatische Etymologie* presents parallels between numerous languages of both continents.

Also Father Ulysses Penafort in his curious book on prehistoric Brazil says he is impressed with the similarities between Tupí words and Indo-European, offering a display of these.

Martius linked Tupí terms with Asiatic and Oceanic ones, allowing a possibility of a common origin.

O-014

AUTHOR: Okladnikov, Aleksei Pavlovich
DATE: 1950
TITLE: Neolit i bronzovyi vek Pribaikaliya [The Neolithic and Bronze Age of the Lake Baikal Region]
IN: Materialy i issledovaniya po arkheologii SSR 18:5-412

Pages 250, 257: From widespread deposits of nephrite in the Baikal area, especially towards the end of the Neolithic, small models or effigies of fish were produced in great quantities. These were used for fish bait and are also known from Eskimos and some North American Indians.

O-017

AUTHOR: Oldham, Charles F.
DATE: 1905
TITLE: The Sun and the Serpent: A Contribution to the History of Serpent-Worship
IMPRINT: A. Constable: London

Page 183: "It seems in the highest degree improbable that this close connexion [discussed earlier with case material] between the Sun and the serpent could have originated, independently, in countries so far apart as China and the west of Africa, or India and Peru. And it seems scarcely possible that, in addition to this, the same forms of worship of these deities, and the same ritual, could have arisen, spontaneously, amongst each of these far distant peoples." There must have been communication from a common center (between the Euphrates and the Indus). Phoenicians were among the carriers; such carriers he terms "the solar race."

O-018

AUTHOR: Oldham, H. Yule
DATE: 1895
TITLE: A Pre-Columbian Discovery of America
IN: Geographical Journal 3:221-233

Argues that (1) it was easier for the Portuguese to sail across the Atlantic in the 15th century than to coast to or from West Africa; (2) Portuguese official policy kept discoveries secret; (3) evidence justifies concluding that Newfoundland had been discovered by them before 1492; and (4) before 1492 they were aware of a continent to the southwest of the Cape Verde Islands. Followed by a summary of the discussion which ensued when the paper was read, most commentators disagreeing with his conclusions. [See T-019.]

O-019

AUTHOR: Oldham, H. Yule
DATE: 1973 [1895-1896]
TITLE: The Importance of Mediaeval Manuscript Maps in the Study of the History of Geographical Discovery
IN: Cartographica 17:101-104 [Reprinted from the *Report of the Sixth International Geographical Congress* (London 1895-1896), 703-706]

Early maps included information prior to its appearance in print. Case: Bianco's map dated 1447 shows a coastline that must be Brazil. But Batalha-Reis in comments following this paper cautions that maps may have later unacknowledged additions after the nominal date.

O-021

AUTHOR: Oleson, Tryggvi J.
DATE: 1955
TITLE: The Vikings in America: A Critical Bibliography
IN: The Canadian Historical Review 36/2:166-173

This survey was originally an appendix to a paper read by the author to the Canadian Historical Association meeting (1954) and printed in the *Annual Report*. It covers primarily works published between 1939 and 1954. Selectively incorporated into this bibliography.

O-022

AUTHOR: Oleson, Tryggvi J.
DATE: 1964
TITLE: Early Voyages and Northern Approaches, 1000-1632
IMPRINT: The Canadian Centenary Series, vol. 1 (McClelland and Stewart: Toronto; and Oxford University Press: New York)

A history of pre-Columbian voyages to North America which submits evidence of some cultural intermixing of peoples from Iceland with the Dorset people of the Canadian Arctic.

O-023

AUTHOR: Olmsted, David L.
DATE: 1964
TITLE: Lexicostatistics as "Proof" of Genetic Relationship: The Case of "Macro-Manguean"
IN: VI Congrès International des Sciences Anthropologiques et Ethnologiques (Paris, 1960), 2/2:69-73

Demonstrates that Swadesh's failure to establish historical patterns of phonology before identifying "cognates" renders this case of reconstruction of a proto-language unbelievable. [Thus it serves as a methodological warning about possible problems with other lexicostatistical interpretations that appear to apply, pro or con, to discussions of diffusion.]

O-024B

AUTHOR: Olson, Dana
DATE: 1987
TITLE: Prince Madoc: Founder of Clark County, Indiana
MPRINT: The Author: Jefferson, Indiana

Self-explanatory title.

O-029

AUTHOR: Olson, Ronald L.
DATE: 1929
TITLE: The Possible Middle American Origin of Northwest Coast Weaving
IN: American Anthropologist 31:114-121

Weaving in this area may be due to any of five reasons: (1) independent development, at least in the case of the two-bar loom and spindle; (2) early European influence; (3) Asiatic origin; (4) elaboration of general northern North American weaving; (5) being an outpost of weaving technique from the civilizations to the south. Each hypothesis has evidence in its favor; the matter cannot be settled.

Page 119: The use of the balsa in British Columbia is probably linked with similar craft elsewhere in the Americas.

O-030

AUTHOR: Olson, Ronald L.
DATE: 1927
TITLE: Adze, Canoe and House Types of the Northwest Coast
IN: University of Washington Publications in Anthropology 2:1-38

Page 29: "Various views are held on the possibility of historic relationship of houses of northwest America and northeast Asia. Steensby thinks it probable that the plank house of America is of Asiatic origin. Jochelson argues for a connection" in the underground dwellings.

Page 30: "Its occurrence in Polynesia in a form almost identical with the elbow adze of America suggests a hoary age and extra-American origin" for the Northwest Coast tool.

O-031

AUTHOR: Olson, Ronald L.
DATE: 1930
TITLE: Chumash Prehistory
IMPRINT: University of California Publications in American Archaeology and Ethnology 28:1-21

Page 21: Briefly discusses possible transfer of Oceanic culture elements to North America and especially to southern California.

O-033

AUTHOR: Onffroy de Thoron, Enrique
DATE: [before 1900]
TITLE: Recherches philologiques et historiques sur la langue Quichua de Perou [Philological and Historical Researches on the Quechua Language of Peru]
IN: Bibliotheca Ludovigi Lugiani Bonaparte: Paris

See O-034.

O-034

AUTHOR: Onffroy de Thoron, Enrique
DATE: 1868
TITLE: Voyages des flottes de Salomon et d'Hiram en Amérique [Voyages of Solomon's and Hiram's Fleets to America]
IMPRINT: Maisonneuve: Geneva

The biblical land of Ophir was on the Japura river in South America.

O-035

AUTHOR: Onffroy de Thoron, Enrique
DATE: 1869
TITLE: Antiquité de la navigation de l'ocean: voyages des vaisseaux de Salomon au fleuve des Amazones, Ophir, Tarschisch et Parvaim [The Antiquity of Ocean Navigation: Voyages of Solomon's Ships to the Amazon River, Ophir, Tarshish and Parvaim]
IMPRINT: Carey: Geneva

See O-034.

O-036

AUTHOR: Onffroy de Thoron, Enrique
DATE: 1889
TITLE: Les Phéniciens à l'île de Haïti et sur le continent américain [The Phoenicians on the Island of Haiti and on the American Continent]
IMPRINT: C. Peeters: Louvain

Jews/Phoenicians reached Haiti and Mexico around 600 B.C. causing the Votan tradition. Phoenicians earlier reached Ophir/Tarshish/Parvaim at the mouth of the Amazon. Dighton Rock resulted from another medieval voyage. Gives a list of 100 Taino words for which he finds Hebrew equivalents.

O-037

AUTHOR: Oppenheim, A. Leo
DATE: 1944
TITLE: The Mesopotamian Temple
IN: Biblical Archaeologist 7:54-63

Royal use of the litter in the Bronze Age.

O-038

AUTHOR: Oppenheim, A. Leo
DATE: 1954
TITLE: The Seafaring Merchants of Ur
IN: Journal of the American Oriental Society 74:6-17

Bronze Age vessels in the Indian Ocean.

O-038B

AUTHORS: Oppenheimer, Monroe, and Willard Wirtz
DATE: 1989
TITLE: A Linguistic Analysis of Some West Virginia Petroglyphs
IN: West Virginia Archaeologist 41:1-6

Heavily criticize Fell's transcription and decipherment of West Virginia petroglyphs [see F-053].

O-039

AUTHOR: Orchiston, D. Wayne
DATE: 1968
TITLE: The Practice of Mummification among the New Zealand Maori
IN: Journal of the Polynesian Society 77:186-189

Historical and ethnological documentation shows that mummification was widely known on New Zealand's North Island in pre-European times.

O-040

AUTHOR: Orchiston, D. Wayne
DATE: 1971
TITLE: Maori Mummification in Protohistoric New Zealand
IN: Anthropos 66:753-766

True mummification by the Maori has only recently been proven indisputably, after involved debate early in this century. The practice also has been reported from eastern Polynesia. "Recent interest in circum-Pacific and Melanesian mummification" prompts this review of the New Zealand evidence and its meanings. Nothing more is said in the piece by way of comparison.

O-042

AUTHOR: Orcutt, Phillip Dana
DATE: 1953
TITLE: A Stone Carving on the Galapagos
IN: American Antiquity 18:270

A two-meter-high face not very distinctly carved in basal stone on one of the Galapagos is pictured and briefly reported. There is no indication whether it is prehistoric in date or not.

O-042B

AUTHORS: Orlove, Benjamin S., and David W. Guillet, editors
DATE: 1985
TITLE: Convergences and Differences in Mountain Economies and Societies, a Comparison of the Andes and Himalaya
IN: Mountain Research and Development, vol. 5, no. 1. Proceedings of a Workshop Organized by the American Anthropological Association in Washington, D.C., 4 December 1982 (United Nations University, and International Mountain Society: Boulder, Colorado)

Ecological- and functional-induced similarities, not diffusion.

O-043

AUTHORS: O'Rourke, D. H., B. K. Suarez, and J. D. Crouse
DATE: 1985
TITLE: Genetic Variation in North Amerindian Populations: Covariance with Climate
IN: American Journal of Physical Anthropology 67:241-250

Gene frequency patterns reflect climatic selection, resulting in latitudinal patterns which would mask historical factors.

O-044

AUTHOR: Orr, Rowland B.
DATE: 1913
TITLE: Pre-Columbian Copper in Ontario
IN: Proceedings of the 18th International Congress of Americanists (London, 1912), 313-316

After emphasizing that copper in Canada was native and hammered only, he contrasts Mexico and the west coast of South America which had craftsmen in gold, silver, and copper "of the highest order." "We must remember that the Latins, Gauls, Teutons, and Celts who came to the American continent were looking for everything in the line of precious metals, and they early learned that by securing native copper they could soon transform it into bronze, and return it to those from whom it was pilfered at four times the price."

O-047

AUTHOR: Orta Nadal, Ricardo
DATE: 1964
TITLE: La intuición del espacio y del tiempo en la tradición cultural de China [The Intuition of Space and Time in the Cultural Tradition of China]
IN: Anales de Arqueología y Etnología 19:7-139 (Universidad Nacional de Cuyo, Mendoza, Argentina)

Page 78: Did the Chinese possess a doctrine of eras or ages of the world? They appear not to have had an integral time-and-world view of this type like those so evident in India and Mesoamerica.

Page 107: In long discussions before and after this point, the author believes that he establishes that in China this world view indeed was present but in later times existed only in disintegrated form. He finds Chinese parallels to Mesoamerican and Indian features of calendar and of music associated with dynasties, a myth of the collapse and re-erection of heaven, belief in cyclical destructions of the world especially by flood and fire, a new fire ceremony, the ethical-juridical character of the destructions, etc. He does not end up making a specific historical interpretation from the parallels.

O-048

AUTHOR: Orta Nadal, Ricardo
DATE: 1967
TITLE: El panorama mental de la protohistoria en José Imbelloni [The Mental Panorama of Protohistory in José Imbelloni]
IMPRINT: Facultad de Filosofia, Universidad Nacional del Litoral: Rosario, Argentina [Reprinted *Cuadernos de Antropología* (Departmento de Antropología, Universidad Nacional del Litoral: Rosario, Argentina, 1968)]

Thirteen essays on the works of Imbelloni, published between 1939 and 1946.

O-048B

AUTHOR: Osborn, Alan J.
DATE: 1988
TITLE: Limitations of the Diffusionist Approach: Evolutionary Ecology and Shell-tempered Ceramics
IN: The Transfer and Transformation of Ideas and Material Culture, edited by P. J. Hugill and D. B. Dickson (Texas A & M University Press: College Station, Texas), 23-44

Methodological. The study illustrates the complex, inobvious nature of human behavior and its interrelationships with nature. Idealist archeologists for many decades have been concerned to explain the rise and decline of Mississippian culture in terms of innovation diffusion, however such theory cannot explain the patterns of shell-tempered ceramics in the archeological record. [Innovation diffusion may be involved in providing a knowledge base,] but variability of incidence can be explained primarily in terms of natural selection, that is, environmental constraints.

O-049

AUTHOR: Osborne, George Black
DATE: 1937
TITLE: The Voyage of the "Girl Pat"
IMPRINT: Hutchinson: London [Reprinted George Mann: Maidstone, England, 1974]

From England to British Guiana in a fishing vessel with three companions, navigating only with the aid of a "sixpenny atlas."

O-050

AUTHOR: Oswalt, Wendell
DATE: 1952
TITLE: Pottery from Hooper Bay Village, Alaska
IN: American Antiquity 18:18-29

Supports De Laguna's suggestion of a direct northeastern Asian origin for pottery of this particular area.

O-051

AUTHOR: Oswalt, Wendell
DATE: 1953
TITLE: Northeast Asian and Alaskan Pottery Relationships
IN: Southwestern Journal of Anthropology 9:395-407

The distinctive pottery from the Bristol Bay-Norton Sound region of Alaska is relatively recent. All its designs are reported from northeastern Asia, not from elsewhere in Alaska. The oldest parallel is with Proto-Jomon of northern Japan. Some Proto-Jomon wares survived throughout Jomon and could have influenced later Kurile and Kamchatka wares. Two motifs are the same in Japan and Alaska but absent in the Kuriles or Kamchatka. It is tempting to suggest an Aleutian route for their arrival in

Alaska, but the absence of any pottery in that chain makes the suggestion speculative.

O-052

AUTHOR: Ottolenghi, Aldo
DATE: 1980
TITLE: Civilizaciones americanas prehistóricas [Prehistoric American Civilizations]
IMPRINT: Hachette: Buenos Aires

He illustrates and discusses a series of archaeological materials in Brazil, Paraguay, Chile, Peru, and Bolivia (Tiahuanaco, by Posnansky) which he takes to represent scripts ancestral to the oldest Middle Eastern writing. These include a Brazilian statuette attributed to the explorer Colonel Fawcett which he relates specifically to the Etruscans. He concludes that these manifestations of scripts are descended from "south Semitic" writing of c.1250 B.C.

O-053

AUTHOR: Oxenstierna, Eric C. Gabriel
DATE: 1965
TITLE: The Norsemen
IMPRINT: New York Graphic Society: Greenwich, Connecticut [From the Swedish, *Så levde Vikingarna* (Forum: Stockholm, 1959)]

Profusely illustrated account for the general reader.

Pages 245-263: Northern voyages, Greenland, and the voyages to America. The skraeling are considered Indians, the Kensington Stone is a fraud, and the so-called Viking burial remains on Lake Nipigon, Ontario, are Norwegian of later date. The Ingstads' work is discussed.

O-054

AUTHOR: Oyarzun, Aurelio
DATE: 1927
TITLE: Dos puntas de lanzas paleolíticas de la Isla de Pascua encontradas en un cementerio prehistórica de la costa de Chile [Two Paleolithic Lance Points from Easter Island Found in a Prehistoric Cemetery on the Coast of Chile]
IN: Museo de Etnología y Antropología de Chile 4:273-275

Somewhat generalized features are compared.

O-054B

AUTHOR: Oyarzun, Aurelio
DATE: 1939
TITLE: Las balsas de cuero de lobo de las costas de Chile [The Rafts of Sea Lion Skins on the Coasts of Chile]
IN: Revista del Museo Histórico Nacional de Chile 1/1:129-133

A bibliographical review with commentary on L-302B.

P-002

AUTHOR: Padden, R. C.
DATE: 1973
TITLE: On Diffusion and Historicity
IN: American Historical Review 78:987-1004

A review of Cyrus Gordon's *Before Columbus* and *Man across the Sea*. Gordon is said to reveal by his chronological discrepancies and gratuitous assumptions a lack of understanding of Mesoamerican culture. *Man across the Sea* should mark "the end of traditional transoceanic diffusionist postulation" of Gordon's sort although why he thinks that would ensue is not explicated.

P-003

AUTHOR: Palavecino, Enrique
DATE: 1926a

TITLE: Elementos lingüisticos de Oceánia en el Quechua
[Linguistic Elements from Oceania in Quechua]
IN: Appendix to La Esfinge indiana, by José Imbelloni (El Ateneo, Libreria científica y literaria: Buenos Aires)

He lists 75 words he considers shared between Quechua and Maori.

P-004

AUTHOR: Palavecino, Enrique
DATE: 1926b
TITLE: Elementos oceánicos en el Quechua
[Oceanic Elements in Quechua]
IN: Gaea 2:256ff. (Buenos Aires)

See P-005.

P-005

AUTHOR: Palavecino, Enrique
DATE: 1928a
TITLE: Glosario comparado Kichua-Maori
[Comparative Quechua-Maori Glossary]
IN: Proceedings of the 22nd International Congress of Americanists (Rome, 1926), 2:517-525

He says that more than 30% of Quechua words are formed of Polynesian phonological elements.

P-006

AUTHOR: Palavecino, Enrique
DATE: 1928b
TITLE: Los origenes americanos y la lingüistica
[American Origins and Linguistics]
IN: Nosotros 62/233:65-72 (Buenos Aires)

Rebuts criticism by Argentinian grammarian Costa Alvarez against lexical comparisons used by Rivet and Palavecino. The latter has pointed out over 50 lexical analogies between Maori and Kichua. The critic's knowledge of linguistics and logic is said to be limited and his objections groundless.

P-006B

AUTHOR: Palmer, David A.
DATE: 1967
TITLE: A Study of Mesoamerican Religious Symbolism
IN: Newsletter and Proceedings of the Society for Early Historic Archaeology 103:1-6 (Provo, Utah) [Reprinted in C-230]

Finds conceptual relationships and artistic conventions connected six ancient Mesoamerican symbols: the tree of life, serpent, fire, water, snail or sea shell, and stepped fret. concludes that these symbols point to the serpent as the foundation sign of the set and that anciently a well-defined theology surrounded the serpent deity. All the symbols except the stepped fret were found in Palestine or Mesopotamia before their appearance in America. Independent invention of such a set in the two areas is improbable; diffusion from the Old World to the New is apparent.

P-007

AUTHOR: Palmer, Jock P.
DATE: 1967
TITLE: Jade
IMPRINT: Spring Books: London

Includes refutation of Fischer's 19th century theory that all jade comes from Asia.

P-008

AUTHOR: Palop Martínez, Josefina
DATE: 1970
TITLE: Distribución mundial de la trepanación prehistórica
[World Distribution of Prehistoric Trepanation]

IN: Revista española de antropología americana [continuing Trabajos y Conferencias] 5:51-66 (Madrid)

Page 52: The author's bibliography has over 300 items [only some are incorporated here].

Page 63: Provisionally she concludes that the materials from Asia, Africa, Australia, and North America fail to show successful, institutionalized, intentional trepanation. The practice is sure from three areas only: Nuclear America (chiefly the Andean zone but also in early Oaxaca) [she mistakenly dates this area phenomenon from only A.D. 500], Oceania, and Western Europe/ Mediterranean (including the Canaries). The earliest cases are European (3000 B.C.), the next American, and the latest Oceanic, leading logically to a diffusionary conclusion from east to west across the Atlantic [in agreement with Alcina Franch] and beyond America into the Pacific.

P-009

AUTHOR: Pan Li Chuang
DATE: 1963
TITLE: Panpipes of Ancient China
IMPRINT: Monograph 4, Institute of Ethnology (Academia Sinica: Nankang, Taiwan)

Describes a particular type of panpipe known in Han China and perhaps earlier which is also found on the coast of Ecuador at around 250 B.C. It continued in use in China until recent times and also occurs among Motilon Indians of Colombia.

P-011

AUTHOR: Panhuys, Louis Constant van
DATE: 1925
TITLE: Observations on the Name Bacove
IN: Proceedings of the 21st International Congress of Americanists (Part 2, Gothenburg, Sweden, 1924), 321-332

Convoluted, heavily-documented discussion of terms for plantain and banana and the related name *bacove* in relation to the question of the pre-Columbian presence or Spanish introduction of those plants in tropical America. The issue is not clear; systematic mapping of terms will be required.

P-012

AUTHORS: Pantin, A. M., and P. C. Junqueira
DATE: 1951
TITLE: Blood Groups of Brazilian Indians
IN: Nature 167/4259:998

Preliminary announcement of the absence of the Duffy blood group in a sample of 73 "pure-bred Brazilian Indians in the interior of the Mato Grosso." The authors point out that the lack of Duffy-positive Indians in Brazil (other peoples show high incidences) may prove to be of considerable anthropological importance as showing differentiation among "American Indians."

P-013

AUTHOR: Panton, J. A.
DATE: 1903
TITLE: Ruins on the Islands in the Pacific Attributed to the Mayans of Central America
IN: Victorian Geographical Journal 21/12:98-104

Speculative and uninformed.

P-016

AUTHOR: Paravey, Charles Hippolyte de
DATE: 1835
TITLE: Mémoire sur l'origine japonaise, arabe et basque, de la civilisation des peuples du plateau de Bogota d'après les travaux de Humboldt et Siebold
[Memoir on the Japanese, Arab, and Basque Origin of the Civilization of the Peoples of the Bogota Plateau

According to the Works of Humboldt and Siebold]
IMPRINT: Dondey-Dupré: Paris

He loosely compares Chibchan or Muyscan with Japanese and the other indicated languages, based on publications of Humboldt and Seybold.

P-018

AUTHOR: Paravey, Charles Hippolyte de
DATE: 1844
TITLE: L'Amérique, sous le nom de pays de Fousang, est-elle citée, dès le 5e. siècle de notre ère, dans les grandes annales de la Chine et, dès lors, les Samanéens de l'Asie centrale et du Caboul y ont-ils porté le bouddhisme, ce qu'a cru voir le célèbre M. De Guignes, et ce qu'ont nié Gaubil, Klaproth et M. de Humboldt? Discussion ou dissertation abrégée, où l'affirmative est prouvée
[America, under the Name of Fu-sang, Is It Cited as Early as the Fifth Century of our Era in the Great Annals of China and, Since Then, Have the Samaneans of Central Asia and Kabul Brought Buddhism There, Which the Celebrated Mr. De Guignes Thought He Detected, and Which Gaubil, Klaproth, and M. de Humboldt Denied? Abridged Discussion and Dissertation, Where the Affirmative Is Proved]
IMPRINT: Treuttel et Wurtz: Paris
[Reprinted from *Annales de philosophie chrétienne*, (Feb. 1844)]

Title more than self-explanatory!

P-019

AUTHOR: Paravey, Charles Hippolyte de
DATE: 1847
TITLE: Nouvelles preuves que le pays du Fou-sang mentionné dans les livres Chinois est l'Amérique
[New Proofs That the Country of Fu-sang Mentioned in Chinese Books Is America]
IMPRINT: E. Bautruche: Paris
[Translated in V-057, pages 66-70]

Title self-explanatory.

P-020

AUTHOR: Paravey, Charles Hippolyte de
DATE: 1849
TITLE: Réfutation de l'opinion émise par Jomard que les peuples de l'Amérique n'ont jamais eu aucun rapport avec ceux de l'Asie
[A Refutation of the Opinion Put Forth by Jomard that the People of America Never Had any Contact with Those of Asia]
IMPRINT: H. V. de Surey: Paris
[Reprinted from *Annales de philosophie chrétienne* (May 1849)]

Mexico was Fu-sang.

P-021

AUTHOR: Paredes, Angél Modesto
DATE: 1924
TITLE: Sociología general aplicada a las condiciones de América
[General Sociology Applied to the Conditions of America]
IMPRINT: N. Romero Díaz: Quito

Biblical Hamites were the settlers of America; American civilization is of Egyptian origin.

P-023

AUTHOR: Paris, François E.
DATE: 1882-1908
TITLE: Souvenirs de marine; collection de plans ou dessins de navires et de bâteaux anciens ou modernes, existants ou disparus, 6 vols.
[Souvenirs of a Sailor; a Collection of Plans or Designs for Ships and

Boats, Ancient or Modern, Existing or Lost]
IMPRINT: Gauthier-Villars: Paris

Includes the earliest detailed illustrations of Ecuadorean balsa rafts.

P-024

AUTHOR: Paris, Pierre
DATE: 1942-1943
TITLE: L'Amérique précolombienne et l'Asie méridionale [Pre-Columbian America and South Asia]
IN: Bulletin de la société des études indochinoises 17/2:1-36; 18/1:1-25 (Hanoi)

A substantial and well-documented paper. Notes the quasi-racism of American scholars who insist that the[ir own ancestral] Europeans were the first from the Old World to reach and affect the pristine Americas. Is this "Monroe doctrine," which is especially held by North American scholars, a manifestation of vanity or a result of "the science of man" (i.e., anthropology)? Or is it due to ignorance, in total negation of physical anthropology (quoting ten Kate). Paris' position is that American pre-Columbian civilizations were indeed largely autonomous but that they had a basic Far Eastern origin and during their existence there were intermittent relations with that area, probably across the Pacific. The elephant, the personage on Stela B at Copan compared with the dvàrapàla figure of Cambodia, turbans of Tonkin and Central America, the churning of the sea of milk (Maya and Khmer), Quetzalcoatl and Buddha, and other iconographic features are compared; other data include mano and metate with Indian and Siamese parallels, identical means of coastal and riverine shipping, the planghi and ikat dyeing techniques, and a shared plant ("the importation of American kapok to Indonesia in the 10th century"). He concludes that the Asian area affected the Maya. A brief discussion is added on Indonesian relationships, and the question is asked whether India too had direct influence on America. Chinese parallels are considered briefly in a list of specifics. Transpacific navigation is considered to have been feasible.

The second article (part) is an extended catalog of evidences of Asian and American influences. Provides commentary and considerable documentation on each. Features: elephants, turbans, earplugs (lobe stretchers), poncho (Chinese Fou Nan), Quetzalcoatl (including the cross), lingam, chronology of the peak of Maya civilization fitting the time most likely for Indo-Khmer contact, various Indonesian iconographic parallels, "the horned eye" art motif, various direct Indian iconographic connections (e.g., Smith's Ganesa-God B similarity), various Chinese influences (e.g., the great wall of the Chimu; Chinese relationships are more obvious in Peru than in Mexico), lexical comparisons, Melanesian- or Papuan-looking skulls in America, oars from the Gulf of Siam and of the upper Amazon, bells, ceramic trumpets in the shape of a marine shell [presumably Spondylus], tortoise-effigy ceramic whistles from Siam and Peru, volador (many details), and diseases (citing Fonseca, Soper, Nicolle on parasites). There is also a short section, "Transatlantic Relations?", which quotes from Mortillet regarding the frequent representation of Maya God B shown with torches in his hands like those held by assistants in Mithraistic bull sacrifices.

P-026

AUTHOR: Paris, Pierre
DATE: 1955
TITLE: Esquisse d'une ethnographie navale des peuples annamites [Sketch of an Ethnography of Shipping among the Annamites (Vietnamese)]
IMPRINT: Museum voor Land-en Volkenkunde en Maritiem Museum "Prins Hendrik": Rotterdam, Holland

Construction of and nautical practices associated with all the types of vessels used in recent times by the Vietnamese are described: junks, dhows, praus, canoes with and without outriggers, and large and small rafts (some capable of ocean sailing). Maps show the distribution of the various types of vessels typical of eastern and southern Asia, while two tables show similarities between structural components of Indo-Chinese watercraft and those of other parts of the world. In the section on sailing rafts, similarities are pointed out to Peru and Formosa.

P-027

AUTHOR: Parker, Arthur C.
DATE: 1923
TITLE: Seneca Myths and Folk Tales
IN: Buffalo Historical Society Publications 27:81-82 (Buffalo, New York)

Suggests independent origin of the North American motif of Ursa Major as a bear from native observation that it is in "overturned" position in the winter months, like a hibernating bear. [G-084 finds this or any other explanation for independent development to be inconceivable in light of the degree of detail of Asian parallels.]

P-027B

AUTHOR: Parker, John (author of foreword; no other author listed)
DATE: 1955
TITLE: Antilia and America. A Description of the 1424 Nautical Chart and the Waldseemüller Globe Map of 1507 in the James Ford Bell Collection at the University of Minnesota
IMPRINT: James F. Bell Book Trust (University of Minnesota): Minneapolis

Page 2: If the Spaniards had forgotten the exploits of the Norse by the sixteenth century, the natives of Central America had not, for they told their conquerors of the blond, blue-eyed men who came to them from across the sea and returned again.

Page 3: The present map. "As early as 1424 an unknown Venetian cartographer whose name may have been Zuane Pizzigano drew a chart . . . [which] portrayed the Atlantic Ocean as it was known to him." To the west of the Azores the cartographer placed a group of islands, one of which is named "Antylia." There is no earlier document known which uses this name, and indeed, there is no earlier known chart to show any American lands. This is known as the 1424 Nautical Chart.

Page 4: It would not be abnormal for a ship bound for the Azores or the Canaries, if carried beyond them by storms, to be taken to America and returned to Europe by the currents [Gulf Stream]. This is not to preclude the possibility of intentional voyages to Antilia from Europe.

P-028

AUTHOR: Parker, John
DATE: 1972
TITLE: Discovery: Developing Views of the Earth from Ancient Times to the Voyages of Captain Cook
IMPRINT: Scribner's: New York

Intelligent popular book includes "St. Brendan's Islands" and a few pages on the Vikings. No documentation.

P-029

AUTHOR: Parker, W. T.
DATE: 1901
TITLE: The Religious Character of the North American Indian
IN: Open Court 15:46-56

Favors a theory of Israelite origin for the American Indian.

P-030

AUTHOR: Parrot, André
DATE: 1949
TITLE: Ziggurats et Tour de Babel [Ziggurats and the Tower of Babel]

IN: Michel: Paris

Pages 33-36: The tower of Babel was blown down by the wind, according to one tradition. [Compare I-107 for Mexico.]

Pages 211ff.: Temple chamber atop the sacred pyramid as a contact point with the heavens [as in Mesoamerica].

P-030B

AUTHOR: Parry, J. H.
DATE: 1967
TITLE: The Vinland Story
IN: Perspectives in American History 1:417-433

A review article on Ingstad, Jones, and Skelton et al. from the 1960s. An even-handed treatment of major questions, especially the Vinland Map. One real archaeological discovery south of Newfoundland would settle more than all the speculations based on the sagas.

P-031

AUTHOR: Parsonen, G. S.
DATE: 1962
TITLE: The Settlement of Oceania: An Examination of the Accidental Voyage Theory
IN: Polynesian Navigation; A Symposium on Andrew Sharp's Theory of Accidental Voyages, edited by Jack Golson, Memoir 34 (The Polynesian Society: Wellington), 11-63

Cogent criticism of Sharp's evidence and logic. Supposes that Polynesians intentionally sought better lands when local conditions pushed them to do so. Non-random long voyages were indeed made.

P-033

AUTHOR: Parsons, Jeffrey R.
DATE: 1968
TITLE: The Archaeological Significance of Mahamaes Cultivation on the Coast of Peru
IN: American Antiquity 33:80-85

Sunken pits or basins in the coastal area, called *mahamaes* in Chilca, Peru, are a significant method of irrigation agriculture today and in the archaeological past on the coast of Peru within a 3-5 mile zone parallel to the beach. [Compare Polynesia.]

P-034

AUTHOR: Parsons, Lee A.
DATE: 1961
TITLE: A Fiji-Iroquois War Club
IN: Expedition 4/1:12-13 (Philadelphia)

Refers to a museum item apparently once connected with a circus and probably thus misleadingly labelled as Iroquois though patently Fijian or vice versa.

P-037

AUTHOR: Passarge, Siegfried
DATE: 1926
TITLE: Die politisch-geographischen Grundlage des Südseegebietes vor dem Eintreffen der Europäer [The Political-Geographical Fundamentals of the South Sea Region before Contact with Europeans]
IN: Petermanns Geographische Mitteilungen 72:209-212

Voyagers are unlikely to have been able to cross the Pacific Ocean to America in pre-European times.

P-038B

AUTHOR: Patino, V. M.
DATE: 1963
TITLE: Plantas cultivadas y animales domesticos en América equinoccial

[Cultivated Plants and Domesticated Animals in Equinoctial America]
IMPRINT: Cali, Colombia

The coconut was present and used before the arrival of the Spaniards.

P-039

AUTHOR: Patrón, Pablo
DATE: 1897
TITLE: Origen del Kechúa y del Aymará [Origin of Quechua and Aymara (Languages)]
IMPRINT: Gil: Lima

Claims a Sumerian origin.

P-040

AUTHOR: Patrón, Pablo
DATE: 1901
TITLE: El Perú primitivo; los dioses de la tempestad [Primitive Peru; the Gods of the Storm]
IN: Anales de la Sociedad Científica Argentina 51:145-153

Sumerian and Assyrian words, motifs, and divinities are compared with Quechua.

P-043

AUTHOR: Patrón, Pablo
DATE: 1907
TITLE: Nuevos estudios sobre las lenguas americanas: origen del Kechua y del Aimará [New Studies Concerning the American Languages: The Origin of Quechua and Aymara]
IMPRINT: F. A. Brockhaus: Leipzig

Compares Quechua and Aymara with Sumerian and Assyrian.

P-044

AUTHOR: Patrón, Pablo
DATE: 1908
TITLE: Un huaco con caracteres chino [An Idol with Chinese Characters]
IN: Boletín de la Sociedad Geográfica de Lima 23:241-250

A metal "idol" found among other objects in a cave in Peru in 1865 bears Chinese characters on two constituent metal tablets. The idol figure rests on a snake of a type that did not exist in America but probably belonged to Indochina or Egypt. [Compare L-274 and L-323 which read the characters and consider this a genuine piece.]

P-046

AUTHOR: Patterson, George
DATE: 1892
TITLE: Beothik Vocabularies, with a few Notes on [a] Paper on the Beothiks in "Transactions of the Royal Society of Canada" for 1891
IN: Royal Society of Canada Transactions 10/2:19-32

Beothuk is lightly compared with Malayo-Polynesian. Includes by John Campbell, "Remarks on Preceding Vocabularies."

P-049

AUTHOR: Paulsen, Allison C.
DATE: 1977
TITLE: Patterns of Maritime Trade between South Coastal Ecuador and Western Mesoamerica, 1500 B.C.–A.D. 600
IN: The Sea in the Pre-Columbian World: A Conference at Dumbarton Oaks, October 26th and 27th, 1974, edited by Elizabeth P. Benson (Dumbarton Oaks: Washington, D.C.), 141-160

Methodology. Surveys the evidence for long-distance sea trade along the west coast of the Americas and finds it persuasive for several points in time. The subsequent discussion involving Coe shows, however, the complexity of interpreting such evidence; whether features shared between Mesoamerica and Ecuador are due to diffusion or independent invention is not clear.

P-052

AUTHOR: Paulson, Ivar
DATE: 1952
TITLE: The "Seat of Honor" in Aboriginal Dwellings of the Circumpolar Zone, with Special Regard to the Indians of Northern North America
IN: Indian Tribes of Aboriginal America; Selected Papers of the 29th International Congress of Americanists (New York, 1949), edited by Sol Tax (University of Chicago Press: Chicago), 63-65

This seating spot or holy corner is known widely in Siberia, Central Asia, and Northeastern Europe. The idea is also manifested in North America, Mexico, and Central America.

P-054B

AUTHORS: Payak, M. M., and J. K. S. Sachan
DATE: 1988
TITLE: Maize in Somnathpur, an Indian Mediaeval Temple
IN: Nature 335:773-774

They rebut the initial claim by Johannessen (J-091B) to have found sculptured representations of maize in India.

P-054C

AUTHORS: Payak, M. M., and J. K. S. Sachan
DATE: 1993
TITLE: Maize Ears not Sculpted in 13th Century Somnathpur Temple in India
IN: Economic Botany 47:202-205

They reject the entire contention of Johannessen and Parker [J-095] that maize ears are visible on a sculpture in India, on linguistic, religious, sculptural, archaeological, agricultural, and botanical grounds. The sculptures do not represent maize but an imaginary fruit bearing pearls with a name in Sanskrit. They also rebut criticisms of P-054B by Veena and Sigamani [V-022B].

P-057

AUTHOR: Peabody, Charles
DATE: 1927
TITLE: Red Paint
IN: Journal de la société des américanistes de Paris 19:207-244

European links of these people of northeastern North America?

P-058

AUTHORS: Peabody, Charles, and Warren K. Moorehead
DATE: 1906
TITLE: The So-Called "Gorgets"
IN: Bulletin 2, Department of Archaeology (Phillips Academy: Andover, Massachusetts)

They suggest three possible comparisons in form and meanings of ornaments in Peru and the upper Amazon with eastern Asia, and also between southern Bolivia and Neolithic Portugal.

P-059

AUTHOR: Pearlstone, Zena
DATE: 1973
TITLE: Sujang: A Stirrup Spout Vessel from Nigeria
IN: American Antiquity 38/4:482-486

R-192 published two-stirrup spout vessels from central Africa, which are believed to have been made by the same potter in Mangbetu country around 1930 and which share many features with vessels of the Cupisnique culture of Peru. To

Rowe this constituted a case of independent invention which illustrated the possibility that other Old World cases might be found of this supposedly American shape. F-224 had argued against Rowe's notion. Pearlstone agrees that two "isolated pots, made by the same potter, which have many similarities to Cupisnique types, do not constitute a strong case for the independent invention of the type." More likely modern information had spread [via a Peruvian postage stamp showing such a vessel?] that provided a stimulus or model for the African potter. Other examples from Nigeria are now reported, of unknown date, which are broadly speaking "stirrup-spout vessels" but which have little specific similarity to anything Peruvian. The author concludes that this makes "plausible the suggestion that the [concept of the] stirrup spout and the double spout and bridge forms could have been invented more than once."

P-063

AUTHOR: Pearson, Richard J.
DATE: 1968
TITLE: Migration from Japan to Ecuador: The Japanese Evidence
IN: American Anthropologist 70:85-86

Accuses Meggers, Evans, and Estrada, only on the basis of the literature they cite, of gross ignorance of "Kyushu archaeology." [See M-252 for a discussion of their actual sources, based on museum visits to Japan.]

P-064

AUTHOR: Pedersen, Asbjorn
DATE: 1971
TITLE: Aspectos de la metalurgía indígena americana prehispánica: la huayra y su empleo en el proceso de fundición [Aspects of Native Prehispanic American Metallurgy: The "huayra" and Its Use in the Process of Smelting]
IN: Etnia 14 (Julio/Dic.): 5-10 (Buenos Aires)

A review of chronicle descriptions of metalworking in prehispanic America suggests probable Asiatic influence.

P-065

AUTHOR: Pedersen, Johannes
DATE: 1946
TITLE: Israel, Its Life and Culture, 4 volumes
IMPRINT: Oxford University Press: London; and Branner og Korch: Copenhagen [Translated from Swedish edition of 1920. First published in English by Oxford University Press in 1926; later reprints also exist]

Volumes 3-4:

Page 246: Incense smoke hides from sight a holy object in the temple. [Compare S-053.]

Page 357: Incensing material considered the "blood" of the tree from which it was collected, obtained only after ritual preparation. [Compare T-139, page 142.]

Page 484: Fires and their smoke for Israelite kings at death are implied to serve as a way for the soul's ascent. [Compare B-031 and K-080, for Mesoamerica.] And at Ras Shamra incense was often used at funerals.

P-067

AUTHOR: Peet, Stephen Denison
DATE: 1887a (?)
TITLE: The Religious Beliefs and Traditions of the Aborigines of North America
IMPRINT: Privately printed: n.p. [Apparently from *Transactions of the Victoria Institute*]

There are many symbols, customs and traditions in America which are analogous to those in the east and the Bible: cross or sacred tau, serpent, tree, ark, cloven tongue, pyramids, circumcision, baptism, vestal virgins, tradition of the flood, etc. This proves, perhaps, some common origin long ago.

P-068B

AUTHOR: Peet, Stephen Denison
DATE: 1887b
TITLE: The Serpent Symbol
IN: American Antiquarian and Oriental Journal 9:133-163

Traditions about the serpent associated with both continents (hemispheres) are striking. Examples are cited. "It is possible that we shall find the oriental tradition still connected with the American symbol."

P-069

AUTHOR: Peet, Stephen Denison
DATE: 1888a
TITLE: Animal Worship and Sun Worship in the East and the West Compared
IN: American Antiquarian and Oriental Journal 10:70-95

After considering the serpent, the lion, winged circles, and other symbols associated with the sun in the Old World, he concludes that a human figure seated on a double-headed lion throne represented by John Lloyd Stephens represents "the advent of a Brahman or a Buddhist priest in America."

P-070

AUTHOR: Peet, Stephen Denison
DATE: 1888b
TITLE: The Pyramid in America
IN: American Antiquarian and Oriental Journal 10:221-245

Compares "pyramids" of the Near East and the New World as to symbolism and function and sees a number of points suggesting diffusion to America.

P-071

AUTHOR: Peet, Stephen Denison
DATE: 1888c
TITLE: The Cross in America
IN: American Antiquarian and Oriental Journal 10:292-315

The cross was a sun and weather symbol in ancient North America which commonly appears in petroglyphs and mound artifacts; it was not a Christian symbol.

P-072

AUTHOR: Peet, Stephen Denison
DATE: 1890a
TITLE: The Great Serpent and Other Effigies
IN: American Antiquarian and Oriental Journal 12:211-228

Effigy mounds of Ohio, Wisconsin, etc., display a set of symbols known in the Indo-European area of the Old World: cross, crescent, circle, bird in circle, serpent, and horse shoe-shaped altars.

P-073

AUTHOR: Peet, Stephen Denison
DATE: 1890b
TITLE: Were the Druids in America?
IN: American Antiquarian and Oriental Journal 12:294-302

Sees "Mound-Builder" cults as including cup marks, animal figure pipes offered to the sun, serpent effigy, sun circle and crescent, phallic symbols, cremation, etc., "all the elements of the eastern faiths—Druidic, Phoenician, Hittite."

P-074

AUTHOR: Peet, Stephen Denison
DATE: 1891
TITLE: The Touch of Civilization among the Mound-Builders
IN: American Antiquarian and Oriental Journal 13:174-177

Suggests a possible relationship of mound-building peoples of eastern North America with "civilized races."

P-076

AUTHOR: Peet, Stephen Denison
DATE: 1892
TITLE: The Borrowed Myths of America
IN: American Antiquarian and Oriental Journal 14:336-343

Emphasizes the rule of psychic unity which he briefly applies to explain similarities in stone tools between America and the Old World.

P-076B

AUTHOR: Peet, Stephen Denison
DATE: 1893
TITLE: Commemorative Columns and Ancestor Worship
IN: American Antiquarian and Oriental Journal 15:261-280

Notes cremation and the erection of columns with protruding tongues in the midst of cemeteries as features shared by New Zealand and the Northwest Coast.

P-077

AUTHOR: Peet, Stephen Denison
DATE: 1894a
TITLE: Was There Contact with Asiatic Countries?
IN: American Antiquarian and Oriental Journal 16:175-179

After mentioning various analogies between Asia and America, he issues a challenge. He is willing to forego as evidence the possible elephant trunk(s) or the trunk-like Chinese hook (on the corners of Mesoamerican temples) which he had discussed. However "the law of parallel development will not account" for the [Mayan] globe and animal-headed throne with figure seated cross-legged, Buddha-like, placed in particular orientation to the sun. Likewise unexplainable by that means are the svastika or Hindoo fire-generator and the Maltese cross. Also unexplainable is the priestly costume of a tiger or lion skin found in Egypt, Central America, and the mounds of Ohio. The burden of proof in these matters rests on the autocthonists.

P-079

AUTHOR: Peet, Stephen Denison
DATE: 1894b
TITLE: Sabaeanism or Sky Worship in America
IN: American Antiquarian and Oriental Journal 16:217-237

We find striking relationships of several aboriginal American religions to ancient religions of the East. In regard to the "sky worship" complex, he discusses twelve component elements, including orientation, division of the heavens, sacred mysteries and secret societies, divination, etc., giving American examples. Yet this is only the general religion ("the oldest and most primitive form of nature worship") of "the agricultural races" without particular historical communication being indicated.

P-080

AUTHOR: Peet, Stephen Denison
DATE: 1894c
TITLE: The Zodiac and Orientation in America
IN: American Antiquarian and Oriental Journal 16:245-252

"The constellations were also known in America and were regarded as parts of the zodiac and were given names which resembled those common in the east." Yet he is loath to be definite regarding diffusion, although regarding the solstitial orientation of structural complexes "here we find the analogy between the Egyptian and American systems very startling."

P-082

AUTHOR: Peet, Stephen Denison
DATE: 1894d
TITLE: Secret Societies and Sacred Mysteries
IN: Memoirs of the International Congress of Anthropology, (held in Association with the World Columbian Exposition, Chicago, 1893), edited by C. Staniland Wake (Schulte: Chicago), 176-198

Were such organizations in America part of a single order or did they arise independently among various tribes? "The similarity is due wholly to the identity of psychological action, the same ideas rising from similar impressions in New as in Old World ideas." He pays detailed attention to an address by Garrick Mallery [M-062] in which he compared Israelite practices with those of the Indians, recounting many of Mallery's points, but he insists with Mallery that these have no historical significance, however striking they may appear. Tribes with secret societies were devoted to "nature worship," while sun-worshippers lacked such organizations.

P-083

AUTHOR: Peet, Stephen Denison
DATE: 1895
TITLE: The Story of the Creation among the American Aborigines: A Proof of Prehistoric Contact
IN: American Antiquarian and Oriental Journal 17:127-150

Compares North American and Asiatic creation accounts.

P-085

AUTHOR: Peet, Stephen Denison
DATE: 1901
TITLE: Stone Circles in Europe and America
IN: American Antiquarian and Oriental Journal 23:371-377

Comparison of works at Portsmouth, Ohio, with Avebury, England.

P-086

AUTHOR: Peet, Stephen Denison
DATE: 1902a
TITLE: Human Figures in American and Oriental Art Compared
IN: American Antiquarian and Oriental Journal 24:109-124

Pages 119-120: Now contradicts his view in P-077. The cosmic egg, serpent, swastika hooked cross, etc., "are all so indefinite and so varied, that they only confuse rather than give force to the argument, so that at present it must be left an open question, whether there was contact between the two continents in prehistoric times or not."

P-088

AUTHOR: Peet, Stephen Denison
DATE: 1902b
TITLE: Double-headed Serpent and the Migration of Symbols
IN: American Antiquarian and Oriental Journal 24:482-483

Comparative discussion of a symbol [the amphisbaena] on the Northwest American coast with attention to its mythic background, including Old World occurrences.

P-089

AUTHOR: Peet, Stephen Denison
DATE: 1903
TITLE: The Migration of Symbols
IN: American Antiquarian and Oriental Journal 25:318-337

Comparison of prehistoric American symbols with those from Asia and North Africa.

P-090

AUTHOR: Peet, Stephen Denison
DATE: 1905a

TITLE: Myths and Symbols; or, Aboriginal Religions in America
IMPRINT: Office of the American Antiquarian: Chicago

A book compiled from Peet's writings in the *American Antiquarian* including such as P-081 and P-089. His general view is that the frequent "analogies" he points out between Old and New World cultures are the result of natural, evolutionary developments acting independently in each hemisphere. In America particularly many of the symbols seen were "personifications of the powers of nature."

P-091

AUTHOR: Peet, Stephen Denison
DATE: 1905b
TITLE: The Story of the Deluge
IN: American Antiquarian and Oriental Journal 27:201-216

Comparative study of flood myths in both hemispheres, to no definite end.

P-093

AUTHOR: Pendlebury, J. D. S.
DATE: 1939
TITLE: The Archaeology of Crete
IMPRINT: Metheun: London [Reprinted Bilbo and Tanner: New York, 1963]

Pages 130, 270: Use of the litter in Minoan Crete.

P-094

AUTHOR: Pell, Herbert
DATE: 1948
TITLE: The Old Stone Mill, Newport
IN: Rhode Island History 7:105-119

The tower was the work of shipwrecked mariners, most likely Cortereal and companions.

P-095

AUTHOR: Pelliot, Paul
DATE: 1925
TITLE: Quelques textes chinois concernant l'Indochine hindouisée [Some Chinese Texts about Hinduized Indochina]
IN: Publications de l'École française d'Extrême-Orient 20, Études asiatiques 2:243-263

Pages 255-260: A Chinese source from A.D. 300 speaks of four-masted ships of India which were 50 meters long and capable of carrying 600-700 men and 1000 tons of cargo.

P-096

AUTHOR: Pendergast, David M.
DATE: 1957
TITLE: Further Data on Pacific Coast Fired Clay Figurines
IN: American Antiquity 23:178-180

A ceramic figurine from Washington [like those reported by S-430 to be of Japanese origin] is related to similar objects from northern California. The California instance is assumed to be an independent invention of the figurine concept.

P-098

AUTHOR: Peralta, Jesús T.
DATE: 1980
TITLE: Ancient Mariners of the Philippines
IN: Archaeology 33/5:41-48

Wooden remains of three balanghai-type boats are reported, up to 15 meters long. C-14 dating puts one at A.D. 320, another at A.D. 1250. Essentially similar boats are still used in the Philippines and Indonesia.

P-099

AUTHOR: Pérez, José
DATE: 1862

TITLE: Mémoire sur les relations des anciens Américaines avec les peuples de l'Europe, de l'Asie, et de l'Afrique [Memoir on Contacts between Ancient Americans and Peoples of Europe, Asia, and Africa]
IN: Revue orientale et américaine 8:162 (Paris)

Includes a section on knowledge of America supposedly possessed by the Chinese (Fu-sang).

P-100

AUTHOR: Pérez Aranda, Conrado
DATE: 1895
TITLE: Memoria sobre las imigraciones a la América en general y cuáles hayan llegado al actual territorio mexicano [Memoir Concerning Immigrations to America in General and Those That Reached the Present Territory of Mexico]
IMPRINT: Privately printed: Alamos, Sonora, México

See P-101.

P-101

AUTHOR: Pérez Aranda, Conrado
DATE: 1897
TITLE: Imigraciones a la América en general y cuales hayan llegado al actual territorio mexicano [Immigrations to America in General and Those That Reached the Present Territory of Mexico]
IN: Proceedings of the 11th International Congress of Americanists (Mexico, 1895), 324-356

A rambling concatenation of observations which concludes: There were numerous immigrations from Asia both by land (Bering Strait) and by sea (the North Pacific current). A few immigrations came via the Atlantic current, from (North) Africa, and there were very rare arrivals from the Pacific islands via the equatorial counter-current. The first immigrants to Mexico were Otomis via California and Maya speakers via Chiapas, both arriving from East Asia by way of the North Pacific current. Later the Chichimecs, Nahoas, and barbarous tribes of the North came from Asia by land.

P-102

AUTHOR: Pérez Castro, Federico
DATE: 1971
TITLE: La "inscripción" fenicio-cananea de Paraiba (Brasil) (La polémica Gordon/Friedrich-Cross). Estado de la cuestión [The Phoenician-Canaanite "Inscription" of Parahyba (The Gordon/Friedrich-Cross Polemic). State of the Question]
IN: Anuario de estudios atlánticos 17:307-333 (Madrid) [Primer Simposio internacional sobre posibles relaciones trasatlánticas precolombinas (Islas Canarias, 1970)]

An attempt at an objective analysis of the opposing arguments about this inscription, without reaching a conclusion. Features a lengthy technical commentary on details of Gordon's proposed decipherment. Includes references not incorporated in the present bibliography.

P-103

AUTHOR: Pérez de Barradas, José
DATE: 1946 (1947)
TITLE: Origen oceánico de las culturas arcaicas de Colombia [Oceanic Origin of the Archaic Cultures of Colombia]
IN: Boletín de la Academía de Historia 120:249-259 (Madrid)

Holds for Australian and Melanesian migrations to America based on 62 parallels he lists from Rivet, Graebner, and Nordenskiöld.

P-104

AUTHOR: Pérez de Barradas, José
DATE: 1954
TITLE: Orfebrería prehispánica de Colombia [Prehispanic Gold Work from Colombia]
IMPRINT: Talleres Gráfico "Jura": Madrid [2nd edition 1958]

Pages 310, 320ff.: Notes parallels between the sculptures of San Agustin and those of Easter Island, the Marquesas, and Samoa, and of a special type of collar made of cylindrical, anthropomorphic stone beads with double perforation which is similarly shared.

P-105

AUTHOR: Pérez de Barradas, José
DATE: 1956
TITLE: Viejas y nuevas teorías sobre el origen de la orfebrería prehispánica en Colombia [Old and New Theories Concerning the Origin of Prehispanic Gold Working in Colombia]
IMPRINT: Banco de la República: Bogotá

Reviews theories concerning the origin of Colombian goldworking, from that of Rivet, who places the origin in the Guianas, to that of Heine-Geldern, who postulates a series of migrations across the Pacific.

Favors the latter theory because of the absence from the New World of the earlier stages in the development of Old World metallurgy and because of the resemblances noted by Heine-Geldern between Old and New World art.

P-106

AUTHOR: Pérez de Vega, Francisco
DATE: 1952
TITLE: Afinidades lingüísticas del Japonés y el Karibe; apuntes para el estudio de una correlación fonética, morfológica y sintáctica de dichos idiomas [Linguistic Affinities of the Japanese and the Caribs; Notes for the Study of a Phonetic, Morphologic, and Syntactic Correlation of Said Languages]
IMPRINT: Grafolit: Caracas

Words and particles combine with the Diego blood-group factor to show a relation between the two areas.

P-107

AUTHOR: Pérez de Vega, Francisco
DATE: 1957
TITLE: Las lenguas aborígenes; contribución a la lingüística comparativa e histórica de los idiomas aborígenes americanos y su correlación con las lenguas orientales [Aboriginal Languages: Contribution to the Comparative and Historical Linguistics of the Aboriginal Languages of America, and Their Relation with the Languages of the Orient]
IMPRINT: Editorial "Daily Journal": Caracas [2nd edition, corrected and expanded, Editorial Ciencia: Madríd and Caracas, 1960]

An attempt to classify American Indian languages according to whether they contain l and/or r sounds, and to relate them to oriental languages on this odd basis.

P-108

AUTHOR: Pericot y García, Luís
DATE: 1936
TITLE: Historia de América y de los pueblos americanos, vol 1: América indígena, el hombre americano, los pueblos de América [History of America and of the American Peoples, vol. 1: Native America, American Man, the American Peoples]

IMPRINT: Salvat, Barcelona
[Revised edition *América indígena* (Salvat: Barcelona, 1962)]

[Revised edition.] The third chapter faithfully reviews every theory of the origin of American Indians, whether scientific, fantastic, or biblical. Probably the most detailed survey of theories of American origins, but it is not accompanied by much of a critical sense, and it lacks developments since 1950. Many of its references are incorporated into the present bibliography.

P-109

AUTHOR: Pericot y García, Luís
DATE: 1954
TITLE: Sobre el problema de las relaciones preneolíticas entre España y Marruecos
[Concerning the Problem of the Pre-Neolithic Relations between Spain and Morocco]
IN: I Congreso Arqueológico del Marruecos Español (Tetuán, 1954) (Servicio de Arqueología: Tetuán), 57-65

Possible drift boats to America.

P-110

AUTHOR: Pericot y García, Luís
DATE: 1955
TITLE: Algunos nuevos aspectos de los problemas de la prehistoria de Canarias
[Some New Aspects of Problems of the Prehistory of the Canaries]
IN: Anuario de estudios atlánticos 1:579-619

Page 595: Obsidian-studded clubs of the Nicarao and the macuahuitl of the Aztecs have a striking similarity in Canary Island clubs (with a roughly similar name).

P-111

AUTHOR: Pericot y García, Luís
DATE: 1962
TITLE: El punto de vista de un arqueólogo europeo ante los problemas de la prehistoria americana
[The Point of View of a European Archaeologist with Respect to the Problems of American Prehistory]
IN: Jornadas Internacionales de Arqueología y Etnografía: Segunda Mesa Redonda International de Arqueología y Etnografía, vol. 2: La Arqueología y Etnografía Argentina y sus Correlaciones Continentales y Extracontinentales (Nov./Dic. 1960): 10-18, Comisión Nacional Ejecutiva, 150o. Aniversario de la Revolución de Mayo, Buenos Aires

Pages 17-18: He is delighted that the anti-isolationists of the European schools (Schmidt, Rivet, Heine-Geldern) have "triumphed" over the isolationist North Americans. Passage of cultural features via the Atlantic must surely have played a role. Even though he is not very sympathetic to Heyerdahl, he credits him with breaching the mental barrier that crossing the ocean had been for most scholars.

P-112

AUTHOR: Pericot y García, Luís
DATE: 1963
TITLE: Africa y América: el problema de sus posibles contactos pre-colombinos
[Africa and America: The Problem of Their Possible Pre-Columbian Contacts]
IMPRINT: Instituto de Estudios Africanos: Madrid

Pages 8-9: Compares petroglyph themes between Old and New Worlds. Many Bronze Age motifs found from Ireland through Iberia and the Canaries to the Atlas Mountains are widespread in the Americas. He supposes that accidental voyages carried people and those motifs to America.

P-114

AUTHOR: Pericot y García, Luís
DATE: 1971a
TITLE: El problema del Atlántico en la prehistoria
[The Problem of the Atlantic in Prehistory]
IN: Anuario de estudios atlánticos 17:21-31 (Madrid)

See P-115.

P-115

AUTHOR: Pericot y García, Luís
DATE: 1971b
TITLE: El problema de los contactos prehistóricos afroamericanos
[The Problem of Prehistoric Afro-American Contacts]
IN: Revista de Indias 31/123-124:173-181 (Madrid)

Urges the need for serious study of possible contacts between the African continent and pre-Columbian America, directly or through the Canary Islands.

P-117

AUTHORS: Pericot y García, Luis, and Juan Maluquer de Motes
DATE: 1970
TITLE: La humanidad prehistórica
[Prehistoric Humanity]
IMPRINT: Salvat Editores: Estella, Navarra, Spain

Neolithic developments were connected to the "New World Neolithic" down to the time of the Phoenicians and Greeks.

P-117B

AUTHORS: Pericot García, Luis, and A. Venturina
DATE: 1930
TITLE: Aborígenes de Sudamérica
[Aborigines of South America]
IMPRINT: Los aborígenes de América, Cervantes: Barcelona

See P-108.

P-118

AUTHOR: Perkins, Dixie L.
DATE: 1979
TITLE: The Meaning of the New Mexico Mystery Stone
IMPRINT: Sun Publishing: Albuquerque

A translation of the Los Lunas Stone which claims that it tells in Greek the story of an exile from Greece. [See a strong critique in L-167C.]

P-120

AUTHOR: Perry, William James
DATE: 1915
TITLE: The Geographical Distribution of Terraced Cultivation and Irrigation
IN: Memoirs and Proceedings of the Manchester Literary and Philological Society 60/6:1-22

Methods and uses in the Near East, South Asia, China, Malaysia, Polynesia, and America, which were introduced by Egyptians and Phoenicians, with an addition by Elliot Smith on pages 23-25.

P-122

AUTHOR: Perry, William James
DATE: 1919
TITLE: The Significance of the Search for Amber in Antiquity
IN: Journal of the Manchester Egyptian and Oriental Society 8:71ff.

Egyptian desire to obtain amber is reflected in American civilizations which also treasured the substance.

P-123

AUTHOR: Perry, William James
DATE: 1921
TITLE: The Development and Spread of Civilization
IN: Nature 107:146-148

"In only one region of the world—the Near East—can progressive development of culture be established in ancient times. In that region civilisation probably first appeared." "Everywhere in the world outside the area directly and continuously influenced by this region, the story from the beginning is one of uninterrupted degeneration in arts and crafts."

P-124

AUTHOR: Perry, William James
DATE: 1923
TITLE: The Children of the Sun: A Study in the Early History of Civilization
IMPRINT: Dutton: New York; and Methuen: London

Following Elliot Smith's "heliolithic theory" the writer derives the civilizations of the world from the Sixth dynasty of Egypt. The Phoenicians, from their reputed homeland in the Persian Gulf, are given the major credit for transporting (elements of) Egyptian culture through the Pacific and to the New World. A chapter is devoted to a potpourri of comparative data on many topics: dual organization, totemic clan system, exogamy, the underworld, mother-right doctrine of "theogamy," sky-gods as life-givers, etc.

P-125

AUTHOR: Perry, William James
DATE: 1925
TITLE: Pearls and Pearl-shell in the Pacific
IN: Man 25:37-41

Another valuable sought by the Egyptians in Oceania and America.

P-126

AUTHOR: Perry, William James
DATE: 1928
TITLE: The Children of the Sun
IN: Man 28:163-164

A continuation of interchange via the letters column in this journal between Perry and critics. Here Perry comments on four cases of supposed independent invention produced by Hutton at Perry's challenge: fire piston, bull roarer, use of adrenalin as arrow poison and use of suggestion in medicine and magic [H-509]. Perry clumsily points out some of the problems with over-simple thinking about this problem manifested by Hutton. Anticipates a few points more fully raised much later in C-158.

P-127

AUTHOR: Perry, William James
DATE: 1931
TITLE: The Coming of the Warriors
IN: The Making of Man, edited by V. F. Calverton (Modern Library: New York), 306-330

The warriors, the "Children of the Sun," brought the sun cult, developed agriculture, and cities to many areas of Asia, Oceania, and America. Behind much mythology in, e.g., North America, we can see a political revolution in which the peaceful and enlightened Children of the Sun and their sun gods were replaced by others, less advanced in civilization but more warlike.

P-128

AUTHOR: Perry, William James
DATE: 1932
TITLE: The Age of the Gods
IN: The Frazer Lectures, 1922-1932, by Divers Hands, edited by Warren R. Dawson (Macmillan: London)

Among examples of the migrational impact of "The Children of the Sun," who first appear in Egypt during the Fifth Dynasty, he includes the civilizations of Peru and Mexico and the Natchez Indians of Louisiana.

P-128B

AUTHOR: Pertek, Jerzy
DATE: 1957
TITLE: Polacy na szlakach morskich swiata [Poles on the High Seas]
IMPRINT: Zaklad Narodowy im. Ossolinskich we Wroclawiu: Gdansk, Poland [In English, *Poles on the High Seas* (same publisher: Warsaw, 1978)]

Poland's leading authority on naval history mentions Polish traditions of Atlantic sailings by "Iohannes Scolnus" or "John of Kolno," a Pole, who has been supposed to have reached America.

P-129

AUTHOR: Pesce, Hugo
DATE: 1951
TITLE: Lepra en el Perú precolombiano [Leprosy in Pre-Columbian Peru]
IN: Conferencia de Ciencias Antropológicas (Lima, 1951), 1:171-187

A highly-documented and well-argued evaluation of types of evidence which might show the pre-Columbian presence of leprosy, from chroniclers, linguistics, mummies, and pottery effigies. So far no good evidence exists for leprosy, but there is conclusive evidence for leishmaniasis, verruga, and syphilis. A case can be made also for tuberculosis and exanthematic typhus. All these show some consequences which might be confounded with leprosy. Work on mummies is called for.

P-130

AUTHOR: Peschel, Oscar
DATE: 1894 [1874]
TITLE: The Races of Man, and Their Geographical Distribution
IMPRINT: D. Appleton: New York [Translated from the German 2nd edition, 1874, of a volume not named by the author in the preface]

A long section (pages 400ff.) on "The Aborigines of America" argues at length on evolutionary grounds that ethnological features in the New World were independent developments, for the most part, and that the lesser level of development resulted from smaller population, less variety of environments and natural species, etc., which allowed "the struggle for existence" to go only so far.

Pages 440-441: Reciting a few examples, he argues that occasional mariners would not have had civilizing effect upon arriving in America, rather, they would have become barbaric themselves if not slain.

P-131

AUTHOR: Peterken, E.
DATE: n.d. [c. 1880]
TITLE: L'homme blanc et la croix en Amérique [The White Man and the Cross in America]
IN: Proceedings of the 3rd International Congress of Americanists (Brussels, 1879), 1:507-518

The presence of white men in America is independent of voyages from Europe. Skin color was caused by environment, and at times in North (and southern South) America white skins were produced on the same basis as in Europe. But Phoenicians and Etruscans may also have arrived.

P-132

AUTHOR: Peterson, Betty C.
DATE: 1988
TITLE: More on Bat Creek

IN: NEARA [New England Antiquities Research Association] Journal 23/1, 2:26-28

Summarizes conventional and recent diffusionist and other discussions of this inscription (McCulloch, Carter, Traveller Bird, Kling).

P-133

AUTHOR: Peterson, C. Stewart
DATE: 1946
TITLE: America's Rune Stone of A.D. 1362 Gains Favor
IMPRINT: Hobson: New York

Testimonials and standard arguments in favor of the authenticity of the Kensington Stone.

P-135

AUTHOR: Petersen, E. Allen
DATE: 1954
TITLE: In a Junk across the Pacific
IMPRINT: Elek: London

A couple plus two hands sail a small junk from Shanghai to California, along the coast to Peru, then to New Guinea where war interrupts them.

P-135B

AUTHORS: Petersen, K. S., K. L. Rasmussen, J. Heinemeier, and N. Rud
DATE: 1992
TITLE: Clams before Columbus?
IN: Nature 359 (October 22): 679

Shell of the American soft-shell clam (Mya arenaria) was discovered off the Danish coast, contrary to received opinion to now. A radiocarbon date in the 13th century for this shell leaves only "very slight probability" of its dating after Columbus. Since the transfer had to be by humans, it "could have been transferred from North America to Europe by the Vikings."

P-136

AUTHOR: Petitot, Émile Fortuné Stanislas Joseph
DATE: 1875
TITLE: Les Esquimaux et les Déné-Dindjiés [The Eskimos and the Dene-Dindjie (People)]
IN: Proceedings of the 1st International Congress of Americanists (Nancy, 1875), 1:329-339; 2:13-37, 245-256

The middle portion offers 29 parallels to demonstrate that the Dene of northwestern America had an "Asiatic" origin. The "Asiatic" material is most often drawn from the Old Testament (e.g., circumcision). His final portion argues passionately for the unity of American and Asian peoples and their general relation to the biblical account of the creation of man.

P-138

AUTHOR: Petitot, Émile Fortuné Stanislas Joseph
DATE: 1878-1879
TITLE: Six légendes américaines identifiées à l'histoire de Moïse et du peuple hébreu [Six American Legends Identified with the History of Moses and the Hebrew People]
IN: Les Missions Catholiques de Lyon 10/491–11/510:476-478, 488-491, 499-502, 512-514, 583-586, 605-607, 616-620, 3-5, 21-22, 32-35, 45-48, 57-59, 68-71, 81-83, 93-95, 115-119, 131-134, 156-158

Very vague parallels to portions of the Old Testament from Creek, Blackfoot, and Tzendal myths. Conclusion: A majority of the great American family of the Dindjié-dènè-nabajos-aztèques are remnants of the Israelites taken captive to Chaldea, or rather ancient proselytes to Judaism immigrated from Asia via the Aleutian Islands, most anciently in the sixth or fifth centuries B.C.

P-139

AUTHOR: Petitot, Émile Fortuné Stanislas Joseph

DATE: 1879

TITLE: De l'origine asiatique des Indiens de l'Amérique arctique [On the Asiatic Origin of the Indians of the American Arctic]

IN: Les Missions Catholiques de Lyon 10/543–550: 529-532, 540-544, 550-553, 564-566, 576-578, 589-591, 600-604, 609-611 [Reprinted 1884 in *Société philologique, Alençon, Actes* 10:170-192]

Gives a series of parallels (artifacts, myths, customs, cranial features) which he considers indicate an Asian origin for the Dènè (examples: boomerang, trident, bowl, spoon, javelin, canoe, iron).

P-140

AUTHOR: Petitot, Émile Fortuné Stanislas Joseph

DATE: 1880

TITLE: Légendes américaines identifiquées à l'histoire de Moïse et du peuple hébreu [American Legends Identified with the History of Moses and the Hebrew People]

IN: Annales de la propagation de la foi pour la province de Québec (février): 10:33-79

See P-138.

P-141

AUTHOR: Petitot, Émile Fortuné Stanislas Joseph

DATE: 1883

TITLE: Parallèle des coutumes et des croyances de la famille caraïbo-esquimaude avec celles des peuples altaïques et puniques [Customs and Beliefs of the Carib-Eskimo Family Parallel with Those of the Altaic and Punic Peoples]

IN: Association française pour l'avancement des Sciences, Rouen, 12e. session, 1883, séance du 23 août, 686-697

In addition to a comparison of customs and beliefs, various Eurasiatic language comparisons are made. Celtic elements are in Algonquian language as well as Semitic features among Eskimo.

P-142

AUTHOR: Petitot, Émile Fortuné Stanislas Joseph

DATE: 1884

TITLE: De la prétendue origine orientale des Algonquins [On the Claimed Oriental Origin of the Algonquians]

IN: Société d'anthropologie de Paris, Bulletins et Mémoires, Séance du 20 mars, Série 3e., 78:248-256

They were ultimately Semites.

P-143

AUTHOR: Petitot, Émile Fortuné Stanislas Joseph

DATE: 1889-1890

TITLE: Théogonie des Danites américains [The Theogeny of the American Danites (Déné)]

IN: Revue des religions (1889): 206-220; (1890): 116-134

The Déné were originally the Israelite tribe of Dan.

P-144

AUTHOR: Petitot, Émile Fortuné Stanislas Joseph

DATE: 1890a

TITLE:	Accord des mythologies dans la cosmogonie des Danites arctiques [Agreement of the Mythology with the Cosmogony of the Arctic Danites]
IMPRINT:	Emile Bouillon: Paris

Again, the supposed Israelite connection of the Déné.

P-145

AUTHOR:	Petitot, Émile Fortuné Stanislas Joseph
DATE:	1890b
TITLE:	Origine asiatique des Esquimaux [The Asiatic Origin of the Eskimos]
IMPRINT:	D'Esperance Gagniard: Rouen

Contains a lexical table showing similarities he sees between words of the Old and New Worlds, including a number of Athabascan languages.

P-146

AUTHOR:	Petitot, Émile Fortuné Stanislas Joseph
DATE:	1892
TITLE:	Origine asiatique des Esquimaux [Asiatic Origin of the Eskimos]
IN:	Proceedings of the 8th International Congress of Americanists (Paris, 1890), pages 296-297 [Also 1890, Société normande de géographie de Rouen, Bulletin, 33]

Only a summary. He relies on word comparisons between Eskimo and Turanian, Altaic, Uralo-Altaic, Tartar and Scythian.

P-147

AUTHOR:	Petrie, W. M. Flinders
DATE:	1907
TITLE:	Soul-houses in Egypt
IN:	Records of the Past 6:195-201

Ceramic models of houses are reprised. They were "originally placed upon the surface of the grave, to give shelter to the soul when it came out in search of sustenance." [Compare Chinese and West Mexican ceramic houses, W-197?]

P-148

AUTHOR:	Pettazzoni, Raffaele
DATE:	1924
TITLE:	The Chain of Arrows: The Diffusion of a Myth Motive
IN:	Folklore 35:151-165

This widespread motif involves one or more persons climbing from earth to heaven and sometimes descending again. It is distributed on the Northwest Coast, in California and among the Zuñi, and in South America among the Tupí, as well as in Melanesia, but not in Polynesia, Asia, Australia, nor Africa. In fact a related motif (involving spears) is found in Australia where the bow and arrow were lacking. Concludes that the presence of a myth motif does not necessarily mean that the entire culture complex to which it originally belonged had diffused with it. And when a motif spreads from its original culture complex to a foreign one, it normally is adapted to the new milieu, i.e., it is acculturated.

P-151

AUTHOR:	Phebus, George F.
DATE:	1974
TITLE:	"Konapee's Money?" Elicits Smithsonian Response
IN:	Screenings 23/2:2-3 (Oregon Archaeological Society, Portland)

Concerning Asiatic coins found in the Northwest.

P-152

AUTHOR:	Phene, John S.
DATE:	n.d. [c. 1880]
TITLE:	Les mounds d'Amérique qui simulent des formes animales, comparés à ceux de même genre trouvés en Europe et en Asia [The Mounds of America Which Simulate Animal Forms Compared

to Those of the Same Type Found in Europe and in Asia]
IN: Proceedings of the 3rd International Congress of Americanists (Brussels, 1879), 2:36-41

From his own visits and from the literature, he describes mounds in the shape of snakes, elephant, etc., found in North America, China, and Europe and the Mediterranean. Some are natural, some artificial, and some natural but modified by men. These became the seat of cults to those animals. Leaves it unclear if he involves diffusion, but it appears not.

P-153

AUTHOR: Philips-Birt, Douglas
DATE: 1966
TITLE: Ships and Boats: The Nature of Their Design
IMPRINT: Studio Vista: London [German edition Delius/Klasing: Bielefeld, 1979]

Pages 56-57: Reports an 1893 voyage of a reconstructed Viking ship to North America.

P-155

AUTHOR: Philipson, David
DATE: 1905
TITLE: Are There Traces of the Ten Lost Tribes in Ohio?
IN: American Jewish Historical Society Publications 13:37-46

A rhetorically embellished narration of Wyrick's discovery of the Newark Holy Stone and subsequent controversy. They were proven frauds after Wyrick's death by the discovery in his office of stones on which he had been practicing engraving Hebrew characters.

P-157

AUTHOR: Phillipps, William John
DATE: 1965
TITLE: The Tomoyé, a Japanese Symbol
IN: Journal of the Polynesian Society 74:486-487

"It is of interest to record that the Tomoyé appears to have correspondence with the three armed swastika found in North America and elsewhere in Asia. The conception of all swastika forms as being symbols of good fortune appears to be world wide."

P-158

AUTHOR: Phillips, L. L.
DATE: 1976
TITLE: Cotton
IN: Evolution of Crop Plants, edited by N. W. Simmonds (Longmans: London), 196-200

Summarizes theories of the origin of cotton. His conclusion on American cotton: "Origin of the New World amphidiploid probably took place since the start of the Pleistocene in northern South America following oceanic drift of an A genome propagule from Africa." G. tomentosum is unique to Hawaii; no cotton resembling it is from America. [S-246 gives a different picture.]

P-159

AUTHOR: Phillips, Philip
DATE: 1966
TITLE: The Role of Transpacific Contacts in the Development of New World Pre-Columbian Civilizations
IN: Archaeological Frontiers and External Connections, edited by Gordon F. Ekholm and Gordon R. Willey, volume 4 of Handbook of Middle American Indians (University of Texas Press: Austin), 296-315

Primarily a rebuttal of Heine-Geldern, in the same volume, denying contacts to explain cultural similarities between Mesoamerica and Southeast Asia. The theoretical orientation and logic are orthodox for the 1930-40s. What is important, we are told, is whether transpacific "contacts could have been determinant at critical moments in the development of American culture," that is, whether any contacts there might have been "decisive in the development of Nuclear American civilizations." The issue is also put as concerning "the unity of New and Old World civilizations." [Whether it is sound to speak of a monolithic "American culture" or "Nuclear American civilizations" is not discussed.]

He treats "plant domestication" and "the first appearance of pottery" with special concern for whether Woodland pottery could be of Asiatic origin. (Reasoning: "Woodland is after all a refocalization of Asiatic traits that came into eastern North America not as a complex but separately and at different times." "Whatever the ultimate origins, it is becoming clear that the earliest diffusion of pottery in North America was in a nonagricultural context, and this may have been true for Nuclear America as well." Hence, "the effect of an admission of remote Asiatic origin of pottery on the integrity of Nuclear American civilizations would be just about nil.")

Other brief discussions turn aside diffusionist claims often on grounds of chronology and always on the ground that the supposed importation had no demonstrated significance for "the development" of the American cultural expression in question. Treatments are given on jade and turquoise, tripod pottery, figurines, ceremonial/temple centers, monumental architecture, pyramidal mounds, metallurgy, writing, numeration, the calendar, art styles, etc., often specifically confronting diffusionist arguments. [See M-109 for a strong critique.]

P-160

AUTHOR: Piankoff, A.
DATE: 1934
TITLE: The Sky-goddess Nut and the Night Journey of the Sun
IN: Journal of Egyptian Archaeology 20:57-61

The sun and the dead were "swallowed" by Nut in the evening and born again in the morning. As far back as the pyramid texts the dead, born again, would reach the sky, and "his lot would be like that of the celestial bodies." [Compare N-107 and K-110.]

Page 61: Piankoff argues that the Egyptian conception was that the sun at night moves above Nut for its return journey. Notes in the Jewish Baraita Pesahim (94 b) the statement, "The learned of Israel say, 'The sun moves by day beneath the firmament, and by night above the firmament; the learned of the nations [gentiles] say 'The sun moves by day beneath the firmament, and by night beneath the earth.' " (Citation to *Jewish Encyclopedia,* "Astronomy," page 248.)

P-161

AUTHORS: Piazza, A., P. Menossi, and L. L. Cavalli-Sforza
DATE: 1981
TITLE: Synthetic Gene Frequency Maps of Man and Selective Effects of Climate
IN: Proceedings of the National Academy of Sciences 78:2638-2642 (Washington)

Climatic selection results in latitudinal variation of peoples, which would tend to hide or dilute evidence of any historical factors in the form of genetic or phenotypical characteristics.

P-163

AUTHOR: Pickersgill, Barbara
DATE: 1972
TITLE: Cultivated Plants as Evidence for Cultural Contacts
IN: American Antiquity 37:97-103

Finding "the same" plant in two locations is not necessarily good evidence of human contact. At least species must be identified, for different groups of people have separately cultivated different species of the same genus, and even the same species, independently in different areas.

Only after these botanical possibilities for independent invention have been eliminated can one confidently suppose cultural contact. [For a critical comment see J-080.]

P-163B

AUTHOR: Pickersgill, Barbara
DATE: 1976
TITLE: Pineapple
IN: Evolution of Crop Plants, edited by N. W. Simmonds (Longman: London and New York), 14-18

"The pineapple has been supposed to support theories of pre-Columbian trans-oceanic contacts. Heyerdahl claimed that pineapples were present in the Marquesas before Europeans discovered Polynesia. Merrill (1954) discounted this and stated that the first record of the pineapple in Polynesia was 1769 when Captain Cook sowed pineapple seeds in Tahiti. Pineapples have also been identified on wall carvings in ancient Assyria, on pottery models in Egyptian tombs and on murals at Pompeii, but the reproductions that have been published are not convincing and the pre-Columbian presence of the crop in the Old World remains non-proven."

P-164

AUTHORS: Pickersgill, Barbara, and A. H. Bunting
DATE: 1969
TITLE: Cultivated Plants and the Kon-Tiki Theory
IN: Nature 222/5190:225-227

Gaps in botanical knowledge are great, but today Heyerdahl has less support from botany than when he published first. The most telling argument is negative (absence of shared crop plants). They briefly discuss evidence for sweet potato, coconut, cotton, and bottle gourd. The diffusionists' case is "often speculative and open to alternative interpretation."

P-165

AUTHOR: Pidgeon, Harry
DATE: 1932
TITLE: Around the World Single-handed: The Cruise of the "Islander"
IMPRINT: D. Appleton: New York [Reprinted R. Hart-Davis: London, 1950; reprinted DeGraff: New York, 1960]

From Los Angeles in 1921 to the Marquesas, across the Pacific and Indian Oceans, and to the U.S. via St. Helena.

P-167

AUTHORS: Pierson, Larry J., and James R. Moriarty
DATE: 1980
TITLE: Stone Anchors: Asiatic Shipwrecks off the California Coast
IN: Anthropological Journal of Canada 18:17-23

Heavy stones discovered in the ocean off Redondo Beach were anchors from Chinese ships or rafts, they believe. [Compare F-212.]

P-168

AUTHOR: Piétri, J. B.
DATE: 1949
TITLE: Voiliers d'Indochine, nouvelle edition [Sailboats of Indochina, new edition]
IMPRINT: Société des imprimeries et libraries Indochinoises: Saigon

A superb description and album of drawings of scores of types of Indochinese junks and rafts, including details of rigging, sails, anchors, etc.

P-169

AUTHOR: Pijl, L. van der
DATE: 1938

TITLE: Disharmony between Asiatic Flower-birds and American Bird-flowers
IN: Annales du jardin botanique de Buitenzorg 68/1:17-26

A difference typically distinguishes American and Asiatic bird-pollinated flowers. The American ones are placed in such a way that they can be reached by a pollinating bird from the air while hovering directly outside the blossom, while the latter are reached only by a bird sitting on the foliage. Some Old World species of hibiscus are enigmatic exceptions to this rule. In their most specialized adaptations they differ to such a degree that, in many instances, mutual relations in Asia are questionable. "I dare not say that the above results point to an American origin of H. rosa sinensis, but it is certain that both [the anomalous Asian] Hibiscus-species . . . would fit very well" if we assumed that they were originally adapted to the behavior of humming birds, which are native to America.

P-170
AUTHOR: Pilling, James C.
DATE: 1891
TITLE: Some Queer American Characters
IN: Analostan Magazine 1:58-67

Description of various hieroglyphs, alphabets, and syllabaries in use among the Indians.

P-170B
AUTHOR: Pillot, Gilbert
DATE: 1972
TITLE: Did the Greeks Sail the Atlantic? The Secret Code
IMPRINT: Abelard-Schuman: London and New York
[Translated from *Le Code Secret de l'Odyssée* (Robert Laffont: Paris, 1969)]

The Odyssey reached the Canaries, Madeira, the Hebrides, and Iceland, but nothing is said of America.

P-172
AUTHORS: Piña Chan, Román, and Luis Covarrubias
DATE: 1964
TITLE: El pueblo del jaguar (Los olmecas arqueológicos)
[The People of the Jaguar (The Archaeological Olmecs)]
IMPRINT: Consejo para la Planeación e Instalación del Museo Nacional de Antropología: México

Asiatic ceramic influences from the Siberian Neolithic, along with mounds, arrived in Mexico by 1700 B.C., having earlier appeared in the Northeast U.S. in Vinette I.

P-173
AUTHOR: Pinches, T. G.
DATE: 1951
TITLE: Architecture (Assyro-Babylonian)
IN: Encyclopedia of Religion and Ethics, edited by James Hastings, (Scribner's: New York), 1:689-692

Ziggurats were occasionally used for burials/tombs [as were Mesoamerican temple mound structures].

P-174
AUTHOR: Ping-ti Ho
DATE: 1955
TITLE: The Introduction of American Food Plants into China
IN: American Anthropologist 57:191-201

The aggregate Chinese evidence on the peanut, the sweet potato, and maize definitely upholds the orthodox view of the post-Columbian introduction of American plants into East Asia rather than the notion of an earlier diffusion.

P-175
AUTHOR: Pino, Inés del
DATE: 1981

TITLE: Tipologías arquitectónicas precolombinas en el Ecuador [Pre-Columbian Architectonic Typologies in Ecuador]
IMPRINT: Universidad Centrál del Ecuador, Ediciones CAE-FAU: Quito

Originally a thesis thus laden with jargon. Her survey of the literature leads her to accept strong Mesoamerican influences by sea as well as some features from Asia. Of greatest value is the array of photographs and drawings of house models, many with the upturned roof-ends and "pagoda" form suggested by Estrada and others as indicative of direct Asian sea-borne influence, especially in the La Tolita and Jama-Coaque cultures (500 B.C.-A.D. 500).

P-176
AUTHOR: Pinto, A. Augusto de S.
DATE: 1924
TITLE: Cultos americanos [American Cults]
IN: Proceedings of the 20th International Congress of Americanists (Rio de Janeiro, 1922), 1:96-98

Inexplicit, undocumented parallels in American and Eurasian rites, beliefs, and deities.

P-176B
AUTHOR: Pissurlancar, Panduranga S. S.
DATE: 1920
TITLE: Recherches sur la decouverte de l'Amérique par les anciens hommes de l'Inde [Researches on the Discovery of America by the Ancient Men of India]
IMPRINT: Rau and Irmaos: Sanquelim-Goa, India

Certain cultural comparisons and sailing possibilities.

P-177
AUTHOR: Pistilli S., Vicente
DATE: 1978
TITLE: Vikingos en el Paraguay: la aldea vikinga-guaraní en la cuenca del Plata [Vikings in Paraguay: The Viking-Guarani Village in the Plate River Basin]
IMPRINT: Ediciones comuneros: Asunción

Compare M-048.

P-178
AUTHOR: Pittioni, Richard
DATE: 1969
TITLE: Robert Heine-Geldern
IMPRINT: Almanach für das Jahr 1968, Österreichische Akademia der Wissenschaften: Vienna

A necrology which evaluates Heine-Geldern's diffusionist studies.

P-179B
AUTHOR: Plancarte y Navarrete, Francisco
DATE: 1923
TITLE: Prehistória de México
IMPRINT: Asilo "Patricio Sanz": México

After studying the myths of Cadmus in the Mediterranean and Quetzalcoatl in Mexico he considers that this myth had passed to Mexico from the Old World by means of a maritime migration.

P-179C
AUTHOR: Plancarte y Navarrete, Francisco
DATE: 1934
TITLE: Tamoanchan. 2a. ed.
IMPRINT: Editorial El Escritorio: México

Pages 156-190: After studying the similarities between cultures in the Old and New Worlds, such as the cult of stone instruments, axes and spears, the deposit of votive axes of copper, stamp seals, spindle whorls, ceramic figurines, obsidian instruments, burials, deformations, etc., he comes to the conclusion that neolithic migrations from North Africa by Berbers reached Mexico; according to tradition these were the Ulmecas who arrived at Pánuco.

P-180

AUTHOR: Plant, William J.
DATE: 1984
TITLE: The Origin, Evolution, History and Distribution of the Domestic Fowl, Part 2: Chicken Bone Recoveries
IMPRINT: Privately printed: Maitland, New South Wales, Australia

A mimeographed booklet of unpolished but informative writings on all aspects of the topic. He copies and cites obscure literature and reproduces letters from knowledgeable, often unconventional experts.

Pages 12-16: Treats purported North and South American recoveries, but he is unable to confirm positively any pre-Columbian occurrences.

P-181

AUTHOR: Plant, William J.
DATE: 1985
TITLE: The Origin, Evolution, History and Distribution of the Domestic Fowl, Part 2: Chicken Bone Recoveries, Supplement
IMPRINT: Privately printed: Maitland, New South Wales, Australia

See P-180. Correspondence quoted includes further information on possible pre-Columbian occurrences of domestic fowl bones in America.

P-182

AUTHOR: Plant, William J.
DATE: 1986
TITLE: The Origin, Evolution, History and Distribution of the Domestic Fowl, Part 3: The Gallus Species
IMPRINT: Privately printed: Maitland, New South Wales, Australia

A 98-page addition to P-181. Contains more information on the Araucanian fowl, and also three pages of "Comments on Possible Occurrence of Pre-Columbian Contacts with the Americas," which, however, reach no definite conclusions.

P-182B

AUTHOR: Plant, William J.
DATE: 1989
TITLE: Random Notes on the Chicken in the Pacific Area
IMPRINT: Privately printed: Maitland, New South Wales, Australia
[Copies of all four of Plant's papers are in Sorenson's possession]

Gives bits of information from informants on fowl in Fiji, Saipan, and Polynesia. He believes two distinct species are represented throughout the Pacific, Gallus gallus, the ordinary jungle fowl, and the Malayoid, G. giganteus, or game fowl. Robert Langdon in a lecture before the Magellan Society in 1988 suggested that chickens may have travelled from Kyushu to Valdivia, Ecuador, with early voyagers.

P-184

AUTHOR: Plaut, W. Gunther
DATE: 1953
TITLE: A Hebrew-Dakota Dictionary
IN: American Jewish Historical Society Publication 42:361-370

The dictionary referred to is by Samuel W. Pond (1842).

P-186

AUTHOR: Plischke, Hans
DATE: 1953
TITLE: Thor Heyerdahls Kon-Tiki Theorie und ihre Problematik

[Thor Heyerdahl's Kon Tiki Theory and Its Problematic Nature]
IN: Universitas, Zeitschrift für Wissenschaft, Kunst und Literatur 8:837-846 (Stuttgart)

The key to Polynesian culture is Southeast Asia, not America.

P-188

AUTHOR: Plischke, Hans
DATE: 1957a
TITLE: Vom Ursprung der polynesischen Kultur [On the Origin of Polynesian Culture]
IN: Saeculum 8:404-408

Southeast Asia was the source of Polynesian culture. A Polynesian voyage that picked up the sweet potato is admissible but not Heyerdahl's argument overall.

P-189

AUTHOR: Plischke, Hans
DATE: 1957b
TITLE: The Colonization of Polynesia: A Reply to Thor Heyerdahl
IN: Universitas 1/2:405-413 (Stuttgart)

Page 409: Mentions two 19th-century scholars claiming American influence on Polynesia, Topinard and botanist G. Volkiens. Nevertheless, he supposes that psychic unity explains any parallels. Lack of kites in America is decisive against contacts. Heyerdahl is wrong.

P-190

AUTHOR: Plischke, Hans
DATE: 1961
TITLE: Peruanische Tonkrüge auf europäischen Südseeschiffen, Auseinandersetzung mit Thor Heyerdahl [Peruvian Pottery on European South Sea Ships, Dispute with Thor Heyerdahl]
IN: Zeitschrift für Anthropologie, Ethnologie und Urgeschichte 86:303-310

He attacks Heyerdahl's interpretation of his archaeological finds on the Galapagos, claiming that the South American pottery found had been brought by Spanish buccaneers during the 16th to 18th centuries.

P-191B

AUTHOR: Ploszajski, J. A.
DATE: 1963
TITLE: A History of Ships and Boats of Japan
IN: Bulletin van het Etnografisch Museum Delft 5-6:85-120

Little attention has been paid in Western literature to the development of Japanese native craft. In-country in recent years groups have worked to counteract that neglect, culminating in Kenji Ishii's admirable Nippon-no-Fune [Vessels of Japan] published in 1957 in Japanese. The present author is not a historian nor naval architect but hopes to contribute. Tungusic and Mongoloid peoples immigrated about 4000 B.C. to join Ainu-like post-Paleolithic inhabitants and hasten development of the local Neolithic. One group of these migrants was culturally close to South China, the other to Korea and the Amur Basin. Ships are evidenced in the historical claim to conquest of southern Korea about A.D. 200. Refers then to Nishimura on early craft: logs lashed into rafts, reed bundles and rafts, rafts given buoyancy by calabashes, pots or inflated skins, basket boats, tub boats, bark canoes, logs forming catamarans and dug-outs.

The earliest archaeological specimen, from a peat bog, dates to the early Jomon period before 3000 B.C. Later Jomon specimens are mentioned. Migrants from the continent arrived in the middle of Jomon. Boat building improved with the advent of metal tools ca. 300 B.C. From the third century on fairly large ocean-going boats were built. After the Mongol invasion of the 13th century Japanese ship-building advanced rapidly; Chinese influence is clear. A large chronological table compares the Japanese types he has discussed with world events and nautical development elsewhere. This table lists, around A.D. 500, "Probable crossing of Pacific by Chinese."

P-192

AUTHOR: Plumet, Patrick
DATE: 1968
TITLE: Vikings et Tunit
[Vikings and Tunit]
IN: Inter-Nord 10:303-308 (Paris)

A detailed critique of previous work toward identifying Norse sites in America, especially that of Thomas Lee, and Plumet's definition of problems entailed from present archaeological knowledge. "Tunit" of course refers to the people mentioned by Eskimo and claimed by some to be remnants of the Norse.

P-193

AUTHOR: Plumet, Patrick
DATE: 1969
TITLE: Archéologie de l'Ungava: le problème des maisons longues à deux hémicycles et séparations intérieures
[Archaeology of Ungava: The Problem of the Long Houses with Two Curved Portions and Interior Separations]
IMPRINT: Contribution 7, Centre d'études arctiques et Finno-Scandinaves (Paris)

Following a history of archaeological research in Ungava and a discussion (critique) of Thomas Lee's 37 arguments aimed at proving that the Vikings left structural remains in the area, he reports his own work. He finds sufficient Dorset culture parallels in the structures to deny that Lee's explanation of Norse construction should be accepted.

P-194

AUTHOR: Plumet, Patrick
DATE: 1976
TITLE: Les Vikings en Amérique: la fin d'un mythe
[The Vikings in America: The End of a Myth]
IN: Les Vikings et leur civilisation, problèmes actuels, edited by Regis Boyer (Mouton: Paris), 61-73

An historical perspective on "romantic" attempts to locate the Norse at various places in northeastern North America. Recaps Lee's and Ingstad's works and imagines that they mark the end of the romantic era, now replaced by serious, discussible archaeology.

P-195

AUTHOR: Plumet, Patrick
DATE: 1985
TITLE: Archeologie de l'Ungava: le site de La Pointe aux Belougas (Qilalugarsiuvik) et les maisons longues dorsetiennes
[The Archaeology of the Ungava: The Site of Beluga Point (Qilalugarsiuvik) and the Dorset Long Houses]
IMPRINT: Laboratoire d'Archéologie de l'Université du Québec à Montréal: Montreal

Elaboration of P-193.

P-196

AUTHOR: Plumet, Patrick
DATE: 1987
TITLE: Le développement de l'approche archéologique dans l'Arctique.
[The Development of the Archaeological Approach in the Arctic]
IN: L'Anthropologie 91/4:859-872

The nature and scope of relations between the Norse from Greenland and the Dorset or Thule peoples have been re-evaluated in light of finds of Norse artifacts in the Arctic archipelago. The contacts no longer seem rare, fortuitous or conflictual, as the sagas would indicate.

P-197

AUTHOR: Plummer, Katherine
DATE: 1984
TITLE: The Shogun's Reluctant Ambassadors—Sea Drifters
IMPRINT: Lotus Press: Tokyo

Considers the fate (usually disastrous) of those prior to the mid-19th century who drifted in the north Pacific on disabled vessels, some reaching America. One chapter is on winds and currents of that ocean.

P-200

AUTHOR: Pohl, Frederick J.
DATE: 1945
TITLE: Was the Newport Tower Standing in 1632?
IN: New England Quarterly 18:501-506

In a 1632 colonial paper a passage occurs referring to soldiers and a tower, which Pohl argues is a reference to an already existing structure that must be the Newport Tower. [See M-405 to the contrary.]

P-201

AUTHOR: Pohl, Frederick J.
DATE: 1948a
TITLE: A Key to the Problem of the Newport Tower
IN: Rhode Island History 7:75-83

Argues that the builders of the tower used a Norse standard of measurement.

P-202

AUTHOR: Pohl, Frederick J.
DATE: 1948b
TITLE: Leif Ericsson's Visit to America
IN: American Scandinavian Review 36:18-29

Cape Cod is identified as Leifur's landfall as proved by mooring holes.

P-203

AUTHOR: Pohl, Frederick J.
DATE: 1950a
TITLE: The Newport Tower: An Answer to Mr. Godfrey
IN: Archaeology 3:183

See G-123. Criticizes Godfrey's methods in arriving at the conclusion that the tower was colonial in date.

P-204

AUTHOR: Pohl, Frederick J.
DATE: 1950b
TITLE: The Sinclair Expedition to Nova Scotia in 1398
IMPRINT: Pictou Press: Pictou, Nova Scotia

Identifies Henry Sinclair, Earl of Orkney, as the Zighmni of the Zeno account, which is here considered genuine.

P-206

AUTHOR: Pohl, Frederick J.
DATE: 1952
TITLE: The Lost Discovery: Uncovering the Track of the Vikings in America
IMPRINT: Norton: New York
[Probably the same, in French, *La découverte de l'Amérique par les Vikings* (Laffont: Paris, 1954)]

Describes his search for mooring holes on Cape Cod and his uncritical attempt to locate various places mentioned in the sagas.

P-207

AUTHOR: Pohl, Frederick J.
DATE: 1954
TITLE: Plaster under the Tower
IN: American Antiquity 19:275-277

Claims a flaw in Godfrey's [G-124] interpretation of Newport Tower dating.

P-209

AUTHOR: Pohl, Frederick J.
DATE: 1960
TITLE: Further Proof of Vikings at Follins Pond
IN: Massachusetts Archaeological Society Bulletin 21/3-4:48-49

He reports a 1952 find of evidence for a location where a ship was shored long ago which was of the same dimensions as a Viking ship; this is the spot where he supposes Leif wintered in Vinland.

P-210

AUTHOR: Pohl, Frederick J.
DATE: 1961
TITLE: Atlantic Crossings before Columbus
IMPRINT: Norton: New York

Sections on: Did the Phoenicians reach North America? Brendan; the Heavener runestone; Leif and Thorfinn; Madoc; Newport Tower; runic inscriptions; Kensington Stone; and Sinclair the Sea-King. Leif's house was located at Follins Pond, Massachusetts.

P-211

AUTHOR: Pohl, Frederick J.
DATE: 1964
TITLE: Riddle of the Stone Beehives
IN: Bulletin, Massachusetts Archaeological Society 25/3-4:72-76

Certain semi-underground stone structures were not pre-Columbian but were early colonial defense refuges against Indian attacks. Explains why other explanations will not do.

P-212

AUTHOR: Pohl, Frederick J.
DATE: 1966a
TITLE: Leif Erickson's Campsite in Vinland
IN: American-Scandinavian Review 54:25-29

Pohl mainly recaps his own activities and writings with no other documentation. Claims the Follins Pond site meets 18 geographical requirements for locating Leif's camp site in Vinland plus six supporting archaeological facts.

P-213

AUTHOR: Pohl, Frederick J.
DATE: 1966b
TITLE: The Viking Explorers
IMPRINT: Thomas Y. Crowell: New York

A popular summary of his arguments to date.

P-215

AUTHOR: Pohl, Frederick J.
DATE: 1969
TITLE: The Location of Southern Outposts
IN: American-Scandinavian Review 57:250-259

Vikings in the southeastern United States.

P-216

AUTHOR: Pohl, Frederick J.
DATE: 1972
TITLE: The Viking Settlements of North America
IMPRINT: Clarkson N. Potter: New York [Reviewed 1973, *American Antiquity* 75:195]

A tour through the sagas giving his particular interpretations—geographical (with many local maps), geological, botanical, historical, biographical—of the texts. Newfoundland was Helluland, Nova Scotia Markland, southern New England Vinland, and Hop was in Virginia. In addition he supposes that they could also have reached the Mississippi Valley, via the Gulf of Mexico.

P-217

AUTHOR: Pohl, Frederick J.
DATE: 1973
TITLE: Did Ancient Romans Reach America?
IN: New Diffusionist 3/10:23-37

An intelligently written roundup of material on the question. He notes that even if we assume that no more than 50 Roman ship sailings occurred in the Atlantic each year, the total for the centuries of the Empire would be 25,000. It is not unreasonable that several times in each century one of those would be swept southwestward into the grasp of the trade winds and that some could have reached the Caribbean or Brazil. In 1576 Sir Humphrey Gilbert wrote that a Spanish chronicle reported finding "in the Gold Mynes of America, certain peeces of Money, ingraved with the image of Augustus Caesar." They were sent to the Pope. Also reports the find of a Roman lamp in an Indian mound in Connecticut, subsequently said by Cambridge University savants to have been made in the Aegean islands. A Roman coin and possible parts of an ancient ship were found on an island off Massachusetts in 1950. A Latin inscription on a ledge in Maine could be related. Other coin finds are mentioned. The pineapple at Pompeii was a subject of Pohl's personal investigation, with the help of Dr. Casella, the botanical expert there; Pohl is convinced that it is authentic.

P-218

AUTHOR: Pohl, Frederick J.
DATE: 1974
TITLE: Prince Henry Sinclair: His Expedition to the New World in 1398
IMPRINT: Potter: New York

Ardently defends the reality of a voyage by Sinclair, the landing point being at Pictou, Nova Scotia, where he claims to have located geologic and geographic sites corresponding to those of the narrative. He also claims that the travelers had definite influence on Algonquin Indians of the area.

P-218B

AUTHOR: Pohl, Frederick J.
DATE: 1986
TITLE: The New Columbus
IMPRINT: Security-Dupont Press: Rochester, New York

Columbus was a rediscoverer of superior mapping and navigation knowledge long lost. An appendix gives Gordon's reading of the Parahaiba Stone.

P-219

AUTHOR: Poindexter, Miles
DATE: 1930
TITLE: The Ayar-Incas, 2 volumes
IMPRINT: Horace Liveright: New York

While the author's position is basically racist ("Aryan" civilizers spread anciently throughout the world), he also displays knowledge of considerable scientific literature in discussing Polynesian migrations to Peru, ocean currents affecting Polynesian voyaging (vol. 2, pages 89-90, cites information about changes in currents and winds in the eastern Pacific [now known as the El Niño phenomenon, anticipating F-099]), comparisons of Andean peoples to those of the trans-Himalayan area, Chinese connections, Elliot Smith and elephants, prehistoric white voyagers, the zodiac, Quechua words from various Old World languages (particularly Sanskrit, Sumerian, and "Aryan"), English words in Maya, and religious similarities.

P-220

AUTHOR: Poindexter, Miles
DATE: 1938
TITLE: Peruvian Pharaohs
IMPRINT: Christopher Publishing House: Boston

Title page: "It is sufficient for the purpose of this book to say that man's manner of life—what we call his culture—among those who rule and those who have ruled the civilized countries, in pre-Columbian America as well as elsewhere, is of one continuous growth, evolved from one seed-bed in Central Asia, and carried under the leadership of the Aryan caste to all the other continents."

In America the white immigrant leadership was submerged in the mass of the darker races. "The Peruvian traditions clearly relate that these ancestral chiefs and 'civilizers' were white men." The secret speech of the Incas was called *runa,* from runes, which came to Europe in pre-hellenic times from Asia. Melanesian slaves were brought into Peru by the white rulers there. Etc.

P-221

AUTHOR: Poirier, Jean
DATE: 1950
TITLE: Une hypothèse de travail: les migrateurs nordiques ont-ils atteint, entre le XI et le XIV siècle, la Polynésie orientale?
[A Working Hypothesis: Did the Nordic Migrations Reach Eastern Polynesia between the XIth and XIVth Centuries?]
IN: Journal de la société des océanistes 6:253-254

A professor of letters in Madagascar briefly sketches a working hypothesis that Vikings arrived in Polynesia via America. Sketchy backing is provided from physical anthropology, languages, and mythology. [See also S-214.]

P-222

AUTHOR: Poirier, Jean
DATE: 1952
TITLE: L'élément blond dans l'éthnie polynésienne
[The Blond Element in the Ethnic Polynesians]
IN: Journal de la société des océanistes 8:81-116
[Reprinted as a separate in 1953 with a slightly different title]

Response to S-214 which had criticized P-221.

P-223

AUTHOR: Poirier, Jean
DATE: 1953
TITLE: L'élément blond en Polynésie et les migrations nordiques en Océanie et en Amérique
[The Blond Element in Polynesia and Nordic Migrations in Oceania and in America]
IMPRINT: Société des oceanistes, Musée de l'Homme: Paris
[Reprinted 1952 from *Journal de la société oceanistes* 8:81-116]

Data on apparent "white" persons and groups in Oceania and America.

P-224

AUTHOR: Pokorny, Rudolf
DATE: 1982
TITLE: La cultura de las pyramides cosmicaorientadas [*sic*]
[The Culture of the "Cosmic-oriented" Pyramids]
IN: Abstracts of papers, 44th International Congress of Americanists (Manchester, 1982), (School of Geography, Manchester University: Manchester, England), 210

Pyramids worldwide are connected; the mandala of pyramids.

P-225

AUTHOR: Polakowsky, H.
DATE: 1897
TITLE: Diskussion über präkolumbischen Aussatz und verstümmelte

peruanischen Thonfiguren [Discussion on Pre-Columbian Leprosy and Silent Peruvian Figurines]
IN: Verhandlungen der Berliner Gesellschaft für Anthropologie, Ethnologie und Urgeschichte 29:612-621

Are the effects of leprosy shown on Peruvian figurines? [An Old World disease, leprosy is supposed not to have been present in the New before Columbus. See L-134.]

P-226

AUTHOR: Polakowsky, H.
DATE: 1898
TITLE: Präkolumbische Lepra [Pre-Columbian Leprosy]
IN: Verhandlungen der Berliner Gesellschaft für Anthropologie, Ethnologie und Urgeschichte 30:486-488

Reiterates what he said the same year in Petermann's Geographische Mitteilungen opposing the view that leprosy was present in America.

P-227B

AUTHOR: Polansky, Jon
DATE: 1985
TITLE: A Heuristic Approach to Evaluating Epigraphic Evidence: A Historical View and Future Implications
IN: Epigraphic Society Occasional Papers 21:14-20

Contrasts heuristic method, which stays open to learning as one goes along, with eristic methods which are those typically employed to win debates and popular approval for a viewpoint or legal position, often involving polemics in "intellectual combat." Some in academic archaeology use the latter; they have wished to dismiss as expeditiously as possible any evidence of pre-Columbian exchanges between the cultures of Asia, Europe, and Africa with those in the Americas. The author recounts how his interest in epigraphy was awakened by Fell and how his later attempt to build collaboration with Robert Heizer at Berkeley, which was cut short by the latter's illness and death after a first expression of interest. Polansky has proceeded with various site investigations with emphasis on archaeoastronomy. He also tells of an approach to Richard Adams at the Smithsonian which holds marginal promise. "It will probably require another 5 to 10 years to be able to critically examine the epigraphic evidence." He hopes that ESOP will provide "a heuristic testing ground" toward that goal.

P-228

AUTHOR: Pollitzer, William S.
DATE: 1969
TITLE: Ancestral Traits, Parental Populations, and Hybrids
IN: American Journal of Physical Anthropology 30:415-420

The Melungeons of mountainous Virginia and Tennessee (claimed by some to be descendants of European arrivals in pre-Columbian times) are studied. In general they resemble whites more than Indians or Negroes. Using ABO and other blood genetic materials, several hypotheses of racial ancestry (single and combined) were tested. The data best fit a picture of 90% Portuguese with some Indian and Negro admixture. But the author emphasizes that "with several possible parental populations, different answers are equally likely."

P-230

AUTHOR: Polunin, Nicholas U.
DATE: 1960
TITLE: Introduction to Plant Geography and Some Related Sciences
IMPRINT: McGraw-Hill: New York

Page 181: During work in 1936 in southwestern Greenland he noted living descendants of plants which had evidently been introduced from North

America by Norsemen. "As certain of these plants are of known but restricted distribution (in two instances barely overlapping) on the eastern North American seaboard, they give a clear indication of where their ancestors probably came from, and where, accordingly, Viking relics should be sought which would prove once and for all that North America was known to Europeans long before the birth of Columbus." [After thus tantalizing, he provides no further reference.]

P-230B

AUTHOR: Pompa y Pompa, Antonio
DATE: 1958
TITLE: Dos meditaciones acerca de la protohistoria americana [Two Meditations on American Protohistory]
IN: Memorias y Revista de la Academic Nacional de Ciencias (formerly, Sociedad Científica Antonio Álzate) 58/1-2:45-73 (México)

Argues with some passion about the importance of transpacific migrations in forming Mexican ancestry. A loose survey cites some materials from Heine-Geldern and Ekholm, Covarrubias, and other literature current in the 1950s but adds nothing original. Sees the Pacific Ocean as a "universal zone of integration" across which routes of ocean travel had profound effect. In a second part, beginning on page 59, he discusses "Was there a megalithic horizon?" and concludes that evidence such as from Easter Island "suggest an archaeological horizon earlier than the preclassic."

Pages 56: Mentions a statement by Paul Kirchhoff and/or Wigberto Jiménez Moreno of a tradition of immigration by sea to Jalisco, citing the "Crónica miscelánea" of Fray Antonio Tello.

P-232

AUTHORS: Ponce Sanginés, Carlos, and Enrique Linares Iturralde
DATE: 1966
TITLE: Comentario antropológico acerca de la determinación paleoserológica de grupos sanguineos en momias prehispánicas del altiplano boliviano [Anthropological Commentary Concerning the Paleoserological Determination of Blood Groups in Prehispanic Mummies from the Bolivian Altiplano]
IN: Academía Nacional de Ciencias de Bolivia, Publicación 15 (La Paz)

Finds that blood groups in mummies and native tribes of Bolivia agree, which he presumes indicates continuity of population from past to present.

P-233

AUTHOR: Porras Garcés, Pedro I.
DATE: 1966
TITLE: Posibles contactos culturales precolombinos entre América del Centro y América del Sur, de manera especial el Ecuador: a la luz de los estudios realizados por arqueólogos ecuatorianos y extranjero, a partir del año de 1955 [Possible Pre-Columbian Cultural Contacts between Central and South America, Especially Ecuador: In the Light of Studies Done by Ecuadorian and Other Archaeologists since 1955]
IN: Humanitas 6/1:194-195 (Quito)

Summary of work to date on the question of seaborne interamerican and transpacific contacts on coastal Ecuador.

P-234

AUTHOR: Porras Garcés, Pedro I.
DATE: 1980
TITLE: Arqueología del Ecuador [Archaeology of Ecuador]

IMPRINT: Impresa Editorial "Gallocapitán": Otavalo, Ecuador
[Second editon enlarged, 1980]

A handbook presenting basic information on each identified archaeological culture in Ecuador.

Pages 30-31: Lathrop makes the "interesting proposal" of a possible African origin for the earliest cultivators in lowland South America; if they came, they might have moved upriver to Ecuador over a relatively short period of time without leaving much evidence as they would have used mainly perishable materials for artifacts.

Pages 74-76: Summarizes Meggers and Evans on Japanese origin for Valdivia; states four evidences for and four against without taking a position himself but he cannot accept Lathrap's claim for an Amazonian origin. He cites Piña Chan (no reference) regarding Mexican figurines similar to those of Valdivia.

Page 145: Transverse flutes appear archaeologically in Guangala culture.

Page 153-154: Cites arguments by Estrada and Meggers [E-108] about Asian features in Bahia phase but notes much continuity with earlier phases also; possibly this phase saw the first balsa rafts, very similar to those used in Southeast Asia.

Pages 268-273: Follows Olaf Holm in stating that the tradition of an Inca voyage by balsa into the Pacific could not have been from Peru but must have left Ecuador. Holm has examinaed the Galapagos ceramic material and agrees that some of it is unquestionably pre-Columbian (citing H-380).

P-234B

AUTHOR: Porras Garcés, Pedro I.
DATE: 1987
TITLE: Nuestro Ayer: Manual de Arqueología Ecuatoriana
[Our Yesterday: Manual of Ecuadorian Archaeology]
IN: Pontificia Universidad Católica del Ecuador, Centro de Investigaciones Arqueológicas: Quito

A substantially revised version of P-234. Criticism of Meggers and Evans on a Jomon connection is toned down. On page 51 a table lists the 24 traits claimed to be shared between Jomon and Valdivia, eleven of which also appear in early Peurto Hormiga (Colombia) ceramics and seven in Monagrillo (Panama).

P-235

AUTHOR: Porter, Muriel N.
DATE: 1953
TITLE: Tlatilco and the Pre-Classic Cultures of the New World
IN: Publications in Anthropology 19, The Viking Fund/Wennergren Foundation

Pages 84-85: Rocker-stamping decoration "does seem very likely" to be historically related to Asian occurrences, which include c. 2000 B.C. in Mongolia and Korea but much later in Indo-China.

P-236

AUTHORS: Portugal, Maks, and Dick Edgar Ibarro Grasso
DATE: 1956
TITLE: Antropología física de los indios bolivianos
[Physical Anthropology of the Bolivian Indians]
IN: Khana 4/3:19-20, and 4/4:18-43 (La Paz, Bolivia)

Review of the literature on South American Indian races, and especially the writings of D'Orbigny, Posnansky, and Imbelloni. They accept an origin or influence from the Pacific.

P-236B

AUTHOR: Posnansky, Arturo
DATE: 1914

TITLE: Una metrópoli prehistórica en la América del Sur [A Prehistoric Metropolis in South America]
IMPRINT: Berlin

See P-236D.

P-236C

AUTHOR: Posnansky, Arturo
DATE: 1942
TITLE: ¿Es o no oriundo el hombre americano en América? [Is American Man Native to America or not?]
IN: Proceedings of the 27th International Congress of Americanists (Part 1, Mexico, 1939), pages 99-118

In the cordillera of South America were located the Collas, a superior, non-mongoloid racial element (of "interior Asia" type). They extended to Central America and as far as Canada. Under them Tiahuanacu was the culmination of ancient American culture. The other American race was the "Aruwak," mongoloids, who populated most of the hemisphere. Both types were autocthonous, the predecessors showing up in early fossil and semi-fossil American specimens.

P-236D

AUTHOR: Posnansky, Arturo
DATE: 1958
TITLE: Tiahuanacu, the Cradle of American Man, vol. 3/4
IMPRINT: Ministerio de Educación de Bolivia: La Paz

This was a center of civilization until a cataclysm occurred after 15,000 B.C. The visible monuments are very old.

P-238

AUTHOR: Poutjatine, Pablo Arsenievitch
DATE: 1892
TITLE: De développement d'empreintes de produits textiles sur les poteries russes et leur conformité avec les produits similaires de l'Amérique de Nord [The Development of Textile Imprints on Russian Pottery and Their Resemblance to Similar Products of North America]
IN: Proceedings of the 8th International Congress of Americanists (Paris, 1890), 507-513

Textile marking on pottery strikes him as similar between Russia and North America. Immediately following, on pages 512-513, is a report that Thomas Wilson displayed at the ICA samples of pottery from the eastern U.S. on which were textile markings very similar to those of Poutjatine, however most observers felt there could not be a connection, given the absence of any textile- marked pottery in the western and northwestern part of the continent.

P-239

AUTHOR: Poutrin, Léon
DATE: 1913a
TITLE: Le peuplement de l'Amérique [The Peopling of America]
IN: L'Anthropologie 24/1:51-55

People surely came via the Bering Strait and very probably also across the Pacific borne by the currents.

P-240

AUTHOR: Poutrin, Leon
DATE: 1913b
TITLE: L'origine chinoise des anciennes civilizations du Mexique et du Pérou [The Chinese Origin of the Ancient Civilizations of Mexico and of Peru]

IN: Journal de la société des américanistes de Paris 10:303-304

A very brief report on excavation of a tomb by W. Niven, R. Meña, and M. Conway at Teotihuacan "at the base" of the Pyramid of the Sun. They found a ceramic statuette seven inches high representing an individual of very clear "mongolic type." The clothing represented was that of a Chinese and included the insignia of a mandarin. Niven says the figure dates well before the Aztecs. The statuette was clearly a portrait of the individual buried. He wore a necklace of green jade stones, which are unknown in Mexico. Niven thinks he has discovered vestiges of a Chinese navigator.

P-240B

AUTHOR: Powell, Mary Lucas
DATE: 1992
TITLE: Health and Disease in the Late Prehistoric Southeast
IN: Disease and Demography in the Americas, edited by John W. Verano and Douglas H. Ubelaker (Smithsonian Institution Press: Washington, D.C.), 41-53

The old concept of the aboriginal New World as a "disease-free paradise" is passé. Virulent acute infectious diseases were limited because settlement and population sizes did not favor their spread, but New World peoples still were exposed to a wide variety of diseases primarily affecting animals, with humans as secondary hosts, plus fungi and staphylococcal and streptococcal environmental pathogens. There were two widespread chronic infectious diseases, tuberculosis and treponematosis. Sampling limits our knowledge but there was no doubt much variation in their expression due to social and ecological factors. The presence of such diseases had profound implications for life and death in earlier times and for the results of exposure to related Old World pathogens after 1492.

Summarizes the competing views of the history of treponematosis (syphilis, yaws, pinta). Evidence on tuberculosis incidence is also summarized. Earliest documented cases of the latter are from Chile (160 B.C., Allison). North American cases postdate A.D. 850 (Ontario and Georgia through Arkansas to the Southwest). Treponematosis dates as early as 3300 B.C. in Florida. Finally, the suggestion is made that aborigines previously sensitized to the various diseases mentioned stood at higher risk from reactivation of latent disease when newly exposed to different strains brought by Europeans; the reciprocal was true in the Old World.

P-242

AUTHOR: Powers, Stephen
DATE: 1874
TITLE: Aborigines of California: An Indo-Chinese Study
IN: Atlantic Monthly 33:313-323

He thinks he has linguistic evidence of a Chinese colony on the Russian River in California.

P-243

AUTHOR: Premm, Hanns J.
DATE: 1979
TITLE: Methodische Forderungen an den Nachweis transpazifischer Kulturkontakte [Methodological Challenges in Proving Transpacific Culture Contact]
IN: Archiv für Völkerkunde 33:7-14

Criticizes the use of ethnological literature since deficient evaluation of early colonial sources diminishes their value as "proof."

P-244

AUTHOR: Prescott, William Hickling
DATE: 1843
TITLE: History of the Conquest of Mexico
IMPRINT: Lippincott: Philadelphia [Many later editions, e.g., Bantam Matrix Edition: New York, 1964]

Vol. 1, page 417: In Mexico, "there was a vulgar tradition . . . that on removal of part of the walls [of the temple at Cholula] the god would send forth an inundation to overwhelm his enemies." [Compare Ezekiel 47 regarding issuance of underground waters from beneath the capping temple.]

Vol. 3, page 402: "The coincidences are sufficiently strong to authorize a belief, that the civilization of Anahuac was, in some degree, influenced by that of Eastern Asia."

P-245

AUTHOR: Prescott, William Hickling
DATE: 1900
TITLE: Origin of the Mexican Civilization—Analogies with the Old World
IMPRINT: Collier: New York

From pages 683-706 in the 1964 edition cited in P-244: Originally written as an appendix to P-244 but not published there; it did appear in editions from 1846, then finally as this separate in 1900. He arrives at the same judgement about the origin of the Mexicans as John Lloyd Stephens—caution. Explicates here some parallels he sees with Asia and the Near East—traditions, beliefs, myths, customs, architecture, and so on. Takes these as positive indication of communication from East Asia to Mexico, but they are far from showing identity, probably due to the very remote period of the contact. "Whichever way we turn, the subject is full of embarrassment."

P-247

AUTHOR: Pretty, Graeme L.
DATE: 1969
TITLE: The Macleay Museum Mummy from Torres Straits: A Postscript to Elliot Smith and the Diffusion Controversy
IN: Man 4:24-43

A critique on historical grounds of Elliot Smith's analysis of a mummy from Torres Straits in 1913 which he had used as the basis for a comparison with Egyptian mummification. [See J-088 and K-161.]

P-248

AUTHOR: Preuss, Konrad Theodor
DATE: 1901
TITLE: Phantesideen über die Grundlagen der Kultur [Fantastic Ideas on the Fundamentals of Culture]
IN: Globus 80:9-12

A review of Nuttall [N-118] which he considers in large part fantastic.

P-249

AUTHOR: Preuss, Konrad Theodor
DATE: 1906
TITLE: Der dämonische Ursprung des kriegischen Dramas, erläutert durch mexikanische Parallelen [The Demonic Origin of the War Drama, Explained by Mexican Parallels]
IN: Neue Jahrbucher für das klassische Altertum, Geschichte und Deutsch Literatur und für Pädagogik 9:161-193 (Leipzig)

Psychological convergence provides an explanation for parallels.

P-250

AUTHOR: Preuss, Konrad Theodor
DATE: 1908
TITLE: Die astral Religion in Mexiko in vorhispanischer Zeit und in der Gegenwart [Astral Religion in Mexico in Prehispanic Times and Now]
IN: Third International Congress of Religion, Transactions 1:36-41

Basically a psychic unity treatment of Old-New World parallels.

P-251

AUTHOR: Preuss, Konrad Theodor

DATE: 1909

TITLE: Dialoglieder des Rigveda im Lichte der religiösen Gesänge mexikanischer Indianer [Dialogue Songs of the Rig Veda in Light of the Religious Songs of Mexican Indians]

IN: Globus 95:41-46

A mainly structural, not historical, comparison is made between the Rig Veda and Cora-Huichol ritual poesy.

P-252

AUTHOR: Preuss, Konrad Theodor

DATE: 1928

TITLE: Die Christusmythe und andere Sonnenmythen der Mexicano [The Myth of Christ and Other Sun Myths of the Mexicano]

IN: Festschrift: Publication d'hommage offerte au P. W. Schmidt, edited by Wilhelm Koppers (Mechitharisten-congregations: Vienna), 570-582

Similar to P-250.

P-252B

AUTHOR: Price, Edward T.

DATE: 1951

TITLE: The Melungeons: A Mixed-Blood Strain of the Southern Appalachians

IN: The Geographical Review 42:256-271

A superior survey of the present distribution of this "people" with nothing explicit to say about origin. Assumes they are "mixed blood," that is, a Negro-White mix.

P-254

AUTHOR: Priest, Josiah

DATE: 1833

TITLE: American Antiquities and Discoveries in the West: Being an Exhibition of the Evidence That an Ancient Population of Partially Civilized Nations, Differing Entirely from Those of the Present Indians, Peopled America, Many Centuries before Its Discovery by Columbus. And Inquiries into Their Origin, with a Copious Description of Many of Their Stupendous Works, now in Ruins . . . . Third edition revised

IMPRINT: Packard, Hoffman and White: Albany [1st and 2nd editions also 1833; 5th edition 1841]

A sample of second- or third-hand material that he reports from his period:

Pages 110-113: A large catacomb was found near Lexington, Kentucky, from which hundreds of mummies, wrapped like those of Egypt and probably prepared by people from Egypt, were destroyed by white men some time previously.

Pages 134-135: Brass rings and an ivory image of a mother and child, perhaps of (medieval) Catholic origin, came from a mound of bones near Cincinnati.

Pages 138-144: A cavern on the Ohio River in Indiana contains many hieroglyphics as well as human figures dressed in clothing like the Greeks or Romans.

Pages 176-177: At Marietta, Ohio, a mound yielded remains of a copper helmet and half a steel bow. On following pages he reports an iron blade from Ohio, a copper cross, and brass weapons in many parts of America, "all of which go to prove that this country was once peopled with civilized, industrious nations" (page 224). These were Norwegians, Welch, and Scots, at least.

Pages 282ff.: Opinions of antiquarians respecting the original inhabitants of America are given, particularly Dr. Samuel L. Mitchell who says that probably Malays, Tartars, and Scandinavians arrived in America.

P-255

AUTHOR: Prince, Carlos
DATE: 1915
TITLE: Origen de los Indios de América [Origin of the Indians of America]
IMPRINT: Privately printed: Lima

Pages 91-93: Claims the Chinese believed that they had passed through the Annian [Bering] strait to Quivira and thence to Mexico, Panama, and Peru, based on toponyms and recorded beliefs. Alexander Darley, a priest who had done historical studies in the Orient, said that in 207 B.C. a Chinese ship, named Hi-Li, landed on the Pacific coast near Monterey, California. The captain returned and for over a hundred years ships made innumerable expeditions to the Pacific coast. Also, on the Alaskan coast, Indians have found an ancient tomb in which were read the Chinese characters for the name Li-Hei-Lau. Other relics demonstrate that the Chinese lived in Alaska many years before the Christian era. And some Chinese scholars suppose that the North American Indians are descended from the crew of a Chinese ship wrecked on the North American coast over 20 centuries before.

P-256

AUTHOR: Pritchard, Jackie L.
DATE: 1972
TITLE: Kwakiutl Potlatching and Ponapean Feasting: An Examination of the Potlatch and Potlatching Parallels
IMPRINT: Unpublished; M.A. thesis, Ohio State University

Thesis itself not seen but the abstract reads: "Most anthopologists consider the potlatch institution to be exclusively a Northwest Coast phenomenon. Yet a minority of workers claim to find it elsewhere. This thesis examines this issue in depth. The conclusion is that the potlatch does not exist outside the Northwest Coast of America."

P-257

AUTHOR: Pritchard, L. A.
DATE: 1923
TITLE: Chinese Junks
IN: Mariner's Mirror 9:89-90

Describes a voyage from Shanghai to San Pedro, California in 1912-1913. See also notes in the same volume by H. Szymanski, page 312, and G. A. Ballard, page 316.

P-258

AUTHOR: Probst, Peter S.
DATE: 1963
TITLE: Mirrors of Ancient China and Pre-Columbian America
IMPRINT: Unpublished; M.A. thesis, Columbia University

Suggested and supervised by Gordon Ekholm, although the M.A. degree awarded was in "Political Science." The author credits the advantage of using an extensive file of notes which Marshall Saville had prepared for writing a history of mirrors in the New World. The three sections of the thesis are: the role and history of mirrors in pre-Columbian America, the same for ancient China, and conclusion.

The oldest mirrors in the New World are from Huaca Prieta, Peru, dating around 2500 B.C. Next oldest are (postulated) from La Venta [now many are known from Oaxaca and San Lorenzo of the same age as La Venta]. In China mirrors are described in documents from the Chou period, but literary references place the device before 2600 B.C. The Valdivia-Jomon ceramic similarities suggest that diffusion was possible across the Pacific even at the early dates for the mirrors.

Pages 29-30: A possible extension of New World mirrors may be evidenced in Polynesia. Bennett excavated fine-grain circular "basanite" mirrors on the island of Kauai, Hawaiian Islands, which physically resemble certain Mesoamerican biconically perforated mirrors. Earlier Brigham described similar mirrors reported used in Hawaii and having supposed medicinal powers. They were wetted when used to reflect, the same as polished stone mirrors of British Columbia.

Pages 47-50: Conclusion. Mirror features shared in China and America: most common shape was circular; backs often decorated with scenes and design motifs; worn suspended about the neck (but differences in the mode of suspension); traditional grave offerings, sometimes on the chest of the corpse (Han period prominence of this custom, and in Guatemala about A.D. 500); uses include, instruments of prophecy, in medicine, as insignia of rank, and for igniting sacred state fires. Function as a looking glass in both places was secondary. Other areas also had mirrors however; Syria "at an early date," and First Dynasty Egypt, as well as the Romans and Greeks.

P-259

AUTHOR: Proctor, V.

DATE: 1968

TITLE: Long-distance Dispersal of Seeds by Retention in Digestive Tract of Birds

IN: Science 160/3825:321-322

He suggests that birds may hold seeds in their digestive tracts then drop them after long flights to a distant location; however this notion is based on observations concerning wild, not crop, seeds. [If actual, this might explain some crop distributions without involving human contacts.]

P-260

AUTHOR: Proskouriakoff, Tatiana

DATE: 1971

TITLE: Classic Art of Central Veracruz

IN: Handbook of Middle American Indians, vol. 11, part 2, Archaeology of Northern Mesoamerica, edited by Gordon F. Ekholm and Ignacio Bernal (University of Texas Press: Austin), 558-572

Page 571: Unfortunately we cannot reconstruct the history of the Classic Veracruz style. "Many observers have noted striking similarities between some of the Veracruz designs and those that were used on early Chinese bronzes. Not only are the two sets very similar in general conception, with their dragon forms almost lost amid intricate tracery, but there are specific and complex forms in the two styles so nearly alike that it is hard to believe that they were independently invented. . . .

"Whether the similarities are completely fortuitous or the result of convergence due to basically similar original formulations, whether they indicate repeated contact with the Orient, or whether they are rooted very deeply in the past and stem from early Asiatic migration into America, are questions to which we cannot at present envision even the possibility of an answer."

P-261

AUTHOR: Prufer, Olaf H.

DATE: 1964

TITLE: Hopewell versus Meso-America and Asia

IN: Proceedings of the 35th International Congress of Americanists (Mexico, 1962), 1:113-120

Systematic and critical survey of evidences for inter-area influence. He acknowledges that evidence exists, but there are difficulties of chronology and of focus. Concludes that similarities are few and evidence of connections is open to diverse interpretations. In relation to an Asian source, he ends by quoting G-228, which see.

P-262

AUTHOR: Prufer, Olaf H.

DATE: 1965

TITLE: The McGraw Site: A Study in Hopewellian Dynamics

IN: Scientific Publication 4 (Cleveland

Museum of Natural History: Cleveland)

Purple dye use in Hopewell culture.

P-263

AUTHOR: Puleston, Dennis
DATE: 1979
TITLE: An Epistemological Pathology and the Collapse, or, Why the Maya Kept the Short Count
IN: Maya Archaeology and Ethnohistory, edited by Norman Hammond and Gordon R. Willey (University of Texas Press: Austin), 63-71

Argues that "history" among the Maya was powerfully shaped by cyclic, astronomical, calendrical forecasts of fate. [Potentially comparable to views of "history" and fate in archaic civilizations of Eurasia.]

P-264

AUTHOR: Purseglove, John W.
DATE: 1963
TITLE: Some Problems of the Origin and Distribution of Tropical Crops
IN: Genetica Agraria 17:105-122

See P-266.

P-265

AUTHOR: Purseglove, John W.
DATE: 1965
TITLE: The Spread of Tropical Crops
IN: The Genetics of Colonizing Species, Proceedings of the First International Union of Biological Sciences Symposia on General Biology, edited by H. G. Baker and G. L. Stebbins (Academic Press: New York), 375-390

See P-266.

P-266

AUTHOR: Purseglove, John W.
DATE: 1968
TITLE: Tropical Crops: Dicotyledons
IMPRINT: Longmans: London

Page 13: Only three crops were common to both Old and New Worlds before 1492: the gourd, sweet potato, and coconut. In addition Old World cotton must have reached South America to cross with wild diploid New World cotton to produce tetraploid G. barbadense, but it is *not* (author's emphasis) necessary to invoke the aid of man in the transport of these crops between the hemispheres. Merrill properly notes that some 1800 cultivated species were *not* (author's emphasis) common to both hemispheres.

Page 80-81: On the sweet potato, he had suggested in 1963 that I. batatas had been independently brought into cultivation in South America and in the Pacific, but he here abandons that view. He now considers that "sweet potato capsules float in water and that seeds . . . germinate after immersion in sea water;" thus sweet potato capsules were carried by currents from the New World to Polynesia. Or vines may have been carried across attached to a branch or log. Once the plant had become established in Polynesia, where most of their staple foods were root crops, "it could easily have been taken into cultivation." " 'Pacific Regattas' do not seem to be necessary, therefore, to carry Gossypium and Ipomoea batatas across the Pacific." As to the reputed shared name between South America and Polynesia, "evidence based on vernacular names is not always very reliable and I do not regard this as conclusive."

P-267

AUTHOR: Purves, Libby, editor
DATE: 1982
TITLE: Adventures under Sail; Selected Writings of H. W. Tilman
IMPRINT: Gollancz: London

A selection of the writings of an indefatigable small-boat man in crossing the North and South Atlantic.

P-268B

AUTHOR: Putnam, Charles E.
DATE: 1886
TITLE: The Davenport Tablets
IN: Science 7:119-120, 437-439

A defense on behalf of the Davenport Academy against attacks on the legitimacy of the Davenport Stone, of which they were custodians.

P-269B

AUTHOR: Putnam, Frederick Ward
DATE: 1884-1887
TITLE: Semi-Annual Meeting, April 28, 1886
IN: American Antiquarian Society, Proceedings (n. s.) 3-4:62-64

Exhibits and comments on specimens of "jade" from Old and New Worlds (including one from "a mound in Michigan"). He says that since no jade has been found in situ in America, all varieties of it must have come from Asia. Appends a letter from the Chemical Laboratory of Harvard College informing him that the three Central American specimens he had had tested there were "unquestionably Chinese Jade."

P-271

AUTHOR: Putnam, Frederic Ward
DATE: 1899
TITLE: A Problem in American Anthropology
IN: Proceedings of the American Association for the Advancement of Science (Columbus, Ohio, August 1899), 1-17
[Reprinted 1901 in *Smithsonian Institution Annual Report for 1899,* pages 473-498]

Page 9: Could the pre-Inca Peruvians have come across the Atlantic, considering the resemblance of older Andean art to that of the early Mediterranean, to which it seemingly has a closer resemblance than to any part of the American continent? Or should it be considered a "psychical coincidence," as some writers would have us believe? The nearness of sailing abilities (the Canaries on the one side of the ocean and Caribbean sailing on the other) suggests a possible means of communication.

He quotes Lewis Henry Morgan at the 1857 meeting of the Association regarding the (Iroquois) pattern of matrilineal descent: "Whether this code of descent came out of Asia or originated upon this continent is one of the questions incapable of proof; and it must rest, for its solution, upon the weight of evidence or upon probable induction. Its existence among American races whose languages are radically different, and without any traditional knowledge among them of its origin, indicates a very ancient introduction; and would seem to point to Asia as the birthplace of the system."

Q-001

AUTHOR: Quaife, Milo M.
DATE: 1934
TITLE: The Myth of the Kensington Rune Stone: The Norse Discovery of Minnesota 1362
IN: New England Quarterly 7:613-645

A rebuttal of Holand's special pleading, but less than the coup de grace Quaife intended. [See H-359 for a long rebuttal.]

Q-002

AUTHOR: Quaife, Milo M.
DATE: 1947
TITLE: The Kensington Myth Once More
IN: Michigan History 31:129-161

An attack on Holand's logic, internal inconsistencies, and evidence. Carefully destroys the reliability of most of the claimed Norse artifacts which Holand had discussed in a recent book as "corroborative finds."

Q-003

AUTHOR: Quatrefages de Bréau, J. L. Armand de

DATE: 1864

TITLE: Les Polynésiens et leurs migrations [The Polynesians and Their Migrations]

IMPRINT: Claye: Paris [Reprinted, amplified, from *Revue des deux mondes* 49 (1864): 521-547, 858-901. Revised edition Bertrand: Paris, 1866]

See Q-004.

Q-004

AUTHOR: Quatrefages de Bréau, J. L. Armand de

DATE: 1878

TITLE: Das Menschengeschlecht [The Human Species]

IMPRINT: F. A. Brockhaus: Leipzig [Reprinted Kegan Paul: London, 1879; reprinted D. Appleton: New York, 1881]

Vol. 1, chapter 17, pages 217-232: Arguing against "autocthony," as maintained by some scholars regarding the American natives, he here examines Polynesian migrations by sea as a case providing support for his theory of the ability to migrate far by sea. He concludes that the Polynesians, coming from Malaya spread by means of voluntary migrations and accidental dispersion from west to east to cover their area of the South Pacific.

Vol. 1, chapter 18, pages 233-249: "Migrations to America by Sea." Voyaging by way of the "kouro-sivo" current across the North Pacific was not particularly difficult. The equatorial current across the Atlantic from Africa offers the same possibilities, and rare evidence suggests the possibility that wrecks crossed there. Chinese and Japanese vessels and people crossed a number of times. Isolated black populations have been found in America, and some wrecks might have been a cause. But the "white type" is more widely represented in America than the black, as on the Northwest Coast, and in Peru the Charazanis resemble the Canary Islanders while differing from all surrounding tribes, etc. "The presence of Semitic types in America, certain traditions of Guiana, and the use in this country of a weapon [the Aztec maccuahuitl?] entirely characteristic of the ancient Canary Islanders," can be explained by boats borne on currents. In 1731 and 1764, small ships passing within the Canaries were driven by storms to America.

Of course there are more Asiatics represented in America, because the way from there, via the Bering Strait as well as by vessels, is easier than on the Atlantic side. He argues for Paravey's view of Fou-Sang as America, contra Klaproth; Paravey has published a facsimile of a Chinese drawing representing a llama, which must be the horse mentioned in the Fu-Sang stories. After discussing the Vikings, using some different "facts" than are usually cited, he argues that if smallish Viking vessels could reach America, large Polynesian ones would have done so more easily. (Same text in the American printing, 1881, is on pages 199-213.)

Q-006

AUTHOR: Quatrefages de Bréau, J. L. Armand de

DATE: 1887

TITLE: Introduction à l'étude des races humaines, vol. 1 [Introduction to the Study of Human Races, vol. 1]

IMPRINT: A. Hennuyer: Paris

Page 553: Among those populating America were whites of European origin as well as blacks.

Pages 557-560: Chinese knowledge of the compass and better ships than in the occident meant that transpacific voyages by them would have been possible earlier than might be thought from documents alone. He mapped spots on the North American coast where Japanese ships had been blown (over 60 cases from the 17th century to 1850). Accepts that voyages had been made and Buddhist missionaries had reached America (Fu-sang).

Q-007

AUTHOR: Quatrefages de Bréau, J. L. Armand de
DATE: 1891
TITLE: The Peopling of America
IN: Popular Science Monthly 38:305-313
[An address at the 8th International Congress of Americanists, Paris, 1890, translated from *Revue scientifique*]

America was settled by a series of migrations, via the Bering Strait of course, but also there are reasons to think that intermittently Europe, Africa, Asia, and Oceania "have sent to America a number of involuntary colonists, more considerable, probably, than one would be ready to suppose."

Q-008

AUTHORS: Quezada D., Ricardo Delfín, and Eula Luna Rivas
DATE: 1981
TITLE: La navegación entre los Mayas: una actividad económica
[Navigation among the Maya: An Economic Activity]
IN: Boletín, Escuela de ciencias antropológicas de la Universidad de Yucatán 9/50-51:43-51

Review of the literature, including early Spanish Yucatan material on boats in the Maya area.

Q-009

AUTHOR: Quigley, Carroll
DATE: 1956
TITLE: Aboriginal Fish Poisons and the Diffusion Problem
IN: American Anthropologist 58:508-525

On the basis of distribution of fish poisons, he believes that there was diffusion of matrilineal, root-planting, rain-forest cultures across the South Atlantic from Africa to South America.

Q-010

AUTHOR: Quijada Jara, Sergio
DATE: 1955
TITLE: Algunas comidas típicas del Valle del Mantaro
[Some Typical Food from the Valley of Mantaro]
IN: Archivos peruanos de folklore 1/1:86-93 (Cuzco)

Peruvian cooking in an oven with hot rocks was followed with a "ritual banquet," as in Polynesia.

Q-011

AUTHOR: Quimby, George I.
DATE: 1948
TITLE: Culture Contact on the Northwest Coast, 1785-1795
IN: American Anthropologist 50:247-255

Historical sources indicate that during this period European and American vessels trading on the coast included Chinese, Hawaiians, Negroes, and natives of the Philippines, and they left genes and could have left some features of culture behind. Heizer has compiled (unpublished) data on the presence of Japanese, via disabled craft, on this coast at this time and perhaps earlier. Chinese smiths were employed to manufacture articles for trade with the Indians. Chinese coins and buttons were carried as trade goods. In 1788 a Nootka Indian living near Canton China (he had also visited Hawaii) was given passage back to the Northwest Coast. [Compare K-026D.]

Q-012

AUTHOR: Quimby, George I.
DATE: 1985
TITLE: Japanese Wrecks, Iron Tools, and Prehistoric Indians of the Northwest Coast
IN: Arctic Anthropology 22/2:7-15

Iron blades used by prehistoric Indians of the Northwest Coast likely came from Japan. This survey of wrecks looks at survivors, cargoes, and Indian treatment of the wrecks and survivors. Ship iron was thus obtained. On the basis of historical data for the 18th and 19th centuries, Quimby estimates that "some thousands of disabled vessels reached American shores during the first 17 centuries of the Christian era." Voyages lasted one to two years.

Q-013

AUTHOR: Quimby, George I.
DATE: 1989
TITLE: Consequences of Early Contacts between Japanese Castaways and Native Americans: A Hundred Year Old Problem Still with Us
IN: Reprint Proceedings, Circum-Pacific Prehistory Conference, Seattle, August 1-6, 1989, part VIII: Prehistoric Trans-Pacific Contacts (Washington State University Press: Pullman), articles separately paginated

Abstract only printed. See Q-012. "What are the consequences of such early contacts and why is this problem unresolved?" "The ocean is not a barrier for human movement. It is interesting to seek more evidence of such contacts and cultural influence from Japan and other parts of Asia to the American continents."

Q-013B

AUTHOR: Quinn, David Beers
DATE: 1936
TITLE: Edward IV and Exploration
IN: Mariner's Mirror 21:282-284

Discussion of the apparent knowledge in western Europe in the decades before Columbus of lands to the west, which led to many exploratory voyages.

Q-014

AUTHOR: Quinn, David Beers
DATE: 1961
TITLE: The Argument for the English Discovery of America between 1480 and 1494
IN: The Geographical Journal 127:277-285 (London)

A "fragile" case is made for English discovery of North America in the decade before Columbus. [Compare R-197 and V-043.]

Q-014B

AUTHOR: Quinn, David Beers
DATE: 1967
TITLE: John Day and Columbus
IN: The Geographical Journal 132:205-209

See Q-014.

Q-014C

AUTHOR: Quinn, David Beers
DATE: 1989
TITLE: Atlantic Islands
IN: Atlantic Visions (Proceedings of the First International Conference of the Society of Saint Brendan, September 1985, Dublin and Kerry), edited by John de Courcy Ireland and David C. Sheehy (Boole Press, Dún Laoghaire, Co.: Dublin, Ireland), 77-93

Up-to-date summary of scholarship on the Fortunate Isles, Brasil, Antillia, etc., with reproductions of the most important maps.

Q-015

AUTHOR: Quinn, David Beers
DATE: 1972
TITLE: The Vinland Map, I: A Viking Map of the West?
IN: Saga-Book of the Viking Club. Viking Society for Northern Research 17/1:63-72 (London)

Page 71: Considering Marston and Skelton's information, "it might . . . appear to be ultra-sceptical to suggest that the map could still be a forgery."

Q-016

AUTHOR: Quinn, David Beers
DATE: 1974
TITLE: England and the Discovery of America, 1481-1620
IMPRINT: Knopf: New York

Uses recently found historical evidence to argue that men from Bristol, England, found North America in the 1480s while searching for the isle of "Brasil."

Q-018

AUTHOR: Quinn, David Beers, editor
DATE: 1979
TITLE: America from Concept to Discovery
IMPRINT: Arno Press: New York

Analyzes several medieval accounts which have been used as evidence for pre-Columbian voyages across the Atlantic and rejects them as not representing sound history. Includes excerpts from such medieval records as that of Adam of Bremen.

Q-020

AUTHOR: Quiroga, Adán
DATE: 1901
TITLE: La cruz en América [The Cross in America]
IMPRINT: Imprenta y Litografía "La Buenos Aires": Buenos Aires [Reprinted Editorial americana: Buenos Aires, 1942]

The cross is a symbol of water throughout the Americas. It has no connection with Old World notions of the cross.

Q-021

AUTHOR: Quiroga, Adán
DATE: 1897
TITLE: Calchaquí
IMPRINT: Imprenta española: Tucumán [Reprinted *Calchaquí* ("La Cultura Argentina": Buenos Aires, 1923)]

Lexical similarities of Quechua all over the world.

R-001

AUTHOR: Radicati di Primeglio, Carlos
DATE: n.d. [1979?]
TITLE: El sistema contable de los Incas: yupana y quipu [The Counting System of the Incas: Abacus and Quipu]
IMPRINT: Libreria Studium: Lima

A competent survey of the literature on the yupana or "abacus," the somewhat related taptanas used in games of chance, and the quipu, all of the Andean area. How they functioned and their history. An excellent history of the literature on quipus.

Page 27: The form of board game played with the taptanas apparatus "was the same as that used by the Egyptians of the pharaonic era and also of the ancient Assyrians, whose game boards show great similarity with those we believe were the taptanas of the Incas," citing Contenau, *Manuel d'archéologie orientale* 2:233, 1947. (Taptanas also relate to the question of "bean writing," for they appear to have been in use in scenes on Mochica pots involving beans.) The same can be said of a game played by the Yao of Mozambique today. While never clear, he seems more inclined to suppose the similarities due to independent invention than to diffusion.

R-002

AUTHOR: Radin, Paul
DATE: 1927
TITLE: The Story of the American Indian
IMPRINT: Boni and Liveright: New York [Reprinted 1937, 1944]

Includes the notion that Northwest Coast culture derives in part either from neolithic southeastern Siberia or Oceania.

R-003

AUTHOR: Radin, Paul
DATE: 1929
TITLE: History of Ethnographical Theories
IN: American Anthropologist 31:9-33

Considering the Rivers-Smith-Perry school, the author says that "personally we think the facts they have adduced interesting but [they are] so uncritically and unintelligently presented that no conclusions can possibly be drawn." "Until [the theory] has radically purged itself, it can hardly be intelligently discussed. Yet . . . it possesses the merit that it will force us to re-examine the whole concept of independent development, of psychic unity, and the nature of culture dissemination." He proposes a theory combining diffusion with the psychological approach. It holds that independently developed beliefs or objects remain latent until the presence of intruders makes them "socially functional."

R-005

AUTHOR: Rafn, Carl Christian, compiler
DATE: 1837
TITLE: Antiqvitates Americanae; sive, Scriptores septentrionales rerum ante-columbianarum in America; Samling af de i Nordens Oldskrifter indeholdte Efterretninger om de gamle Nørdboers Opdagelsesreiser til America fra det 10de til 14de Aarhundrede [American Antiquities; or, Northern Writings Regarding Pre-Columbian America . . .]
IMPRINT: Societas Regia Antiqvariorum Septentrionalium: Hafniae (Copenhagen) [Reviewed by Edward Everett, *North American Review* 46 (1838): 161-203. Reprinted Otto Zeller: Osnabrück, Germany, 1968. French edition, La société royale des antiquaires du nord: Copenhagen, 1845]

A Danish antiquary publishes for the first time in accessible form many of the sagas relating to Vinland. He was the first to locate Vinland specifically so as to encompass Rhode Island, citing in proof Dighton Rock and Newport Tower. However, his extreme enthusiasm led to scholarly skepticism over the next half century.

Texts of the sagas are in Icelandic, Danish, and Latin; introductory material is in Danish and Latin.

Several English translations of portions of this work exist.

R-006

AUTHOR: Rafn, Carl Christian
DATE: 1838
TITLE: America Discovered in the Tenth Century
IMPRINT: W. Jackson: New York

Though considerably smaller than his *Antiqvitates Americanae* (only 32 pages long, it originally served as an introduction to the larger work), this was actually more popular and influential: by 1865 it had already appeared in English, German, French, Dutch, Polish, Russian, Spanish, Portuguese, Italian, and even Magyar.

R-009

AUTHOR: Rafn, Carl Christian
DATE: 1864-1865
TITLE: On Indian Place-names
IN: Proceedings of the Massachusetts Historical Society, series 1, 8:193-198

Writing in 1839, he mentions derivation of Indian place names from Icelandic, proof to him that "ancient Northmen" inhabited New England for several centuries.

R-010

AUTHOR: Raglan, Fitzroy Richard Somerset (Lord)
DATE: 1939
TITLE: How Came Civilization?
IMPRINT: Methuen: London

An absolute diffusionist explains (or, rather, asserts) his views. His dogmatic position is exemplified by the statement, "since the chief medium of civilization, the alphabet, was diffused from one centre, civilization itself was diffused from one centre" (page 4). An example of this thinking applied to America: "The principle of glaze (on pottery) was not understood in the New World, yet Wissler . . . tells us that in the Pueblo area a true glaze was used. . . . It seems impossible to explain this fact except on the supposition that the art of glazing was introduced from across the Pacific, but failed to establish itself [more than locally]" (page 108).

Includes chapters on inventiveness, the beginnings of culture, the machinery of diffusion, and selected cases (e.g., the bow, pottery, the kite). Chapter 17 considers "Problems of America," "The whole case for culture diffusion, as opposed to multiple independent invention, depends on America." An immediate problem with "psychic unity" is that "if men's minds always work alike, they must work alike in adjacent villages as well as in widely separated continents," so why is there local variation? And if men's minds do not work the same nearby, why should they at a distance? "There is, of course, no direct evidence for the derivation of American . . . culture from the Old World" but the circumstantial evidence falls under five headings: (1) American culture has no (known) beginnings; (2) it is fundamentally ill-balanced, (3) all the centers of civilization were on or near the Pacific Coast, (4) all the close cultural parallels are with Eastern Asia or the Pacific islands, and (5) the religion of Mexico is heavily tinged with Asiatic, and particularly Buddhist, conceptions." Ends with Spinden's florid rhetoric: "the sky-line of Tikal with its terraced pyramids rises as a mirage out of the past only to find a splendid counterpart in the terraced skyline of New York." "Both are a hundred per cent American, and no more need be said," Raglan chuckles ironically.

R-011

AUTHOR: Raglan, Fitzroy Richard Somerset (Lord)
DATE: 1956
TITLE: The Hero: A Study in Tradition, Myth, and Drama
IMPRINT: Vintage: New York; and Isaac Pitman: London [Reprinted Greenwood: Westport, Connecticut, 1975]

The thesis is that traditional narratives are never history but merely myths, told in connection with a rite, and that standard versions have diffused widely. Among examples treated: King Arthur, Robin Hood, Troy, and the Norse sagas.

Pages 65-69: An excursus on Leif the Lucky supposes that all versions are merely variant tales without historical basis for the differences and likely none for the person ("if a man called Leif really discovered America").

Pages 200-201: Quetzalcoatl too was represented as a hero, a sky god, the living representative of a line of priestly rulers, an idol (part man, part bird-serpent), and certain animals—quetzal-bird and serpent. Five elements of the Quetzalcoatl story are found also in the hero of the tribes of the Sudan as well as in Horus, Attis, and Dionysos.

R-012B

AUTHOR: Raglan, Fitzroy Richard Somerset (Lord)
DATE: 1957
TITLE: Some Aspects of Diffusion
IN: Journal of the Royal Anthropological Institute 87:139-148

Page 139: "Except for developments within the same culture area, that is to say where people with the same cultural background were making similar experiments, no invention has been made twice," whether in material culture or in symbolic matters. No inventions were made during the entire Paleolithic, short of a few slight improvements in technique.

R-013

AUTHOR: Raglan, Fitzroy Richard Somerset (Lord)
DATE: 1964
TITLE: The Temple and the House
IMPRINT: Routledge and Paul: London; and Norton: New York

Pages 196-200: Emphasizes the conservatism of cultures, contrary to Wissler and other inventionists; in fact innovation is often actively discouraged. The native Americas are often cited as a prime example of inventiveness; he disagrees. Points out the inadequacy of Ogburn's list of alleged simultaneous inventions, which T. Chandler has critiqued devastatingly. Most if not all culture traits had a single origin.

R-014

AUTHOR: Rainey, Froelich
DATE: 1953
TITLE: The Significance of Recent Archaeological Discoveries in Inland Alaska
IN: Asia and North America: Transpacific Contacts, Memoirs of the Society for American Archaeology, No. 9. Supplement to American Antiquity 18/3, Part 2:43-46

After years of archaeological research in Alaska, he finds an "astonishing lack of any evidence for human occupation in the north during just that period when, we have assumed, ancestors of the American Indian were infiltrating into North America." To assume that primitive settlers could cross this daunting area but to question the ability of early settlers to cross the much more congenial ocean is to "strain at a gnat and swallow a camel."

R-015

AUTHOR: Rainey, Froelich
DATE: 1971
TITLE: The Ipiutak Culture: Excavations at Point Hope, Alaska
IN: Current Topics in Anthropology, Addison-Wesley Modular Publications, Module 8, pages 1-32

Point Hope, 200 miles north of Bering Strait, is an interception point for migrating whales, walrus, and seals.

Page 15: A wrought iron or steel blade remnant was found in an engraving tool. Similar thin-slotted knife handles from Okvik and Old Bering Sea sites indicate that fully developed Eskimo culture, as we know it in Siberia and Alaska, had access to limited quantities of wrought iron.

Page 25: Small, thin chipped blades very like Ipiutak have been found in the Urals around the junction of the Volga and Kama Rivers in the province of Perm, with a distinctive art style clearly related to Ipiutak. Bronze objects in fantastic shapes there resemble Ipiutak openwork ivory carvings. These are believed to be "shamanistic," as they compare favorably to items on shaman costumes in Siberia. [Compare S-008 through S-017.]

V. Chernetsov (1935) reported an ancient coast culture based on sea-mammal hunting, especially walrus, on Yamal Peninsula, just north of this Urals center (Bronze-Iron Age date). People there lived in houses not unlike those at Ipiutak and had harpoons and kayaks like the Eskimo. They also had metal: a brooch in the style of the Volga-Kama region confirms the theory of expeditions sent from that region to the far north, traveling down the Ob River for furs, fish, and probably walrus ivory. At Ipiutak Rainey found a similar bear-head figure and a rakelike object. Now Larsen finds rakelike objects from Ipiutak were part of a circumpolar bear cult, used to comb polar bear fur on skins as part of elaborate ceremonial treatment of dead bears.

Page 26: Specific Ipiutak traits cited relate to the "Siberian Animal Style" (Scythians). He suggests possible trade in walrus ivory and rawhide line, since walrus ivory in Asia was believed to have supernatural qualities (e.g., able to stop bleeding) and was highly prized for dagger handles, while rawhide line cut in one long spiraling strip was the strongest line known before invention of the steel cable. The two most strategic places in the world to intercept walrus were the Yamal peninsula and Point Hope.

Page 27: Chinese records suggest that iron was widely used on the steppes of Asia no earlier than about 500 B.C. Bronzes like Ipiutak style dated to near the time of Christ; Ipiutak dates about the same time.

R-015B

AUTHOR: Rainey, Froelich
DATE: 1992
TITLE: Reflections of a Digger: Fifty Years of World Archaeology
IMPRINT: University Museum of Archaeology and Anthropology, University of Pennsylvnia: Philadelphia

Pages 81-82: Reprises R-014.

Page 85: "Seven years of searching in the Arctic proved nothing about these hypothetical Bering Strait migrations that are supposed to have peopled America at an unknown time in the past. That theory is still accepted as fact, although no real proof has yet turned up in the Bering Strait region. My guess is that in the future some other theory will replace it to explain the origin of the American Indian. Theories about the ancient past rarely last for long."

R-016

AUTHOR: Rallier du Baty, Raymond
DATE: n.d.
TITLE: 15,000 Miles in a Ketch
IMPRINT: Thomas Nelson: London

In 1907-08 a crew of six in a 50-foot ketch sailed from France to Brazil, then to Australia by way of Tristan da Cunha and the Kerguelen Islands.

R-016B

AUTHOR: Ramos, Bernardo de Azevedo da Silva
DATE: 1939
TITLE: Inscripçoes e tradições da America prehistorica, especialmente do Brasil, 2 volumes [Inscriptions and Traditions of Prehistoric America, Especially of Brazil]
IMPRINT: Rio de Janeiro: Imprensa Nacional [Portions appeared in 1930 as *Inscripções da America prehistorica, Rio de Janeiro,* and again, apparently as a single volume, in 1932 with the present title]

A massive compendium (over 1050 pages) of original chapters, reprinted scholarly papers, accounts of lectures, and newspaper articles. Originally he found an inscription on a rock in the mountains behind Rio de Janeiro which he read as Phoenician. Other Brazilians claimed it was not even writing but only natural cracks or marks. Thus challenged, he worked for 30 years to locate over 3000 inscriptions in Brazil and other countries which he compared to Old World materials. [Compare S-160.] Includes many drawings and a few indistinct photographs of hundreds of rock inscriptions found in Brazil (chiefly), Colombia, Peru, Mexico, North America, and various other New World areas. He gives a reading of most of these as in Greek language. Few of the materials are found in the international literature. His prime thesis is that Greek and Phoenician voyagers reached Brazil and left actual cities and hundreds if not thousands of inscriptions. A little attention is paid to Egyptian influence also.

The final 55 pages consists of reprints of talks or papers given by him in Brazil and of press reports of the same.

R-017

AUTHOR: Ramos, Demetria

DATE: 1971

TITLE: Los contactos transatlánticos decisivos, como precedentes del viaje de Colón
[The Decisive Transatlantic Contacts as Precedents for the Voyage of Columbus]

IN: Anuario de estudios atlánticos 17:467-532 (Madrid)
[Separately, 1972, same title, as Cuadernos Colombinos 2 by Casa-Museo de Colon, Seminario de Historia de America de la Universidad de Valladolid]

Alludes to a possible accidental voyage to America and return, which provoked a seriously organized expedition by Diego de Teive in 1452, patronized by the Portuguese king. This expedition traveled more than 150 leagues southwest of the Azores and was caught in the Sargasso but managed to get out and made the great circle voyage north then east to Ireland to return. This itinerary seems to represent a replica of an accidental voyage a little earlier. The pilot of the expedition, Vázquez de Palos had occasion to talk with Columbus and Pinzón and no doubt reported that trip. Another voyage, in 1462, by Tavira, reached unknown islands west-northwest of the Canaries and Madeira, which could have been Bermuda, before returning. Accidental voyages of vessels swept westward from the Canaries are noted.

Page 3: A footnote discusses the statements of Sarmiento de Gamboa, who lived in Mexico from 1555-1557. He speculated that Ulysses' voyage went into the Atlantic and reached Yucatan, offering a little evidence for a crossing but stating that the Indians had "anciently" preserved "a ship anchor which they venerated as an idol."

Pages 4-5: Makes a distinction between "tact" and "contact," the latter prevailing only with a return voyage. Ramos believes transoceanic voyages were made but not until the late 15th century was there a return.

Page 44: Humboldt made passing reference to vessels in 1731 and 1764 navigating between islands of the Canary archipelago which were swept to America.

R-018

AUTHOR: Randall, Betty Uchitelle

DATE: 1949

TITLE: The Cinderella Theme in Northwest Coast Folklore

IN: Indians of the Urban Northwest, edited by Marian W. Smith (Columbia University Press: New York), 243-285

Cross-cultural survey of Northwest Coast variants of the Eurasian Cinderella folktale, supposing convergence.

R-020

AUTHOR: Rands, Robert L.

DATE: 1953

TITLE: The Water Lily in Maya Art: A Complex of Alleged Asiatic Origin

IN: Smithsonian Institution, Bureau of American Ethnology Bulletin 151 (Washington, D.C.), 75-153

An examination of the religious symbolism of the water lily and the iconographic uses to which it was put by the Maya. He does not find evidence for transpacific importation of the theme, although conceptual parallels to Southeast Asia are striking.

Grants "truly remarkable parallels" in representations of the water lily and its symbolic associations between Chichén Itzá/Palenque and Amaravati, India, but finds almost no evidence of an intrusion into Mesoamerican art history corresponding to Heine-Geldern and Ekholm's thesis. A naturalistic convergent explanation for the parallels cannot be ruled out.

The water lily forms part of a complex with the Long-Nosed God and beings perhaps related to the Serpent Bird. "To explain the elaborated water lily as of Asiatic derivation, it would appear necessary to postulate a complex series of waves of fundamental influence which accounted for new traits on various time levels." The possible basic relationship between Old and New World theocracies, and the cursive tendencies in Maya and Indian art, may explain the parallels in Maya and Hindu-Buddhist depictions.

R-021

AUTHOR: Rands, Robert L.
DATE: 1957
TITLE: Comparative Notes on the Hand-eye and Related Motifs
IN: American Antiquity 22:247-257

He discusses occurrence of a number of versions of the symbol of the open eye on the open hand in Mesoamerica, the Southern Cult, Adena, the Northwest Coast, and elsewhere in North America. A diffusionist explanation for the North American and Mesoamerican examples might be possible, although he urges fuller study before the issue could be settled. He particularly thinks that such study ought to consider visually similar Pacific Basin examples (from East Asia to Peru) cited by C-402, D-183, S-147 and S-148.

R-022

AUTHORS: Rands, Robert L., and Carroll L. Riley
DATE: 1958
TITLE: Diffusion and Discontinuous Distribution
IN: American Anthropologist 60:274-297

They reexamine certain concepts relating to patterning and discontinuous distributions: pattern elaboration, complex demand, and complex nucleus. An example is the treatment of the Asian and American blowgun, which superficially fulfills Tylor's rule demonstrating diffusion, while actually it represents independent cases of complex demand springing from a familiarity with hollow reeds, canes, or bamboo.

Further, in both areas a distinctive and rather curious way of holding the blowgun in firing is so unusual that it has been supposed an arbitrary element in a diffused complex, but actually that stance also is "a product of complex demand."

R-023

AUTHOR: Ranking, John
DATE: 1827
TITLE: Historical Researches on the Conquest of Peru, Mexico, Bogata, Natchez, and Talomeco, in the Thirteenth Century, by the Mongols, Accompanied with Elephants
IMPRINT: Longman, Rees, Orme, Brown, and Green: London

He supposes that Manco Capac, first Inca ruler, was a son of Kubla Khan, and that Montezuma's ancestor was a Mongol noble, perhaps from Assam. Virtually all the evidences of civilization in America owe to them. The quipu and a type of abacus (using grains of maize for counters), both used in China, are adduced as evidence. Draws heavily on Peruvian stories recorded by the Spaniards.

R-024

AUTHOR: Rashidi, Runoko
DATE: 1987
TITLE: Men out of Asia: A Review and Update of the Gladwin Thesis
IN: African Presence in Early America, edited by Ivan van Sertima (n.p.: n.p.), 248-263
["Incorporating Journal of African Civilizations, Dec. 1986, vol. 8, no. 2." "All inquiries should be addressed to Transaction Books, Rutgers—the State University, New Brunswick, New Jersey"]

Offered as "a critical review and reassessment of the 'Gladwin Thesis' from an Afrocentric perspective." Pygmies, Australoids, "the Clovis-Folsom Point Blacks," Algonquins ("the first American arrivals who are not known to have been of a Black or Africoid phenotype"), Eskimos (first of the Mongoloids to reach America). Nothing is added to the Gladwin argument and no critique or reassessment is made.

An "Africoid mask" of basalt of unknown age found on the North Canadian coast is shown on page 263.

R-025

AUTHOR: Rashidi, Runoko
DATE: 1990
TITLE: Introduction to the Study of African Classical Civilization
IMPRINT: Karnak House: London

Includes detailed examination of evidence for the appearance of black people as aboriginals at various times in Europe, America, and India.

R-027

AUTHOR: Rath, Julius
DATE: 1942
TITLE: Ein altperuanisches Batikmuster [An Old Peruvian Batik Design]
IN: Paideuma 2:239-242

Southeast Asia comparison.

R-028

AUTHOR: Ratzel, Friedrich
DATE: 1896-1898
TITLE: The History of Mankind
IMPRINT: Macmillan: London
[First edition, *Völkerkunde,* 3 vols. (Bibliographischen Instituts: Leipzig, 1885-88). Second edition, revised, 1894-1895, in two volumes, from which the English translation was made]

Vol. 1, pages 146-147: American natives are the most easterly extension of the Asians, but largely independent in development because of distance.

Page 148: Topinard refers the mass of Polynesians to North America with conquerors coming among them from the Celebes, but we do not yet possess evidence to prove this view. In any case the idea of a single immigration of Polynesians from Asia does not fit the observed facts of racial variety.

Page 149: Zuñiga asserted the South American origin of the Tagals (Philippines), claiming a likeness between Tagalese and Chileans, but Friederici rejects this.

Page 150: The masks of New Ireland remind us strikingly of those of the Haidas. And it is not always neighboring peoples who show the closest relations; the Dyak loom resembles that of the Northwest Coast and head-hunting, skull cult, and human hair for ornamentation are common to both. The ornament of Malay fabrics is remarkably like that of the early Americans. Calchaqui (Peruvian-like) decoration reminds us of Malay work.

Page 154: Evidence for Japanese influence increases as we go north along the Pacific Coast of America. The Chinese land to the east [Fu-sang] can only refer to Northwest America.

Vol. 2: A number of comparisons are made of American civilizational characteristics directly to the Old World beyond Oceania.

R-029

AUTHOR: Ratzel, Friedrich
DATE: 1912
TITLE: Anthropogeographie, 2nd edition [Anthropogeography]
IMPRINT: J. Engelhorn: Stuttgart [4th edition, 1921-22]

Vol. 2, page 25: "Until 1492 America was, ethnographically, the Far East, its relations point to Asia and Polynesia, not to Europe or Africa; its union with the Old Continent was not established by way of the Atlantic but of the Pacific."

Page 575: Clubs of New Zealand and the Northwest Coast are so similar that they must evidence cultural contact.

R-030

AUTHOR: Rau, Charles
DATE: 1882
TITLE: Cups and Circles
IN: Nature 26 (June 8): 126-129

Describes "cup" depressions in rocks in parts of America and Old World. Their function may be utilitarian and ornamental in part, but religious conceptions associated with the feature seem sometimes involved and deserve further study as possible evidence of interhemispheric movement.

R-031

AUTHOR: Ravines, Roger, compiler and editor
DATE: 1978
TITLE: Tecnología andina [Andean Technology]
IMPRINT: Instituto de Estudios Peruanos: Lima

A reader reprinting articles such as well-known pieces by Gayton, Tello, Lechtman, Lothrop, Kosok, the Aschers, and Hrdlicka. Bibliographies are omitted, but some convenience results in access to basic material on quipus, trepanation, navigation, the bridge at Sarhua, and so on.

R-032

AUTHOR: Ravines, Roger
DATE: 1982
TITLE: Panorama de la arqueología andina [Panorama of Andean Archaeology]
IMPRINT: Instituto de Estudios Peruanos: Lima

Page 67: Is not persuaded of a Japanese connection at Valdivia.

R-033

AUTHOR: Rawson, A. L.
DATE: 1891
TITLE: The Ancient Inscription on a Wall at Chatata, Tennessee
IN: New York Academy of Sciences Transactions 11:26-29

Some 872 characters were found on a sandstone "wall" in Tennessee that had been intentionally buried after the characters were engraved. "Accidental imitation of oriental alphabets are numerous." The site was reported in a Smithsonian publication. [See W-213B.]

R-034

AUTHOR: Rawson, A. L.
DATE: 1892
TITLE: The Ancient Inscription of Chatata, Tennessee
IN: American Antiquarian and Oriental Journal 14:221-223

Discusses the 1891 discovery of a half-buried "wall" of sandstone 1060 feet long on which was an inscription containing characters vaguely like "Near Eastern" writing. [See W-213B.]

R-035

AUTHOR: Ray, G. Whitfield
DATE: 1951
TITLE: The American Indian—Who Is He?

IMPRINT: Meador: Boston

An impassioned argument for the autocthony of native Americans, against all claims of Bering Strait or voyaging origins.

In the foreword, "Methewayob" (Scott H. Peters), listed as Chief of Chiefs, Indian Council Fire, apparently representing a group of Indian tribes, welcomes this book by an adopted Indian (who is also a F.R.G.S.), for, he says, "We do not believe that our 'family tree' was ever rooted in Asia, nor are we in any sense ethnologically connected with the Orient. In all our many Tribes and languages, there is no legend of our having crossed the sea from Asia. Even the western tribes of our people have no such folklore or tradition." The book is without bibliography but intelligently cites in text a great deal of current popular and scientific literature.

R-036

AUTHOR: Raynaud, Georges
DATE: 1901
TITLE: Les nombres sacrés et les signes cunéiformes dans la moyenne Amérique précolombienne [The Sacred Numbers and Cuneiform Signs in Pre-Columbian Middle America]
IN: Revue de l'histoire des religions 44:235-261

So-called crosses and sacred numbers (3, 4, 7, 13, etc.) do not mean the same thing as what are sometimes taken as European equivalents. The "cross" in at least some form is probably from Asia out of Buddhist influence on American civilizations.

R-037

AUTHOR: Read, C. Hercules
DATE: 1917
TITLE: Siberian Bronzes and Chinese Jade
IN: Man 17:1-4

Shows a stylistic affinity between a jade carving of a monstrous animal which recalls Chinese style in jade, and Siberian or Scythian bronzes. [In turn related to ivory carvings of Alaska; see R-015.] Read also notes similarities with art representations of strange creatures in Peru.

R-037B

AUTHOR: Reader's Digest (Principal Adviser and Editorial Consultant, Michael D. Coe)
DATE: 1986
TITLE: Mysteries of the Ancient Americas: The New World before Columbus
IMPRINT: Reader's Digest Association: Pleasantville, New York

Over 20 short chapters and many sidebars (no authors are attributed) discuss not only conventional archaeological interpretations but topics of interest in regard to transoceanic contacts. The material is well-written, based on intelligent literature, and generally even-handed. Excellent illustrations accompany the discussions.

The first six sections are grouped under the heading "Voyagers of Legend."

Pages 10-21, "Visitors from Lands Beyond": Includes discussions of Le Plongeon, G. Elliot Smith, Brasseur de B ourbourg, R. A. Jairazbhoy, Robert Marx, B. Fell, the Ra Expedition, the Paraiba Stone, von Däniken, and M. Reiche.

Pages 22-31, "Mirrors of Culture": Valdivia, Fu-sang, tripod cylinders, Ekholm and Heine-Geldern, patolli, calendar similarities, Heyerdahl, accidental voyages, wheeled toys, anchor stones, and "elephants." Illustrations: a fat, narrow-eyed male figurine [apparently from the early Xochipala tradition in Mexico]--"Could it be modeled on a Japanese Sumo wrestler?" Also shown is a Mochica pot picturing use of a captive cormorant in fishing.

Pages 32-41, "Lost Tribes in the New World": Madoc, the Mandans, Ten Lost Israelite Tribes, Lord Kingsborough, Manasseh ben Israel,

Quetzalcoatl, beards, the Book of Mormon, and Melungeons.

Pages 42-49, "Islands in the Mist": early maps, Brandan, Tim Severin, "Seven Cities" of Brazil, Atlantis, and Lemuria.

Pages 50-65, "Vinland the Good": Eric, Leif, Greenlnd, "the Arctic mirage," "GRAPES," "Viking hoaxes" (Kensington Stone and Vinland Map), skraelings, and L'Anse aux Meadows.

Pages 66-107, "In Search of Early Man."

Page 103: "Hawaii's Mysterious Cotton."

Pages 104-105: Lathrap's idea of early Africans arriving in South America.

Pages 166-187, "Clues to a Forgotten Past": Mound Builders and earthworks.

R-038

AUTHOR: Redmond, Jeffrey R.
DATE: 1979
TITLE: "Viking" Hoaxes in North America
IMPRINT: Carlton Press: New York

A short book (30 pages of actual text) which cites evidence against the authenticity of the Kensington Stone, Newport Tower, Norse halberds, the Vinland Map, Oklahoma, runes and various other claimed Viking productions. Wahlgren's foreword lays out the line: "Persons known and unknown have 'enlarged our knowledge' of early Scandinavian exploration through the planting of artifacts or through elaborately preposterous interpretations of the finds." But Science is triumphant despite such obstacles.

Incidentally Wahlgren considers Thomas E. Lee's case for Norse Ungava Peninsula ruins to rest on "impressive arguments." Of special interest are two appended letters from Lee to the author, dated 1977, indicating perhaps his final views on the subject. To the end Lee remained independent and highly opinionated (e.g., Haugen and Morison have "tightly closed minds"; "opinions from men like these mean nothing"; and Fell "is not to be believed"), but these letters include, and call for, new data on Newport, Kensington, etc.

R-039

AUTHOR: Reed, Alma M.
DATE: 1966
TITLE: The Ancient Past of Mexico
IMPRINT: Crown: New York

Pages 7-14: A journalist reasonably acquainted with Mesoamerican cultural materials reprises the independent invention vs. diffusionist positions, displaying only partial control of sources but grinding no axes either way. Summarizes F-062, which introduces (page 10) a brief report on a project initiated by Ferguson in 1964 in which Morris Swadesh and assistants compared "a few hundred words of indigenous languages of Mexico with Hebrew." Swadesh is quoted as commenting: "I was surprised at the number and closeness of the parallels between the Sawi-Zaa [which includes Zapotec] and the Semitic languages." Ferguson had reported that the Zapotec vocabulary sampled contained from 18 to 20 percent recognizable Hebrew words. [See also A-032.] He has compiled a list of 311 cultural elements common to the Near East and Middle America.

Page 11-14: The flowing vase, symbolizing the Milky Way, and the Tree of Life symbol are shared by Near Eastern cultures and Mayan and Izapan art. Altars too are similar, and the six-pointed star of David, found as early as the seventh century B.C. in Phoenicia, appears at Uxmal with a pennated tail attached, like Assyrian, Phoenician, and Persian orbs. Brendan elements are discussed also.

Pages 41-46: A bit of Ekholm, Heine-Geldern, and Kirchoff is sketched. Quotes Mesoamericanist Eulalía Guzman on her reaction to visiting Peking and discovering concordances between the Chinese cultural remains and what she knew already from Mexico. [This mirrors sinologist Joseph Needham's experience in Mexico.] In her view "Three or four sections of the old Winter Palace in the heart of Peking are the same as those of the Palace of Atetelco at Teotihuacan. Exact parallels are to be seen in the two constructions. . . . Since these dramatic resemblances exist, why not, considering the time element, believe that the influence traveled westward from the American continent to Asia." Furthermore, "I was astonished to see from the day of my arrival marked resemblances everywhere to motifs prevalent in our own archaeological discoveries. Every fret I knew from the codices or the Monte Albán jewels, I found in Peking, sometimes on the friezes, again in the furniture or on other objects." The fat dogs shared by the China and West Mexico support the idea.

Pages 265-270: In description and illustrations, she recaps some of the key comparisons made by Ekholm and others between Mayan culture and those of India and Cambodia.

R-040

AUTHOR: Reed, Charles A.
DATE: 1977
TITLE: Origins of Agriculture: Discussion and Some Conclusions
IN: The Origins of Agriculture, edited by Charles A. Reed (Aldine: Chicago), 879-953

Pages 930-937: Surveys and evaluates the status of theories for the American origin of agriculture. "I like Lathrop's concept of trans-Atlantic voyages by fishermen in dugout canoes from western Africa to eastern Brazil." He thinks that Carter's case for American chickens tips the scale to acceptance.

R-041

AUTHOR: Reed, Erik K.
DATE: 1961
TITLE: Diffusionism and Darwinism
IN: American Anthropologist 63:375-377

"Unilinear evolution" is far from Darwinism. Biological evolution supposes variation according to local circumstances, not universal stages through which all of a species must pass. Rather, "the extreme diffusionists probably are closer to corresponding with biological evolution."

R-042

AUTHOR: Reed, T. Edward
DATE: 1967
TITLE: The Evidence for Natural Selection Due to Blood Groups
IN: Proceedings of the World Population Conference (Belgrade, 1965) (United Nations: New York), 2:498-502

The evidence is substantial, undermining the value of blood groups as historical indicators.

R-043

AUTHOR: Rees, Fallis F.
DATE: 1968
TITLE: Juxtlahuaca Cave Paintings of Mexico
IN: All Points Bulletin 5/4:3-7 [Denver Chapter, Colorado Archaeological Society]

Based on Carlo Gay's report on an Olmec wall painting 3400 feet inside this cave in the Mexican state of Guerrero, Rees makes a comparison with an Egyptian cult scene. At Juxtlahuaca a large figure dressed in jaguar skin brandishes two implements toward a smaller seated figure seen as having a black face. He believes this represents the Egyptian rite of "opening the mouth."

Comparisons he makes: feline pelt with spotted tail hanging between legs of the standing figures; ritual adz; trident or forked flint instrument, known to be used in Egypt in this ceremony; painted black face and chin beard; "corn measure" hat; underground locale (Osirian connection).

Farther inside the cave is a feline-serpent hybrid figure including several signs, notably a cross-in-circle, with an Egyptian meaning.

Ends abruptly thus: "And so ends the story of the negroes, the bearded white men and the mongols on gulf coast Mexico on that fall day c. 600 B.C., when the integrated crew of Pharaoh Necho's navy landed there."

R-044

AUTHOR: Reeves, Arthur Middleton
DATE: 1895
TITLE: The Finding of Wineland the Good: The History of the Icelandic Discovery of America, Edited and Translated from the Earliest Records
IMPRINT: Henry Frowde: London [Reprinted Burt Franklin: New York, 1967(?)]

Based upon research in Iceland, the author critically examines what the extant texts say about the discovery of Vinland and related lands. He identifies and traces the history of the relevant manuscripts, noting inconsistencies among them and discriminating concerning their likely value as historical documents. (The oldest surviving document was written not later than 1334.)

He assails Rafn (1837) for allowing his zeal to bring recognition to the Viking discoverers to lead him into "many dubious theories and hazardous conjectures," which most students of the subject since then have pursued rather than what the texts have to say. "If the authenticity of the Icelandic discovery of America is to be determined by runic inscriptions or other archaeological remains left by the discoverers, it is altogether probable that the discovery will never be confirmed."

The latter part of the volume shows photographs of each of the manuscripts along with annotated printed transliterations. Reeves' English translations are in chapters 2 and 3.

Pages 159-192: This section of his notes includes judicious comments on not only the sagas but the interpretive literature, such as the possible affiliations with Eskimo or Indian languages of the words attributed to the skraelings.

R-045

AUTHOR: Reeves, Arthur Middleton
DATE: 1906
TITLE: The Norse Discovery of America: A Compilation in Extenso of all the Sagas, Manuscripts, and Inscriptive Memorials Relating to the Finding and Settlement of the New World in the Eleventh Century
IMPRINT: Norroena Society: London

Reprints the first six chapters of R-044 and argues his case along essentially the same lines.

R-045B

AUTHORS: Reeves, R. G., and Paul C. Mangelsdorf
DATE: 1959
TITLE: The Origin of Corn. V. A Critique of Current Theories
IN: Harvard University, Botanical Museum Leaflets 18:428-440

Includes what they consider a definitive critique against claims for pre-Columbian occurrence of corn in Asia.

R-046

AUTHOR: Regamey, Felix
DATE: 1896-1897
TITLE: Poterie américaine et japonaise [American and Japanese Pottery]
IN: Journal de la société des americanistes de Paris 1:89-90

Briefly compares (illustrates) Japanese effigy pottery in the form of a duck with such from the Mississippi Valley and finds the similarity striking.

R-048B

AUTHOR: Reichel-Dolmatoff, Gerardo
DATE: 1978
TITLE: The Loom of Life: A Kogi Principle of Integration
IN: Journal of Latin American Lore 4/1:5-27

Shows the cosmic model of the Kogi Indians of northern Colombia displayed in their house and temple structures and looms. He relates it to their astronomy, calendar, and key myths. Their origin he is inclined to see in Central America under influence of the Maya. He concludes: "The symbolism of the Loom of Life, of the Great Weaver, of life and death interlacing the strands of the tapestry of destiny, appears in many societies the world over. From prehistoric Egypt to the modern Dogon, from the ancient Sumerians to India; from Plato's spindle of Necessity to the nameless prehistoric Indians of the coast of Ecuador, we find the same basic constellation of ideas, symbols, and metaphors. The reason for this lies in the fact that all these peoples were agriculturalists and weavers and that all of them were anxiously watching the sun, bringer of rain or drought, tracing with his course the limits of sacred space. The loom and the calendric outlines of solstices and equinoxes coincide in so many aspects of form and process that a basic image came to be shared by different societies through the ages."

[In contrast, David H. Kelley, personal communication to Sorenson, August 1995, comments regarding the Kogi: "They seem to have a poor man's version of a Buddhist stupa, are near vegetarians, believe in reincarnation, have the Saturnian Nine so emphasized in Buddhism (although I haven't seen it identified as Saturn in Buddhism), serpent-footed god, Maun as centre/zenith, Owl in appropriate position—massive amounts of stuff linking to India on the one hand and Mesoamerica on the other."]

R-050

AUTHORS: Reichlen, Henry, and Paule Reichlen
DATE: 1950
TITLE: Recherches archéologiques dans les Andes du haut Utcubamba [Archaeological Researches in the Andes of Upper Utcubamba]
IN: Journal de la société des américanistes de Paris 39:219-246

Report a burial mode which struck Rivet as having "extraordinary similarity" to a practice in Celebes.

R-051

AUTHOR: Reinman, Fred M.
DATE: 1968
TITLE: Tuna Tagging and Shell Fishhooks: A Comment from Oceania
IN: American Antiquity 33:95-98

Consideration of the uses of single-piece shell fishhooks in Oceania leads him to doubt Landberg's [L-016] guess that tuna might have carried such hooks to the Pacific Coast of the Americas, for tuna are fished for with a quite different hook, so Landberg's view is improbable.

R-052

AUTHOR: Rejón García, M.
DATE: 1905
TITLE: Los Mayas primitivos [The Primitive Maya]
IMPRINT: Imprenta de la Loteria del Estado: Mérida, Yucatan

Discusses the etymology of Maya place-names and seeks on linguistic, religious, and archaeological grounds to prove that the Mayas descended from the ancient Egyptians.

R-052B

AUTHOR: Reko, Blas Pablo
DATE: 1919

TITLE: De los nombres botánicos aztecas
IN: El México antiguo 1 (5 Dic.): 113-157

Page 115: Indigenous plant and animal names are among the most ancient relics of a people and comparative study of them worldwide could open up a very distant perspective on the mythological traditions about prehistoric migrations and the origin of certain cultivated species. "The name 'toloache,' which coincides with the Chinese name 'tolo-wan' for the same plant (Datura strammonium), could indicate transpacific communications."

R-054

AUTHOR: Reko, Blas Pablo
DATE: 1934a
TITLE: Einführung in die vergleichende Astralmythologie [Introduction to Comparative Astral Mythology]
IN: El México antiguo 3/3-4 (Diciembre): 15-47

Compares data on star names and their meanings for various Mesoamerican groups and for Japan, China, India, Mesopotamia, Egypt, the Hebrews, and additional areas. He supposes that only a diffusionist position will explain the similarities.

R-055

AUTHOR: Reko, Blas Pablo
DATE: 1934b
TITLE: The Royal Stars of the Hebrews, Aztecs and Quiches
IN: El México antiguo 3/3-4 (Diciembre): 49-56

Four directionally associated constellations or stars were noted by Humboldt. "The four royal stars of the Hebrews and the Aztecs were not only identical but . . . two of their names had even the same meaning. More remarkably, in both places the two solstices were represented by the most conspicuous constellation of northern and southern heavens respectively." Inca and Chinese compare also in regard to symbols for the solstices. Further, the Popol Vuh gives names of the four royal houses of the Quiches related to the foregoing star names. "The similarity of the myths of all parts of the world is so great and convincing that it can never be explained by a convergence of the human mind as expressed in the theory [of psychic unity] of Bastian, but proves conclusively a common origin."

R-056

AUTHOR: Reko, Blas Pablo
DATE: 1935-1938
TITLE: Star Names of the Chilam Balam of Chumayel
IN: El México antiguo 3/9-10: 1-51; 3/11-12: 13-84; 4/1-2: 21-67; 4/3-4: 95-129; 4/5-6: 163-178; 4/7-8: 255-285

Immensely detailed data on the nomenclature and associations of native American stars, constellations, months, zodiac, rulers, and so forth, with many comments on Eurasian parallels. A large fold-out chart in the first issue correlates zodiac signs with Babylonian, Egyptian, Hindu, Chinese, Japanese, Incan, Zapotec, Mayan, Aztec, and Tarascan months/rulers/symbols.

R-057

AUTHOR: Reman, Edward (edited by A. G. Brodeur)
DATE: 1949
TITLE: The Norse Discoveries and Explorations in America
IMPRINT: University of California Press: Berkeley

An experienced Norwegian sailor critically reinterprets the sagas, concluding that Karlsefni's Markland was around Ungava Bay and his ultimate landing on the west side of Hudson Bay, while Leif's Markland was Newfoundland and Maine was his Vinland. He decries the faking of "evidence," including the Kensington Stone.

R-058

AUTHOR: Remington, Judith Ann

DATE: 1981

TITLE: Mesoamerican Archaeoastronomy: Parallax, Perspective, and Focus

IN: Archaeoastronomy in the Americas, edited by Ray A. Williamson, Ballena Press Anthropological Papers No. 22 (Ballena Press: Los Altos, California), 193-204

Discusses the forcing engaged in by older Mesoamericanists in an effort to preserve an old paradigm— "a determined and often defiant adherence to assumptions that were no longer tenable was characteristic of the second generation of Mesoamericanists." Meanwhile, new discoveries wreak havoc with old hypotheses. "Nonetheless, the hypotheses were presented as theories and defended fiercely." Now a third generation comes on the scene more willing "to consider the possibility of truly alien methods of organizing the 'same' data."

Page 202: For example, "Talking about the possibility of diffusion was not quite nice; Jomon pottery was discussed in hushed tones, and the suggestions of connections between the calendars and constellations of the Americas and Asia was considered to be in rather bad taste."

R-059

AUTHOR: Renaud, A. Etienne B.

DATE: 1928

TITLE: Comparison of Indian and Papuan Skulls

IN: El Palacio 25:409-410 (Santa Fe, New Mexico)

Paul A. F. Walter, the editor of *El Palacio,* provides a very brief report of a paper on this topic delivered by Renaud at a meeting of the Colorado-Wyoming Academy of Science. A skull from a burial mound in Illinois "fits into the series of head types of some African and Oceanian peoples, particularly the Papuan-Australian group."

R-060

AUTHOR: Renaud, A. Etienne B.

DATE: 1929

TITLE: Prehistoric Female Figurines from America and the Old World

IN: Scientific Monthly 28:507-512

Female figurines are everywhere "statuettes of the goddess of fecundity and life" which "betray the same psychology in primitive men of different continents."

R-061

AUTHOR: Renaud, A. Etienne B.

DATE: 1933

TITLE: Rassemblances des cultures préhistoriques de l'Ancien et du Nouveau Monde [Resemblances of Prehistoric Cultures of the Old and New World]

IN: Revue anthropologique 43:468-476

The general similarity in implements of paleolithic and neolithic type and then the same sequence of stages in the development of civilization in both America and the Old World attests to the remarkable similarity of human psychology in all lands.

R-063

AUTHOR: Renaud, A. Etienne B.

DATE: 1953

TITLE: The Negroid Elements among Prehistoric Indians

IN: Southwestern Lore 19/2:25-29

He has pointed out previously "a strong Proto-Negroid factor in the Southwest and in many districts of both North and South America [as at Lagoa Santa], associated in places with a rather primitive state of culture" and preceding the arrival of brachycephals.

R-064

AUTHOR: Rendón, Silvia

DATE: 1953

TITLE: ¿Fué el maíz originario de América? [Was Maize Native to America?]
IN: América indígena 13:223-230

Reviews selected linguistic and historic data with the conclusion that maize is not American in origin but that it probably originated in the Danube basin or Transcaucasia.

R-065

AUTHOR: Rensberger, Boyce
DATE: 1981
TITLE: Black Kings of Ancient America
IN: Science Digest 89:74-77, 122

Popular-level summary of van Sertima [S-194].

R-067

AUTHOR: Retzius, Anders
DATE: 1860
TITLE: Present State of Ethnology in Relation to the Form of the Human Skull
IN: Annual Report of the Board of Regents of the Smithsonian Institution . . . [for] 1859, pages 251-270

Finds vague analogies in skulls between American Indians, Guanches, Tuaregs and Copts. The dolichocephals he terms American Semites while the brachycephals are American Mongolidae of Asiatic and South Sea origin.

R-068

AUTHOR: Réville, Albert
DATE: 1855
TITLE: Les religions du Mexique, de l'Amérique Centrale et du Pérou [The Religions of Mexico, Central America and Peru]
IMPRINT: Fischbacher: Paris [English, Scribner's: New York, 1884. Reprinted AMS: New York, 1983]

Page 48, note: The Aztec term for temple, *teocalli,* can be compared with Greek *theokalias,* house of god.

R-069

AUTHORS: Reynolds, Earle, and Barbara Reynolds
DATE: 1962
TITLE: All in the Same Boat: An American Family's Adventures on a Voyage around the World in the Yacht Phoenix
IMPRINT: McKay: New York

An American anthropologist with wife and three children sails a 50-foot ketch from Japan around the world.

R-070

AUTHOR: Ribeiro, Darcy
DATE: 1968
TITLE: The Civilizational Process
IMPRINT: Smithsonian Institution Press: Washington

Page 25: "Each technological revolution will follow a different history in a new context from that of its original context. Thus a great variety in expression is to be expected since (1) change is more often brought about by diffusion than it is generated internally; (2) diffusion does not make available to receiving societies all the elements originally developed, nor are these elements acquired in their original order or with the same associated elements."

R-070B

AUTHOR: Ricci, Clemente
DATE: 1923
TITLE: La civilización preincasica y el problema sumerológico [Pre-Incan Civilization and the Sumerological Problem]
IN: Verbum (Sept.): 52-69 (Buenos Aires)

The key to Asian civilization is the Sumerians. Where did they come from? Because of well-defined affinities between them and American civilizations, he maintains that they went from America to central Asia and then to Mesopotamia. Link cited: the Mexican solar cult of Tonatiuh and the lunar cult of Metztli or Tecciztecatl have been found completely similar in essentials to Sumerian religion. Giant stone remains at Tiahuanaco are reflected in later Egypt.

R-071

AUTHOR: Richards, Cara E.
DATE: 1958
TITLE: Of Vikings and Longhouses: A Reply to A. H. Mallery
IN: American Anthropologist 60:1199-1203

Mallery [M-060] claimed that Iroquois and Scandinavian longhouses were very similar, the former being derived through the Norse voyagers from the latter. Richards points out that only some of the claimed similarities are correct and that the remaining ones are quite generic.

R-072

AUTHOR: Richardson, Edward A.
DATE: 1960
TITLE: The Builders of the Newport (R.I.) Tower
IN: Journal of the Surveying and Mapping Division, Proceedings of the American Society of Civil Engineers 86:541ff.

Not a pre-Columbian structure.

R-072B

AUTHOR: Richter, Elise
DATE: 1928
TITLE: Zu Leo Wiener's Africa and the Discovery of America [On Leo Wiener's Africa and the Discovery of America]
IN: Anthropos 23:436-447

A substantial refutation of W-128 especially in the matter of claimed Old World pre-Columbian tobacco.

R-074

AUTHOR: Richthofen, B.
DATE: 1932
TITLE: Zur Frage der archäologischen Beziehungen zwischen Nordamerika und Nordasien [On the Question of Archaeological Relations between North America and North Asia]
IN: Anthropos 27:123-151

Despite inadequacies in data and treatment, he provides a general basis for comparison of pottery between the Baltic area and Woodland area of the eastern U.S., between which he finds suggestive similarities.

R-074B

AUTHOR: Rickard, Thomas Arthur
DATE: 1932
TITLE: Man and Metals, Volumes I and II
IMPRINT: Whittlesey House: New York [Reprinted Arno Press: New York, 1974]

Reprint edition, pages 652-653: Garcilaso de la Vega said that a pilot, Alonzo Sánchez, who sailed from Huelva in 1484, was blown off his course between the Canaries and Madeira and in 28 days reached an island believed to be Santo Domingo or Haiti. Five of the crew of 17 returned to Terceira, the Azores, where they talked to Columbus before dying. Gomara, Oviedo and Acosta repeated this story. There is plenty of evidence that oriental people reached California before the Europeans arrived in North America. It is easy to sail in an almost straight line from China to California without being far from shore (maximum open sea is only 200 miles).

R-074C

AUTHOR: Rickard, Thomas Arthur
DATE: 1939
TITLE: The Use of Iron and Copper by the Indians of British Columbia
IN: The British Columbia Historical Quarterly 3/1:25-50

Supposes shipwrecks to have been a significant source of metal. Repeats the story that marooned Japanese were purchased from the Haidas and given their freedom. [Keddie's research questions that this happened.]

R-075

AUTHOR: Rickard, Thomas Arthur
DATE: 1941
TITLE: The Strait of Anian
IN: British Columbia Historical Quarterly 5/3:161-183

Pages 167-170: A substantial, documented discussion of facts and sources about the so-called Finn-men, probably Eskimos, who reached northwestern Europe in kayaks.

R-076

AUTHOR: Rickey, Don G., Jr.
DATE: 1978
TITLE: Potential Relationship of Two Southwestern Pre-Columbian Inscription Petroglyph Sites with Some Bronze Age Fertility Concepts
IN: Ancient Vermont: Proceedings of the Castleton Conference, edited by Warren L. Cook (Castleton State College: Rutland, Vermont), 50-56

Written by a professional archaeologist who has no connection to the "epigraphers." Two inscriptions on stones, from New Mexico and Colorado, have been found by professional researchers. These appear to represent, respectively, Celtic writing referring to a fertility rite and North African writing with somewhat similar subject matter. Sketches of both inscriptions are included as well as ancillary documentation. The one in New Mexico is only a short distance from where the Flora Vista tablet was found.

R-077

AUTHOR: Ricks, Welby W.
DATE: 1964
TITLE: A Purported Phoenician Inscription in New Mexico
IN: Papers of the 15th Annual Symposium on the Archaeology of the Scriptures, edited by Ross T. Christensen (Brigham Young University Extension Publications: Provo, Utah), 94-100

An inscription found along a dry stream bed near Los Lunas, New Mexico, was claimed locally to be a Phoenician-written version of the Ten Commandments. Field investigation in the early 1950s by several Mormon scholars concluded that it was probably not ancient but is fraudulent.

R-078

AUTHORS: Ridgway, John, and Chay Blyth
DATE: 1967
TITLE: A Fighting Chance
IMPRINT: Hamlyn: London

A running commentary on a 91-day row-boat voyage from Cape Cod to Ireland, with some detail on equipment and stores.

R-079

AUTHOR: Ridler, Donald
DATE: 1972
TITLE: Erik the Red; the Atlantic Alone in a Home-made Boat
IMPRINT: William Kimber: London

Describes the author's voyage in 1971 in the 26-foot dory Erik the Red from Falmouth, England, to Spain, the Azores, Antigua, Bermuda, and back home.

R-080

AUTHOR: Ridley, Frank
DATE: 1960
TITLE: Transatlantic Contacts of Primitive Man: Eastern Canada and Northwestern Russia
IN: Pennsylvania Archaeologist 30/2:46-57

Hypothesizes entry of Old World cultural traditions into eastern North America via both Bering Strait and the north Atlantic. Early pottery came via Asia, but a second influence came from across the Atlantic introducing the bulk of Woodland wares from northern Europe. Cites a substantial number of cultural parallels.

R-081

AUTHOR: Riefstahl, Elizabeth
DATE: 1943
TITLE: Doll, Queen, or Goddess?
IN: Brooklyn Museum Journal 44:7-23

An Egyptian 25th Dynasty bronze of a nude female with movable arms is shown; a total of 15 examples of movable-limb figures are known. A Syrian source is suggested, from Astarte, connoting fertility. [Compare American movable-limb figures, B-277.]

R-082

AUTHOR: Riesenfeld, Alphonse
DATE: 1951
TITLE: [Kon Tiki and Pacific Migration—comments on a letter to the editor]
IN: Natural History 60:50, 96

Concludes that "Heyerdahl's merit lies not only in his demonstration of the feasibility of a raft voyage across the Pacific, but also in the fact that he has added a few more traits to the long list of already well-known similarities between America, the Pacific, and the Old World."

R-083

AUTHOR: Riesenfeld, Alphonse
DATE: 1955
TITLE: Bronze-age Influence in the Pacific
IN: Internationales Archiv für Ethnologie 47:215-255

Aberrant stone adzes of Polynesia, as Duff called them, are shown to be in the same form as socketed bronze axes/adzes of Eurasia. A continuity of types can be shown to exist from the Asiatic mainland across the various islands of the Pacific to Easter Island. A connection between such axes and bird symbolism is also discussed and its distribution given. Fewkes [F-085] noted stone axes with bird heads from the Antilles. Riesenfeld is unable to say this is more than coincidence but considers the similarity to Javanese and An-yang specimens "certainly remarkable." Fewkes pointed out that the form of these American axes reminded him of Old World (European) specimens. Riesenfeld reports an exotic stone axe form in Nicaragua which seems to deserve consideration as related to the Antillean ones. Heine-Geldern has pointed also to Peruvian socketed copper axes and other artifacts which he connects with the Dongson culture. A final section discusses the problem of American influence on Pacific Islands adze types; he argues that detailed differences rule out that possibility.

R-084

AUTHOR: Rieth, Adolf
DATE: 1967
TITLE: Vorzeit Gefälscht [Prehistoric Fraud]
IMPRINT: Wasmuth: Tübingen [English translation, *Archaeological Fakes* (Barrie and Jenkins: London; and Praeger: New York, 1970)]

Pages 160-168: Faked Runic Inscriptions, emphasizing the Kensington Stone [sources used are very thin].

Pages 169-174: The "Viking" Turkeys in Schleswig Cathedral. Gives a history of the painting of these American fowl by restorers (1888, 1890, 1938), which led to claims of the pre-Columbian presence of the fowl in Europe.

R-085

AUTHOR: Riley, Carroll L.
DATE: 1952
TITLE: The Blowgun in the New World
IN: Southwestern Journal of Anthropology 8:297-319

Taking a worldwide view, he sees the blowgun invented two or three times. Traits of the complex in America and Southeast Asia are "remarkably similar," yet the similarities were "the inevitable development" from the basic idea of the blowgun, not due to diffusion.

R-087

AUTHOR: Riley, Carroll L.
DATE: 1963
TITLE: Color-Direction Symbolism: An Example of Mexican-Southwestern Contacts
IN: América indígena 23:49-60

After posing two possible explanations for notable similarities in this feature between China and America (diffusion or "pattern elaboration" of basic concepts), the author ends up with no more than a distribution study of Southwestern and Mesoamerican color symbolism. Answers about significance are years away, he says.

R-088

AUTHOR: Riley, Carroll L.
DATE: 1978
TITLE: Interhemispheric Contacts? Comments on a Controversy
IN: Archaeology 31:59-61

A small review article on diffusion over the years and particularly recently. He finds van Sertima not very convincing although some of his examples may prove correct. He finds little that is persuasive in Fell, although some of his data may be of value. We require epistemological ground rules if we are to make progress in this area.

R-089

AUTHORS: Riley, Carroll L., J. Charles Kelley, Campbell W. Pennington, and Robert L. Rands, editors
DATE: 1971
TITLE: Man across the Sea: Problems of Pre-Columbian Contacts
IMPRINT: University of Texas Press: Austin [For a selection of these articles in Japanese see the title mentioned in J-073]

Papers from the landmark symposium at the SAA meeting in Santa Fe in 1969. Includes 21 papers and three commentaries, virtually all of which are included in this bibliography under their respective authors. An indispensible source.

R-089B

AUTHORS: Riley, Carroll L., J. Charles Kelley, Campbell W. Pennington, and Robert L. Rands
DATE: 1971
TITLE: Conclusions
IN: Man across the Sea: Problems of Pre-Columbian Contacts, edited by Carroll L. Riley, J. Charles Kelley, Campbell W. Pennington, and Robert L. Rands (University of Texas Press: Austin), 445-458

Emphasize the seriousness of the topic as seen by most participants in the symposium which their volume reports; it is of crucial, not trivial, significance to answer the question of the significance of transoceanic contacts. They summarize in turn the results of the conference regarding each of the five topics they outlined as important in their introduction: "[1] hard evidence for contacts, [2] similar traits in the two hemispheres, [3] linguistic resemblances, [4] plant evidence, and [5] theoretical implications."

Page 449: "The lack of absolute evidence for transhemispherical contact is, of course significant . . . and zero evidence of an artifactual type must be explained. We must be careful, however, not to overemphasize negative evidence. For one thing . . . archaeological evidence, by its very nature, is incomplete, not only because of the natural attrition of time but also because many important contacts may be nonmaterial in nature. In addition, archaeological exploration, to date, is far from complete—in fact, certain crucial regions in both the New World and the Old World (western Mexico and much of Southeast Asia, for example) are hardly known at all. The possibility must also be considered that actual artifacts *may* have been discovered but discarded, misunderstood, or incompletely reported."

The use of linguistic evidence remains highly indeterminate. They are not optimistic that human biological comparisons could yield significant evidence of contacts. Botanists at this conference found that "*there is no hard and fast evidence for any pre-Columbian human introduction of any single plant or animal* across the ocean from the Old World to the New World, *or vice versa*" (emphasis in the original). This is emphatically not to say that it could not have occurred." [The statement is untrue in regard to intestinal parasites.]

Page 457: "The underlying problem that must be solved is that of the origins of New World civilization. Clearly, the present status of our knowledge of American archaeology does not allow us to attribute the origins of New World civilization to diffusion from the Old World with assurance. Equally, however, it does not demonstrate the independent origin of New World high culture. Just as the zero occurrence of artifacts originating in the Old World and found in America may be taken as a strong argument against the diffusionist explanation, so the early occurrence of a complex of Old World-like trait—often very sophisticated—in early levels of Nuclear American civilization casts a strong reflection against the independent origins hypothesis."

R-092

AUTHOR: Ritchie, William A.
DATE: 1966
TITLE: Early Trans-Atlantic Contacts between the Old and New Worlds: Fact or Fiction?
IN: Proceedings of the 36th International Congress of Americanists (Barcelona and Seville, 1964), 1:107

(Abstract only.) He opposes recent efforts to argue for a contact from Europe to northeastern North America (i.e., Greenman, Ridley). "Recent studies" (unspecified) have shown that the supposed parallels are explainable in America as either autochthonous developments or from Asiatic sources.

R-093B

AUTHOR: Ritter, Chris
DATE: 1967
TITLE: Did the Romans Visit Maine?
IN: NEARA [New England Antiquities Research Association] Journal 2:16-18

A local archaeological society has found a Latin inscription (worn and obscure) carved in a ledge by the sea. (Ten miles away in 1960 three pieces of bronze were found attached to a big chunk of coastal flotsam and these have been identified as Roman coinage of c. A.D. 237.) A transcription and translation are presented. Reasons are given why the pieces are not likely to have been modern or medieval. Suggests it may have resulted from a Roman ship blown from the Iceland route.

R-093C

AUTHOR: Riva Aguero, José de la
DATE: 1937
TITLE: Los precursores de Colón [Columbus' Predecessors]
IN: Opúsculos 1:103-148 (Lima)

Surveys diverse diffusionist and migrationist views that have been put forward.

R-097

AUTHORS: Rivero y Ustáriz, Mariano Eduard de, and Juan Diego de Tschudi
DATE: 1851
TITLE: Antigüedades peruanas, 2 vols. [Peruvian Antiquities]
IMPRINT: Imprimerie Imperial de la Corte y del Estado: Vienna [American edition, Putnam: New York, 1853]

Missionaries of Brahma or Buddha affected civilized America. Accept the claim of Chinese visits to Peru and of Norse voyages to North America. Plate 33 shows what they see as an Oceanic artifact found in Peru.

R-098

AUTHOR: Rivers, William Halse Rivers
DATE: 1911
TITLE: The Ethnological Analysis of Culture
IN: Nature 87:356-360 [Reprinted 1911, *Science* 34 (September 29): 385-397, and also in *Nature* (Sept.) 14:356-360. An edited version was reprinted 1921 as "The Analysis of Blended Cultures," in *Introduction to the Science of Sociology*, by Robert E. Park and Ernest W. Burgess (University of Chicago Press, Chicago), 746-750]

His address as section president to the British Academy. Contrasts the British and German diffusionist schools. His work in Melanesia has led him to see social structure as the most enduring feature or shaper of culture. To him the final aim of anthropology is "understanding the history of human institutions." To do that the complex history must be disentangled through social relations, not through artifacts or customs.

R-100

AUTHOR: Rivers, William Halse Rivers
DATE: 1923
TITLE: Psychology and Politics
IMPRINT: Harcourt, Brace: New York

Using data collected by Elliot Smith, the writer argues that distributional evidence from ethnology that there were adequate sea craft is not necessary to demonstrate transpacific contacts. Also, the disappearance of cultural features is well documented historically, hence absences do not argue strongly against diffusion. [Compare R-101.]

R-101

AUTHOR: Rivers, William Halse Rivers
DATE: 1931 [1912]
TITLE: The Disappearance of Useful Arts
IN: Source Book in Anthropology, revised edition, edited by A. L. Kroeber and T. T. Waterman (Harcourt, Brace: New York), 524-535 [Originally in *Festskrift Tillägnad Edvard Westermarck,* (Helsingfors, 1912), 109-130]

Shows "that arts of the highest utility have disappeared in Oceania." Canoes, pottery, and bow and arrow are particularly treated. Material, social and magico-religious causes for these losses are presented.

Pages 534-535: "Mr. Joyce has lately argued against any influence of people from the Pacific Ocean upon South America on the grounds that along the whole of the coast of South America nothing but the most primitive raft was found. The facts I have brought forward deprive this argument of its cogency."

R-102

AUTHOR: Rivet, Paul
DATE: 1909

TITLE: Recherches anthropologiques sur la Basse Californie [Anthropological Researches on Lower California]
IN: Journal de la société des américanistes de Paris 6:147-253

Remains of presumed Pericu Indians closely resemble those from Lagoa Santa and likewise people from Melanesia and Australia.

R-103
AUTHOR: Rivet, Paul
DATE: 1920
TITLE: A propos du mot "sampan" [About the Word "Sampan"]
IN: Journal de la société des américanistes de Paris 12:253-254

Says that Loayza [L-274] claims "sampan" to be an aboriginal word in Peru.

R-103B
AUTHOR: Rivet, Paul
DATE: 1921
TITLE: [Untitled note, signed "P.R."]
IN: Journal de la société des américanistes de Paris 13:319-320

In the Brazilian state of Goyaz on an enormous area flooded by the Argauya River is a plant with "an extraordinary resemblance to common rice" but with grains somewhat unlike normal rice. Citation: *Revue économique franco-brésilienne* (Nov. 1921): 16.

R-105
AUTHOR: Rivet, Paul
DATE: 1925a
TITLE: Les Mélano-Polynésiens et les Australiens en Amérique [The Melano-Polynesians and the Australians in America]
IN: Anthropos 20:51-54

Gives 21 words for which equivalents are shown in two columns: "Melano- Polynesien" and "Hoka" (Hokan). He does not specify from which particular languages the terms are taken. [One of his "Melano-Polynesien" words is "himene," i.e., hymn, sing, a missionary-introduced term throughout Oceania.]

He also gives a list of 26 words in columns headed "Australien" and "Tson" (of Patagonia). For the Australian terms, again nothing is specified about which particular languages [a point made by Schmidt, whose Australian vocabularies Schmidt considered Rivet to have misused—see S-109]. Besides the lexical comparisons, only a few comments are made citing such as Quatrefages, Graebner, and Nordenskiöld.

R-106
AUTHOR: Rivet, Paul
DATE: 1925b
TITLE: Les Australiens en Amérique [Australians in America]
IN: Bulletin de la société de linguistique de Paris 36:23-63

Gives basic linguistic material comparing his "Tson" group of languages in southern South America with his composite of Australian languages. A touch of ethnographic comparison is appended.

R-107
AUTHOR: Rivet, Paul
DATE: 1925c
TITLE: Les éléments constituifs des civilisations de Nord-Ouest et de l'Ouest Sud-Américain [The Constituent Elements of the Civilizations of the North-West and West of South America]
IN: Proceedings of the 21st International Congress of Americanists (Part 2, Gothenburg, Sweden, 1924), pages 1-20

The basic population of the area came in various waves from the eastern lowlands. He identifies eight migrations. The first was Arawak-speaking. The second also came from the east, and he identifies it with Malayo-Polynesians [who had reached the Amazon area earlier, obviously]. The second group extended also into Mexico, Central America, and as far south as northern Chile and Argentina. They appeared in Peru in the age of Proto-Nazca, Proto-Lima, Proto-Chimu, and Proto-Chancay. Cultural element markers of their presence: atlatl (propulseur), labret, panpipe, trophy-head taking, and blowgun. The eighth and last to arrive were the Incaic group.

R-109

AUTHOR: Rivet, Paul
DATE: 1926a
TITLE: Les Malayo-Polynésiens en Amérique [Malayo-Polynesians in America]
IN: Journal de la société des américanistes de Paris 18:141-278

A short survey of ethnographic parallels is followed by lengthy linguistic material. Lexical comparisons are made between Hoka(n), Melanesian, Polynesian, Micronesian and Indonesian. [But the effect is badly weakened by the potpourri forming his categories. For example his "Hoka" draws on 25 languages and his Melanesian on 263, hence his comparisons are able to pick and choose among all those phonetic variants as though only a single language were involved.]

R-110

AUTHOR: Rivet, Paul
DATE: 1926b
TITLE: Le peuplement de l'Amérique précolombienne [The Peopling of Pre-Columbian America]
IN: Scientia 40:89-100 (Bologna)

Emphasizes the variability, not the uniformity of biological characteristics of American Indians. Bering Strait theory explains some things, but not all. Briefly recaps the diffusionist studies of interest to him (Nordenskiöld, Graebner, Schmidt) particularly his own. The intrusions of an Australian element and of Melanesians in America are shown by linguistics, physical anthropology, and ethnography. There may have been other elements arrive too. For example, the Maya civilization seems to him to have a different source.

R-111

AUTHOR: Rivet, Paul
DATE: 1926c
TITLE: Recherche d'une voie de migration des Australiens vers l'Amérique [Research on a Migration Route of the Australians to America]
IN: Compte-rendu sommaire de la société de biogéographie de Paris 3/18:11-16

See R-116.

R-112

AUTHOR: Rivet, Paul
DATE: 1927a
TITLE: Relations commerciales précolombiennes entre l'Océanie et l'Amérique [Pre-Columbian Commercial Relations between Oceania and America]
IMPRINT: Compte-rendu sommaire de la société de biogéographie de Paris 4/29:65-68 [Reprinted *Festschrift: Publication d'hommage offerte au P. W. Schmidt*, edited by Wilhelm Koppers (Mechitharisten-Congregation: Vienna, 1928), 583-609; reprinted in *Anales de la Facultad de ciencias de la educación* (Paraná, 1928), 3:165-193; reprinted in *Boletín de la Junta histórica y numismática americana* (Buenos Aires), 4:213ff.]

Same material in brief form appears as chapter 9 in R-122. [Also see K-137.]

A recapitulation of evidence for Polynesian and Melanesian contact with South America. He supposes that the contacts were frequent and "commercial," hence influential.

R-113

AUTHOR: Rivet, Paul
DATE: 1927b
TITLE: Le groupe océanien [The Oceanian Group]
IN: Bulletin de la société linguistique 27/3:141-168 (Paris)

Same as R-115.

R-115

AUTHOR: Rivet, Paul
DATE: 1928a
TITLE: Le groupe océanien [The Oceanian Group]
IN: Proceedings of the Third Pan-Pacific Science Congress (Tokyo, 1926) 2:2332-2353, National Research Council of Japan, Tokyo

Mainly compares words from "Australian-Tasmanian" and "Oceanian" (including Mon Khmer and Munda) in his characteristically oversimplified parallel lists. Mere mention that Oceanians reached America.

R-116

AUTHOR: Rivet, Paul
DATE: 1928b
TITLE: Migration australienne en Amérique [Australian Migration to America]
IN: Proceedings of the Third Pan-Pacific Science Congress (Tokyo, 1926) 2:2354-2356, National Research Council of Japan, Tokyo

Based on his previous comparison of Australian languages with those of Tierra del Fuego and Patagonia. He agrees that Australians could not have reached America by direct voyaging, as they lacked the technical ability. But they may have moved along the coast of the Antarctic continent during the postglacial optimum, around 6000 years ago, when conditions were much warmer. [Compare M-275 and L-201B.]

R-117

AUTHOR: Rivet, Paul
DATE: 1929
TITLE: Sumérien et Océanien [Sumerian and Oceanian]
IN: Collection linguistique publiée par la société de linguistique de Paris 24 (Librairie Ancienne Honoré Champion: Paris)

Based on very generalized lexical comparisons, he believes that from a Southeast Asian center speakers of a single language family spread by maritime means to Japan (Ainu), Tasmania, the Mediterranean, Africa, and America. In the section called "Vocabulaire comparatif Suméro-Océanien," he lists "Sumerian" words then gives a series of words with related meanings under the headings Melanesian, Polynesian, Indonesian, Munda, Mon-Khmer, Australian, Tasmanian, and Ainu, without specific languages being further identified.

R-119

AUTHOR: Rivet, Paul
DATE: 1932a
TITLE: Les "Océaniens;" étude des grandes migrations humaines dans le Pacifique [The "Oceanians;" a Study of the Great Human Migrations in the Pacific]
IN: Bulletin de la société d'océanographie de France 12/63:1121-1130

Not seen but probably the same as R-120.

R-120

AUTHOR: Rivet, Paul

DATE: 1932b

TITLE: Les Océaniens
[The Oceanians]

IN: The Frazer Lectures 1922-32 by Divers Hands, edited by Warren R. Dawson (Macmillan: London), 321-327
[The Frazer Lectures reprinted *Books for Libraries*, (Freeport: New York, 1967); reprinted 1932, *Revista del Instituto de Etnología de la Universidad de Tucumán* 2:185-187; reprinted 1932, *Praehistoria Asiae orientalis* 1:5-46 (Premier Congrès de Préhistoriens d'Extreme-Orient, Hanoï); reprinted 1933, *Annales de l'Université de Hanoï* 1:32-45; reprinted 1933, *Journal asiatique* 112:235-256 (Paris); reprinted 1934, *Contribution à l'étude de peuplement zoologique et botanique des îles du Pacifique* 4:226-248 (Société de biogéographie, Paris); reprinted 1934, *Annais da Faculdade de ciencias do Porto 18*]

A comprehensive recapitulation of his previous statements on movements from Australia, Melanesia, and Polynesia to South America.

R-121

AUTHOR: Rivet, Paul

DATE: 1939

TITLE: Orígenes del hombre americano
[Origins of American Man]

IN: Revista de la Academía colombiana de ciencias exactas, físicas y naturales 9-10:156-164 (Bogotá)

Argues against Hrdlicka regarding the unity of "the Indians" and Ameghino re. autocthonist evolution. Summarizes and supports Mendes-Correa's view of Australians reaching southern South America ca. 4000 B.C. via islands and Antarctic peninsulas during a climatic optimum.

R-122

AUTHOR: Rivet, Paul

DATE: 1943

TITLE: Les origines de l'homme américain
[The Origins of American Man]

IMPRINT: Gallimard: Paris
[Reviewed by Georges Pottier in *Bulletin de la société de linguistique de Paris* 44 (1947-1948): 229-230. Canadian edition in French, Les éditions de l'arbe: Montreal, 1943; 3rd French edition, 1957. Spanish editions, Ediciones Cuadernos Americanos, no. 5: México, 1945; and Fondo de Cultura Económica: México, 1960. Brazilian editions, Instituto Progreso Editorial: São Paulo, 1948; and Anhambi: São Paulo, 1960]

An extremely influential book for decades, yet brief and basically not very satisfactory from the point of view of its handling of evidence and treatment of the literature.

Chapter 1: The geology of America; Atlantis and Wegener disposed of.

Chapter 2: The antiquity of man in America, early hunters.

Chapter 3: The peopling of America from Asia, including material on the basic Asiatic affiliation of the Amerindians in terms of physical anthropology, ethnology, and linguistics.

Chapter 4: The Eskimo problem (they stand rather too much and too long in the way to allow for often-presumed migrations across the Bering Strait).

Chapter 5: Australians in America—anthropological, ethnological, and linguistic evidences.

Chapter 6: Melanesians in America.

Chapter 7: The Norse in America.

Chapter 8: "Commercial relations between Polynesia and America," in which he cites his usual material to support the idea that voyaging was frequent between the two.

Page 124: In a footnote, citing Velasco (1841-1843), he notes that when the first Europeans visited the Galapagos, they found charcoal from fires in several caves, which suggests pre-Columbian voyages/landings.

R-125

AUTHOR: Rivet, Paul
DATE: 1956
TITLE: Las relaciones antiguas entre Polinesia y América [Ancient Relations between Polynesia and America]
IN: Diogenes 4/16:107-119

Rivet's most lucid late statement. The word *kumara* for sweet potato is limited to the northern dialects of Quechua (north Peru and Ecuador), attested from 1582 in cited dictionaries. Material is also presented on names for yams, taro, and hibiscus and other shared crop plants. The incidence of the toki axe and the patu patu club in America is sketched, but no word exchange is evidenced, only the artifacts. The Polynesian earth oven occurs in Chile, Peru, and Mexico. Polynesian navigation is impressive. Legends in Oceania and America of arrivals and departures by seas are noted. However, the Atlantic was a virtual wall against contacts.

R-126

AUTHOR: Rivet, Paul
DATE: 1958
TITLE: L'élément blanc et les pygmies en Amérique [The White Element and Pygmies in America]
IN: Proceedings of the 33rd International Congress of Americanists (San José, Costa Rica, 1958), pages 587-593

Summary of mentions of blondism and beards in living American Indians, their mummies, and their art, interpreted as the result of a special migration across the Bering Strait of people with these characteristics. Reports of Indians of pygmy size led Rivet to two speculations: (1) if African pygmies are the result of a mutation, the same mutation could occur in the Americas; or (2) a group of Old World pygmies could have constituted one of the multiple migrations into the New World.

R-126B

AUTHORS: Robbins, Roland Wells, and Evan Jones
DATE: 1959
TITLE: Hidden America
IMPRINT: Alfred A. Knopf: New York

"A remarkably successful pick-and-shovel historian tells how he has uncovered some of the buried landmarks of our heritage." Topics include "Viking encampments on Cape Cod," "the Kensington Rune Stone," and "Newport's mysterious Tower."

R-127

AUTHOR: Roberts, Helen H.
DATE: 1926
TITLE: Ancient Hawaiian Music
IN: Bernice P. Bishop Museum Bulletin 29 (Honolulu)

Pages 322-346: Comparison of American Indian with Polynesian, African, and other musical forms.

R-128

AUTHORS: Roberts, Kenneth G., and Philip Shackleton
DATE: 1983
TITLE: Canoe: A History of the Craft from Panama to the Arctic
IMPRINT: International Marine Publishing: Camden, Maine; and Macmillan: Toronto

Historically, ethnographically, and artistically a superior volume. One wants more depth but is still rewarded (e.g., page 32, 1855 traveller Squier reported dugouts from ceiba tree trunks in Central America seven and a half feet across). Covers rafts and floats, the dugout (sections separately on the Caribbean, Central America, Mexico of the Aztecs, Maya, Florida, Eastern Seaboard, the Mississippi and Westward, Northward—Coast to Coast, the North Pacific—to Bering Strait, and California); the skin boat (kayak, umiak, and bull boat family); the bark canoe; and the modern canoe. Not footnoted but the bibliography by section is extensive, and there are a modest index and good map.

R-129

AUTHOR: Roberts, Warren
DATE: 1966
TITLE: International Folktales among the North American Indians
IN: Acta Ethnographica, Academiae Scientiarum Hungaricae 15:161-166

As important as is Stith Thompson's index [T-082], it includes only those folktale types borrowed in post-Columbian times more or less directly from European immigrants. "There remains a large number of stories which have entered North America probably mostly from Asia in pre-Columbian times."

In regard to adaptation, there are tales known only for a short time which have been extensively adapted to an Indian culture, while a tale known for a long time has undergone little assimilation, thus the form a tale takes says little about when it was received. Regarding those which seem to have entered North America from Asia in pre-Columbian times, they give no indication of external derivation [i.e., from where] and are thoroughly adapted. Because of the possibility of similar tales arising independently and the lack of materials for some areas, these tales present many baffling problems. Example: The War of the Pygmies and the Cranes, which is classical Greek, Finnish, Lappish, Turkish, Gilyak, and Yenisei Ostyak. Also Cherokee, Apache, and Crow, but most often Northwest Coast (Tsimshian). The similarities are so specific that it seems unlikely we are dealing here with a tale that has arisen independently in Eurasia and North America. The fact that there are many such parallel tales makes it likely that such a spread over great distances has taken place, ranging from Lappland to the southeastern United States.

R-130

AUTHOR: Robertson, John S.
DATE: 1987
TITLE: The Origins of the Mamean Pronominals: A Mayan/Indo-European Typological Comparison
IN: International Journal of American Linguistics 53:74-85

Similarities in the polite/familiar distinction in Mam and some nearby Mayan languages are explicated by reference to the same sort of distinction in Indo-European languages, where history gives us a clearer picture of process. The parallel tendencies in the two language groups "are not due to chance, borrowing, or genetic filiation," but to "universal tendencies of language change."

R-131

AUTHOR: Robinson, Eugene
DATE: 1942
TITLE: Shell Fishhooks of the California Coast
IN: Bernice P. Bishop Museum Occasional Papers 17/4:57-65

A study of collections of hooks from the Santa Barbara Channel Islands and the nearby California coast. Polynesian-Micronesian hooks are "similar in pattern" to those of the Chumash. The shell hook is "not a very ancient element" on the California coast. Barbed shell hooks may imitate European ones and might have been used by Hawaiian sailors on American vessels in the early 1800s. [Compare S-275.]

R-131B

AUTHOR: Robinson, Lila
DATE: 1969
TITLE: Linguistic and Folkloric Analyses of Cashibo Narrative Prose
IMPRINT: Unpublished; Ph.D. dissertation, University of Texas, Austin

This inland Peruvian tribe has a tradition of coming from across the (Pacific) ocean on the west.

R-132

AUTHOR: Robinson, George L.
DATE: 1951
TITLE: High Place
IN: Encyclopedia of Religion and Ethics, edited by James Hastings (Scribner's: New York), 6:678-681

[Mesoamerican parallels exist for the following:]

Page 681: Beneath the high place (sacred mound) at Gezer were found 20 jars each containing a skeleton of an infant. Compare Isaiah 57:5, Micah 6:7. There was also a bell-shaped pit near the sacred cave. A cave lies beneath the central area of 'Ain Shems (Beth-Shemesh) [compare the cave beneath Teotihuacan's Pyramid of the Sun?].

Near Eastern stelae, a double row is at Taanach, and ten in a row, north-south, at Gezer.

R-133B

AUTHOR: Robinson, Victor
DATE: 1938
TITLE: Did Columbus Discover Syphilis?
IN: British Journal of Dermatology and Syphilis 50:593-605

A resumé of the early Spanish literature attributing the origin of European syphilis to Columbus and his crew in Haiti. He finds no viable alternative to this, while acknowledging that arguments, to him unpersuasive, have been made that it had been known in Europe previously. His references section mentions the key sources on the subject to 1938.

R-134

AUTHOR: Robinson, William Albert
DATE: 1932
TITLE: Deep Water and Shoal
IMPRINT: J. Cape: London [Several reprintings]

Small-crew sea voyaging.

R-135

AUTHOR: Robinson, William Albert
DATE: 1972
TITLE: Return to the Sea
IMPRINT: John de Graff: Tuckahoe, New York

Sailed from Massachusetts to Tahiti in 1945 in a 70-foot brigantine. He also describes a round trip he made from Tahiti to Bangkok and back using in part the Equatorial Counter Current.

R-136B

AUTHOR: Rock, Barbara Holley
DATE: 1993
TITLE: Ancient Egyptians of New Mexico, Part 1
IN: The Ancient American 1/3:26-28 (Colfax, Wisconsin)

In 1991 an inscription was found on a stone in New Mexico (illustrated by a photo). [Characters show some relation to others in the western states discussed by Paul Cheesman at Polansky's San Francisco meeting as having possibly a Hmong connection. See H-091B.] She translates these characters as Egyptian.

R-137

AUTHOR: Röck, Fritz
DATE: 1914
TITLE: Die Skorpionmenschen in Babylonien und bei den Maya von Jukatan

[The Scorpion Men in Babylonia and among the Maya of Yucatan]
IN: Mitra, Monatschrift für vergleichende Mythenforschung 1:177-187 (Vienna)

Pictures mythical or divine scorpion men in Near Eastern art and Mayan codices and compares some characteristics. Coincidence or psychic unity will not do as an explanation.

R-139
AUTHOR: Röck, Fritz
DATE: 1919-1920
TITLE: Die Götter der sieben Planeten im alten Mexico und die Frage eines alten Zusammenhanges toltekischer Bildung mit altweltlichen Kultursystemen
[The Gods of the Seven Planets in Ancient Mexico and the Question of an Ancient Connection of Toltec Form with Old World Cultural Systems]
IN: Anthropos 14/15:1080-1098

See R-140.

R-140
AUTHOR: Röck, Fritz
DATE: 1922
TITLE: Kalender, Sternglaube und Weltbilder der Tolteken als Zeugen verschollener Kulturbeziehungen zur Alten Welt
[Calendars, Astrology, and World Conceptions of the Toltecs as Evidence of a Lost Cultural Connection to the Old World]
IN: Mitteilungen der anthropologischen Gesellschaft in Wien 52:43-136
[Reviewed by F. Bork, *Zeitschrift für Ethnologie* 56 (1924): 223-225]

Claims that calendar features (the Venus calendar which originated in Assyria, the notion of astrology, schematic cosmograms of Mexico, day names, etc.) found in Middle America were transmitted to the Toltecs from Southeast Asia, by way of Polynesia. [His "Toltecs" are chronologically earlier than the Maya.] Compares Polynesian calendars with the Mexican.

R-141
AUTHOR: Röck, Fritz
DATE: 1924a
TITLE: Altamerikanische Kulturbeziehungen zwischen Nord-, Mittel-, und Südamerika
[Ancient American Cultural Relations between North, Central, and South America]
IN: Proceedings of the 21st International Congress of Americanists (Part 1, The Hague, 1924), pages 200-211

The same theme as R-142 but with fuller documentation.

R-142
AUTHOR: Röck, Fritz
DATE: 1924b
TITLE: Ein mythisch religiöses Motiv der alten Maya Kunst
[A Mythical Religious Motif in Ancient Mayan Art]
IN: Proceedings of the 21st International Congress of Americanists (Part 1, The Hague, 1924), pages 270-273

The two-headed snake or sisiutl motif in art and myth was widespread and ancient in the Americas, in Maya and Chavin art and among surviving groups from Alaska to Argentina. [This motif has parallels in East Asia.]

R-144
AUTHOR: Röck, Fritz
DATE: 1928
TITLE: Kalenderkreise und Kalenderschichten im alten Mexiko und Mittelamerika

[Calendar Circle and Calendar Strata in Ancient Mexico and Middle America]

IN: Festschrift: Publication d'hommage offerte au P. W. Schmidt, edited by Wilhelm Koppers (Mechitharisten-congregations: Vienna), 610-628

See K-137.

R-145

AUTHOR: Röck, Fritz

DATE: 1930

TITLE: Neunmalneun und Siebenmalsieben [Nine Times Nine and Seven Times Seven]

IN: Mitteilungen der anthropologischen Gessellschaft in Wien 60:320-330

Calendar similarities between China and Southeast Asia on the one hand and Mesoamerica on the other.

R-146

AUTHOR: Roehrig, F. L. O.

DATE: 1873

TITLE: Language of the Dakota or Sioux Indians

IN: Annual Report of the Board of Regents of the Smithsonian Institution . . . [for] 1871, pages 434-450

Compares Dakota to Indo-European, very tentatively suggesting that it might be related with Turanian (Ural-Altaic).

R-146B

AUTHOR: Rogers, Everett M.

DATE: 1983

TITLE: Diffusion of Innovations, 3rd edition

IMPRINT: Free Press: New York

Historical case studies illustrate his discussion of theoretical points on why innovations (including, of course, those from "diffusion") may or may not be accepted in a host culture. Emphasizes resistance to adoption.

R-147

AUTHOR: Rogers, Spencer Lee

DATE: 1940

TITLE: The Aboriginal Bow and Arrow of North America and Eastern Asia

IN: American Anthropologist 42:255-269

He classifies and shows the distribution of forms of bows and arrows and methods of arrow release, the first major comparative study of these matters. Details are given, but in general American features are simpler than, though basically parallel to, those of Asia, with a likelihood of diffusion from the latter for certain items. By implication, though not explicitly, this would have been "early" and via Bering Strait.

R-148

AUTHOR: Rogers, Spencer Lee

DATE: 1944

TITLE: Disease Concepts in North America

IN: American Anthropologist 46:559-564

A map, revised from Clement, shows the distribution of six disease concepts in North and Central America. Contrary to Lowie, the soul loss concept does not appear to differ much in antiquity from the spirit intrusion doctrine. The former is better developed in the north, probably because of Asiatic influence, or perhaps the reverse. The scattered distribution of the various concepts suggests to the author the need for caution in making any historical interpretation.

R-149

AUTHOR: Rogers, Spencer Lee

DATE: 1963

TITLE: The Physical Characteristics of the Aboriginal La Jollan Population of Southern California

IN: San Diego Museum Papers No. 4 (Museum of Man: San Diego)

Page 29: While he finds that this population falls within the normal morphological range of other California Indian groups, he notes "impressive similarity . . . between representative La Jollan measurements and those of a prehistoric population from the Island of Kyushu, Japan," without clarifying the significance he sees in this.

R-150

AUTHOR: Rogers, Spencer Lee
DATE: 1937
TITLE: A Comparison between Aboriginal Archery in Western North America and Eastern Asia
IMPRINT: Unpublished; Ph.D. dissertation, University of Southern California [Partially published in *American Anthropologist* 42 (1940): 255-269]

Begins an intercontinental comparison of the form and construction of bows and arrows and methods of arrow release. Tentative conclusions: American archery was not as elaborate as Asiatic. What was brought by migrators was apparently only the self bow. The sinew-lined North American bow is so different that it does not argue for diffusion from Asia. Rather there are strong autochthonous tendencies.

R-151

AUTHOR: Ronan, Colin A., abridger
DATE: 1986
TITLE: The Shorter Science and Civilisation in China: An Abridgement of Joseph Needham's Original Text, Volume III, A Section of Volume IV, Part 1 and a Section of Volume IV, Part 3 of the Major Series
IMPRINT: Cambridge University Press: Cambridge

Aside from the general topic of Chinese nautics, pages 153-159 present Needham's basic position and summary data favoring Chinese-American relations in pre-European times.

R-152

AUTHOR: Romero, Javier
DATE: 1951
TITLE: Monte Negro, centro de interés antropológico [Monte Negro, Center of Anthropological Interest]
IN: Homenaje al Doctor Alfonso Caso, edited by Juan Comas, et al. (Imprenta Nuevo Mundo: México), 317-329

Page 318: Trepanation in Monte Alban I phase (500-200 B.C.)

R-154

AUTHOR: Romero, Jesús C.
DATE: 1949
TITLE: La ofrenda alimenticia a la memoria de los muertos, entre nuestros indígenas, es de origen Egipcio [Food Offerings as a Memorial to the Dead, among our Native People, Is of Egyptian Origin]
IN: Yikal Maya Than 10/123:115-116, 129-131 (Mérida)

A paper given to the Sociedad Folklórica Mexicana in 1943 which asserts the proposed relationship in passing but offers no substance.

R-155

AUTHOR: Roney, J. G., Jr.
DATE: 1966
TITLE: Paleoepidemiology: An Example from California
IN: Human Paleopathology, edited by Saul Jarcho (Yale University Press: New Haven), 99-107

Evidence for pre-Columbian presence of tuberculosis in a California skeleton.

R-156 See now D-098B

R-158

AUTHOR: Roosevelt, Anna

DATE: 1984

TITLE: Problems Interpreting the Diffusion of Cultivated Plants

IN: Pre-Columbian Plant Migration. Papers Presented at the Pre-Columbian Plant Migration Symposium, 44th International Congress of Americanists, Manchester, England, edited by Doris Stone (Harvard University, Peabody Museum of Archaeology and Ethnology: Cambridge), 1-18

A good discussion of problems, including archaeological ones, in obtaining and interpreting plant remains related to diffusion questions.

Page 10: Pollen finds do not definitely identify the presence of cultivated maize as opposed to wild relatives. Early pollen finds in Mexican and Panamanian lake sediments may represent "wild" maize (quotation marks in the original), early cultivated maize, teosinte, or some other near relative.

R-158B

AUTHORS: Roosevelt, Anna C., R. A. Housley, M. Imazio da Silveira, S. Maranca, and R. Johnson

DATE: 1991

TITLE: Eighth Millennium Pottery from a Prehistoric Shell Midden in the Brazilian Amazon

IN: Science 254/5038:1621-1624

[This early material could potentially be relevant to the proposal by Lathrap and others of early agriculturists crossing the south Atlantic, see L-077B.]

R-159

AUTHOR: Root, William C.

DATE: 1961

TITLE: Pre-Columbian Metalwork of Colombia and Its Neighbors

IN: Essays in Pre-Columbian Art and Archaeology, edited by Samuel K. Lothrop (Harvard University Press: Cambridge), 242-257

Metalworking gradually moved northward from Peru, developing as it went; it is not likely to have been introduced from the Old World.

R-161

AUTHOR: Rooth, Anna Birgitta

DATE: 1957

TITLE: The Creation Myths of the North American Indians

IN: Anthropos 52:497-508 [Reprinted in *Sacred Narrative: Readings in the Theory of Myth,* edited by Alan Dundes (University of California Press: Berkeley, 1984), 166-181]

Based on 300 creation myths of North American Indians, she sets up eight types. The Earth Diver is the widest distributed of these.

Page 170: Earth Diver type myths on the different continents are genetically related, not separately developed.

Pages 171-173: A map of the World-Parents type shows distribution in Southern California, Arizona, and New Mexico as well as in Japan, China, and Polynesia. This type must have come by way of the Pacific Islands to southern California, "or rather to the Meso-American tradition area, whose northern part includes southern North America."

Page 175: Spider as Creator appears in southern North America and Mexico with parallels in the Pacific Islands, East Asia, and India. Specific details connect China and southern California, so the relationship must be genetic (and is connected with color-direction symbolism). The connection must have been via the Pacific Islands.

Pages 178-179: The Ymir type has the world created from the corpse of a dead giant or a dead man or woman. Its distribution is North America, China, Tibet, East Asia, the Pacific Islands, and Scandinavia.

Page 181: Of the eight types in North America, seven are in Eurasia and are related in details. Four relate to Mexico as the source (for North America) and from Mexico they connect to the Pacific Islands, and East and South Asia. Also the World Egg myth occurs in Peru, the Pacific Islands and East and South Asia.

It appears, then, that there were two channels of communication of these myths into North America, one via Northern Asia and one via the Pacific Islands.

R-162

AUTHOR: Rooth, Anna Birgitta
DATE: 1963
TITLE: The Raven and the Carcass: An Investigation of a Motif in the Deluge Myth in Europe, Asia, and North America
IN: FF [Folklore Fellows] Communications No. 186 (Suomalainen Tiedeakatemia: Stockholm)

The distribution is presented of the motif of a raven being released from the deluge-surviving vessel and then eating from a carcass. Its occurrence in America and elsewhere at great distances has been suggested as something that originated spontaneously in connection with the Bible text or that it arose in different places from a sailors' custom. She shows (pages 154ff. and 191) that the latter cannot explain the desert-and-prairie environment for most of the cases, while also arguing that it is a scholastic tradition that is being followed, not an invention by individual writers. She also considers in detail Earth Diver tales in connection with Flood stories. She finds many "Christian influences" which seem to her so thoroughly Indianized that she is doubtful they can have come via post-Conquest European missionizing.

R-164

AUTHOR: Rosendahl, Paul, and Douglas E. Yen
DATE: 1971
TITLE: Fossil Sweet Potato Remains from Hawaii
IN: Journal of the Polynesian Society 80:379-385

A macrofossil sweet potato appears to date within A.D. 1358-1626. Two other occurrences of archaeological specimens in Polynesia are also discussed. Given their dispersal, it seems likely that the sweet potato had to have been present in the center of dispersal well before European discovery.

R-165

AUTHOR: Rosny-Foucqueville, Lucien de
DATE: 1864
TITLE: Étude d'archéologie américaine comparée [Study of American Comparative Archaeology]
IMPRINT: Comité d'Archéologie Américaine: Paris

He finds similarities in names and beliefs between the Popol Vuh and Mexican codices on the one hand and Egyptian concepts on the other.

R-166

AUTHOR: Ross, Alan S. C.
DATE: 1936
TITLE: Preliminary Notice of Some Late Eighteenth Century Numerals from Easter Island
IN: Man 36/120

Ten of the numerals collected by Agüera on Easter Island bear no resemblance to those listed by Cook only four years later, leading him to speculate on their source. [See M-324.]

R-167
AUTHORS: Ross, Anne, and Peter Reynolds
DATE: 1978
TITLE: Antique Vermont
IN: Antiquity 52:100-107

The authors (European archaeologists) attended the October 1977 conference held at Castleton, Vermont. They heard the papers read there by Barry Fell and colleagues, visited some sites, and examined artifacts. They discuss the types of evidence adduced by the speakers then conclude that the evidence for Celtic settlements and writings in pre-Columbian America as presented to date is totally unacceptable.

R-169
AUTHOR: Rossel Castro, Alberto
DATE: 1942
TITLE: Sistema de irrigación antigua del Río Grande de Nasca [Ancient Irrigation System of the Rio Grande de Nazca]
IN: Revista del Museo Nacional 11/2:196-202 (Lima)

Reports chain well or qanat water systems, some of which may be prehispanic.

R-170
AUTHOR: Rossignol, Pére
DATE: 1915
TITLE: Vestiges de traditions bibliques chez les Cris de l'Amérique du Nord [Vestiges of Biblical Traditions among the Cree of North America]
IN: Les missions catholiques 47:130-132 (Lyon)

A re-hash of P-138.

R-176
AUTHOR: Roth, H. Ling
DATE: 1923
TITLE: The Maori Mantle
IMPRINT: Bankfield Museum: Halifax, England

Detailed comparison of mantles leads the author to conclude that while the techniques show coincidental similarities, they "developed independently both in Northwest America and in New Zealand."

R-178
AUTHOR: Rothovius, Andrew E.
DATE: 1963a
TITLE: The Strange Stone Structures of North Salem, New Hampshire
IN: Anthropological Journal of Canada 1/3:19-24

A general description, topographic map, and some cross-sections of the structures on Pattee's Hill ("Mystery Hill"). The role of W. B. Goodwin, who ardently believed that this was part of the Great Ireland of Norse mention and who dug alone and destructively. Bird and Vescelius' later investigation found no basis for Goodwin's claims. Diffusionists now consider that it resembles European "megalithic" remains. It is hoped that responsible investigation will proceed.

R-179
AUTHOR: Rothovius, Andrew E.
DATE: 1963b
TITLE: A Possible Megalithic Settlement Complex at North Salem, New Hampshire, and Apparently Related Structures Elsewhere in New England
IN: New York State Archaeological Association Bulletin 27:2-11

See R-178.

R-180B

AUTHOR: Rothovius, Andrew E.
DATE: 1967
TITLE: A Footnote to "Did the Romans Visit Maine?"
IN: NEARA [New England Antiquities Research Association] Journal 2:46

Refers to R-093B without adding anything substantive.

R-181

AUTHOR: Rothovius, Andrew E.
DATE: 1969
TITLE: Did the Vikings Reach the Pacific Coast?
IN: INFO Journal 2:1-4 [International Fortean Organization, Arlington, Virginia]

Reports a Seri legend from the Gulf of California of a boat of Viking type arriving. Also apocryphal accounts of the remains of "ships" found in the area.

R-181B

AUTHOR: Rothovius, Andrew E.
DATE: 1972
TITLE: The Inscribed Stones of Southwestern Nova Scotia
IN: NEARA [New England Antiquities Research Association] Journal 7:67

The Yarmouth Stone, inscribed with characters which some have thought runic, was discovered in 1812 in southwest Nova Scotia. The author publishes a photo of it and says that eight "related" stones are known from the area. Investigation continues.

R-181C

AUTHOR: Rothovius, Andrew E.
DATE: 1974
TITLE: New Discoveries Supporting Medieval Norse Presence in the Upper Midwest
IN: NEARA [New England Antiquities Research Association] Journal 9:15-16

Insubstantial report about discoveries purported by Marion Dahm of Minnesota to be Norse mooring holes and other stone objects.

R-182

AUTHOR: Rottländer, R.
DATE: 1982
TITLE: Ein metrischer Zusammenhang zwischen einem Mass der XII. Dynastie Ägyptens und Massen vom nordwestlichen Südamerika [A Connection between a Unit of Measure of the 12th Egyptian Dynasty and Measures in Northwestern South America]
IN: Zeitschrift für Ethnologie 107/2:227-232

Standard measures of length are described for ancient Egypt, Tiahuanaco (Bolivia), and China. Comparison shows a high degree of correspondence in units of measure, from which it is concluded that contact between Egypt and China, then between East Asia and South America (probably via a Chinese ship) is demonstrated. This is coordinate with von Hornbostel's relating measurements manifested on panpipes on both sides of the Pacific.

R-183

AUTHOR: Rougé, Jean
DATE: 1981
TITLE: Ships and Fleets of the Ancient Mediterranean
IMPRINT: Wesleyan University Press: Middletown, Connecticut [Translated from, *La marine dans l'antiquité* (Presses universitaires de France: Paris, 1975)]

A short illustrated volume on construction, rigging and gear, ballast and cargo, ports, crews, and the religion of seafarers.

R-184

AUTHOR: Rouget, Gilbert
DATE: 1948
TITLE: La conque comme signe des migrations océaniennes en Amérique [The Conch as a Sign of Oceanic Migrations in America]
IN: Proceedings of the 28th International Congress of Americanists (Paris, 1947), pages 297-305

Surveys the literature on the shell trumpet in India, Japan, Indochina, Melanesia, Polynesia, and nuclear America and concludes that independent invention of usages and meanings is unlikely. Diffusion is supposed.

R-185

AUTHOR: Rouse, Irving
DATE: 1958
TITLE: The Inference of Migrations from Anthropological Evidence
IN: Migration in New World Culture History, edited by Raymond H. Thompson, University of Arizona Bulletin 29/2:63-68

An early version of R-186.

R-186

AUTHOR: Rouse, Irving
DATE: 1986
TITLE: Migrations in Prehistory: Inferring Population Movement from Cultural Remains
IMPRINT: Yale University Press: New Haven

Aims to explain an adequate methodology and illustrate its use in five case studies which combine data from archaeology, physical anthropology, and linguistics. Criticizes Fell for drawing "conclusions from artifacts whose context is not known. . . . Such artifacts tell us nothing about the migrations because we cannot determine empirically who produced, used and deposited them."

R-187

AUTHOR: Rousseau, Jacques
DATE: 1951
TITLE: The Identity of Vinber and Vinland
IN: Rhodora 53:244-245

Remarks on ethnobotanical considerations involved in identity of the Nova Scotia-Maine region as Vinland in terms of whether the vinber of the sagas is a vine, a cranberry, or a red currant.

R-189

AUTHOR: Rousselièrre, G. M.
DATE: 1961
TITLE: The Mystery of Vineland and the Eskimos
IN: Eskimo 58:11-12 (Churchill, Manitoba)

Discusses Gini's [G-099] hypothesis of Vinland on the north shore of Lake Ontario and challenges his contention that skraelings were Eskimo.

R-190

AUTHOR: Rout, Ettie A.
DATE: 1926
TITLE: Maori Symbolism, Being an Account of the Origin, Migration, and Culture of the New Zealand Maori as Recorded in Certain Sacred Legends
IMPRINT: Kegan Paul, Trench, Trubner: London

Pages xxvii-xxviii: certain parallels (a few of which she mentions) persuade her that ancient Mexico and the Maori are related.

Pages 2ff.: Discussion and map of the "Route of Great Migration," from the Caucasus to Spain, the Southeastern U.S., Middle America, Peru, Easter Island, and New Zealand.

Pages 229-234: Ancient Israelites, "the Brown or Brunet Peoples," have spread throughout the world. One stream reached New Zealand as the Maori. At least four irrefutable proofs of this distribution exist: agriculture, tattooing, "Sacred Life-Symbols," and "Native (abdominal and pelvic) Dances, and the realization of their health value."

Pages 261-262: "Bits of old pottery have been found in river-beds in the South Island, which are said to resemble the type of pottery used in Peru, and their presence has not been accounted for." (Cites Frances Del Mar, *A Year among the Maoris*, page 146.)

Pages 275-277: The quipu is taken as related to knotted cords for counting in Peru, West Africa, Zuñi, Hawaii, China, etc.

R-191

AUTHOR: Routledge, Mrs. W. Scoresby
DATE: 1919
TITLE: The Mystery of Easter Island: The Story of an Expedition
IMPRINT: Sifton: London

Her recording of the tradition of Hotu-matua's settling of Easter Island differs significantly from that recorded a generation earlier by Thomson. She concludes that if there is any connection between the island and South America, it would have gone eastward, for there is no evidence that she can discern of South American features on the island.

R-192

AUTHOR: Rowe, John Howland
DATE: 1965
TITLE: Stirrup-spout Bottles from Central Africa
IN: American Antiquity 30:474-476

Modern vessels in this South American form are made in western Africa. See R-193 for his argument.

R-193

AUTHOR: Rowe, John Howland
DATE: 1966
TITLE: Diffusionism and Archaeology
IN: American Antiquity 31:334-337

In an ultra-anti-diffusionist statement, some 60 practices and artifacts common to Mesoamerica and the Mediterranean or Africa are listed, such as entrail-divination, litters, military discipline, board-games, steelyard balance, sandals, retainer-sacrifices, adobe buildings, vertical looms, and pack animals. He argues that since nobody takes these seriously as evidence of cultural contact across the Atlantic, then transpacific diffusionist comparisons, having no more compelling basis, should likewise be explained without calling on diffusion. The author is seriously upset by what he characterizes as "diffusionist fantasies," "nonsense," and the "hardy weed" of diffusionism which continues to "infest" the virgin field of archaeology.

[See J-079 and M-109 for detailed rebuttals.]

R-194

AUTHOR: Rowlett, E. S.
DATE: 1978
TITLE: Review of *America B.C.*, by Barry Fell
IN: Archaeology 31/2:64-65

Finds little merit in the book.

R-195

AUTHOR: Rubens, Alfred
DATE: 1967
TITLE: A History of Jewish Costume
IMPRINT: Vallentine, Mitchell: London

Purple dye used in sacred costumes.

R-196

AUTHOR: Rubín de la Borbolla, S. A.
DATE: 1968
TITLE: Capítulos para una historia de la navegación [Chapters for a History of Navigation]
IN: La palabra y el hombre 45:17-29 (Xalapa, Veracruz)

Page 28: References to "great embarcations" on both coasts of Mesoamerica lead us to suppose that there existed a marine traffic of some significance.

R-197

AUTHOR: Ruddock, Alwyn A.
DATE: 1966
TITLE: John Day of Bristol and the English Voyages across the Atlantic before 1497
IN: The Geographical Journal 132:222-233 (London)

Bristol sailors reached North America somewhat earlier than claimed by Quinn and others. His survey of documentary evidence points to the coast of North America (probably Newfoundland) having been discovered prior to 1480, but with the landfall then lost until re-discovered by Cabot in 1497.

R-198

AUTHOR: Rudler, F. W.
DATE: 1890
TITLE: On the Source of Jade Used for Ancient Implements in Europe and America
IN: Journal of the Anthropological Institute 20:332-342

A survey of the views of Fischer and others claiming an Asian origin for American and European "jade" and reprising the state of knowledge at the time. Sees no evidence for interhemispheric transport of the material.

R-199

AUTHOR: Rudofsky, Bernard
DATE: 1977
TITLE: The Prodigious Builders
IMPRINT: Harcourt Brace Jovanovich: New York

Pages 2186-289: Wind scoops (ventilating columns for houses) are found in Sind, ancient Egypt, and Peru [as well as contemporary Iran].

R-200

AUTHOR: Rudolph, Ebermut
DATE: 1982
TITLE: Das "Andere Ich" des Menschen im Tiere: Ein Beitrag zur Frage des "Lebensgleichlaufes" und anderer psychologischer wie paranormaler Phänomene in der Mensch-Tier-Beziehung [The "Other Self" of Humans in Animals: A Study on the Question of "Parallel Lines" and Other Psychological As Well As Paranormal Phenomena in Human-animal Relationships]
IN: Zeitschrift für Ethnologie 107/1:23-68

Occurrence of the idea of an animal alter ego, especially as manifested in art, is surveyed for South and Middle America, Africa, northern Eurasia, and middle and southeastern Europe. A psychological explanation for similarities is preferred rather than a culture-genetic one.

R-201

AUTHOR: Ruff, Elsie
DATE: 1950
TITLE: Jade of the Maori
IMPRINT: Gemmological Association of Great Britain: London

The hei tiki jade figure of the Maori is similar to a carved figure in Central America.

R-207

AUTHOR: Ruíz Olavarrieta, Alejandro
DATE: 1897
TITLE: Disertación sobre el origen de los pobladores de América [Dissertation Concerning the Origin of the Settlers of America]
IN: Proceedings of the 11th International Congress of Americanists (Mexico, 1895), pages 278-287

A resumé of ideas of Israelite settlement of America (Menasseh ben Israel, Montesinos, Lord Kingsborough, George Jones, etc.), in what the author characterizes as a "modest rhapsody" rather than a scientific study.

R-207B

AUTHOR: Runkle, Gerald
DATE: 1981
TITLE: The Kensington Stone
IN: Good Thinking: An Introduction to Logic, Second edition (Holt, Rinehart and Winston: New York), 286-289

"This account of the Kensington Stone is from Monroe C. Beardsley's *Practical Logic* (second edition, Prentice Hall: Englewood Cliffs, New Jersey, 1961), 548-549. Beardsley himself is indebted to Hjalmar J. Holand, *Westward from Vinland* (Duel, Sloan and Pearce: New York, 1940)."

A case exercise in logic compares three hypotheses to explain the Kensington Stone: the stone was carved by twelfth-century Vikings, or it is a hoax, or it was carved by fourteenth-century Vikings. The "facts" adduced from the sources he consulted lead him to conclude that the third is to be preferred. However, he then goes on to note that "the great historian," S. E. Morison, believes the stone a hoax, and Runkle bows to his authority and that of additional "facts" which Morison asserts.

R-208

AUTHOR: Rusconi, C.
DATE: 1945
TITLE: Tokis líticos de Mendoza [Stone "Tokis" from Mendoza]
IMPRINT: Publicaciones 10 (Instituto de la Arqueología, Linguística y Folklore, Universidad Nacional de Córdoba: Córdoba, Argentina)

More clubs of Polynesian form, as per Imbelloni.

R-209

AUTHOR: Russell, Vincent
DATE: 1938
TITLE: The Serpent as the Prime Symbol of Immortality Has Its Origin in the Semitic-Sumerian Culture
IMPRINT: Unpublished; Ph.D. dissertation, University of Southern California

Using mythology and art, he concludes that in Asia the serpent is a symbol associated with immortality, procreation, knowledge, and the custody of the Waters of Life. It originated from a central "Semitic -Sumerian" point in the Near East and extended to India, China, Tibet, North Borneo, and Ceylon. The same cultural pattern swept over Mexico and the entire North American area as well as South America and reveals the same basic concepts as in Asia. The combination of associated ideas is too complex to be explained on the basis of a presumed generic unity of the human mind nor on the basis of a Freudian or similar thesis. The possibility (notion) of voyaging across the Pacific seems not to have been seriously examined yet, let alone destroyed.

Page 121-122: The early Chimu pottery designs examined in the national museum in Lima in their extraordinary anthropomorphic designs "remind one forcibly of Egyptian motifs. Men are disguised as birds and birds as men, in a fashion reminiscent of the representation of the soul of Osiris." The Weeping God is a phallic serpent associated with signs representing water in

Peru, in the Codex Cortesianus, and among the Zuni as on Chinese neolithic ceramics.

Page 125: The plumed serpent is the central motif of all Indian tribes, in South as in North America. All share deep similarity with Chinese, Indian, and other Asiatic representations. Intertwined serpents are also ancient and shared.

R-210

AUTHOR: Ruz Lhuillier, Alberto
DATE: 1951-1962
TITLE: Exploraciones arqueológicas en Palenque
[Archaeological Explorations in Palenque]
IN: Anales del Instituto Nacional de Antropología e Historia 5:47-66; 6:79-110; 10:69-116, 117-184, 185-240, 241-299; 14:35-90, 91-112 (México)

See R-211.

R-211

AUTHOR: Ruz Lhuillier, Alberto
DATE: 1952
TITLE: Estudio de la cripta del Templo de las Inscripciones en Palenque
[Study of the Crypt in the Temple of the Inscriptions at Palenque]
IN: Tlatoani 1/5-6:2-28 (México)

Pages 12-15: Observations on Old World comparisons of the tomb he excavated. Notes the definitional problems of "pyramid" in comparing Palenque, other Mesoamerican burial and non-burial pyramidal structures, and those in Egypt, Mesopotamia, and southeast Asia. This find shows similarities to the Old World, but chronology and distance lead him to consider them as "vague conceptual parallelisms that demonstrate the essential unity of culture" wherever found.

R-214

AUTHOR: Ruz Lhuillier, Alberto
DATE: 1954
TITLE: La pirámide-tumba de Palenque
[The Pyramid-Tomb of Palenque]
IN: Cuadernos americanos 13/2:141-159

General parallels are cited to China, Cambodia, and the Near East, but in no way does this tomb indicate contact. Egyptian and American civilizations were separated by unbridgeable gaps in space and time.

R-215

AUTHOR: Ruz Lhuillier, Alberto
DATE: 1963
TITLE: La civilización de los antiguos Mayas
IN: Instituto Nacional de Antropología e Historia: México
[Reprinted as the second half of *Aportaciones del mundo prehispánico y esquema de Mesoamérica* (Editorial Universitaria: Guatemala, 1974)]

Chapter 1 includes a lengthy discussion of "The origin of Mesoamerican culture" particularly rejecting Kirchoff's argument that high culture was imported from Asia. He also argues against Ekholm and Heine-Geldern [actually against a simplified, straw-man version of their positions]. In a small work on Maya art he himself has tried to explain stylistic parallels between Khmer, Javanese, and Chinese art and architecture on the one hand and that of Palenque on the other. He found time and space differences so contradictory to a diffusionist view that he chooses to explain the connection on the basis of a "connection in blood and spirit" between peoples of the two areas, together with such factors as enervating heat, earthquakes, and raw nature which produces "sensual exhuberance" in the art. He cites Kroeber approvingly about "certain inherent tendencies in the human mind in certain directions."

R-216

AUTHOR: Ruz Lhuillier, Alberto

DATE: 1968

TITLE: Costumbres funerarias de los antiguos Mayas [Funerary Customs of the Ancient Maya]

IMPRINT: Seminario de Cultura Maya, Universidad Autónoma de México: México

Pages 239-269: Comparison between funerary practices and beliefs of the ancient Maya and those of the Old World. Differences and similarities are spelled out at length from the archaeological and ethnographic literature, from the paleolithic on.

Topics treated include exposure of corpse, retainer sacrifice, burial mounds, orientation of corpse, cremation, secondary burial, offerings, belief in resurrection, red pigment cult of the dead, etc. Funeral forms in the Maya area are highly varied and cannot be considered the result of any evolutionary scheme. It is evident that funerary features among the Maya are "notoriously" similar to those in the Old World.

R-218

AUTHOR: Ruz Lhuillier, Alberto

DATE: 1977

TITLE: La civilización de los antiquos mayas [The Civilization of the Ancient Maya]

IN: Antropología Centroamericana, by David Luna Desola (Editorial Universitaría Centroamericana (EDUCA), Ciudad Universitaría Rodrigo Facio: Costa Rica), 166-177 [Ruz's essay is referred to on page 166 as dating from 1974, but no further information is provided]

He critiques Ekholm on a southeast Asian origin for Mesoamerican civilization, considering that he has little basis ("superficial similarities") for such derivation. He quotes Kroeber, rather, about "certain inherent tendencies in the human mind." Any influences out of Oceania would have been accidental and unimportant.

His note 2 says that when Heine-Geldern visited Chichen Itza with Ruz, the former, seeing for himself the elements on the Castillo that Ekholm considered Asian, discarded any idea of such a relationship.

R-218B

AUTHOR: Ryan, Beverly

DATE: 1991

TITLE: Transpacific Contacts before Columbus

IN: Bulletin of Bibliography 48/4:183-187

A minor effort at bibliography for librarians citing fairly well-known sources (a few misapplied).

R-219

AUTHOR: Rydén, Stig

DATE: 1931

TITLE: Notes on Some Archaeological Whistling Arrow-heads from Peru

IN: Origin of the Indian Civilizations in South America, vol. 8 of Comparative Ethnographical Studies, by Erland Nordenskiöld (Pehrssons: Göteborg), Appendix 5a, pages 115-121 [Reprinted AMS Press: New York, 1979]

Page 120: In discussing specimens of hollow whistling arrowheads, the author notes that Baron Nordenskiöld had discussed this trait in volume 8 of the Contributions, supposing from its distribution that it was invented in at least two different places. Friederici later noted an occurrence in eastern Asia, considering that its presence in America was due to Asiatic influence via Bering Strait. Rydén grants that the presence of the whistling arrow in North America might be due to such a diffusion.

R-221

AUTHOR: Rydén, Stig
DATE: 1956
TITLE: Did the Indians in Chile Know the Use of Sails in Pre-Columbian Times?
IN: Southwestern Journal of Anthropology 12:115-116

Heyerdahl is all wrong on sails, he maintains in a brief note. Indians of South America had no sails until they copied them from Europeans. [See H-278 for a rejoinder.]

S-002

AUTHORS: Sabo, Deborah, and George Sabo III
DATE: 1978
TITLE: A Possible Thule Carving of a Viking from Baffin Island, N.W.T., Canada
IN: Canadian Journal of Archaeology 2:33-42

In a Thule culture house from the Okialivialuk site.

S-001B

AUTHOR: Sabloff, Jeremy A.
DATE: 1989
TITLE: The Cities of Ancient Mexico: Reconstructing a Lost World
IMPRINT: Thames and Hudson: New York

Chapter 9, "The Roots of Mexican Civilization," includes discussion of "several examples that attempt to illustrate external influences on Mexico." Brief comments are given on works by P. Tompkins, Heyerdahl, Von Däniken, Meggers, Van Sertima, and Jairazbhoy. While their arguments are not all equally at fault, all are ultimately flawed due to "misunderstandings of cultural development." "These arguments generally relate to impressionistic comparisons of style, and not to concrete archaeological evidence of contact, and I do not find them convincing." [His interesting, but naive, assumption seems to be widely held by archaeologists that somehow "concrete archaeological evidence" could exist which would not involve "impressionistic comparisons of style."]

S-004

AUTHOR: Sacchetti, Alfredo
DATE: 1965
TITLE: Sobre la dispersión del factor diego en indígenas americanos [On the Dispersion of the Diego Factor in American Natives]
IN: Anales de antropología 2:113-120 (México)

Statistical analysis of data compiled by Juan Comas. There is wide variability and the distribution of the frequencies can be characterized as supernormal [i.e., as supporting either varied genetic ancestry or variable adaptation].

S-004B

AUTHOR: Sacchetti, Alfredo
DATE: 1983
TITLE: Taxa anthropológica de México en el marco mesoamericano [Anthropological Classification in Mexico in the Mesoamerican Framework]
IN: Universidad Autónoma de México, Serie antropológica 28

A substantial discussion of nearly all theories of Amerindian origins.

S-005

AUTHORS: Sachan, J. K. S., and K. R. Sarkar
DATE: 1986
TITLE: Discovery of Sikkim Primitive Precursor in the Americas
IN: Maize Genetics Cooperative Newsletter 60:104-106

Himalayan maize ancestry is linked to very early American maize.

S-006

AUTHOR: Sachs, Curt
DATE: 1929
TITLE: Geist und Werden der Musikinstrumente [Spirit and Development of Musical Instruments]
IMPRINT: D. Reimer: Berlin

A major work in which instruments are logically grouped and attributed to various kulturkreis circles. American instrument types extend beyond the hemisphere. [See S-007.]

S-007

AUTHOR: Sachs, Curt
DATE: 1940
TITLE: The History of Musical Instruments
IMPRINT: Norton: New York

Following Hornbostel, he supposes on musicological grounds that panpipes of South America and Melanesia had to be related historically.

S-008

AUTHOR: Sadovszky, Otto J.
DATE: 1970
TITLE: The Fish and the Prop: A Study in Semantic Reconstruction
IMPRINT: Unpublished; Ph.D. dissertation, University of California at Los Angeles [University Microfilms International Order No. 7103851]

Using linguistic, artistic, archaeological, and other information, the author shows that detailed parallels exist between Ob-Ugrian of western Siberia and California Penutian words, meanings, and practices relating to the central house post, fish, and other concepts.

S-009

AUTHOR: Sadovszky, Otto J.
DATE: 1973
TITLE: The Reconstruction of IE *pisko and the Extension of Its Semantic Sphere
IN: Journal of Indo-European Studies 1:81-100

Semantic associations between animal symbolism and the human body are traced, occurring across linguistic and cultural boundaries in various parts of Eurasia, North Africa, the Middle East, and California.

S-010

AUTHOR: Sadovszky, Otto J.
DATE: 1975
TITLE: The Concept of the "Calf of the Leg" and "Fish Eggs" and the Tattooed Man of Pazyryk
IN: Congressus Tertius Internationalis Fenno-Ugristarum (Tallinn, Esthonian Socialist Soviet Republic, 1970)

Fish eggs and the lower leg or calf of the leg are equated in Indo-European, Finno-Ugric, Altaic, Yukaghir, Arabic, Basque, and California Penutian. The calf muscles in the horizontal position are widely thought to look like the belly of a fish full of roe. Word linkages showing the connection are given. [See also S-016.]

S-011

AUTHOR: Sadovszky, Otto J.
DATE: 1976
TITLE: Report on the State of the Uralo-Penutian Research
IN: Ural-Altaische Jahrbücher 48:191-204 (Wiesbaden)

He has been involved for almost 14 years to establish the genetic relationship between the Uralic language family and California Penutian. While a student at Berkeley he found that even a superficial impression of the structure of Penutian indicated some similarities with western Siberia. Upon reading Callaghan's Proto Miwok article he found about 50 possible cognates with possible sound laws. At Berkeley "we made several attempts" to reconstruct Proto California Penutian without success. Perhaps because of borrowing, unclear and complex soundlaws resulted. Although there is no doubt these languages are related, we still have to restrain ourselves from reconstruction. Concentrating on Costanoan, he concluded that it is a Uralic language and not much more distant than some of the Samoyed languages. In 1967 he wrote a paper, still waiting publication in Hamburg [actually never published], which contained 470 possible cognates plus many grammatical suffixes. He subsequently learned that Viitso had done research independent from his which reached the same conclusion about the genetic relations between the two language families and which presented 86 cognates [V-046].

Continued study has extended into other languages of the Penutian family and has discovered relationships in mythological themes (e.g., eagle as the first "deity," earth diver). Some decoration on ceremonial spoons appears identical; the construction of dwellings, totemism, the Miwok clan system and kinship system, etc., corroborate the linguistic tie. Material cultures are very similar: use of birch bark, prediliction for salmon and sturgeon which they catch with similar fish-traps and weirs, hunting geese with collapsible nets, trapping squirrels and weasels, honoring the bear, hunting deer with bow and arrow, keeping eagles as pets, not knowing pottery or the wheel, lacking a skin drum but utilizing an upside down hollow log by dancing on it and kicking it with their heels. They are skilled boatmen on their primitive boats and rafts. His hypothesis: fishing bands from the Ob and Yenisei rivers drifted north to the Arctic shore and followed the salmon eastward along the shores of Siberia, shifting their fishing camps and utilizing the Arctic current. At the Bering Strait they fished salmon southward until reaching the Carmel-Monterey area where the Arctic current in the Pacific ends.

By now the possible cognates he has recognized amount to thousands. As a demonstration, he lists here 110 possible cognates just with initial p- [most of which are thoroughly obvious as listed, e.g., Mics.: pisuu 'striped squirrel,' and Yr: pinsuu-k 'striped squirrel'].

S-011B

AUTHOR: Sadovszky, Otto J.

DATE: 1978

TITLE: Demonstration of a Close Genetic Relationship between the Wintun Languages of Northern California and the Ob-Ugrian Languages of North-western Siberia; a Preliminary Report

IMPRINT: Unpublished; photocopied manuscript, "Fullerton/Los Angeles, California"
[Copy in Sorenson's possession]

The lengthy bibliography occupies pages 5-31. The text begins on page 32. It is addressed to Uralicists and Penutianists and presents substantial detail through page 119 demonstrating that Wintun, a branch of the California Penutian family, belongs in the Uralic family. He proposes the term Cal-Ugrian to indicate this relationship. The linguistic evidence also shows that the Wintun transferred a substantial amount of their culture from Siberia (for example, Ostyak *hul* [fish], and Wintun *hul* [salmon]; Uralic *pot* [poison], and Penutian *pot-* [poison oa]). Similarities (only some reported here) were found in grammatical structure, grammatical elements, words for parts of the human and animal bodies, kinship terms, names of plants and animals, meteorology, all aspects of the material culture, words connected with spiritual culture, shamanism and totemism, and many verbs. They evidently moved down the Ob and/or other rivers to the Arctic coast, then to the Bering Strait in search of salmon, sturgeon, etc. They followed the salmon south to the Klamath River or San Francisco Bay. A few arguments from culture are offered to support the idea that the Wintun movement to California "could have occurred 3,000 or 4,000 years ago."

S-012

AUTHOR: Sadovszky, Otto J.
DATE: 1984a
TITLE: The Discovery of California: Breaking the Silence of the Siberian-to-America Migrator
IN: The Californians 2/6:9-20

He writes at a popular level on his discovery that California Penutian languages are directly related to Ob-Ugrian languages (Vogul and Ostyak) of western Siberia. He was slow in recognizing the relationship because, like others, he supposed that languages distant in space must also be distant in time. Contrary data were neglected. He has since found that there were several migrations of the California Penutians, not just one, and there was also strong Samoyed (Yurak and Yukaghir) influence.

A number of cognates are given illustrating close ties in both language and culture. Place names and other evidence indicate that the main groups of these Central California Indians entered the area from the ocean via Bodega, San Francisco and Monterey bays. They probably followed salmon down the coast (salmon end near Monterey). Other parallels are in the bear cult, tattoo designs, shamanistic practices, hunting, weapons, etc. Language comparison shows that the migrants left the Ob River area after certain dialect features, but before others, originated. The indicated date is after 500 B.C. [See S-017.]

S-013

AUTHOR: Sadovszky, Otto J.
DATE: 1984b
TITLE: The New Genetic Relationship and the Paleolinguistics of the Central California Indian Ceremonial Houses
IN: Tenth LACUS [Linguistic Association of Canada and the United States] Forum (Quebec City, 1983), pages 516-530 (Columbia, South Carolina)

Discusses the house, sweathouse, and shamanistic trance shared between the Ob-Ugrian language group (Vogul and Ostyak) and the California Penutian-speaking group of Indians and furnishes many cognate pairs.

S-014

AUTHOR: Sadovszky, Otto J.
DATE: 1984c
TITLE: Ob-Ugrian Elements in the Adverbs, Verbal Prefixes and Postpositions of California Wintuan
IN: Congressus Quintus Internationalis Fenno-Ugristarum (Turku, Finland, 1980), 6:237-243

Linguistic evidence indicates that Wintu (as well as Nomlaki) of central California is a Vogul language. About 80% of Wintu root morphemes can be equated with Vogul or Ostyak. California Patwin approaches Siberian Ostyak, as does Miwokan. Costanoan seems to contain Finnic elements. Maiduan is closest to Sayan Samoyed. Yokutsan was strongly influenced by Yukagir. It appears that perhaps several separate migrations by Uralic ancestors roughly duplicated in California the geographical correlations among their original homelands.

S-015

AUTHOR: Sadovszky, Otto J.
DATE: 1984d
TITLE: "Xanti" in California
IN: Forum Linguisticum 8/2:115-128 (Lake Bluff, Illinois)

Wintu (California) and west Siberian Ostyak are compared along new lines.

S-016

AUTHOR: Sadovszky, Otto J.
DATE: 1985a
TITLE: Siberia's Frozen Mummy and the Genesis of the California Indian Culture
IN: The Californians 3/6:9-20

Tombs cut into permafrost in the upper Ob River area of Siberia perhaps 500 B.C. revealed tattooing on perfectly preserved bodies. One tattoo shows the chimera, similar to chimerae of Pacific coastal South and Middle America. California Penutian Indians, all of whom tattooed, have many of the same words for tattooing and associated cultural phenomena as in western Siberia. He discusses a very widespread linkage of terms for "knee" and "generate," throughout most Indo-European and Finno-Ugric languages. The same tie occurs in California Penutian. He adds related similarities in art, notably the relation to fertility of a snake motif tattooed on the calf. The Penutian football game also has perfect equivalents among Finno-Ugrians. Myth parallels are also adduced.

S-017

AUTHOR: Sadovszky, Otto J.
DATE: 1985b
TITLE: Die Zeit der Ankunft der Cal-Ugrier in Kalifornien im Lichte des ugrischen Lautwechsels *k->x->h- [The Time of Arrival of the Cal-Ugrians in California in the Light of the Ugrian Sound Change *k->x->h-]
IN: Congressus Sextus Internationalis Fenno-Ugristarum, Abstracts: Linguistics, 1:19 (USSR Academy of Sciences, Komi Branch: Syktyvkar) [An English version of the complete paper is in Sorenson's possession by the author's courtesy]

Lists 50 cognates between mainly Vogul and Miwok that show k- unchanged between Ugrian and "Cal-Ugrian" (California Penutian languages), and then 100 cognates showing k->x->h- changes. The changes show Cal-Ugrian close to the Eurasian languages of the Proto-Ugrian period that ended around 500 B.C. But irrespective of dating, the "several thousand cognates (both grammatical and lexical) speak . . . of a close relationship between the Ugrian and the Cal-Ugrian languages."

S-018

AUTHOR: Sáenz de Santa María, Carmelo
DATE: 1974
TITLE: Lo cristiano en los libros indígenas del altiplano guatemalteco [What is Christian in the Native Books of the Guatemalan Highlands]
IN: Proceedings of the 40th International Congress of Americanists (Rome and Genoa, 1972), 2:365-370

Considers how Ximénez, through whom the Popol Vuh came to us, could have been influenced (e.g., by Saint Thomas stories) to introduce Europeanisms from the Bible into the Popol Vuh text. Urges preparation of a critical edition considering such matters.

S-019

AUTHORS: Safer, Jane Fearer, and Frances McLaughlin
DATE: 1981
TITLE: Spirals from the Sea: An Anthropological Look at Shells
IMPRINT: Clarkson N. Potter: New York, in association with the American Museum of Natural History

Pages 26-29: On purple shellfish dye among Phoenicians, Jews, Romans, and Japanese, and in Peru, Mexico, and Europe in the Middle Ages—varieties, processes, functions.

S-020

AUTHOR: Safford, William E.
DATE: 1917
TITLE: Food-plants and Textiles of Ancient America
IN: Proceedings of the 19th International Congress of Americanists (Washington, 1915), pages 12-30

Page 16: Lupinus Cruickshanksii (lupine) found in Peru bears close resemblance to Lupinus albus of southern France, and another lupine from Peru is related. "The presence of these lupines in South America, so distinct from the endemic species of that continent and so very similar to those used for food in the Old World is of great interest to the ethnologist."

Page 17: The one species of peanut found in graves at Ancón, Peru, resembles specimens collected by Collins in southern Mexico. The same form is cultivated in China, Formosa, and India, "where it was probably introduced at a very early [pre-Columbian? post-Columbian?] date." One of the most common errors about cultivated plants is the statement that the peanut is of African origin.

Page 18: Cucurbita lagenaria undoubtedly occurred in Europe, Asia, Africa, and Polynesia as well as in America in pre-Columbian times.

Page 19: Presence of specimens of Annona chermoia Miller in graves at Ancón, Peru, refutes the statement of Padre Cobo that the chirimoya was introduced by him into Peru from Guatemala in the early 17th century. [Compare a parallel situation regarding bananas.]

Page 24: Specimens of sweet potatoes come from Ancón graves as well as being represented in ceramics.

Page 26: The use of lime or ashes for chewing coca leaves recalls the similar custom in India and Malaysia of using these substances with the areca nut and with leaves of the betel pepper. Carved bone buttons or toggles resembling the netsukes used by Japanese for suspending their tobacco pouches from their belts have been found in northern Chile along with ornamented lime-holding gourds and spoons of carved bone.

S-021

AUTHOR: Safford, William E.
DATE: 1924
TITLE: The Isolation of Ancient America as Established by the Cultivated Plants and the Languages of Its Aborigines
IN: Proceedings of the 20th International Congress of Americanists (Rio de Janeiro, 1922), 1:167-171
[Reprinted, essentially, as, "The Isolation of Ancient America as Indicated by Its Agriculture and Languages," *Scientific Monthly* 22 (1926): 55-59]

The object of the paper is to point out "the complete isolation of America from the rest of the world before the time of Columbus." "One of the most convincing proofs of this was the fact that every food staple encountered by the discoverers . . . was unknown to the Old World." Especially attacks Wiener on the supposed African origin of tobacco. Regarding language, "not the faintest connection can be traced between them and any languages or stock of languages of the Old World."

S-022

AUTHOR: St. John, Harold
DATE: 1962
TITLE: Origin of the Sustenance Plants of Polynesia, and Linguistic Evidence for the Migration Route of the Polynesians into the Pacific (Abstract)
IN: Proceedings of the Ninth Pacific Science Congress (Bangkok, 1957), volume 3

Page 308: Of the 27 Polynesian crop plants, one, the sweet potato, was of American origin but in prehistoric times was carried by natives as far west as New Guinea. Proposed origin sites of the others are listed. All 27 were in use in the East Indies. Vernacular names do not disagree.

S-023

AUTHOR: Sakaki, Ryozaburo
DATE: 1910
TITLE: Une nouvelle interprétation du pays de Fou-Sang

[A New Interpretation of the Land of Fu-Sang]
IN: Proceedings of the 16th International Congress of Americanists (Vienna, 1908), 1:35-50

Hypothesizes that Fou-sang was located in Japan but that from there sea communication probably reached America.

S-024

AUTHOR: Salaman, Redcliffe N.
DATE: 1949
TITLE: The History and Social Influence of the Potato
IMPRINT: Cambridge University Press: Cambridge

Page 232: Notes the similarity in both form and use of the Peruvian taclla implement and the footplough of Celtic lands.

S-025

AUTHOR: Salas, Julio C.
DATE: 1924
TITLE: Orígenes americanos. Lenguas indias comparadas
[American Origins. Comparative Indian Languages]
IMPRINT: The author: Caracas, Venezuela

Random comparisons of lexical items from mainly Caribbean and lowland South American languages with Mediterranean languages. Sample: Greek Apollo, sun god, is composed of two words, *apo* and *olo* which in specified American Indian languages signify chief and god respectively.

S-026

AUTHORS: Salazar Mallén, Mario, and Teresa Arias
DATE: 1959
TITLE: Consideraciones acerca del origen del hombre americano, desde el punto de vista immuno-hematológico
[Considerations Concerning the Origin of American Man, from the Point of View of Immuno-hematology]
IN: Gaceta médica de México 89/8:721-728

Chinese, Polynesians, Eskimos, and American Indians are considered to be of common stock because of their high R1 (CDe) frequencies and absence of the r(cde) chromosome. Yet on the basis of the lack of the Diego factor in Polynesians and its high frequency in American Indians, these two races show little similarity. Moreover this high frequency of Diego in the Indians suggests that they evolved from a stock near the base of the common paleo-asiatic stem. The lower Diego frequencies of the Chinese are attributed to later admixture with people high in blood groups B and N.

S-027

AUTHOR: Salmony, Alfred
DATE: 1933
TITLE: The Cicada in Ancient Chinese Art
IN: Connoisseur 91:174-179

The cicada signified the idea of resurrection of the dead. One bronze vessel represents a cicada with the head of a monster. Cicada pieces (and also the praying mantis, as well as carvings of the larvae of both insects) were placed on the tongue of a corpse. [Compare Mexico.]

S-027B

AUTHOR: Salmony, Alfred
DATE: 1954
TITLE: Antler and Tongue (supplement to Artibus Asiae)
IMPRINT: Artibus Asiae: Ascona, Switzerland

Sees similarities in Chinese and New World art.

S-027C
AUTHOR: Salmony, Alfred
DATE: 1958
TITLE: With Antler and Tongue
IN: Artibus Asiae 21:29-36

More similarities in Chinese and New World art.

S-028B
AUTHOR: Salter, Leon J.
DATE: 1973
TITLE: The ABO Blood Types: Their Bearing on Amerindian Origins and Britain's Neolithic
IN: Anthropological Journal of Canada 11/4:18-35 [Reprinted 1974, *NEARA (New England Antiquities Research Association) Journal* 9:22ff.]

He supposes that the A, B, and O groups are bedrock, unchanging data. Lack of B in America combined with O in Africa leads him to ask, "Could Tuareg ancestors have rafted to America?" Pages of striking visual comparisons are made between artifacts in Neolithic Britain and North America. He supposes that the North Atlantic could have been crossed by "raft hopping" when sea level was lower.

S-030
AUTHOR: Salzano, Francisco M.
DATE: 1964
TITLE: Genetics of South American Indians and the Origin of American Man
IN: Encontros Intelectuais de São Paulo, II (São Paulo, 1962) (Instituto de Pre-História, Universidad de São Paulo: São Paulo), 371-379

The genetic data give no support to the alleged influence of Australians, Melanesians, Tasmanians, and Protoindonesians in the peopling of the New World. The solution to the problem of Amerindian origins can only be obtained through an international, interdisciplinary approach involving, especially, the populations living in the Asiatic portions of the USSR.

S-031 See now S-042B.

S-033
AUTHOR: Sánchez Calvo, Estanislao
DATE: 1884
TITLE: Los nombres de los dioses . . . indagación acerca del origen del lenguaje y de las religiones á la luz del Eúskaro y de los idiomas turanianos [The Names of the Gods . . . Investigation into the Origin of Language and of Religions in the Light of Basque and of the Turanian Tongues]
IMPRINT: Enrique de la Riva: Madrid

A largely undocumented discourse in which Basque is supposed to be the operative original language or representative thereof. Movement of people from Asia to America must have been before the continents were separated at Bering Strait. No one can tell the remote age when American traditions reveal a common origin with those of the Old World. For example, the emperor of China and the Inca ruler of Peru both broke the ground in the same annual festival to inaugurate cultivation for the year.

Page 323: Perhaps "the Icelander Biorn Abramson" played a divine role among the ancestors of the Aztecs when he lived in the Great Lakes region of Canada.

S-037
AUTHOR: Sanders, Ronald
DATE: 1978
TITLE: Lost Tribes and Promised Lands: The Origins of American Racism
IMPRINT: Little, Brown: Boston

A few pages of general information about Vikings, Madoc, Brendan, generally accepting a role of some consequence for them in the settling of pre-Columbian America.

S-038

AUTHORS: Sanders, William T., and Joseph Marino
DATE: 1970
TITLE: New World Prehistory: Archaeology of the American Indian
IMPRINT: Prentice-Hall: Englewood Cliffs, New Jersey

Treating the prehistory of the entire western hemisphere in evolutionary terms, they give but brief consideration to diffusion. Interpretive rules they say they employ are: (1) entirely different criteria should be used in evaluating evidence of diffusion over great distances as against short distances; (2) it is doubtful that migrations have been common enough in history to have played a major role in cultural development; (3) successful diffusion demands sustained, periodic communication.

S-039

AUTHOR: Sanderson, Ivan T.
DATE: 1956
TITLE: Follow the Whale
IMPRINT: Little, Brown: Boston

In a well-written account of whaling since the Neolithic, the author discusses Norse and Basque whale hunting along with their concepts and technology of sailing. A commonsense view of navigation from a sailor's viewpoint eliminates some of the often-supposed aura of mystery about early maritime achievements. Basques were in the open Atlantic before A.D. 900 and may have reached North America before Columbus. Rather vivid descriptions are also provided about Phoenician sailing and vessels.

S-040B

AUTHOR: Sandison, A. T.
DATE: 1967
TITLE: Parasitic Diseases
IN: Diseases in Antiquity. A Survey of the Diseases, Injuries and Surgery of Early Populations, edited and compiled by Don Brothwell and A. T. Sandison (Charles C. Thomas: Springfield, Illinois), 178-183

From pre-Columbian Mexico and pre-conquest Peru come evidence that round worm was known (as in Eurasia). Some authorities believe that hook worm disease may have existed. Antihelminthics were certainly known in America as in Eurasia. Lice and nits are known from pre-Columbian Mexico and Peru as well as the Mediterranean through China. "Probably malaria also occurred in pre-Columbian America" (page 182).

S-042

AUTHORS: Sandstrom, Alan R., and Pamela Effrain Sandstrom
DATE: 1986
TITLE: Traditional Papermaking and Paper Cult Figures of Mexico
IMPRINT: University of Oklahoma Press: Norman and London

Page 14: Suggestions that specific traits may derive from the Near East or Asia typically are met with derision. A few scholars (e.g., Meggers and Schneider) however, have presented more sophisticated evidence to suggest contact. Among these is Tolstoy's work on the bark paper manufacture complex, but his conclusion is controversial.

S-042B

AUTHOR: San Martín, Hernán
DATE: 1967
TITLE: Nueva teoría sobre el origen del pueblo Araucano y el desarrollo de su cultura [New Theory Concerning the Origin of the Araucanian People and the Development of Their Culture]
IN: Revista del Pacífico 4/4:70-89 (Valparaiso, Chile)

Notes the possibility that we must view the Araucanian Indians as showing strong Oceanic influence.

S-044

AUTHORS: Santillana, Giorgio de, and Hertha von Dechend
DATE: 1969
TITLE: Hamlet's Mill: An Essay on Myth and the Frame of Time
IMPRINT: Gambit: Boston

Shakespeare's Hamlet provides the nominal introduction to this highly erudite study, but Hamlet's prototypical figure was Amlodhi of Icelandic myth, who owned a fabulous mill that ground out peace and plenty. Later, in decaying times, it gave out salt, and now produces rock and sand at the bottom of the sea while creating above a vast whirlpool, the Maelstrom, that leads to the land of the dead. The authors pursue this motif through Scandinavia, Ireland, Italy, Greece, Persia, Egypt, India, China, Oceania, and Mexico.

Reams of interlocking data (including: flood, tree of life, zodiac, pillar, well as plugged access to the abyss or underworld waters, primal mountain, and navel of the earth) are interpreted to mean that all the great myths of the world have a common origin whose geography is celestial, not that of earth. In short, the myths preserved and transmitted astronomical knowledge ("astrology has provided man with his continuing lingua franca through the centuries"), the basic formulation of which goes back to archaic Mesopotamia.

Pages 111, 223-227, 232-234, 247, 317, 410, 437-450 are especially relevant to Old-New World connections. For example: Sanskrit skambha "world tree, pillar, pole, prop, support" —> Finnish sampo "world tree" (Weltbaum) = Grotte = Old Norse Ygdasil ("tree below which Odin's horse grazes") = Sanskrit ashvatta ("below which the horses stand; sacred fig tree"); mandragora = alraun = Mexican quecholli = Huichol and Tarahumara hikuli = "peyote". A Mexican hunting festival celebrates the fall of the gods who had plucked the forbidden flowers in Tamoanchan, "The-House-of-Descending."

S-045

AUTHOR: Sapir, Edward
DATE: 1913
TITLE: Methods and Principles
IN: Current Anthropological Literature 2/2:69-72

A critique of von Hornbostel's [H-409] comparison of musical scales of panpipes between South America and Melanesia. The similarities make a connection "very probable," but independent development cannot be ruled out.

S-046

AUTHOR: Sapir, Edward
DATE: 1925
TITLE: The Similarity of Chinese and Indian Languages
IN: Science 62/1607:xii

A popular note of little substance in support of an enthusiasm of the author's that he never documented. Describes arguments in favor of a Chinese and Tibetan linkage with Nadene languages, citing "tonal accent" and "certain words" that are identical. [See H-517.]

S-048

AUTHOR: Sapper, Karl
DATE: 1934a
TITLE: Der Kulturzustand der Indianer vor der Berührung mit den Europäern und in der Gegenwart [The Cultural Situation of the Indians before Contact with Europeans and at the Present]
IN: Proceedings of the 24th International Congress of Americanists (Hamburg, 1930), pages 73-96

Any Melanesian or Polynesian plants or cultural elements that might have arrived in America were insignificant.

S-049

AUTHOR: Sapper, Karl
DATE: 1934b
TITLE: Geographie der altindianischen Landwirtschaft [Geography of Ancient Indian Agriculture]
IN: Petermanns Geographische Mitteilungen 80:119ff.

Discusses whether the banana was known before the Spanish introduction. Gives names for the plant from many languages and concludes on that basis that yes, the plant had to have been present well before, probably in the first millennium A.D.

S-050B

AUTHORS: Sarkar, K. R., B. K. Mukherjee, D. Gupta, and H. K. Jain
DATE: 1974
TITLE: Maize
IN: Evolutionary Studies in World Crops. Diversity and Change in the Indian Subcontinent, edited by Joseph B. Hutchinson (Cambridge University Press: London), 121-127

Pages 121-124: Early history. A lengthy discussion of the (mainly) botanical literature on possible pre-Columbian maize in India. It is generally believed that the Portuguese introduced it to India from Europe during the early part of the sixteenth century. Little or no real evidence for the existence of maize on the Indian plains in pre-Columbian times is available from the literature of botany, ethnology, or history. There is no authentic Sanskrit name for the plant. The earliest unambiguous reference to the plant is A.D. 1590. However the idea that maize might have been pre-Columbian gained some credence with the discovery of "waxy" maize in western China by Collins. He concluded that it had existed in China for a long time and came from the west. The work of Stonor and Anderson is reprised. Mangelsdorf, Oliver, Reeves, and Merrill disputed the view that maize was early.

The issue of the antiquity of maize in India is reopened by the recent survey of primitive germ plasm by the Indian Agricultural Research Institute. In addition to ethnological and linguistic evidences pointed out, the characteristics raise the question again (results summarized). "The studies on the two Himalayan primitive varieties clearly establish them as distinct entities different from the advanced types as well as (from) the American primitive types. Speculation on the origin and location of these varieties in remote Himalayan regions would be premature at this stage. Nevertheless, they open up an entirely new angle on the origin, evolution and distribution of maize." "It seems that the question of the presence of maize in Asia before 1492 remains open."

Ignoring the Sikkim primitive maizes, there remain two morphologically distinct complexes from India proper. One resembles Mexican and the other "Columbian" [Colombian?] germ plasm.

S-051

AUTHOR: Sasson, J. M.
DATE: 1966
TITLE: Canaanite Maritime Involvement in the Second Millennium B.C.
IN: Journal of the American Oriental Society 86:123-138

Ship technology and navigation capabilities in the Mediterranean.

S-052

AUTHOR: Satterthwaite, Linton, Jr.
DATE: 1944
TITLE: Review of *Archaeological Reconnaissance in Campeche,*

Quintana Roó, and Petén, by Karl Ruppert and J. H. Denison
IN: American Antiquity 10:216-218

"It has been usual to suppose that the principle of the true arch was unknown to the American Indian. . . . If the reader will turn to Figures 22 and 23 and Plates 3b and 4a of this report, I believe he will have no doubt that the Maya at La Muñeca roofed a long room with the true arch, and that they knew exactly what they were doing."

S-053

AUTHOR: Satterthwaite, Linton, Jr.
DATE: 1946
TITLE: Incense Burning at Piedras Negras
IN: University of Pennsylvania, Museum Bulletin 11/4:16-22

Page 21: Incense smoke hid from sight a holy object in the temple. [Compare P-065.]

S-054

AUTHOR: Satterthwaite, Linton, Jr.
DATE: 1948
TITLE: An Unusual Type of Building in the Maya Old Empire
IN: Proceedings of the 26th International Congress of Americanists (Seville, 1935), 1:243-254

An apparent sweathouse at Classic Piedras Negras. [Compare L-305.]

S-055

AUTHOR: Sauer, Carl O.
DATE: 1944
TITLE: Review of *Les origines de l'homme américain* [Origins of American Man], by Paul Rivet
IN: Geographical Review 34:680-681

The Mendes-Corrêa hypothesis of movements from Australia via Antarctica, which Rivet supports, is a fantasy unrelated to the real history of climates and seas. The Melanesian thesis is less unattractive, but oversimplified. But Rivet's handling of the sweet potato question is exemplary.

S-056

AUTHOR: Sauer, Carl O.
DATE: 1950
TITLE: Cultivated Plants of South and Central America
IN: Physical Anthropology, Linguistics and Cultural Geography of South American Indians, vol. 6 of Handbook of South American Indians, edited by Julian H. Steward, Smithsonian Institution, Bureau of American Ethnology Bulletin 143 (Washington, D.C.), 487-543

Very important synthetic source on American flora with observations regarding a considerable number of plants evidently or possibly shared between New World and Old World.

Pages 499-500: Canavalia beans deserve study as possible transoceanic transfers in pre-Columbian times.

Pages 500-503: The Asiatic Phaseolus was also cultivated in America, and the lima bean and Vigna sp. occurred in both hemispheres and should be studied.

Pages 526-527: There is the possibility that some bananas were present in America before the Spaniards.

Page 536: The feral cotton on the Galapagos is of Peruvian type.

S-057

AUTHOR: Sauer, Carl O.
DATE: 1952
TITLE: Agricultural Origins and Dispersals
IMPRINT: Bowman Memorial Lectures, American Geographical Society: New York

[Reprinted MIT Press: Cambridge, 1969]

Page 42: The northern South America cultivating hearth shows many ethnic traits resembling Indonesia (mentioned). Following pages reprise information on major cultigens of the area, including (page 47) the lone New World cultivated yam (Dioscorea trifida).

Pages 54-57: Presents the general hypothesis that both tropical Asian and Andean planting cultures are divergences from one basic way of horticulture. Moreover, the overall configuration of customs and skills are much like those in monsoon Asia, thus we come to the question of common or independent origin.

Diffusion of the pattern around the northern margin of the Pacific should have presented no greater difficulties than its spread westward as far as Africa and Europe. Numerous resemblances in customs between the Northwest coast and Indonesia are familiar. "The burden of denying passage to boat people having the skills mentioned would seem to me to rest on those who object to such diffusion into the New World." We have in North America a number of curiously distributed plants commonly associated with man (sweet flag, the esculent Cyperus, water chestnut, Nelumbium lotus, and Sagittaria sagittifolia) perhaps close to or identical with Old World forms and not likely to have been transported by water or animal. Later there is varied and good evidence of transpacific carriage of plants in low latitudes for which human agency alone appears competent.

Pages 57-60: Summarizes what leads him to think the black-boned, black-meated chicken crossed the ocean in pre-European voyaging times.

Pages 60, 67: The transpacific carriage of cotton, the true gourd, sweet potato, and coconut appears proven, and, even for the coconut, due to the deliberate action of man. Notes especially questions about Cucurbitae in Asia. There has been reluctance to get and weigh the available evidence. Needing clarification: sweet potato, maize in China, bananas, and the chicken, although there are several dozen cultigens that need critical investigation.

Is inclined to believe that maize was carried across the Pacific in pre-Columbian times but cannot guess in which direction.

S-058

AUTHOR: Sauer, Carl O.
DATE: 1959
TITLE: Middle America as a Culture Historical Location
IN: Proceedings of the 33rd International Congress of Americanists (San José, Costa Rica, 1958), 1:115-122

Suggests the possibility that it is the dry-land bias of most modern scholars, rather than the facts about ancient voyaging possibilities, that leads to so much resistance to the idea that pre-modern people could sail long distances.

S-059

AUTHOR: Sauer, Carl O.
DATE: 1962
TITLE: Maize into Europe
IN: Proceedings of the 34th International Congress of Americanists (Vienna, 1960), pages 777-788

How and when was this plant carried to Europe? It may have been in Europe before Columbus.

S-060

AUTHOR: Sauer, Carl O.
DATE: 1968
TITLE: Northern Mists
IMPRINT: University of California Press: Berkeley
[Reviewed 1970 by R. A. Skelton, *Mariner's Mirror* 56:291]

His review of conditions and vessels of the northern and western Atlantic affirms that in the

15th century the Portuguese had sailed from the Azores to North America, but had been preceded by Bristolmen. Even earlier ships of the Hanseatic League in the north and of the Hermandad de las Marismas from the Bay of Biscay were fishing and whaling the North Atlantic. Still earlier were the Norse, but they "followed, mainly or entirely, routes of Irish discovery" to reach the North American mainland.

S-061

AUTHOR: Sauer, Jonathan D.
DATE: 1950a
TITLE: Amaranths as Dye Plants among the Pueblo Peoples
IN: Southwestern Journal of Anthropology 6:412-415

Since ancient times many Old and New World peoples have cultivated several amaranth species as grain crops, pot herbs, ornamentals, fetish plants, and dye plants. Amaranth used for dye is recorded in East Africa and Latin America. He gives some information on dye use by peoples in the U.S. Southwest.

S-062

AUTHOR: Sauer, Jonathan D.
DATE: 1950b
TITLE: The Grain Amaranths: A Survey of Their History and Classification
IN: Annals of the Missouri Botanical Garden 37:561-632

Based on his dissertation at Washington University under Edgar Anderson, he classifies the jumble of reported specimens in America into four species, each characteristic of one area: Mexico and the Southwestern U.S., Guatemala, the Andean region, and Argentina. Two, those from Mexico and the Andean region, are also cultivated in Asia, extending from Manchuria to Iran and India. There is some indication that the Andean species grew in parts of Africa, although the records are feeble. Since in Asia occurrence is largely among marginal and hill peoples with no record of use by the more advanced peoples of the coasts, Sauer supposes that amaranth cultivation was ancient and widespread. An American origin for all the species seems sure and floating of the seeds by sea seems impossible, suggesting a movement by men in pre-Columbian times. He admits the possibility of post-Columbian transfer, however.

S-063

AUTHOR: Sauer, Jonathan D.
DATE: 1967
TITLE: The Grain Amaranths and Their Relatives: A Revised Taxonomic and Geographic Survey
IN: Annals of the Missouri Botanical Garden 54:103-137

[By complete silence on the topic does he imply reluctance to pursue his earlier suggestion of pre-Columbian dispersal of amaranth in Asia?]

S-064

AUTHOR: Sauer, Jonathan D.
DATE: 1968
TITLE: The Problem of Introduction of New World Grain Amaranths to the Old World (Resumé)
IN: Proceedings of the 37th International Congress of Americanists (Mar del Plata, Argentina, 1966), 4:127-128

The North American A. hypochondriacus was one of the main crop and ceremonial plants of Aztec Mexico and extended to Arizona in late prehistoric times. In the 19th century, botanists found the common, white-seeded Mexican amaranth to be established as a grain crop over an enormous, coherent area from Manchuria through China, Burma, the Himalayas, and to Persia with an outlier in the Nilgiri Hills of South India. No archaeological record of it is known from the Old World but a plant with the same common name was in use in 10th century Szechwan. Post-Columbian introduction is hard to imagine.

Another race, with deep red plant color, was a traditional Pueblo Indian dye plant and is widely planted as an ornamental in both the New and Old Worlds; much of its dispersal may be historic (European), although early botanists found it growing among a surprising array of peoples in Africa, Asia, and the Pacific islands. A. Caudatus, an old grain crop in the Andes, was taken to Europe in the 16th century and historically dispersed, yet other races from the Andean complex are also in the Old World and are harder to explain; one was first found by European botanists in Kashmir and Ethiopia where it is planted for grain.

S-065

AUTHOR: Sauer, Jonathan D.

DATE: 1971

TITLE: A Reevaluation of the Coconut as an Indicator of Human Dispersal

IN: Man across the Sea: Problems of Pre-Columbian Contacts, edited by Carroll L. Riley, et al. (University of Texas Press: Austin), 309-319

Discusses evidence for the distribution of Cocos nucifera, concluding that the transpacific distribution of the species is not reliable evidence of human dispersal.

S-066

AUTHOR: Sauer, Jonathan D.

DATE: 1976

TITLE: Grain Amaranths

IN: Evolution of Crop Plants, edited by N. W. Simmonds (Longmans: London), 309-319

Same comment as for S-063.

S-067

AUTHOR: Sauer, Jonathan D.

DATE: 1988

TITLE: Plant Migration: The Dynamics of Geographic Patterning in Seed Plant Species

IMPRINT: University of California Press: Berkeley and Los Angeles

Pages 18-26: Cases are cited of value regarding sea and storm dispersal, or lack of it, of plants such as Lagenaria and Cocos.

Page 229: It is "generally accepted" that the common polyploid species of Gossypium hirsutum originated in the Pleistocene by hybridization on tropical American seacoasts between native diploids and an African diploid whose seeds had dispersed by ocean currents.

S-067B

AUTHOR: Sauer, Jonathan D.

DATE: 1993

TITLE: Historical Geography of Crop Plants: A Select Roster

IMPRINT: CRC Press: Boca Raton, Florida

Include discussions of most of the crops which have been suggested as diffused between Old and New Worlds. Archaeological evidences and origins are sketched usefully with substantial, generally up-to-date, but mainly cautiously conventional, documentation. A good summary of current opinion among botanists, although more an eclectic précis rather than a systematically critical evaluation, of sources and positions. The treatment of origins typically supposes "independent origins" in multiple areas based on taxonomic inferences, although, for example regarding the sweet potato, he notes that one model of the occurrence of the same plant in distant areas (natural spread of seed to Polynesia from South America) need not rule out another model (South American raftsmen introducing the plant).

For example, on page 232, "The possibility of Pre-Columbian presence of maize in various regions of the Old World was actively debated during the 1960s and 1970s. Historical evidence was drawn from early reports now generally interpreted as references to grain sorghum. Archaeological remains were reported only from 15th-century India, but the dating is questionable. New evidence has been drawn from stone carvings in 12th- and 13th-century temples in southern India that depict objects resembling maize ears. The resemblances are intriguing, but other possible models have been suggested, including Pandanus fruits. Moreover, the carvings may not be as old as the temples."

His discussion of amaranth says not a word about his earlier pro-diffusion position (S-062, S-064).

S-068

AUTHORS: Sauer, Jonathan D., and Lawrence Kaplan
DATE: 1969
TITLE: Canavalia Beans in American Prehistory
IN: American Antiquity 34/4:417-424

Review of the occurrence of two domesticated species, C. plagiosperma in Peru and C. ensiformis in Mexico and Arizona; time(s) and place(s) of domestication cannot be designated without additional archaeological and ethnographic evidence. [Compare S-056.]

S-069B

AUTHORS: Saunders, Shelley R., Peter G. Ramsden and D. Ann Herring
DATE: 1992
TITLE: Transformation and Disease
IN: Disease and Demography in the Americas, edited by John W. Verano and Douglas H. Ubelaker (Smithsonian Institution Press: Washington), 117-125

The idea of America as pristine prior to contact has deep roots in the western European mentality as a rationalization of the course of White/Indian relations in the following centuries and continues to validate the paternal role of governments over native populations. Substantial social and population changes predated European contact in Ontario which may already have suffered infectious disease epidemics. European contact just added new pathogens to the established infection load.

They list known diseases: mycobacterium tuberculosis, bacillary and amoebic dysentery, influenza and pneumonia, arthritides, rickettsial and viral fevers, protozoan diseases (leishmaniasis and trypanosomiasis), ascarids and endoparasites, streptococcus, staphylococcus, and salmonella have been identified or suggested seriously to have been present. "Clearly, the introduction of European acute community infections like measles, smallpox, and whooping cough . . . was unlikely to have constituted the first experience of infectious disease among New World peoples." Village life would have created conditions conducive to epidemics. Longhouse living would have been a factor. Migrants due to social disruption also could disseminate different infectious agents.

S-070

AUTHOR: Sauneron, Serge
DATE: 1957
TITLE: Les prêtres de l'ancienne Égypte [The Priests of Ancient Egypt]
IMPRINT: Editions du Seuil: Paris [English edition Grove: New York, 1960]

Page 38: The Egyptian Sm- priest wore a panther skin. [Compare Mayan priests and their jaguar skins?]

S-071

AUTHOR: Sauvageot, Aurèlien
DATE: 1924
TITLE: Eskimo et Ouralien [Eskimo and Uralian]
IN: Journal de la société des américanistes de Paris 16:279-316

Claims a historical relationship between Eskimo and Finno-Ugric languages.

S-072

AUTHOR: Sauvageot, Aurèlien
DATE: 1930
TITLE: Recherches sur le vocabulaire des langues Ouralo-Altaïques [Researches on the Vocabulary of Ural-Altaic Languages]
IN: Collection linguistique 30 (publiée par la société de linguistique de Paris), (Librairie Ancienne Honoré Champion: Paris)

Page xx: Seems open to the idea of a connection between Aymara and Turkic.

Page 141: He believes that similarities beyond coincidence are found between Finno-Ugric and Quechua and Algonkian.

S-073

AUTHOR: Sauvageot, Aurèlien
DATE: 1953
TITLE: Charactère ouraloïde du verbe eskimo [Uralic Character of the Eskimo Verb]
IN: Bulletin de la société de linguistique de Paris 49:107-121

Hammerich's hypothesis of a connection is absurd [see H-051].

S-074

AUTHOR: Savage, Dana C., Jr.
DATE: 1979
TITLE: The Decalogue Tablet, Newark, Ohio
IN: Epigraphic Society Occasional Publications 7/165:193-199

Historical resumé of interpretations of the "Newark Holy Stone."

S-075

AUTHORS: Savage-Smith, E., and Marion B. Smith
DATE: 1980
TITLE: Islamic Geomancy and a Thirteenth Century Divinatory Device
IMPRINT: Undena Publications: Malibu, California

Pages vii-4: Geomancy was very popular in Europe in medieval and renaissance times. It was a distinctly Islamic development which later reached the Byzantine and Latin worlds. In Islam the name means "the science of sand." Names involved are possibly of Buddhist or Berber origin. Geomancy may have originated in the pre-Islamic Near East or India. [For potential comparison to hinted occurrence in the earlier Near East, China, and Mesoamerica compare C-059 and A-045.] A certain North African tribe practiced scapulimancy.

S-077

AUTHOR: Saville, Marshall Howard
DATE: 1897
TITLE: A Primitive Maya Musical Instrument
IN: American Anthropologist (o. s.) 10:389-396

See S-078.

S-078

AUTHOR: Saville, Marshall Howard
DATE: 1898
TITLE: The Musical Bow in Ancient Mexico
IN: American Anthropologist (o. s.) 11:280-284

In S-077 he published on a Maya Indian musical bow. Brinton had written in *American Antiquarian,* January 1897, reporting on four bows from Central America opining that the instrument was pre-Columbian. Mason in the November 1897 *American Anthropologist* agreed. In *Science* (Sept. 16, 1898), Mason reported that Carl Sapper believes the Maya instrument came from Africa (post-Columbian) yet that musical bows were known before the Spanish, since the Lacandon have them. Habel, ten Kate, and Morse are also cited. Here Saville shows what he considers a bow in a depiction of a musical ensemble on a pre-Columbian codex, the Manuscrit du Cacique.

S-079

AUTHOR: Saville, Marshall Howard
DATE: 1899
TITLE: Exploration of Zapotecan Tombs in Southern Mexico
IN: American Anthropologist 1:350-362

Pages 355-356: A lengthy stretch of ceramic drain pipe appears in a mound of Zapotec Classic age. Two other cases in the area are noted. [Compare N-015.]

S-081

AUTHORS: Sawyer, Jack, and Robert A. Levine
DATE: 1966
TITLE: Cultural Dimensions: A Factor Analysis of the World Ethnographic Sample
IN: American Anthropologist 68:708-731

See S-351.

S-082

AUTHOR: Sawyer, P. H.
DATE: 1971
TITLE: The Age of the Vikings
IMPRINT: St. Martin's: New York [First edition, Edward Arnold: London, 1962]

1971 edition, pages 66-85: A judicious summary of the nature, uses, and history of Viking ships, with basic bibliography.

S-083B

AUTHOR: Sayles, E. B. "Ted"
DATE: 1968
TITLE: Fantasies of Gold: Legends of Treasures and How They Grew
IMPRINT: University of Arizona Press: Tucson

Pages 87-89: Account of the "Elephant Slabs" which came in 1950 to the Arizona State Museum where Sayles was on the staff. Archaeologist Earl Morris noted in the museum record that these objects of very hard quartzitic sandstone had been found in a ruin on the Animas River opposite Flora Vista, New Mexico. They had been purchased by A. M. Amsden prior to 1910 from a boy who lived in Flora Vista. Morris visited the ruin and dated it by pottery to A.D. 1100 and later. Morris could see no reason to doubt the authenticity of the slabs but could not explain them. Harold Gladwin noted that most archaeologists who saw them condemned them immediately as fakes. One proposal was that they were Mormon-made. A Navajo told a folklore collector a legend in which two Navajo "Calendar Stones" were buried, and there might be some connection. The slabs are illustrated. Slab B shows unique incised signs which look like some Old World letters and includes two crude drawings of elephants in the midst of the inscription, plus a few other natural forms.

S-085

AUTHOR: Schaefer, F. J.
DATE: 1920
TITLE: Bibliography of the Kensington Rune Stone
IN: Catholic Historical Review 6:387-391

Fifty-two items including newspaper articles, the major ones annotated, in chronological order from 1899 to 1919.

S-086

AUTHOR: Schaeffner, A.
DATE: 1936
TITLE: Origine des instruments de musique [The Origin of Musical Instruments]
IMPRINT: Payot: Paris

Pages 72ff., 249ff., 265, 284, 288ff., and 387: Compares Old World and American instruments.

S-086B

AUTHOR: Schanfield, Moses S.
DATE: 1992
TITLE: Immunoglobulin Allotypes (GM and KM) Indicate Multiple Founding Populations of Native Americans: Evidence of at Least Four Migrations to the New World
IN: Human Biology 64:381-402

Recent discussions on the origin of Amerindians have focused on North American populations. On the basis of GM and KM typing and language, approximately 28,000 Amerindians were divided into four groups of populations: non-Nadene South American (eight [tribal?] groups), non-Nadene North American (seven groups), Nadene (four groups), and Eskaleuts (six groups). These groups were compared to four groups of Asian populations (Chukchi, Ainu, Tungus-Evens, Uralic-KM*1). The distribution of GM haplotypes differed significantly among and within these groups as measured by chi-square analysis. Furthermore, as reflected in a maximum linkage cluster analysis, Amerindian populations in general cluster among geographic divisions, with Eskaleuts and Nadenes clustering with the Asian populations and non-Nadene North American and non-Nadene South American populations forming two additional clusters. The divisions appear to reflect populations descended from groups that entered the New World at different times. Maximum linkage cluster analysis puts Alaskan Athapaskans closest to northwestern Siberian populations and Eskaleuts closest to the Chukchi, their nearest Asian neighbor. These analyses suggest that "at least four separate migrant groups crossed Beringia." It appears likely that the South American non-Nadene entered the New World before 17,000 B.P., the North American non-Nadene in the immediate postglacial, and the Eskaleut and Nadene at a later date.

S-087

AUTHOR: Scheans, Daniel J.
DATE: 1966
TITLE: A New View of Philippines Pottery Manufacture
IN: Southwestern Journal of Anthropology 22:206-219

Methodological. Great local variation is found in the ways in which pottery is manufactured. The functional and historical significance of the use of "the potter's wheel" as against not using it is questionable. [Compare F-145.]

S-087B

AUTHOR: Schedl, Armando
DATE: 1957
TITLE: ¿Negros prehispánicos en América? [(Were There) Prehispanic Negroes in America?]
IN: Revista geográfica americana no. 244:121-124
[Reprinted, translated to Portuguese, in *Eu Sei Tudo* 4 (1958): 69-72, Rio de Janeiro]

Argues that there were, and that they might have been associated with African voyages to America in connection with the Bachofen/Frobenius "Poseidonic" kulturkreis supposedly stemming from African Guinea. [See F-208.]

S-087C

AUTHOR: Schedl, Armando
DATE: 1959
TITLE: Los negros precolombianos
IN: Revista geográfica americana 252:555-565 (Buenos Aires)

An expanded version of S-087B.

S-091

AUTHOR: Schellhas, Paul
DATE: 1904
TITLE: Representation of Deities of the Maya Manuscripts, second edition, revised

IN: Papers 44/1, Peabody Museum of American Archaeology and Ethnology, Harvard University

Page 443: The dog as lightning-beast belongs to the death god. [Compare D-105.]

S-091B

AUTHOR: Schenk, Joseph
DATE: 1982
TITLE: Mystery of the Holy Stones
IMPRINT: Pheasant Run: St. Louis

A compilation of documents about and discussion of the stones from Newark, Ohio, engraved with Hebrew characters.

S-091C

AUTHOR: Scherz, James P.
DATE: 1994
TITLE: The Kingman Coins
IN: The Ancient American 7:32-38

Eight coins found in Wisconsin are illustrated and discussed in part. They appear to be copper and Roman. Further analysis is planned.

S-092

AUTHOR: Schindele, St.
DATE: 1909
TITLE: Hatten die Alten Kunde von Amerika? [Did the Ancients Have Knowledge of America?]
IN: Deutsche Rundschau für Geographie und Statistik 31:241-246 (Vienna)

Short recap of and speculations regarding ancient Greek comments on lands to the west including Atlantis, plus a short discussion of the Norse.

S-094

AUTHOR: Schledermann, Peter
DATE: 1980
TITLE: Notes on Norse Finds from the East Coast of Ellesmere Island, N.W.T.
IN: Arctic 33:454-463

Metal, wool, and oak objects of apparent Norse origin were found in 1978-1980 on the east coast of Ellesmere Island in old Thule culture house ruins. Radiocarbon dates from here and other places where Norse goods have appeared cluster in the vicinity of the 13th century. Either direct trade or second-hand trade, or both, with the Norse are possible explanations.

S-094B

AUTHOR: Schledermann, Peter
DATE: 1981
TITLE: Ellesmere Island: Eskimo and Viking Finds in the High Arctic
IN: National Geographic Magazine 159:574-601

A fragment of chain-mail armor, iron boat rivets, European oak wood, and wool cloth of a Norse sort have all been found in archaeological sites on Ellesmere Island opposite the northwesternmost portion of Greenland in the past three years. They could have come directly or indirectly from the Norse or perhaps across Asia eastward. Also found, a small carved figure probably representing a Norseman and also a copper blade which might be European. Ceramics were worked at one time by Eskimo coming from the west, however they lost that capability, perhaps due to lack of wood to fire pots. They turned to carving soapstone vessels instead.

S-095

AUTHORS: Schledermann, Peter, and Karen McCullough
DATE: 1980
TITLE: Western Elements in Early Thule Culture of the Eastern High Arctic
IN: Arctic 33:833-841

Some features are perhaps of Norse derivation.

S-096

AUTHOR: Schlegel, Gustave
DATE: 1892
TITLE: Problèmes géographiques: les peuples étrangers chez les historiens chinois, I. Fou-sang Kouo: les pays de Fou-sang [Geographic Problems: Foreign Peoples According to Chinese Historians, I. Fu-Sang Kouo: The Countries of Fu-Sang]
IMPRINT: Brill: Leiden [Extract from *T'oung-Pao* 3/2:101-168]

Reasons why an American identification for Fusang will not do.

S-098

AUTHOR: Schlenther, Ursula von
DATE: 1968
TITLE: Conceptos cristianos en textos indígenas de los siglos XVI al XX [Christian Concepts in Native Texts of the 16th to 20th Centuries]
IN: Sociedad mexicana de antropología, Traducciones Mesoamericanistas 2:221-246 [Reprinted from 1965 *Wissenschaftliche Zeitschrift der Humboldt-Universität zu Berlin* 14:176-186]

Refers to texts in Aztec, Maya of Yucatan and Quiché of Guatemala, and also to prayers in Quiché and Kekchi. Cites some texts in the original language. [Compare G-194.]

S-100

AUTHOR: Schlesier, K. H.
DATE: 1965
TITLE: Geschichte der Besiedlung Nordamerikas von den Anfängen bis zum Beginn der christlichen Zeitrechnung [History of the Settlement of North America from Earliest Times to the Start of the Christian Era]
IN: Saeculum 16/1:29-41 (Munich)

Sees nine major migrations, beginning with Neanderthaloid hunters in the Würm era. The second was Solutrean, from Lake Baikal, while the third was Plano hunters from Lake Baikal (Serovo culture) about 3000 B.C. Mongoloid-Europoid hunters from the Gobi brought the microblade tradition ca. 5500 B.C., then from the Siberian tundra the small tool tradition arrived 4000 B.C., followed by the Eskaleut-Chukchis about the same time; the Chukchis later returned to northeast Asia. The last two waves were, respectively, Algonkian and Athapaskans of the second millennium B.C.

S-101

AUTHOR: Schlesinger, Kathleen
DATE: 1939
TITLE: The Greek Aulos
IMPRINT: Methuen: London

Criticizes on methodological grounds Hornbostel's argument that panpipes of Melanesia and South America had to be related.

S-102

AUTHOR: Schlinghoff, D.
DATE: 1982
TITLE: Indische Seefahrt in römischer Zeit [Shipping of India in Roman Times]
IN: Zur geschichtlichen Bedeutung der frühen Seefahrt, edited by Hermann Müller-Karpe, Kolloquien zur Allgemeinen und Vergleichenden Archäologie, Band 2 (C. H. Beck: München), 51-85

Superlative discussion complete with 188 footnotes.

S-103

AUTHOR: Schmeltz, Johannes Diedrich Eduard
DATE: 1898

TITLE: Nouvelles et correspondance, XXXIII. A Patu-patu or Merai from an American Mound
IN: Internationales Archiv für Ethnographie 11:165 (Leiden)

Reports a stone club in the National Museum in Washington said by the curator, Thomas Wilson, to have been dug in 1883 from a mound in Bent County, Colorado. It is very similar to the well-known New Zealand patu-patu type.

S-104

AUTHOR: Schmidt, Max
DATE: 1911
TITLE: Über altperuanische Gewebe mit szenenhaften Darstellungen [On Ancient Peruvian Textiles with Scenic Representations]
IN: Baessler-Archiv 1:1-61

Points out parallels between Peruvian and Near Eastern myths relating to textiles.

S-105

AUTHOR: Schmidt, Max
DATE: 1914
TITLE: Die Paressi-Kabisi: Ethnologische Ergebnisse der Expedition zu den Quellen der Jauru und Juruena im Jahre 1910 [The Paressi-Cabisi: Ethnological Findings of the Expedition to the Sources of the Jauru and Jaruena Rivers in 1910]
IN: Baessler-Archiv 4/4-5:167-240

Fig. 19: Fishing with the assistance of cormorants, known in China, is shown to occur in Peru.

S-107

AUTHOR: Schmidt, Wilhelm
DATE: 1913
TITLE: Kulturkreise und Kulturschichten in Südamerika [Culture Circle and Culture Strata in South America]
IMPRINT: Zeitschrift für Ethnologie 45:1014-1130 [Reprinted as *Etnologia sul-americana, circulos culturäes e estratos culturäes na America do Sul* (Companhia Editora Nacional: São Paulo, 1942)]

This major paper applies Schmidt's kulturkreis schema to America. Several Old World "circles" are identified and discussed, notably the "frei-mutterrechtliche Kulturkreise oder die Bogenkultur" [free-matrilineal culture circle or bow culture], and the "frei-vaterrechtlichen Kulturkreise (polynesische und indonesische Kultur)" [free-patrichineal culture circle (Polynesian and Indonesian culture)]. The last seven pages summarize an arid discussion involving Krause, Ehrenreich, Ankermann, and Schmidt.

S-109

AUTHOR: Schmidt, Wilhelm
DATE: 1933
TITLE: High Gods in North America
IMPRINT: Oxford University Press: Oxford

Pages 14-15: He considers Rivet's evidence for linguistic connection between Fuegians and Australians without value. Rivet took his Australian material from Schmidt's monograph, but from the most disparate Australian languages, often having no affinity whatever with each other.

Page 18: The tribes in the south of North America are quite apart from those to the north (north-central Californians, Algonkins, and "Selish" are the oldest groups in North America). All those with totemism or mother-right (including the Siouans, Iroquois, Muskogian, and Pueblo) originated in Mexico and Central America but ultimately came from Indonesia and Southeast Asia by sea.

Page 27: The high god of the old, northern tribes bears the name Thunder or the like, as in the Old

World, while in America and North Asia not thunder but the Thunder-bird is god.

Page 133: The oldest wave from Asia, those of North-West Central California and some of the North-East Algonkins, came in paleolithic times. [Compare S-012.]

Page 134: A whole series of points of contact in religion is seen between the oldest American tribes and the oldest of north-east Asia: Samoyeds, Koryak, Ainu, extending even as far as the Mongols, Turks, and East Slavs.

S-111

AUTHOR: Schmidt, Wilhelm
DATE: 1937
TITLE: Das Tauchmotif in den Erdschöpfungsmythen Nordamerikas, Asiens and Europas
[The Earth Diver Motif in the Creation Stories of North America, Asia and Europe]
IN: Mélanges de linguistique et de philologie (C. Klinckwieck: Paris), 111-122

Parallels between the Algonkian, Samoyed, and others.

S-112

AUTHOR: Schmidt, Wilhelm
DATE: 1939
TITLE: The Culture Historical Method of Ethnology
IMPRINT: Fortuny's: New York

The first part of the book is a rambling critique and discussion of "the historical method in ethnology" without surprises for anyone knowing Schmidt's views. It includes references to the writings and thought of figures like Wissler, Tylor, Graebner, Ratzel, Dixon, Kroeber, Rivers, Smith, Quatrefages, etc. Explains what the kulturkreislehre has come to mean to Schmidt and what he considers proper methods to be followed for the study of diffusion and development.

S-113

AUTHOR: Schmidt, Wilhelm
DATE: 1948
TITLE: The Central-Algonkin Floodmyth
IN: Proceedings of the 28th International Congress of Americanists (Paris, 1947), pages 317-319

Related to S-111.

S-114

AUTHOR: Schmidt, Wilhelm
DATE: 1964
TITLE: Wege der Kulturen
[Paths of Culture]
IN: Anthropos-Instituts: St. Augustin bei Bonn

A collection of Schmidt's papers intended to represent the range of his anthropological interests, including S-111.

S-115

AUTHORS: Schmidt, Wilhelm, and Wilhelm Koppers
DATE: 1924
TITLE: Völker und Kulturen I: Gesellschaft und Wirtschaft der Völker, Band 3: Der Mensch aller Zeiten
[Peoples and Cultures I: Society and Economy of the Peoples. Vol. 3: Men of all Periods]
IMPRINT: Habbel: Regensberg

Fundamental work for the kulturkreislehre, applying the system worldwide, including America of course.

S-118

AUTHOR: Schmitz, Emile
DATE: n.d. [c. 1880]

TITLE: Vestiges du Christianisme et de l'homme blanc en Amérique avant sa découverte par Christophe Colomb
[Vestiges of Christianity and of the White Man in America before its Discovery by Christopher Columbus]
IN: Proceedings of the 3rd International Congress of Americanists (Brussels, 1879), 1:493-507

Summarizes the Norse in Greenland and northeastern North America. Among the Creeks there was a tradition of the arrival of bearded white men with long robes, sandals, etc. These must have been Scotch-Irish holy men of the Order of St. Columba who had arrived in Vinland via Greenland and reached as far as Florida. In Mexico there was Quetzalcoatl; his doctrines and religious usages were clearly Christian (eucharist, baptism, cross, etc.). Similar ideas were in Brazil and Paraguay (where runic inscriptions have been found). Finally, the Incas had a tradition of white visitors, the cross, and other Christian features.

S-118B

AUTHOR: Schmökel, Hartmut
DATE: 1969
TITLE: Randbemerkungen zur sogenannte Parahyba-inschrift
[Comments on the So-called Parahyba Inscription]
IN: Mélanges de l'Université Saint-Joseph 45 (fasc. 17): 295-306 (Beirut)

Examines critically but with some sympathy the context of the discovery and early reactions to the inscription in Brazil.

S-119

AUTHOR: Schneider, Harold K.
DATE: 1977
TITLE: Prehistoric Transpacific Contact and the Theory of Culture Change
IN: American Anthropologist 79:9-25

Important. Argues that culture-change theory follows a genetic model and that such a model predicts pre-Columbian contact between the hemispheres. That fact is supported by a growing body of data, a sample of which he cites.

S-120

AUTHOR: Schneider, Marius
DATE: 1934
TITLE: Geschichte der Mehrstimmigkeit, vol. 1
[History of Polyphony]
IMPRINT: J. Bard: Berlin

Under the influence of kulturkreis theory, he postulates noncontiguous areas for polyphony in music (South Asia, South America, Micronesia, Polynesia) and gives these areas significance as historical units.

S-122

AUTHOR: Schobinger, Juan
DATE: 1956
TITLE: Las "clavas insignias" de Argentina y Chile; descripción de nuevos ejemplares procedentes de las provincias del Neuquén y Mendoza, y análisis de conjunto
[The "Insignia Clubs" of Argentina and Chile; Description of New Examples from the Provinces of Neuquen and Mendoza, and Analysis of the Group]
IN: Runa 7/2:252-280

General discussion of an unusual form of ceremonial baton or club found in Chile and adjacent Argentina, with detailed description of 11 examples. The author concludes that these objects are the result of Polynesian influence on the south coast of Chile sometime in the prehistoric period. The trait was retained by the later Mapuche culture and diffused throughout the area of Mapuche influence. A map shows the location of recorded finds of these objects.

S-123

AUTHOR: Schobinger, Juan

DATE: 1956-1957

TITLE: Sobre los antecedentes morfológicos de las clavas semilunares océanica-americanas [Concerning the Morphological Antecedents of Oceanic-American Semi-lunar Clubs]

IN: Runa 7/8:270-276

On semi-lunar clubs of Oceania and South America, prototypes of which occur in Formosa and China.

S-124

AUTHOR: Schobinger, Juan

DATE: 1961

TITLE: La arqueología y el Libro de Mormón [Archaeology and The Book of Mormon]

IN: Anales de arqueología y etnología 16:259-265 (Mendoza, Argentina)

A negative critique at about the same level of limited information as W-061.

S-125

AUTHOR: Schobinger, Juan

DATE: 1969

TITLE: Prehistoria de Sudamérica [Prehistory of South America]

IMPRINT: Nueva Colección Labor No. 95 (Editorial Labor: Barcelona)

Pages 265-266: On the background of a population derived from Asia via the Bering Strait, mongoloid contingents commenced to arrive in America from East and Southeast Asia and nearby islands from 3000 B.C. or before. The ancient population was in part displaced and in part absorbed by the new waves, which were a minority in numbers but brought into play a stronger biodynamic. This included the Valdivia manifestation. Then in the first millennium B.C. new elements arrived via the Pacific into the old American temple-bearing cultures.

S-126

AUTHOR: Schobinger, Juan

DATE: 1977-1978

TITLE: Mediterraneos, Semitas, Celtas y Vikingos en America: ojeada sobre algunas modernas expresiones de hiperdifusionismo transatlántico [Mediterraneans, Semites, Celts and Vikings in America: A Review of Some Modern Expressions of Transatlantic Hyperdiffusionism]

IN: Anales de arqueología y etnología 32-33:25-73 (Mendoza, Argentina)

Distressed by what he considers a disappearing tradition of genuine scientific criticism in Argentina, he sets out to slay all the hyperdiffusionist dragons he can reach. After a brief survey of the pre-scientific views (e.g., Grotius) of the topic, he gives light treatments to the Tiahuanacologists, the Parahyba Stone, Gordon, Fell, Honoré, et al., but then quickly focuses on Mahieu's theory of Viking voyages to South America, which he dissects in detail. The one exception to his attack on transatlantic diffusion is Alcina Franch, who does not, in Schobinger's view, belong in the same fantasy category as the others. He considers transpacific diffusion an entirely different subject; he might be persuadable about it. [However, Schobinger is unwilling to criticize anti-diffusionist sources that he cites, such as McKusick, Wauchope, Cole, and Rowe, each of which he happily and entirely accepts.]

S-127

AUTHOR: Schobinger, Juan

DATE: 1980

TITLE: ¿Vikingos en Sudamerica? Ojeada sobre una reciente teoria hiperdifusionista por via transatlántica [Vikings in South America? A

Review of a Recent Hyperdiffusionist Theory via the Transatlantic Route]

IN: La antropología americanista en la actualidad; homenaje a Raphael Girard, tomo II (Editores mexicanos unidos: México), 356-397

He blasts the "fantamazonicas" [fantasy-amazonian] genre of popular archaeological writing in which he includes Von Däniken and Mahieu.

S-128

AUTHOR: Schobinger, Juan

DATE: 1981-1982

TITLE: ¿Vikingos en Sudamerica? Una enojosa polémica [Vikings in South America? An Angry Polemic]

IN: Anales de arqueología y etnología 36-37:177-181 (Mendoza, Argentina)

Schobinger's vigorous response to correspondence from Mahieu who had threatened prosecution for libel, stimulated by S-126 and S-127.

S-129

AUTHOR: Schobinger, Juan

DATE: 1982

TITLE: ¿Vikingos o extraterrestres? Estudio crítico de algunas teorías recientes sobre el origin y desarrollo de las culturas precolombinas [Vikings or Extraterrestrials? A Critical Study of Some Recent Theories on the Origin and Development of the Pre-Columbian Cultures]

IMPRINT: Editorial Huemul: Buenos Aires

Essentially the same content as in S-126, S-127, and S-128.

S-130

AUTHOR: Schoff, Wilfred H., translator

DATE: 1974

TITLE: The Periplus of the Erythraean Sea: Travel and Trade in the Indian Ocean by a Merchant of the First Century

IMPRINT: Oriental Books Reprint Corporation: New Delhi

Outlines nautical technology and conditions attending voyaging on the Indian Ocean during the first century A.D.

S-134

AUTHOR: Schoolcraft, Henry R.

DATE: 1851-1853

TITLE: Information Respecting the History, Condition and Prospects of the Indian Tribes of the United States: Collected and Prepared under the Direction of the Bureau of Indian Affairs per Act of Congress of March 3rd 1847, 6 vols.

IMPRINT: Lippincott, Grambo: Philadelphia

Part 1:

Pages 106-129: "Archaeological evidences that the continent had been visited by people having letters, prior to the era of Columbus." Northmen from Greenland visited Newfoundland, Nova Scotia, Massachusetts, and Rhode Island, "with much probability," and perhaps even reached Florida. Dighton Rock is interpreted in detail here by a local Indian chief as showing conflict between two Indian groups.

A 70-foot high tumulus, Grave Creek mound near Wheeling, West Virginia, yielded a stone inscribed in Celtic rune-like characters. (Page 122: M. Jomard, of Paris, deems it "in the ancient Libyan language.") The stone could have been introduced here after De Soto. Or it "would appear to be some grounds here for the Welsh tradition of Madoc." It is not Indian.

A globular stone found near Grave Creek contains three inscribed characters.

Iroquois tradition (published 1825) preserves the account of the wreck of a vessel on the South Atlantic coast before white men came; this may refer to the Roanoke colony.

Reprise of a reported discovery of a burial in which copper armor was worn by the corpse and thought Carthaginian by some; the author thinks the metal due to 18th-century French trade.

Entire set:

Consult Frances S. Nichols, "Index to Schoolcraft's 'Indian Tribes of the United States,' " Smithsonian Institution, Bureau of American Ethnology Bulletin 152, 1954, under the headings: Asiatics compared with Indian tribes; Aztecs not aborigines; balsa illustration; Celtic inscription (supposed); Chinese element at Uxmal; Chinook resemblance to Japanese; Chippewa compared with Hebrew; Dighton Rock inscription; Hebrew (coin, custom, history, language, origin of Indians); Hindoo; hook-swinging (Hindoo); inscriptions (Runic, Phoenician, Grave Creek compared with Phoenician, supposed Grecian, supposed Scandinavian); Jewish (customs, resemblance); Kingsborough; lost tribes of Israel; Vinland; Welsh.

S-135

AUTHOR: Schori, Dieter

DATE: 1959

TITLE: Das Floss in Ozeanien. Formen, Funktion und Verbreitung des Flosses und flossartiger Schwimmkörper in der Südsee [The Raft in Oceania. Form, Function and Diffusion of Rafts and Raft-like Swimming Aids in the South Seas]

IN: Völkerkundliche Beiträge zur Ozeanistik, Band 1, her. von Erhard Schlesier. In Kommission bei Buchhandlung Dr. LudwigHäntzschel [His dissertation at Georg August-Universität zu Göttingen]

A compendium of ethnographic accounts of rafts, raft-bundle "vessels," and surfing aids in Melanesia, Micronesia, and Polynesia, island group by island group. [The bibliography, while large, omits significant English-language sources, more of the French, and almost all the Spanish.] A tabular word list gathers hundreds of terms connected with rafts (interesting example, a term from Saipan, *batsa* [raft]). Deals with Heyerdahl on rafts at length and the general question of evidences and hypotheses for American-Polynesian contacts cursorily. It would have been possible for a rare Polynesian boat perhaps to reach South America, but raft journeys, in both directions, would be problematic, although the forms of rafts in South America are like Oceanic forms.

S-136

AUTHOR: Schroeder, Gerhard

DATE: 1957

TITLE: Hallazgos de artefactos de piedra en el Perú y los problemas del poblamiento de América [Discoveries of Stone Artifacts in Peru and the Problems of the Peopling of America]

IN: Revista del Museo Nacional 26:290-294 (Lima)

Notes the finding in recent decades of paleolithic-like stone tools in the Andean area and proceeds to apply a 19th century evolutionary model (e.g., lower and higher gatherers) to interpret the cultural status of existing peoples of the hemisphere. But Heine-Geldern and others have also proven that voyaging took place from Southeast Asia to South America long ago. Various parallels with Asia are mentioned (e.g., the Inca ruler's rite of first plowing, use of palanquin, and stepped pyramids). Furthermore, the Tupac Yupanqui expedition on balsas into the Pacific would not have been done without a tradition about lands being out there. From all this it is very probable that the founders of the first high cultures in Peru (Chavin, Chimu and Nazca) arrived via the ocean from Asia, bringing a superior culture which they extended over the inferior cultures of the area.

S-136B

AUTHOR: Schuhmacher, W. W.
DATE: 1974
TITLE: Linguistic Evidence for Amerindian Sea Routes to Polynesia? (A First Approach)
IN: Norwegian Journal of Linguistics (NTS) 28:41-44

A lengthy review of the literature yields no definite support for Heyerdahl's views, but he points out reasons why that does not rule them out totally.

S-137

AUTHOR: Schuhmacher, W. W.
DATE: 1976
TITLE: On the Linguistic Aspect of Thor Heyerdahl's Theory: The So-called Non-Polynesian Number Names from Easter Island
IN: Anthropos 71(5/6): 806-847

Discusses evidence for the hypothesis that Easter Island language and culture had its origin in North and South America, noting especially the words for numbers used in various languages.

S-138

AUTHOR: Schuler-Schömig, Immina von
DATE: 1984
TITLE: Eine chinesisches Porzellenfigürchen aus Oaxaca, Mexico [A Chinese Porcelain Figurine from Oaxaca, Mexico]
IN: Indiana 9:147-157 (Berlin)

A Ming period figurine (A.D. 1550-1600) in the Berlin Museum since 1852, was reportedly excavated at Monte Alban. It is attributed to early Spanish trade.

S-139

AUTHOR: Schuller, Rudolf
DATE: 1907
TITLE: Ergänzungen zur "Monographie bibliographique sur l'île de Pâques, par le Dr. W. Lehmann" [Supplements to the "Bibliographic Monograph on Easter Island," by Dr. W. Lehmann]
IN: Globus 92:270-271

See L-122.

S-140 See now S-137B.

S-142

AUTHORS: Schulte, Martha, and Beverly Seckinger
DATE: 1984-1985
TITLE: The Dating Game: One Last Look at Glottochronology: The Case of Some Arabic Dialects
IN: Atlatl Occasional Papers, no. 5, edited by Barbara Roth and Susannah Heyer (University of Arizona: Tucson), 41-77

A strong critique of glottochronology and any attempts to use it to reconstruct history beyond a single language family. They review the literature on such problems as composition of the test list and rate of change and find striking disagreements. Their own careful analysis here for Arabic confirms previous problems. Thus, "it is certain that there is no . . . constant morpheme decay [process] in basic vocabulary."

S-144

AUTHOR: Schurtz, Heinrich
DATE: 1895
TITLE: Das Augenornament und verwandte Probleme

	[Eye Ornamentation and Related Problems]
IN:	Abhandlungen der philologisch-historischen Classe der königlichen sächsischen Gesellschaft der Wissenschaften 15 (S. Hirzel: Leipzig)

Compares art motifs of the Northwest Coast with those of Indonesia and Oceania, asserting transpacific linkages.

S-146

AUTHOR:	Schuster, Alfred B.
DATE:	1958
TITLE:	The Art of Two Worlds; Studies in Pre-Columbian and European Cultures
IMPRINT:	Mann: Berlin [Reprinted Praeger: New York, 1959]

A comparison of art in the two areas considering their fundamentals, which are taken as similar throughout each area. The American portion is only lightly informed by the literature of the time.

Page 156: In studying America we may neglect outside influences as non- existent or negligible. The recent tendency to find strong Asiatic influences is noted at several points in chapter 2, but "what was made of such material on American soil is absolutely original and sui generis."

S-147

AUTHOR:	Schuster, Carl
DATE:	1951
TITLE:	Joint-marks: A Possible Index of Cultural Contact between America, Oceania and the Far East
IN:	Mededeling no. 94, Afdeling Culturele em Physische Anthropologie, no. 39 (Koninklijk Instituut voor de Tropen: Amsterdam)

Comparative study of an art motif consisting of a squatting human figure with a pair of disks in the spaces between flexed elbows and knees. Examples are cited from the West Indies, Venezuela, Amazonia, the Andes, and Central America, as well as from various parts of the Old World. The question is raised whether these are the result of independent invention or of diffusion from the Old World to the New.

S-148

AUTHOR:	Schuster, Carl
DATE:	1952a
TITLE:	A Survival of the Eurasiatic Animal Style in Modern Alaskan Eskimo Art
IN:	Indian Tribes of Aboriginal America; Selected Papers of the 29th International Congress of Americanists (New York, 1949), edited by Sol Tax (University of Chicago Press: Chicago), 35-45

Agrees with Larsen and Rainey that Ipiutak sculptural art is "a branch of the Eurasiatic or Scytho-Siberian animal style." He points out further similarities. He also suggests the possible spread of certain traits of the style to the south of Alaska, into the Northwest Coast area, including joint marks.

S-149

AUTHOR:	Schuster, Carl
DATE:	1952b
TITLE:	V-shaped Chest-markings; Distribution of a Design Motif in and around the Pacific
IN:	Anthropos 47:99-118

See S-154.

S-150

AUTHOR:	Schuster, Carl
DATE:	1956-1958
TITLE:	Genealogical Patterns in the Old and New Worlds

IN: Revista do Museu Paulista 10:7-123 (São Paulo)

Distribution of an art motif called by Ch'en Ch'i-lu [C-212] figures-joined-limb-to-limb.

S-151

AUTHOR: Schuster, Carl

DATE: 1958

TITLE: Human Figures with Spiral Limbs in Tropical America

IN: Miscellanea Paul Rivet, Octogenario Dicata, Universidad Nacional Autónoma de México, Publicaciones del Instituto de Historia 1/50, [Proceedings of the 31st International Congress of Americanists (São Paulo, 1954)], 2:549-561

Suggests the need to study the decorative feature of bands of highly conventionalized human figures, a possible interhemispheric diffused design, perhaps very old. Also, the New World image of human limbs ending as spirals may have developed early in Western Asia then spread, by means we cannot now determine, to the New World.

S-152

AUTHOR: Schuster, Carl

DATE: 1963

TITLE: Skin and Fur Mosaics from Early Prehistoric Times to Modern Survivals: A Synthesis of Archaeological and Ethnographic Evidence from the Old and New Worlds

IN: 6e. Congrès International des Sciences Anthropologiques et Ethnologiques (Paris, 1960), 2/1:631-632 [Reprinted 1964 in expanded form, as "Skin and Fur Mosaics in Prehistoric and Modern Times," in *Festschrift für Ad. E. Jensen,* edited by Eike Haberland, Meinhard Schuster, and Helmut Straube (Klaus Renner: Munich), 2:559-610]

A decorative technique visible in garments, body-painting, and ceramics in both Old and New Worlds could have arisen separately among different groups who used skin garments. He supposes, however, that it probably had an Upper Paleolithic source and could have spread from there.

S-153

AUTHOR: Schuster, Carl

DATE: 1968

TITLE: On the Distribution and Meaning of Double-Headed Figures in the Old and New Worlds

IN: Proceedings of the 37th International Congress of Americanists (Mar del Plata, Argentina, 1966), 4:129-132

Sees a basic relation of double-headed figures and the double-headed forked house post. Such figures are as early as Valdivia in Ecuador and the Preclassic of Mexico (Tlatilco). Lack of archaeological material prevents a clear conclusion, but he believes that the question of the transmission of this type of representation across or around the Pacific must remain an open question.

S-154

AUTHOR: Schuster, Carl

DATE: 1968-1969

TITLE: V-shaped Chest-markings Reconsidered: A Palaeolithic Figurine as Explanation of Their Wide Modern Distribution

IN: Anthropos 63-64/3-4: 428-440

S-149 noted the distribution of V-shaped chest markings in Southeast Asia, the Pacific islands, and North and South America. One type of marking, composed of two or more parallel rows of dots forming a V, occurs repeatedly in almost every region. An Upper Palaeolithic figurine from Kostienki in south Russia shows this same pattern, which probably represents beads. He thinks it inescapable that this shows us a cultural ancestor of the modern customs. Hence no late diffusion need be supposed to account for the distribution.

S-155

AUTHOR: Schwabacher, W.
DATE: 1962
TITLE: Die Azoren und die Seefahrt der Alten (Eine vergessene schwedische numismatische Entdeckung)
[The Azores and Seafaring of the Ancients (A Forgotten Swedish Numismatic Discovery)]
IN: Numisma (Nov.-Dec.): 9-16

Phoenician coins were found in a Phoenician jar in the Azores.

S-157

AUTHOR: Schweig, Bruno
DATE: 1941
TITLE: Mirrors
IN: Antiquity 15:257-268

A summary history of mirror uses around the world. Brief mention is made of Peruvian, Mexican, Chinese, and Japanese mirrors, the Chinese ones being mentioned in Chinese classics from ca 2000 B.C. No intimation is given here of diffusion. Mirrors were especially well known in Egypt, from which source Phoenicians and Hebrews obtained them; the Pentateuch says that Moses collected brass mirrors to make the brazen laver for the tabernacle. Ceylonese, Syrian, Greek, and Roman mirrors are also mentioned.

S-158

AUTHOR: Schweigger, Erwin
DATE: 1960
TITLE: Vorkolumbianische Seefahrzeuge und Seeschiffahrt in Südamerika
[Pre-Columbian Sea Vessels and Seafaring in South America]
IN: Erdkunde 14/1:46-52 (Bonn)

It was much easier to sail by balsa to Tahiti than to go the reverse direction. Also, a tomb at Ica, Peru, contained a model of a balsa, without a sail.

S-160

AUTHOR: Schwennhagen, Ludovico
DATE: 1928
TITLE: Antiga historia do Brasil, de 1100 a. Chr. até 1500 dep. Chr., primeira parte
[Ancient History of Brasil, from 1100 B.C. to A.D. 1500, Part 1]
IMPRINT: Imprensa Official: Theresina, Brazil

Summarizes and admires Thoron (1876)—who believed that a fleet of Hiram of Tyre and Solomon reached the Amazon ca. 960 B.C.—B. Ramos [S-249], and Candido Costa. It is well established that there existed in the first millennium B.C. a Brasilian civilization, shown by Ramos' 3000 inscriptions found all over Brazil and other American countries which compare with materials from the three old continents [see R-016B]. These were made on stone with iron or bronze instruments or with indelible paints. They generally relate to the Mediterranean area, Phoenician and Egyptian demotic script. There are also inscriptions with Babylonian/Sumerian characters, as well as from Crete, Etruria, Iberia, and Greek and Latin areas. His work discusses the Phoenicians in the Northeast of Brazil, the Tyrrhenians of Marajó, Solomon's and Hiram's activities in the Amazon, the Ionians, the Carians, and others, including Egyptians. Depends heavily on place names [in the manner of Mertz, M-317] and random comparisons of words.

S-161

AUTHOR: Schwerin, Karl H.
DATE: 1966
TITLE: On the Arch in Pre-Columbian Mesoamerica

IN: Current Anthropology 7:89

Suggests that the Oztuma true arch in Mexico was overlooked by B-141 and E-045. He believes the evidence favors a pre-Columbian date for this arch. A short reply by Ekholm follows in which he acknowledges that Oztuma should probably have been mentioned by him.

S-162

AUTHOR: Schwerin, Karl H.
DATE: 1970
TITLE: Winds across the Atlantic
IN: Mesoamerican Studies 6 (University of Southern Illinois: Carbondale)

Considers the possibility that preceramic African farmer-fishermen were blown to the New World between 8000 and 5700 B.C. where they established cultivation of cotton, bottle gourds, and jackbeans.

S-163

AUTHOR: Schwidetzky, Ilse
DATE: 1963
TITLE: La población prehispánica de las Islas Canarias [The Prehispanic Population of the Canary Islands]
IN: Publicación 4 (Museo Arqueológico: Santa Cruz de Tenerife, Canary Islands)

Neolithic settlers arrived around 2000 B.C., obviously by boat. [Such boats were liable to being swept across the Atlantic.] Certain petroglyph motifs relate to Crete.

S-163B

AUTHOR: Science News
DATE: 1996
TITLE: Polynesian Tools Tout Ancient Travels
IN: Science News 149 (March 2): 135

Tools of fine-grained basalt from a quarry on American Samoa have been identified by X-ray tests on both Mangaia, the Cook Islands, and the Marquesas Islands. Radiocarbon dates at the recipient areas establish the usage from "about 3,000 years ago up until about A.D. 330." If this information is further confirmed, it has revolutionary implications about voyaging in such early times. The research involved Marshall Weisler of the University of Otago, Patrick Kirch at Berkeley, and Barry Rolett at Hawaii.

S-164

AUTHOR: Scisco, Louis Dow
DATE: 1924
TITLE: Pre-Columbian Discovery by Basques
IN: Proceedings and Transactions of the Royal Society of Canada, series 3, vol. 18, section 2, pages 51-61

Reviews the history of the "legend" of pre-Columbian Basque discovery of the New World and finds it purely speculative.

S-164B

AUTHOR: Scobie, Alex
DATE: 1975
TITLE: The Battle of the Pygmies and the Cranes in Chinese, Arab, and North American Indian Sources
IN: Folklore 86:122-132

Greek and Roman writers from Homer's time told of a battle of the cranes against the pygmies ("geranomachy"). The Chinese knew the same theme but referred it to the Near East/Mediterranean area. He here reports a similar tale among the Cherokees and another version shared among three Northwest Coast tribes. He finds the situation easiest to explain in terms of multiple independent inventions.

S-165

AUTHOR: Seaby, Peter
DATE: 1978

TITLE: The First Datable Norse Find from North America?

IN: Seaby Coin and Medal Bulletin 724:369-370, 377-382

A "Norse penny" from Maine.

S-166

AUTHOR: Sears, William H.

DATE: 1977

TITLE: Seaborne Contacts between Early Cultures in Lower Southeastern United States and Middle through South America

IN: The Sea in the Pre-Columbian World: A Conference at Dumbarton Oaks, October 26th and 27th, 1974, edited by Elizabeth P. Benson (Dumbarton Oaks: Washington, D.C.), 1-16

Pages 2-4: On the adequacy of vessels and the logic of long hops from South America to Florida. "I have little regard for arguments against long water crossings based on the terrors and dangers of the sea." Survival of small groups in small vessels is much documented by now. In the Antilles and northern South America "there is historical documentation for dugout canoes in the sixty-to-eighty foot range" which could travel safely and at high speed. Linguistic and archaeological data (citing Granberry) demonstrate that such vessels and voyages must predate 2000 B.C. Possible routes are mapped on Figure 2, covering up to thousands of miles. Failure to stop on intermediate islands can be explained.

S-166B

AUTHOR: Secorse, C. R.

DATE: 1991

TITLE: Culture Contact, Continuity, and Change on the Gold Coast, A.D. 1400-1900

IN: African Archaeological Review 10:163-196

Methodological. Documents show that extensive changes took place in the sociopolitical realm, economic relations, etc. Archaeological excavations show a lot of change in technology and material culture, in major part as a consequence of the intrusion of Europeans, but these changes are not clearly correlated with the story according to historical documents. The situation was evidently complicated, and in the area of world view and beliefs, for example, the most marked changes are not manifested in the remains until the 19th century, and even then major continuity prevailed.

S-167

AUTHOR: Seele, Enno

DATE: 1969

TITLE: Galerías filtrantes en el area de Acatzingo-Tepeaca, estado de Puebla [Filtration Galleries in the Area of Acatzingo-Tepeaca, State of Puebla]

IN: Instituto Nacional de Antropología e Historia Boletin 35:3-8 (México)

Chain wells or qanat water systems are suggested as possibly prehispanic.

S-168

AUTHOR: Seemann, Berthold

DATE: 1865-1873

TITLE: Flora vitiensis, 2 vols [Fijian Flora]

IMPRINT: L. Reeves: London [Reprinted in one volume, Cramer: Vaduz, Liechtenstein, 1977]

In volume 1 he was the first to note the similarity of the sweet potato name, kumara/cumar, between Oceania and Ecuador and to suggest South America as the homeland of the Oceanic sweet potato.

S-169

AUTHOR: Seeman, Berthold

DATE: 1866

TITLE: On the Resemblance of Inscriptions Found on Ancient British Rocks with Those of Central America
IN: Anthropological Society of London, Memoirs 2:277-282

Finds notable similarities between petroglyphs of Northumberland and some he had seen in the Chiriqui area of Panama.

S-171

AUTHOR: Seidenberg, A.
DATE: 1960
TITLE: The Diffusion of Counting Practices
IN: University of California Publications in Mathematics 3/4:215-299

Intended as a contribution to Raglan's theory that civilization had an origin in ritual and that it spread by diffusion. Counting practices are among elements so spread and their history is given here, including Old/New World connections.

Pages 244-248: Surveys American systems, finds them varied, and makes observations on possible internal diffusions.

Pages 248-250: The Wawenoc Indians (an Abenaki group) had a unique set of number names. The set cannot have come from any other American Indians. He cites A. H. Keane (in the appendix to *Central America, West Indies and South America*, edited by H. W. Bates, page 543), who says the Wawenoc "have been credited by some ethnologists with a system of numerals which are really Kymric or Old British, brought over by some early [i.e., 17th century] Welsh or Cumbrian settlers. When the memory of their true origin was forgotten, the English-speaking colonists attributed them to the Indians, and they were afterwards used to prove that the Wawenoc Redmen were of British descent." Seidenberg admits that the numerals "appear to bear some resemblance to the Welsh numerals." Finally, on page 250, he concludes that at least "the inventor" of these numerals "knew the Welsh numerals."

Pages 275-276: The class of "flat things" has a special number system in India and North America, but not in some other areas that do have the principle of number classes. "One can scarcely suppose that the mind is led spontaneously to generate this class in some places, whilst in others it is led to generate quite different ones."

Page 277: A common word, *kumi,* is widespread for "ten" in Bantu, Austronesian, Kanitsatka, and in America, Mixtec, Miskito, and Maidu.

S-172

AUTHOR: Seidenberg, A.
DATE: 1986
TITLE: The Zero in the Mayan Numerical Notation
IN: Native American Mathematics, edited by Michael P. Closs (University of Texas Press: Austin), 371-386

He addresses the topic by analyzing Kroeber's logic about diffusion and independent invention of Mayan zero and place-value notation in his 1923 and 1948 textbooks. He points out inconsistencies and biases in Kroeber's discussions. Seidenberg implies that the evidence for diffusion of these traits from the Old World has merit. In any case, after he has finished taking Kroeber apart, he notes, "The Independent Inventionists can regard the Zero with scant satisfaction."

S-173

AUTHOR: Seidenberg, A.
DATE: 1962-1966
TITLE: The Ritual Origin of Counting
IN: Archive for the History of Exact Sciences 2:1-40 (Berlin)

Various unusual features of counting practices [compare *Anthropos* 56 (1961): 986] lead to the supposition of diffusion from a single civilized center. The importance of ritual in archaic society was such that it is probable that counting had a ritual origin, perhaps being elaborated in the Creation rite, as a means of calling participants onto the ritual scene.

S-174

AUTHOR: Seler, Eduard
DATE: 1899
TITLE: Mittelamerikanische Musikinstrumente [Middle American Musical Instrument]
IN: Globus 75/7:109-112

There were no stringed instruments in America, specifically rebutting S-078 in which, he says, Saville badly misinterprets a codex scene.

S-175

AUTHOR: Seler, Eduard
DATE: 1895
TITLE: Über den Ursprung der altamerikanischen Kulturen [On the Origin of Ancient American Cultures]
IN: Preussische Jahrbücher 79:488-502 [Reprinted in *Gesammelte Abhandlungen zur Amerikanischen Sprach- und Alterthumskunde* (A. Asher, Berlin, 1904), 1:3-15. The *Gesammelte* reprinted by Akademische Druck- u. Verlagsanstalt: Graz, Austria, 1960-1967. In English 1991 in *Eduard Seler: Collected Works in Mesoamerican Linguistics and Archaeology,* volume 2, Frank E. Comparato, general editor (Labyrinthos: Culver City, California), 3-9]

Limited seriously by the gaps in reliable information in his day, he explains why parallels between Old and New World civilizations do not justify an explanation that the latter derived from the former. Decisive for him is the lack of cognate languages between the hemispheres and lack of shared cultivated plants.

Page 7 of the 1991 edition: "As far as the facts are now known, the Monroe Doctrine—'America for the Americans'—must hold good for the old American civilizations. And American science would only be the gainer if the fruitless attempts to institute imaginary connections should be given up."

S-175B

AUTHOR: Seler, Eduard
DATE: 1897
TITLE: Nachrichten über den Aussatz in alten mexikanischen Quellen [Leprosy in Old Mexican Documents]
IN: Zeitschrift für Ethnologie 29:609-611 [For other printings, see page 56 of the 1991 English edition of Seler's *Collected Works* referenced at S-175]

"There is no doubt that leprosy . . . was known in Mexico about the middle of the sixteenth century." Names and descriptions of symptoms are given from Molina's dictionary and from Sahagun. While convinced that this disease was pre-Columbian in Mexico, he acknowledges the possibility that "another disease may have been designated in antiquity by teococoliztli, perhaps the jiote, and that they [subsequently] applied this name to leprosy and thus may have spoken falsely of leprosy with reference to antiquity."

S-176

AUTHOR: Seler, Eduard
DATE: 1898
TITLE: Codex Borgia
IMPRINT: Globus 74:297-302, 315-319 [Also in his collected works in several editions and reprints; see S-175 for general citation]

[*Gesammelte,* volume 2] Page 31: Shows a [Mixtecan?] ritual comparable in detail to one in Egypt, although Seler himself makes no such comparison. [The parallel was first pointed out in C-208.] Mictlantecuhtli, sometimes lord of the north, and Mictlancihuatl, together lord and lady of the region of death, pour water in crossed streams over the head of Ixtlilton, the "little black god," a minor healing deity. [See G-039 for Egyptian parallel and comparison in S-361.]

[When shown the Egypt-Borgia comparison, Near Easternist William F. Albright considered the likeness "amazing," and said that had the Mexican example come from an area geographically closer to Egypt, there would be no question but that diffusion should be credited. Personal communication to John L. Sorenson, 1954.]

S-176B

AUTHOR: Seler, Eduard
DATE: 1902
TITLE: Über den Ursprung der mittelamerikanischen Kulturen
IN: Berlin Geological Society, Zeitschrift 37:537-552
[Reprinted in *Gesammelte Abhandlungen zur Amerikanischen Sprach- und Alterthumskunde* (A. Asher: Berlin, 1904), 1:16-30. The *Gesammelte* reprinted Akademische Druck- u. Verlagsanstalt: Graz, Austria, 1960-1967. In English, *Eduard Seler: Collected Works in Mesoamerican Linguistics and Archaeology*, volume 2, Frank E. Comparato, general editor (Labyrinthos: Culver City, California, 1991), 10-17]

Pages 10-11 (of 1991 edition): Reviews basic pros and cons of Old World origin for Mesoamerican civilizations. "The more conversant we become with the ornamentation, the development in art, and the linguistic forms of the Mexicans, Peruvians, and the other ancient Mexican civilized peoples, the further into the background is pushed the possibility of connecting this art development with any of the Old World." "We cannot deny that in some basic elements there is often a surprising uniformity between Old World and New World art" but this is not historically significant. He does not deny that northwestern America evidences "an infiltration of Asiatic elements of civilization, perhaps a mixing of races." Also, "perhaps an introduction of elements of civilization, or an exchange of the same, should also be assumed further to the south, from the South Pacific Ocean."

Page 16 (of 1991 edition): Note that his interpretation is out of a very abbreviated time scale. For example "the golden age of Quiriguá [was] between the end of the thirteenth and the end of the fourteenth centuries."

S-177

AUTHOR: Seler, Eduard
DATE: 1909-1910
TITLE: Die Tierbilder der mexikanischen und der maya-Handschriften [Animal Pictures of the Mexican and Mayan Codices]
IN: Zeitschrift für Ethnologie 41:210-257, 381-457, 784-846; 42:31-97, 242-287

The claimed elephants in Mexican sculptures are tortoises, he says.

S-178

AUTHOR: Seligman, Charles Gabriel
DATE: 1920
TITLE: Bird-chariots and Socketed Celts in Europe and China
IN: Journal of the Anthropological Institute 50:153-158

Ritual wheeled miniatures [for comparison with Mesoamerica]. On the basis of socketed celt distribution, he concludes that both arrived in China via India, not by way of Siberia.

S-179

AUTHOR: Seligman, Charles Gabriel
DATE: 1924

TITLE: An Amerind Type in China in T'ang Times
IN: Man 24:113

In support of Hrdlicka's "important conclusion of the fundamental unity of the American race" and the interchangeability of Amerindians with Asians, this brief note draws attention to T'ang period figures "which so closely reproduce the facial characteristics of the American Indian, that the observer immediately thinks of the latter rather than of a Chinese."

S-180

AUTHOR: Seligman, Charles Gabriel
DATE: 1928
TITLE: Further Notes on Bird-chariots in China and Europe
IN: Journal of the Royal Anthropological Institute of Great Britain and Ireland 58:247-254

Wheeled bird figures he had previously shown to have reached China from the European Bronze Age. They were now toys with former ritual function lost by the time they got to China. [For comparison with Mesoamerica.]

S-181

AUTHOR: Seligmann, Linda
DATE: 1987
TITLE: The Chicken in Andean History and Myth: The Quechua Concept of Wallpa
IN: Ethnohistory 34:139-170

The fowl was a Spanish introduction [but she is unaware of Johannessen's and Carter's work].

S-183

AUTHOR: Selmer, Carl
DATE: 1959
TITLE: Navigatio Sancti Brendani Abbatis
IN: Publications in Mediaeval Studies XVI (University of Notre Dame Press: Notre Dame, Indiana)

A compilation of information and views on Brendan with an interpretation.

S-184

AUTHOR: Semple, Ellen
DATE: 1958
TITLE: Migration Eternal and Universal
IN: Race: Individual and Collective Behavior, edited by Edgar T. Thompson and Everett C. Hughes (Free Press: Glencoe, Illinois), 163-167

General hypotheses, by a geographer, on historical movement, emphasizing differences between migrating "primitive" and "civilized" groups.

S-185

AUTHOR: Serebrennikov, B. A.
DATE: 1986
TITLE: Nostratic Languages
IN: Typology, Relationship and Time: A Collection of Papers on Language Change and Relationship by Soviet Linguists, edited and translated by Vitalij V. Shevoroshkin and T. L. Markey (Karoma: Ann Arbor, Michigan), 66-86 [Translation of: Problema dostatochnosti osnovaniia v gipotezakh kasaiushchikhsia geneticheskogo rodstva iazykov, 3: Nostraticheski iazyki, pages 47-62, in, Teoreticheski osnovy klassifikatsii iazykov mira]

Page 66: "Morris Swadesh tried to forge a genetic connection between the languages of the Old World and those of the New. He suggested the existence of a large macrofamily, which he termed Dene-Finnic (Finnodenean), after the names of the two geographically most widely separated members of this macrofamily." This author renders no judgment on Swadesh's notion, but implies sympathy.

S-187

AUTHOR: Sergi, Giuseppe

DATE: 1906

TITLE: Contributo all'antropologia americana [Contribution to American Anthropology]

IN: Annales della Societa Romana di Antropologia 12/11 [Reprinted from an earlier source]

Three types of American Indian skulls are discussed: Peruvian, indicating a Negrito or Oceanic pigmy element in ancient Peru; Bolivian, showing a Melanesian element; and Mound-builder, representing Asiatic immigration into North America.

S-188

AUTHOR: Sergi, Giuseppe

DATE: 1928

TITLE: Di alcuni caratteri speciali negli indigeni americani; Contributo alla soluzione del problema della loro origine [About Several Special Characteristics among American Natives; Contribution of the Solution of the Problem of Their Origin]

IN: Proceedings of the 22nd International Congress of Americanists (Rome, 1926), 1:155-167

He considers the Americans provisionally autocthonous, but with an overlaid biological stratum from Asia via Bering Strait and another stratum out of Oceania.

S-189B

AUTHOR: Serjeantson, S. W.

DATE: 1989

TITLE: HLA Genes and Antigens

IN: The Colonization of the Pacific: A Genetic Trail, edited by A. V. S. Hill and S. W. Serjeantson (Clarendon Press: Oxford), 120-173

Discusses the possibility of a minor Amerind contribution to the genes in eastern Polynesia. Although the evidence is tenuous, the proposition cannot be excluded.

S-189C

AUTHOR: Serra, Mari Carmen

DATE: 1988

TITLE: Contribuciones de la UNAM al conocimiento del origen del hombre americano

IN: Orígenes del hombre americano (seminario), compiled by Alba González Jácome (Secretaría de Educación Pública: México), 319-331

Summarizes the work on "origins" by various UNAM researchers, including in some detail Bosch-Gimpera, Comas, Genovés, and Martínez del Río, who all suppose that significant Old World groups other than Bering Strait mongoloids reached the New World .

S-189D

AUTHOR: Serra Rafols, Elías

DATE: 1957

TITLE: La navegación primitiva de los mares de Canaria [Primitive Navigation in the Waters of the Canary Islands]

IN: Revista de historia canaria 23/119-120:83-91 (La Laguna)

While the inhabitants of the Canaries had no boats when discovered by the Portuguese, he argues from historical sources that an independent tradition of modest nautics existed along the Moroccan coast south of the zone of Arab influence and that such vessels could and no doubt did reach the islands anciently.

S-190

AUTHOR: Serra Rafols, Elías
DATE: 1965
TITLE: La primera anfora romana hallada en Canarias
[The First Roman Amphora Found in the Canaries]
IN: Revista de historia canaria 29:231-233 (La Laguna)

Title self-explanatory.

S-191

AUTHOR: Serra Rafols, Elías
DATE: 1966
TITLE: Información arqueológica de la zona de Canarias; más ánforas romanas en aguas lanzaroteñas
[Archaeological Information from the Canaries Zone; More Roman Amphoras in Coastal Waters]
IN: Revista de historia canaria 30:255-257 (La Laguna)

Title self-explanatory.

S-192

AUTHOR: Serrano, Antonia
DATE: 1938
TITLE: La etnografía antigua de Santiago del Estero y la llamada civilización Chaco-Santiagueña
[The Ancient Ethnography of Santiago del Estero and the Civilization Called Chaco-Santiagueña]
IMPRINT: Casa Predassi: Paraná, Argentina

Reports views of the Wagner brothers, who had excavated in Santiago del Estero province of north central Argentina, that their materials show numerous analogies with Schliemann's Troy.

S-193

AUTHOR: Serrano S., Carlos
DATE: 1972
TITLE: Una serie de cráneos procedentes de Campeche, México
[A Series of Skulls from Campeche, Mexico]
IN: Anales de antropología 9:175-188 (México)

Describes a series of 14 skulls from the Maya region that have been dated as early 19th century. Comparisons are made with other cranial studies on the Maya. The author supports Comas' contention that peoples of Maya languages are highly variable in their osteological traits.

S-194

AUTHOR: Sertima, Ivan van
DATE: 1976
TITLE: They Came before Columbus
IMPRINT: Random House: New York
[French, *Ils y étaient avant Christophe Colomb* (Flammarion: Paris, 1976)]

Presents about every argument for pre-Columbian cultural and genetic transmission to and from the Americas and Africa: Leo Wiener's tobacco, Jeffrey's maize, 25th dynasty Nubian as well as 12th century expeditions from Mali, negroid representations in art, and features of crania. A good deal of the material is presented uncritically and with chronology largely ignored, yet the writing is vigorous and some of the documentation is of value.

Plate 11 (from a museum model in Mombasa) is a representation of an "East african trading ship" of "great antiquity" said to have sailed to China.

Plate 13 is an artist's impression of a large oar-powered "African power canoe" seen in Gambia by the Portuguese in A.D. 1455. A similar vessel "developed on the Orinoco" A.D. 120 could travel "from Venezuela to Puerto Rico in one day."

S-196

AUTHOR: Sertima, Ivan van, editor
DATE: 1987a
TITLE: African Presence in Early America
IMPRINT: n.p.: n.p. ["Incorporating Journal of African Civilizations, Dec. 1986, vol. 8, no. 2." "All inquiries should be addressed to Transaction Books, Rutgers—the State University, New Brunswick, New Jersey"]

Papers in this volume are abstracted and listed separately.

S-197

AUTHOR: Sertima, Ivan van
DATE: 1987b
TITLE: Ten Years after [an Introduction and Overview]
IN: African Presence in Early America, edited by Ivan van Sertima (n.p.: n.p.), 5-27 ["Incorporating Journal of African Civilizations, Dec. 1986, vol. 8, no. 2." "All inquiries should be addressed to Transaction Books, Rutgers—the State University, New Brunswick, New Jersey"]

The title refers to the period since S-194 was published. He explains what was his intent with that much-criticized book and adds "new facts that undermine or consolidate my case."

Pages 7-10: An excerpt from a taped conversation between the author and Alexander von Wuthenau in 1985 in Mexico City concerning the importance of ceramic figures with non-Amerindian faces.

Pages 10-11: F. Peterson, earlier cited by Sertima in support of a negroid element among the Olmecs, has disavowed such a belief. See the article by Jordan in this volume. Wiercinski is cited.

Pages 11-12: Mention is made of "early maps" claimed as support for pre- Columbian discovery of America.

Pages 12-14: Pyramid measurements as evidence for interhemispheric influence.

The remainder of this piece summarizes Jairazbhoy, tries to rehabilitate Leo Wiener, claims Mandinga voyages to the New World, and illustrates a petroglyph array from the Virgin Islands said to be in Libyan script, along with Fell's decipherment. Finally he argues, paraphrasing Gladwin, that early "Africoids" reached the New World via the Bering Strait; Chandler [C-159] believes that "Negroid" Shang Chinese affected Mesoamerica.

A postscript (pages 26-27) refers to "Abu Bakari, the black king," from Africa arriving in Mexico in 1311 and being taken as Quetzalcoatl in his "rain-god and wind-god aspects."

S-198

AUTHOR: Sertima, Ivan van
DATE: 1987c
TITLE: Egypto-Nubian Presences in Ancient Mexico
IN: African Presence in Early America, edited by Ivan van Sertima, (n.p.: n.p.), 29-55 ["Incorporating Journal of African Civilizations, Dec. 1986, vol. 8, no. 2." "All inquiries should be addressed to Transaction Books, Rutgers—the State University, New Brunswick, New Jersey"] [Reprinted from *Dollars and Sense Magazine* 8(6) (Feb./Mar. 1983)]

A summary of elements from Irwin, Jairazbhoy, Wuthenau, Wiercinski, etc., written in a confrontational mode with the archaeological "establishment" which disputes his picture of an "African presence" as one element in Olmec civilization.

S-198B

AUTHOR: Sertima, Ivan van
DATE: 1995
TITLE: African Presence in Early America

IN: Race, Discourse, and the Origin of the Americas: A New World View, edited by Vera L. Hyatt and Rex Nettleford (Smithsonian Institution Press: Washington), 66-102

The fullest and most carefully phrased presentation yet of his case for substantial influence by African voyagers on ancient American cultures. He hopes that he will "not be judged today on all the positions I held fifteen years ago, but on what I say now. In such a broad-ranging exploration where one is walking on ground that is partly lit and partly hidden in the grayness of antiquity, one is bound to stumble here and there. The important point is to admit it when one discovers one has erred." But his fundamental thesis has not been weakened by new evidence but reinforced.

Reviews reports and traditions about black peoples in the Caribbean at the time of European discovery, sea-going craft and navigation, plants shared between Africa and America, Olmec negroid heads, figurine negroid heads, cultural parallels, and similar materials previously discussed in his works.

S-199

AUTHOR: Service, Elman R.
DATE: 1964
TITLE: Archaeological Theory and Ethnological Fact
IN: Process and Pattern in Culture: Essays in Honor of Julian H. Steward, edited by Robert A. Manners (Aldine: Chicago), 364-375

A survey of thought on the "diffusibility" of the several aspects of culture. He concludes that there are parts of culture best seen as diffusible shreds and patches, others as historically stable, and others as functionally adaptive, but so far we are ignorant about how to distinguish them. Studies of (historical) cases would help us understand "how culture actually does behave."

S-199B

AUTHOR: Service, Elman R.
DATE: 1985
TITLE: A Century of Controversy: Ethnological Issues from 1860 to 1960
IMPRINT: Academic Press: Orlando, Florida

Nothing at all is said about "diffusion," an indicator of how insignificant the topic was in mainline anthropology in 1985.

S-201

AUTHOR: Setchell, William Albert
DATE: 1921
TITLE: Aboriginal Tobaccos
IN: American Anthropologist 23:397-414

He identifies the varieties of Indian-used tobaccos in North America and their areas of use. Characterizes Wiener's theory of the African origin of tobacco as absurd and documents why.

S-202

AUTHOR: Settig, Otto
DATE: 1890
TITLE: Über unfreiwillige Wanderungen im Grossen Ozean [On Compulsory Migrations in the Pacific Ocean]
IN: Petermanns Geographische Mitteilungen 36:161-166, 185-188

An important early source documenting historically that drift voyages in the Pacific were not rare.

S-203

AUTHOR: Settig, Otto
DATE: 1896
TITLE: Compulsory Migrations in the Pacific Ocean
IN: Annual Report of the Board of Regents of the Smithsonian

Institution . . . [for] 1895, pages 519-535

A translation of S-202.

S-204

AUTHOR: Severin, Timothy
DATE: 1977
TITLE: The Voyage of Brendan
IN: National Geographic Magazine 152:770-797

Basic information on the Brendan traditions, which the author followed as far as possible in constructing a vessel and sailing it across the North Atlantic.

S-205

AUTHOR: Severin, Timothy
DATE: 1978
TITLE: The Brendan Voyage
IMPRINT: McGraw-Hill: New York

His book documents the construction of a replica curragh in Ireland and the voyage in it to Newfoundland by a four-man crew. He takes the trip as adequate demonstration that such craft, which were the same as available to St. Brendan, were fully capable of doing what the Navigatio says Brandan did—sail about the North Atlantic and return home again.

S-205B

AUTHOR: Sewall, Rufus King
DATE: 1895
TITLE: Ancient Voyages to the Western Continent. Three Phases of History on the Coast of Maine
IMPRINT: The Knickerbocker Press, G. P. Putnam's Sons: New York

Page 8: Shows "rock tracings" from Monhegan Island and Damariscove Island, Maine, in what might be considered script.

Page 9: It was "early claimed" (footnote: "Frontier Missionary, pp. 246, 247") that of the Monhegan Island markings "six or seven characters are lingual representatives of Runic or Phoenician origin." In 1602 an Englishman met at Damaris Cove certain "Biscay shallops, sailed by natives in European vestments" [*sic*].

S-206

AUTHOR: Shafer, Robert
DATE: 1952
TITLE: Athapaskan and Sino-Tibetan
IN: International Journal of American Linquistics 18:12-19

Limited material in support of a hypothetical relationship suggested by Sapir.

S-207

AUTHOR: Shafer, Robert
DATE: 1957
TITLE: A Note on Athapaskan and Sino-Tibetan
IN: International Journal of American Linguistics 23:116-117

See S-206. Some 24 new morphemes are compared.

S-208

AUTHOR: Shafer, Robert
DATE: 1969
TITLE: A Few More Athapaskan and Sino-Tibetan Comparisons
IN: International Journal of American Linquistics 35:67

A handful more lexical parallels.

S-209

AUTHOR: Shao, Paul (Shao Pang-hua)
DATE: 1976
TITLE: Asiatic Influences in Pre-Columbian American Art
IMPRINT: Iowa State University Press: Ames

An early, and not very satisfactory, version of S-211. Primarily a pictorial essay comparing selected trait complexes seen in east Asian and Mesoamerican (mainly Mayan) sculptures. Details within these art styles are shown to be similar in the two areas, but historical mechanisms of sharing are not seriously proposed.

He points out six main similarities: (1) standing figures holding double-headed serpent bars (amphisbaenas) horizontally or as borders or mouldings round the periphery of shrines and niches; (2) figures with three or many heads, sometimes vertically stacked, sometimes with two faces resolved into one by sharing a common eye; (3) multi-headed, multi-limbed deities (trimurti); (4) postures and gestures often recalling standard yoga positions (e.g., lotus position); (5) one figure, sometimes in armor, treading beneath his feet some demon or evil spirit (lokapala motif); and (6) the long-nose motif, which some have seen related to the elephant. Also notes parallels in the use of loose, heavy ceremonial belts and of deities emerging from flowers.

S-210

AUTHOR: Shao, Paul (Shao Pang-hua)
DATE: 1978
TITLE: Chinese Influence in Pre-Classic Mesoamerican Art
IN: Diffusion and Migration: Their Roles in Cultural Development, edited by P. G. Duke, J. Ebert, G. Langemann, and A. P. Buchner, (University of Calgary Archaeological Association: Calgary), 202-225

An excerpt from his then forthcoming book [S-211] best seen in the book itself.

S-211

AUTHOR: Shao, Paul (Shao Pang-hua)
DATE: 1983
TITLE: The Origin of Ancient American Cultures
IMPRINT: Iowa State University Press: Ames

A greatly expanded version of S-209, still quite impressionistic. Mechanisms of transmission are still not proposed, and the author shows only partial knowledge of previous work on the subject, yet it is a volume that should be carefully considered by anyone treating transpacific comparative art.

S-212

AUTHOR: Shapiro, Harry Lionel
DATE: 1940
TITLE: The Physical Relationship of the Easter Islanders
IN: Ethnology of Easter Island, by Alfred Métraux, Bulletin 160 (Bernice P. Bishop Museum: Honolulu)

This appendix says they are eastern Polynesians, nothing else.

S-214

AUTHOR: Shapiro, Harry Lionel
DATE: 1951
TITLE: Remarques sur l'origine des Polynésiens [Remarks on the Origin of the Polynesians]
IN: Journal de la société des océanistes 7:282-290

Criticism of P-221 which proposed a Viking arrival in Polynesia to account for "white" biological features. Followed by a comment from Poirier.

S-215

AUTHOR: Shapiro, Harry Lionel
DATE: 1964
TITLE: The Peopling of the Pacific Rim (The Thomas Burke Memorial Lecture, 1964)
IMPRINT: Thomas Burke Memorial Washington State Museum: Seattle

[Published also by American Museum of Natural History: New York, 1964. In Spanish, 1964, *Anales de antropología* 4:19-48 (México)]

A panoramic view of the settlement of the "Pacific Ring" or circumpacific lands from Paleolithic times on. More than half the piece is about the diffusion of features from China and Southeast Asia to America. Credits Heine-Geldern with the primary intellectual role in making this idea acceptable and supposes that many scholars now accept it. Mentions illustrative comparisons drawn from Heine-Geldern's writings as well as the Valdivia-Jomon material, Ekholm, Lou, and Schuster. Former skepticism about maritime capabilities has been replaced due to studies of early Chinese vessels. He proposes that the presence of large numbers of even local boats in island Asia would result at least in accidental voyages in significant numbers to America over the centuries. Focuses on reasons why China was the propulsion platform to America, not, say, India. Reviews Heyerdahl with skepticism but acknowledges that there is something there.

S-216

AUTHORS: Shapiro, Harry Lionel, and Robert C. Suggs
DATE: 1959
TITLE: New Data for Polynesian History
IN: Man 59:12-13

Includes a critique of Heyerdahl and his Easter Island views.

S-216B

AUTHORS: Sharma, B. D., and Vishnu-Mittre
DATE: 1969
TITLE: Studies of Post-Glacial Vegetational History from the Kashmir Valley, 2. Baba Rishi and Yus Maidan
IN: The Palaeobotanist 17/3:243ff. (Lucknow)

Report finding subfossil maize pollen from deposits in Kashmir which may indicate pre-Columbian occurrence of the plant there.

S-217

AUTHOR: Sharp, Andrew
DATE: 1956
TITLE: Ancient Voyagers in the Pacific
IMPRINT: Memoir 32, Polynesian Society: Wellington
[Reprinted Penguin Books: Harmondsworth, 1957; reviewed 1958 by B. A. L. Cranstone, *Man* 58:103-104; reviewed 1958 by Katherine Luomala, *American Anthropologist* 60:776-778. Revised edition with new title: *Ancient Voyagers in Polynesia* (Paul's Book Arcade: Hamilton, New Zealand, 1963)]

Pages 85-90 (of Penguin edition): He reviews the evidence known to him of an American connection for Polynesian people, language and culture and finds it not credible. He still would allow occasional voyages, especially from America westward, but without significant impact. His prime thesis is that Polynesians settled their islands exclusively by means of accidental voyages. Their nautical capabilities were much more limited than romanticists have represented.

S-219

AUTHOR: Sharp, Andrew
DATE: 1961
TITLE: Polynesian Navigation to Distant Islands
IN: Journal of the Polynesian Society 70:219-226

The supposed use of star paths for navigation, suggested by H. Gatty, is fallacious. Deliberate settlement of Hawaii and New Zealand by Polynesians was impossible. There is no valid theory of Polynesian long navigation.

S-220

AUTHOR: Sharp, Andrew
DATE: 1966
TITLE: David Lewis's Experimental Voyage
IN: Journal of the Polynesian Society 75:231-233

Lewis [L-197] has proved nothing significant about Polynesian ability to conduct planned voyages.

S-221

AUTHOR: Sharp, Andrew
DATE: 1968
TITLE: Review of *Sea Routes to Polynesia,* by Thor Heyerdahl
IN: Journal of the Polynesian Society 77:317-319

"It seems evident that migrants from America did come occasionally into Polynesia in prehistoric times, although I do not think there is any valid evidence that they were dispersed widely or that any of them got back to America."

S-222

AUTHOR: Sharp, Andrew
DATE: 1969
TITLE: Prehistoric Voyages and Modern Experimenters
IN: Oceania 39:231-233

The latter he sees as not relevant to the former, in his terms.

S-223

AUTHOR: Shaw, Thurston
DATE: 1960
TITLE: Early Smoking Pipes in Africa, Europe, and America
IN: Journal of the Royal Anthropological Institute of Great Britain and Ireland 90:272-305

Clay smoking pipes dug from a site in Ghana [unknown date] have the closest prototypes near the northern coast of the Gulf of Mexico. It is possible that Sir John Hawkins' seamen, after they had been in contact with the Florida area, introduced this type of stem-socket pipe into West Africa.

S-225

AUTHOR: Sherwin, Reider Thorbjorn
DATE: 1940-1956
TITLE: The Viking and the Red Man; the Old Norse Origin of the Algonquin Language, 8 volumes
IMPRINT: Funk and Wagnalls: New York, vol. 1, 1940; vol, 2, 1942. Vols. 3-8, The author: Bronxville, New York, 1944-1956

Approximately 5,000 old Norse words are compared with Algonqian languages. [See negative reviews, S-242 and H-336.]

S-226

AUTHORS: Sherzer, Joel, and Richard Bauman
DATE: 1972
TITLE: Areal Studies and Culture History: Language as a Key to the Historical Study of Culture Contact
IN: Southwestern Journal of Anthropology 28:131-152

A methodological discussion of problems and possibilities in studying linguistic diffusion. "One current of opinion in historical linguistic theory argues that linguistic structure—semantic, syntactic, and phonetic—is rarely affected by diffusion. Increasingly, however, examples of diffusion from all . . . aspects of language are being documented." Examples are given of the diffusion of numerals, of vocabulary indicating ecological adaptation, etc. Students of pidginization and creolization provide increasing evidence that linguistic diffusion occurs at all levels of language.

S-227

AUTHOR: Shetelig, Haakon
DATE: 1948
TITLE: Roman Coins Found in Iceland
IN: Antiquity 22:161-163

Three coins, dating between A.D. 270-305, give no reason to suspect fraud. The circumstances surrounding the find are rather persuasive that they could have come from a Roman visit. They raise an interesting question concerning early navigation of the North Atlantic.

S-229

AUTHORS: Shevoroshkin, Vitalij V., and T. L. Markey, editors and translators
DATE: 1986
TITLE: Typology, Relationship and Time: A Collection of Papers on Language Change and Relationship by Soviet Linguists
IMPRINT: Karoma: Ann Arbor, Michigan

The foreword by the editors provides an up-to-date discussion of attempts by linguists (especially Soviets) to demonstrate distant genetic relationships at great time-depths ("megalo-comparisons"). It is important since the work and thinking discussed challenge many conventional notions that informed older (binary) language comparisons. Nostratic, the conception of an early relationship among Indo-European, Semitic, Uralic, Dravidian, etc., is among the topics whose literature is updated. Mention is made of a paper by S. Nikolaev [omitted from the bibliography in this poorly-edited volume] "on Dene-Caucasian (he later added Na-Dene languages to Sino-Caucasian, thereby significantly broadening the horizons of this macro-family, which is now termed Dene-Caucasian)." See pages xxxvi-xxxvii.

Page xv: They comment on a reason for the resistance to or ignorance of these long-range comparisons among North American linguists, few of whom now "pass through the demanding mill of Indo-European studies," consequently, these shallowly trained scholars believe, "any broad-scale comparison between seemingly (on the surface) disparate languages is ultimately doomed to failure, an adventure into the realm of whimsy." Not only have American linguists in the midst of this anti-historical, anti-comparative climate failed to use or cite Soviet publications on Nostratic from the last two decades, other scholarship on remote linguistic affiliations have likewise been consigned to a conspiracy of silence, notably the many very revealing comparisons (albeit largely without proper reconstructions) by Joseph H. Greenberg are relegated to the great dustbin of linguistic history.

Page xlii: They assert that, "Both O. Sadowski [Otto Sadovszky] and V. Ivanov have erroneously defined Penutian as closely related to Uralic, which, in turn, belongs to the Nostratic macro-family."

Page 50: In the article by Dogopolsky in the same volume, mention is made that S. Nikolaev considers Chukchee-Kamchatkan "to belong to a different macro-family [from East Nostratic], namely, 'Macro-Dene-Caucasian,' along with Yenisseian, Sino-Tibetan, North-Caucasian, Athapascan, Salishan, Wakashan and Algonquian languages. On the other hand, Eskimo-Aleut languages seemingly belong to Nostratic."

B. A. Serebrennikov's article, "Nostratic Languages," pages 66-86, discusses, among other topics, the question "Is genetic relationship ever really proven?" without answering it. He does say (p. 69) that, "It is well known that, insofar as the genetic relationship of languages may be determined, the material relationship of grammatical formants is more relevant than a comparison of lexical roots."

S-232

AUTHOR: Shipley, Marie Adelaide (Brown), Mrs.
DATE: 1887

TITLE: The Icelandic Discoverers of America; or, Honor to Whom Honor Is Due
IMPRINT: Privately printed: London [Privately printed: Boston, 1888; John B. Alden: Boston, 1890]

Insists that "justice" must be done to the Norse discoverers. "The Church of Rome" knew about those discoveries but concealed knowledge of them; that organization has, after all, "the genius for deceit, for trickery," etc. Properly "the Scandinavian North will . . . resume its true rank" as the "intellectual and moral leader of the civilized world," as in Leif's day.

[The 1891 printing contains a 27-page appendix: "Confirmation from Roman Catholic authorities of the statements made in this book; namely, that in the Vatican and other monastic libraries of Europe, are the records and documents that will fully establish the fact that America was discovered by Leif Erikson in the year 1000, and that Norse colonies existed there for several centuries; extracts from Centennial discourse delivered by Rev. Wm. F. Clark, S.J., at St. Joseph's Church, Philadelphia, July 4th, 1876."]

S-233
AUTHOR: Shipley, Marie Adelaide (Brown), Mrs.
DATE: 1892
TITLE: The Missing Records of the Norse Discovery of America
IN: Proceedings of the 8th International Congress of Americanists (Paris, 1890), pages 190-200

The Catholic Church undoubtedly has records about the Christianization of North America (Vinland). That area was abandoned by the church-dominated Norwegians when the colonists refused to continue in church ways. Some Catholic scholars understand the need to search these things out at the Vatican, but scientists and historians ignore the challenge. Crediting Columbus with discovery is a Romish plot to deny proper credit.

S-234
AUTHOR: Shipp, Bernard
DATE: 1897
TITLE: The Indian and Antiquities of America
IMPRINT: Sherman: Philadelphia

Attempts to show that American mounds were similar to works in Europe and Asia. Concludes that communication existed between the two hemispheres in very remote times.

S-236
AUTHOR: Shook, Charles A.
DATE: 1910
TITLE: Cumorah Revisited, or "The Book of Mormon" and the Claims of the Mormons Re-examined from the Viewpoint of American Archaeology and Ethnology
IMPRINT: Standard: Cincinnati

An attack on the claim that Indian traditions parallel Hebrew history or The Book of Mormon account.

S-238
AUTHOR: Shook, Edwin M.
DATE: 1952
TITLE: Lugares arqueológicos del altiplano meridional central de Guatemala [Archaeological Sites of the South Central Highlands of Guatemala]
IN: Antropología e historia de Guatemala 4/2:3-40

Rows of standing stones, apparently aligned astronomically, date to Middle and Late Preclassic times, especially at the site of Naranjo. [Compare Near Eastern cult centers.]

S-241
AUTHOR: Short, John T.
DATE: 1882

TITLE: North Americans of Antiquity: Their Origin, Migrations and Type of Civilization Considered, 3d edition
IMPRINT: Harper and Brothers: New York [First edition 1880]

Among topics addressed are:

Chapter 3: "Diversity of Opinion as to the Origin of the Ancient Americans"—Early Spanish fathers, Atlantis, Kingsborough, Phoenicians, Greek and Egyptian theories, the Tartars, Japanese and Chinese theories (Fu-sang), the Mongol theory, the Irish, the Northmen, the Welsh; none of these views impress the author. Head flattening probably began in central Asia then spread, probably via Polynesia, to America.

Chapter 5: "Origin of the Maya Nations"—Votan (probably of Old World origin) and the Quiché seem related to Mediterranean peoples because of their worship of the morning star. Las Casas' account of Hunab Ku, "the only God," shows so many striking likenesses to Christ's life that this must be an introduction from the Old World, thus he is inclined to believe that the Maya peoples are of transatlantic origin.

Chapter 6: "Origin of the Nahua Nations"—The Toltec account of a deluge is remarkably similar to the Near Eastern version of a great flood; the name Quetzalcoatl may originally have been applied to an intelligent princely foreigner cast upon the shores of the region.

Chapter 8: "Supposed Old World Analogies"—The Nahuas and Mayas were probably descendants of foreign stock but their civilization was developed indigenously, with only some few analogies elsewhere.

Chapter 9: "Other Analogies"—Calendar, analogies in history (Asiatic and Jewish), Buddhism in the New World, Scandinavian, and Greek parallels.

Chapter 10: "Languages"—Quotes Le Plongeon (letter) that one-third of the Maya language is Greek and contains words from almost every language [he also sees a sculpture of a bear's head at Uxmal!], then gives at length a letter from Brasseur to Rafn claiming analogies between Mayan languages and those of northern Europe—especially Scandinavian. He is impressed by Najera's similarities between Otomí and Chinese as well as Forchhammer [F-127] which connects southeastern U.S. tongues to Ural-Altaic. Finally, the Maya family was at least influenced by if not originated from transatlantic sources, while Nahua may have connections to Asia.

Chapter 11: "The Probabilities that America Was Peopled from the Old World, Considered Geographically and Physically."

S-241B

AUTHOR: Shuang, Shaohua B.
DATE: 1992
TITLE: Chinese Ancestors Opened up America
IMPRINT: Heilongjiang Press: Heilongjiang, China

Not seen but referred to by Xu [X-001]. Connects the origin of the Olmec culture to refugees from the Shang dynasty of China. He reads inscriptions on the six jade celts from Offering No. 4 at La Venta as matching the names of ancestors and kings of the Shang dynasty.

S-241C

AUTHOR: Shutler, Richard, Jr.
DATE: 1983
TITLE: The Australian Parallel to the Peopling of the New World
IN: Early Man in the New World, edited by Richard Shutler, Jr. (Sage Publications: Beverly Hills), 43-46

Supposes both groups originated in China and "both groups entered new continents through restricted entrances." Isolation then evolved distinct biological features. The Australian example has shown that water [that is, the open ocean distance between the Sunda shelf and

Australia] was not a barrier (ca. 50,000 years ago) "and some of us feel that the same applies for North America."

S-242

AUTHOR: Siebert, Frank T., Jr.
DATE: 1941
TITLE: Review of *The Viking and the Red Man, the Old Norse Origin of the Algonquin Language*, by Reider T. Sherwin
IN: American Antiquity 7:89-90

Quickly demonstrates that Sherwin's [S-225] linguistic thesis is naive. Any two unrelated languages show a few purely fortuitous correspondences; a few in Sherwin are interesting, but not significant historically. "Not a single one of Sherwin's Algonquian-Norse 'cognates' are convincing. Many are ridiculous and the remainder, although they may seem plausible to the layman, are demonstrably false." In all probability the Norsemen did reach the North American continent, but their cultural and linguistic influence was slight.

S-243

AUTHOR: Siers, James
DATE: 1977
TITLE: Taratai: A Pacific Adventure
IMPRINT: Millwood Press: Wellington, New Zealand

An account of the building of an experimental vessel with an outrigger and the attempt to show how deliberate voyages eastward from Tonga (contra Sharp and Heyerdahl) could account for Polynesian settlement. The boat's performance was laden with problems.

S-244

AUTHOR: Siers, James
DATE: 1978
TITLE: Taratai II: A Continuing Pacific Adventure
IMPRINT: Millwood Press: Wellington, New Zealand

Using lessons learned in building and sailing Taratai I, the author had a second vessel built, but it was lost due to damage to the outrigger.

S-245

AUTHOR: Signorini, Italo
DATE: 1969
TITLE: The Heine-Geldern Theory at [*sic*] the Light of Recent Radiocarbon Dating
IN: Proceedings of the 38th International Congress of Americanists (Stuttgart-Munich, 1968), 1:467-469

Heine-Geldern had wanted to compare Chavin with Chou motifs, based on then extant chronology. Three C-14 dates for Chavin now push it back to between 1200-1000 B.C. This strengthens the case for a transpacific connection, for, actually, Shang stylistic affinities of that date are more apt than Chou. Phillips' article in the Handbook of Middle American Indians [P-159] arguing against transoceanic diffusion takes an unscientific tack by avoiding the (theoretically) more dangerous comparisons while picking out easy targets for criticism. Diffusion theory needs improvement, but it does not need to be maliciously harassed.

[Actually the C-14 dates Signorini urges have proved too early in the light of other chronological data, hence Heine-Geldern's position stands.]

S-245B

AUTHOR: Sigstad, J. Steve
DATE: 1989
TITLE: "Ogam" and Rock Art in Southeastern Colorado
IN: Rock Art of the Western Canyons, Memoir No. 3 (Colorado Archaeological Society and Denver

Museum of Natural History: Boulder, Colorado), 171-178

After visiting purported Ogam sites with McGlone et al., he believes the markings have nothing to do with any form of writing. If Ogam, he asks, where are the European-type sites and artifacts in the area that should connect with them?

S-245C

AUTHOR: Silliman, Horace F.
DATE: 1967
TITLE: The Copper Breast Plates of the New England Indians
IN: NEARA [New England Antiquities Research Association] Journal 2/4:64

Gives historical documentation supporting the idea that English copper and brass was traded with Indians on the Atlantic coast of North America (they were reported as having an abundance of it at one point in that period), perhaps from Newport Tower, between about 1570 and 1620. (Zinc brass was first made in modern times in England in 1568.)

S-245D

AUTHOR: Silliman, Horace F.
DATE: 1968
TITLE: The Newport Tower, Sir Walter Raleigh and the Hansa
IN: NEARA [New England Antiquities Research Association] Journal 3:86-93

Offers considerable circumstantial evidence for a theory that the tower was built by Englishmen late in the 16th century to serve as a base for contraband trade with Indians while searching for gold in the surrounding territory.

S-245E

AUTHOR: Silliman, Horace F.
DATE: 1970
TITLE: Further Notes on New England Indians' Copper Breast Plates
IN: NEARA [New England Antiquities Research Association] Journal 5:14-17

Further historical information along the lines of S-245C.

S-245F

AUTHOR: Silliman, Horace F.
DATE: 1981
TITLE: The Background of the Newport Tower: The English Elizabethan Solution
IN: NEARA [New England Antiquities Research Association] Journal 16:50

See S-245D.

S-246

AUTHOR: Silow, R. A.
DATE: 1949
TITLE: The Problem of Trans-Pacific Migration Involved in the Origin of the Cultivated Cottons of the New World
IN: Proceedings, Seventh Pacific Science Congress 5:112-118

A fundamental synthesis of knowledge of the history of cotton to the time of writing of the article, this remains one of the most cogent statements of evidence for human transport of a crop plant across the Pacific. Explains in easy-to-understand cytogenetic terms why no other explanation is acceptable for New World cultivated tetraploid cottons except transfer of G. arboreum from South Asia, most likely India, to America where it hybridized with a native diploid cotton. New World domesticated cottons occur exclusively with the same type of spindle "used by the fine spinners of Dacca muslin in India and the looms also are identical with those used in the Old World," "involving at least eleven independent technical inventions." "It seems most unlikely that such an assemblage of developments, identical with that which had occurred in the Old World, should have appeared in the New World by independent invention." Hawaiian wild tetraploid G. tomentosum can be explained only as derived from American cotton "which reached Hawaii only after the establishment of civilization in tropical America" being "perhaps a degenerated escape from early attempts at cultivation [in Hawaii]." Decisive arguments are presented why chance transfer by seed floating from Asia to America is not acceptable. Of the eight wild species in the Americas, only one, G. raimondii, is suitable to explain characteristics of the subsequent hybrid domesticated (tetraploid) cottons (G. barbadense and G. hirsutum). G. raimondii is limited to northwestern South America, which is then indicated as the home of the earliest tetraploid hybrid. The most plausible explanation is the transference of the Asiatic diploid parent by humans across the entire Pacific.

Page 118: "It may well [also] be that detailed biosystemateic investigations of other domesticated crops, similar to that which has been undertaken [beginning 1934] for cotton, will contribute further towards a solution of the highly controversial problem of the origin of civilization in the New World."

S-247

AUTHOR: Silva Galdames, Osvaldo
DATE: 1977
TITLE: Prehistoria de América, 3d edition, corrected and enlarged [Prehistory of America]
IMPRINT: Editorial Universitaria: Santiago, Chile

Pages 9-12: In a reasonably up-to-date but compact summary of the culture history of Mesoamerica and Peru, this section is on transoceanic diffusion. It is held that evidence cited by diffusionists, such as Meggers on Shang-Olmec links, can be interpreted as resulting from convergence and independent invention, since the diffusionist position lacks explanation of means of communication, etc. In any case, any diffused elements could not have been important.

S-248 See now R-016B.

S-249 See now R-016B.

S-250

AUTHOR: Silva Sifuentes, Jorge E.
DATE: 1978
TITLE: Instrumentos musicales pre-colombinos [Pre-Columbian Musical Instruments]
IN: Serie investigaciones no. 2, Gabinete de Arqueología, Colegio Real (Universidad Nacional Mayor de San Marcos: Lima, Peru)

Some interhemispheric comparisons of music and instruments.

S-251

AUTHOR: Silverberg, Robert
DATE: 1968
TITLE: Mound Builders of Ancient America: The Archaeology of a Myth
IMPRINT: New York Graphic Society: New York

A generally well written, semi-popular history of speculation and scholarship on the Mound Builders. The crucial part is chapter 5 recounting the role of Cyrus Thomas at the Smithsonian in the "deflation of the myth" from the early 19th century of an exotic Mound Builder race. Mentions purple dye use by Hopewellians.

S-252

AUTHOR: Siméon, Rémi
DATE: 1880
TITLE: Dictionnaire de la langue nauatl ou mexicaine

[Dictionary of the Nahuatl or Mexican Language]
IMPRINT: Imprimerie nationale: Paris [Reprinted Akademische Druck- und Verlaganstalt: Graz, 1963]

In this huge dictionary he notes incidentally a similarity between a Nahuatl verb and one in Sanskrit.

S-252B

AUTHOR: Simmonds, Norman W.
DATE: 1965
TITLE: The Grain Chenopods of the Tropical American Highlands
IN: Economic Botany 19:223-235

Page 234: Old World people also used chenopods as grains, shown by Iron Age bog burials of Jutland (Chenopodium album) and many other places in Europe and in Asia, although it never became important as a crop.

S-253

AUTHOR: Simmonds, Norman William, editor
DATE: 1976
TITLE: Evolution of Crop Plants
IMPRINT: Longmans: London

A unique compendium in which botanists review each of some 88 crops or classes of related crops, generally giving introduction, cyto-taxonomic background, early history, recent history and prospects, with a limited (95% botanical) bibliography. The brief historical portions generally take a very conservative position regarding possible pre-Columbian transfers. Thus amaranth in the Old World is said to be only post-Columbian (J. Sauer; contrast his older view in S-062); evidences that pineapples were present in Assyria, Egypt and Pompeii are not convincing (B. Pickersgill); "there is no evidence (some earlier writings notwithstanding) that maize moved out of the western hemisphere" before the Spanish conquest (Gregory and Gregory); there is no hint of domesticated pre-Columbian barley in America (Harlan); for bananas "there is no good evidence of pre-Columbian presence in the New World" (Simmonds).

Some exceptions: Yen gives several sides to the sweet potato matter, courteously downplaying his own position which unquestionably calls for pre-Columbian spread from America to Polynesia; Whitehead agrees that coconut spread "might have been assisted by man" across the Pacific; while the possible interhemispheric history of cotton is left completely indeterminate by Phillips.

Page 16: While the pineapple is old in the New World on distributional grounds, the only archaeological record for it consists of seeds and bracts found in coprolites from caves in the Tehuacan valley of Mexico dated about 200 B.C.-A.D. 700.

Page 67: Lagenaria siceraria, gourd, is likely indigenous to Africa south of the equator, and it has been identified in Egyptian tombs dated at about 3300-3500 B.C., yet it was in the western hemisphere, probably as a cultivated plant, as early as 7000 B.C.

S-254

AUTHOR: Simmons, Roy T.
DATE: 1962
TITLE: Blood Group Genes in Polynesians and Comparisons with Other Pacific Peoples
IN: Oceania 32:198-210

Blood grouping data indicate that contributions to the Polynesian stock have undoubtedly come from Tonga, Samoa, Indonesia, and South America to form a common gene pool and single, different physical type. Population additions from the coast of America would have represented a voyage of no-return.

Four points of similarity are tabulated with American Indians, two with Australian aborigines, one with Indonesians, and none with Melanesians, Micronesians or Ainu. It appears, then, that American Indians and Polynesians shared in a common gene pool, more so than Polynesians and races to the west and north-west.

S-255

AUTHOR: Simmons, Roy T.
DATE: 1965
TITLE: The Blood Group Genetics of Easter Islanders (Pascuense) and Other Polynesians
IN: Reports of the Norwegian Archaeological Expedition to Easter Island and the East Pacific, vol. 2, Miscellaneous Papers, edited by Thor Heyerdahl and Edwin N. Ferdon, Jr., Monographs of the School of American Research and the Museum of New Mexico, and the Kon-Tiki Museum, no. 24, part 2 (Rand McNally: Chicago), 333-343

Finds Polynesians have more points of similarity with American Indians than with other neighboring peoples, however, he is pessimistic that historical conclusions can be drawn from the data available now or likely to be available.

S-256

AUTHOR: Simmons, Roy T.
DATE: 1976
TITLE: The Biological Origin of Australian Aborigines: An Examination of Blood Group Genes and Gene Frequencies for Possible Evidence in Populations from Australia to Eurasia
IN: The Origin of the Australians, edited by R. L. Kirk and A. G. Thorne (Australian Institute of Aboriginal Studies: Canberra; and Humanities Press International: Atlantic Highlands, New Jersey), 307-328

After 35 years of work, he concludes that studies on blood groups in Oceania have created a picture of great genetic heterogeneity, uncorrelated with the geographical, cultural, and linguistic variability found there, hence great caution should be observed in trying to use blood groups in historical reconstruction.

S-257

AUTHORS: Simmons, Roy T., and J. J. Graydon
DATE: 1957
TITLE: A Blood Group Genetical Survey in Eastern and Central Polynesia
IN: American Journal of Physical Anthropology 15:357-366

A discussion of the absence of the Diego antigen in Polynesia and how it pertains to the relationship between Polynesians and American Indians.

S-258

AUTHORS: Simmons, Roy T., J. J. Graydon, N. M. Semple, and E. I. Fry
DATE: 1955
TITLE: A Blood Group Genetical Survey of Cook Islanders, Polynesia, and Comparisons with American Indians
IN: American Journal of Physical Anthropology 13:667-690

Simple measures taken to limit the sample of persons from whom blood was drawn to natives of "pure" ancestry were no doubt insufficient, as they probably have been in most studies of Pacific island populations. Nevertheless, the conclusions reached by Heyerdahl relative to American Indians and Polynesians on the basis of A-B-O blood groups alone have not been contradicted by Graydon utilizing three blood group systems for comparison, or by Mourant who compiled all the available blood group data to the end of 1953. Cook Island data here reported do not invalidate the position that there is a close blood genetic relationship between American Indians and Polynesians and that no similar relationship is evident when Polynesians are compared with Melanesians, Micronesians, and Indonesians, except mainly in adjacent areas of direct contact.

S-260

AUTHOR: Simoons, Frederick J.
DATE: 1961
TITLE: Eat Not This Flesh: Food Avoidances in the Old World
IMPRINT: University of Wisconsin Press: Madison

Dogs were sacrificed and eaten in China as early as Shang times. [Compare evidence for eating dogs at Olmec San Lorenzo, C-284, and see F-089]

S-262

AUTHOR: Simpson, George Gaylord
DATE: 1970
TITLE: Uniformitarianism: An Inquiry into Principle, Theory and Method in Geohistory and Biohistory
IN: Essays in Evolution and Genetics in Honor of Theodosius Dobzhansky, edited by Max K. Hecht and William C. Steere (Appleton-Century-Crofts: New York), 43-96

An important essay by a distinguished natural scientist arguing from biological models and principles that diffusion has to be an important process in human evolution and history.

S-262B

AUTHOR: Sinclair, Andrew
DATE: 1992
TITLE: The Sword and the Grail. Of the Grail and the Templars and a True Discovery of America
IMPRINT: Crown: New York

Indian maize and an aloe cactus are carved in stone on Rosslyn Chapel in England which is of pre-Columbian date. Illustrated.

Page 134: The Zeno and St. Clair voyages are considered.

Page 148: The Micmac have traditions of a culture bearer from across the ocean.

S-262C

AUTHOR: Singh, Bhag
DATE: 1977
TITLE: Races of Maize in India
IMPRINT: Indian Council of Agricultural Research: New Delhi

Notes the presence of stone carvings that represent what appear to be ears of maize on medieval temples near Mysore, India. [Compare J-095.]

S-263

AUTHOR: Singh, G.
DATE: 1964
TITLE: Preliminary Survey of the Post-Glacial Vegetational History of the Kashmir Valley
IN: The Paleobotanist 12:73-108

Maize pollen was reported from two cores in mire in Kashmir [see V-062]. Dating was estimated only to be "post glacial" in one case but radiocarbon indicated for the other a date before 800 B.C. [However, Johannessen and Parker (J-095) cite a personal communication from Vishnu-Mittre questioning whether the pollen grains classified as Zea mays were properly identified.]

S-264

AUTHOR: Singhal, D. P.
DATE: 1969
TITLE: India and World Civilization, vol. 2
IMPRINT: Michigan State University Press: East Lansing

Chapter 2, pages 35-79, is entitled "Red Indians or Asioamericans—Indian Foam on Pacific Waves." Mentions Maya and Indian zero, stylistic parallels between Maya and India and Cambodia from the first half of the first millennium A.D. to the 12th century, similarity between the Brahma-Visnu-Siva trinity and Mexican Huitzilopochtli-Tlaloc, the umbella, a goddess who spits out precious stones, and characteristics of Quetzalcoatl.

Page 65: An ascending series of sequentially destroyed world ages, the first one 4800 divine years long and each with a symbolic color, occur in the same order in India and Mesoamerica.

S-265

AUTHOR: Sinor, Denis
DATE: 1961
TITLE: On Water-transport in Central Eurasia
IN: Ural-Altaische Jahrbücher 33:156-179

In a comprehensive survey of names and boat types among Turkic, Tunguz, and Mongol peoples he found no evidence to corroborate a statement by Hornell that "the coracle was a distinctive feature of early Mongolian culture and in general use by them before a wave of Mongolian migration carried numbers of this race across the sea to the shores of North America."

S-266

AUTHOR: Sinoto, Yosihiko H.
DATE: 1983
TITLE: The Huahine Excavation: Discovery of an Ancient Polynesian Canoe
IN: Archaeology 36/2:10-15

Excavation in the Marquesas shows that "great vessels" were being built there at least in the ninth century A.D.

S-267

AUTHOR: Sinoto, Yosihiko H.
DATE: 1989
TITLE: Accidental Cross-Pacific Drift Voyages to the Americas from Japan
IN: Reprint Proceedings, Circum-Pacific Prehistory Conference, Seattle, August 1-6, 1989, part VIII: Prehistoric Trans-Pacific Contacts, (Washington State University Press: Pullman), articles separately paginated

Only a long abstract. Citing chiefly Brooks, he notes that "similar incidents could have happened in prehistoric times, though the survival rate would have been considerably smaller" than in the historic period. Recently dugout canoes and bones of deep-sea fish have been recovered from Early Jomon mounds on the Pacific coast of Japan, and a unique Jomon stone tool has been uncovered from prehistoric sites in Alaska, perhaps transferred by drifting Jomon people.

S-268B

AUTHOR: Sittig, Otto
DATE: 1896
TITLE: Compulsory Migrations in the Pacific Ocean
IN: Smithsonian Institution, Annual Report for 1895, pages 519-535 [Translated from *Petermanns Mitteilungen* 36, 1890, VII, VIII]

A comprehensive survey of what the sources have said about dismasted ships and their voyages. Most cases given are in the western Pacific. A few relate to North America, but none to South America, although he considers such not impossible.

S-268C

AUTHOR: Sittinger, Auguste
DATE: 1982
TITLE: Trésor des templiers et découverte de l'Amérique [Treasure of the Knights Templar and the Discovery of America]
IN: Kadath: Chroniques des civilisations disparues, no. 47:5-10 (Brussels) [Reprinted from *Nouvel Europe Magazine*]

A basic recapitulation of the thesis of Mahieu [M-049]. At Tiahuanaco and in Mesoamerica are remnant evidences of voyagers from Europe. In

Indian languages of Guatemala are found roots of words in old German, English and French. A list is given, following Brasseur, of some French roots he claims he found in Quiché Maya. There were three European waves which reached America: Irish monks, Vikings, and Templars (late 13th century). The Portuguese voyagers were influenced by the Templar tradition.

S-270

AUTHOR: Skaare, Kolbjorn
DATE: 1979
TITLE: An Eleventh Century Norwegian Penny Found on the Coast of Maine
IN: Norwegian Numismatic Journal 2:4-17

Self-explanatory title.

S-270B

AUTHORS: Skeat, Walter William, and Charles Otto Blagden
DATE: 1906
TITLE: Pagan Races of the Malay Peninsula, 2 vols.
IMPRINT: Macmillan: London

Authors note the resemblance between the Malacca Mantra belief that the sun, personified as a female tied by a string to her unidentified lord who pulls her along, and Polynesian and Bella Coola (Northwest Coast) beliefs.

S-272

AUTHOR: Skelton, R. A.
DATE: 1966
TITLE: The Vinland Map
IN: Geographical Journal 132:336-339

A letter responding critically to C-427. Skelton holds that the map must be either a remarkable fifteenth century one or else a twentieth century fabrication. No other explanation will do. In a short letter immediately following, Crone continues gently to disagree that these are the only possibilities.

S-272B

AUTHOR: Skelton, R. A.
DATE: 1967
TITLE: The Vinland Map and the Tartar Relation
IN: Geographical Magazine 38:662-668

A general description in which he emphasizes the value and novelty of the source. Greenland is shown with remarkable accuracy. "Had it been forged," the forger would have taken a different tack. [See, as of 1996, W-028.]

S-273

AUTHORS: Skelton, R. A., Thomas E. Marston, and George D. Painter
DATE: 1965
TITLE: The Vinland Map and The Tartar Relation
IMPRINT: Yale University Press: New Haven [Reviewed by O. Jensen in *American Heritage* 16 (1965): 4-11, and *American-Scandinavian Review* 53 (1965): 361-374; reviewed by Arthur Davies in *Geography* 51 (1966): 259-265; reviewed by J. G. Pounds in *Journal of American History* 53 (1966): 107-108; reviewed by Wilcomb E. Washburn in *American History Review* 71 (1966): 927-928. For responses by Skelton, see *Geographical Journal* 132:177-178, 336-339, and 448-450]

First description of this manuscript map and text which, it was claimed, were copied about 1440 from lost originals. It covers the western Atlantic with representations of Iceland, Greenland, and Vinland. They discuss questions about its authenticity. [See A-179B and W-028.]

S-274

AUTHOR: Skinner, Henry Devenish
DATE: 1917
TITLE: Mummification among the Maoris

IN: Journal of the Polynesian Society 26:188-189

He affirms that the canoe is closely associated with burial rites among the Maori (or Moriori) and the weight of the evidence points to a connection with Egypt. It is possible to argue that these arose independently, but he considers that unlikely.

S-275

AUTHOR: Skinner, Henry Devenish
DATE: 1930
TITLE: Review of *Pacific Islands Records: Fish Hooks*, by Harry F. Beasley
IN: American Anthropologist 32:309-312

A hook on Plate 34, the reviewer believes, while tentatively allotted to New Zealand, "may probably be assigned to the American Northwest coast." Six hooks on Plates 62 and 63 he also rejects as Polynesian, "in spite of the fact that the barbed points of five of them are extraordinarily like one type of New Zealand point." He suggests that they also are of the Northwest Coast. [The fact that similarities are so close as to cause disputes about provenance is suggestive.]

Beasley does not speculate about extra-Oceanic relationships of hook forms shown in the volume, "but an American student could hardly avoid conjecture on the point. What are we to think of the hooks of the Santa Barbara islands, or of those attributed to the Peruvian coast? Is Gudger's suggestion of relationship between the Ruvettus hook of Polynesia and the halibut hook of the Northwest coast justified by other known cultural features? We are now in a position to attack these and other allied problems."

S-276

AUTHOR: Skinner, Henry Devenish
DATE: 1931
TITLE: On the Patu Family and Its Occurrence beyond New Zealand
IN: Journal of the Polynesian Society 40:183-196

See S-280.

S-277

AUTHOR: Skinner, Henry Devenish
DATE: 1942
TITLE: A Classification of the Fish-hooks of Murihiki
IN: Journal of the Polynesian Society 51:256-286

Pages 261-262 and figures 68, 70: Fishhooks of the Santa Barbara, California, region are classed as a distinct type and are compared to Polynesian examples.

S-278

AUTHOR: Skinner, Henry Devenish
DATE: 1955
TITLE: Easter Island Masonry
IN: Journal of the Polynesian Society 64:292-294

He argues that the often-cited similarity between Peruvian stone masonry and that of the facing blocks of Easter Island ahus is due to convergence. The Easter Island work follows the technique of plank work used in Polynesian canoes, yielding only a veneer, unlike Peruvian walls.

S-279

AUTHOR: Skinner, Henry Devenish
DATE: 1967
TITLE: Cylindrical Headdress in the Pacific Region
IN: Polynesian Culture History: Essays Presented in Honor of Kenneth P. Emory, edited by Genevieve Highland, et al., Special Publication 56 (Bernice P. Bishop Museum: Honolulu), 167-190

Anciently this form of headdress was widespread in Asia, impinging at an undetermined date on western Oceania (New Britain, Solomons) and in Polynesia and the American Northwest Coast. He believes that the cylindrical artifacts of red tufa occurring on the heads of human figures on Easter Island are such headdresses. Examples are shown but no explanation is offered for the distribution. The source for the Northwest Coast headdress "is not at present known."

S-280

AUTHOR: Skinner, Henry Devenish [edited by Peter Gathercole, Foss Leach, and Helen Leach]

DATE: 1974

TITLE: Comparatively Speaking: Studies in Pacific Material Culture, 1921-1972

IMPRINT: University of Otago Press: Dunedin, New Zealand

His paper on the patu in the Pacific [S-276], included in this volume, compares this club form, which is characteristic of New Zealand and the Chatham Islands, with examples from elsewhere in Polynesia, the Solomons, Taiwan, South China, Japan, and the Northwest Coast of America. [See M-231.]

S-281

AUTHOR: Skinner, J. Ralston

DATE: 1886-1887

TITLE: The Identification of the British Inch as the Unit of Measure of the Mound Builders of the Ohio Valley

IN: Journal of the Cincinnati Society of Natural History 9:115-127, 142-162, 231-243

Self-explanatory title.

S-282

AUTHOR: Skogman, C.

DATE: 1854

TITLE: Fregatten Eugenies Resaomkring Jorden Åren 1851-1853 [The Frigate Eugenie's Voyage around the World in 1851-1853]

IMPRINT: Stockholm [Translated to German by Anton von Etzel as *Erdumsegelung der Königlichen Schwedischen Fregatte Eugenie, in den Jahren 1851 bis 1853* (Berlin, 1856)]

German edition, page 216: Reported South American balsa rafts "sixty to seventy feet long" that made voyages "even to the Galapagos Islands."

S-283

AUTHOR: Skottsberg, Carl J. F., editor

DATE: 1920

TITLE: The Phanerogams of Easter Island, vol. 1 of The Natural History of Juan Fernández and Easter Island

IMPRINT: Almquist and Wiksells Boktryckeri: Uppsala, Sweden

Vol. 1, pages 13: Irrigating of small cultivated plots dug below ground level [has a South American parallel—mahamaes, see L-072 and M-432].

In the two crater lakes on Easter Island were two freshwater plant species: the totora reed, widely used for house covering and boat manufacture, and a medicinal plant called tavari. Both grow at Lake Titicaca, Bolivia, where the same uses occur. Both are unknown elsewhere in the Pacific. On the moist margin of the island's lakes grew also another American species, a Cyperus (vegetus) with edible roots; its homeland was Peru. The only wild Easter Island shrub had edible berries and could also have come from Peru. One heavily-used tree not found elsewhere in Oceania is the toromiro, traditionally said to have been imported by early migrants; it is the same species as Chilean toromiro.

S-284

AUTHOR: Skottsberg, Carl J. F.

DATE: 1934

TITLE: Le peuplement des îles pacifiques du Chili; contribution a l'étude du peuplement zoologique et botanique des îles du Pacifique [The Peopling of the Pacific Islands of Chile: Contribution to the Study of the Zoological and Botanical Populating of the Pacific Islands]
IN: Journal de la société de biogéographia 4:271-280

Lists in the "elément américain" of the flora of Easter Island seven species, four "non endémiques," and four "endémiques." It is possible that they represent remnants of an ancient [shared] endemic flora.

S-284B

AUTHOR: Skupin, Michael
DATE: 1989
TITLE: The Los Lunas Errata
IN: Epigraphic Society Occasional Publication 18:249-252

If this inscription is ever to reveal anything, it will be by carefully analyzing its errors in grammar and so on in the light of expectable Hebrew. He points out some interesting anomalies in relation to the supposed source in Exodus in the Bible, come of which could point to an Alexandrian Jewish source.

S-285

AUTHOR: Skvortzov, B. V.
DATE: 1920
TITLE: On Some Varieties of Peanuts Grown in China
IN: Journal of the North China Branch, Royal Asiatic Society 51:142-145

Supposes the peanut present before European influence.

S-286

AUTHOR: Slack, Kenneth E.
DATE: 1966
TITLE: In the Wake of the Spray
IMPRINT: Rutgers University Press: New Brunswick, New Jersey

An admirer of Captain Joshua Slocum's yawl "Spray," in which Slocum circled the globe in 1895-1898, documents everything about the vessel, its performance, and its many imitations. [Compare S-289.]

S-288

AUTHOR: Slobodin, Richard
DATE: 1978
TITLE: W. H. R. Rivers
IMPRINT: Leaders of Modern Anthropology Series (Columbia University Press: New York)

Pages 148-160: "Diffusionism." Demonstrates that Rivers' (and to some extent G. Elliot Smith's) view of the topic was much more sophisticated and less doctrinaire than critics (particularly Edmund Leach) have made it out to be. Appreciates that current discussions of diffusionism (citing Heine-Geldern, Ekholm, Jett, etc.) are much better informed than in Rivers' day.

S-289

AUTHOR: Slocum, Joshua
DATE: 1900
TITLE: Sailing Alone around the World
IMPRINT: Century: New York [Reprinted DeGraff New York, 1952; reprinted Dover: New York, 1956; reprinted Naval Institute Press: Annapolis, 1985]

Classic story of the first single-handed voyage around the world (46,000 miles), in a 37-foot yawl, "Spray," 1895-1898, by a man who could not swim! Earlier, he had built an open 35-footer—all he could afford after an earlier vessel was lost—in Brazil and used it to take him, his wife, and two small children 5500 miles from Brazil to South Carolina. But in 1909 he was lost at sea in the Spray.

His course was from Newport to Morocco, then to Brazil, around the Horn, the Marquesas, Fiji, Tasmania, the Cape, and to Brazil again.

S-290

AUTHOR: Smith, A. Ledyard
DATE: 1940
TITLE: The Corbelled Arch in the New World
IN: The Maya and Their Neighbors, edited by Clarence L. Hay, et al. (Appleton-Century: New York), 202-221
[Reprinted Dover: New York, 1977]

Origin and development, spread and distribution of the corbelled arch in Middle America. Other types of roofs are considered briefly. [The corbelled arch has been claimed as diffused from the Old World.]

S-291

AUTHOR: Smith, Barbara B.
DATE: 1960
TITLE: Music of Polynesia
IN: Proceedings of the Centennial Workshop in Ethnomusicology Held at the University of British Columbia, Vancouver, June 19 to 23, 1967, edited by Peter Crossley-Holland (Government of the Province of British Columbia: Vancouver), 94-101
[Reprinted Center for Continuing Education, University of British Columbia: Vancouver, 1970]

Considers in some detail problems in discussing Polynesian and American Indian musical relations. In particular she notes that little is known about truly early native music so that the very basis for comparison is weak; furthermore, she emphasizes the variety that characterized "Polynesian culture." Considering Polynesian navigational accomplishments, it is not inconceivable that one or more voyages could have reached America, or vice versa, but probably music would not have been transferred under such conditions. The same may be said of possible connections between Peru and eastern Polynesian islands.

Pages 100-101: In the summary of discussion following this paper, Dr. Ida Halpern asks about comparison of Northwest Coast and Polynesian sculpture; Prof. Smith responds that examples she had seen in the Vancouver museum had a rib structure similar to examples from the Marquesas but the number of fingers differed. Dr. George List, who had given a paper on Hopi music and poetics, observes that Polynesian chants in which chanters dropped to a lower pitch then came back on it was also characteristic of the Hopi, and the Hopi had terminal glides just as strongly as the Maori. Also the slit-drum and nose flute seemed similar.

S-292

AUTHOR: Smith, Benjamin E.
DATE: 1953
TITLE: A Report on the Follins Pond Investigation
IN: Bulletin of the Massachusetts Archaeological Society 14:82-88

Negative on a purported Viking site.

S-292B

AUTHOR: Smith, Bruce D.
DATE: 1995
TITLE: The Emergence of Agriculture
IN: Scientific American Library/W. H. Freeman: New York

A relatively popular but highly useful and completely up-to-date book that emphasizes explanation of techniques and methods used in addressing the topic. Critiques some faulty (too early) dating for certain New World crop remains.

S-293

AUTHOR: Smith, C. Earle, Jr.
DATE: 1965
TITLE: Agriculture, Tehuacan Valley
IN: Chicago Natural History Museum, Fieldiana, Botany 31/3

He describes for this Mexican valley the pre-Columbian use of a system of tunnels and air vents as part of the irrigation system, comparing them generally with the "chain well" system of the Negev of Palestine, though not calling them qanats.

Page 97: No archaeological evidence exists that a[ny] plant had been carried from the Old World to the New World or vice versa. Botanical evidence regarding the sweet potato indicates that it was carried "apparently by Polynesian explorers who visited the west coast of South America." "All other supposed introductions from one area or the other can be shown to be erroneous conclusions due to misunderstanding of some of the broad biological implications of the facts."

S-294

AUTHORS: Smith, C. Earle, Jr., and Richard S. MacNeish
DATE: 1964
TITLE: Antiquity of American Polyploid Cotton
IN: Science 143/3607:675-676

The presence in the Tehuacan Valley of cotton, maize, beans, and squash removes the possibility that any of those crops could have arrived from the Old World, since voyaging that early would have been out of the question.

S-295

AUTHOR: Smith, C. H.
DATE: 1902
TITLE: Arms, Armor
IN: The Popular and Critical Bible Encyclopedia and Scriptural Dictionary, edited by Samuel Fallows, 2 vols. (Howard-Severance: Chicago)
[1904, 3 vols., same publisher]

Page 158: "Shirion" of II Chronicles 26:14 and Nehemiah 4:16 is interpreted as quilted textile armor. Metal leaf armor, slings, shields, javelins, and bows and arrows are also treated. [Mesoamerican comparisons possible.]

S-299

AUTHOR: Smith, Grafton Elliot
DATE: 1915a
TITLE: The Migrations of Early Culture; A Study of the Significance of the Geographical Distribution of the Practice of Mummification as Evidence of the Migrations of Peoples and the Spread of Certain Customs and Beliefs
IMPRINT: University of Manchester Publications No. 52; Ethnological Series No. 1; Manchester Memoirs 59/10 (Manchester University Press: Manchester; also Longmans Green: London)
[Said to be reprinted from S-304, despite dates. Reprinted from *Memoirs and Proceedings of the Manchester Literary and Philosophical Society, Session 1914-1915*, and reprinted again 1929 with index added. Reviewed by Henry D. Skinner, *Journal of the Polynesian Society* 25 (1916): 122-124]

See S-304.

S-300

AUTHOR: Smith, Grafton Elliot
DATE: 1915b
TITLE: Pre-Columbian Representations of Elephants in America
IN: Nature 96/2404:340-341; 2407:425; 2413: 93-595

Argues that the carved figures near the top of Stela B at Copan represent Indian elephants ridden by turbaned mahouts, giving detailed anatomical and cultural evidences. Also sees Indian elephants in Maya and Aztec manuscripts.

S-301

AUTHOR: Smith, Grafton Elliot

DATE: 1915c

TITLE: The Evidence Afforded by the Winged-disc in Mexico and Central America for the Egyptian Origin of Certain Elements of the Pre-Columbian Civilization [abstract]

IN: Memoirs and Proceedings of the Manchester Literary and Philosophical Society 60: xvi-xvii

Self-explanatory title. [See also S-316, pages 97-98.]

S-302

AUTHOR: Smith, Grafton Elliot

DATE: 1915d

TITLE: Further Notes on Pre-Columbian Representations of the Elephant in America [abstract]

IN: Memoirs and Proceedings of the Manchester Literary and Philosophical Society 60: xx-xxi

See S-316, pages 11-34.

S-303

AUTHOR: Smith, Grafton Elliot

DATE: 1915e

TITLE: Discussion on the Influence of Ancient Egyptian Civilization on the World's Culture; Opening Statement

IN: Report of the British Association for the Advancement of Science, pages 667-669 (Manchester)

See S-315.

S-304

AUTHOR: Smith, Grafton Elliot

DATE: 1916a

TITLE: The Influence of Ancient Egyptian Civilization in the East and in America

IMPRINT: Bulletin of the John Rylands Library 3:48-77 (Manchester) [As a separate by Manchester University Press, 1916. S-299 says it is a reprint of this item, despite the dates. Reprinted as *The Making of Man, An Outline of Anthropology*, edited by V. F. Calverton (Modern Library: New York, 1931), 393-420]

"I am calling attention to a mass of evidence which seems to prove that, towards the close of the period of the New Empire . . . a great many of the most distinctive practices of Egyptian civilization suddenly appeared in more distant parts of the coastlines of Africa, Europe, and Asia, and also in course of time in Oceania and America; and to suggest that the Phoenicians must have been the chief agents. . . ." This trade between the eastern Mediterranean and India began some time after 800 B.C. and continued for many centuries.

The stream of culture that reached America, however, had been much modified, with additions from Indonesia, Melanesia, and Polynesia as well as China and Japan. Also, from India America took over the major part of her remarkable pantheon, including practically the whole of the beliefs associated with the worship of Indra. The primary evidences are: mummification cult, megalithic monuments, idols with many associated beliefs (including deluge, divine origin of kings, and origin of the chosen people from incestuous unions), worship of the sun, circumcision, tattooing, massage, piercing and distending the earlobes, skull deformation and perhaps trephining and dental mutilations, linen weaving, use of purple dye, pearls and conch-shell trumpets, certain metallurgical methods, intensive agriculture including terracing, phallic ideas, swastika, boomerang, beliefs about heavenly twins, couvade, certain games, etc.

Use of winged discs in which a grotesque face with bulging eyes and no lower jaw is shown to be widespread in America and East Asia.

S-305

AUTHOR: Smith, Grafton Elliot
DATE: 1916b
TITLE: Sulle migrazioni dei marinai mediterranei in Oceania e in America nei tempi pre-colombiani [Concerning Migrations of Mediterranean Sailors in Oceania and in America in Pre-Columbian Times]
IN: Rivista de antropologia 20:3-6

Compare S-304.

S-306

AUTHOR: Smith, Grafton Elliot
DATE: 1916c
TITLE: The Origin of the Pre-Columbian Civilization of America
IN: Science 44:190-195

This is "a crude sketch of views which I have set forth in greater detail elsewhere." Civilization arose from the drab, universally "primitive" background in only one place—Egypt. There a unique concatenation of favorable environment and influences from neighboring areas crystallized the higher level of life. Eventually the influence of Egypt was handed on from place to place. "Links which all ethnologists recognize as genuine bonds of union can with . . . certainty be joined up into a cultural chain uniting Egypt to America." Here he mentions only a small portion of the "extraordinary cargo of bizarre practises and beliefs with which these ancient mariners . . . set out from the African coast more than twenty-five centuries ago on the great expedition that eventually led their successors some centuries later to the New World. At every spot where they touched and tarried, whether on the coasts of Asia, the islands of the Pacific or on the continent of America, the new culture took root and flourished in its own distinctive manner, as it was subjected to the influence of the aborigines or to that of later comers." The first great cultural wave must have begun some time after B.C. 900.

S-306B

AUTHOR: Smith, Grafton Elliot
DATE: 1917a
TITLE: The Origin of the Pre-Columbian Civilization of America
IN: Science 44:241-247

Response to a letter to the journal by Goldenweiser and Means calling on Smith to answer certain questions of substance and method in the wake of S-306. This defensive response adds little. [His continued condemnation of Tylor's "psychic unity" or independent invention to explain cultural parallels put Smith at increased odds with the British anthropological establishment, for Tylor had recently passed away and was then being honored as a founding father.] Smith notes that the writings of the German diffusionists were completely unknown to him when he formulated his own position.

S-307

AUTHOR: Smith, Grafton Elliot
DATE: 1917b
TITLE: Mummification in New Zealand
IN: Journal of the Polynesian Society 26:71-74

See O-040.

S-308

AUTHOR: Smith, Grafton Elliot
DATE: 1917c
TITLE: Ships as Evidence of the Migrations of Early Culture
IMPRINT: Manchester University Press: London
[Reprinted from the *Journal of the*

Manchester Egyptian and Oriental Society 5 (1916): 63-102]

Certain features of Oceanic vessels recall Egyptian ships and ship customs.

S-309

AUTHOR: Smith, Grafton Elliot
DATE: 1917d
TITLE: Ancient Mariners
IN: Journal of the Manchester Geographical Society 33/1-4:1-22

Citing only his own writings, he gives his version of the role of voyaging in the "great Oriental drift of Western culture" which he had already described as stemming from Egypt. The reason this influence did not make itself visible at certain points (e.g., China) must be that the avid search for gold and pearls that motivated the voyagers found little of interest there. Australia had such wealth but the migrators evidently could not get the aboriginals ("with their mental limitations") to work for them so gave up; yet in Melanesia ("people akin to the Australians") they were able to impress their culture more deeply on the locals. In Polynesia they were the first inhabitants, hence the descendants look more "Mediterranean." "These hardy and adventurous mariners continued to push east until they reached the coast of America, where they found in abundance the pearls, the gold and silver and the other treasures they had kept constantly before their gaze." Meanwhile the earliest inhabitants of the New World (had) made their way via Bering Strait to America, having already encountered those adventurous relatives who had branched off to the Yenisei in northeastern Asia, so they (the overland migrants) "naturally brought with them from the Old World the customs and (heliolithic) beliefs" of that area, but that movement did not begin before 25 centuries ago.

S-310

AUTHOR: Smith, Grafton Elliot
DATE: 1918
TITLE: An American Dragon
IN: Man 18:161-166

Describes a pot from Honduras showing a deer/fish monster, a concept invented in Babylonia in connection with the god Ea, who wears a fish skin and is related to pictures of a god emerging from an Oceanic deity and which interchanges with the makara and naga in India and Indonesia.

S-312

AUTHOR: Smith, Grafton Elliot
DATE: 1919a
TITLE: Dragons and Rain-gods
IN: Bulletin of the John Rylands Library 5:317-380

Pages 324-344: Relations and transformations of the makara and other Asiatic "dragons" to the elephant-headed god in Mesoamerica. Specifically, e.g., Codex Troano shows Chac treading on a serpent head and pouring water from a vessel—"Here we find depicted with childlike simplicity and directness, the Vedic conception of Indra overcoming the demon Vritra." In Seler's works, "not only is practically every episode of the dragon-myth of the Old World graphically depicted, but also every phase and incident of the legends from India (and Babylonia, Egypt, and the Aegean, he notes) that contributed to the building up of the myth" (as he explains on his pages 317-324). "The Maya Chac is, in fact, Indra transferred to the other side of the Pacific and there only thinly disguised by a veneer of American stylistic design." "The god who controls the rain, Chac of the Mayas, Tlaloc of the Aztecs, carried the axe and the thunderbolt like his homologues and prototypes in the Old World." "Hardly any incident in the history of the Egyptian falcon or the thunder-birds of Babylonia, Greece or India fails to reappear in America and find pictorial expression in the Maya and Aztec codices." "Essentially the same material reached America in manifold forms," hence its confused state to our eyes. Some versions came via the Bering Strait, as well as through "ancient mariners (who) began to coast along the Eastern Asiatic littoral" and along the Aleutian Route, and through Polynesia, etc. From this jumble, "the local priesthood of Central America built up a system of beliefs which is distinctively American, though . . . borrowed from the Old World."

S-313

AUTHOR: Smith, Grafton Elliot
DATE: 1919b
TITLE: The Evolution of the Dragon
IMPRINT: John Rylands Library/University of Manchester Press: Manchester

Compare S-310.

Pages 83-92, 154: The significance of the American elephant representations.

S-314

AUTHOR: Smith, Grafton Elliot
DATE: 1921
TITLE: Anthropology
IN: Encyclopedia Britannica, 12th edition, 1:143-154

Opposes an independent invention explanation for the origin of American civilizations.

S-315

AUTHOR: Smith, Grafton Elliot
DATE: 1923
TITLE: The Ancient Egyptians and the Origin of Civilization, new and revised edition
IMPRINT: Harper: London [First edition *The Ancient Egyptians and Their Influence upon the Civilization of Europe* (Harper: London, 1911)]

Civilization originated in Egypt and from there agriculture, irrigation, metallurgy, linen-weaving, carpentry, masonry, architecture, shipbuilding, the solar calendar, circumcision, couvade, skull deformation, tattooing, earlobe distension (along with lobe perforation, this relates to the sun), boomerang, similar ceramic forms, ritual assassination of the monarch, priests wearing a costume made of the skin of their victims, the idea of dragons, certain games, flood tradition, the swastika, year of 360 plus five unlucky days, four world elements, and mining techniques, were carried throughout the world by an identifiable physical type. The objective of this dispersion was the search for precious minerals. Elements reached Central America and Peru via Polynesian voyagers about the beginning of the Christian era.

S-316

AUTHOR: Smith, Grafton Elliot
DATE: 1924
TITLE: Elephants and Ethnologists: Asiatic Origins of the Maya Ruins
IN: Kegan Paul, Trench, Trubner: London; and Dutton: New York [Reviewed in *Nature* 114 (1924): 923-925]

Probably the best single source on his thought and research.

Pages 1-2: By 1915 he was convinced that pre-Columbian civilization in America was not wholly indigenous but was "inspired mainly by immigrants" during the first twelve centuries of the Christian era, and perhaps two or three centuries before, who crossed the Pacific and planted in Honduras and elsewhere "the germs of Old World culture," which with the aid of locals developed in a distinctive New World manner.

Page 3: Map showing lines of diffusion in the Pacific, via Micronesia and Polynesia.

Page 5: Concentrates here on the Indian elephant and associated figures and concepts, omitting Egypt entirely from the diffusion question for clarity.

Pages 11-19: Summarizes 25 items in the literature dealing with the representation of elephants in Mesoamerican art with special attention to Stela B at Copan, pointing out inconsistencies and contradictions in interpretation by Schellhas, Seler, Spinden, Tozzer, etc., who see macaw, tortoise, tapir or bat.

Pages 20-34: Gives a detailed analysis of Copan Stela B representations showing a number of stylistic details (e.g. ear-plugs, pendants, bracelets, anklets, girdles, shells) matched in Indian and Indonesian representations and beliefs about elephant-associated deities. Emphasizes the composite nature of elephant representations in southeast Asia involving the makara or mythical "crocodile" and the naga serpent from whose mouth emerges the head of a rain god. (Page 32: This conception originated in Babylonia in beliefs regarding Ea and Marduk.)

Pages 34-40: Other evidence of Indian influence in America, beginning with Tylor on patolli-pachisi. Tylor in 1894 noted the "complete identity of the experiences of the soul in four scenes of the Buddhist purgatory, depicted on Japanese temple scrolls, and those of the Mexican journey to the spirit land" in the Vatican codex. Tylor also noted Humboldt's argument from calendars and mythic catastrophes in Mexico and Asia, as well as metal-work and games.

Pages 51ff.: Codex Cortesianus has a representation of a snake enclosing rain in a sac-form that is compared with Indra-associated serpent Vritra who caught and kept rain from falling to earth. Also makes comparisons of Tlaloc with India, seeing elephant-connected Indra the prototype of the Chacs and Tlaloc.

Pages 52-82: Discusses the origin and senses of the makara or "dragon," which includes elephant characteristics, along with serpent, shark, deer, turtle, tiger, etc., reminiscent in part of the Mexican cipactli. (Page 69: Ultimately, he hints, from the Babylonian tiamat dragon representing the Great Deep.)

Pages 81ff.: The celestial dog, death associated, connected with flaming thunder weapons, for both Mayans and Chinese.

Pages 83-95: The spiral ornament on the Copan stela elephant representation and its associations in India and the Near East. Also the lion-headed couch and the Phrygian cap worn by deity as connected with this spiral.

Pages 95-97: Animal vehicles upon which deities ride or are enthroned, Mayan and South Asian.

Pages 97-98: Winged disc representation.

Pages 102-103: Mexican figurines from beneath a layer of lava approximately 2000 years old [Cuicuilco?] were shown in 1921 by Zelia Nuttall to Indianists; they identified the turbans on the figurines as distinctive of certain regions of India.

Pages 117-129: All the evidence points clearly to Indo-China as the chief source of Maya civilization. Comparisons in this portion focus on that area rather than India.

S-317

AUTHOR: Smith, Grafton Elliot
DATE: 1927
TITLE: The Diffusion of Culture
IN: Culture: The Diffusion Controversy, edited by Grafton Elliot Smith, et al. (Norton: New York), 9-25

In Central America, Mexico, and Peru, civilization appeared suddenly and fully developed. It conformed in almost every respect to that peculiar civilization that flourished in the southeastern corner of Asia at the time when it made its appearance in Central America. The whole series of arts and crafts, customs, and beliefs introduced in the New World bear unmistakable evidence of Asiatic origin, particularly from Cambodia and Java. The only additions in transit across the Pacific were features distinctive of Melanesia and Polynesia. Polynesian sailors must surely have landed repeatedly on the shores of America for ten centuries or more.

The discussion of the writings of Robertson, Prescott, and Tylor shows in part the history of the development of the view through the 19th century that American civilization was independent, which notion, of course, Smith was combatting.

S-318

AUTHOR: Smith, Grafton Elliot
DATE: 1928
TITLE: In the Beginning: The Origin of Civilization (The Thinker's Library, No. 29, new edition, revised and enlarged)
IMPRINT: Howe: London
[Published as *En el comienzo de la civilización* (Nova: Buenos Aires, 1945)]

Another brief potboiler. Nothing new except some phrasing. At the end: "For a hundred and fifty years ethnologists have been discussing this issue [of diffusion to America or not] without reaching any general agreement. The American problem remains the crux of the whole dispute regarding diffusion." No one "who has freed his mind of the scholastic formula" can fail, upon examining the "overwhelming mass of exact evidence" available, to recognize "the derivation of the cultural capital of America from South-eastern Asia," though ultimately from Egypt.

S-320

AUTHOR: Smith, Grafton Elliot
DATE: 1933
TITLE: The Diffusion of Culture
IMPRINT: Watts: London

This book is more polemical than descriptive or didactic.

Page 68: In his book *Human History* (1929), he concentrated on the central importance of Greek culture, which reached India (modified of course) by the first century A.D. then to the East Indies (further modified) by the fifth to eight centuries. While in that volume he said virtually nothing about America, now he asserts that, "The identical phase suddenly appeared in Central America" in the seventh and eighth centuries. Notes the "unmistakably Indian [i.e., Asiatic] aspect" of the "earliest culture of Mexico, Central America, and Peru" (page 77).

Pages 72-73: Absent cultural features following a diffusionary episode may be accounted for easily by examining historical cases which teach us about the frequent loss of both practical and esoteric arts.

Pages 84-111: "The Enigma of Prescott" is that after Prescott noted a number of particular cultural parallels of American civilizations to the Old World, such as the calendar and games, he could bring himself to depend on the idea of essential autocthony.

Pages 112-175: Treats Tylor in the same way, but in more detail and harsher. Quotes at length from Tylor's strong arguments for diffusion from parallels, yet he always hedged and seems definitively to have "recanted" his diffusionist views in his last publication, in the 1910 Encyclopedia Britannica [T-178]. Some of Smith's often-published distribution maps are interspersed in this section, notably, on page 127, ear deformation worldwide, and page 129, head deformation.

S-320B

AUTHOR: Smith, Grafton Elliot
DATE: 1969
TITLE: ¿El elefante en América? [The Elephant in America?]
IN: El mundo de la arqueología (Destino: Barcelona), 383-388

See S-300; this must be a translation of one of his early publications.

S-323

AUTHOR: Smith, Hale G.
DATE: 1955

TITLE: Archaeological Significance of Oriental Porcelain in Florida Sites
IN: Florida Anthropologist 8/4:111-116

Brief description of three Florida Indian sites of historic date, supplementing A-030.

S-324
AUTHOR: Smith, Joseph Lindon
DATE: 1956
TITLE: Tombs, Temples and Ancient Art
IMPRINT: University of Oklahoma Press: Norman

Notes "striking features in common between the cultures of the Egyptians and of the Maya," including the flowing vase which symbolized an early Mesopotamian myth of the Milky Way as the life-power of deity, the serpent, and the Tree of Life.

Page 300: He saw no reminder of Maya temples in Cambodia, but in Egypt he found the use of space similar, at least impressionistically.

S-325
AUTHOR: Smith, Joshua Toulmin
DATE: 1839
TITLE: The Northmen in New England, or America in the Tenth Century
IMPRINT: Hilliard, Gray: Boston

A long discussion of the matter cast in the form of a dialogue among fictional gentlemen in Massachusetts, hung on an argument over "Columbus' alleged discovery" of America, the substance based on the Antiqvitates Americanae. A map shows the Vinland areas identified in Massachusetts and Rhode Island. The Irish were also acquainted with the southern parts of North America about the same time that the Northmen discovered the northern parts. Moreover, the Norse sent out explorers who probably reached as far as Carolina and may well have heard about Mexico. Newport Tower, of course, is a Norse ruin.

S-326
AUTHOR: Smith, Marian W.
DATE: 1947
TITLE: House Types of the Middle Fraser River
IN: American Antiquity 12/4:255-267

Ties between northeastern Asia and northwestern America are frequently postulated but have never been satisfactorily worked out in detail. Pit and plank houses have been suggested as evidence for such movement. Her fieldwork suggests that pit houses might once have reached the Pacific Coast in the Lower Fraser valley of British Columbia, hence future discussions of Asiatic-American relations will have to take into consideration the presence of pit houses within easy reach of the sea [thus of diffusion by boat, impliedly].

S-327
AUTHOR: Smith, Marian W.
DATE: 1952
TITLE: Culture Area and Culture Depth: With Data from the Northwest Coast
IN: Indian Tribes of Aboriginal America; Selected Papers of the 29th International Congress of Americanists (New York, 1949), edited by Sol Tax (University of Chicago Press: Chicago), 80-96

Page 95: An early substratum of Arctic traits underlies Northwest Coast culture, and it may have extended into Asia across the northern Pacific. "The distribution of traits across the northern Pacific unequivocally attests to contacts between Northwest Coast and northeastern Asia. The parallels in these regions are specific, unlike those rather shadowy and unsatisfactory (though intriguing) trans-Pacific parallels which are sometimes suggested for more distant areas."

S-328
AUTHOR: Smith, Marian W.
DATE: 1953

TITLE: The Theory behind the Kon-Tiki Expedition
IN: Journal of the Royal Geographical Society 119:471-476

A review of *American Indians in the Pacific,* by Thor Heyerdahl.

Pages 474-475: Supposes that neither the theories of Heyerdahl nor Heine- Geldern can be accepted in toto. Yet "there is no doubt that resemblances in practice exist in areas separated by the Pacific. Some of these, such as the making-of-man cult, are elaborate complexes of associated phenomena; some, like self-torture by hanging from pegs thrust under the muscles of the back, are simpler and may, when full examined, prove to have quite different histories. In either case, the more striking resemblances are those which relate Melanesia or continental Asia with interior sections of the Americas. Thus the problem is even a greater one than that of bridging the Pacific."

A peculiarly stylized facial form in human sculptures appears in Bihar, central India, among the Coast Salish of Washington, and among the Cuna of Panama (citing Archer 1947, plates 13, 14, 44, 45). It is unlike facial forms in other sculptures in those areas and there is no proof that it developed locally. Though we cannot establish contact from such data, the question remains.

Anthropologists have tended to criticize views like Heyerdahl's on very narrow grounds. She as an expert on the Northwest coast can assert that hardly a single one of Heyerdahl's statements about that area is both accurate and complete. Yet considerations such as this should not prejudice readers against his writing which at best is very good.

S-329

AUTHOR: Smith, Michael E.
DATE: 1977-1978
TITLE: A Model for the Diffusion of the Shaft Tomb Complex from South America to West Mexico
IN: Journal of the Steward Anthropological Society 9:179-204 (Urbana, Illinois)

Methodology. Detailed review of the features characterizing the shaft tomb complex of northwestern South America (Panama and Venezuela to Peru, dated from ca. 550 B.C. to the 20th century) and West Mexico (dated only ca. 140 B.C.-A.D. 400) establishes that they are probably directly related. Ethnological parallels are adduced to clarify tomb usages and the meaning of paraphernalia. His model of contact sees the complex carried by sea from South America to West Mexico by a group of traders and shamans around the second century B.C., or by some such "intense, relatively 'noise-free' " communication between the two areas. The ceramics accompanying the tombs rule out the possibility of a large-scale migration of people from Ecuador. Stopping places in Panama and other coastal areas along the way are to be expected. Apparently, however, the shaft tomb complex did not "take" widely throughout Mesoamerica and eventually died out, particularly when Teotihuacan influence penetrated West Mexico.

S-331

AUTHOR: Smith, Robert F.
DATE: 1986
TITLE: Ramses II BYU Exhibit: Supplementary Comments on the Artifacts
IMPRINT: Foundation for Ancient Research and Mormon Studies: Provo, Utah

Page 4: Compares the androgynous Mayan god Itzam-Na (Iguana-House) to Nephthys, NBt-hwt (Lady of the House). The wife of Itzam-Na was the red goddess of painting, Ixchel/Ixchebelyax (compare Mayan "Black and Red" land of writing, Tlillan and Tlapallan, while Egyptians used red headings and black for normal text, terming writing as "words of God; sacred writing.")

Page 5: A Mexican ceramic figure, "The scribe of Cuilapan" (Cuilapan = place of writing) dating to Monte Alban 2 period (circa the time of Christ), displays a seating pattern like that of Egyptian scribes.

Page 6: Fish, symbols of rebirth in Islam and among early Christians, appear on Izapa Stela 5, interpreted by Norman as generally referring to rebirth.

Page 12: Rosettes and radial-whorl designs associated with feline deities in the Old and New Worlds are a symbol of fertility and eternal life in Christian and contemporary non-Christian usage. [Compare the "spiral ornament" of S-316, page 83, and K-007 on the lion rosette.]

S-336

AUTHORS: Smith, Stanley, and Charles Violet
DATE: 1952
TITLE: The Wind Calls the Tune: The Eventful Voyage of the Nova Espero
IMPRINT: Van Nostrand: New York

Small-crew sea voyage.

S-337

AUTHOR: Smith, T. Scott
DATE: 1981
TITLE: Teaching the History of Astronomy; or Seven Challenges for Archaeoastronomy
IN: Archaeoastronomy in the Americas, edited by Ray A. Williamson, Ballena Press Anthropological Papers No. 22 (Ballena Press: Los Altos, California), 350-354

Page 353: One could never accept a totally diffusionistic model for archaeoastronomy like that applied to astro-myth in S-044, but such a book does include interesting suggestions that may serve as hypotheses to be tested by a more intensive study of early astronomies. Two examples: the origin of the worldwide earth-deluge myth in astronomical precession, and the diffusion of the strong-man figure plus animal jawbone motif evident in ethnographic data on the Orion, Taurus, and Hyades region of the sky. The final answer must be some combination of naturally arising ideas fitting local conditions, in conjunction with adoption and modification of ideas from outside.

S-338

AUTHOR: Smith, Watson
DATE: 1971
TITLE: Review of *Man across the Sea: Problems of Pre-Columbian Contacts,* edited by Carroll L. Riley, et al.
IN: Science 174:484

Finds great value in this compendium, but emphasizes the need in any further study of transoceanic diffusion for more "sophisticated theoretical, methodological, and evidentiary standards for handling" the data in broad perspective that transcends isolated element comparison. "The [old] controversy happily now seems to have reached a plane of rationality on which everyone may stand prepared to accept at least the plausibility if not the certainty of transoceanic contacts." Potential implications of the issue are tremendous.

S-339

AUTHOR: Smith, Woodruff
DATE: 1978
TITLE: The Social and Political Origins of German Diffusionist Ethnology
IN: Journal of the History of the Behavioral Sciences 14:103-112

Diffusionism is shown to have had roots in trends of political and social development in 19th century Germany. Several important features of diffusionism, especially the concepts of Lebensraum, of colonization as a natural process, and of the primacy of agriculture in cultural development, in part developed out of conservative political ideologies and reflected the social origins of the early diffusionists in preindustrial segments of the German middle class.

S-339B

AUTHOR: Smithana, Don
DATE: 1990
TITLE: America, Land of the Rising Sun
IMPRINT: The author: Los Angeles

Page 13: A "student of the Japanese language" believes the name *es-kimo* (originally supposed to mean "people who eat sea lions") comes from an archaic language of Japan representing a parent language used by marine immigrants who later spread to North America. He discovered during World War II that Native Americans were able to communicate with Japanese prisoners. Words common among "North American natives" have the same meaning in the ancient language of Japan (e.g., the "Native American" term for corn, that is, maize, was derived from archaic Japanese meshi—meaning "corn porridge").

S-339C

AUTHOR: Smole, William J.
DATE: 1980
TITLE: Musa Cultivation in Pre-Columbian South America
IN: Historical Geography of Latin America, ed. William V. Davidson and James J. Parsons, Geoscience and Man 21:47-50 [special issue]

Presents evidence that some Musa (bananas/plantains) were cultivated in the New World in pre-Columbian times, contrary to the usual view. His ecological and ethnographic studies among the Yanoama Indians in Brazil/Venezuela provide convincing basis for him that their current heavy dependence on plantain cultivation is an old, conservative feature. Cultivated plantains relate to a variety of wild Musa forms in the vicinity. Credible evidence from the Tertiary of Colombia also indicates the presence of a banana [see B-175]. He re-examines the Spanish chroniclers and finds their statements support the indigenous view rather than that the Spaniards exclusively introduced bananas. The evidence overall is not incontrovertible but does support the hypothesis.

S-342

AUTHOR: Snodgrass, Adrian
DATE: 1985
TITLE: The Symbolism of the Stupa
IMPRINT: Cornell University Southeast Asia Program Studies on Southeast Asia: Ithaca, New York

According to the Preface, in 1984 the author was finishing a doctoral dissertation, using Chinese, Indic, pre-Columbian, African, Christian, and Islamic materials to analyze how temporal concepts and cycles of time are incorporated in buildings.

[Many parallels are evident between Mesoamerica and ideas discussed here and deserve careful comparison:] symbolism of the center, sun as center, symbolism of measuring, symbolism of spatial directions, altar, lotus, circle, square, sacred enclosure, axis and pillar, mountain, tree, symbolism of the dome (womb, egg, lotus, cross, mountain), levels, sun door, ascension, parasol, etc.

S-344

AUTHOR: Snow, Dean R.
DATE: 1980
TITLE: The Archaeology of New England
IMPRINT: Academic Press: New York

Brushes aside claims that remains of pre-Columbian European visitors exist in New England, feeling that "the problem [of such 'myths'] will go away if simply ignored."

S-344B

AUTHOR: Snow, Dean R.
DATE: 1968

TITLE: Fact and Fantasy in American Prehistory
IN: NEARA [New England Antiquities Research Association] Journal 3:36

A list of 21 groups supposed by someone or other to be ancestral to the Indians or groups purported to have visited America before Columbus. He says there is no evidence to confirm their presence except in the case of the Norse.

S-345

AUTHOR: Society for Early Historic Archaeology
DATE: 1984
TITLE: Symposium Report
IN: Newsletter and Proceedings of the Society for Early Historic Archaeology 158:7-10 (Provo, Utah)

Pages 9-10: Reports a presentation by B. Urrutia where the Spangler Nodule (a small piece of iron ore) was treated (illustrated). Found about 1800 in Ohio, it bears five inscribed characters. He reads these as "YHWWY" in archaic Hebrew.

S-345B

AUTHOR: Society for Nautical Research
DATE: 1932
TITLE: Report of Meeting: Primitive Craft—Evolution or Diffusion
IN: Mariner's Mirror 18:303-317

February 24th meeting featured a paper by H. H. Brindley, plus other papers and comments of little reported substance by A. C. Haddon, James Hornell, G. S. Laird Clowes, and Lt. Commander Vaughn.

The rivalry of the "evolution" and "independent invention" positions was put initially by Pitt-Rivers and Balfour some years ago. They urged that we not accept an evolutionary explanation for cultural parallels until diffusion had been proven unlikely. They emphasized the innate conservatism of humans, not their inventiveness.

Page 306: Case: the "monitor" type of bark canoe, pointed at both ends under water, without the point feature having any known function, occurs in the Amur River basin and among the Kootenay of British Columbia and Washington, but nowhere else on either continent. Another case: The inverted "V" mast, first appearing in Old Kingdom Egypt, on Borobudur sculptures of the 6th-7th centuries, in Borneo and Eastern Siberia today, on 16th-century balsas of Ecuador and Peru, and still on Lake Titicaca. Another puzzling distribution: deep-cleft in the stem head of canoes, among western Eskimo and in Kamchatka, Hawaii, Samoa, and through to Madagascar (after Müller-Wismar—maybe he was too enthusiastic). But this is something unlikely to have been invented twice. Distribution questions are complicated by "lost arts" as discussed by Pitt-Rivers.

A discussion of sails, the outrigger canoe, balsas, and other "primitive craft" follows, accompanied by a fold-out chart showing a conjectural "genealogy" of some of the forms. Notes the general New World absence of sails. Those on Peruvian balsas are due to Asiatic influence, while on the Eskimo umiak European influence is to be credited. The jangada sail is "doubtless" Portuguese. Certain basic craft, such as the dugout, could arise independently.

S-345C

AUTHOR: Sodders, Betty
DATE: 1991
TITLE: Michigan Prehistory Mysteries, 2 vols.
IMPRINT: Avery Color Studios: Au Train, Michigan

A local enthusiast's report on her decades-long investigation of the Newberry Stone and other artifacts revealed in Michigan in the late 19th century. [See M-319.]

S-345D

AUTHOR: Sodders, Betty
DATE: 1994
TITLE: McGruer's Gods and the Newberry Stone
IN: The Ancient American 1/5:24-26 (Colfax, Wisconsin)

Discusses the history of the finding of and early reporting on human effigy figures found with the Newberry Tablet. Gives Fell's translation of the tablet which he claims was in "Hittite-Minoan" language. There are vague similarities in the "statues" to figures from archaeological cultures in the Balkans.

S-348

AUTHOR: Solari, Benjamín T.
DATE: 1928
TITLE: Ensayo de filología; breve vocabulario Español-Guaraní con las relaciones etimológicas del idioma americano
[Essay in Philology: Brief Spanish-Guaraní Vocabulary with Etymological Relations of the American Language]
IMPRINT: "Coni": Buenos Aires [2nd edition 1944]

He finds Sanskrit, Latin, Greek, and Arabic roots in Guaraní.

S-351

AUTHOR: Solheim, Wilhelm G., II
DATE: 1968
TITLE: "World Ethnographic Sample . . ." A Possible Historical Explanation
IN: American Anthropologist 70:569

A letter to the editor comments on S-081. The authors had observed in their factor analysis of Murdock's World Ethnographic Sample a puzzling clustering of characteristics for four regions: South America, Insular Pacific, East Eurasia, and Africa. They could see no basis for a diffusionary connection so put down the "striking congruence" as unexplainable.

Solheim suggests that if Southeast Asia is considered as a diffusion source linking East Eurasia with Africa (via Madagascar especially), and also with Oceania and on to South America, an explanation of the similarities by diffusion becomes acceptable. If a new cluster analysis were to be done, he would expect Southeast Asia to fall in the middle, validating his hypothesis of diffusion.

S-355

AUTHOR: Soper, Fred L.
DATE: 1927
TITLE: The Report of a Nearly Pure "Ancylostoma duodenale" Infestation in Native South American Indians and a Discussion of Its Ethnological Significance
IN: American Journal of Hygiene 7:174-184

Distribution suggests that the intestinal parasite A. duodenale was introduced to South America by ancient migrations from Indonesia or Polynesia. Cold climate in the Arctic would have interrupted the life cycle of the parasitic organism and thus precludes the possibility that the introduction to America came by way of Bering Strait.

S-357

AUTHOR: Sorenson, John L.
DATE: 1952
TITLE: Evidences of Culture Contacts between Polynesia and the Americas in Precolumbian Times
IMPRINT: Unpublished; M.A. thesis, Brigham Young University

After a chapter on the problem of diffusion to America, a history of thought on the topic involving Polynesia, and criteria for evidence, materials are laid out in nine chapters under headings derived from the Human Relations Area Files.

Pages 22-36: A linguistically naive but provocative list of nearly 200 Polynesian morphemes [the author had previously written a grammar of a Polynesian language, Rarotongan] with sound-alike equivalents in many American Indian and some Old World languages ("to draw to the attention of competent linguists a large body of possible evidence of inter-cultural contact" which they might well investigate).

Pages 37ff.: Documented items discussed include, in part, poetic parallelistic couplets, quipu, signalling by fire/smoke, signal drums or gongs, digging stick, fertilizer use, terracing, irrigation, pits excavated to water level for planting, ethnobotany (cotton, sweet potato, gourd, plantain, banana, coconut, Pachyrrhizus, hibiscus, Dioscorea alata, Heliconia bihai, Argemone alba, and others), fattened (non-barking, "hairless") dogs for food, shell fish hooks (single-piece and composite), fish poisoning, several food-preparation artifacts, storage pits, masticated fermented drinks, poncho, feather cloaks, mosaics of glued feathers, turbans and other headdresses, various ornaments including earplugs (sometimes in distended ear holes), composite comb, plaited fan, parasol, skull deformation, tattooing, bark-cloth complex, weaving/loom, coiled basketry, twined-root textile weaving, slab stone work, stone ditch, stone balls, stone weapon forms from metal prototypes, pumpdrill, houseforms, wooden pillows and seats, sliding panel door, polished stone mirrors, sacred plazas, stepped mounds and related features, astronomical function of mounds (sighting), men's house, fortification features, moon goddess/weaving/jade/female complex, Quetzalcoatl-Lono parallels, idols/oracles, reptilian links with water, bird deities, moth/butterfly/souls, shark god, tree of life/world tree, layered heavens, omphalos, stone burial cist, canoe burial, mummification, attendants slain on death of master, codex/rongorongo burial with priest, sacrifice complex, circumcision (insection), "turning the mat" rite, life-cycle rites, isolation of virgin girls, taboo breach causing illness—confession producing cure, divination methods, fire-walking, many sports/games, gambling, stamped designs, negative "painting," bead drilled from two directions, double-headed figures, exaggerated eye-ring on stone figures, panpipe and other musical instruments, stilts in ceremonial dancing, marionettes, sacred number five, numeration systems, calendar features, various water craft, litter, carrying pole, blood groups. Word comparisons are pointed out for each topic where applicable. Chronological data for America are given where possible.

Concludes that abundant parallels seem to call for diffusionist explanations, at least in part, yet the lack of consistent geographical clustering leaves the picture unclear. Finally, with a number of qualifiers attached, he proposes at least a "basic Oceanic" connection with the Andean and tropical forest areas by 1000 B.C., possible movement from Ecuador westward between A.D. 300 and 700, and possible contact from the Northwest Coast to Hawaii in the first centuries of the Christian era.

S-358

AUTHOR:	Sorenson, John L.
DATE:	1955
TITLE:	Some Mesoamerican Traditions of Immigration by Sea
IN:	El México Antiguo 8:425-439 (México)

A review of accounts reporting settlement in Mesoamerica via navigation across the sea, such as from Ixtlilxochitl, Sahagun, and Torquemada.

[Victor von Hagen enlightens us about this piece and its author in a footnote in his potboiler, *The Aztec: Man and Tribe*: "This was written by a resident of Utah and a Mormon. There are two aspects of this church, one the respected community of hard-working, God-fearing, God-in-my-heart people, and the other, the history-twisters. They attempt, as this book *(sic)* exemplifies, using every device in archaeology, to 'prove' that the American Indians were Jews. . . . Any theory which advances the cause of 'peopling the Americas' by sea, rafts, balsas, they pursue to delirium. Every natural and explainable Indian motif is transmuted into symbols which will prove the theme of 'The American Indians are Jews.' " Moreover, he claims that the Mormons support their archaeological work in Mexico by selling gold plates!]

S-361

AUTHOR: Sorenson, John L.

DATE: 1971

TITLE: The Significance of an Apparent Relationship between the Ancient Near East and Mesoamerica

IN: Man across the Sea: Problems of Pre-Columbian Contacts, edited by Carroll L. Riley, et al. (University of Texas Press: Austin), 219-241

The paper aims chiefly to point out the theoretical and methodological significance of evidences for diffusion from the Near East to Mesoamerica, and to make public a neglected body of that evidence by citing an extensive literature.

The model employed is derived from the studies of Kroeber and Hewes who characterized an Old World cultural ecumene (oikoumene) extending, finally, from Iberia to Japan. They describe that diffusion sphere in terms of hundreds of traits which had come to be generally shared throughout it by the 15th century. Sorenson asks whether those ecumenical traits can be found in Mesoamerica and notes other features of the same order of complexity and arbitrariness where they appear in both Near Eastern and Mesoamerican culture areas.

Of the 200 features used by Hewes and Kroeber to characterize the Old World ecumene, one in eight reappear in Mesoamerica and another one tenth may prove shared as well. The author believes that this suggests "at least a generic connection between the two areas, although not a strong one." Moreover the shared features are in many cases culturally central, not merely peripheral. This evidence makes it "plausible, and perhaps necessary, to interpret the rise of civilization in Mesoamerica as significantly dependent upon communication from . . . Eurasia."

If significant historical connections link the two areas, "then there can be no ultimately satisfying scientific answer to the question of how men became civilized, for there will be but a single case of the phenomenon," not two which could serve as controls on each other. He also commends Kroeber's dictum that an assumption of independent invention calls for as much supporting evidence as does one of diffusion or migration, a point almost universally neglected in studies of American cultures. Finally, "an evolutionary . . . anthropology that fails to control for historical diffusion seems to rest on grounds potentially as weak as . . . unrestrained diffusionism."

Shared features listed in an appendix, each with introductory documentation, include: 22 elements under the heading "Temple and Its Platform"; at least 17 elements under the heading "Astronomy, Calendar, Writing"; 13 under "Burial"; 19 under "Incense and Incense Furniture"; 4 under "Standing Stones as Cult Objects"; 8 under "Figurines"; 20 under "Sacrifice Complex"; 11 under "Lustration"; 3 relating to "Divination"; 9 under "Snake Symbolism"; 5 under "Feline Symbolism"; 4 under "Mountain/Rain/Cloud Divinity"; 8 connected with "Tree"; 24 connected with "Aesthetic Features and Motifs"; 9 involving cosmological features; 11 under "Kingship Complex"; more than 25 under "Technology"; and others.

S-362

AUTHOR: Sorenson, John L.

DATE: 1971-1972

TITLE: A Collection of References to Trans-oceanic Contacts with the Americas before the Recognized Discoveries

IN: NEARA [New England Antiquities

Research Association] Journal 67:38-40, 78-80

Superseded by the present bibliography.

S-363

AUTHOR: Sorenson, John L.
DATE: 1976
TITLE: The Book of Mormon as a Mesoamerican Codex
IN: Newsletter and Proceedings of the Society for Early Historic Archaeology 139 (December): 1-7 (Provo, Utah)

Discussion and a table show that a large number of stylistic features, motifs, concepts and beliefs were shared in Mesoamerica, the Near East, and the text of The Book of Mormon.

S-364

AUTHOR: Sorenson, John L.
DATE: 1977
TITLE: Review of *America B.C.,* by Barry Fell
IN: Brigham Young University Studies 17:375-377

Appreciative of the enterprise but critical of the methods, logic, and resulting interpretations.

S-365

AUTHOR: Sorenson, John L.
DATE: 1981
TITLE: Wheeled Figurines in the Ancient World
IN: Preliminary Report SOR-81, Foundation for Ancient Research and Mormon Studies, Provo, Utah

A substantial, though unpolished, survey of the literature is given under the headings "The Mesoamerican Wheeled Figurines," "Function," "Wheels and Movement in Mesoamerican Belief," and "Wheeled Figurines in the Old World." In Mesoamerica the dates range from at least 100 B.C. to the time of the Spanish Conquest. In the Old World, they began around 3500 B.C. and continued through the medieval era, the earliest specimens being from Mesopotamia.

In both hemispheres a variety of animal figures are directly wheeled or (in the Old World) pull a wheeled wagon or chariot: dogs, deer, felines (underworld-associated in both areas), horses, and hybrids. In both hemispheres strong solar connection is evident, obviously tied with the wheel itself as well as with movement across the sky (also with Tlaloc and his rings/circles).

Animal companions for the deceased into the underworld are clearly represented in both hemispheres; for example, the figurines are often burial/tomb/death connected, and a solar regeneration/resurrection sense is plain. An Egyptian and Mexican parallel is the notion of death as the eating of the sun/corpse/companion animal, followed the next cycle by birth/ regeneration from the womb of either the overarching sky goddess, Egyptian Nut, or Aztec underlying earth-goddess Tlaltecuhtli. Corpses (or deity figures?) are carried in Old World chariots, presumably to the west/underworld; in Mesoamerica examples are known that have a human figure (figurine) riding atop a wheeled platform or vehicle, presumably in some sort of cultic action. (At the same time showing that the concept of a functional wheeled vehicle, not a mere "toy," was grasped.) Also, in the Old World the dead sometimes rode on an animal to the underworld/death, and in Mesoamerica several representations of humans astride animals are known.

The number of elements involved in what seems a cultic complex associated with death/regeneration/sun/guardian animal in both hemispheres calls for a diffusionist explanation.

S-366

AUTHOR: Sorenson, John L.
DATE: 1985

TITLE: An Ancient American Setting for the Book of Mormon
IMPRINT: Foundation for Ancient Research and Mormon Studies, and Deseret Book: Salt Lake City

While laying out a "plausible" model for articulating the picture of culture and society presented in the Book of Mormon with the history and culture of central Mesoamerica, at one point the author recapitulates material in S-361.

There is some added information, e.g., page 186, compares Hebrew *pol* (bean), and Mayan *bol* or *bul* (bean); and page 279, cites literature showing that reconstructed morphemes for "metal" in three Mesoamerican language families are dated by the respective linguists to the second millennium B.C., two millennia prior to the conventional date for the beginning of metallurgy.

S-366B

AUTHORS: Sorenson, John L., and Martin H. Raish
DATE: 1990
TITLE: Pre-Columbian Contact with the Americas across the Oceans: An Annotated Bibliography, vol. 1
IMPRINT: Research Press: Provo, Utah

Pages x-xi. This portion of the introduction is headed "Interim Conclusions." The following points are made briefly by the authors: (1) technological capability to cross the oceans successfully has been available at a number of possible departure points in the Old World fairly often in the past; (2) it is both plausible and probable that numerous voyages did cross the oceans at several points; (3) the substantial evidence available can be mustered to support this view; (4) too little theory is available to conclude how substantial were the impacts of those crossings on cultures in America; (5) instances of convergence or independent invention probably did take place aside from diffusion/migration.

S-367

AUTHOR: Soto Hall, Máximo
DATE: 1937
TITLE: Los Mayas [The Mayas]
IMPRINT: Editorial Labor: Barcelona

Claims that the Egyptians were Mayas transplanted to the Nile, which is a Maya name.

S-369

AUTHOR: Soustelle, Jacques
DATE: 1967
TITLE: Mexico (Archaeologia Mundi)
IMPRINT: Nagel: Geneva; and World: Cleveland and New York

Pages 169-170: We are left with a number of similarities between Mexico and the Old World which cannot be explained away as mere chance resemblances, as shown by Tylor, Graebner, Hentze, Rivet, Heine-Geldern, and Ekholm. Indians derived from prehistoric Asia via the Bering Strait invented for themselves the basics of their civilizations, yet the origins of the advanced civilizations of Mexico, and of the Olmec in particular, still remain mysterious. "We certainly cannot exclude the possibility that particular cultural features may have travelled from the Old World to the New."

S-371

AUTHOR: Spaulding, Albert C.
DATE: 1946
TITLE: Northeastern Archaeology and General Trends in the Northern Forest Zone
IN: Man in Northeastern North America, edited by Frederick Johnson (Phillips Academy: Andover, Massachusetts), 143-167

On the basis of parallels evident between artifacts spread from northeastern Europe all the way to northeastern North America, he supposes that the northern boreal zone has been a medium of long-continued contacts between Eurasia and North America.

S-373

AUTHOR: Speck, Frank G.
DATE: 1941
TITLE: Art Processes in Birchbark of the River Desert Algonquin, a Circumboreal Trait
IN: Smithsonian Institution, Bureau of American Ethnology Bulletin 128, Anthropological Paper 17 (Washington, D.C.), 229-274

Curvilinear treatments of plants and animals were definitely present earlier despite frequent statements in the literature that such treatments only originated under the influence of modern European invaders.

S-375

AUTHOR: Speiser, Ephraim
DATE: 1935
TITLE: Excavations at Tepe Gawra, vol. 1
IMPRINT: University of Pennsylvania Press: Philadelphia

Plate LXXIV, page 204: An object the same shape as a Mesoamerican mushroom stone [incense cloud?]

Pages 68-76: "Chariot models" and wheeled animal figurines found at the site, dating as early as early Copper Age, are discussed. The prototype animal seems to be a haltered dog.

S-376

AUTHOR: Spence, Lewis
DATE: 1907
TITLE: The Mythologies of Ancient Mexico and Peru
IMPRINT: Archibald Constable: London

Pages 71-76: The Skraelings met by the Norse had none of the characteristics of "the Red Man," so they must have represented a race with Eskimo affinities whom the Mongoloid Red Indians replaced after A.D. 1000, at least on "the prairies of North-east America." There is a slight possibility that Buddhist priests from Asia visited Central America in the fifth century. However, the religions of Mexico and Peru were of indigenous origin and are explicable by "the well known law" that similar environments produce through evolution similar religious beliefs in widely separated areas. As to the reported "white man," Quetzalcoatl, he thinks that it would be interesting to consider him in light of European myths which speak of men who set out for America and of "white tribes" in America. The Irish might be involved or Madoc.

S-378

AUTHOR: Spence, Lewis
DATE: 1914
TITLE: The Myths of the North American Indians
IMPRINT: Crowell: New York

Summarizes theories of Indian origin, including Welsh and Jewish connections as well as "evidence of Asiatic intercourse." Norse contacts are discussed in a standard manner.

Page 248: He takes folklore about small people as a record of "perhaps the last vestiges of a pigmy folk who at one time inhabited the eastern portion of North America."

S-378B

AUTHOR: Spence, Lewis
DATE: 1925
TITLE: Atlantis in America
IMPRINT: Ernest Benn: London

His thesis is that notable cultural similarities between Eurasia and America involved Atlantis from which those features moved both eastward and westward when the continent sank (he scoffs at Elliot Smith's "children of the sun"). In the course of his argument he presents information on supposed parallels which could have meaning for some diffusionists apart from the Atlantean supposition. On his treatment of witchcraft (pages 122-133) see S-379, a fuller treatment. Other sections discuss interesting, if at times imaginative and undocumented, bodies of information on lore and legend, religion (including mysteries and secret societies), mummies, "ethnology" (i.e., biological groups), and art and architecture.

S-379

AUTHOR: Spence, Lewis
DATE: 1930
TITLE: The Magic and Mysteries of Mexico; or, the Arcane Secrets and Occult Lore of the Ancient Mexicans and Mayas
IMPRINT: Rider: London
[Reprinted under title *Arcane Secrets and Occult Lore of Mexico and Mayan Central America; A Treasury of Magic, Astrology, Witchcraft, Demonology, and Symbolism* (B. Ethridge: Detroit, 1973)]

Pages 129-136: The cult of the witch was as general in Mexico as in Europe and Asia, and in its American form it bore so startling a resemblance to the witchcraft of the Old World that it is difficult not to believe that both can be referred back to a common origin. The patroness of the witches, Tlazolteotl, flew through the air on a broomstick and was depicted as a traditional European witch with peaked bark hat, accompanied by an owl, revelling at a cross road, etc. The "exact parallel" of these features accompanying the Haunting Mothers and their patroness seems complete and should provide those who regard witchcraft as European with considerable food for thought. Some similarities also prevail to Siberian shamanism.

Page 140: It is strange that in America, where no horse suitable for riding was known, the notion of riding on the broom is found, which looks like it had been an imported notion.

Page 142: Believes that Mexican witchcraft originated from the Azilian area of Spain (chief home of the broom-riding witch-cult in late Middle Age Europe) and the shamanism of Siberia. And there may have been influence from Druidic Britain, where, according to Caesar in the first century, the British peoples were capable of building ships much larger and more seaworthy than those of the Romans. May not Quetzalcoatl have been a Druid priest?

Page 274: The mysteries of Mexico display a decided resemblance to those of the Old World and were the same in essence as in the eastern hemisphere, though with novel features. We must think of the cult of Quetzalcoatl as a mystery cult; Quetzalcoatl seems like Dionysus or Osiris. In Mexico we find as nowhere else but Persia a distinct dualism of good and evil, together with a ball-game between the good and evil deities which figures so large in Iranian as in Mexican belief.

S-380

AUTHOR: Spence, Lewis
DATE: 1951
TITLE: Divination (American)
IN: Encyclopedia of Religion and Ethics, edited by James Hastings (Scribner's: New York), 4:780-783

Astrology in Old and New Worlds. Divination among Aztecs by flight and song of birds [as in the Mediterranean].

S-381

AUTHOR: Spence, Lewis
DATE: n.d. [c. 1953]
TITLE: Folk-lore of "The Popol Vuh"
IN: Proceedings of the 30th International Congress of Americanists (Cambridge, England, 1952), pages 50-53

"In its pages very numerous folk-lore commonplaces such as are to be encountered in European, Asiatic, and African folk-tales and sagas make their appearance." The gods Hurakan and Gucumatz have several analogies in European and Asiatic myth, more especially in

Celtic and Teutonic. Twin deities are familiar in European and Asiatic myth, identified as sun and moon. Xquiq, goddess of fertility, is associated with the underworld as in European myth. Toothache-caused-by-worm was also in Babylonia and Scotland. The ball-game has quite a number of analogies in European games, and has stellar significance. Pickaxes and hoes working automatically for Hunahpu reminds one of European and Asiatic fairy stories. The list of royal regalia is precisely what we would expect to find in Europe or Asia: throne, mantle, dais, jewelry, feathers, standards, etc. [Compare H-398.]

S-382

AUTHORS: Spencer, Joseph E., and G. A. Hale
DATE: 1961
TITLE: The Origin, Nature, and Distribution of Agricultural Terracing
IN: Pacific Viewpoint 2/1:1-40

Note common presence of elaborate agricultural terraces in China and Peru. The feature could have spread to America across either Pacific or Atlantic.

S-382B

AUTHOR: Spennemann, Dirk H. R. (text by)
DATE: 1988
TITLE: Pathways to the Tongan Past: An Exhibition of Three Decades of Modern Archaeology in the Kingdom of Tonga (1957 to 1987)
IMPRINT: Tongan National Centre: Nuku'alofa, Tonga [Booklet prepared by the Research School of Pacific Studies, Australian National University]

Page 13: Domesticated animals in Lapita times (1500 B.C.) included chicken and pig, but not dogs until much later. [No date is given for introduction of the sweet potato.]

Page 20: The famous stone gateway structure, Ha'amonga-'a-Maui on Tongatapu, was constructed in the 12th century A.D. [it is cited by some diffusionists as "megalithic"].

Page 22: The earliest Tongan canoe type was double-hulled with fixed bow, which could not tack against the wind and was unwieldy to handle. It was replaced only in the 17th century by a more versatile type built by Samoan craftsmen.

S-384

AUTHOR: Spier, Leslie
DATE: 1927
TITLE: Review of *Culture, the Diffusion Controversy*, by Grafton Elliot Smith, et al.
IN: Journal of American Folk-Lore 40:415-416

A condescending treatment showing the reasonableness of Spier and the three orthodox writers in the volume under review as against the "mechanical" picture of diffusion Smith is said to support.

S-385

AUTHOR: Spier, Leslie
DATE: 1929
TITLE: Review of *The Building of Cultures*, by Roland B. Dixon
IN: American Anthropologist 31:140-145

Considers it a good sketch of orthodox Americanist thought of that day, while scorning "the almost ribald heliolithic theory" as well as kulturkreislehre. Also rejects Wissler's environmentalism and expresses interest in more rigorous data. He thinks Kroeber's piece on stimulus diffusion "swung too far" in opening the gates to diffusion.

S-386

AUTHOR: Spier, Robert F. G.
DATE: 1951
TITLE: Some Notes on the Origin of Taro

IN: Southwestern Journal of Anthropology 7:69-76

It is probable that the plant (Colocasia) has been cultivated in Southeast Asia during the past 2000-2500 years, and it likely originated there, perhaps in Assam. It was used in Egypt and China by the beginning of our era. It is used now in the U.S. and West Indies, where "its presence is in no sense aboriginal." [Others claim that taro in America was aboriginal.]

S-387

AUTHORS: Spiess, Gerry, and Marlin Bree
DATE: 1982
TITLE: Alone against the Atlantic
IMPRINT: Souvenir: London

Voyage in a small boat from Norfolk, Virginia, to England in 1979.

S-388

AUTHOR: Spinden, Herbert J.
DATE: 1916a
TITLE: Pre-Columbian Representations of the Elephant in America
IN: Nature 96/2413:592-593

Argues that the "elephant" figures near the top of Stela B at Copan represent macaws.

S-389

AUTHOR: Spinden, Herbert J.
DATE: 1916b
TITLE: The Question of the Zodiac in America
IN: American Anthropologist 18:53-80

"In all his papers Mr. Hagar has not presented a single sound and convincing argument . . . that the classical zodiac was introduced from the Old World into America." He even doubts "dependable proof of the existence of any sort of zodiac in the New World." "There are a small number of anthropologists, such as Graebner, who have assumed an historical explanation for the close similarities in ideas, in social and religious structures, and in material art that are found between otherwise distinct peoples in the New and Old Worlds. The weight of evidence indicates that these similarities should be explained by psychic unity and convergent evolution, rather than by contact and transmission." [See H-020 for the original work and H-023 for a rejoinder.]

S-390

AUTHOR: Spinden, Herbert J.
DATE: 1917
TITLE: The Origin and Distribution of Agriculture in America
IN: Proceedings of the 19th International Congress of Americanists (Washington, 1915), pages 269-276

Pages 271-272: It behooves us not to assume lightly that any cultivated plant was common to both the Old World and the New before the coming of Columbus until botanists establish the fact beyond doubt. The weight of anthropological science is strongly against over-sea transmission as an easy explanation of enigmas in human culture. Lagenaria vulgaris and Gossypium, yes, but they are fitted by nature to be distributed long distances by wind and water thus from Old to New World. The case for the coconut made by Cook is not convincing, and Laufer explained away the claims for pre-Columbian use of maize in China before Collins made them.

S-391

AUTHOR: Spinden, Herbert J.
DATE: 1924
TITLE: New World Correlations
IN: Proceedings of the 21st International Congress of Americanists (Part 1, The Hague, 1924), pages 76-86

If American civilizations were independent of those in the Old World "in all the higher reaches of achievement," then he feels that "such parallels as do occur . . . have a tremendous bearing on the innate potentialities of mankind." His generalized comparisons of agriculture, textiles, metals, the calendar, diseases ("It does not appear that a single important disease of parasitic type was common" to the two areas), etc., leads him to conclude that American Indians were notably inventive and that they "achieved by far the greater portion of their culture in the New World without occult [*sic*] help from the dominant civilization of the Old World."

Specifics: glazing on pottery was used in the New World to a limited extent [it has often been said that it did not occur at all], as a kind of self-glazing pottery in Salvador and southern Guatemala [plumbate], and a true glaze paint used by Pueblo tribes of New Mexico. In Costa Rica a light bluish color paint on pottery was possibly from the purpura shell fish. Mentions American indigo "distinct from Asiatic indigo," as well as the cochineal and purple dye from a species of Murex ("a nice example of the independent seizing of similar resources in nature. The American murex differs in species from the Mediterranean and Indian ones, and could not have been transported.") Another parallel with the Old World was the preparation of rubber from the coagulated latex of the Castilla elastica [in fact this was not Old World].

S-392

AUTHOR: Spinden, Herbert J.
DATE: 1928
TITLE: Origin of Civilization in Central America and Mexico
IMPRINT: Privately printed: New York

See S-393.

S-393

AUTHOR: Spinden, Herbert J.
DATE: 1933
TITLE: Origin of Civilizations in Central America and Mexico
IN: The American Aborigines: Their Origin and Antiquity, A Collection of Papers by Ten Authors, Assembled and Edited by Diamond Jenness. Published for Presentation at the Fifth Pacific Science Congress (Canada, 1933), (University of Toronto Press: Toronto), 217-246 [Reprinted Russell and Russell: New York, 1972]

Students of the higher civilizations of the American tropics are "beset with diffusionist doctrines" with which he has no patience. Surely, the "American civilizations rise from a Neolithic platform." "The fact that no food plant is common to the two hemispheres is enough to offset any number of petty puzzles in arts and myths."

S-395

AUTHORS: Spjeldnaes, Nils, and Kari E. Henningsmoen
DATE: 1938
TITLE: Littorina littorea: An Indicator of Norse Settlement in North America?
IN: Science 141:275-276

It is suggested that the originally European species of the mollusk Littorina littorea, was introduced to North America by Norse settlers about A.D. 1000. Its subfossil distribution might be used to trace the extent of Norse travel in this region, for L. littorea is a hardy species that can survive for a long time in the bottom water of open boats.

S-396

AUTHOR: Spoehr, Alexander
DATE: 1951
TITLE: A Close Look at "Kon-Tiki"
IN: Chicago Natural History Museum Bulletin 22/7

Page 6: Strongly critical.

S-397

AUTHOR: Spranz, Bodo, editor
DATE: 1984
TITLE: Boote: Technik und Symbolik; die Schiffahrt in aussereuropäischen Kulturen [Ships: Technique and Symbolism; Voyaging in Non-European Cultures]
IN: Veröffentlichungen 5-6 (Museum für Völkerkunde der Stadt: Freiburg im Breisgau)

A good museum handbook with sections written by museum staff on the Near East, South Asia, Southeast Asia, North Asia, East Asia, Oceania (the three -nesias separate), Australia, North America, South America, and Africa, with an additional treatment of magical-religious aspects of boats. Discussions are brief—the section on Micronesia covers a dozen pages. Illustrations often use artifacts or models from the museum.

S-398

AUTHOR: Sprengling, Martin
DATE: 1933
TITLE: Scapulimantia and the Mongols
IN: American Anthropologist 35:134-137

A 12th century Syriac commentary on an obscure term in Leviticus 19:31 relating to soothsaying says that Israelite diviners read the shoulder blades of sheep. Sprengling believes that knowledge about the Mongol court coming into western Asia at the time the commentater wrote explains this attribution of scapulimancy to ancient Israel. [Scapulimancy is sometimes cited as an interhemispheric parallel.]

S-399

AUTHOR: Spriggs, Matthew
DATE: 1984
TITLE: Early Coconut Remains from the South Pacific
IN: Journal of the Polynesian Society 93:71-76

Radiocarbon dates on coconut remains excavated on Aneityum Island, Vanuatu, reach the fourth millennium B.C., prior to human settlement. Other possible early coconut remains are discussed. These dates support the idea that coconuts were distributed by natural means [at least in the western Pacific]. They also suggest an Indo-Pacific source for this plant rather than a Central American one with human carriage of the seed, as claimed by Heyerdahl.

S-400

AUTHOR: Sprinzin, Noemie G.
DATE: 1930
TITLE: The Blowgun in America, Indonesia, and Oceania
IN: Proceedings of the 23rd International Congress of Americanists (New York, 1928), pages 699-704

She points out similarities between Indonesian and New World blowguns and other elements of a "complex." For example, wadding for the dart, poison, and use in hunting small game. Based on material in the USSR Museum of Anthropology and Ethnography, she extends Friederici's work. Forms, materials, and uses in the two hemispheres are very similar. A map is included based on Friederici. Recommends careful comparative study of relevant names, as those provided by Friederici for America are mostly European derived.

S-401

AUTHOR: Spuhler, J. S.
DATE: 1979
TITLE: Genetic Distances, Trees, and Maps of North American Indians
IN: The First Americans: Origins, Affinities, and Adaptations, edited by William S. Laughlin and Albert B. Harper (Gustav Fischer, New York), 135-183

Gene frequencies for 53 groups are arranged as genetic trees in comparison with languages and culture area. The associations are not, of course, perfect. In fact, genetic distances classify tribes into their culture area only 58.5% of the time. [Thus significant biological variation occurs among culture sharers. Compare C-328, C-334.]

S-403

AUTHOR: Squier, Ephraim G., editor
DATE: 1860
TITLE: Carta dirijida al Rey de España; Collection of Rare and Original Documents and Relations Concerning the Discovery and Conquest of America; Chiefly from the Spanish Archives
IMPRINT: Charles B. Norton: New York

Page 71: In Central America, blood was collected from a sacrificed animal and scattered ritually over the area about the altar. [Compare Leviticus 4:5-7.]

S-404

AUTHOR: Squier, Ephraim G.
DATE: 1870
TITLE: The Primeval Monuments of Peru Compared with Those in Other Parts of the World
IN: American Naturalist 4:1-17

Compares chullpas (circular stone towers) of Peru with cromlechs, dolmens, etc., of Europe and Asia. These were erected by a population in Peru "identical in degree and stage of development" with people in the Old World who built stonework. [Whether diffusion is intended as an explanation is not clear; probably not.]

S-405

AUTHOR: Squier, Ephraim G.
DATE: 1871-1872
TITLE: The Arch in America
IN: Journal of the Anthropological Institute of New York 1:78-80

Cites impostures of true arches. There is only one genuine arch that he knows of, in the ruins of Pachacamac, Peru, a building of Inca origin: "a perfect, well-turned arch." "It is said that arches are also found among the aboriginal monuments in the vicinity of Tumbez, Northern Peru," but at present he considers these "entirely enigmatical." Given even one example, however, he asks how could use of the principle not have been more widespread?

S-406

AUTHOR: Squire, John
DATE: 1952
TITLE: The Theory behind the Voyage of the Kon Tiki
IN: Illustrated London News 221/5913 (16 August): 248

Strongly negative.

S-407

AUTHOR: Stafford, Harry E.
DATE: 1959
TITLE: The Early Inhabitants of the Americas
IMPRINT: Vantage: New York

A kind of handbook of American Indians a la John Collier with the section on "origin" being an uncritical Book of Mormon summary.

S-408

AUTHORS: Standley, Paul C., and Salvador Calderón
DATE: 1925
TITLE: Lista preliminar de las plantas de El Salvador [Preliminary List of the Plants of El Salvador]
IMPRINT: Tipografía La Unión, Dutriz Hermanos: San Salvador

Page 213: They consider Cucurbita ficifolia (chilacayote) to be of Asiatic origin, although it has since been considered American by Vavilov and others.

S-408B

AUTHOR: Stanton, Kevin

DATE: 1990

TITLE: Visitors to America in pre-Columbian Time

IMPRINT: Unpublished; M.A. Thesis, University of Arizona [University Microfilms International, Order No. 1340264]

Done under Vine Deloria in the American Indian Studies program. Competently surveys conventional archaeologists' picture of Amerindian origins, the variety of diffusionist/migrationist proposals, and mentions tribal traditions which picture autocthonist origin. Treats the history of nineteenth-century American views culminating in the Smithsonian Institution's establishing the dogma of no ocean-borne visitors before Columbus. He then continues a history-of-science critique up to current issues.

The Bat Creek Tablet episode is reprised and the revival of concern due to Mertz, Mahan, and Gordon. In the course of that treatment, Stanton reports Traveler Bird's claim that the Sequoyah script was adapted from an earlier native writing system. Stanton checked that point with Dr. Robert Thomas, "a member of the Cherokee tribe and an expert on the history of the syllabary," who affirmed that Sequoyah was indeed the inventor and Bird's claim was "a fraud." He also recapitulates McCulloch's work, observing, "Will the Bat Creek tablet be, for the Hebrews and other Old World visitors, what L'Anse aux Meadows was for the Norse?" "The whole Bat Creek sequence presents serious problems indicating that perhaps mound evidence has not been properly handled." His investigations (which involved site visits—including Crack Cave on his won—and interviews with scholars) "revealed an apparent contempt and nearly total disregard fostered by most rank and file establishment scientists against pre-Columbian contact research."

Other positive but judicious treatments are of Fell, epigraphy, rock art (especially labyrinth and Tanit motifs), ogam, the "Oklarado" archaeoastronomy sites, Farley, New England stone chambers, the "Blanchard Stone" of Vermont, Peterborough, Lake Superior copper mining, a North Atlantic Archaic maritime cultural continuum, Valdivia, and, at some length, the Los Lunas Stone and the Tucson artifacts. The literature cited is broad-based if not completely up-to-date and comprehensive.

S-409

AUTHORS: Stanton, W. R., and F. Willett

DATE: 1963

TITLE: Archaeological Evidence for Changes in Maize Type in West Africa: An Experiment in Technique

IN: Man 63:117-123

An attempt at refutation of Stonor and Anderson and Jeffreys that Asia and Africa had maize before Columbus.

S-411

AUTHOR: Starr, Chester G.

DATE: 1941

TITLE: The Roman Imperial Navy, 31 B.C.–A.D. 324

IMPRINT: Cornell University Press: Ithaca [2nd edition, Barnes and Noble: New York, 1960. Reprinted Greenwood: Westport, Connecticut, 1975]

Page; 152-155: Comment on "the unsuitability of Mediterranean craft in the [open Atlantic] ocean." Roman warships reached as far as the northern end of Britain only once, according to the documents.

Page 175: Roman naval operations in the Red Sea were unsuccessful and in the Indian Ocean were impractible.

S-412

AUTHOR: Starr, Frederick
DATE: 1900
TITLE: Mexican Paper
IN: American Antiquarian and Oriental Journal 22:301-309

Sees significance in the similarity of Polynesian, Tlingit, and Mexican bark-beaters. They are reinforcing, but not strong, evidence of borrowing.

S-413

AUTHOR: Starr, Richard F. S.
DATE: 1937, 1939
TITLE: Nuzi; Report on the Excavation at Yorgan Tepe near Kirkuk, Iraq, Conducted by Harvard University in Conjunction with the American School of Oriental Research and the University Museum of Philadelphia, 1927-1931, 2 vols.
IMPRINT: Harvard University Press: Cambridge, Massachusetts

Vol 1: Crudely made "votive chariots" were commonly found throughout the site, indiscriminately in temple, palace, and houses. Wheels were found at three other sites.

Pages 374-375: Archaeological evidence of plantings on ziggurat terraces. [Compare K-095.]

Vol. 2, plate 114E: shows a conical bronze incense burner stand with three reclining feline figures on the rim. [Compare B-275.]

S-414

AUTHOR: Stebbins, G. Ledyard
DATE: 1947
TITLE: Evidence on Rates of Evolution from the Distribution of Existing and Fossil Plant Species
IN: Ecological Monographs 17:149-158

China may have served as a way-station in the transmission of cotton between the hemispheres in pre-Columbian times.

S-415

AUTHOR: Stecchini, Livio Catullo
DATE: 1971
TITLE: Notes on the Relation of Ancient Measures to the Great Pyramid
IN: Secrets of the Great Pyramid, by Peter Tompkins (Harper and Row: New York), Appendix (pages 287-382)

Page 297: Discusses the ancient Square of Pegasus concept used in mapping the sky in Egypt and elsewhere. [For illustrations, see S-044, pages 434-435] This rectangular "fishpond" symbol (enclosing or not fish and water) is found all over the world. [George F. Carter, personal communication to Sorenson, notes that one of the illustrations in S-044 is from a Mimbres, Arizona, pot, though not so identified.] Stecchini chides Santillana and von Dechend for timidity in interpreting the significance of the distribution of the symbols they report. If the volume were accepted at face value it "should have the impact of a Copernican revolution on current conceptions of the development of human culture."

His mass of numerical evidence, chiefly on Egypt and classical Mediterranean lands, shows that the inhabitants of the ancient world were acquainted with the rate of precession of the equinoxes and attached major significance to it. [Compare B-097.]

S-417

AUTHOR: Steche, Theodor
DATE: 1935
TITLE: Die normannischen Fahrten nach Vinland und ihre Nachwirkungen [The Norse Voyages to Vinland and Their Consequences]

N: Zeitschrift für deutsche Philologie 60:121-173

Claims traces of the Norse in Aztec mythology.

S-418

AUTHOR: Steede, Neil

DATE: 1984

TITLE: Catálogo preliminar de los tabiques de Comalcalco: una colección de inscripciones mayas inexplicables / Preliminary Catalogue of the Comalcalco Bricks: An Unexplicable Collection of Maya Inscriptions

IMPRINT: Published in coordination with Municipio de Cárdenas, F.R.A.A. [Foundation for Research on Ancient America], and S.A.R.H. [Secretaría de Agricultura e Recursos Hidraúlicos], Centro de Investigación Precolombina: H. Cárdenas, Tabasco, México

In Spanish with parallel English translation.

Contains drawings of approximately 350 bricks from the Maya site of Comalcalco display grafitti, Mayan writing characters, and what he believes to be Phoenician, Greek, Tifinag, and other inscriptions, following the ideas of Barry Fell.

S-418B

AUTHOR: Steede, Neil

DATE: 1985

TITLE: Comalcalco, the Brick City of the Mayas

IN: Epigraphic Society Occasional Publications 14:116-128

See S-418C.

S-418C

AUTHOR: Steede, Neil

DATE: 1993

TITLE: Ogam in Mesoamerica

IN: The Eclectic Epigrapher, edited by Donald L. Cyr (Stonehenge Viewpoint: Santa Barbara, California), 122-125

Claims that Ogam characters occur scratched on various bricks at the site of Comalcalco, and there are similar marks on stone monuments at La Venta. He supposes that Comalcalco ("already quite occupied by the Maya civilization") was settled by "refugees from the Old World" 500 years after the last La Venta monuments were carved. These newcomers were responsible for both the Comalcalco "Ogam" marks and those they belatedly scratched on La Venta monuments.

S-418D

AUTHORS: Steele, D. Gentry, and Joseph F. Powell

DATE: 1992

TITLE: Peopling of the Americas: Paleobiological Evidence

IN: Human Biology 64:303-336

Notes the surprising neglect and denigration of the value of ancient skeletal material in America. It is commonly held that American Indians vary biologically over only a narrow range, which is based on (unsystematic) comparison of superficial bodily features in living groups rather than on osteological and dental features on ancient specimens, which indicate, to some scholars, much more variability. Given these perceptions and methodological penchants "physical anthropologists consistently conclude that modern American Indians evolved from one or more modern human populations from northern Asia" not very long ago. The authors examine that question by multivariate analysis of accessible Paleo-Indian specimens. Their result sees craniofacial similarities to southern Asians and Europeans. When braincase and face are considered together "the Paleo-Indian samples lie outside the central tendencies of northern Asians and North American Indians." The reason is uncertain. Contra C. Turner, they see the Paleo-Indians as not classically sinodont but appearing much like modern south Asians. Could adaptation be part of the answer?

S-419

AUTHOR: Steensby, Hans Peder
DATE: 1924
TITLE: The Norsemen's Route from Greenland to Wineland
IN: Meddelelser om Grønland 56:151-202 (Copenhagen) [Also, Proceedings of the 20th International Congress of Americanists (Rio de Janeiro, 1922), 1:99-102]

He makes the St. Lawrence River the chief area of Norse action. [See T-046.]

S-421

AUTHOR: Stefansson, Vilhjalmur
DATE: 1938
TITLE: The Three Voyages of Martin Frobisher in Search of a Passage to Cathay and India by the Northwest, A.D. 1576-8
IMPRINT: Argonaut: London

The introduction contains a discussion of the voyages to Iceland, the Greenland colony and its disappearance, and pre-Columbian knowledge in Europe of lands west of the Atlantic.

S-423

AUTHOR: Stefansson, Vilhjalmur
DATE: 1947
TITLE: Great Adventures and Explorations from the Earliest Times to the Present, as Told by the Explorers Themselves
IMPRINT: Dial: New York

Contains a chapter on the Vinland voyages with mention of the Kensington Stone and Newport Tower. He thinks it may be possible that the former is genuine and the latter very likely of Norse age.

S-424

AUTHOR: Steinen, K. von den
DATE: 1903
TITLE: Marquesanische Knotenschnüre [Marquesan Knotted Strings]
IN: Correspondenz-Blatt, Deutschen Gesellschaft für Anthropologie 34:108-114 (München)

Knotted strings are used by Marquesan priests as mnemonic devices to aid recall of technical terms, legends and songs, ancestral names, etc. Emphasizes the suggestive analogy to Peruvian quipus.

S-425

AUTHOR: Steiner, Stan
DATE: 1979
TITLE: Fusang, the Chinese Who Built America
IMPRINT: Harper and Row: New York

His chapter 3, "Ancient Mariners," appeared previously in the magazine *Natural History.* A popular, well-written survey of Chinese voyaging which is willing to see Fusang in America.

S-427

AUTHOR: Steinman, David
DATE: 1988
TITLE: Goodbye, Columbus? Were the Chinese the First to Discover the New World? The Evidence Could Be Buried in San Pedro Bay
IN: Random Lengths; Harbor Community News 9/4, 5, 6 (April, May, June), page 1 of each tabloid issue (San Pedro, California)

A well-researched journalistic treatment of the claimed "Chinese anchor stones" off the southern California coast. [See P-167 and F-212.] All sides are presented. Emphasis goes to comments from several interviewed experts saying that only a major, extensive set of mineralogical tests would settle the matter; these have not been, and are not likely to be, performed.

The ideas of Paul Chace, an archaeologist from Escondido, California, are featured in the final segment. He maintains that a reasonable case can be made (which is more than can be said for any other theory) that the stones owe to the activities of Portuguese whalers in the last decades of the nineteenth century.

S-428

AUTHOR: Steinmann, G.
DATE: 1924
TITLE: Zur Urbesiedelung Amerikas [On the Original Settlement of America]
IN: Proceedings of the 21st International Congress of Americanists (Part 1, The Hague, 1924), pages 63-70

Opposes the idea that voyagers could have crossed the Pacific.

S-429

AUTHOR: Stempell, W.
DATE: 1908
TITLE: Die Tierbilder der Mayahandschriften [Pictures of Animals in Maya Codices]
IN: Zeitschrift für Ethnologie 40:704-718

A zoologist claims on technical evidence that the trunked animal in the Maya codices is undoubtedly an elephant, and that those on Copan Stela B could not be tapirs, but are mammoths, Elephas Columbi.

S-429B

AUTHOR: Stender, Walter
DATE: 1988
TITLE: The Cross of the Inca
IN: Epigraphic Society Occasional Publications 17:179-186

The cross with four arms of equal length is identified in illustrative materials from Incan and earlier Peru and Mesoamerica [including an example mistakenly labeled mesoamerican which is from the Southern Cult in the U.S. Southeast]. In the Old World the form is said to go back to the Sumerians. He speculates that from "Sumerian Ur as a starting point, a white and bearded people emigrated to South America and founded in the Titicaca region a sun worshipping culture" which was kept "stable from the middle of the third millennium B.C. up to the middle of the first millennium A.D.," in addition to migrating to "the Pacific islands" and Mesoamerica.

S-430

AUTHOR: Stenger, Alison T.
DATE: 1989
TITLE: Japanese Influenced Ceramics in Pre-contact Washington State: A View of the Wares and Their Possible Origin
IN: Reprint Proceedings, Circum-Pacific Prehistory Conference, Seattle, August 1-6, 1989, part VIII: Prehistoric Trans-Pacific Contacts (Washington State University Press: Pullman), articles separately paginated

Discusses ceramic wares (apparently locally made) from southwest Washington dating to ca. A.D. 1400. There is no ethnographic record of ceramics in this region. Lack of surface burning characterizes over 90% of the 200 finely-textured specimens examined, which distinguishes them from wares produced in most other areas of the U.S. and indicates a formal kiln firing environment. Included are tabular figurines, vessels, tobacco pipes, pendants, and fragmentary unidentified specimens, including heads sculpted in clay. The figurines are similar in form to Alaskan slate figurines (one Alaskan site has clay figurines). Decoration is paralleled in coastal sites in Korea and the Russian maritime area, both areas showing Japanese influences in late prehistoric times. One motif is apparently duplicated in America only at Mayapan (Yucatan). [Compare W-232.]

S-431

AUTHOR: Stephens, John Lloyd
DATE: 1841
TITLE: Incidents of Travel in Central America, Chiapas, and Yucatan
IMPRINT: Harper: New York [Many editions]

Page 20: Regarding a local boat he rode in Belize, "This is the same fashion of boat in which the Indians navigated the rivers of America before the Spaniards discovered it. European ingenuity has not contrived a better. . . . [It is] about forty feet long, and six wide in the centre, running to a point at both ends, and made of the trunk of a mahogany-tree. Ten feet from the stern, and running forward, was a light wooden top, supported by fanciful stancheons, with curtains for protection against sun and rain."

He is impressed by the resemblance of animals on Stela B at Copan to elephants. But he scoffs at the idea of Old World origins for Mesoamerican civilization.

S-432

AUTHOR: Stephens, Stanley G.
DATE: 1947
TITLE: The Cytogenetics of Gossypium and the Problem of the Origin of New World Cottons
IN: Advances in Genetics 1:431-432

A history of the taxonomy of Gossypium and genetic studies on it. It is now believed that South America was the scene where genes doubled to produce the American forms. G. tomentosum in Hawaii is the only one remaining of proposed endemics in Polynesia after elimination of those in the Marquesas, Fiji, and Galapagos. Those three are actually American cottons. A chance crossing by air or ocean currents is possible but seems unlikely over such immense distances as would be required for this tropical plant. Cottonseed loses viability quickly in moist air. Gossypium does not survive in the wild. The facts all suggest that American cottons may have been used by man at the outset and not independently developed from wild ancestral species. In general he ends up cautious about the question of Old World ancestry for American cotton, although inclined to accept it.

S-433

AUTHOR: Stephens, Stanley G.
DATE: 1963
TITLE: Polynesian Cottons
IN: Annals of the Missouri Botanical Garden 50:1-22

He sees the wide distribution of Gossypium in the Pacific islands as a result of at least three independent introductions. The earliest, G. tomentosum Nutt., came into the Hawaiian Islands, most likely by oceanic drift (perhaps on a "natural island" of vegetation, such as a mass of trees), where it became endemic. Wild hirsutum, scattered in southern Polynesia, was introduced much more recently. It is difficult to account for its disjunct distribution (Caribbean, Central America, South Pacific) by ocean drift alone. Possibly it entered by 16-17th century Spanish expeditions, some of which carried and even planted cotton. The final introduction was by missionaries.

S-434

AUTHOR: Stephens, Stanley G.
DATE: 1966
TITLE: The Potential for Long Range Oceanic Dispersal of Cotton Seeds
IN: American Naturalist 100:199-210

Proposes that unopened bolls of wild cotton with hard-coated seeds can float in seawater and remain viable. Thus ocean currents could have carried Old World cotton to America, and American cotton to Polynesia.

S-435

AUTHOR: Stephens, Stanley G.
DATE: 1967
TITLE: Evolution under Domestication of the New World Cottons (Gossypium spp.)
IN: Ciencia e cultura 19/1:118-134

See S-436.

S-436

AUTHOR: Stephens, Stanley G.
DATE: 1971
TITLE: Some Problems of Interpreting Transoceanic Dispersal of the New World Cottons
IN: Man across the Sea: Problems of Pre-Columbian Contacts, edited by Carroll L. Riley, et al. (University of Texas Press: Austin), 401-415

"Wild" species of cotton have been found on all the continents with suitable climates; if seeds could thus be naturally carried, then presumably natural means could also have carried cultivated species. Also, historically the Spaniards and later Europeans in the Pacific islands spread many cottons in a very short period of time, further complicating any interpretation of history from distribution. Difficulties in reliable identification of cotton varieties from archaeological materials are also discussed. In two situations, the Cape Verdes and the Marquesas, presence and distribution of wild American cotton suggests human transmission in pre-Columbian times, although the evidence is not conclusive.

The problem of how a cotton with Central American affinities became established in southern Polynesia remains an open question.

S-439

AUTHOR: Sternberg, Leo
DATE: 1906
TITLE: Bemerkungen über Beziehungen zwischen der Morphologie der giljakischen und amerikanischen Sprachen
[Observations on Connections between the Morphology of the Gilyak and American Languages]
IN: Proceedings of the 14th International Congress of Americanists (Stuttgart, 1906), 1:137-140

Only a few rather general grammatical points of similarity are mentioned.

S-442B

AUTHOR: Stevenson, Ian
DATE: 1974
TITLE: Twenty Cases Suggestive of Reincarnation
IMPRINT: University of Virginia Press: Charlottesville
[Second edition, revised and enlarged, 1974. First edition, 1966, as vol. 26 of the *Proceedings of the American Society for Psychical Research*]

Pages 216-223: Introductory comments to Seven Cases Suggestive of Reincarnation among the Tlingit Indians of Southeastern Alaska. [The author, a psychiatrist at the University of Virginia, has long investigated first hand such cases around the world.] The Tlingit, Haida, Tsimsyan, Athapaskans of Alaska, Eskimos, and Aleuts all believe in reincarnation. Also, "The Incas of Peru believed in reincarnation, but into the same fleshly body, not into a new one. Their belief somewhat resembled that of the ancient Egyptians and similarly led to the practice of mummification of the physical body after death. In contrast, the Alaskan Tlingits who believed in reincarnation into a new body practiced cremation. . . . However, some Eskimos of southeastern Alaska practiced mummification (into the nineteenth century) and also believed in rebirth into a new physical body."

Most anthropologists believe the Tlingits and neighboring peoples were the last to cross over from Asia, as evidenced particularly by "the fact that the art/ architecture, customs, and beliefs of the peoples of northeastern Siberia resemble much more closely those of the natives of northwest America than those of other American tribes." They also believe that migrations and contacts from Asia to America ceased thousands of years before the Christian era, but some evidence suggests that considerable contact persisted well into the Christian era and possibly until shortly before the beginning of the historical period in Alaska in the 18th century. Evidence he cites on this point comes from Barbeau [B-037, B-039, B-040]: funeral dirges and other mourning rite elements of apparent Chinese or Mongolian Buddhist form, some word similarities in words, the Hwui Shan story, and the unearthing of several objects of oriental origin. "The Tlingit belief in reincarnation is by no means as fully elaborated as the doctrines on this subject in Hinduism and Buddhism. But it does include concepts somewhat similar to that of karma."

"Whether or not Buddhism actually reached Alaska we cannot say with certainty. But I find this possibility quite plausible to contemplate." The close similarity "compels attention although not conviction." Their closeness suggest further that the ancestors of the Tlingits imported rather than invented their ideas on reincarnation.

S-443

AUTHOR: Stevenson, Robert
DATE: 1952
TITLE: Music in Mexico: A Historical Survey [cover adds subtitle: The Only Complete History of Mexican Music from Aztec Times to the Present]
IMPRINT: Thomas Y. Crowell: New York

Page 12: None of the aboriginal peoples of North or South America possessed a stringed instrument, although some investigators have thought it strange that the Aztecs and Mayas never stumbled upon so simple an idea as the use of the hunter's bow for a musical instrument. [This supposed absence has been frequently contradicted.]

Page 66: Uncertain whether a marimba-type instrument existed in pre-Columbian Guatemala. He says it came from African slaves of the Spaniards, but there are claimants on both sides of the issue.

Pages 76-77: The Bonampak murals show pairs of long vertical trumpets. In Guatemala ethnographic parallels of such trumpets are used to "invoke . . . deity." Other sources report Mesoamerican paired vertical trumpets. He notes that in the Bible, Numbers 10:1 mentions trumpet instruments in ritual, which scholars (*Jewish Encyclopedia,* 1916, 12:268) say were long and of silver. In both places the instruments lack any finger holes.

Page 79: A Mesoamerican copper instrument is described in the documents was apparently a metal gong struck with a metal hammer and sounded like a bell.

S-444

AUTHOR: Stevenson, Robert
DATE: 1968
TITLE: Music in Aztec and Inca Territory
IMPRINT: University of California Press: Berkeley

A basic source for interhemispheric comparisons of music and instruments.

S-445

AUTHOR: Steward, Julian H.
DATE: 1929
TITLE: Diffusion and Independent Invention: A Critique of Logic
IN: American Anthropologist 31:491-495

A methodological/epistemological discussion, proposing that when closely similar cultural traits are found in two or more localities, the probability of independent invention as an explanation is directly proportional to the difficulty of communication between the places and to the uniqueness of the element. The probability is inversely proportional to the number of elements shared, and to the elapsed time since the feature appeared in either locality.

S-446

AUTHOR: Steward, Julian H.
DATE: 1949a
TITLE: Review of *Men out of Asia,* by Harold S. Gladwin
IN: American Anthropologist 51:113-115

After an even-handed summary, Steward says that while Americanists will cringe at the conclusions, Gladwin has touched a sore spot in that little is known from archaeology at this point about the origins of American civilizations.

S-447

AUTHOR: Steward, Julian H.
DATE: 1949b
TITLE: South American Cultures: An Interpretive Summary
IN: The Comparative Ethnology of South American Indians, volume 5 of Handbook of South American Indians, edited by Julian H. Steward, Smithsonian Institution, Bureau of American Ethnology Bulletin 143 (Washington, D.C.), 669-772

Under "Theoretical Considerations," beginning page 742, he discusses the general issue of diffusion in relation to the history of South American cultures. Eliott Smith, Perry, Graebner, Schmidt, and Rivet are adjudged "among the more influential and serious writers."

"Few American anthropologists deny the possibility of transoceanic influence on New World cultures, though most of them repudiate the theories that bring total cultures from overseas. At one extreme evidences such as matrilineal descent are worthless, being merely classificatory labels. At an opposite extreme are actual American domesticated plants, whose identity and genetic connection with Old World species can be established beyond reasonable doubt: sweet potatoes, Pachyrrhizus, Lagenaria, cotton, plantains, and perhaps peanuts and coconuts. Between these extremes are doubtful cases involving subjective judgements."

"Among traits which might with some plausibility be argued as evidence for transoceanic diffusion: blowgun, bark cloth, panpipes, chewing lime with a narcotic, star-headed clubs, trepanning, the venesection bow, and ikat weaving, if chronology and transportation possibilities could be shown suitable. A good many of them might have been introduced to America by individual boatloads of voyagers in the course of settlement of the Polynesian Islands during the Christian Era. But the history of these items is not very important to understanding the American cultures, which were basically formed before any conceivable trans-Pacific navigation could have taken place."

S-448

AUTHORS: Steward, Julian H., and Louis C. Faron
DATE: 1959
TITLE: Native Peoples of South America
IMPRINT: McGraw-Hill: New York

Page 43: They list fifteen parallels between South America and Asia which they consider of interest. It is conceivable that even a preponderance of cultural traits might have been derived from Asia, but even if that were the case, social and political forms still had to develop locally. Imports could not have been more than "superficial embellishments" on "the basic patterns."

S-449

AUTHOR: Stewart, Dorothy N.
DATE: 1952
TITLE: Geometric Implications in Construction of the Caracol: Greek Measures in Maya Architecture
IN: El Palacio 59/6:163-174

Believes the so-called Pythagorean proportions, the "golden section" of the Greeks, was known and employed by Maya builders, either through their "innate ability" or through Asiatic instructors. [The author's concept of racial instinct and her evidence for a 1.618 constant in Maya building are unconvincing.]

S-449B

AUTHOR: Stewart, Ethel G.

DATE: 1991

TITLE: The Dene and Na-Dene Indian Migration 1233 A.D. (Escape from Genghis Khan to America)

IMPRINT: ISAC Press: Columbus, Georgia

Claims that the Dene peoples of North America (the Athapaskans) and the NaDene (the linguistically related Haida and Tlingit of British Columbia) fled to America from conquest and oppression at the hands of the Mongol hordes. Details of this flight were supposedly preserved in oral tradition. She relies heavily on traditions recorded by Father Emil Petitot [see P-136 through P-146].

S-450

AUTHOR: Stewart, Joe D.

DATE: 1974

TITLE: Mesoamerican and Eurasian Calendars

IMPRINT: Unpublished; Ph.D. dissertation, University of Calgary

Mesoamerican and Eurasian lists of calendar symbols show a high degree of sequential and other patterned similarity ("extensive and detailed similarities"). Some Mesoamerican and Eurasian lists are more similar to each other than are certain Eurasian lists long thought to have common origins. The Mesoamerican system appears to derive from the area of northwestern India between 400 and 100 B.C. "More than superficial effects on Mesoamerican civilization" must be seen resulting from this transmission. One of his aims, which he attains, was "to show that historical interdependence [particularly in the case of Mesoamerica and Old World centers of civilization] is a major reality that cannot be ignored in the study of cultural developments."

Critics of his thesis demand evidence for other borrowings which "must have" accompanied the direct transmission he supposes for these calendar elements. Where are the language comparisons? The wheel? The Kama Sutra? Material objects from the Old World found in Mesoamerica? But, he replies, where is similar evidence for, say, Mesoamerican and South American contacts, which are fully recognized, and over a long period of time at that?

His conclusion gives a summary of D. Kelley's work and position on these calendrical matters. Stewart differs in details which he sees reconciling even more of the comparisons among the historical systems.

S-451

AUTHOR: Stewart, Joe D.

DATE: 1978a

TITLE: A Research Strategy for the Study of Star Lore

IN: Diffusion and Migration: Their Roles in Cultural Development, edited by P. G. Duke, et al. (University of Calgary Archaeological Association: Calgary), 144-166

Outlines how one may study the ethnoastronomy of an area, which may shed light on problems of intercommunication including diffusion. Using a sample of data on North American Indian societies from a belt between 39 and 41 degrees north latitude from Pacific to Atlantic oceans, he shows what ethnoastronomically-relevant questions to ask of the data sources and summarizes some results.

Page 149: In passing he notes that in eastern North America an association of bear, litter, death and mourning appears that is quite similar in Hebrew and Arabian lore. "It is tempting to conclude from [cited] examples [of the Milky

Way and Pleiades] that the widespread similarities in symbolism reflect independent, parallel creations of the human mind, rather than diffusion or the retention of a very ancient body of ideas." However this fails to explain why certain "obvious" North American ideas have wide distributions outside the New World at the same time that other equally "obvious" ideas have restricted distributions. Possibly because ideas that tend to arise repeatedly tend also to diffuse easily.

Table 2 (10 pages) lists 107 star identifications from 37 societies of his sample with meanings associated with particular stars, plus references.

S-452

AUTHOR: Stewart, Joe D.
DATE: 1978b
TITLE: A Consideration of the Posthole Murder Motif
IN: Diffusion and Migration: Their Roles in Cultural Development, edited by P. G. Duke, et al. (University of Calgary Archaeological Association: Calgary), 226-235

A motif shared in detail between Micronesia and Guatemala. [See S-453.]

S-453

AUTHOR: Stewart, Joe D.
DATE: 1984a
TITLE: Ethnohistorical Implications of a Mythological Theme in Micronesia and Mesoamerica
IN: Canadian Journal of Anthropology/Revue canadienne d'anthropologie 4/1:23-37

The posthole murder motif is unique enough that contact between the two areas is quite certain. What is uncertain is when and how. The possibility is considered of native sailors on Spanish ships as a diffusion mechanism, but pre-Columbian movement is also to be considered.

S-454

AUTHOR: Stewart, Joe D.
DATE: 1984b
TITLE: Structural Evidence of a Luni-solar Calendar in Ancient Mesoamerica
IN: Estudios de cultura nahuatl 17:171-191

A calendar of 12-13 "moons" in ancient Mesoamerica is almost presumable on general grounds. Specific evidence is discussed in this paper making the supposition virtually certain. The complex Mesoamerican calendar system may have superseded it.

S-455

AUTHORS: Stewart, Joe D., and David H. Kelley
DATE: 1970
TITLE: The Eurasian Origin of the Mesoamerican Calendar System
IMPRINT: Unpublished; typescript, 9 pages [Photocopy in files of John Sorenson]

A summary of the present state of the problem, under these headings: reliability of the evidence, its significance, processes of change and variation, nature of the evidence, and conclusions. "The Mesoamerican calendar derives from one of the Eurasian systems of lunar mansions, more like the Indian system than the Chinese or the Greco-Coptic-Arabian system. The particular system is not recorded. It is the same one from which, at an earlier date, the alphabet was derived." "It is not impossible that certain associated traits may have originated in the New World and spread back to Eurasia."

S-456

AUTHOR: Stewart, Thomas Dale
DATE: 1939
TITLE: Negro Skeletal Remains from Indian Sites in the West Indies
IN: Man 39:49-51

A caution on B-484 which had claimed that a Negroid physical type inhabited the Virgin Islands in pre-Columbian times. That is contrary to accepted findings of science. He uses known Negro skulls from the Antilles found in an Indian site to show that these were unquestionably Negro, not Negroid, and were quite surely intrusive post-Columbian burials.

S-460

AUTHOR: Stewart, Thomas Dale
DATE: 1958
TITLE: Stone Age Skull Surgery: A General Review, with Emphasis on the New World
IN: Annual Report of the Board of Regents of the Smithsonian Institution . . . [for] 1957, pages 469-491

Employs the following subheadings: distribution (Europe, South America, North America, Africa, Asia), motives for operating, surgical techniques, sites of operation, outcome of operation. Includes data on skulls in the Tello (Peruvian) collection of ceramics in the Peabody Museum of Harvard University and certain North American specimens.

His estimate of the number of trephined skulls recovered in Peru is about 1000, a number perhaps higher than for all the rest of the prehistoric world. Twelve putative examples from North America give the impression of only beginning to experiment with trephining, and Middle America not much better.

S-461

AUTHOR: Stewart, Thomas Dale
DATE: 1960
TITLE: A Physical Anthropologist's View of the Peopling of the New World
IN: Southwestern Journal of Anthropology 16:259-273

Page 263: While certain ancient American bones have been tested serologically and tentatively labelled as showing blood type A, other researchers, with whom the author clearly agrees, do not trust the accuracy of methods for doing this. High variability in Diego factor results on the living suggest some unrecognized selection factor at work (rather than purely genetic history).

Page 264: He emphasizes the homogeneity of American aborigines. The possibility of transpacific contacts at a late date does not alter the picture because few individuals would have been involved.

Page 265: Emphasizes disease isolation of the Americas. Tuberculosis may be the only disease carried (across Bering Strait) in prehistoric times, but even its presence is uncertain.

Page 269: Melanesians and Australians have been placed in America, quite illogically, on very little more evidence than skull typing.

S-462

AUTHOR: Stewart, Thomas Dale
DATE: 1973
TITLE: The People of America
IMPRINT: Scribner's: New York; and Weidenfeld and Nicolson: London

In the course of a general semi-scientific presentation on the physical anthropology of American Indians, the author has a chapter on "theories and misconceptions about American origins" (i.e., lost tribes of Israel, Mormons, Atlantis, Vikings, Antarctic route) and summaries of Meggers and Evans and Rivet.

Page 187: Head deformation on the Northwest Coast "can be accounted for only on the basis of independent invention or trans-Pacific contact" (drift junks implied).

Pages 38-44: Summary discussions of malaria, syphilitic diseases, and tuberculosis are related to arguments about the separate disease history of the western hemisphere in pre-Columbian times. He opts for nearly total separation as well as racial homogeneity throughout the hemisphere while allowing the possibility of insignificant incursions by sea.

Pages 193-197: Trephining. Peru was the center, with a success rate of 55-60% (perhaps due to use of coca as an anaesthetic), but in Middle and North America the procedure was little developed. [Confined to mainly English language sources, omits consideration of an important segment of the polygenesis literature cited, for example, in C-321 and C-325.]

S-464

AUTHORS: Stewart, Thomas Dale, and John R. Groome
DATE: 1968
TITLE: The African Custom of Tooth Mutilation in America
IN: American Journal of Physical Anthropology 28:31-42

Tooth mutilation in Mesoamerica goes back to c. 1400-1000 B.C., citing Romero. It spread from there to the coast of Ecuador and the middle Mississippi valley. Shortly after the conquest, the custom disappeared. Lignitz has shown that tooth mutilation was common over Africa from coast to coast in the tropics. Its age is unknown. Probably no contact between the two occurred. The custom was in Japan in ancient times (citations); the possibility exists that it spread from Asia to both the New World and to Africa. The African pattern was chipping teeth; the New World of filing edges or of drilling cavities to insert inlays. A great variety of details occurred on both continents. African slaves spread tooth mutilation to a few Indian tribes after the Conquest, but only very simple pointing. The article reports on a case found on a Negro skull on Grenada. [Obviously "tooth mutilation" is merely a modern conceptual category, not a singe ancient complex.]

S-465

AUTHORS: Stewart, Thomas Dale, and Marshall T. Newman
DATE: 1951
TITLE: An Historical Resume of the Concept of Differences in Indian Types
IN: American Anthropologist 53:19-36

An essential source on the history of ideas concerning the unity or plurality of American Indians: Humboldt, Morton, Putnam, Brinton, Dixon, Hrdlicka, Hooton, etc. Before 1920 authorities favored a single homotype. In Europe since 1880 migrationism has been uncritically used to interpret Amerind biological variation. Genetic interpretations have been almost entirely ignored to date.

S-466

AUTHORS: Stewart, Thomas Dale, and Alexander Spoehr
DATE: 1952
TITLE: Evidence on the Paleopathology of Yaws
IN: Bulletin of the History of Medicine 26:538-553

They suggest that syphilis may have evolved from yaws in the Caribbean area just prior to the discovery of America and thus may have been ready for distribution by the Spanish to susceptible populations in both hemispheres.

S-466B

AUTHOR: Stickel, E. Gary
DATE: 1983
TITLE: The Mystery of the Prehistoric "Chinese Anchors": Toward Research Designs for Underwater Archaeology
IN: Shipwreck Anthropology, edited by Richard A. Gould (University of New Mexico Press and School of American Research: Albuquerque), 219-244

A programmatic paper which recaps the controversy in S-427, critiques cogently the undocumented assumptions of the pro-"Chinese anchor" people, and specifies a detailed research design that could test their position.

S-466C

AUTHOR: Stiebing, William
DATE: 1984
TITLE: Ancient Astronauts, Cosmic Collisions and Other Popular Theories about Man's Past
IMPRINT: Prometheus: New York

Critical of claimed Ogam inscriptions and other purported Old World evidences.

S-467

AUTHOR: Stieglitz, Robert Raphael
DATE: 1971
TITLE: Maritime Activity in Ancient Israel
IMPRINT: Unpublished; Ph.D. dissertation, Brandeis University [University Microfilms International Order No. 7130153]

The extent and impact of maritime activity on the Israelites from ca. 1200-600 B.C. Bible tradition has the Israelite tribes which were close neighbors to the Phoenicians (Dan, Asher, and Zebulun) as seafarers already in the period of the Judges (1200-1000 B.C.) The first of two parts here deals with nautical terminology in the Bible: the sea in mythology, the sea in nature, topographical and geographical terms connected with maritime activity, types of ships, parts and equipment of ships, personnel, and materials and products associated. Special attention is given to the alphabetic cuneiform texts from Ugarit since in many cases they illuminate lexical items in the Bible. The second part outlines historical developments of maritime activity in Israel. The result indicates that the nautical dimension was important. Finally, he examines the role of the Phoenicians in developing Israelite interests in maritime trade and shipping.

S-467B

AUTHOR: Stieglitz, Robert Raphael
DATE: 1975
TITLE: Did Ancient Jews Reach America?
IN: The New Diffusionist 5/19-20:54-59

The Bat Creek Stone is characterized. On palaeographic grounds the letters belong around the period of Bar-Kokhba's revolt, ca. A.D. 100. He gives his reading of it, generally agreeing with Gordon. Shows that the Jews at that time had a significant naval force which was defeated by the Romans.

S-468

AUTHOR: Stieglitz, Robert Raphael
DATE: 1976
TITLE: An Ancient Judean Inscription from Tennesseee
IN: Epigraphic Society Occasional Publications 3/65

The Bat Creek stone is reprised. Its script is ancient Hebrew and closest to characters on coins from the period of rebellions against the Romans (66-135 A.D.). Those rebellions involved a Jewish naval force, which explains how the makers of this stone could reach America.

S-469

AUTHOR: Stieglitz, Robert Raphael
DATE: 1984
TITLE: Long-distance Seafaring in the Ancient Near East
IN: Biblical Archaeologist 47/3:134-142

The Bronze Age resulted in the dissemination of people, materials, and ideas across the Indian Ocean. Some discussion of ships.

S-470

AUTHOR: Stierlin, Henri
DATE: 1964
TITLE: Living Architecture: Mayan
IMPRINT: Grosset and Dunlap: New York

Pages 14-15: He considers preposterous certain old ideas that the great pre-Columbian civilizations originated outside America. The evidence used to support such notions (including Ruz's Palenque tomb which looks so Egyptian) are superficial and "ignore historical and material data." The "most disturbing links," however, connect Mesoamerica and South-east Asia, as between Palenque and Angkor. "These are astonishing parallels." And "the same decorative principles and graphic treatment of surfaces are found all around the Pacific basin, in archaic China, among the primitive peoples of Siberia and New Zealand, in Alaska, Melanesia—and in the lands of the Maya."

S-471

AUTHOR: Stirling, Matthew W.
DATE: 1923
TITLE: Indonesia and the Middle American Calendar
IN: American Anthropologist 25:228-246

A critique of R-140 which connected Meso-american calendar features to Asia. Stirling argues for no connection, since "practically every item in the calendar" can be "satisfactorily traced to an origin much nearer home."

S-472

AUTHOR: Stirling, Matthew W.
DATE: 1938
TITLE: Historical and Ethnological Material on the Jivaro Indians
IMPRINT: Smithsonian Institution, Bureau of American Ethnology Bulletin 117 (Washington D.C.)

Pages 80-81: Suggests that use of the blowgun among the Jivaro and other South American groups resulted from post-Columbian introduction from the Old World, perhaps via Philippine natives on Manila galleons. [He ignores sources showing use already at the time of the Spanish Conquest such as R-085.]

S-473

AUTHOR: Stirling, Matthew W.
DATE: 1940
TITLE: Great Stone Faces in the Mexican Jungle
IN: National Geographic Magazine 78:309-334

Page 317: "Night cap" shown worn on a figure at Tres Zapotes. [Compare A-044.]

Page 327: Toes of footgear point upward. [Compare A-044.]

S-474

AUTHOR: Stirling, Matthew W.
DATE: 1943
TITLE: Stone Monuments of Southern Mexico
IMPRINT: Smithsonian Institution, Bureau of American Ethnology Bulletin 138 (Washington D.C.)

Page 59: Stone sarcophagus with rope border. [Compare I-098.]

S-475

AUTHOR: Stirling, Matthew W.
DATE: 1961
TITLE: The Olmecs: Artists in Jade
IN: Essays in Pre-Columbian Art and Architecture, edited by Samuel Lothrop (Harvard University Press: Cambridge), 43-59

Page 43: Notes China-Mesoamerica parallels with regard to jade use: emphasis; the word for the stone means precious, verdant; an esteemed person was said to have a heart of jade.

S-476

AUTHOR: Stirling, Matthew W.
DATE: 1962
TITLE: Wheeled Toys from Tres Zapotes
IN: Amerindia 1:43-49 (Montevideo)

Noting and illustrating "toys" with wheels, the author asks whether this represents diffusion from the Old World or an independent invention in the New. Speculates on why the discovery was apparently not utilized practically.

S-477

AUTHOR: Stirling, Matthew W.
DATE: 1968
TITLE: Aboriginal Jade Use in the New World
IN: Proceedings of the 37th International Congress of Americanists (Mar del Plata, Argentina, 1966), 4:19-28

The finest jade known is brilliant emerald green from Burma. This type of jade was used at La Venta, the first known occurrence outside Burma, long before it was known in Burma or exported from there to China. Jade was used in the Lake Baikal region by about 2000 B.C. Lavish use of red paint with burials was characteristic of this Siberian period, a practice that later accompanied mortuary use of jade both in China and Middle America.

By 1000 B.C., jade was extremely popular in burials in China (Chou dynasty). The early Chinese, like natives of Middle America, classed as jade many stones of more or less similar appearance that were neither jadeite nor nephrite. Both used the term for jade to indicate fine qualities of any sort. The apparent everlasting quality of jade suggested its connection with immortality, and like the Chinese, the early Mexicans frequently placed a piece of jade in the mouth of the dead.

He considers the American centers of jade working to have been separate entities, although this is a subject "which will long produce controversy between the diffusionists and the advocates of independent invention."

S-479

AUTHOR: Stocker, Terrance L.
DATE: 1991
TITLE: Discussion: Empire Formation, Figurine Function and Distribution
IN: The New World Figurine Project, vol. 1, edited by Terrance Stocker (Research Press: Provo, Utah), 145-165

If the similarities between Valdivia and Jomon are explained by reason of their being merely "simple designs," as some have claimed, how did both cultures hit upon the same simple designs when scores of other simple designs were absent in both? With Stenger's material in this volume [compare S-430], there seems little doubt that a figurine style somehow diffused from Japan to Washington, but was it a concept, a people, or what that made the move? And what happened to the makers of these figurines from Lake River? Absorbed, exterminated? K-042 and J-095 are powerful further indicators that real movements of some sort took place across the ocean.

S-479B

AUTHORS: Stodder, Ann L. W., and Debra L. Martin
DATE: 1992
TITLE: Health and Disease in the Southwest before and after Spanish Contact
IN: Disease and Demography in the Americas, edited by John W. Verano and Douglas H. Ubelaker (Smithsonian Institution Press: Washington D.C.), 55-73

Pandemic disease appears to have preceded direct European contact. Diseases thought to have been present: several viruses (staphylococcal and streptococcal), forms of herpes and hepatitis, poliomyelitis, pertussis, rhinoviruses, tick-borne fevers, rabies, sylvatic plague, tularemia, giardiasis, amoebic dysentery, coccidioido-mycosis, and perhaps salmonella and shigella. At least eight species of helminthis parasites appear in coprolites. Treponemal disease has also been identified. Over (prehistoric) time the rate of infection among the Mogollon increased. In the protohistoric period endemic problems of drought and famine were superimposed on economic disruption caused by the Spanish. It is likely that either the pathogenicity or prevalence or both of tuberculosis and treponematosis were increased due to demographic disturbance, warfare, famine, malnutrition, and population structure. [Thus the often-presumed drastic effects of new diseases introduced by immigrants from Europe in Columbus' day may have less to do with the newness of the pathogens than with attendant social and environmental conditions.]

S-481

AUTHOR: Stokes, John F. G.
DATE: 1932
TITLE: Spaniards and the Sweet Potato in Hawaii and Hawaiian-American Contacts
IN: American Anthropologist 34:594-600

Joins Dixon [D-142] in denying early Spanish contact with Hawaii as a believable source for the sweet potato. He also points out the close similarity in the Hawaiian stone "flat-iron" type of poi-pounder and its use to American implements as possibly, though not clearly, showing contacts between Hawaii and Central America. Also, a legend is repeated which he sees as perhaps referring to a voyage to a land to the east of Hawaii.

S-483

AUTHOR: Stolp, Karl
DATE: 1888
TITLE: Indianische Zeichen aus der Cordillere Chiles aufgefunden von Karl Stolp [Indian Signs from the Chilean Cordillera Discovered by Karl Stolp]
IN: Verhandlungen der deutschen Wissenschaft Verein zu Santiago 2/1:35-37 (Santiago, Chile)

Translated into English in B-340.

High on a wall in a remote cave he found signs painted in black, red, and white. The marks remind the author "of the old Egyptians" in general. His drawing is reproduced by Carter in C-097 and B-340. [Ray Matheny, Brigham Young University archaeologist, personal communication, reports visiting the cave in 1993. The signs are scattered on the cave wall; they do not, as implied by Stolp, form a consistent inscription.]

S-484

AUTHOR: Stolywho, Kazimierz
DATE: 1952
TITLE: The Antiquity of Man in the Argentine and the Survival of South American Fossil Mammals until Contemporary Times
IN: Indian Tribes of Aboriginal America; Selected Papers of the 29th International Congress of Americanists (New York, 1949), edited by Sol Tax (University of Chicago Press: Chicago), 353-360

He agrees with Mendes-Corrêa's theory of a crossing from Australia via Antarctica and summarizes that view while also accepting Imbelloni and Rivet. The Bering Strait route was, of course, available much earlier, since the southern, transpacific way had to await sailing capability. Pleistocene mammals survived until very recent times.

S-484B

AUTHORS: Stone, Doris, and Carlos Balser
DATE: 1967
TITLE: Aboriginal Metalwork in Lower Central America
IMPRINT: The authors: San José, Costa Rica

Pages 43-44: They list nine features connected with the art of metal casting, all of which appeared in Asia much earlier than in America. They also give ten "decorative elements and artifacts [types] of metal which are found in both Asia and America," citing H-154. Taken together and "associated as they are with the complex of metalwork, the likelihood of their being historically related is greatly increased. They appear late, and if they do indicate connections, a long continuance of transpacific contacts would be implied."

S-486

AUTHOR: Stone, William L.
DATE: 1878
TITLE: The Moundbuilders: Were They Egyptians, and Did They ever Occupy the State of New York?
IMPRINT: A. S. Barnes: New York [Reprinted from *The Magazine of American History* 2 (1878): 533-539]

A smoking pipe dug up at Seneca Falls, N.Y., in 1877 has atop it a carved figure (illustrated) which he feels is "almost an exact representation" of the [Egyptian] Colossus of Memnon and very different from anything Indian. Finds of a copper and a "bronze" spear (head) are also reported. He takes these as supporting the "Atlantic theory" for the origin of American civilization put forward by Brasseur de Bourbourg.

S-486B

AUTHOR: Stonebraker, Jay
DATE: 1982
TITLE: A Decipherment of the Los Lunas Decalogue Inscription
IN: Epigraphic Society Occasional Publication 10/239:74-81

Fell has presented "awesome epigraphic and numismatic evidence" for the presence of Mediterranean seafarers reaching the interior of North America via both the Atlantic and Pacific Oceans. Here he deals with "the linguistic evidence in transcription, identification, transliteration, analysis, and decipherment of the Los Lunas text." The decipherment is his own; he seems unaware of other attempts. Supposes the language is Hebrew and the script Phoenician of roughly the 10th century B.C.

S-488

AUTHORS: Stonor, C. R., and Edgar Anderson
DATE: 1949
TITLE: Maize among the Hill Peoples of Assam
IN: Annals of the Missouri Botanical Garden 36:355-404 [Reviewed 1950 by John H. Hutton, *Man* 50:153-154]

Page 392: Canavalia, the sword bean, cultivated throughout the Pacific and considered of Old World origin, is found in preceramic Huaca Prieta on the Peruvian coast before 1000 B.C. People in the hill country of Assam and northern Burma grow maize widely. They say they have had it from time immemorial, although they have no written language nor permanent records. The folk customs connected with its cultivation and its use as a green vegetable, for bread and brewing, and as animal food would indicate that they have had it for a long time. These varieties differ from those of Middle America and are closer to those of South America. They also differ sharply from the varieties now widely distributed in eastern China and the Philippines, which presumably came via the Spaniards from Mexico. There is also a persistent rumor that corn came into China from the west. Consequently the authors conclude that maize crossed the Pacific, perhaps more than once, long before 1492.

S-491

AUTHOR: Storm, Gustav
DATE: 1887
TITLE: Studier over Vinlandsreiserne, Vinlands Geografi og Ethnografi [Research on Voyages to Vinland] [in Icelandic]
IN: Aarboger for Nordisk Oldkyndighed og Historie (2. raekke) 2:293-372 (Copenhagen)

This Danish history professor lays out for the first time beyond question the documents establishing Norse discovery of America; he places Vinland in Nova Scotia. His scholarship rebutted much skepticism that had arisen in the wake of R-005. T-117 maintains that he shed baleful influence on clarity by his insistence that the sagas were laced with factual errors, such as the presence of grapes.

S-492

AUTHOR: Storm, Gustav
DATE: 1888
TITLE: Studies on the Vineland Voyages
IMPRINT: Memoires de la société royal des antiquaires du nord, 307-370 (Copenhagen)
[Reprinted Theile: Copenhagen, 1889]

Asserts that Norsemen never reached within the present boundaries of the United States. [His book created ill-will in Scandinavian-American circles, stimulating debate about the voyages.]

S-494

AUTHOR: Stothert, Karen E.
DATE: 1975
TITLE: The Early Prehistory of the Santa Elena Peninsula, Ecuador: Continuities between the Preceramic and Ceramic Cultures
IN: Proceedings of the 41st International Congress of Americanists (Mexico, 1974), 2:88-94

Downgrades or denies immigration by sea in Valdivia times because pre- Valdivia cultures are now known.

S-495

AUTHOR: Stowell, H. W.
DATE: 1961
TITLE: Mystery Inscription
IN: New Mexico: Magazine of the Land of Enchantment 39/8:24-27

Popular speculation about the purported Phoenician inscription near Los Lunas, New Mexico.

S-497

AUTHORS: Strake, Gail, and Steven Strake
DATE: 1981
TITLE: Ogam on the Susquehanna
IN: Epigraphic Society Occasional Publications 9/224:178-179

The authors maintain that stones in Pennylvania reported by J. Witthoft as having been grooved by serving as shaft polishers bear Ogam inscriptions.

S-498

AUTHOR: Strandwold, Olaf
DATE: 1939
TITLE: Runic Rock Inscriptions along the American Atlantic Seaboard
IMPRINT: Privately printed: Prosser, Washington
[Second edition as *Norse Inscriptions on American Stones* (M. Bjorndal: Weehauken, New Jersey, 1948)]

Attributes many American inscriptions to Norse visitors.

[Moltke says of this work that it "shows that this author lacks the most elementary knowledge of Scandinavian languages; he is able to find runes in any crevice or groove and decipher them."]

S-499

AUTHOR: Stromsted, Astri A.
DATE: 1974
TITLE: Ancient Pioneers: Early Connections between Scandinavia and the New World
IMPRINT: Erik J. Friis: n.p.

A melange of Vikings and much earlier (Trojan, Sumerian, Egyptian, Solomonic, etc.) "sea kings" or their representatives who reached not only northeastern North America but Mexico (Toltec intruders) and South America. Utilizes, then outdoes, Reider Sherwin [S-225] in finding place names of Norse and many other peoples/tongues all over the hemisphere. No bibliography.

S-500

AUTHOR: Strong, William Duncan
DATE: 1951
TITLE: Cultural Resemblances in Nuclear America: Parallelism or Diffusion?
IN: The Civilizations of Ancient America; Selected Papers of the 29th International Congress of Americanists (New York, 1949), edited by Sol Tax (University of Chicago Press: Chicago), 271-279

Methodology. After summarizing the sequences for Nuclear America (Meso- and Andean South America), the author concludes, without substantive argumentation, "that the marked resemblances in all known stages of the development of culture in the northern and southern portions of Nuclear America are due to original historical unity and later indirect diffusion, rather than to independent, parallel or convergent evolution." He stresses the indirect nature of the contact involved—it was by "peoples in trouble jostling other peoples until the trouble or idea spread, rather than by actual migrations, that the higher cultures of the American continent kept in step." "There is too much in common to believe otherwise."

As against the common elements, quoting Kroeber favorably, "it matters little that Mexico grew cacao and the agave, Peru the potato and the peanut, that Mexico alone developed lime mortar and cement, a day count calendar, writing and paper, Peru, wool spinning and the balance. Many Mexican peoples, the Maya and Tarasca for instance, differ almost as much among themselves." That developments of New World civilization seem "remarkably similar to those which, several millennia earlier, led to the development of Old World civilizations opens important theoretical vistas."

S-501

AUTHOR: Stross, Brian
DATE: 1986
TITLE: Some Observations on T585 (Quincunx) of the Maya Script
IN: Anthropological Linguistics 28:283-311

Sound similarities between words for wind, moon, and star in Mayan languages and wind, sun, and moon in Zapotec, are connected with the quincunx symbol in both cases. "Oddly, E. A. Wallis Budge. . . , [Egyptianist], during the early years of this century, supplies an economically stated linkage between wind, sun, and Venus," quoting him on occurrence of "wind crosses" in Peru and Mexico which possess solar or stellar character. [However Budge meant nothing diffusionistic in his mention.]

S-502

AUTHOR: Stubbs, Brian
DATE: 1988
TITLE: Elements of Hebrew in Uto-Aztecan: A Summary of the Data
IMPRINT: Preliminary Report STU-88 (Foundation for Ancient Research and Mormon Studies: Provo, Utah)

A technical paper by a linguist with substantial experience in both Uto-Aztecan and Semitics concludes that Hebrew is one ancestor language of Uto-Aztecan. A quite consistent pattern of sound correspondences emerges. More than 40% of the sets in W. Miller's Uto-Aztecan Cognate Sets are referred to. A considerable amount of Hebrew morphology is also apparent in Uto-Aztecan, some of it still productive but most fossilized. Semitic roots often include diverse, not-obviously-related semantic dimensions which are also found in UA stems. The material presented here involves over 200 roots; an expanded paper will add 250 more having apparent reflexes in UA. Much non-Semitic material is also present in UA, of course, leading the author to suggest the possibility of creolization.

S-503

AUTHOR: Stucken, Eduard

DATE: 1913

TITLE: Der Ursprung des Alphabets und die Mondstationen [The Origin of the Alphabet and of Observatories]

IMPRINT: J. C. Hinrich's Buchhandlung: Leipzig

Origin of the alphabet in relation to astronomy with mention of New World connections.

S-504

AUTHOR: Stucken, Eduard

DATE: 1927

TITLE: Polynesisches Sprachgut in Amerika und in Sumer [Polynesian Linguistic Heritage in America and Sumer]

IN: Mitteilungen der Vorderasiatisch-aegyptischen Gesellschaft 31/2 (Leipzig)

Strained language comparisons: Polynesian, American, Sumerian.

S-505

AUTHOR: Stunkel, Kenneth R.

DATE: 1967

TITLE: Review of *Maps of the Ancient Sea Kings,* by Charles H. Hapgood

IN: Geographical Review 57:440-442

He believes that Hapgood's "superstructure of inference [i.e., reading early maps as showing ancient exploration of America] is too heavy for the base of evidence on which it rests." Stunkel observes in passing that Mexico appears to have "learned from Pacific cultures." The Aztecs had myths about bringers of culture from the west.

S-507

AUTHOR: Sturtevant, William C.

DATE: 1969

TITLE: Agriculture on Artificial Islands in Burma and Elsewhere

IN: Proceedings of the 8th International Congress of Anthropological and Ethnological Sciences (Tokyo and Kyoto, 1968), 8:195

The chinampas of Mexico are very similar to Kashmir and Burmese systems of cultivation, although he does not intend this in a diffusionist sense.

S-509

AUTHOR: Suggs, Robert C.

DATE: 1960

TITLE: The Island Civilizations of Polynesia

IMPRINT: New American Library: New York

Page 218: Objects to Heyerdahl's theory of settlement of Polynesia from South America in part on the ground that sails were not used on that continent until European times. Heyerdahl's work is without merit.

S-511

AUTHOR: Suggs, Robert C.

DATE: 1967

TITLE: A Reanalysis of Galapagos Ceramics Data

IN: Zeitschrift für Ethnologie 92:239-247

Depending on only the published material, he applies quantitative methods and concludes that resemblances between Galapagos and Viru Valley (Peru) sherds are insignificant and explainable by chance. Association of historic and prehistoric wares indicates a high mathematical probability of simultaneous arrival. Heyerdahl's claim that there were pre-Spanish visits is seen as resulting from faulty use of archaeological methods. He argues against any pre-pirate occupation of the islands and claims that European vessels carried "aboriginal pottery" in substantial amounts. [See now P-234.]

S-512

AUTHOR: Sullivan, Louis R.
DATE: 1922
TITLE: The "Blond" Eskimo—A Question of Method
IN: American Anthropologist 24:225-228

A critique of J-061. Sullivan denies the validity of the criteria employed by Jenness. Neither Jenness nor Stefansson have given data able to shed significant light on the question of possible Norse influence on Eskimo "blonds."

S-514

AUTHORS: Sullivan, Louis R., and Milo Hellman
DATE: 1925
TITLE: The Punin Calvarium
IN: Anthropological Papers of the American Museum of Natural History 23:307-337

The Punín, Ecuador, skull is of definitely Australoid type and akin to Melanesian skulls.

S-515

AUTHOR: Sullivan, Michael
DATE: 1967
TITLE: A Short History of Chinese Art
IMPRINT: University of California Press: Berkeley

Page 57: The Shang people had cultural affinities with the peoples of Alaska, British Columbia, and Central America. The similarities between certain Shang designs and those, for example, in the art of the West Coast Indians of North America are too close to be accidental.

Pages 60-61: Shang carving in ivory relates to the fact that elephants roamed North China in prehistoric times and probably were still to be found north of the Yangtse in the Shang Dynasty. At least one Shang emperor kept one as a pet. "Like the bronzes, these bone and ivory carvings show striking similarities with the art of the West Coast Indians of North America. For years scholars have toyed with the fascinating possibilities that these similarities have opened up, but as yet no archaeological connecting links have been found to account for them."

S-516

AUTHOR: Sullivan, Michael
DATE: 1973
TITLE: The Arts of China
IMPRINT: University of California Press: Berkeley [Third edition, 1984]

Page 40: T'ao-t'ieh and other designs on bone and ivory, as on bronzes, "show striking similarities with the art of the Northwest Coast Indians of North America."

S-517

AUTHOR: Sullivan, Walter
DATE: 1982
TITLE: Rio Artifacts May Indicate Roman Visit
IN: New York Times, October 10, page 3

Underwater archaeologist Robert Marx found a semi-buried Roman amphora of 2nd century B.C. type, partly buried in mud and coral, in a bay near Rio de Janeiro harbor. [Compare M-146 and M-146B.]

S-517B

AUTHOR: Sundby-Hansen, Harry
DATE: 1923
TITLE: Leif Ericson Conquering America
IN: American-Scandinavian Review 11:538-547

The increasing popularity of tributes to Leif Ericson at this time is traced primarily to the adroit public relations move of sailing the replica ship "Viking" across the Atlantic to reach Chicago for the opening of the 1893 Chicago World's Fair. Meanwhile three simultaneous replicas of Columbus' vessels had to be towed across the Atlantic. [Heyerdahl's Kon Tiki expedition may be seen as a similar public relations breakthrough for diffusionism.]

S-518

AUTHORS: Suto, T., and Y. Yoshida
DATE: 1956
TITLE: Characteristics of the Oriental Maize
IN: Land and Crops of Nepal Himalaya: Scientific Results of the Japanese Expeditions to Nepal Himalaya 1952-1953, volume 2, edited by H. Kihara (Fauna and Flora Research Society, Kyoto University: Kyoto), 375-530

A comparative study of Asiatic maizes, including 20 races from North China, revealing that "Caribbean" types, which prevail on the coasts of China and presumably were introduced by Europeans in the 16th century, had crossed with "Aegean" types which predominate now in China, particularly far inland. Although at the present stage of research it cannot be positively asserted that the inland maize was present in pre-Columbian times, it is suggestive. The Chinese naturalist Li Shih-Chen stated that a pod-like maize was introduced to China from India via Tibet in 1368. Others question his date.

S-519

AUTHOR: Swadesh, Morris
DATE: 1952
TITLE: Review of *Athapaskan and Sino-Tibetan,* by Robert Shafer
IN: International Journal of American Linguistics 18:178-181

Appreciates Shafer's independent effort, then passes on what he noted and recalls of a Sapir lecture on the subject that went beyond what Sapir published.

S-520

AUTHOR: Swadesh, Morris
DATE: 1959a
TITLE: Linguistics as an Instrument of Prehistory
IN: Southwestern Journal of Anthropology 15:20-35

Page 30: One of the earliest statements on the logic and use of lexicostatistics, i.e., comparing standard basic word lists to establish the degree, and thus the inferred chronology, of divergence of languages which shared a common origin. "The use of a borrowed culture term almost always implies the diffusion of the corresponding culture trait and is therefore a fairly direct clue to a fact of prehistory."

S-521

AUTHOR: Swadesh, Morris
DATE: 1959b
TITLE: Mapas de clasificación linguística de México y de las Americas [Linguistic Classification Maps of Mexico and the Americas]
IN: Cuadernos del Instituto de Historia, Serie antropológica 8, Universidad Nacional Autónoma de México

Proposes a Vascodéné network of tongues (Basque to Na-Dene) including Uralic and Eskimo-Aleut but not Indo-European. Na-Dene is said to be closest to Wakashan, Kutenai, and Japanese and somewhat less close to Macro-Hokan, Hamitic, and Indo-European.

S-522

AUTHOR: Swadesh, Morris
DATE: 1960a
TITLE: On Interhemisphere Linguistic Connections
IN: Culture and History: Essays in Honor of Paul Radin, edited by Stanley Diamond (Columbia University Press: New York), 894-924

He considers serious several attempts to compare New and Old World languages. Sapir's comparison of Nadene and Sino-Tibetan is supported by extensive material in Sapir's files beyond the little that he published. Others deserving attention: Eskimo-Aleutian in relation to Ural-Altaic, Nahua with Sanskrit and Indo-European, and Rivet on "Tsonekan" related to Australian and Hokan to Malay-Polynesian. Some of these may relate to this article, while "others would seem to represent later levels of affinity."

Page 896: "New languages probably came into America in the late millennia just before Columbus, but their speakers must have been absorbed . . . without leaving any language that has continued to modern times."

Here he discusses lexical, morphological, and phonological evidences for a partially-reconstructable Ancient American base language of perhaps 15,000 years ago.

S-523

AUTHOR: Swadesh, Morris

DATE: 1960b

TITLE: Tras la huella lingüística de la prehistoria [Beyond the Linguistic Trail of Prehistory]

IN: Suplementos del Seminario de Problemas Científicos y Filosóficos 26:97-145 (México?)

See S-520.

S-524

AUTHOR: Swadesh, Morris

DATE: 1961

TITLE: Los supuestos Australianos en América [The Supposed Australians in America]

IN: Homenaje a Pablo Martínez del Rio, edited by Ignacio Bernal, et al. (Instituto Nacional de Antropología e Historia: México), 147-161

A trenchant critique of Rivet's supposed lexical similarities between "Chon" and "Australian" in terms of lexicostatistics. Considers the probable linguistic situation in both South America and Australia on the order of 5000 years ago by choosing distantly, but visibly, related languages within each of those areas to set limits to the likely lexicon of the period. He presents his comparisons in detail. The conclusion is that the observed similarities between the languages on the separate continents must have been due to connection on the order of 18,000 years ago or more, not 5000. Clearly the similarities hark back to a common source in Asia rather than to direct boat-borne contact or migration.

S-525

AUTHOR: Swadesh, Morris

DATE: 1962a

TITLE: Afinidades de las lenguas amerindias [Affinities of the Amerindian Languages]

IN: Proceedings of the 34th International Congress of Americanists (Vienna, 1960), pages 729-738

See S-520.

S-526

AUTHOR: Swadesh, Morris

DATE: 1962b

TITLE: Linguistic Relations across Bering Strait

IN: American Anthropologist 64:1262-1291

A detailed study of relationships between Eskimo-Aleut and Chukchi-Koryak-Kamchadal. Grammatical similarities plus systematic and detailed comparative phonology based on a large number of comparisons.

S-527

AUTHOR: Swadesh, Morris
DATE: 1964
TITLE: Linguistic Overview
IN: Prehistoric Man in the New World, edited by Jesse D. Jennings and Edward Norbeck (published for Rice University by the University of Chicago Press: Chicago), 527-556

The last extant language to enter the New World was the ancestor of Eskimo-Aleutian, about 5000 years ago. On the basis of glottochronology, he supposes a sequence of earlier migrations from Asia represented by surviving language groupings, including: Macro-Cariban, Macro-Arawakan, Macro-Quechuan (including Zuñi and Tarasco), Macro-Mayan, and finally Bask-Dennean, which overall includes many Eurasian languages. As to transoceanic movements, the linguistic materials neither support nor disprove such contacts.

S-528

AUTHOR: Swadesh, Morris
DATE: 1965
TITLE: Lingvisticheskie sviazi Ameriki i Evrazii [Linguistic Connections of America and Eurasia]
IN: Etimologiia 5:271-322

Written in 1960. Proposes a Finno-Déné grouping.

S-530B

AUTHORS: Swadesh, Morris, and Madalena Sancho
DATE: 1966
TITLE: Los mil elementos del mexicano clásico: base analítica de la lengua nahua [The Thousand Elements of Classical Mexicano: Analytical Base of the Nahua Language]
IMPRINT: Instituto de investigaciones históricas, Universidad Nacional Autónoma de México

Pages 24-26: Note a resemblance between Aztec and Latin but do not pursue it.

S-532

AUTHOR: Swanton, John R.
DATE: 1916
TITLE: Notes on the Aboriginal Name "Aje"
IN: Journal of the Washington Academy of Sciences 6:136-137

In relation to the presence of the crop plant Dioscorea sp. in both hemispheres.

S-532B

AUTHOR: Swanton, John R.
DATE: 1940
TITLE: The First Description of an Indian Tribe in the Territory of the Present United States
IN: Studies for William A. Read: A Miscellany Presented by Some of his Colleagues and Friends, edited by Nathaniel M. Caffee and Thomas A. Kirby (Louisiana State University Press: Baton Rouge), 326-338 [Reprinted, Books for Libraries Press: Freeport, New York, 1968]

Page 326: Peter Martyr gives an account drawn from conversations he had in Santo Domingo with an Indian known as Francisco of Chicora, who had been carried there from the territory of present South Carolina in 1521. His report was that a settlement near Chicora was inhabited by "white men" with brown hair which hung to their heels.

Page 334: References to "white men" among the Indians in the sense of white tribes are fairly numerous. Nothing more is signified than the fact that they had, or were believed to have had, a relatively fairer complexion.

S-534

AUTHOR: Swauger, James
DATE: 1976
TITLE: The Stone Structure of Mystery Hill, North Salem, NH, USA
IN: Almogaren 7:191-198 [Also 1986 in *NEARA Journal* 20:65]

Against claims for early "megalithic" settlers from Europe.

S-535

AUTHORS: Swauger, James, and Mark Milburn
DATE: 1976-1977
TITLE: Grooved Petroglyph Sites in West Virginia and the Sahara
IN: Arkansas Archaeologist 16-18:81-84

A brief argument to show why certain sites in Arkansas, West Virginia, New Guinea, and Africa are tool-sharpening sites and grooves resulting in rocks are not petroglyphs as such.

S-537

AUTHOR: Sydow, C. W. von
DATE: 1948
TITLE: Selected Papers on Folklore
IMPRINT: Rosenkilde and Bagger: Copenhagen

Shows that tales may diffuse by jumping over large geographical areas without leaving an intervening trace.

S-538

AUTHOR: Sykes, Egerton
DATE: 1962
TITLE: Some Inscribed Stones from West Virginia
IN: New World Antiquity 9/1-2:12-15

Article not signed but surely by the editor, Sykes.

Three inscribed stones with inscriptions in "semitic script" have been found in the state in 1838, 1932, and 1956 (respectively, Grave Creek, Braxton, and Ohio County Stones). Unless opponents of early voyaging can explain these as a series of forgeries extending over almost 120 years, which seems illogical, they must be taken seriously.

S-539

AUTHOR: Sykes, Egerton
DATE: 1965a
TITLE: The Diffusion of Cultures
IN: New World Antiquity 12/7-8:83-84

This is an offer to sell copies of "a remarkable series of [apparently unpublished] papers on various aspects of diffusion," 68 in number, by Rendel Harris and/or H. T. Sherlock. Among the titles: "Egypt and the Atlantic"; "Voyage of Hanno"; "Go West"; "St. Kilda, the Azores and Brazil"; "Who Discovered North America?"; and "A Temple in Tennessee." [None of these has been seen for this bibliography.]

S-540

AUTHOR: Sykes, Egerton
DATE: 1965b
TITLE: Diffusion or Sterility
IN: New World Antiquity 12/7-8:67-71

Reviewing the strong interest in seafaring in the Mediterranean and Atlantic for thousands of years, he considers that it would be absurd to think that no vessels had crossed to America, whatever effect their crews might have had.

S-541

AUTHOR: Sykes, Egerton
DATE: 1965c
TITLE: Dr. S. R. Varshavsky and Pre Columbian Travellers
IN: New World Antiquity 13/7-8:75-80

Primarily translations to English of two letters by a Russian geographer briefly presenting his case for voyages from Europe to North America, one by an unknown merchant adventurer in 1271, as evidenced by an inscription found in Connecticut in 1964, and the other by Nicolas of Lynn in 1330. The extended argument constituted a manuscript of 309 pages which had been translated to English by an associate of Sykes but never published.

S-542

AUTHOR: Sykes, Egerton
DATE: 1968
TITLE: These Roman Artifacts
IN: New World Antiquity 15/7-8:75-77

Comment on the clay head reported in H-176.

S-542B

AUTHOR: Sykes, Egerton
DATE: 1976
TITLE: Egypt in America
IN: New World Antiquity 23:62-82

A rambling survey of what he sees as multiple Egyptian influences manifest in sites and monuments of the East Coast of North America, the Mississippi Valley, Florida, and the West Indies.

S-543B

AUTHOR: Syverson, Earl
DATE: 1979
TITLE: Norse Runic Inscriptions: With Their Long-forgotten Cryptography
IMPRINT: Vine Hill Press: Sebastopol, California

Dozens of examples are reprised of what he purports are cryptographic inscriptions in runes from both sides of the Atlantic.

S-544B

AUTHOR: Szasz, Ferenc M.
DATE: 1982
TITLE: Pre-Columbian Contacts in the American Southwest: Theories and Evidence
IN: New Mexico Humanities Review 5/1:43-58

Surveys capably a number of scholarly, pseudo-scholarly, and journalistic treatments of several inscriptions which "play a major role in the current debate over pre-Columbian contacts," notably the Heavener rune stone and Los Lunas stone. Cites a number of obscure sources not listed in this bibliography. Believes in the possibility that the Los Lunas inscription originated in the 18th century from a certain guide for the Dominguez-Escalante expedition who was in that vicinity at one point in time. Concludes that until a scientific means to date the inscriptions is found, the issue of these inscriptions will remain controversial.

S-545

AUTHOR: Szaszdi, Adam
DATE: 1978
TITLE: En torno a la balsa de Salango (Ecuador) que capturó Bartolomé Ruiz [Regarding the Balsa from Salango (Ecuador) Which Bartolome Ruiz Captured]
IN: Anuario de estudios americanos 35:453-554 (Sevilla)

Detailed characteristics of an early balsa raft.

S-548

AUTHORS: Szathmary, Emöke J. E., and N. S. Ossenberg
DATE: 1978
TITLE: Are the Biological Differences between North American Indians and Eskimos Truly Profound?
IN: Current Anthropology 19:673-701

Eskimos and Indians of the Na-Dene linguistic phylum represent offshoots of the same population base at c. 10,000 B.P. Also lightly reviews theories of Eskimo origin, emphasizing the variety of views. Commentators point out many complications in the interpretation offered by the authors (one of which is that the genetic distance separating East and West Greenland is as great as between West Greenland and the Navaho).

S-549

AUTHOR: Szemerényi, Oswald
DATE: 1987[?]
TITLE: Hounded out of Academe . . . : The Sad Fate of a Genius
IN: Studi di Storia e di Filologia Anatolica Dedicati a Giovanni Pugliese Carratelli (Elite [Edizioni Librarie Italiane Estere]: Florence), 257-294

Biographical summary and appreciation of the Hittitological accomplishments of Emil O. Forrer, a Swiss citizen who lived his last four decades in El Salvador [see F-135]. In 1946, while reading in the Variae Historiae of Claudius Aelianus (ca. A.D. 175-235), he was struck with a reported conversation between King Midas and Silenus which referred to a continent beyond the Old World. He then decided to move to Central America where he could "prove the accuracy and truth of the Silenus story about the volcano Anostos and the early trans-Atlantic contacts."

T-001

AUTHOR: Taboada Terán, Alvaro
DATE: 1982
TITLE: Mesoamérica: de su origen al modo de producción asiático [Mesoamerica: Of Its Origin in the Asiatic Mode of Production]
IMPRINT: Editorial Casa de la Cultura Ecuatoriana: Quito

A Nicaraguan educated at Tulane and relying heavily on Canals Frau recaps some of the "alocthonist" theories of American origins as well as the conventional "autocthonist" view. He concludes that diffused elements from Asia and Oceania indeed arrived in America where they were culturally important despite the relatively small numbers of bearers involved. But the high civilizations, characterized by the marxian (Godelierian) "Asiatic mode of production," were independent developments upon the Formative base.

T-002

AUTHOR: Talmage, James E.
DATE: 1911
TITLE: The Michigan Relics: A Story of Forgery and Deception
IN: Bulletin 2, Deseret Museum (Salt Lake City)

A geologist (and Mormon church leader), on the basis of field work in 1909, asserts that inscribed objects found in Michigan since 1874 were fraudulent. [Compare M-319 and C-267.]

T-005

AUTHOR: Tanner, Väinö
DATE: 1941
TITLE: Ruinerna på Sculpin Island (Kanayoktok) i Nains skärgård, Newfoundland-Labrador [Ruins on Sculpin Island (Kanayoktok) and the Place of Reefs in Newfoundland-Labrador]
IN: Geografisk Tidsskrift 44:129-155

Examines house ruins, which some have claimed to be Norse, and finds that they are Eskimo.

T-008

AUTHOR: Täuber, Carl [Karl]
DATE: 1925
TITLE: Algunas hipótesis vasco-indoeuropeo-indio [Some Basque-Indoeuropean-Indian Hypotheses]
IN: Gaea 1:200ff. (Buenos Aires)

An undocumented, arm-waving hypothesis of the spread of people from the Pyrenees to the Altai mountains to North America. Furthermore, "among the most advanced of the Indians there are cultural indications that show contact with the most advanced peoples who lived about 2000 B.C. in the angle formed by the three continents Europe, Asia and Africa" and who came to South America by circumnavigating Africa.

T-009

AUTHOR: Täuber, Carl [Karl]
DATE: 1928a
TITLE: Die neuesten Forschungen über die Herkunft der Indianer [The Latest Research on the Origin of the Indians]
IN: Petermanns Geographische Mitteilungen 74:90ff.

A concise summary of then-current sources and thinking about transpacific movements and influences into America. Recaps ethnographic, linguistic, legendary, physical anthropological, etc., evidences adduced by proponents of transpacific voyaging. A large map shows by lines and arrows routes proposed by Hrdlicka (Aleutian), Imbelloni, Rivet, Palavecino, and others.

T-010

AUTHOR: Täuber, Carl [Karl]
DATE: 1928b
TITLE: Polynesisches Sprachgut in Amerika und im Sumer [Polynesian Linguistic Heritage in America and Sumer]
IN: Petermanns Geographische Mitteilungen 74:283

A concise summary of then current sources and thinking about transpacific movements and influences into America. Recaps ethnographic, linguistic, legendary, physical anthropological, etc., evidences adduced by proponents of transpacific voyaging. A large map shows by lines and arrows routes for immigration proposed by Hrdlicka (Aleutians), Imbelloni, Rivet, Palavecino, and others.

T-011

AUTHOR: Täuber, Carl [Karl]
DATE: 1932
TITLE: Entwicklung der Menschheit von der Ur-Australien bis Europea auf Grund der neuesten Forschungen über die Wanderungen der Ozeanier [Development of Mankind from Primeval Australia to Europe Based on the Latest Research on the Migrations of the Oceanians]
IMPRINT: Grethlein: Zurich

He says his conclusions coincide remarkably with those expounded by Rivet in R-120. [See T-009, T-013, and T-014.]

T-013

AUTHOR: Täuber, Carl [Karl]
DATE: 1935
TITLE: Die Melanesier—das erste Kapitel der Weltgeschichte [The Melanesians—the First Chapter in World History]
IN: Bulletin der schweizerische Gesellschaft für Anthropologie und Ethnologie 11:16-22

See T-014.

T-014

AUTHOR: Täuber, Carl [Karl]
DATE: 1937
TITLE: Diffusion de la culture et de la langue des proto-Mélanésiennes dans toutes les régions du globe [Diffusion of the Culture and the Language of the Proto-Melanesians throughout all the Regions of the Globe]
IN: Scientia (May): 124-131

In the last few years two groups of scientists have focused on the movements of ancient peoples: (a) a Paris-Zürich group (Rivet, Täuber, Hevesy) and (b) a Viennese group (Eickstedt, Menghin,

Heine-Geldern). The former, on the basis of "a vast ensemble of facts," conclude that a major movement took place out of Indonesia-Australia via oceanic navigation. The latter group, on the contrary, following "ingenious speculations," see Interior Asia as the cradle of humanity. Anthropology, ethnology, and linguistics combine to eliminate the oppositions between these two groups. He then compares certain words which clarify the movements along the lines of Rivet's publications.

T-015

AUTHOR: Taylor, Andrew
DATE: 1955
TITLE: Geographical Discovery and Exploration in the Queen Elizabeth Islands
IMPRINT: Memoir 3, Geographical Branch (Canada Department of Mines and Technical Surveys: Ottawa)

Includes a brief discussion of the evidence for a Norse presence in the islands, including Ellesmere Island, in the late Middle Ages.

T-016

AUTHOR: Taylor, Archer
DATE: 1944
TITLE: American Indian Riddles
IN: Journal of American Folklore 57:1-15

Anthropologists have declared that American Indians lacked riddles, although riddles are known everywhere else in the world. Upon examining the published material, the author concludes that probably some American Indians did have riddles of their own.

T-017

AUTHOR: Taylor, Douglas
DATE: 1949
TITLE: The Interpretation of Some Documentary Evidence on Carib Culture
IN: Southwestern Journal of Anthropology 5:379-392

Page 386: "Botanists usually describe yams (Dioscorea spp.) as of Old World origin, but it now seems certain that a species of Dioscorea trifida, known to the Carib as kúsu, and formerly much employed by them, was American."

T-018

AUTHOR: Taylor, Douglas
DATE: 1962
TITLE: Review of *Papers in Caribbean Anthropology*, compiled by Sidney W. Mintz
IN: American Anthropologist 64:179-186

Regarding M-215 the reviewer agrees that while sails were first introduced by Europeans, use of raised plank sides on large dugouts was probably pre-Columbian for Taino and Island Carib. Taylor furnishes original information on terminology: while the words for sail show borrowing from Spanish, all words referring to parts found only in canoes with built-up sides appear to be native. Data are given on dimensions of the impressive Island Carib vessels.

T-019

AUTHOR: Taylor, E. G. R.
DATE: 1926
TITLE: A Pre-Columbian Discovery of America
IN: Geographical Journal 67:282-283

A critical note on O-018 which would rob the argument there of validity if the criticism is correct.

T-020

AUTHOR: Taylor, E. G. R.
DATE: 1956
TITLE: The Haven-finding Art: A History of Navigation from Odysseus to Captain Cook

IMPRINT: Hollis and Carter: London [Second edition, 1971]

Excellent information on many aspects of navigation for Phoenicians, Greeks, Irish, Norse, medieval Europeans, Arabs, and later sailors.

Page 79. Norse voyages to the Faroes, Iceland and Greenland were made in round-built merchant ships, and not in the long-oared Viking ships which were used for pirate raids and war, of which alone specimens have been preserved.

T-021

AUTHOR: Taylor, E. G. R.
DATE: 1964a
TITLE: A Fourteenth-Century Riddle and Its Solution
IN: Geographical Review 54:573-576

A narrative tells of a fisherman's experiences in a rich country, more than 1000 miles west of the Faroes, about A.D. 1354-1380, which he here considers to have been the coasts of Labrador and Newfoundland, with Markland the southern half of Labrador.

T-022

AUTHOR: Taylor, E. G. R.
DATE: 1964b
TITLE: Imaginary Islands: A Problem Solved
IN: Geographical Journal 130:105-109

He gives reasons for accepting as real the islands represented in medieval maps of the Atlantic.

T-023

AUTHOR: Taylor, E. G. R.
DATE: 1965
TITLE: The Fisherman's Story, 1354
IN: Geographical Magazine 37:709-712 (London)

Account of a fisherman from the Faroes, blown by a gale to Labrador. After several years there in the Norse colony of Markland (Estotiland) and in captivity among the Algonkian Indians, he returned home in 1380. His story was recounted in a purported letter by a Venetian visitor to the Faroes and published by Nicolo Zeno in 1558. A recurring, though infrequent, meteorological situation over the North Atlantic produces an east-northeasterly flow for up to 10 days which could drive a square-rigged vessel from Europe to North America between 50 and 60 degrees North.

T-024

AUTHOR: Taylor, Gordon D.
DATE: 1953
TITLE: Some Crop Distributions by Tribes in Upland Southeast Asia
IN: Southwestern Journal of Anthropology 9:296-308

Pages 300-301: Some scholars such as Sauer argue for pre-Columbian introduction of maize into Southeast Asia; others favor a post-Columbian date. A clue may come from present-day distribution, mapped on page 300, that shows higher prevalence in the eastern than in the western half of upland Southeast Asia. This may indicate that maize spread predominantly from China.

T-025

AUTHOR: Taylor, Herbert C., Jr.
DATE: 1971
TITLE: Vinland and the Way Thither
IN: Man across the Sea: Problems of Pre-Columbian Contacts, edited by Carroll L. Riley, et al. (University of Texas Press: Austin), 242-254

The "Vinland Map and the Tartar Relation" documents do not appear authentic. Such cartographic and documentary items hold poor prospects for shedding light on Norse contacts with North America.

T-027

AUTHOR: Taylor, William E.
DATE: 1964
TITLE: The Prehistory of the Quebec-Labrador Peninsula
IN: École Pratique des Hautes Études, Bibliothèque arctique et antarctique 2:181-210 (Paris) [Also in French, 1964, Anthropology Papers 7 (National Museum of Canada: Ottawa)]

Discusses Archaic, Woodland, and Eskimo Pre-Dorset, Dorset, and Thule cultures, reviewing major sites and remains. A brief Viking occupation around 1000 is considered possible.

T-028

AUTHOR: Taylor, William E.
DATE: 1965
TITLE: The Fragments of Eskimo Prehistory
IN: The Beaver 295:4-17 (Winnipeg)

In a broad survey, discounts the theory of a Dorset-Norse blending to produce the Thule culture.

T-029

AUTHOR: Tee, Garry J.
DATE: 1980
TITLE: Evidence for the Chinese Origin of the Jaguar Motif in Chavin Art
IN: Asian Perspectives 21/1:27-29 (Honolulu)

Comparison of feline-shaped vessels of Chavin and Early Chou shows such close similarities as to imply transpacific influence.

T-030

AUTHOR: Teeter, Karl V.
DATE: 1964
TITLE: Lexicostatistics and Genetic Relationship
IN: Language 39:638-648

Questions the postulates of lexicostatistics and especially use of the scheme to construct supposed linguistic history. Lexicostatistics is not a key to history but a ground-clearing operation prior to historical research.

T-032

AUTHOR: Tekiner, Roselle
DATE: 1974a
TITLE: Trans-Pacific Contact: The Evidence of the Panpipe
IN: Proceedings of the 40th International Congress of Americanists (Rome and Genoa, 1972), 2:31-38

Reference to the panpipe as evidence of transpacific contact has been based primarily on criteria suggested by musicologists von Hornbostel and Sachs. To them the similarities between panpipes of the Solomon Islands and western Brazil could not have been due to chance. Subsequent studies by Bukofzer and Schlesinger cast doubt on the significance of the parallels. Form parallels were also mentioned, as well as alternation in sequential notes between the two sides of the instrument, as in China, Burma and the Andes. The Bahia culture of coastal Ecuador has panpipes comparable to southeastern Asia.

The author examined 850 panpipes, critically evaluating the proposed parallels in detail as evidence for contact. Important as methodology. Her conclusion is that a number of features provide interesting evidence for transoceanic contact, but not in the absolute sense claimed by von Hornbostel [see H-410, H-411]. [See T-033 for a fuller treatment.]

T-033

AUTHOR: Tekiner, Roselle
DATE: 1974b
TITLE: The Panpipe as Indicator of Culture Contact: A Test of Tolstoy's Method in Long Range Comparison

IMPRINT: Unpublished; Ph.D. dissertation, City University of New York [University Microfilms International Order No. 7419488]

A world-wide inventory of panpipe traits was compiled from museum collections and publications. Types were defined for South America and the Pacific islands based on those traits. Andean and Melanesian types resemble each other in musical features more than any two other types. The parallels were analyzed according to Tolstoy's criteria [T-108]. The results do not successfully demonstrate the probability of a relationship between Andean and Melanesian panpipes due to unsuitability of the available data.

However, a demonstration of the likelihood of a relationship between panpipes of the Pacific and South America was made by separate comparisons of traits that determine musical characteristics and those that do not. Coefficients of similarity were derived for all possible pairs of types, from which clusters of types were constructed. Clustering on the basis of musical traits is supported by distribution patterns, but not by morphological traits unrelated to music making. The results suggest that musical traits are the more reliable indicators of cultural affiliations.

T-034

AUTHOR: Tekiner, Roselle

DATE: 1977

TITLE: The Evidence of the Panpipe for Trans-Pacific Contact

IN: Archiv für Völkerkunde 31:7-132

Essentially the same as T-033.

T-035

AUTHOR: Tello, Julio C.

DATE: 1909

TITLE: La antigüedad de la sífilis en el Perú [The Antiquity of Syphilis in Peru]

IMPRINT: Sanmarti: Lima [Universidad Mayor de San Marcos, Faculdad de Medicina]

Syphilis, for which he gives a Quechua name, was ancient here.

T-036

AUTHOR: Tello, Julio C.

DATE: 1913

TITLE: Prehistoric Trephining among the Yauyos of Peru

IN: Proceedings of the 18th International Congress of Americanists (London, 1912), pages 75-83

Page 83: Details of trephining are illustrated and discussed. In a collection of 400 crania with artificial openings in the dome, 250 showed that the operation had succeeded, an astonishing success rate.

T-038

AUTHOR: ten Kate, Hermann

DATE: 1892

TITLE: Sur la question de la pluralité et de la parenté des races en Amérique [On the Question of the Plurality and Relatedness of American Races]

IN: Proceedings of the 8th International Congress of Americanists (Paris, 1890), pages 288-294

Reviewing and criticizing statements by scholars of the day about the origin of American Indians, he insists that they are broadly Mongoloid (including Melanesians and Polynesians in that category), although only the Dene and others of northwestern North America are unmistakably and directly derived from Asiatics now visible to us.

T-039

AUTHOR: ten Kate, Hermann

DATE: 1897-1898

TITLE: Geographical Distribution of the Musical Bow
IN: American Anthropologist (o.s.) 11:93-94

Reports buying a simple musical bow (called "koh'lo") in 1896 from a Tehuelche (Patagonian) Indian. Compares the name of the bow in the Solomon Islands ("kolove"). He believes such an instrument is very old and nearly worldwide thus independently invented in a number of localities.

A note following, by O. T. Mason, points out that his position on invention has been given in several articles—simple ones with few parts (like this bow) might arise independently, but devices with many parts are less likely to do so. In any case the horsehair string of the Tehuelche specimen could not have been pre-Columbian; the device may not be older than the European-introduced horse.

T-039B

AUTHOR: ten Kate, Hermann
DATE: 1884
TITLE: Matériaux pour servir a l'anthropologie de la presqu'ile californienne [Materials Contributing to the Anthropology of Baja California]
IN: Bulletin de la société d'anthropologie de Paris, 3e serie, 7:551-569

"The native race which exists in Eastern [Baja] California and the adjoining islands forms a link between Melanesian and American races" and ties to the Lagoa Santa specimen of Brazil.

T-040

AUTHOR: Tentori, Tullio
DATE: 1947
TITLE: Su alcuni pestelli dell'Oceania e della costa nord occidentale dell'America settentrionale [About Some Pestles from Oceania and the North West Coast of South America]
IN: Rivista di antropologia 35:421-423

Grain- or root-grinding pestles of exactly the same shape are found in parts of Oceania and South America.

T-041

AUTHOR: Termer, Franz
DATE: 1951
TITLE: Die "Hühner" der Azteken [The "Fowl" of the Aztecs]
IN: Zeitschrift für Ethnologie 76/2:205-215

16th- to 18th-century observers reported domestic fowl in Middle America when actually they meant turkeys. The author finds no evidence for pre- Columbian chickens there, nor for fowls introduced via the Pacific from southern Asia. [Contrast C-089.]

T-042

AUTHOR: Terrell, John
DATE: 1986
TITLE: Prehistory in the Pacific Islands: A Study of Variation in Language, Customs, and Human Biology
IMPRINT: Cambridge University Press: Cambridge

A superior discussion of how, and how not, to learn about the past from archaeological study using Pacific Island materials. Of special relevance is his careful discussion of what Heyerdahl and Skjölsvold found on the Galapagos Islands and the various, inconclusive, ways in which this may be interpreted. It does not mean that they demonstrated that pre-Spanish South Americans voyaged to the Galapagos.

T-043

AUTHOR: Te-tzu Chang
DATE: 1983

TITLE: The Origins and Early Cultures of the Cereal Grains and Food Legumes
IN: The Origins of Chinese Civilization, edited by David N. Keightley (University of California Press: Berkeley), 65-94

Page 81: A single statement says the peanut was a foreign introduction but leaves unclear whether the author considers it [with K. Chang] pre-Columbian.

T-044

AUTHOR: Thalbitzer, William Carl
DATE: 1913
TITLE: Four Skraeling Words from Markland (Newfoundland) in the Saga of Erik the Red (Eirikr Rauti)
IN: Proceedings of the 18th International Congress of Americanists (London, 1912), pages 87-95

He accepts Nova Scotia as Vinland; identifies four non-Norse words in Icelandic accounts and tries to show they are Eskimo.

Page 94: Defends traditional interpretations against Nansen's revisionism that considers Vinland mythical.

T-045

AUTHOR: Thalbitzer, William Carl
DATE: 1914-1923
TITLE: The Ammassalik Eskimo, I-II
IN: Meddelelser om Grønland 39-40

First Part: Suggests several Japanese influences on the Eskimo.

Second part, pages 577-580: Notes similarities between Eskimo and Kerek (Chukotan) languages.

T-046

AUTHOR: Thalbitzer, William Carl
DATE: 1924a
TITLE: Hans Peter Steensby's Paper on the Norsemen's Route from Greenland to Wineland
IN: Proceedings of the 20th International Congress of Americanists (Rio de Janeiro, 1922), 1:99-102

Steensby had planned to give a paper but his death precluded it. Thalbitzer communicates the main lines of his intent. Steensby went through the descriptions in the sagas in relation to modern maps, supplemented by his personal observations from Quebec around to southern Newfoundland. The coast of Labrador and into the St. Lawrence estuary is where we find Helluland to Wineland, the latter being the St. Lawrence valley.

T-047

AUTHOR: Thalbitzer, William Carl
DATE: 1924b
TITLE: Parallels within the Culture of the Arctic Peoples
IN: Proceedings of the 20th International Congress of Americanists (Rio de Janeiro, 1922), 1:283-287

Circumpolar resemblances, from the Lapps through Siberia to East Greenland, are so marked that one wonders about a common origin. The forked lifting stick from Greenland, for example, is so much like the Lapp hammer that he feels there must be some sort of connection between them.

T-048

AUTHOR: Thalbitzer, William Carl
DATE: 1925
TITLE: Cultic Games and Festivals in Greenland
IN: Proceedings of the 21st International Congress of Americanists (Part 2, Gothenburg, Sweden, 1924), pages 236-255

Page 254: Reports what he considers an Ainu-Japanese loan word in Eskimo. He had suggested earlier a probable connection of the Eskimo term for human being with a Japanese origin myth. H. G. Steensby supposed Japanese influence on neo-Eskimo culture in the neighborhood of Bering Strait in whaling and skin (umiak) boats. Japanese fishermen are supposed to have visited the northerly whaling districts during centuries prior to 1641.

T-049

AUTHOR: Thalbitzer, William Carl
DATE: 1928a
TITLE: Die kultischen Gottheiten der Eskimos
[The Ritual Gods of the Eskimos]
IN: Archiv für Religionswissenschaft 26:364-430

Nansen supposed that the gods of the Greenland Eskimo were derived from the Norse because of notable similarities. Here the author traces the Eskimo roots rather to Central Asia, received via Alaska. The Norse gods had their own ties to the common Asiatic source.

T-050

AUTHOR: Thalbitzer, William Carl
DATE: 1928b
TITLE: Is There Any Connection between the Eskimo Language and the Uralian?
IN: Proceedings of the 22nd International Congress of Americanists (Rome, 1926), 2:551-567

Critiques previous approaches to this question, particular those of Uhlenbeck and Sauvageot, concluding that there is only a faint possibility of a relationship in language between Eskimo and Ugro-Finnish, or any nearer languages.

T-052

AUTHOR: Thalbitzer, William Carl
DATE: 1944
TITLE: Uhlenbeck's Eskimo-Indoeuropean Hypothesis
IN: Traveaux de cercle linguistique de Copenhagen 1:66-96

Serious and largely sympathetic evaluation of the hypothesis, which looked to convergence, plus some mutual ancient Asiatic contact, rather than genetic relationship. Krauss describes it as "the most important discussion in print on that subject."

T-053

AUTHOR: Thalbitzer, William Carl
DATE: 1948
TITLE: On the Eskimo Language
IN: Proceedings of the 26th International Congress of Americanists (Seville, 1935), 1:403-406

Notes Uhlenbeck's theory of Indo-European roots in the Eskimo lexicon. Also, a handful of Eskimo words with apparent parallels in Yakut, Tungus, Dakota, and Algonkin, but these similarities, "astonishingly few," may be fortuitous.

T-054

AUTHOR: Thalbitzer, William Carl
DATE: 1951a
TITLE: Two Runic Stones, from Greenland and Minnesota
IMPRINT: Smithsonian Institution Miscellaneous Collections 116/3 [Reviewed 1953 by W. S. Godfrey, Jr., *American Anthropologist* 55:275-276]

A translation of "To fjaerne runestene frå Grønland og Amerika," *Danske Studier,* 1946-1947.

A runological study of a west Greenlandic stone with the one from Kensington finds significant resemblances between the two, but he hedges by saying that while both may be authentic, the authenticity of the Kensington piece is uncertain.

T-055

AUTHOR: Thalbitzer, William Carl
DATE: 1951b
TITLE: The Voyage of Powell Knutsson; a Lost Expedition to Greenland—and Further to Vinland?
IN: Linden-Museum für Länder- und Völkerkunde, Jahrbuch, Neue Folge, 1:92-97
[A modification and translation from Danish of an article published in *Det Grønlandske Selskabs Årsskrift,* 1948, Copenhagen]

A translation of and comments on King Magnus' letter of 1354 ordering Knutsson to go to Greenland to support the Christian faith. He reached the colony, then went farther but vanished. Rare fur products reached Europe in the Middle Ages from America. In 1347 a Greenland ship with a crew of 17 that had been in Markland, happened to be driven straight to Iceland by storms.

T-056

AUTHOR: Thalbitzer, William Carl
DATE: 1952
TITLE: Possible Early Contacts between Eskimo and Old World Languages
IN: Indian Tribes of Aboriginal America; Selected Papers of the 29th International Congress of Americanists (New York, 1949), edited by Sol Tax (University of Chicago Press: Chicago), 50-54

Only a few loan-words between Chukchee-Koryak and Eskimo can be noted. There is no genetic relationship to neighboring Asiatic languages. Over the past 50 years he has sought Eskimo loan-words or "inner" resemblances among the languages of North American Indians, Ainu, Japanese, Turkish, Tungus, and even more distant peoples and gives the meager findings (e.g., Eskimo Asiak, deity of rain; Aztec, Asiak, rain-god). He concludes that Eskimo is not related to any other language in the world.

T-056B

AUTHOR: Thapa, J. K.
DATE: 1966
TITLE: Primitive Maize with the Lepchas
IN: Bulletin of Tibetology 3:29-31 (Namgyal Institute of Tibetology, Gangtok, Sikkim)

A "primitive" race of maize found in Sikkim in 1962 by Sprague and Dhawan bears "the closest resemblance to the wild maize of which an actual specimen in fossil was uncovered (1960) in the lower levels of San Marcos Cave in Mexico" as reported by Mangelsdorf. There is a possibility to find archaeological remains of maize in the Himalayas and Trans-Himalayas if archaeology could be undertaken there. Furthermore, there is "more than an element of chance that adequate references to maize plants may be found in ancient Tibetan literature" and one such reference is known to occur in the rGyal-Bod-yig-tshang (text) which "dates back to a period before the discovery of America." A date of 1368 for the introduction of maize to China through Tibet as recorded by the Chinese naturalist Li Shih-Chen cannot be ruled out at this time [see S-518].

T-056C

AUTHOR: Thayer, Marshall
DATE: 1980
TITLE: Motivational Aspects of Early Norse Exploration
IN: Anthropological Journal of Canada 18/4:16-17

Tries to follow Norse thinking about exploration and concludes that they would have set no arbitrary southern limit but would tend to follow a coast as far as time and inclination permitted. They could well have explored Hudson Bay. A footnote by T. E. Lee, the editor, commends the extensive, generally inaccessible materials (in Icelandic in manuscript) by the late Jon Duason as of much value on these matters [see D-184]. Lee further notes that informants have reported to him possible Viking ship remains and structures on the west of Hudson Bay.

T-057

AUTHOR: Thomas, Cyrus W.
DATE: 1884
TITLE: Origin of the Indians
IN: American Antiquarian and Oriental Journal 16:3-14, 99-105

It is highly probable that Polynesian and Melanesian influences reached the Pacific slope of America. Emphasizes Haida-Polynesian comparisons. An earlier, darker ("Papuan") race could have preceded the Polynesians and also reached America.

T-058

AUTHOR: Thomas, Cyrus W.
DATE: 1886
TITLE: The Davenport Tablet
IN: Science 7:10-11, 189-190

Points to apparent contradictions in the proceedings published by the Davenport Academy of Science on the Davenport Stone. These may indicate fraud and need investigation and explanation. A response by F. H. Putnam for the Academy on pages 119-120 condemns the refusal by Thomas or others in Washington to come investigate first hand. Thomas responds on pages 189-190; he "prefers" to use the proceedings as his basis, so a visit is not necessary. Putnam further defends his position against Thomas' charges on pages 437-439.

T-059

AUTHOR: Thomas, Cyrus W,
DATE: 1894a
TITLE: Polynesian Types in Mexico and Central America
IN: American Antiquarian and Oriental Journal 16:99-105

Continues T-057 giving additional evidence for Polynesian and Melanesian influences, especially as related to the origin of some peculiar features of Mexican and Central American civilization. Compares features of the Hawaiian calendar, including animals associated with day names [anticipating D. Kelley and Moran]. That influence must have come directly to Mexico/Central America, for it does not appear elsewhere in America.

T-060

AUTHOR: Thomas, Cyrus W.
DATE: 1894b
TITLE: The Maya Year
IN: Smithsonian Institution, Bureau of American Ethnology Bulletin 18 (Washington, D.C.)

Points out similarities between the Maya and Polynesian calendar systems, from which he infers dependence of the Maya on the latter and the ultimate Asiatic derivation of both.

T-061

AUTHOR: Thomas, Cyrus W.
DATE: 1894c
TITLE: Tennessee Mound Explorations
IN: Twelfth Annual Report of the Bureau of Ethnology to the Secretary of the Smithsonian Institution, 1890-91

Includes his account of obtaining what has come to be known as the Bat Creek stone, on which is an inscription that Thomas considered Cherokee, in Sequoyah's syllabary [but which has been claimed (G-169, G-171, M-197) as Hebrew].

T-062

AUTHOR: Thomas, Cyrus W.
DATE: 1896
TITLE: The Vigesimal System of Numeration
IN: American Anthropologist (o.s.) 9:409-410

There are indications that a vigesimal system preceded in Southeast Asia the commoner decimal one. Analyzes some Polynesian data and concludes that an older (vigesimal) system was also used in Polynesia, probably derived from Malaysia. The Maya method of numeration was very similar to the early Polynesian one.

T-063

AUTHOR: Thomas, Cyrus W.
DATE: 1898
TITLE: Maya and Malay
IN: Journal of the Polynesian Society 7:89-100

A series of similarities is noted in the two languages, particularly related to the calendar or astronomy. They seem inexplicable except on the theory that a strong Malay element has been infused into the Maya family. More could be given if there were space to draw at length on the Hindu Mahabharata, the ultimate source of the Malay epics. [See also T-144.]

T-064

AUTHOR: Thomas, N. W.
DATE: 1901
TITLE: Note on Some American Parallels to European Agricultural Customs
IN: Journal of the Anthropological Institute 31:155-156

From Florida, the Papago, Pawnee, Prussian Slavs and Woguls he draws examples of use of a slain animal (skin) hung in a tree together with foodstuffs as an offering. "The corn-spirit which we know in Europe reappears almost unchanged in America." Nothing is said of diffusion; one supposes he follows Fraser.

T-065

AUTHOR: Thomas, Norman D.
DATE: 1956
TITLE: A Revision of the Distribution of Armor in Native North America
IMPRINT: Unpublished; M.A. thesis, University of New Mexico

Of three North American areas where armor was used, the Alaskan was essentially like Asiatic plate armor and was late in the Alaskan sequence. It was significantly separated from and largely unrelated to other North American armors. Alaskan slat armor, the New World type most often proposed to be connected to plate armor, has a much closer affinity to New World rod armor of western North America. An eastern states rod armor shows no connection to that in the west.

T-066

AUTHOR: Thomas, Stephen D.
DATE: 1985
TITLE: The Sons of Palulep: Navigating without Instruments in Oceania
IN: Oceanus 28/1:52-58

Page 56: Piailug of Satawal, Micronesia, teaches a yachtsman his methods. Piailug knows star paths for all islands of the Carolines, Hawaii, California, South America, Tahiti, Samoa, Marquesas, Tuamotus, Cooks, Marshalls, Tonga, Japan. He learned these from his grandfather "from long, long ago" (the author supposes some of these were learned, however, through Micronesians aboard European sailing ships late in the last century). Bodies of knowledge supplementing star paths are also discussed.

T-067

AUTHOR: Thompson, Almose A., Jr.
DATE: 1975

TITLE: Pre-Columbian Black Presence in the Western Hemisphere
IN: Negro History Bulletin 38:452-456

Believes that "sometime during the first few centuries following the death of Jesus Christ, black African explorers began voyages to the New World; perhaps as a part of a world wide trade network." Uses mainly older sources.

T-068

AUTHOR: Thompson, Claiborne W.
DATE: 1975
TITLE: Crooning his Own Quaint Runes: The Professional Runologist and the Enthusiastic Amateur
IN: Man in the Northeast 9:2-8

Asserts that no authentic rune stones have been found anywhere in North America; all were either forged or produced by natural means.

T-069

AUTHOR: Thompson, Gunnar
DATE: 1989
TITLE: Nu Sun: Asian-American Voyages 500 b.c.
IMPRINT: Argonaut: Fresno, California

On the basis primarily of isolated motifs from the two areas, he maintains that Asians (led by one Nu Sun who was backed by fanatical Korean mercenaries) sailed to Guatemala and Honduras by 500 B.C. and established a trading colony among "the primitive Mayan tribes." The Mayans, hitherto "wallowing in the backwaters of Olmec domination," welcomed these civilizers, for they offered cultural and political means for withstanding the Olmecs who had been taking slaves, tribute, and sacrificial victims. The new colony permitted the "first great commercial alliance in the Americas" with trade routes between there and China and Indonesia by which the Mayans gained literary, artistic, religious, and political inspiration that allowed them to endure as a civilization for more than a thousand years. The visitors shared the blowgun and bow with the natives, while Taoist mystics amazed them with such devices as magical mirrors, smoking pipes (for herbs and opium), magnetic needles, iron knives, oil lamps, mercury, and dragon kites. Evidence can be seen, for example, in Izapa Stela 5 which displays 13 Asian elements such as paired fishes, serpent/turtle, and parasol. By A.D. 800-900, the golden age of this Mayan confederacy, there were further or renewed Asian contacts, evidenced by such items as corbelled vaults, colonnades, atlantean figures, and elephant images.

T-069B

AUTHOR: Thompson, Gunnar
DATE: 1992
TITLE: American Discovery—The Real Story
IMPRINT: Argonauts Misty Isles Press: Seattle

Illustrated by the author's sketches of comparative artifacts and motifs, although he is less than meticulous about details put into his drawings based on original and secondary sources. At points strains logic and fails to criticize sources utilized, which range from odd-ball to sound without his noting the difference. He accepts unquestioningly materials other diffusionists question, yet he casts a wide net to dig up obscure information some of which may prove of value.

Pages xvi-xvii: In a chronological table he shows bamboo rafts with A-mast sail and single-person reed raft before 25,000 B.C. Totora reed boat, skin basket, and dugout canoe with woven reed sail before 12,000 B.C. Skin boat with hide sail and dugout canoe with a bark-fiber sail on a V-mast in the Neolithic, between 12,000 and 5000 B.C. Reed ship with woven flax sail and sewn plank-extended dugout with secured steering paddle by 3000 B.C. Plank ships: junk with lug sail, and galley with square cotton sail before 1000 B.C. "From 3000 B.C. onward, all the world's major civilizations had plank-built boats which were capable of sailing to America" (no documentation).

Page 2: "Ancient Routes to America." In addition to migrants by land 150,000 to 100,000 years ago, who reached South America by 60,000 B.C., he sees maritime hunters sailing around the North Pacific rim between 12,000 and 3000 B.C. and Northern European "Red Paint People" following migratory seabirds to America between 9000 and 2000 B.C.

Pages 14-15: His sketches of skulls claim to demonstrate "that America's Native Peoples were the world's most cosmopolitan 'race.' " "Greenberg's (linguistic) analysis supports theories of three major Asian maritime [*sic*] migrations."

Pages 25-45: "Japanese Voyagers." "Japanese epigrapher Nobuhiro Yoshida identified the exodus of a maritime tribe, the Azumi, from Kyushu, Japan, between the 8th and 13th centuries. He believes the tribe sailed to America and . . . became the ancestors of the Zuni" (citation: Japan Petrograph Society, "Semitic Inscriptions Found in Japan," 1991). Prof. Orozco identifies the Purépecha [Tarascan] tribe of Western Mexico as probable descendants of Japanese islanders. He reported similar Purépechan and Japanese folktales (the example given: foxes and coyotes have weddings during storms, hence mothers admonish their children to stay indoors) (page 41, citation: "Professor Cecilio Orozco, California State University, Fresno, and Domingo Valdez [1990]," personal communication?). Rice came from Japan. "During the formative phase of developing civilizations, from 3000 B.C. to 500 B.C., rice served as a primary food source. Mayan rice farmers built extensive canals in the midst of the jungle for rice farming. . . . After maize farming superseded rice farming circa A.D. 500, the canals were no longer necessary, and they were abandoned. Archeologists were baffled when they uncovered canals in the Mayan region" (page 44).

Pages 47-69: "Ancient Mariners (10,000 B.C.-1000 B.C.)." Atlantis, Red Paint people, "Babylonian maps and traditions of a western continent," reed ships, Old World scripts in South America, lotus symbol, four quarters, stepped pyramid, myths, plant diffusion (bottle gourd, cotton, henna, pineapple), batik, cylinder seal, etc.

Pages 71-89: "Egyptian Explorers (5000 B.C.-350 B.C.)." Jairazbhoy, Olmec faces, mathematics and astronomy, Bes, ankh knot, reed ships, inscriptions, serpent apron, trephining, embalming, etc.

Pages 91-105: "Black African Creators (1000 B.C.-A.D. 1500)." Olmec heads, Abubakari's voyage, African ships, van Sertima, Wuthenau, black African languages in South America, plants and animals (yam, jackbean, "hogs" distinguished from peccary, the former claimed found in but not indigenous to the Americas), etc.

Pages 107-137: "Chinese Merchants (3000 B.C.-A.D.1850)." Ships, Fu Sang, world maps, coins, inscriptions, yin-yang, Paul Shao's symbols, quipu, balsa raft, Ekholm, Asian dogs in America, rice farming, the first horses in America were from China, smoking pipes, jade/cinnabar, myths and beliefs, cylindrical pots, bow and arrow, plants (peanut, tobacco, anona, chili, sweet potato, maize, hibiscus), 18-month calendar with 20-day month, etc.

Pages 139-163: "Minoans & Phoenicians (3400 B.C.-146 B.C.)." Ships, Lake Superior copper trade, maze design, purple, coins, inscriptions, Parahyba.

Pages 165-191: "Greco-Roman Traders (146 B.C.-A.D.900)." Ships, maps, shipwrecks, amphoras, coins, metal implements, lamps, Roman figurines, symbols, Hebrew refugees (Bat Creek), inscriptions, Los Lunas stone, Newark stones, star of David, Hebrew words, Calalus, burnt bricks and mason's marks, fortified cities, colonnade, pineapple, barley, pumpkin, beans, bubonic plague.

Pages 193-215: "Welsh & Irish Rovers (3000 B.C.-A.D.1200)." Megaliths, Brendan, ogam, legends, ships, metal tools, potatoes, wine grapes from Europe, Madoc, Mallery's iron, etc.

Pages 217-241: "Hindu Seafarers (A.D. 100-1500)." Hindu and Indonesian ships, elephant, symbols, chickens, blowguns, panpipe, wheeled toys, "printing wheels," patolli, "monster doorway," iron tools, sun pillar, memorial stelae, niche temple, tumbaga/tembaga name, calendar, bark cloth, paper, maize in India, pineapple, tomato, typhus, cholera, hookworm, etc. (Concerning cholera he states, "In the 9th century, cholera or a similar pandemic devastated Mayan cities throughout Central America causing the collapse of the Mayan Confederacy. At least ten million Mayans perished from this epidemic" page 236.)

Pages 243-263: "Pacific Island Voyagers (2000 B.C.-A.D. 1500)." Ships, legends, bark cloth, physical types, animals and plants, much Heyerdahl.

Pages 265-287: "The Vikings (1700 B.C.-A.D. 1400)."

Pages 289-309: "Merchants of Arabia (A.D. 630-1492)."

Pages 311-337: "Vanguard of Conquest (Late Medieval Europe A.D. 1200-1480)." Maps, Basques, Sinclair, Zenos, Antilia, Quetzalcoatl, diseases, horses.

T-070

AUTHOR: Thompson, Homer C.
DATE: 1923
TITLE: Vegetable Crops
IMPRINT: McGraw-Hill: New York [Second edition 1931; another edition 1949]

Page 373: The sweet potato, a native of tropical America, "was carried to the islands of the Pacific very early. It was apparently known in China early in the Christian Era."

T-071

AUTHOR: Thompson, Henry O.
DATE: 1967
TITLE: Tell el-Husn—Biblical Beth-shan
IN: Biblical Archaeologist 30/4:110-135

The Late Bronze Age Temple of Mekal [shows features reminiscent of later Mesoamerica]: lion figure is thought to signify deity status; the lion itself commonly in the Near East is associated with kings and gods. Here the figure is Nergal, Sumerian god of disease and war, the devourer, associated with death and burial; Nergal was feline lord of the underworld—the sun god who was spending the night in the underworld. Also he had fertility and war associations, and his cult symbols included snakes. He was worshipped from Sumerian times at least to third century Phoenicia. The dog as protector and healer is also represented here.

Page 117: A radial star on the lion's shoulder [compare K-007] represents deity in Ugarit, Egypt, and Mesopotamia. [See G-026 for Mesoamerica.]

Page 122: Stelae at Beth-shan syncretistically combine Mesopotamian and Egyptian elements.

Pages 123ff.: Abundant animal figurines are associated with the cult of Nergal/ Mekal/Set (lion/underworld) and perhaps with necromancy. Feline relation to temples, kings, gods. A fertility connection is seen in Nergal's marriage to Ereshkigal, the goddess of the underworld. He carried a mace with two lions on it, symbolizing his double role. Lotus as a symbol of life in Egypt.

T-072

AUTHOR: Thompson, John Eric S.
DATE: 1927
TITLE: The Elephant Heads in the Waldeck Manuscripts
IN: Scientific Monthly 25:392-398

If these are elephants, then this would show late Asiatic influence, but all this is uncertain. Even if Waldeck were reliable, and he is not, this would only slightly modify autocthonist views.

T-073

AUTHOR: Thompson, John Eric S.
DATE: 1928
TITLE: The "Children of the Sun" and Central America
IN: Antiquity 2:161-167

Most of the piece is a put-down of Elliot Smith and Perry in the orthodox manner. In two final paragraphs Thompson opens a slight door for diffusion.

Monsters, dragons, and double-headed serpents found in Mesoamerica appear to have little connection with basic Maya religion ("plain nature worship"), and when they appear in late old empire times they "have an Asiatic air" about them. True turbans are seen (citing specifically a figurine in Blom and La Farge, *Tribes and Temples,* 1926, figure 81). The elephant controversy is too deep to get into, "nevertheless the Yalloch vase is a difficult thing to be explained away by non-believers."

Patolli-pachisi and purple dye are other interesting points, but comparison of temple mounds with Egyptian pyramids won't do. "As a working hypothesis" we might see autocthonous Maya civilization "at some period towards the close of the old empire" receiving Asiatic influence, introducing new religious concepts, some changes in apparel, and possibly metalworking. More excavation is needed to check this possibility.

T-074

AUTHOR: Thompson, John Eric S.
DATE: 1933
TITLE: Mexico before Cortes: An Account of the Daily Life, Religion, and Ritual of the Aztecs and Kindred Peoples
IMPRINT: Scribner's: New York

Page 232: Remarks on the similarity of coca-chewing in America and betel- chewing in southeast Asia.

Page 290: Regarding some images of animals in Mesoamerican art, in a few cases "the trunks are certainly very elephantine," which he thinks came from "a half-forgotten tradition of the mastadon."

T-075

AUTHOR: Thompson, John Eric S.
DATE: 1934
TITLE: Sky Bearers, Colours and Directions in Maya and Mexican Religion
IN: Carnegie Institution of Washington Contributions to American Archaeology 2/10:209-242

A basic source for potential comparisons with Asia. [See also T-077.]

T-076

AUTHOR: Thompson, John Eric S.
DATE: 1949
TITLE: Canoes and Navigation of the Maya and Their Neighbors
IN: Journal of the Royal Anthropological Institute 79:69-78

Evidence from archaeological and documentary sources indicates a greater mastery of navigation than hitherto supposed, including use of sails, raised gunwales, possibly the double canoe with sail, crotch-headed paddle, calabash and reed rafts, etc.

T-077

AUTHOR: Thompson, John Eric S.
DATE: 1954
TITLE: The Rise and Fall of Maya Civilization
IMPRINT: University of Oklahoma Press: Norman

Page 40-41: No specialist supposes America was populated by immigrations across either ocean, "although the possibility of late influences having reached the New World from Polynesia cannot be ruled out." After citing with near approval Hooton's suggestion that the ancestors of the Classic Mayas were mongoloid-modified "second cousins once removed to peoples such as the Sumerians," he wonders if parallels in civilization, such as astronomy and pyramids, were fortuitous. "Did the Maya and others of their race carry the seeds of such ideas with them when they crossed to the New World?"

Pages 42-43: He sees the possibility that "the last arrivals who may have left Siberia as late as the beginning of the Christian Era brought with them certain religious concepts which survive in eastern Asia to this day," such as the association of colors and celestial dragons with four world quarters, "ideas which I think are too complex and unnaturalistic to have been evolved independently in both Asia and America." "These later immigrants from the Old World may . . . have brought with them the idea of agriculture," though not the principal crops. Yet the presence of cotton, the bottle gourd and perhaps the sweet potato in both hemispheres before A.D. 1492 is an important matter.

Page 70: Piedras Negras features stelae showing "gods seated in niches in Buddha-like poses."

T-078

AUTHOR: Thompson, John Eric S.
DATE: 1958
TITLE: Symbols, Glyphs, and Divinatory Almanacs for Diseases in the Maya Dresden and Madrid Codices
IN: American Antiquity 23:297-308

Ixchel, the Maya patroness of childbirth, connotes procreation, growing crops, "our mother," "lady," etc. She was symbolized by a curl of hair. [Compare F-167 for Near Eastern parallel.]

T-079

AUTHOR: Thompson, John Eric S.
DATE: 1960
TITLE: Maya Hieroglyphic Writing: An Introduction, revised edition
IMPRINT: University of Oklahoma Press: Norman
[First edition 1950, Publication 589, Carnegie Institution of Washington]

Pages 61-62: "There are close parallels in Maya transcriptions of the colonial period, and, I am convinced, in the hieroglyphic texts themselves to the verses of the Psalms, and the poetry of Job."

Page 73: The water lily was intimately associated with the crocodile monster in the underworld sea, symbolizing an aspect of abundance. [Compare the water lily as the Egyptian symbol of primordial abundance.]

Page 83: Strong dualism in Mayan culture.

Page 99: Multiple heavens.

Page 134: The jaguar was a symbol of the night aspect of the sun in the underworld. [Compare T-071.]

T-080

AUTHOR: Thompson, John Eric S.
DATE: 1970
TITLE: Maya History and Religion
IMPRINT: University of Oklahoma Press: Norman

[Potential comparisons in the Mediterranean include:] sacred fire, virgin fire, vestal virgins, mother superior attached to temples. Numbers themselves were deities [compare G-168]. Ancestor cults. Dogs lead souls of the dead to the underworld. Diseases introduced by Europeans include tuberculosis, influenza, malaria, hookworm, dysentery.

Page 370: The Pandora's box motif may be pre-Columbian, brought anciently from the Old World.

T-082

AUTHOR: Thompson, Stith
DATE: 1919

TITLE: European Tales among the North American Indians: A Study in the Migration of Folktales
IN: Colorado College Publications 100-101 (Language Series 2) 34:319-471

Type-by-type comparative analysis of twenty-seven North American Indian and European narratives and story categories. Attempts to show how Indians transformed the folklore they acquired from European colonial sources. [But includes materials considered by Hultkrantz, Count, Utley, and others as unquestionably pre-Columbian.]

T-084

AUTHOR: Thompson, Stith
DATE: 1946
TITLE: The Folktale
IMPRINT: Dryden: New York

Makes a general appeal to psychic unity to explain North American and Greek Orpheus myth parallels, despite surprising resemblance. They were not borrowed from European colonists.

T-086

AUTHOR: Thompson, Stith
DATE: 1968
TITLE: Icelandic Parallels among the Northeastern Algonquins: A Reconsideration
IN: Nordica et Anglica: Studies in Honor of Stefán Einarsson, edited by Allan H. Orrick (Mouton: The Hague), 133-139

Critique of L-153, deciding that suggested Icelandic parallels are invalid.

T-087

AUTHOR: Thompson, Stith
DATE: 1970
TITLE: Analogues and Borrowings in North and South American Indian Tales
IN: Languages and Cultures of Western North America: Essays in Honor of Sven S. Liljeblad, edited by Earl H. Swanson, Jr. (Idaho State University Press: Pocatello), 277-288

Includes a list of 181 "North and South American Indian Motifs Known in Other Continents." Some are general but others are "very specific stories with practically worldwide occurrence," such as the theft of fire. He does not try to account for the parallels.

T-088

AUTHOR: Thomsen, Harriette H.
DATE: 1960
TITLE: Occurrence of Fired Bricks in Pre-Conquest Mexico
IN: Southwestern Journal of Anthropology 16:428-441

The belief was long held that fired bricks were unknown in America before the Spaniards arrived. Her assessment of the evidence for Mesoamerica shows that they were widespread, at Comalcalco (Tabasco), Coixtlahuaca (Oaxaca), central Mexico (Cholula, Tizatlán), Tula, and Chalchihuites (Zacatecas). Identification is complicated because clays harden under atmospheric conditions.

T-089

AUTHOR: Thomson, William J.
DATE: 1891
TITLE: Te Pito te Henua, or Easter Island
IN: Report of the United States National Museum for the year ending June 30, 1889, Part 3, Number 2, pages 447-552

Substantial information on traditions, including the arrival of invader Hotu Matua and a large group bringing various plants with them.

T-090

AUTHOR: Thorarinsson, Sigurdur
DATE: 1942
TITLE: Vinlandsproblemet; Några reflexioner med anledning av V. Tanners skrift [The Vinland Problem; Some Retrospective Considerations with Regard to V. Tanner's Paper]
IN: Ymer 62:39-46

A resume of various theories advanced by scientists other than Tanner [T-005?]. The confusion because of the name "Vin"land is discussed along with its geographical location. The distribution of the bog-myrtle (Myrica gale) and other plants on both sides of the North Atlantic is speculated upon, including the possibility of their being carried by the Norse.

T-091

AUTHOR: Thórdarson, Matthias
DATE: 1930
TITLE: The Vinland Voyages
IN: Research Series No. 18 (American Geographical Society: New York)

A brief, general summary of the saga material. He follows closely Steensby's readings of the sagas and geography. Vinland/Hop was along the coast of Maine.

T-096

AUTHOR: Tibbetts, G. R.
DATE: 1971
TITLE: Arab Navigation in the Indian Ocean before the Coming of the Portuguese, Being a Translation of Kitab al-Fawaid fi usul al-bahr wal-qawaid of Ahmad b. Majid al-Najdi; Together with an Introduction on the History of Arab Navigation, Notes on the Navigational Techniques and on the Topography of the Indian Ocean, and a Glossary of Navigational Terms
IMPRINT: Royal Asiatic Society of Great Britain and Ireland: London [Reprinted 1981]

Translation and extensive analysis of medieval Arab documents on voyaging and navigation from the Arabian peninsula to India and southeast Asia.

T-099

AUTHOR: Tilman, H. W.
DATE: 1968
TITLE: Mischief Goes South
IMPRINT: Hollis & Carter: London

The author's voyage alone in his small boat Mischief in 1966-1967 from England to Montevideo, Punta Arenas, and South Georgia.

T-099B

AUTHOR: Tisseuil, J.
DATE: 1974
TITLE: Le syphilis vénérienne n'est pas d'origine américaine [Venereal Syphilis Is Not of American Origin]
IN: Bulletin de la société de pathologie exotique 67:40-44

Omitting nearly all the up-to-date literature he argues that endemic syphilis was widespread in Europe in the Middle Ages ("by cutaneous transmission"), mainly among the deprived classes. At the end of the 15th century, movements of armies and populations favored an epidemic explosion of venereal syphilis in Europe which was promptly carried to the New World.

T-100

AUTHOR: Tobler, Arthur J.
DATE: 1950
TITLE: Excavations at Tepe Gawra, vol. 2
IMPRINT: University of Pennsylvania Press: Philadelphia

Page 167: Wheeled model vehicles evidenced in the form of loose wheels, the earliest in Late Ubaid [nowadays, c. 3900-3500 B.C. conservatively, but as much as 500 years earlier by some C-14-related reckoning].

T-102 See now C-217B.

T-103

AUTHOR: Tolstoy, Paul
DATE: 1953
TITLE: Some Amerasian Pottery Traits in North Asian Prehistory
IN: American Antiquity 19:25-29

In his own words, he attempts "to outline the Old World distributions of a limited number of ceramic elements and to make a case for their introduction into North America, specifically the Eastern Woodland, some 3000 to 4000 years ago." Surveys fairly completely the type of data only sketched by Griffin and Krieger [G-232]. He gives time and space distribution for Russian Asia of such decorative features of pottery as cord-marking, fabric marking and paddling. While noting, belatedly, "staggering inadequacies" of the data, he makes clear that he very much wants to correlate the highly scattered Asian occurrences of the third millennium B.C. with Woodland North American pottery. He finds enough correlation to persuade himself of "the diffusion of a ceramic complex in prehistoric times from the Old World [Northern Asia] to the New [Eastern North America]."

T-104

AUTHOR: Tolstoy, Paul
DATE: 1958a
TITLE: The Archaeology of the Lena Basin and Its New World Relationships, Part I
IN: American Antiquity 23:397-418

See T-105.

T-105

AUTHOR: Tolstoy, Paul
DATE: 1958b
TITLE: The Archaeology of the Lena Basin and Its New World Relationships, Part II
IN: American Antiquity 24:63-68

Beyond comparison of earlier portions of the sequences, the main emphasis is on the Neolithic of the Lena drainage and Archaic to Early Woodland developments in eastern North America. The survey of literature on the North American side is comprehensive.

"Rather extensive similarities in nonceramic inventories" between the two areas are presented, as well as "numerous resemblances between Neolithic and Early Bronze pottery in the Lena Basin and Early and Middle Woodland ceramics in eastern North America," that is, "a large number of features pertaining to vessel manufacture, paste, surface treatment and decoration" that "actually make up the majority of recognizable variations in pottery" on both sides. The Lena features date at about 2000-1500 B.C., while receipt of the traits in eastern North America appears to begin at about 1000 B.C., with first appearance of some features lagging as late as the beginning of our era. "The Arctic was a major obstacle to the transmission of pottery from the Old World to the New." We may never be able to pick up, archaeologically, the intervening threads.

In the light of this material, the author offers some "remarks" about, rather than a full theory of, diffusion (pages 75-77) [although these statements are more powerful and apt than many more labored treatments].

T-106

AUTHOR: Tolstoy, Paul
DATE: 1963
TITLE: Cultural Parallels between Southeast Asia and Mesoamerica in the Manufacture of Bark Cloth

IN: Transactions of the New York Academy of Sciences 25:646-662

The methods are explained which he is using in a world-wide study of bark-cloth manufacture still in progress. Notable similarities between the industries of Southeast Asia and Mesoamerica are highly indicative of historical relationship. The author thinks that the technology was introduced into Mesoamerica in the early part of the first millennium B.C. [This is arguably the most comprehensive and most persuasive of all analyses of a trait or complex yet offered as evidence for transoceanic contact.]

T-107

AUTHOR: Tolstoy, Paul

DATE: 1964

TITLE: Review of *A Survey of Peruvian Fishing Communities,* by E. A. Hammel and Y. D. Haase

IN: American Antiquity 30:109

"A slight quarrel might be picked with the authors' view of the manner in which some of the problems they raise should be, or will be solved. Like Foster before them, they seem overly inclined to assume that, when Spanish and post-Columbian types are shared in an area and pre-Columbian evidence is lacking, the types are of European origin. . . . If outside evidence is examined, other areas besides the western Mediterranean can be considered. . . . It is important to know something of the world distribution of the traits in question (if only to judge whether a certain kind of trait is rare, like the fire piston, or widespread, like the bow and arrow), and also to know something of their aboriginal distribution in the New World or along the rim of the Pacific."

T-108

AUTHOR: Tolstoy, Paul

DATE: 1966

TITLE: Method in Long-range Comparison

IN: Proceedings of the 36th International Congress of Americanists (Barcelona and Seville, 1964), 1:69-89

The procedures and concepts used to verify claims for transpacific diffusion of traits are delineated and applied to a test case elaborated for bark cloth and beaters from Southeast Asia, South and Middle America. [With T-106, probably the most sophisticated statement and demonstration of sound methodology in diffusion research yet to appear.]

T-109

AUTHOR: Tolstoy, Paul

DATE: 1972

TITLE: Diffusion: As Explanation and as Event

IN: Oceania and the Americas, volume 3 of Early Chinese Art and Its Possible Influence in the Pacific Basin; A Symposium Arranged by the Department of Art History and Archaeology, Columbia University, New York City, August 21-25, 1967, edited by Noel Barnard in collaboration with Douglas Fraser, 3 vols. (Intercultural Arts Press: New York), 3:823-841 [Reprinted Hsün-Mei Publishing Co.: Taipei, Taiwan; and Hong Kong Bookstore: Hong Kong, 1974]

Methodological and theoretical issues are examined by looking at the possibility that paper-making was brought from Southeast Asia to Mesoamerica in pre-Columbian times. One conclusion: a need in a society intense enough to induce borrowing may not suffice to compel invention, but we cannot guess at the intensity of past "needs."

T-110

AUTHOR: Tolstoy, Paul

DATE: 1974a

TITLE: Mesoamerica

IN: Prehispanic America, edited by Shirley Gorenstein (St. Martin's: New York), 29-64

Page 45: Like the Ocos style of the Isthmus of Tehuantepec, Tlatilco hints at maritime contacts between western Mesoamerica and remote portions of the Pacific rim.

T-111

AUTHOR: Tolstoy, Paul
DATE: 1974b
TITLE: Transoceanic Diffusion and Nuclear Mesoamerica
IN: Prehispanic America, edited by Shirley Gorenstein (St. Martin's: New York), 124-144

Once we acknowledge that there were transpacific contributions to native American culture at all, we have no basis but empirical research for limiting the scope of those contributions. He would allow from five to fifty percent or more of the overall list of characteristics of Mesoamerican civilization as coming from Southeast Asia, with no clear way to settle a figure within that broad range.

Mentions: plants (gourd, cotton, peanut, coconut, plantain, sweet potato, hibiscus), chickens, hairless dog.

Discusses for South America: Valdivia-Jomon pottery (these parallels show "a remarkable degree of clustering in time and space"), coca/betel chewing, bark cloth, intrusive complexes of Asian ceramic parallels (in Ecuador), metallurgy, tie-dyeing, poncho, panpipes, sailing raft, neckrest, coolie yoke, blowgun, backstrap loom, patu clubs, flasks.

For Mesoamerica: zodiac and associated deities, zero, calendrics, books and writing, paper, world ages and quarters, color symbolism, patolli, sacrifice usages, incense, volador, symbolism of felines, snakes and trees, litters, parasols, fans, ceramic features, jade, mirrors, wheeled figures, attributes of rulership, Ekholm's Complex A from Southeast Asia, diving god, sun disk.

Includes a bibliographic essay, pages 140-144.

T-111B

AUTHOR: Tolstoy, Paul
DATE: 1975
TITLE: From the Old World to the New World via Bering Strait
IN: North America, edited by Shirley Gorenstein (St. Martin's Press: New York), 165-185 (chapter 6)

A good brief summary of highlights of the then sparse finds relevant to the question. Despite typological similarities in Asian and the earliest North American Woodland pottery, he now doubts a connection because of the "vast geographic gap" separating the two manifestations. Kehoe's proposal for a crossing of the North Atlantic to introduce pottery from early Europe is, however, even less attractive "on the face of it."

T-111C

AUTHOR: Tolstoy, Paul
DATE: 1986
TITLE: Asia and the Americas. Trans-Pacific Contacts: What, Where and When?
IN: The Quarterly Review of Archaeology 7/2-3 (September-December): 1, 6-11

A lengthy summary and review of N-016. Points out some ways in which the authors might have pursued other lines, and in the discussion contributes significant information and ideas involving, for example, Asian/American calendars, drawing particularly on the work of J. Stewart and D. Kelley as well as his own case study on bark cloth. His methodological cautions and suggestions are valuable. Particularly urges effort to overcome the catalogue approach, that is, merely listing traits. Instead he wishes to relate sets of the transoceanic parallels into larger contexts (e.g., a rabbit-in-moon complex involving moon, licentiousness, calendar, etc.), against the easy folly of anti-diffusionists who consider fragmented evidence dismissible.

In the second part of the review an important semi-independent essay is presented addressing three questions: (1) Do different kinds of phenomena differ in value as evidence for diffusion? (2) What are the implications of the evidence in N-016 as to the what, when and where of contacts from Asia?, and (3) What is the importance of the entire problem for New World archaeology? His summary answer to the last asserts that we cannot know a priori. It remains to be seen, once good faith efforts have examined the contacts question competently, what the consequences for New World development appear to have been; they might have been of substantial significance.

T-111D

AUTHOR: Tolstoy, Paul
DATE: 1991
TITLE: The Maya Rediscovered: Paper Route
IN: Natural History 100:6-8, 10, 12-14

Further consideration of the bark-cloth complex apparently brought to Mesoamerica from Malaysia.

T-112

AUTHOR: Tompkins, Peter
DATE: 1976
TITLE: Mysteries of the Mexican Pyramids
IMPRINT: Harper and Row: New York

History of the exploration of Mesoamerican sites, from ancient explorers to recent archaeological projects, stressing architectural layout and archaeoastronomy. Gives some weight to unconventional theories about the origins of New World societies.

T-113

AUTHOR: Toribio Medina, José
DATE: 1912a
TITLE: Monedas usadas por los Indios de América al tiempo del descubrimiento según los antiguos documentos y cronistas españoles [Money Used by the Indians of America at the Time of the Discovery According to the Ancient Documents and Spanish Chroniclers]
IN: Proceedings of the 17th International Congress of Americanists (Buenos Aires and Mexico, 1910), pages 556-567

Regarding the concept of money, which is comparable in its ramifications—less struck coins only—to what prevailed in the Old World.

T-114

AUTHOR: Toribio Medina, José
DATE: 1912b
TITLE: El supuesto descubrimiento de Chile por los Frisios en el siglo XI [The Supposed Discovery of Chile by the Frisians in the 11th Century]
IN: Proceedings of the 17th International Congress of Americanists (Buenos Aires and Mexico, 1910), pages 603-604

Little more than an abstract, with notes on discussion by Seler and others. Cites older literature on the Frisian proposition; the only specific evidence he offers is the double-headed eagle design. (A commentator claims that freak double-headed birds occur in nature and could have suggested the motif.)

T-115

AUTHOR: Tornöe, Johannes Kristoffer
DATE: 1944
TITLE: Lysstreif over Norgesveldents Historie [Focussing on Norse History]
IN: Norges Svalbard- og Ishavs-Undersokelser, Meddelelser 56 (Oslo)

With English summary. On the long-distance voyaging of Greenlanders and Icelanders. He identifies Vineland as on the Gulf of St. Lawrence. [After a trip to America he revised this view to that seen in T-116.]

T-116

AUTHOR: Tornöe, Johannes Kristoffer
DATE: 1964
TITLE: Early American History: Norsemen before Columbus
IMPRINT: Univcrsitetsforlaget: Oslo [Also, George Allen & Unwin: London, 1965. Also in 1965, with title inverted, Humanities: New York]

Argues that Norse settlements ranged from Nova Scotia to Chesapeake Bay, including one on Manhattan Island. "The sagas . . . can be interpreted as factual reports of historical events." His reconstruction may be the most literally-based thus far, and in the book he displays his reasoning clearly on crucial navigational and geographical points.

Includes the North American voyages of Herjulfsson, the Eirikssons and Karlsefne, with a chapter on the construction and sailing speed of Viking ships. Bjarne, driven off course on an Iceland-Greenland voyage, sailed along the Baffin-Nova Scotia coasts in 986 but did not land. Leiv's Budir settlement is placed near Falmouth, Cape Cod, and Vinland's northern limit at the Gulf of St. Lawrence. The skraelings were Indians. [Critically reviewed 1965 in *Arctic* 18:142-143.]

T-117

AUTHOR: Tornöe, Johannes Kristoffer
DATE: 1965
TITLE: Columbus in the Arctic?, and the Vineland Literature
IMPRINT: A. W. Broggers: Oslo

Evaluates favorably the Russian discovery in 1959 of a purported secret letter from Ferdinand and Isabella to Columbus indicating Columbus' awareness of Norse discoveries. His possible participation in the Scolvus expedition of 1476-77 is discussed. A plausible time-table is offered for this trip north following Cortereal's return to Lisbon from the Pining expedition of 1471-73, and it is supposed that Scolvus/ Columbus sailed to Greenland, Labrador, and the Caribbean. H. Ingstad's finds at L'Anse aux Meadows are considered a late 13th century Norse settlement.

T-119

AUTHOR: Torres González, Yolotl
DATE: 1972
TITLE: Algunos aspectos del culto a la luna en el México antiguo [Some Aspects of the Moon Cult in Ancient Mexico]
IN: Estudios de cultura náhuatl 11:113-127

Among other similarities between Old World and Mexican moon beliefs and practices, she notes Aztec association of the moon with the pulque deities and parallel among the Indo-Iranian peoples in which the sacred homa-soma drink had a totally lunar character and was personified by autonomous deities. [Compare W-119.]

T-121

AUTHOR: Totten, Norman
DATE: 1976
TITLE: Implications of the Figuig Decipherment
IN: Epigraphic Society Occasional Publications 3/47:1-10

The inscription referred to in F-041 he dates, without giving external evidence, in the period "429-535 A.D." when Vandals were in North Africa. The voyage supposed to be the subject of this inscription must have taken place about A.D. 480, the voyagers fleeing Vandals.

T-122

AUTHOR: Totten, Norman
DATE: 1978
TITLE: Numismatic Evidence for Pre-Columbian Voyages
IN: "Ancient Vermont:" Proceedings of the Castleton Conference, edited by Warren L. Cook (Castleton State College: Rutland, Vermont), 44-46

Brief comments accompanying an illustrated lecture which showed a number of coins which are putatively European and which have been found randomly in eastern North America. [Without being able to see any images the comments are of little value.]

T-123

AUTHOR: Totten, Norman
DATE: 1981
TITLE: Epigraphic Research in America; Reply to Archeologists' Denunciations
IN: Epigraphic Society Occasional Publications 9/215:71-115

A compendium of the most slashing attacks on Fell's competence and results is given in the form of excerpts, with Totten's defense immediately following each.

T-124

AUTHOR: Totten, Norman
DATE: 1985
TITLE: Documentary Evidence for Writing in the Pre-Inca Andes
IN: Epigraphic Society Occasional Publications 13:63-66

Summary of statements from the Spanish chroniclers and Ibarra Grasso about proposed Incan and earlier writing. Best seen in Spanish in, e.g., J-030B, but conveniently in English here.

T-125

AUTHOR: Totten, Norman
DATE: 1988
TITLE: Categories of Evidence for Old World Contacts with Ancient America
IN: The Book of Mormon: The Keystone Scripture. Papers from the First Annual Book of Mormon Symposium, edited by Paul R. Cheesman (Brigham Young University Religious Studies Center: Provo, Utah), 187-205

A short rundown on a limited range of diffusionist ideas and data.

T-125B

AUTHOR: Totten, Norman
DATE: 1992
TITLE: King Juba Remembered?
IN: Epigraphic Society Occasional Publications 21:165-175

A progress report of research and hypothesis of possible Berber influence on the origin of Tiwanaku and Moche civilizations. A human effigy-head pot is pictured which the author bought from a dealer in 1978. Marks around the large headdress are read by Fell as in corrupt Greek and referring to King Juba II in North Africa. Some cultural features supporting a connection between North Africa and Peru (and other areas in the Americas) are pictured and discussed.

T-127

AUTHOR: Toung-Dekien
DATE: 1924
TITLE: De l'origine des Américains précolombiens [On the Origin of Pre-Columbian Americans]
IN: Proceedings of the 20th International Congress of

Americanists (Rio de Janeiro, 1922), pages 3-47

A free-ranging presentation of data on and interpretation of mythic and language similarities between China and America, Fu-sang, Atlantic voyages, etc. Supposes Buddhist missionaries, shipwrecks and voyagers, as well as Bering Strait movements.

Page 45: Fifth century Chinese coins were found in Indian burial mounds near Vancouver, British Columbia. Says that D. Charnay found at Tula fragments of faience, porcelain, and Roman glass [citing Lettre au Trait d'union du 28 Aout 1880, Archives des Missions Scientifiques 7].

T-128

AUTHOR: Toung-Dekien
DATE: 1927
TITLE: Origen de los Americanos precolumbianos [Origin of the Pre-Columbian Americans]
IN: Memorias de la Sociedad científica "Antonio Alzate" 48:67-147

See T-127.

T-129

AUTHORS: Touny, A. D., and Steffen Wenig
DATE: 1969
TITLE: Der Sport im alten Aegypten [Sport in Ancient Egypt]
IMPRINT: Edition Leipzig: Leipzig [English edition Kunst und Wissenschaft: Leipzig, 1969]

Page 48: Religious texts in pyramids of the 6th dynasty include the statement, "Hit the ball to the field of Apis," which would appear to mean that ball playing was a recreation of the sacred dead in heaven. [Compare Mesoamerican ballgame?]

T-129B

AUTHOR: Towe, Kenneth M.
DATE: 1990
TITLE: The Vinland Map: Still a Forgery
IN: Accounts of Chemical Research 23:84-87

Concurs with McCrone [M-196C] that the best tests indeed show the ink to be modern.

T-130

AUTHOR: Towle, Jerry
DATE: 1973
TITLE: Jade: An Indicator of Trans-Pacific Contact?
IN: Yearbook of the Association of Pacific Coast Geographers 35:165-172

Notes similarities between Chinese and Mesoamerican methods of prospecting for jade as well as working (sawing, drilling, and polishing with abrasives) and using it. Ethnographic documentation (but not ancient sources) from both areas show belief that "exhalations" from the mineral helped prospectors locate it.

T-131

AUTHOR: Towle, Margaret Ashley
DATE: 1952
TITLE: The Pre-Columbian Occurrence of Lagenaria Seeds in Coastal Peru
IN: Harvard University Botanical Museum Leaflets 15/6:171-184

A study of Lagenaria seeds from two sites, with a review of the literature on the archaeological occurrence of the gourd in Peru. Concludes with a discussion of the possibility of the diffusion of the plant by oceanic drift; she thinks it likely.

T-133

AUTHOR: Towle, Margaret Ashley
DATE: 1961
TITLE: The Ethnobotany of Pre-Columbian Peru
IN: Viking Fund Publications in Anthropology 30 (Wenner-Gren

Foundation for Anthropological Research: Chicago)

First major work in English on the ethnobotany of pre-Columbian Peruvian materials arranged so that it is of value to botanists, archaeologists, and ethnologists. Discussions by plant groups, then by archaeological epochs in major geographical areas.

Page 97: Accepts the pre-Spanish presence of the plantain as evidence of interhemispheric contacts.

T-134

AUTHOR: Townsend, Charles H. T.
DATE: 1925
TITLE: Ancient Voyages to America
IN: Brazilian American 12 (4 July): five unnumbered pages

Offers a "working hypothesis" still to be tested and elucidated. Phoenicians guided Solomon's fleet from the Red Sea around Africa to Ophir and Parvaim which he says were up the Amazon. Three years later the fleet reached home via the Mediterranean. Later they returned to Tardshish [*sic*] in the same area, then made many voyages. The Kishua language came originally from Asia Minor and is related to Chaldaic, Semitic, and Egyptian. The names of the fleet's cargo (as listed in the Bible) are traceable to Kishua words. There were no more transatlantic voyages, however, after the fall of Carthage in 143 B.C.

Plants in use: When Columbus arrived he found in use plantains, bananas, coconuts, and cotton, while rice and barley were both growing in parts of South America. The sweet potato is a distinct case. All eight of these plants were known in the Old World from ancient times. At least some were undoubtedly taken to America by the pre-diluvial inhabitants of Atlantis. The Mexican boll weevil and the Peruvian square weevil attack no other plant in nature and have evidently been adapted to local cotton for tens of thousands of years. As they are not carried in the seed, they would not have been transported to the Eastern Hemisphere when the seed was taken there originally from America. Rice has been found in a wild state in parts of South America under circumstances which quite preclude its escape from cultivation since the date of European conquest. Barley: 16 species of Hordeum are known in the temperate and subtropical regions of the Northern Hemisphere and in extra-tropical South America.

Add to the eight cultivated plants indigo and cactus, both known from remote times in both hemispheres. Opuntia and all Cactaceae are of American origin and have been in Asia and Africa from remote times. If oats and hops were not originally native to both hemispheres, we may lay their dispersion to the Norsemen. Reasons are given why unique American plants, like quinoa, were not transferred to the Old World.

East and West evidently dovetailed in settling and civilizing America. The route from India to China and across the Pacific vied with that from India to Asia Minor and across the Atlantic.

T-135

AUTHOR: Townsend, Richard Fraser
DATE: 1982
TITLE: Pyramid and Sacred Mountain
IN: Ethnoastronomy and Archaeoastronomy in the American Tropics, edited by Anthony F. Aveni and Gary Urton (New York Academy of Sciences: New York), 37-62

Astronomical features are tied to Mexican mountains and pyramids sacred to Huitzilopochtli and Tlaloc, and at the sacred hill of Tetzcotzingo ideas of sustenance or fertility, orientation, cosmic plan, paths, ritual bathing/purification and dynastic ruling lines are shown to be conceptually linked. [Compare Near Eastern and East Asian complexes with similar elements.]

Page 48: Thelma Sullivan notes that Tlaltecuhtli, Lord or Lady Earth, was the source of life, her hair the source of vegetation. Her numerous eyes were springs, fountains, and small caves. She was said to have eyes and mouths at the limb joints. [Compare eyes/faces at joints noted by S-147 and C-402.]

T-136B

AUTHOR: Tozzer, Alfred M.
DATE: 1913
TITLE: A Preliminary Study of the Ruins of Nakum, Guatemala
IN: Harvard University Peabody Museum Memoirs 5:137-201

Pages 167-168: "The two lateral doorways have what may truthfully be called concrete arches. They are the first and only examples of the true arch which I have met in Maya buildings."

T-137

AUTHOR: Tozzer, Alfred M.
DATE: 1916
TITLE: Pre-Columbian Representations of the Elephant in America
IN: Nature 96/2413:592

The writer argues that the carved figures near the top of Stela B at Copan are either blue macaws or the "long-nosed god," not elephants as argued by Smith.

T-138

AUTHOR: Tozzer, Alfred M.
DATE: 1933
TITLE: Zelia Nuttall
IN: American Anthropologist 35:475-482

A necrology. Nuttall's idea of "undeniable similarities and identities between the civilization of both hemispheres . . . fell upon the receptive ear of Professor Putnam [at Harvard], who held throughout his life a conviction that the Americas received their greatest cultures through Asia, and he was very proud that his Museum could publish her paper." Her diffusionist oriented book [N-118] had considerable influence in attracting several students to the Middle American field.

T-139

AUTHOR: Tozzer, Alfred M., translator and editor
DATE: 1941
TITLE: Landa's Relacion de las Cosas de Yucatan: A Translation
IN: Papers of the Peabody Museum of Archaeology and Ethnology, vol. 18 (Harvard University: Cambridge)

[Old World parallels exist:] Pages 26-27, 42-43: Shortly before the coming of the Spaniards Maya priest Ah Cambal prophesied that his people would soon be subjugated by a white, bearded race coming from the east who would preach to them one God and the power of a tree represented by a cross. [Stimulated by a previous European contact?]

Pages 104, 142: Burned offering consisting of cereal mixed with incense. [Compare Leviticus 2:1-3.]

Pages 104, 123: Sacrifice of criminals.

Page 113: Blood-letting rite. [Compare 1 Kings 18:28, Deuteronomy 18:1.]

Pages 116, 184: Sacrifice by pushing off a tall structure to be crushed by the fall. [Compare H-507.]

Page 120: Communion with deity by worshippers eating part of sacrifice.

Pages 129-130: Burial of retainers with lord.

Pages 142-143: Incense material a gum termed the "blood" of the tree producing it. [The same terminology occurs for Arabian frankincense.] Incense was collected only after ritual preparation. [Compare P-065, page 357.]

Pages 144, 148: Maize meal or parched grain offered as a sacrifice with the heart of a deer or iguana flesh. Balche liquor as a sacrificial libation.

Pages 153, 155, 158: Incense to be burned only with holy (special) fire. [Compare Leviticus 10:1.]

Page 196, note 1055; also page 199, note 1086: Dioscorea alata, a plant supposedly introduced by the Spaniards, is here suggested as indigenous and is described in Landa's book.

Pages 117, 226: Sickness of an important person led to alleviatory sacrifice. [Compare Leviticus 4:22 and 14:15, Numbers 19.]

Page 226: Scapegoat principle. An old woman was taken outside town by priests and people, confessed sins, was killed, and people buried her with rocks; thus sin was removed from the community. [Compare Leviticus 16.]

T-142

AUTHOR: Traveller Bird
DATE: 1971
TITLE: Tell Them They Lie: The Sequoyah Myth
IMPRINT: Westernlore: Los Angeles

A Cherokee Indian maintains that the syllabary credited to Sequoyah really was a prehistoric script used by his people and which Sequoyah only adopted or adapted.

T-144

AUTHOR: Tregear, Edward
DATE: 1898
TITLE: Notes on Maya and Malay
IN: Journal of the Polynesian Society 7:101-108

Supports Thomas [T-063]'s comparisons of words from Sanscrit, "Malay Archipelago," and Oceania and says that Thomas is on sound etymological ground in his comparisons to Maya, including words for hill, water, sky, king, chief, earth, hand, breast, wall, shore, fort, sacred, fish, tiger, etc. He concludes that the agreements are remarkable enough that either the Mayans and Malay are of the same linguistic stock or else they share numerous loan words.

T-147

AUTHOR: Trento, Salvatore Michael
DATE: 1978
TITLE: The Search for Lost America: The Mysteries of the Stone Ruins
IMPRINT: Contemporary Books: Chicago [Also Penguin: New York, 1979]

A study of megalithic monuments, primarily in the eastern United States. His stated purpose is not to make a case for any people monopolizing the American continent in pre-Columbian times but rather to point out that a variety of stonework and scripts exists which seems to have more in common with Old World ancient cultures than with known Indian and historic European societies.

Sympathetic to B. Fell's views, the author argues that construction techniques and forms of stone structures in the northeastern U.S. are similar in detail to early European structures and reports radiocarbon dates which he interprets to support his position.

T-148

AUTHOR: Triana, Miguel
DATE: 1951
TITLE: La civilización chibcha [Chibchan Civilization]
IMPRINT: Ministerio de Educación Nacional: Bogotá

Pages 39ff.: Amid suggestions that Fu-sang was Mexico and that Phoenicians may have reached America, he claims that Chibchan civilization had its ultimate origins in transatlantic voyagers who entered South America at the mouth of the Orinoco.

Pages 237ff.: "Indications of writing," including a sketch of "Greek letters of the hieroglyphic of Pandi," "archaic Chinese characters," a "cuneiform inscription on a Babylonian brick found in Duitama," and reports of other inscriptions, including Semitic writing.

T-148B

AUTHOR: Trigger, Bruce G.
DATE: 1990
TITLE: A History of Archaeological Thought
IMPRINT: Cambridge University Press: Cambridge

Negative about all attempts to link American cultures substantively with Old World predecessors, supposing racism as a motive in such proposals.

T-150

AUTHOR: Trimborn, Hermann
DATE: 1959
TITLE: Das Alte Amerika [Ancient America]
IMPRINT: Fretz und Wasmuth: Zürich

Pages 122ff.: This general introductory book offers a brief but balanced discussion of possible Asiatic influence on America.

T-151

AUTHOR: Trimborn, Hermann
DATE: 1963
TITLE: Die indianischen Hochkulturen des alten Amerika [Advanced Indian Civilizations of Ancient America]
IMPRINT: Springer: Berlin

Pages 143-145: A short popular work takes brief note of Heyerdahl, Heine-Geldern and Ekholm, Graebner, and Hentze, without commitment about substance.

T-152

AUTHOR: Troll, Carl
DATE: 1963
TITLE: Qanat-Bewässerung in der Alten und Neuen Welt: ein Kulturgeographisches und Kulturgeschichtliches Problem [Qanat-Irrigation in the Old and New Worlds: A Cultural-Geographical and Ethnological Problem]
IN: Mitteilungen der Österreichischen geographischen Gesellschaft, Festschrift Hans Bobek, Teil II, Band 105:313-330

Qanat or chain wells in the Old and New Worlds: are they due to pre-Columbian diffusion? After the problem is outlined, no answer can be given.

T-153

AUTHOR: Trombetti, Alfredo
DATE: 1905
TITLE: L'unità d'origine del linguaggio [The Single Origin of Language]
IMPRINT: Libreria Treves di Luidi Beltrami: Bologna

He is amused at F-004 (which derives Andean languages from Sumerian and Assyrian) and its type of interpretation, yet he is convinced of the origin of all languages from a single source, and he compares vocabulary and grammatical forms widely around the world, including America, to support his idea.

T-154

AUTHOR: Trombetti, Alfredo
DATE: 1907
TITLE: Come si fa la critica de un libro, con nuovi contributi alla dottrina della monogenesi del linguaggio e alla glottologia generale comparata [How a Book Is Criticized, with New Contributions to the Doctrine of the Monogenesis of Language and to General Comparative Linguistics]
IMPRINT: L. Beltrami: Bologna

Pages 188ff.: He cites evidence for a linkage between languages of Australia and Tierra del Fuego.

T-156

AUTHOR: Trombetti, Alfredo
DATE: 1924-1925
TITLE: Lingue oceaniche in America? [Oceanic Languages in America?]
IN: Rendiconto delle sessioni della Reale Accademia delle Scienze delle Instituto de Bologna, Classe di Science Morali 9 [Also published separately by Coop. Tipografica Azzoguidi: Bologna, 1925]

Rejects migrations from Oceania.

T-157

AUTHOR: Trombetti, Alfredo
DATE: 1928
TITLE: Origine asiatica delle lingue e popolazione americane [Asiatic Origins of the American Languages and Populations]
IN: Proceedings of the 22nd International Congress of Americanists (Rome, 1926), 1:169-246

Languages of Indo-china, and especially the "Munda-Kmer" group, provided the trunk from which American Indian languages sprang. That group occupied all east Asia prior to the presence of the Altaic languages there. Oceania was only settled later so could not have been significant as a connector between Southeast Asia and America.

Includes mention of Basque words in Amerindian languages. He connects Basque with Caucasic, Indochinese languages, and Paleoasiatic, thence with North American Indians.

T-160

AUTHOR: True, F. W.
DATE: 1884
TITLE: Babiroussa Tusks from an Indian Grave in British Columbia
IN: Science 4:34

These were found by J. G. Swan of the Smithsonian in the grave of a shaman (death estimated c. A.D. 1840) excavated on Graham Island in the Queen Charlotte group. They came ultimately from the Celebes.

T-161

AUTHOR: Tsai Yuan Pei
DATE: 1924
TITLE: Analogie entre l'écriture des nombres chez les anciens Américaines et chez les anciens Chinois [Analogy between the Writing of Numbers among the Ancient Americans and among the Ancient Chinese]
IN: Proceedings of the 21st International Congress of Americanists (Part 1, The Hague, 1924), pages 281-284

Illustrates Chinese use of lines and dots to represent numbers and compares them very loosely to Mesoamerican numeration. He also compares one decorative motif, several pot forms, and some glyphic characters.

T-163B

AUTHOR: Tuck, James
DATE: 1975
TITLE: The Northeastern Maritime Continuum: 8000 Years of Cultural Development in the Far Northeast
IN: Arctic Anthropology

A "highly advanced" Archaic maritime culture (including the Red Paint culture) existed in coastal northeast Canada perhaps from as early as 7500 B.C. The first inhabitants were probably paleo-hunters who came along the now-submerged coast from the south and quickly adapted to local conditions basing their culture on sea mammal hunting.

[S-408B reports contacting Tuck about the significance of similar cultural features—artifacts, economies, burial customs—in Ireland, Britain, Spain, and Siberia, as claimed by some. Tuck vehemently denied that there could be any connection.]

T-164

AUTHOR: Tucker, Tim M.
DATE: 1964
TITLE: A Comparative Study of Ancient Mesoamerican and Mesopotamian Temple-towers
IN: Papers of the Fifteenth Annual Symposium on the Archaeology of the Scriptures (Society for Early Historic Archaeology: Provo, Utah), 79-89

Origin, architecture, materials, use, and beliefs are discussed. The Mesoamerican version is similar in essentials to the ziggurat, with partial similarity to the Egyptian pyramid. No specific diffusionary proposal is made.

T-168

AUTHORS: Turner, Christy G., II, and Doris R. Swindler
DATE: 1978
TITLE: The Dentition of New Britain West Nakanai Melanesians, VIII: Peopling of the Pacific
IN: American Journal of Physical Anthropology 49:361-372

Crown morphology traits and size here are unlike those of other Melanesians, as well as Micronesians and Polynesians, and even less like what is known for modern and Neolithic Southeast Asians. [The variability suggests that attempts at historical reconstruction, especially using gross population categories like "Melanesian," are subject to doubt.]

T-169

AUTHOR: Turner, Geoffrey
DATE: 1955
TITLE: Hair Embroidery in Siberia and North America
IMPRINT: Pitt-Rivers Museum Occasional Papers on Technology 7 (Oxford University Press: Oxford)

Occurred from western Siberia to eastern Canada and could have gone from either continent to the other within the last 2000 years.

T-170

AUTHOR: Tushingham, A. Douglas
DATE: 1966
TITLE: The Beardmore Relics, Hoax or History?
IMPRINT: University of Toronto Press: Toronto

Links the "Norse axe" from Ontario with the Kensington Stone as truly Norse.

T-171

AUTHOR: Tylor, Edward B.
DATE: 1861
TITLE: Anahuac; or Mexico and the Mexicans, Ancient and Modern
IMPRINT: Longman, Green, Longman and Robert: London

Pages 278-280: Notes reports of visitors to ancient Mexico from the east, Aztec customs like Old World ones, including Christian analogies (e.g., the cross, monasteries, nunneries, penance, confession, dedicated bread eaten as sacrifice). "Perhaps these peculiar rites, with the Mexican system of astronomy, (were) from Asia; or perhaps the white bearded men from the East may have brought them." No consistent theory can now be offered.

T-171B

AUTHOR: Tylor, Edward B.
DATE: 1870
TITLE: Researches into the Early History of Mankind and the Development of Civilization, 2d edition
IN: J. Murray: London

Points out various Old and New World cultural parallels which he implies could be due to diffusion, but he does not make his view clear.

T-171C

AUTHOR: Tylor, Edward B.
DATE: 1871
TITLE: Primitive Culture. Researches into the Development of Mythology, Philosophy, Religion, Art, and Custom
IN: J. Murray: London

Spells out certain parallels between American and Old World cultures but hedges by also talking about "tendencies of the human mind."

T-172

AUTHOR: Tylor, Edward B.
DATE: 1878a
TITLE: Geographical Distribution of Myths
IN: Researches into the Early History of Mankind and the Development of Civilization, by Edward B. Tylor (Estes and Lauriat: Boston), 333-371

Page 339: Evidence of an Asiatic connection with America comes from correspondences in myths.

T-173

AUTHOR: Tylor, Edward B.
DATE: 1878b
TITLE: Backgammon among the Aztecs
IN: Macmillan's Magazine 39:142-150 (London)
[Reprinted 1879, *Eclectic Magazine* (February); reprinted 1879, *Popular Science* (February); reprinted in *The Games of the Americas: A Book of Readings: Part 1, Central and South America,* edited by Brian Sutton-Smith (Arno Press: New York, 1975), not paginated]

A relatively popularized comparison of Asiatic pachisi and Aztec patolli.

"We often hear Mexican culture talked of as self-produced, with its bronze and gold work, its elaborate architecture," etc. He holds, rather, that "the higher art and life of the whole Central American district is most rationally accounted for by a carrying across of culture from Asia." "It may very well have been the same agency which transported to Mexico the art of bronze-making, the computation of time by periods of dogs and apes, the casting of nativities, and the playing of backgammon. . . . The Asiatic communication to be traced in the culture of the Aztec nation may not have been very ancient or extensive; all we can argue is that communication of some sort there was."

T-174

AUTHOR: Tylor, Edward B.
DATE: 1878c
TITLE: On the Game of Patolli in Ancient Mexico, and Its Probably Asiatic Origin
IN: Journal of the Anthropological Institute 8:116-131
[Reprinted in *The Games of the Americas: A Book of Readings: Part 1, Central and South America*, edited by Brian Sutton-Smith (Arno Press: New York, 1975), not paginated. Excerpted and combined with T-177 in Kroeber and Waterman, see T-177]

"Lot-backgammon as represented by tab, pachisi, etc., ranges in the Old World from Egypt across Southern Asia to Burma. As the patolli of the Mexicans is a variety of lot-backgammon most nearly approaching the Hindu pachisi . . .

its presence seems to prove that it had made its way across from Asia. Now if any item of culture, even a matter so trifling as a game, can be distinctly made out to have passed over from Asia and established itself [first in Mexico and then] among the rude tribes of North America, this opens a way by which various other features of their culture may be fairly accounted for as due to Asiatic influence." In discussion, Hyde Clark suggested that the Tarahumara language "is related to remarkable languages of the Old World" and that other features in abundance now assure us of a specific migration.

T-174B

AUTHOR: Tylor, Edward B.
DATE: 1879
TITLE: Remarks on the Geographical Distribution of Games
IN: Journal of the Anthropological Institute 9:23-30

Repeats some previous information on parallels between Asia and America in games, including cat's cradle. Kite-flying and its cultural accompaniments are discussed also, in China, Siam, India, Japan, New Zealand, the Society Islands, and America. Implies diffusion as an explanation.

T-175

AUTHOR: Tylor, Edward B.
DATE: 1883-1884
TITLE: Old Scandinavian Civilisation among the Modern Eskimaux
IN: Journal of the Anthropological Institute 13:348-357

Certain features appear to have been borrowed from Scandinavians when they met the Skraelings (Eskimo) in North America as well as in Greenland. Among the culture traits so affected are four games.

T-176

AUTHOR: Tylor, Edward B.
DATE: 1894
TITLE: On the Diffusion of Mythical Beliefs as Evidence in the History of Culture
IN: Report of the British Association, page 774-775

A long abstract of a delivered paper. A model (although he does not use the term) is laid out illustratively by showing how two mythical beliefs [motifs]—weighing souls in a balance, and bridge of death—extend from Egypt (oldest) to western Christendom and also through south Asia to eastern Buddhism. Of the same kind are evidences of Asiatic influences under which the pre-Columbian culture of America took shape. In Mexico four great scenes are faced in the journey of the soul in the land of the dead: crossing a river, passage between two mountains which clash together, climbing a mountain set with obsidian knives, and dangers of the wind carrying such knives on its blast. Buddhist and Mexican analogues are so close and complex as to preclude any explanation other than direct transmission. Combined with Humboldt's argument from calendars and mythic catastrophes in Mexico and Asia as well as correspondence in Bronze Age metal work and in games, "anthropologists might well feel justified in treating the nations of America as having reached their level of culture under Asiatic influence."

T-177

AUTHOR: Tylor, Edward B.
DATE: 1896
TITLE: On American Lot-games as Evidence of Asiatic Intercourse before the Time of Columbus
IN: Internationales Archiv für Ethnographie 9 (supplement): 55-67 (Leiden)
[Reprinted 1931, combined with excerpts from T-174, as "American Lot-games as Evidence of Asiatic Intercourse," in *Source Book in*

Anthropology, revised edition, compiled by Alfred L. Kroeber and T. T. Waterman (Harcourt, Brace: New York), 388-397]

Quotes the Spanish chroniclers regarding how the Aztec game of patolli was set up and played. The Apache game called tze-tiehl, played with stones and sticks, is so much like the Chinese-Korean game of nyut that the Indians might as well have learned it directly from modern Chinese workers in the U.S., yet it was known long before they were about. The complexity of the various parts of patolli and pachisi from India (or related Eurasian games) which are analogous to each other must be due not to separate inventions but to "communication across the Pacific from Eastern Asia."

T-178

AUTHOR: Tylor, Edward B.
DATE: 1910
TITLE: Anthropology
IN: Encyclopedia Britannica, 11th edition, 2:108-119

Here he appears in the course of 14 years since his last statement on the subject to have become a backslider regarding diffusion [as Smith accused him], pronouncing now against it as explanation.

U-001

AUTHOR: Ubbelohde-Doering, Heinrich
DATE: 1934
TITLE: Archäologische Grabungen in Peru, 1931-1932 [Archaeological Excavations in Peru, 1931-1932]
IN: Proceedings of the 1st International Congress of Anthropological and Ethnological Sciences (London, 1934), pages 237-239 (London)

Wooden posts of the Atarco region in the Nazca zone of Peru are carved with figures of the ancestors like posts used in the Admiralty Islands.

U-002B

AUTHOR: Ubelaker, Douglas H.
DATE: 1992
TITLE: Patterns of Demographic Change in the Americas
IN: Human Biology 64:361-379

On the effects of disease from the "Columbian Exchange." "The evidence suggests that after 1492 population reduction was caused not by continental pandemics but by localized or regional epidemics augmented by social and economic disruption." Some demographers (notably Dobyns), assuming continental disease devastation, project back to hypothesize a very high pre-Conquest American population figure, while others see much less disease effect hence a much lower pre-European population (Ubelaker is one of these). This is a contrast in interpretive frameworks between those who think of prehistory as "paradise" vs. those who think it much less ideal. [Relevant to the question of how epidemiologically isolated the pre-Columbian New World was from the Old prior to the age of European discovery.]

U-003

AUTHOR: Uhle, Max
DATE: 1922
TITLE: Fundamentos étnicos y arqueologícos de Arica y Tacna, 2a. edición [Ethnic Fundamentals and the Archaeology of Arica and Tacna]
IMPRINT: Universidad Central: Quito

A toy vessel fitted with a square sail was found in a [presumably pre-Spanish] grave from the "primitive fisher population" of northern Chile.

U-007

AUTHOR: Uhle, Max
DATE: 1930
TITLE: Desarrollo y origen de las civilizaciones americanas

[Development and Origin of the American Civilizations]
IN: Proceedings of the 23rd International Congress of Americanists (New York, 1928), 1:31-43

Cites some fairly generalized, and a few specific, cultural parallels between South and North America as evidence of a former unitary civilization in Central America from which those elements had spread in both directions. Since some of the features are also Asiatic (e.g., calendar), Asia must have been the source of the original Central American high culture, by diffusion (implies by ocean-crossing).

U-008
AUTHOR: Uhle, Max
DATE: 1942a
TITLE: Procedencia y origen de las antiguas civilizaciones americanas [Source and Origin of the Ancient American Civilizations]
IN: Proceedings of the 27th International Congress of Americanists (Part 2, Lima, 1939), 1:355-368

See U-009.

U-009
AUTHOR: Uhle, Max
DATE: 1942b
TITLE: La marcha de las civilizaciones [The March of Civilizations]
IN: Proceedings of the 27th International Congress of Americanists (Part 2, Lima, 1939), 1:369-382

Around 1250 B.C. dragon figures began appearing on the coast of China, representing personification of the rains. Along with the dragon was another cult figure with "thick, protruding upper lip" and prominent teeth. These are later seen in images of Tlaloc in Mexico and earlier in Maya vases and on the facade of the temple of Quetzalcoatl at Teotihuacan. He also sees stylistic parallels between proto-Chinese vases of the ninth century B.C. and others in Mexico, both bearing butterfly images. The Mexican calendar too was from China, having appeared first in Babylonia. The early Chinese elements reached Mesoamerica by a migrating party around 1200 B.C. It first appeared in Mexico but later reached Peru by way of the Chorotega area of Nicaragua.

U-012
AUTHOR: Uhlenbeck, Christianus Cornelis
DATE: 1942-1945
TITLE: Ur- und altindogermanische Anklänge im Wortschatz des Eskimo [Proto-Indogermanic and Old Indogermanic Echoes in the Vocabulary of the Eskimo]
IN: Anthropos 37-40:133-182

His full presentation of linguistic comparisons which he believes show a connection between old Indo-European and Eskimo languages.

U-014
AUTHOR: Ulloa, Louis
DATE: 1934
TITLE: La pré-découverte de l'Amérique par Colombe et l'origine Catalane de celui-ci [The Pre-Discovery of America by Columbus and his Catalonian Origin]
IN: Proceedings of the 24th International Congress of Americanists (Hamburg, 1930), pages 3-18

Columbus visited Iceland, Greenland, Labrador, Newfoundland, and Florida in the company of Danish corsairs (in 1477) years before he asked for the support of the Spanish rulers for his expedition. It was he who gave birth to the legend of Jean Scolvus. The conventional history results from a scandalous cover-up beginning with the

Spaniards and abetted by subsequent scholars who have ignored or downgraded abundant documents proving this case.

U-015

AUTHOR: Underwood, Horace C.
DATE: 1933
TITLE: Korean Boats and Ships
IN: Asiatic Society of Korea, Transactions No. 6 (complete issue) [Reprinted Chosen Christian College: Seoul, 1934; reprinted Yonsei University Press: Seoul, 1979]

A "preliminary study" which includes eye-witness descriptions and illustrations of Korean ships of today, construction, associated rites and customs, history, and the 1592-1598 naval campaign. Concludes that no ships are documented usefully until near our era, although no doubt some existed before. There is no indication of travel to any distance.

U-015B

AUTHOR: Underwood, L. Lyle
DATE: 1982
TITLE: The Los Lunas Inscription
IN: Eqigraphic Society Occasional Publication 10/237:57-67

Another description of the scene and the inscription (with a translation) accompanied by some confident but inaccurate statements. Says that Frank Hibben saw the stone in 1936 when it already "was old" in appearance. Conjectures regarding King Solomon's ships' crew as makers of the inscription.

U-017

AUTHOR: United Press International
DATE: 1983
TITLE: Atlantic in a Barrel Is His Claim to Fame
IN: Deseret News [Salt Lake City, Utah], February 10

A man claims to have crossed the Atlantic from the Canary Islands to Guadeloupe alone in a 6-foot barrel in 46 days. Another man had done the same in 85 days.

U-018

AUTHOR: Urban, Manfred
DATE: 1961
TITLE: Die Haustiere der Polynesier: Ein Beitrag zur Kulturgeschichte der Südsee [Domesticated Animals of the Polynesians: A Contribution to the Ethnology of the South Sea]
IMPRINT: Ludwig Häntzschel: Göttingen

Exhaustive consideration of domesticated animals (i.e., pig, dog, and chicken) in Polynesia in culture historical terms leads him specifically to exclude any contact with the New World.

U-019

AUTHOR: Urban, Manfred
DATE: 1966
TITLE: Zur Herkunft der polynesischen Kultur; Bemerkungen aus der Sicht der Ethnobotanik und Ethnozoologie des pazifischen Raumes [On the Origin of Polynesian Culture; Observations from the Viewpoint of Ethnobotany and Ethnozoology in the Pacific Region]
IN: Mitteilungen zur Kulturkunde 1:169-178 (Wiesbaden) [Constituting also *Paideuma,* Band 12]

Polynesians probably crossed to America, but no cultural items of much importance were brought by them on their return.

U-020

AUTHOR: Urban, Manfred
DATE: 1968-1969

TITLE: Das Alter der Süsskartoffel in der Südsee
[The Antiquity of the Sweet Potato in the Pacific]
IN: Anthropos 63-64:395-408

The sweet potato was introduced to Micronesia and Melanesia directly or indirectly by the Spanish, but Polynesia had received it between perhaps A.D. 1000 and 1400.

U-021
AUTHOR: Urbanski, Edmund Stephen
DATE: 1962
TITLE: Where Is the Cradle of Indo-American Civilization?
IN: América indígena 22:143-154

A general discussion of the question of transpacific diffusion. Believes some communication across the Pacific is indicated by recent publications, but more study is needed to clarify the matter.

U-023
AUTHOR: Urrutia, Benjamin
DATE: 1974
TITLE: Additional Evidence for the Precolumbian Migration of Black Africans to the American Continent
IN: Journal of Human Evolution 3/3:265

In a paragraph, he complains that were the same criteria applied to judge the evidence, African as much as Asian presence in pre-Columbian America would have to be granted. [See also S-345.]

U-024
AUTHOR: Urteaga, Horacio H.
DATE: 1917
TITLE: El arte de navegar entre los antiguos peruanos
[The Art of Navigation among the Ancient Peruvians]
IMPRINT: Revista histórica 5:363-391 (Lima)

Accepts, with Lothrop and Means, Xerez's 16th-century description of aboriginal square-sail rigged rafts.

U-025
AUTHOR: Urteaga, Horacio H.
DATE: 1919
TITLE: Las antiguas civilizaciones y razas del Perú
[The Ancient Civilizations and Races of Peru]
IN: Boletín, Sociedad geográfica de Lima 35:245-292
[Article with same title in *Proceedings of the 20th International Congress of Americanists (Rio de Janeiro, 1922)*, 2:423-450]

Immigrants to Peru, as in the traditions preserved on the Peruvian coast, must have come from Asia via the oceanic islands or by way of a former continent now submerged.

U-026
AUTHOR: Urteaga, Horacio H.
DATE: 1978 [1919]
TITLE: El arte de navegar entre los antiguos peruanos
[The Art of Navigation among the Ancient Peruvians]
IN: Tecnología andina, edited by Roger Ravines (Instituto de estudios peruanos: Lima), 659-676

Recapitulates quite fully statements by the Spanish chroniclers about Andean area ships (rafts) and their uses.

U-027
AUTHOR: Utley, Francis Lee
DATE: 1960
TITLE: Noah, his Wife and the Devil
IN: Studies in Biblical and Jewish Folklore, edited by Raphael Patai, Francis Lee Utley, and Dov Noy,

Indiana University Folklore Series, no. 13, Memoir Series of the American Folklore Society, vol. 51, (Indiana University Press: Bloomington), 59-91

Pages 61-62: The Earth Diver story he calls indigenous to America, but it occurred from Ontario all around the Arctic to European Russia.

U-028

AUTHOR: Utley, Francis Lee
DATE: 1974
TITLE: The Migration of Folktales: Four Channels to the Americas
IN: Current Anthropology 15:5-27

Detailed survey of folklore and mythic features shared between Old and New Worlds, such as Earth Diver, Magic Flight, and more. Appends comments by prominent scholars including Earl Count. Very important.

U-029

AUTHOR: Utsurikawa, N.
DATE: 1934
TITLE: Distribution of Patu Type of Stone Implements in the Pacific Area and Similar Stone Objects Discovered in Formosa
IN: Shigakka-Nenpo (Annual Bulletin of the Department of History, Taikohu Imperial University), no. 1

Found also in South America.

V-001A

AUTHOR: Vacher de Lapouge, Georges
DATE: 1896
TITLE: Les sélections sociales: cours libre de science politique [Social Selections: A Free Course in Political Science]
IMPRINT: A. Fontemoing: Paris

Supposes the presence of a pre-Columbian black race in America.

V-001B

AUTHOR: Vaillant, George C.
DATE: 1931
TITLE: A Bearded Mystery
IN: Natural History 31:243-244

Shows a bearded head from a ceramic figurine from the Balsas Valley of Mexico notably similar to representations of the god Melkarth of Phoenicia. [See comparative illustrations in I-098.]

V-002

AUTHOR: Vaillant, George C.
DATE: 1935
TITLE: Excavations at El Arbolillo
IMPRINT: American Museum of Natural History, Anthropological Papers 35:136-279

Page 245: Turquoise mosaic in use in Mexico before 1000 B.C. [Compare W-233 on Sumerian use.]

V-002B

AUTHOR: Valdiosera Berman, R.
DATE: 1975
TITLE: Quetzalcoatl Vikingo [The Viking Quetzalcoatl]
IMPRINT: Editorial associación: México

Self-explanatory title.

V-004

AUTHOR: Valentini, Philipp J. J.
DATE: 1881
TITLE: Two Mexican Chalchihuites, the Humboldt Celt and the Leyden Plate
IN: Proceedings of the American Antiquarian Society 1:283-302

Diffusionist treatment of jades supposed to show Asian sources.

V-005

AUTHOR: Vallaux, V.
DATE: 1926
TITLE: L'entrée de l'Océan Pacifique dans le cadre de l'histoire [Entry of the Pacific Ocean in the Framework of History]
IN: Scientia 40:163ff.

Voyaging across the Pacific before European discovery was likely impossible.

V-006

AUTHOR: Vallette, Marc F.
DATE: 1915
TITLE: American Mythology as Related to Asiatic and Hebrew Tradition
IN: American Catholic Quarterly Review 40:584-601

Comparison of American Indian myths and ceremonials, especially in the treatment of the dead, to those of Oceania and the Near East. Summarized in V-007, pages 307ff.

V-007

AUTHOR: Vallette, Marc F.
DATE: 1920
TITLE: Is the American Indian of Asiatic Origin?
IN: American Catholic Quarterly Review 45:294-320

Summarizes the views of Father Petitot [see P-136 to P-146] thus: One race who occupied the north were tall with small heads and receding foreheads who reached America by way of the Aleutians, fleeing before another race which had held them in bondage and who followed them to this continent. This first group were the Dené; their customs were of a Hebrew or Chaldean character and they practiced circumcision, but were intermingled with a foreign, uncircumcised group. Their pursuers were virtually a race of giants, with abnormally large heads deformed artificially. They wore no clothing [*sic*], had weapons of metal, wore helmet and cuirass, and took trophy heads. They were expert canoemen. They strongly resembled, physically, the Celtic peoples of the early Iron Age of northern Europe. The Dené regarded the latter groups as a "race of dogs" or "nation of women." Part of the Dené remained longer in Asia where they mingled with foreign elements before reaching America by way of Bering Strait. All this took place no earlier than the fifth or sixth century B.C. They seem related to the Israelite ten tribes or perhaps the Jews. There are many points of contact between the migrations of the later Dené and the Toltecs and other Mexican races. On the other hand the "Caraibo-Inneck" people are descended from Ham and are in customs most like "the Phoenico-Egyptian nations." Vallette then proceeds to "examine some of the arms and utensils" of prehistoric Europe and compare them with those of American aborigines [based on totally outdated sources]. He then repeats the material of V-006, involving especially belief that American cremation practice all began in India.

V-010

AUTHOR: Van Blerkom, Linda Miller
DATE: 1979 [issued 1981]
TITLE: A Comparison of Maya and Egyptian Hieroglyphics
IN: Katunob 11/3:1-8 (Greeley, Colorado)

Compares the principles of Maya writing with those of Egyptian hieroglyphs; the Maya glyphs were formed and used according to the same specific, enumerated principles as those of which applied in the Egypt system.

V-011

AUTHOR: Van Buren, Elizabeth Douglas
DATE: 1933

TITLE: The Flowing Vase and the God with Streams
IMPRINT: H. Stoetz: Berlin

Representations in the Near East show a deity at the center of the Milky Way, which is represented as an overflowing vase with streams flowing away in opposite directions. [Compare C-403, Plate 50 for a Palenque equivalent and Zapotec representations in W-040, pages 144-145.]

V-011B

AUTHORS: Van der Veen, M., and P. Moerman
DATE: 1978
TITLE: Protocartographie de l'Amérique [Early Cartography of America]
IN: Kadath: Chroniques des civilisations disparues, no. 30:38-39 (Brussels)

Comments on M-046, which immediately precedes it.

V-012

AUTHOR: Van Pelt, Dina
DATE: 1988
TITLE: Poles May Be Clue to Lifting Stones
IN: Insight 4 (17 April 25): 54 (Washington)

John Cunningham, art professor at Skidmore College, theorized in an article in *Nature* about how the ancients might have lifted heavy stones. Sets of poles, shown in Egyptian artwork and tested experimentally by him, were placed beneath large stones, then lifted incrementally at their ends which caused them to bend slightly without breaking. If each pole end is progressively propped up with small stones during this process, the stone is slowly lifted to the desired height. He posits that Egyptians and Incas both built stone structures using this method.

V-013

AUTHOR: VanStan, Ina
DATE: 1957
TITLE: A Peruvian Ikat from Pachacamac
IN: American Antiquity 23:150-159

This resist-dyeing technique was until recently thought to have been unknown in pre-Columbian Peru [and America generally], citing publications dating 1916, 1928, 1931. The first publication of a Peruvian example was 1930. Presently- known examples are surveyed, including some which date to the late Middle period [A.D. 800?]. No comment of a diffusionist nature is made [although diffusionists have noted the similarity of the technique to that in Southeast Asia—compare B-442].

V-014

AUTHOR: VanStan, Ina
DATE: 1963
TITLE: A Problematic Example of Peruvian Resist-dyeing
IN: American Antiquity 29:166-173

Claims that batik-type dyeing has not yet been proven present before European discovery, but the likelihood is that it was present in Peru.

V-015

AUTHOR: VanStan, Ina
DATE: 1979
TITLE: Did Inca Weavers Use an Upright Loom?
IN: The Junius B. Bird Pre-Columbian Textile Conference, May 19th and 20th, 1973, edited by Ann Pollar Rowe, Elizabeth P. Benson, and Ann-Louise Schaffer (The Textile Museum and Dumbarton Oaks: Washington, D.C.), 233-238

Discovery of a tiny ceramic model of a loom, which forms part of the ornamentation at the top of one section of a bridged blackware jar found at Pachacamac, has raised new questions about pre-Columbian looms in Peru. What is shown has two upright posts planted in the ground and a round crossbar cradled in the cutout tops of the posts. Women are weaving on both sides. One may be seated in a pit. The date is late Inca, but the excavator is convinced that it is pre-Spanish. No other evidence for such a loom in pre-Spanish America is known. But a pre-Columbian replica in silver of another type of fixed-frame loom has been exhibited. Thus a number of frame-loom types might have existed.

V-016

AUTHOR: Varnhagen, Francisco Adolphe de
DATE: 1876
TITLE: L'origine touranienne des Américains Tupis-Caraïbes et des anciens Egyptiens, indiquée principalement par la philologie comparée: traces d'une ancienne migration en Amérique, invasion du Brésil par les Tupis
[The Turanian Origin of the Tupí-Carib Americans and Ancient Egyptians, Indicated Principally by Comparative Philology: Traces of an Ancient Migration to America, Invasion of Brazil by the Tupís]
IMPRINT: de Faes and Frick: Vienna

Title self-explanatory.

V-017

AUTHOR: Varron, A.
DATE: 1942
TITLE: The Umbrella as an Emblem of Dignity and Power
IN: Ciba Review 9:42

Distribution of the umbrella in the Mediterranean, Near East, and South and East Asia with symbolic associations. It is reflected in the use of a royal canopy or pavilion in Israel (Jeremiah 43:10). Also on coins of Herod Agrippa and in Athenian ritual, as well as among Assyrians. Symbolic of dignity, power, divinity, nobility. [American parallels.]

V-018

AUTHOR: Varshavsky, S. R.
DATE: 1961
TITLE: Appearance of American Turkeys in Europe before Columbus
IN: New World Antiquity 8/8:104-105

A letter from a Russian geographer points out an error in the literature on this topic: (American) turkeys on friezes at Schleswig Cathedral, supposedly of the 13th century, were actually put there by an artist doing restoration in 1920 (citations to obscure literature are included). Yet an article on ornithology recently published in Hungary reports turkey bones of 13th century date (Bökönyi and Janossy, 1959, *Aquila, Annales Inst. Ornithologici Hungarici* 65:265-269, includes English text). This agrees with similar finds of bones in Switzerland (Middle Ages) and Budapest (14th century). Furthermore, three signet rings indubitably depicting turkeys, have been found in 10th-13th century graves in the Central Danube lowlands.

V-019

AUTHOR: Vaux-Phalipau, Mme.
DATE: 1937
TITLE: Le mythe des mélusine à travers le monde et son type le plus Complet; la mélusine des Lusignan
[The Melusine Myth throughout the World and Its Most Complete Type: The Melusine of the Lusignan]
IN: L'Ethnographie 33/34:105-107

The myth (including five distinct motifs) probably originated in Asia but expanded to Europe and even to America. No data are given in support of the statement re. America.

V-021

AUTHOR: Vayda, Andrew P.
DATE: 1958
TITLE: A Voyage by Polynesian Exiles
IN: Journal of the Polynesian Society 67:324-329

Detailing a late 19th-century case of exile (from the Northern Cook Islands) due to status rivalry, he believes it probable that purposive voyages by Polynesian exiles, including women, occurred in the past.

V-023

AUTHOR: Vega, Carlos
DATE: 1934
TITLE: La flauta de pan andina [The Andean Panpipe]
IN: Proceedings of the 25th International Congress of Americanists (La Plata, Argentina, 1932), 1:333-348

A mysterious term used in Peru to denominate the panpipe is apparently Polynesian. Other possible relationships in music-related names are shown, including the shell trumpet. He believes his work should be carefully considered by linguists who can render final judgement. Together with what Imbelloni and Palavecino have shown on the use of introduced Polynesian words, he is sure that culture elements from that area reached South America, yet he is cautious about how important the contacts may have been.

V-024

AUTHOR: Végréville, P.
DATE: n.d. [c.1880]
TITLE: Notes philologiques [Philological Notes]
IN: Proceedings of the 3rd International Congress of Americanists (Brussels, 1879), 2:586-624

Favors the idea that there were multiple immigrations to America. Gives tables which compare vocabulary and certain grammatical features of Assiniboine and Cree with Western European languages; there are some rough equivalences.

V-025

AUTHOR: Vélez, Baltasar
DATE: 1894
TITLE: Descubrimiento precolombino de la América: ensayo crítico histórico [Pre-Columbian Discovery of America: A Critical Historical Essay]
IMPRINT: Garnier Hermanos: Paris

Of no substantive significance. Brief notes on Vikings, Fu-sang, and the like.

V-026

AUTHOR: Vélez López, Señora L. R.
DATE: 1924
TITLE: ¿Existió la escritura entre los Yungas? [Did Writing Exist among the Yungas?]
IN: Proceedings of the 21st International Congress of Americanists (Part 1, The Hague, 1924), pages 87-88

Montesinos claimed that writing existed among the Chimus before Inca domination. This is shown by finds from Peru assumed to be ancient and shown here in three plates, all of them containing patent or possible Chinese characters. She reports the presence of signs in lineal forms, like those of Chinese, cuneiform and Phoenician writing, on Peruvian ceramics and shells. [Compare J-030B.]

V-026B

AUTHOR: Venkateswarlu, J.
DATE: 1962
TITLE: Origin of Maize
IN: Proceedings of the Summer School of Botany—Darjeeling, edited by P. Mekeshwari, B. M. Johri, and I. K. Vasil (Council of Scientific and Industrial Research, Government of India: New Delhi), 494-504

Hypothesizes an Asian origin for maize.

V-026C

AUTHOR: Verano, John W.

DATE: 1992

TITLE: Prehistoric Disease and Demography in the Andes

IN: Disease and Demography in the Americas, edited by John W. Verano and Douglas H. Ubelaker (Smithsonian Institution Press: Washington, D.C.), 15-24

Much of the early debate over syphilis and leprosy was based on artistic depictions more than skeletal remains; subsequent research has failed to produce unequivocal evidence for either disease. Tuberculosis has been positively identified. There is some evidence that leishmaniasis (uta), an insect-borne disease, afflicted prehistoric Andean populations. Coprolites from coastal Peru show intestinal parasites: tapeworm (by 2700 B.C.), pinworm (approximately 2300 B.C.), whipworm (by 2700 B.C.), and roundworm. Hookworm (Ancylostoma duodenale) also comes from a mummy. [Compare F-120.]

Selectivity of museum collections of skeletal materials make it difficult to make reliable statements about disease frequency. Allison and associates have documented chronic infectious diseases in Peruvian and Chilean mummies: tuberculosis, blastomycosis, broncho-pneumonia and lobar pneumonia. Pneumonia was the major cause of death for all time periods. Health conditions before the Spanish advent deteriorated in the long term on the central coast of Peru with increasing sedentism, agricultural intensification, and population growth. When European diseases hit, local effects varied greatly.

V-027

AUTHOR: Verdoorn, Frans, editor

DATE: 1946

TITLE: Merrilleana: A Selection from the General Writings of Elmer Drew Merrill

IN: Chronica Botanica 10/3-4 (Waltham, Massachusetts)

Merrill admits for the first time that the sweet potato reached Polynesia from America before Europeans.

He believes that crops were rapidly disseminated by commerce virtually worldwide immediately after the European discovery of America. Maize arrived in China only 25 years after being introduced into Spain. The Portuguese carried it to Goa from Brazil whence it spread to Assam by overland dispersal in a couple of decades. [F-092 wonders why this grain, which became of major importance in Asian agriculture thereafter, should first have been cultivated in remote Assam rather in much more likely India, if indeed it arrived via Goa. Compare T-217B.]

V-028

AUTHOR: Verhoog, P.

DATE: 1958

TITLE: De Ontdekking van Amerika vóór Columbus
[The Discovery of America before Columbus]

IMPRINT: Uitgeverij C. De Boer Jr.: Hilversum, The Netherlands

Popular treatment, documented to a considerable extent, although the sources are a curious mix of outdated and current materials. Nothing new: Brendan, Madoc, the Norse, Fu-sang, Heine-Geldern, etc.

V-029

AUTHOR: Verity, William E.

DATE: 1966

TITLE: Solo Trans-Gulf Crossing in the "Nonoalca"

IN: Florida Anthropologist 19/4:145-153

A round trip from Florida to Veracruz in a 12-foot sloop. Mayans would have had no trouble duplicating such a trip. "I believe that at least five culture heroes came to the Americas (by sea). One [not further explained] was very early, possibly 500 B.C., and others followed through the centuries until Cortes."

V-029B

AUTHOR: Verlinden, Charles
DATE: 1970
TITLE: A Precursor of Columbus: The Fleming Ferdinand Van Olmen (1487)
IN: The Beginnings of Modern Colonization: Eleven Essays with an Introduction, by Charles Verlinden (Cornell University Press: Ithaca, New York), 181-195

As early as 1462 a knight of the Portuguese court had been granted rights over two islands to be found west of the Azores, and in 1474 similar rights were conferred on a member of the royal council, including mention of the Island of the Seven Cities or Antilia. In 1486 the Portuguese king decreed that Ferdinand van Olmen, a Fleming who had been given permission to colonize in the Azores, should undertake voyages to the west in hopes of finding a large island, or islands, or the coast of a continent where it was thought the Seven Cities were to be found, and he expected to find them within a 40-day voyage. The phrasing indicates that voyages had already been made that had sighted land but without taking possession. He set out northwesterly, toward Newfoundland, but seems to have perished on the voyage.

V-030

AUTHOR: Verneau, René
DATE: 1889
TITLE: Le papyrus egyptien, la tapa océanienne et le papier des ancien Mexicains [Egyptian Papyrus, Oceanian Tapa and the Paper of the Ancient Mexicans]
IN: La nature 17/1:43-44

Brief descriptions of the Mexican and Polynesian methods of preparing amate (bark) paper on the one hand and tapa (bark cloth) on the other. The stone beaters (illustrated) are similar. Early Chinese paper was done in the same way and Egyptian papyrus too was handled the same. Vaguely implies, but does not concretely claim, connections among the cultures mentioned.

V-032

AUTHOR: Verneau, René
DATE: 1924
TITLE: Crânes d'Indiens de la Colombie; l'élément Papoua en Amérique [Indian Skulls of Colombia; the Papuan Element in America]
IN: L'Anthropologie 34:353-386

Skulls unearthed at Lagoa Santa, Brazil, and others from Baja California differ radically from ordinary Indian skulls but closely resemble skulls of natives of the New Hebrides, New Caledonia, and other parts of Melanesia.

V-032B

AUTHOR: Verneau, Rene, and Paul Rivet
DATE: 1924
TITLE: Ethnographie ancienne de l'Equateur [The Ancient Ethnography of Ecuador]
IMPRINT: Gauthier-Villars: Paris

Includes evidence for somatological similarities between Melanesia and South America. Clubs with heads of stone in the shape of stars or rings are in Polynesia as in Ecuador.

V-035

AUTHOR: Vernet Ginés, Juan
DATE: 1971
TITLE: Textos arabes de viajes por el Atlántico [Arab Texts of Voyages in the Atlantic]

IN: Anuario de estudios atlánticos 17:401-427 (Madrid)

Since before the 12th century, (Arab) ships of Cordoba, which had stood off the Normans since A.D. 844, had been inspired architecturally by Mediterranean ships. They travelled in the area between Britain and Negro Africa. In the middle 10th century one Persian document reports the presence of an Iberian ship in the Persian Gulf, implying the circumnavigation of Africa. Other accounts of Arab voyaging through the 15th century are summarized.

V-036

AUTHOR: Verrill, A. Hyatt

DATE: 1929

TITLE: Old Civilizations of the New World

IMPRINT: Bobbs Merrill: New York [Reprinted New Home Library: New York, 1942. Spanish editions 1945, Mexico City; and 1947, Buenos Aires]

An archaeologist of the old adventurous sort writes a popular work laced with some documentable (but not here documented) facts relevant to interhemispheric diffusion, as well as more dubious assertions. For example: Easter Island is a remnant of an archipelago that existed in comparatively recent times; among nearly all tribes of western South America we find scores of words of the same meanings in Oceanian dialects; the strange bearded Sirionos have typically Oceanian features but not the faintest resemblance to any other known Indian tribe.

V-038

AUTHORS: Verrill, A. Hyatt, and Ruth Verrill

DATE: 1953

TITLE: America's Ancient Civilizations

IMPRINT: Putnam's: New York [Reprinted Capricorn: New York, 1967]

This is an archaeological last will and testament, as it were, of a pair of unorthodox researchers, intellectual successors of Le Plongeon. It illustrates how convoluted a set of arguments determined diffusionists can construct.

Pages xvi-xvii: Their view of the Old World origins of ancient American civilizations depends heavily on R. Verrill's unpublished manuscript study, "Gods Who Were Men," which she has circulated widely and which she interprets as having been "commended and accepted" by such people as Junius Bird and Gordon Ekholm.

Pages 9-11, 14-21: Expressed in terms even darker than Gladwin's, their view is that academic "die-hards" have not only opposed the idea of Old World influences but have covered up evidence favoring it. But now it is possible to talk about the subject. She is implied to have been the first to call attention to the similarity of a small figurine from the Rio Balsas in Mexico [compare V-001B, I-098] with the Mediterranean, where a stone image from Cyprus has an identical beard and facial expression.

Among the Sumerian records now deciphered by Mrs. Verrill, we learn of the establishment of colonies in a far Sunset Land and conquests there by Sargon, King Menes, etc. Numerous finds in America appear to verify this, particularly the presence in the Colorado River area of pictographs and glyphs cut and painted on cliffs and caves that are not the accepted North American type.

Pages 92ff.: The ancestors of the ancient Mexicans came from Peru, first exploring up into the Colorado River drainage to Chaco Canyon and beyond. The Seven Caves of the Aztecs he may have found near Kanab, Utah. Nearby an amateur archaeologist discovered a set of obsidian disks or "coins" bearing hieroglyphs on both sides which are similar to Hittite, Sumerian and pre-dynastic Egyptian writing. (A "Smithsonian Institution archaeologist" to whom these were shown is reported to have said the only similar items were from Egypt.)

Pages 101ff.: The Plumed Serpent, Quetzalcoatl, was Naram-sin, who arrived in Mexico by sea. A mace head found beneath Lake Texcoco is "almost identical" in shape with those that belonged to Naram-sin and Sargon.

Pages 109ff.: The clinching evidence is the representation of the Plumed Serpent on the Santa Rita frescoes in British Honduras. Mrs. Verrill reads "the many odd ornaments, decorations, etc." which appear thereon as "archaic Sumerian script" concerning overseas visitors.

Pages 132-133: A figurine they excavated at Coclé, Panama, is described as "strikingly and obviously elephantine."

Pages 294-296: Sumerians of 2000 B.C. possessed ocean-going ships rigged with large sails and three decks. Their records speak of boats nearly 100 feet long. Ancient Sumerian explorers, including Sargon, his son Menes, and Naram-Sin, son of Menes, actually visited Peru. A stone tablet found at Sachuayacu, 150 miles north of Cuzco, bears a famous inscription of 22 characters (an almost identical inscription was found in Bolivia). Mrs. Verrill identifies the writing as "the Gangetic (India) form of Archaic Sumerian Linear Script" and gives a reading. Etc.

Pages 299ff.: Who was Wira Kocha? Either Sargon or Menes. Many cultural features manifest Near Eastern influence on the Andean area: fitted stone walls with handling projections left attached, massive door lintels, metal keys locking stones together, foot hoes, slings, a wooden shield of peculiar form, star-shaped maces, balances, steelyards, shears, and more.

Pages 310-312: A list of 42 of these important features that were identical or very nearly so.

Pages: 312-315: The book ends abruptly with a listing of "duplicate or very similar words . . . that have the same meanings in the Sumerian and Peruvian languages."

V-039B

AUTHOR: Vescelius, Gary S.
DATE: 1982-1983
TITLE: The Antiquity of Pattee's Cave
IN: NEARA [New England Antiquities Research Association] Journal 17:2-16 (Part I); 17:28-42 (Part II); 17:59-69 (Part III)

A comprehensive report on excavations at the North Salem/Pattee/Mystery Hill site(s) in Massachusetts. Although the remains "resemble certain Old World megalithic ruins, the similarities are not in themselves great enough to warrant belief in an historical relationship." All the thousands of artifacts excavated, furthermore, "appear, to my unpracticed eye, to date from the late eighteenth or nineteenth century." "The historical evidence is such as to suggest that the Caves were built by Jonathan Pattee, who lived at the site during the period 1826-1948." "They were not built by Irish monks."

In a footnote the author notes that F. Glynn, in a short unpublished manuscript, has pointed to a number of specific parallels between this architecture and that of certain early Maltese sites, but Vescelius offers alternative interpretations for the similarities.

V-040

AUTHOR: Vignaud, Henri
DATE: 1902
TITLE: Toscanelli and Columbus: The Letter and Chart of Toscanelli on the Route to the Indies by Way of the West, Sent in 1474 to the Portuguese Fernam Martins, and Later on to Christopher Columbus
IMPRINT: Sands: London [Reprinted Books for Libraries: Freeport, New York, 1971]

Letters purporting to be from Toscanelli to Columbus which appear to give the latter information about westward navigation are here claimed to be a fraud, in which Columbus knowingly participated, although the information actually made no substantial difference to the success of his project.

V-041B

AUTHOR: Vignaud, Henri
DATE: 1920
TITLE: The Columbian Tradition on the Discovery of America and the Part Played Therein by the Astronomer Toscanelli
IMPRINT: Clarendon Press: Oxford

See V-040.

V-042

AUTHOR: Vignaud, Henri
DATE: 1922
TITLE: Le probléme du peuplement initial de l'Amérique et de l'origine éthnique de sa population indigéne [The Problem of the Initial Peopling of America and the Ethnic Origin of Its Native Population]
IN: Journal de la société des américanistes de Paris 14:1-63

The Canaanites (Jebusites) fled the Israelites under Joshua and reached America via North Africa. An inscription in Mauritania documents their passage.

V-043

AUTHOR: Vigneras, Louis André
DATE: 1956
TITLE: New Light on the 1497 Cabot Voyage to America
IN: Hispanic American Historical Review 36:503-509

Columbus may have heard of transatlantic voyages from an "unknown pilot." Bristol sailors knew of this information, which Columbus may have learned about when he was in England in 1477.

V-046

AUTHOR: Viitso, Tiit-Rein
DATE: 1971
TITLE: Preliminary Data on the Relation of California Penutian to Uralic and other Nostratic Languages
IN: Soviet Fenno-Ugric Studies 7/2:119-128

The Nostratic concept has been around since 1903 but has been worked on mainly since 1960. "It is . . . possible that there are some more language families both in Asia and America that are related to Nostratic." Shows here California Penutian comparisons with Uralic and other Nostratic languages through 83 "word articles" (morpheme comparisons). Acknowledges that von Sadovszky has been working on "Costanoan and Uralic." [See S-011.]

V-047

AUTHOR: Villacorta Cifuentes, Jorge Luís
DATE: 1976
TITLE: Historia de la medicina, cirugía y obstetricia prehispánicas [History of Prehispanic Medicine, Surgery and Obstetrics]
IMPRINT: n.p.: Guatemala

A medical doctor presents well-documented discussions on pre-Columbian pathologies based on art, traditions, chronicles, colonial reports, and modern studies.

Page 44: The old picture presented the New World as victimized by the importation by the Spaniards and their slaves of previously unknown, terribly destructive diseases. "Nevertheless, recent studies have permitted demonstration that at the moment of discovery and conquest neither of the hemispheres were free of the great majority of them [diseases]."

Pages 44-82: Each major disease entity is discussed in turn and evidence about pre-Columbian occurrence is examined, with citations. Yellow fever quite certainly was present in the reservoir provided by monkeys, and there is evidence that periodically, under certain ecological conditions, it had severe effects on humans.

Measles and smallpox: The Spanish terminology is confused, nevertheless, it appears that measles was a pre-Columbian disease (representations on figurines remove all doubt), but smallpox was indeed the most damaging Spanish import. Exanthematic typhus was also present.

Tuberculosis: it was once thought that only tuberculosis of the bones was present, but discovery of pulmonary lesions in a Peruvian mummy now leaves no doubt about that form also being present.

Leprosy: The evidence tends to be against its presence, but the case is arguable.

Syphilis: There is no question of its presence in both New and Old Worlds before the Spanish Conquest. Yaws (mal del pinto) also was in America.

Malaria: The preponderance of evidence is against this being present, however, the fact that the Peruvians knew of the value of quinine as an agent against it in colonial times leaves a question.

V-048

AUTHOR: Villamil de Rada, Emeterio
DATE: 1888
TITLE: La lengua de Adán y el hombre de Tiahuanaco
[The Language of Adam and the Man of Tiahuanaco]
IMPRINT: Imprenta de "La Razon": La Paz
[Reprinted Imprenta Artística: La Paz, 1939]

Aymara was the language of the Garden of Eden.

V-049

AUTHOR: Villiers, Alan John
DATE: 1937
TITLE: Cruise of the Conrad: A Journal of a Voyage round the World, Undertaken and Carried out in the Ship Joseph Conrad, 212 Tons, in the Years 1934, 1935 and 1936 by Way of Good Hope, the East Indies, the South Seas and Cape Horn
IMPRINT: Scribner's: New York

An experienced salt tells much of nautical interest about small-vessel voyaging.

V-050

AUTHOR: Villiers, Alan John
DATE: 1940
TITLE: Sons of Sinbad: An Account of Sailing with the Arabs in Their Dhows, in the Red Sea, around the Coasts of Arabia, and to Zanzibar and Tanganyika
IMPRINT: Scribner's: New York
[Reprinted Scribner's: New York, 1969]

Indian Ocean sailing ways.

V-052

AUTHOR: Villiers, Alan John
DATE: 1957
TITLE: Wild Ocean: The Story of the North Atlantic and the Men Who Sailed It
IMPRINT: McGraw-Hill: New York

In chapters 2 and 3 this supremely experienced sailor scoffs at shore-bound critics who doubt that Phoenicians could circumnavigate Africa, or 15th- century Portuguese could sail the Atlantic to Newfoundland. They could and did, but they were close-mouthed about it: "no one hired the Phoenicians to write a book." Interesting points: Tenerife in the Canaries can be seen a hundred miles away on a clear day; in Cardiff Museum are fragments of ancient Roman pottery dredged up from the shallow fishing bank called the Porcupine, far out in the North Atlantic beyond the coast of Ireland; the connection of Ireland with Iceland by voyagers was an ancient one, at least by the sixth century A.D., and the Brandan stories were persistent. He takes pleasure in recounting the sailing of the model Viking ship to Chicago in 1893, impressed with its superior characteristics for ocean travel.

V-055

AUTHOR: Vilmundarson, Thórhallur
DATE: 1966
TITLE: Reflections on the Vinland Map
IN: American-Scandinavian Review 54:20-24

Many questions about the Vinland Map are so complex that it will take the collaboration of many scholars years to answer, if they ever can be. He considers that the map is not obviously a forgery. Skelton et al. [S-273] were not sufficiently deep into or current with relevant scholarship in preparing their book, although it is still valuable.

V-056

AUTHOR: Vincent, Joseph E.
DATE: 1961
TITLE: [Tupí-Polynesian Similarities]
IN: Science of Man 1/5:173-174

The author (as editor of the periodical) reports identification of a number of words purportedly gathered by writer James Norman Hall in the Tuamotus in 1922-23, and considered by Hall anomalous in Polynesian, to be Tupí, of Brazil. [Compare H-034; M-336 shows that this business was a hoax.]

V-057

AUTHOR: Vining, Edward P.
DATE: 1885
TITLE: An Inglorious Columbus; or, Evidence that Hwui Shan and a Party of Buddhist Monks from Afghanistan Discovered America in the Fifth Century, A.D.
IMPRINT: D. Appleton: New York

An extensive survey of the literature on the Fu-sang matter, reprinting most of the substantive material and arguments, pro and con. He concludes in chapter 37, pages 684-710, "Recapitulation," by systematically summarizing what he considers the evidences favoring the thesis that Fu-sang was Mexico which have survived the critics. These include: mirrors, silk, pyramids, architecture, arts, religious structures, religious customs and beliefs, idols, marriage ceremonies, dress, food, books, games, metallurgy, suspension bridge, and calendar.

V-058

AUTHOR: Vinson, Julien
DATE: 1875
TITLE: La langue basque et les langues américaines [The Basque and American Languages]
IN: Proceedings of the 1st International Congress of Americanists (Nancy, 1875), 2:46-80

After long-labored comparisons, he concludes that Basque is not related to Algonquian languages, except some elements from an early common source.

V-059

AUTHOR: Virchow, Rudolf
DATE: 1883
TITLE: Das Gräberfeld von Koban im Lande der Ossten, Kaukasus [The Cemetery of Koban in the Land of Ossten, Caucasia]
IMPRINT: Asher: Berlin

Notes striking similarity between bronze needles of the Caucasus and needles of the Andean region. (Comparing Ernest Chantre, *Recherches anthropologiques dans le Caucase*, vol. 2. *Période protohistorique,* Paris, 1886.)

V-060

AUTHOR: Virchow, Rudolf
DATE: 1889
TITLE: Crania americana ethnica [American Ethnic Crania]

IN: Mitteilungen der Anthropologische Gesellschaft in Wien 19:138-140

Peruvians were descended from the Malays.

V-061

AUTHOR: Vishnu-Mittre
DATE: 1966
TITLE: Kaudinyapur Plant Economy in Protohistoric and Historic Times
IN: The Paleobotanist 15:152-156 (Lucknow)

Reports the apparent impression of a maize ear rolled over a clay pot prior to its being fired ca. A.D. 1435 in Madhya Pradesh, India. [See also *Palaeobotanist* 15 (1966): 142.]

Page 155: ". . . it would appear that the evidence of maize in India is not in any case later than 1435 A.D. which . . . tends to establish its pre-Columbian age."

[Johannessen, personal communication to Sorenson, found in 1992 that the impressions failed tests for having been made by maize kernels.]

V-061B

AUTHOR: Vishnu-Mittre
DATE: 1974
TITLE: [The Beginnings of Agriculture:] Palaeobotanical Evidence in India
IN: Evolutionary Studies in World Crops: Diversity and Change in the Indian Subcontinent, edited by Joseph B. Hutchinson (Cambridge University Press: London), 3-30

Archaeological evidences and radiocarbon dates are adduced and mapped, crop by crop, to document the earliest agriculture in India.

Pages 22-23: Maize. Pollen evidence from the Kashmir Valley, citing V-062, "is dated by conservative estimate to the fifteenth century A.D." Impressions on a potsherd from Kaundinyapur, Madhya Pradesh, and dated archaeologically to about A.D. 1435, have created a difference of opinion among the experts; the opinions seem determined by adherence to one or the other school about the pre-Columbian occurrence of maize in Asia (not so much by the facts). Richard McNeish and James Griffin opined that the impression could have been made by a piece of basketry or textile, but experiments conducted by George Carter disproved that. "This discovery tends to support a pre-Columbian introduction" of maize to India. In any event, Jeffreys is to be believed, on the basis of names for maize in India (which mean "Mecca sorghum" or "grain of Mecca"), that the Arabs were responsible for the introduction, not the Portuguese.

"Apart from the problem of its introduction, the enigmatic living fossil maize in Sikkim perhaps tends to suggest a reconsideration of the occurrence of maize there." Several distinct varieties of it are grown by aborigines in Siam, Burma, Assam, Sikkim, China, Tibet, etc. "It seems to have been grown there for a long time. It can hardly have been introduced by the Arabs through the inland caravan routes," and local names do not indicate any such thing. The variety of the names (some cited) suggests a rather long period of cultivation and that it was an introduced crop.

Page 28: Conclusion. "Evidence presented suggests reconciliation with the view that maize was introduced into India in the pre-Columbian era and probably by the Arabs—a case of transatlantic diffusion, though the source of the enigmatic maize of Sikkim and Assam remains unknown." [See V-061.]

V-062

AUTHORS: Vishnu-Mittre, and H. P. Gupta
DATE: 1966
TITLE: Pollen Morphological Studies of Some Primitive Varieties of Maize (Zea mays L.) with Remarks on the History of Maize in India
IN: The Paleobotanist 15:176-185 (Lucknow)

They found maize pollen in mire which they interpret [contradictorily], on indirect evidence, as indicating cultivation beginning in the 13th-14th century, or, alternatively, not "more than four hundred years old." Considering this subfossil maize pollen and the alleged maize imprints on a potsherd from Madhya Pradesh, as well as ten primitive maize forms from Assam, they admit the possibility that this crop spread to India in pre-Columbian times as a result of transpacific contacts with South America.

V-063

AUTHOR: Vivante, Armando
DATE: 1941
TITLE: La escritura de los mochica sobre porotes
[Mochica Writing on Beans]
IN: Revista de geografía americana 15/92:297-310 (Buenos Aires)

What Larco Hoyle believed to be a Peruvian system of writing on beans looks to this author like part of a game.

V-064

AUTHOR: Vivante, Armando
DATE: 1942
TITLE: El juego mochica con pallares
[The Mochica Game with Beans]
IN: Revista de geografía americana 18/110:275-280 (Buenos Aires)

See V-063.

V-065

AUTHOR: Vivante, Armando
DATE: 1963
TITLE: Estado actual de la discusión sobre pigmeos americanos
[Present State of the Discussion Concerning American Pygmies]
IN: Revista del Museo de La Plata, Sección de Antropología 5:193-263

A summary of materials in support of the idea. [See also I-023.]

V-066

AUTHOR: Vivante, Armando
DATE: 1967
TITLE: El problema de los negros prehispánicos americanos: notas sobre los melanodermos precolombinos
[The Problem of the American Prehispanic Negroes: Notes Concerning the Pre-Columbian Darkly-Pigmented People]
IN: Revista del Museo de La Plata, Sección de Antropología 6:281-333

Asks why more attention has not been paid to the possibility of Atlantic crossings in the populating of America and mentions the main scholars who have considered it. He then does a detailed ransacking of about every writing on the possible presence of (African) negroes in America before Columbus [unearthing more small bits of interesting information than Comas, C-317]. While obviously accepting some African contacts, he ends leaving the question open for further investigation.

V-069

AUTHORS: Voegelin, Carl F., and F. M. Voegelin
DATE: 1964
TITLE: Extinction of American Indian Languages before and after Contact Periods
IN: Anthropological Linguistics 6/6:46-58

As opposed to Lamb, the authors give their opinion that there was no wholesale extinction of North American languages prior to the European conquest. Alien languages were adopted by populations because of relatively greater prestige, or extensive inter-marriage, but evidence for extinction is weak. [Should this view or Lamb's apply to languages perhaps brought by transoceanic migrants?]

V-070

AUTHOR: Voegelin, Erminie W.
DATE: 1947
TITLE: Three Shasta Myths, Including "Orpheus"
IN: Journal of American Folklore 60:52-58

The Orpheus theme is not a European loan but "of native origin."

V-071

AUTHOR: Voget, Fred W.
DATE: 1975
TITLE: A History of Ethnology
IMPRINT: Holt, Rinehart and Winston: New York

Pages 340-341: Summarizes Nordenskiöld's culture historical studies of South American Indians and his isolationist conclusions.

Pages 343-348: The rise and decline of diffusionism in Britain: Smith, Perry, Rivers.

Pages 348-355: German-Austrian Kulturkreis theoreticians: Ratzel, Frobenius, Graebner, Schmidt, Koppers.

Pages 355-358: The treatments of the positions and settings for the works of the major figures are essentially descriptive. They provide little substance for understanding the corpus of diffusionist work, the reasons for its development, or the decline of diffusionism.

V-072

AUTHOR: Vogt, Evon Z.
DATE: 1964
TITLE: Ancient Maya Concepts in Contemporary Zinacantan Religion
IN: Sixth International Congress of Anthropological and Ethnological Sciences (Paris, 1960), 2/2:497-502 (Paris)

Cites and parallels generally H-377. Maintains that Tzotzil beliefs about sacred mountains, etc., are functionally similar and close to those about ancient Maya pyramids. [The beliefs are parallel to those of Eurasia at a number of points.]

V-073

AUTHORS: Voitov, V. I., and D. D. Tumarkin
DATE: 1967
TITLE: Navigational Conditions of Sea Routes to Polynesia
IN: Archaeology at the Eleventh Pacific Science Congress (Tokyo, 1966), edited by Wilhelm G. Solheim II, Asian and Pacific Archaeological Series, No. 1 (Social Science Research Institute, University of Hawai: Honolulu), 88-100 [Reprinted 1969 in *Asian Perspectives* 10]

The South Equatorial Current and southeastern trade winds favor drift voyages from some areas of South America to the Tuamotus and Marquesas but not to Easter Island. Conclude that as far as winds and currents are concerned, Polynesia could have been colonized via either Micronesia or Melanesia. [While their opinion is not new, it is based on more refined oceanographic data than available before and counters the views of Heyerdahl, at least in reference to drift voyages.]

V-074

AUTHOR: Vokes, Emily H.
DATE: 1963
TITLE: A Possible Hindu Influence at Teotihuacan
IN: American Antiquity 29:94-95

Some of the shells depicted on the facade of the Temple of Quetzalcoatl at Teotihuacan can be identified, according to the author, as the West Indian Chank, a shell closely related to the

"Sacred Chank" of India. This ceremonial use of the same kind of shell in the two areas may be significant.

V-074B

AUTHOR: Vollgraff-Roes, Anne
DATE: 1953
TITLE: The Lion with Body Markings in Oriental Art
IN: Journal of Near Eastern Studies 12:40-49

A corrective to what she says is great over-simplification in Kantor's treatment of the rosette or whorl on the shoulder of the lion [K-007]. Emphasizes the spread of the feature into Asia via Achaemenid art influence. Her Fig. 15 (page 49) shows a wooden lion from a modern piece of Japanese furniture with the rosette on the shoulder [and which overall is rather like the Palenque example; see J-129].

V-075

AUTHOR: Von Der Porten, Edward P.
DATE: 1984
TITLE: The Drake Puzzle Solved
IN: Pacific Discovery 37 (July-September): 22-26

Methodology. After a hundred years of speculation, uncertainty, and false artifact leads, at last meticulous analysis of porcelain sherds from Drake's Bay, California (and from a nearby Miwok Indian site), conclusively demonstrates that Drake's ship landed in 1579 right where most scholars had supposed in the absence of the decisive archaeological material.

[A letter in the following issue, page 3, from Robert H. Power, challenges Von Der Porten's conclusion. While the technological analysis reported indeed demonstrates that the sherds in question came from China, they tell us nothing definite about whether they arrived in Drake's ship or another. Power holds for San Francisco Bay as the Drake site. The dispute speaks to the indeterminacy of much archaeological research concerning specific historical events.]

V-076

AUTHOR: Von Hagen, Victor W.
DATE: 1944
TITLE: The Aztec and Maya Papermakers
IMPRINT: J. J. Augustin: New York

Assumes no Old World influence. [Contrast T-106.]

V-078

AUTHOR: Von Hagen, Victor W.
DATE: 1958
TITLE: The Aztec: Man and Tribe
IMPRINT: New American Library: New York

See S-358.

V-079

AUTHOR: Von Hagen, Victor W.
DATE: 1965
TITLE: The Desert Kingdoms of Peru
IMPRINT: New York Graphic Society: Greenwich, Connecticut

Page 56, Plates 35, 36: Shows a ventilator or architectural wind scoop on Mochica ceramic house models [a feature of Near Eastern architecture].

Pages 140ff.: A long discussion of balsa rafts and Topa Inca Yupanqui's expedition into the ocean concludes that he could only have gone north and explains at length why Heyerdahl is wrong about voyages to the Galapagos.

V-080

AUTHOR: Voss, J. C.
DATE: 1903
TITLE: The Voyage of the Indian War Canoe "Tilikum" across the Pacific from Canada to Australia

IMPRINT: Printed at the Caxton Office: Invercargill, New Zealand [Reprinted as *The Venturesome Voyages of Captain Voss* (DeGraff, New York, 1955)]

Transoceanic voyages in a Northwest Coast Indian craft.

V-081

AUTHOR: Vreeland, James M., Jr.
DATE: 1980
TITLE: Anthropological and Historical Perspectives
IN: Mummies of Peru, by James M. Vreeland, Jr., and Aidan Cockburn, chapter 9 in Mummies, Disease, and Ancient Cultures, edited by Aidan Cockburn and Eve Cockburn (Cambridge University Press: Cambridge), 135-157

Page 141ff.: Cloth shrouds or ponchos cover mummies dating to the Middle Horizon and Inca Period (page 153). [The poncho has been cited as a transpacific parallel, but for Peru it has also been claimed as a post-Conquest innovation.]

W-001

AUTHOR: Waal Malefijt, Annemarie de
DATE: 1974
TITLE: Images of Man: A History of Anthropological Thought
IMPRINT: Knopf: New York

Pages 160-180: Chapter on "diffusion and migration" offers only greatly simplified ideas about Smith, Perry, Graebner, etc.

W-001B

AUTHOR: Wächtel, N.
DATE: 1971
TITLE: La visión des vaincus [Vision of the Vanquished]
IMPRINT: Gallimard: Paris

Includes traditions of a white god bringing civilization to South America.

W-002

AUTHOR: Waddell, Lawrence A.
DATE: 1929
TITLE: The Makers of Civilization in Race and History
IMPRINT: Luzac: London

Sumer was the focus of all Asiatic civilization and its influence reached America.

W-003

AUTHORS: Wagner, Emile R., and Duncan L. Wagner
DATE: 1934a
TITLE: La civilización Chaco-Santiagueña [The Chaco-Santiagueña Civilization]
IN: Proceedings of the 25th International Congress of Americanists (La Plata, 1932), 2:221-225

A summary of finds resulting from 30 years of study of this Argentine area, which contains thousands of mounds. Claims that links to the most ancient civilizations of both hemispheres are visible here.

W-004

AUTHORS: Wagner, Emile R., and Duncan L. Wagner
DATE: 1934b
TITLE: La civilización Chaco-Santiagueña y sus correlaciones con las del Viejo y Nuevo Mundo [The Chaco-Santiagueña Civilization and Its Correlations with Those of the Old and New Worlds]
IMPRINT: Compañia impresora argentina: Buenos Aires

They claim analogies between their sites in Argentina and materials from Troy published by

Schliemann. They posit existence of an empire of the llanos before that of the highlands (i.e., Tiahuanaco) and of human-bird-reptilian divinity which was known throughout America and in Greece, Etruria, and Troy. [See W-005.]

W-004B

AUTHORS: Wagner, Emile R., and Duncan L. Wagner
DATE: 1940
TITLE: Los aborígenes de Santiago del Estero
[The Natives of Santiago del Estero]
IN: Relaciones de la Sociedad Argentina de antropología 2:79-115 (Buenos Aires)

See W-004 and W-005.

W-005

AUTHORS: Wagner, Emile R., and Olimpia L. Righetti
DATE: 1946
TITLE: Arqueología comparada: resumen de prehistoria; una divinidad primordial y universal
[Comparative Archaeology: A Resumé of Prehistory; A Primordial and Universal Divinity]
IMPRINT: n.p.: Buenos Aires

The civilization they found was at as high a level as any in the New World. It all began on a continent in the Pacific now submerged, from which settlers pushed by submergence reached Asia and spread civilization throughout Eurasia and Africa. A branch returned via Bering Strait to America. The key to identifying these strands is their deity of generation (fecundity). They establish commonality thus in the iconography of Egypt, Assyria, Akkad, and the Mayas, and of course Santiago del Estero. For example, on page 41 they illustrate metal figurines from Tihuanacu and from their area in Argentina which are said to have all the attributes of Egyptian Isis.

W-005B

AUTHOR: Wagner, Henry R.
DATE: 1937
TITLE: The Cartography of the Northwest Coast of America to the Year 1800, vol. 2
IMPRINT: University of California Press: Berkeley

Page 455: Obsolete Place Names. Fou-Sang. Identified as being in America by de Guignes about 1750, then Buache adopted the idea in a 1753 book. [K-026C notes the name on maps of the Northwest coast in the next 20 years, probably echoing de Guignes.]

W-006

AUTHOR: Wahlgren, Erik
DATE: 1952
TITLE: The Runes of Kensington
IN: Studies in Honor of Albert Morey Sturtevant (University of Kansas Press: Lawrence), 57-70

A refutation of H-027.

W-007

AUTHOR: Wahlgren, Erik
DATE: 1958
TITLE: The Kensington Stone: A Mystery Solved
IMPRINT: University of Wisconsin Press: Madison

Rejects claims that the stone was Norse made. He says his historical detective work has demonstrated that the stone was carved in the 1890s by an uneducated but intelligent Minnesotan, Olof Ohman, as a hoax. He describes the circumstances among the Norwegian American minority in America which supposedly called forth and welcomed this hoax and its aftermath.

W-010B

AUTHOR: Wahlgren, Erik
DATE: 1982
TITLE: American Runes: From Kensington to Spirit Pond
IN: Journal of English and Germanic Philology 81:157-185

See W-010C.

W-010C

AUTHOR: Wahlgren, Erik
DATE: 1986
TITLE: The Vikings in America
IMPRINT: Thames and Hudson: London

In a comprehensive treatment, he discounts all evidence for Norse involvement with the Kensington Stone, Newport Tower, the Vinland Map, and Spirit Pond and all resulting intimations that the Norse penetrated deeply into North America. L'Anse aux Meadows plus his interpretation of archaeology to date and the land forms indicated in the sagas leads him to consider Vinland to have consisted of only parts of Newfoundland and Nova Scotia.

W-011B

AUTHOR: Waisbard, Simone
DATE: 1980
TITLE: L'origine de Naymlap, roi de Lambayeque [The Origin of Naymlap, King of Lambayeque]
IN: Kadath: Chroniques des civilisations disparues, no. 39:7-13 (Brussels)

This culture hero was reported to have arrived with a fleet of rafts and to bear Tiahuanaco culture. Quotes Jorge E. Adoum, National Director of Culture in Ecuador, in UNESCO Courier, April 1974, as accepting connection of balsas of fifth century B.C. China with those of Vietnam and South America.

W-011C

AUTHOR: Waisbard, Simone
DATE: 1981
TITLE: Les écritures "perdues" de l'ancien Pérou (1ere partie) [The "Lost" Writing Systems of Ancient Peru (first and second parts)]
IN: Kadath: Chroniques des civilisations disparues, no. 43:37-49; no. 44:37-47 (Brussels)

A resumé of the question of whether there was "writing." With some illustrations, treats various petroglyphs (including the "letters" of Sahuaracu and an "inscription" on an adobe wall at Huaycan), painted stones, bean writing, the quipu, textile designs and colors with possible ideographic significance. Inca libation vases (keros) are interpreted by de la Jara as showing a sort of cartouche. [See J-030B.]

W-012

AUTHOR: Waisberg, Leo
DATE: 1976
TITLE: Lost Sherds and Sunken Ships: Paradigm in the Jomon-Valdivia Case
IN: Journal of Anthropology at McMaster 2/1:43-59 (Hamilton, Ontario)

This is an alarmed response to the apparent flourishing of diffusionism as shown at the Santa Fe meetings of the Society for American Archaeology, 1969. Typological comparison, the most common and widely accepted tool of North American archaeologists, has been pushed past its logical limit by the diffusionists in their acceptance of a Jomon-Valdivia pottery connection. Diffusionist theories are essentially a product of the confusion between the presence of certain motifs and the totality of style (specifically following M-458). Grants and recounts six distinct strengths of the Jomon-Valdivia connection at the trait level. "The ingenuity of this argument rests on the difficulty of contradicting statements concerning cultural processes." Archaeological knowledge and technique continue to change, and should in this case. Paradoxically concludes "diffusionists, who have so boggled matters, can be thrust aside in favour of more contemporary exponents of quite new fallacies."

W-013

AUTHOR: Wake, C. Staniland
DATE: 1873
TITLE: Origin of Serpent Worship
IN: Journal of the Anthropological Institute 2:373-390

Compares the Egyptian uraeus symbol with the plumed serpent of the Aztecs.

W-014

AUTHOR: Wake, C. Staniland
DATE: 1904a
TITLE: American Origins
IN: American Antiquarian and Oriental Journal 26:105-115

Connections across the ocean to America from Asia and via the Phoenicians across the Atlantic.

W-015

AUTHOR: Wake, C. Staniland
DATE: 1904b
TITLE: Traits of an Ancient Egyptian Folk-Tale Compared with Those of Aboriginal American Tales
IN: Journal of American Folk-lore 17:255-264

The Two Brothers tale in ancient Egypt has notable parallels in America, however direct communication is not necessary to explain this, although doubtless there was indirect contact via the Phoenicians. The tale probably spread from a Central Asian source to both America and Egypt. A few other parallels to the Old World are briefly noted.

W-016

AUTHOR: Wake, C. Staniland
DATE: 1907a
TITLE: A Widespread Boy-Hero Story
IN: Journal of American Folk-Lore 20:216-219

Gives Norwegian and Skidi Pawnee versions of a story in which an orphan boy performs great deeds and becomes a chief. "It can hardly be doubted that either one of the peoples referred to has derived it from the other, directly or indirectly, or both stories have been derived from a common source."

W-017

AUTHOR: Wake, C. Staniland
DATE: 1907b
TITLE: Cambodia and Yucatan
IN: American Antiquarian and Oriental Journal 29:244-248

Assumes a connection with but little critically-considered evidence.

W-019

AUTHOR: Wales, H. G. Quaritch
DATE: 1953
TITLE: The Mountain of God
IMPRINT: Bernard Quaritch: London

Pages 8-16: A model of the universe was represented in the ziggurat: underworld, heavens, earth and water, the bond between heaven and earth. The cosmic axis was tied to the zenith at the point of divine communication, the sanctum on the ziggurat's summit. The most important associated divinity was lord of the earth (Enlil) with Tammuz, represented by a serpent, as the fertility aspect of the god. The sacred cedar, tree of the mountains, was also symbolic of the cosmic axis. The Egyptian pyramids shared a mixture of key ideas with the ziggurat despite their differences. [A number of these features also characterize Mesoamerican temple-pyramids. Compare W-139, W-140.]

W-020

AUTHOR: Walk, L.
DATE: 1933
TITLE: Die Verbreitung der Tauchmotivs in den Urmeerschöpfungs (und Sintflut-) Sagen
[The Diffusion of the Diving-God Motif in the Ocean Creation (and Flood) Myths]
IN: Mitteilungen der Anthropologischen Gesellschaft in Wien 63:60-76

Earth Diver myth distribution in both hemispheres.

W-022

AUTHORS: Wallace, Ben J., and William M. Hurley
DATE: 1968
TITLE: Transpacific Contacts: A Selected Annotated Bibliography
IN: Asian Perspectives 11:157-175

A short list now superseded.

W-023

AUTHOR: Wallace, Birgitta Linderoth
DATE: 1971
TITLE: Some Points of Controversy
IN: The Quest for America, edited by Geoffrey Ashe (Praeger: New York; and Pall Mall: London), 155-174

Reviews the Kensington Stone, "mooring holes," "Norse weapons," and the Newport Tower and tells why they should not be accepted as proponents of Norse visits claim.

W-024

AUTHOR: Wallace, Birgitta L.
DATE: 1982
TITLE: Viking Hoaxes
IN: Vikings in the West, edited by E. Guralnick (Archaeological Institute of America: Chicago), 53-76

A systematic survey of purported Norse finds (halberds, mooring holes, runic stones, etc.). Each is weighed and all the prominent ones are rejected as without sufficient foundation if not frauds or errors.

W-024B

AUTHOR: Wallace, Birgitta Linderoth
DATE: 1991
TITLE: The Vikings in North America: Myth and Reality
IN: Social Approaches to Viking Studies, edited by Ross Samson (Cruithne Press: Glasgow), 207-220

For Carnegie Museum the author investigated first hand 52 sites, 73 artifacts and over 100 inscriptions alleged to be Norse. Concludes that most of the reputed evidence is based on wishful thinking, not rational research—an example of "cult archaeology." A page on Newport Tower, one on the Kensington Stone, and half a page on halberds indicates the scope of the report. Much more space goes to L'Anse aux Meadows, which of course is considered solid evidence, and some discussion also is devoted to certain apparent real finds in native sites on the Arctic islands.

W-025

AUTHOR: Wallace, Howard
DATE: 1961
TITLE: Leviathan and the Beast in Revelation
IN: Biblical Archaeologist Reader, edited by G. Ernest Wright and David Noel Freedman (Quadrangle: Chicago), 290-298

The primordial sea beneath the earth and its reptilian inhabitants. [Compare Mesoamerica.]

W-026

AUTHOR: Wallace, W. S.
DATE: 1939
TITLE: The Literature Relating to Norse Voyages to America

IN: Canadian Historical Review 20:8-16

A survey of writings on the subject with some comments on the Kensington Stone and the Beardmore relics. He does not enter into the question of authenticity of the latter but as to the former, he "finds it easier to believe that the Kensington rune-stone is genuine than that it is a modern forgery."

W-027

AUTHOR: Wallis, Helen

DATE: 1967

TITLE: Review of *Maps of the Ancient Sea Kings*, by Charles H. Hapgood

IN: Geographical Journal 133:394-395

Gently skeptical of Hapgood's interpretations, which she considers nautically naive.

W-028

AUTHORS: Wallis, Helen, F. R. Maddison, G. D. Painter, D. B. Quinn, R. M. Perkins, G. R. Crone, A. D. Baynes-Cope, Walter C. McCrone, and Lucy B. McCrone

DATE: 1974

TITLE: The Strange Case of the Vinland Map: A Symposium

IN: Geographical Journal 140:183-214

An introduction and seven papers consider the map's discovery, evaluate the "Tartar Relation" that accompanied it, and judge its authenticity based on cartography and ink analysis ("grave doubts" that it is ancient). A bibliography of discussions of the map since 1966 is given.

[An Associated Press article in *The (Salt Lake City) Deseret News,* Feb. 14, 1996, reports that Yale University Press has just published a new edition of *The Vinland Map and Tartar Relation* (see S-273 and W-047) "which explains how historians and scientists analyzed the map to re-establish its authenticity," according to W. E. Washburn of the Smithsonian. McCrone's counter opinion is noted. But "in 1985, physicists at the University of California at Davis performed particle-induced X-ray emission tests on the ink and paper to identify the elements they contained." They concluded that the earlier test results, relied upon by McCrone and such critics, were erroneous, because the new tests found traces of titanium, supposed by the critics to be an ingredient of only modern ink, also present on many other medieval documents.]

W-029

AUTHOR: Wallis, Wilson D.

DATE: 1912

TITLE: Review of *Where Animals Talk*, by Robert H. Nassau

IN: Current Anthropological Literature 1:207-208

Cautions against inferring culture contact from correspondences in folktales, giving the example of a surely independent, convergent, detailed pairing: Hopi tales of Coyote compared with Mpongwe (Africa) stories of Leopard.

W-030

AUTHOR: Wallis, Wilson D.

DATE: 1917

TITLE: Similarities in Culture

IN: American Anthropologist 19:41-54

A general treatment of the process of convergence. "Myth-making is so universal that if the similarity in two myths of widely separated tribes is such as to imply borrowing, it is because of the number of similar accidental traits." He has difficulty thus explaining "puzzling parallels" between the Hopi (and Sioux) and the African Thonga; not only are many incidents held in common but beliefs regarding the moon and morning star also are.

Sewed, pitched bark canoes are found in northern Australia and Algonkian territory, but they could not be connected. So too with the almost simultaneous arising of messianic movements, the Ghost Dance of North America, and Mahdiism of Sudan.

W-031

AUTHOR: Wallis, Wilson D.
DATE: 1925
TITLE: Diffusion as a Criterion of Age
IN: American Anthropologist 27:91-99

A theory of evolution changes when it must face the possibilities of diffusion. Distribution cannot be read as diffusion, which must be checked with historical documentation if we are to know what the distribution means.

W-032

AUTHOR: Wallis, Wilson D.
DATE: 1928
TITLE: Probability and the Diffusion of Culture Traits
IN: American Anthropologist 30:94-106

A critique of C-266, which demonstrated a statistical method for determining "special cultural relationships" between peoples, by which diffusion is implied. Wallis points out flaws in the analysis by using the same sample of data as C-266 (on Polynesia) but handling it according to different presuppositions and reaching different results. A useful cautionary contribution to method in studying diffusion.

W-033

AUTHOR: Wallis, Wilson D.
DATE: 1929
TITLE: Magnitude of Distribution, Centrifugal Spread, and Centripetal Elaboration of Culture Traits
IN: American Anthropologist 31:755-771

On the inapplicability almost everywhere of Wissler's principle of centrifugal diffusion based on Old World cases.

W-034

AUTHOR: Wallis, Wilson D.
DATE: 1945
TITLE: Inferences of Relative Age of Culture Traits from Magnitude of Distribution
IN: Southwestern Journal of Anthropology 1:142-159

An acerbic critique of a commonly assumed "principle" in ethnological and archaeological reconstruction. The idea is untestable. "If it has been established that in . . . 98% of the cases distribution is an index of age, the . . . vital thing is . . . to know that the case we are pondering is in the group of 98% rather than in the group of 2%," but we cannot learn this from geography.

W-037

AUTHOR: Walters, M. I.
DATE: 1956
TITLE: New and Old Discoveries in America
IMPRINT: Georgetown University Forum: Washington, D. C.

See M-060.

W-039

AUTHOR: Ward, John A.
DATE: 1984
TITLE: Ancient Archives among the Cornstalks
IMPRINT: Privately printed: [Vincennes, Indiana (?)]

A layman discusses his discovery that stones bearing "strange markings" that had been considered plow marks actually are inscriptions. Written in "ancient Lybian" and said to date to "c. 726 B.C.," they tell of voyagers from Africa who came to conduct commerce with "Nubians" in what is now Indiana.

W-040

AUTHORS: Warren, Bruce W., and Thomas Stuart Ferguson
DATE: 1987
TITLE: The Messiah in Ancient America

IMPRINT: Book of Mormon Research Foundation: Provo, Utah

Warren, a Mesoamerican archaeologist, extensively revises and updates Ferguson's F-062. Included are discussions of the early culture hero Quetzalcoatl as Jesus Christ, Izapa Stela 5 parallels to the Near East, and pages 201-230 which list 184 "religious and cultural parallels" between Mesoamerica and the Old World (a revision and expansion of Ferguson's 1958 list), with nods to Carter, Jett, Doran, Kelley, Shao, etc.

Pages 86-94: Combines Hamlet's Mill with elements from Mesoamerican codices to demonstrate a "model of the universe" involving sun, moon, and five visible planets plus two eclipse signs (forming an Ennead). A table on pages 90-92 compares details of these elements for Greece, Egypt, Syria, Mesopotamia, India, and Mesoamerica.

Pages 132-133: Another table compares aspects of the Maya baptismal rite as reported by Landa with Israelite purification rituals (including the scapegoat) from the book of Leviticus.

W-041

AUTHOR: Warren, Lyman O.
DATE: 1972
TITLE: Treponematosis
IN: Florida Anthropologist 25/4:175-188

A concise, well-informed summary ending in a hypothesis accommodating both worldwide occurrence of the disease before Columbus and the serious consequences for Europeans after Columbian sailors carried back a particularly debilitating local venereal variety from the Caribbean.

W-042

AUTHOR: Warren, William F.
DATE: 1898
TITLE: Paradise Found: The Cradle of the Human Race at the North Pole
IMPRINT: Houghton Mifflin: Boston

There was a common source for the pyramids in Mesopotamia, Egypt, and America.

W-043

AUTHOR: Warren, William W.
DATE: 1898
TITLE: Traditions of Descent
IN: DeLestry's Western Magazine 3/12:40-47

Attempts to prove that North American Indians are the lost tribes of Israel by citing an Ojibwa tribal origin myth and religious practices.

W-044

AUTHOR: Washburn, Mabel Thatcher Rosemary
DATE: 1932
TITLE: Were There Fourteenth Century Christian Europeans in the Land That Became the United States?
IN: Journal of American History 26:121-145

A reasonable summary of the Norse Vinland episode and of the Kensington Stone controversy. She concludes that Holand had mainly turned aside his critics. A fairly continuous interest in the American continent existed in Viking Europe from the end of the 10th century to the second half of the 14th. She argues from the documents that there was an expedition led by Paul Knutson that reached the American mainland in the mid-14th century. Illustrates various "battle axes" found in Minnesota.

W-045

AUTHOR: Washburn, Richard Kirk
DATE: 1987
TITLE: Another Reading of the Anubis Panel
IN: NEARA [New England Antiquities Research Association] Journal 21/4

Critiques Fell's translation of the Oklahoma inscription [F-055] and offers an alternative.

W-047

AUTHOR: Washburn, Wilcomb E., editor
DATE: 1971
TITLE: Proceedings of the Vinland Map Conference, Smithsonian Institution, 1966
IMPRINT: University of Chicago Press: Chicago

Compare S-273. Scholars studied the authenticity of the Vinland Map and Tartar Relation without reaching a clear conclusion, although there is considerable skepticism about their authenticity. [Now see W-028 about a 1996 reaffirmation of authenticity.]

W-048

AUTHOR: Wassén, S. Henry
DATE: 1931
TITLE: The Ancient Peruvian Abacus
IN: Origin of the Indian Civilizations in South America, vol. 9 of Comparative Ethnographical Studies, by Erland Nordenskiöld (Pehrssons: Göteborg), 189-205
[Reprinted AMS Press: New York, 1979]

Huaman Poma told of a device here described functionally and compared in general terms with East Asian "computing tablets," but without intimation of historical connection.

W-049

AUTHOR: Wassén, S. Henry
DATE: 1940
TITLE: An Analogy between a South American and Oceanic Myth Motif and Negro Influence in Darien
IN: Etnologiska Studier 10:69-79 (Göteborg)

Cites his previous publications on the world- or life-tree motif (when chopped down this tree yields from its top water, fish, and all kinds of fruit). In one he drew a parallel between this motif from Palau in Micronesia and the Kuna (Cuna) and Chocó of Panama and Colombia respectively. He sees "a direct parallel." Here he notes "another special analogy," from the Chocó and from Palau: a man visits the underworld where he casts fruit into the water to attract fish so that the water will be cleared of them and the sun can go down in it. Also, the sun's hut is plentifully equipped with food. Associated with the tale is the mythical birth of twins out of a woman's knee (for which there are African parallels). The parallels raise the possibility of a direct communication in pre-Columbian times, but he has insufficient information to test that point.

In a footnote, he says that Krämer, the source of the Palau material, has written to him that he has not heard of this fish-clearing motif anywhere else and finds the Chocó case very interesting since "other Palau traditions are found farther east in Oceania." Wassén also relates a Chocó "myth theme" of a person being swallowed by a sea monster which is destroyed by fire after its mouth is propped open with a pole. Ehrenreich [E-029, page 96] had mentioned this as a special analogy between Polynesia and South America. Notices Nordenskiöld's long list of "Oceanian culture elements" found in Colombia and Panama [N-103].

W-050

AUTHOR: Wassén, S. Henry
DATE: 1949
TITLE: Contributions to Cuna Ethnography
IN: Etnologiska Studier 16:3-139 (Göteborg)

He includes a generally non-interpretive discussion of striking parallels between South American and circumpolar culture traits. [See W-051.]

W-051

AUTHOR: Wassén, S. Henry
DATE: 1954
TITLE: Viss Parallellism Mellan Lapska och Indianska Födelse-föreställningar [Parallels between Lapps and American Indians]
IMPRINT: Västerbotten (Sweden?)

Parallels between Lapps and Cuna and other Indians.

W-053

AUTHOR: Wasson, Robert Gordon
DATE: 1968
TITLE: Soma: Divine Mushroom of Immortality
IMPRINT: Ethnomycological Studies No. 1 (Mouton: The Hague)

Page 163: After briefly noting general similarities between northern Eurasian and Middle American mushroom usages and beliefs, he comments that to harbor a thought of genetic (historical) relation between Mesoamerican mushroom practices and the Old World would be hazardous. Both patterns are autonomous and both are very old.

W-054

AUTHOR: Wasson, Robert Gordon
DATE: 1980
TITLE: The Wondrous Mushroom: Mycolatry in Mesoamerica
IMPRINT: McGraw-Hill: New York

He overstated the autonomy of the bodies of knowledge and practice in the Old and New Worlds in his 1968 book [W-053]. Subsequently he has allowed himself to be guided and stimulated by Levi-Strauss [L-186] who supposed a connection likely. Now he believes and has evidence that for centuries, perhaps millennia, Ojibway and other Algonkian Indians had known and used the fly agaric "in full panoply," as in Siberia. Whether this diffused to them, or they themselves came, via northeastern Asia or northwestern Europe matters not, for he has shown that the pattern was virtually circumpolar, "wherever the birch or appropriate conifers thrived" on which the hallucinogenic organism grew.

The Quiché of Guatemala equate Amanita muscaria with the thunderbolt ("mushroom of the lightning-bolt," although they do not eat it, instead consuming Psylocybe species), as in Eurasia and as do the Ojibway.

W-055

AUTHORS: Wasson, Valentina Pavlovna, and Robert Gordon Wasson
DATE: 1957
TITLE: Mushrooms, Russia, and History, vol. 2
IMPRINT: Pantheon: New York

Pages 215-329: Nahua mushroom use.

Page 418: An index of relevant terms in eight Mesoamerican languages.

Pages 215-216: Mushrooms are also consumed for psychic effects in New Guinea, though very little is known of this.

Pages 274ff.: Discussion and illustration of archaeological "mushroom stones" which they consider evidence of the presence of a mushroom belief system going way back [B.C. times] in southern Mesoamerica.

Pages 316ff.: Distant parallels in mythology involving mushrooms.

Page 317: "Independent genesis" of the link between lightning and fungal procreation is highly improbable. Did the idea diffuse (implies within recent centuries) over the vast distance involved? But where and when?

The possibility that attracts him is that this belief is a "surviving trace of an early cosmology elaborated when the ancestors of the Zapotecs and Greeks and Semites and Polynesians and

Chinese [all of whom have a similar notion] were all neighbors" in the Eurasian homeland.

Page 318: There are "startling parallels" between the use of fly amanita in Siberia and the divine mushrooms of Middle America (e.g., the substance is said to "speak" to the eater).

W-056

AUTHOR: Watanabe, Hitoshi
DATE: 1989
TITLE: The Northern Pacific Maritime Culture Zone: A Viewpoint on Hunter-Gatherer Mobility and Sedentism
IN: Reprint Proceedings, Circum-Pacific Prehistory Conference, Seattle, August 1-6, 1989, part III: Development of Hunting-Fishing-Gathering Maritime Societies on the Pacific, Part One, section B: Development of Hunting-Fishing-Gathering Maritime Societies in Northeast Asia (Washington State University Press: Pullman), articles separately paginated

This zone, extending from Japan to the Northwest Coast, is divided into four zones displaying local features while sharing many common elements. "The main purpose of this paper is to suggest the importance of interconnections or contacts between northern Pacific maritime cultures and of the northern Pacific maritime route of culture diffusion." [Little relevant detail is given, however.]

W-057

AUTHOR: Waterman, T. T.
DATE: 1927
TITLE: The Architecture of the American Indians
IN: American Anthropologist 29:210-230

A slapdash survey, with minimal documentation, of structure types hemisphere-wide.

Pages 228-230: He has read Vining on Fu-sang and it cannot refer to Mexico. In any case a single person, or ship, could not have noticeable influence on a culture. Only "trade and business relations" would be noticeable. If any Asiatic people had been here seriously, they would have brought rice, tea, and porcelain and would have taken back maize, potatoes, and tobacco.

W-058

AUTHOR: Waterman, T. T.
DATE: 1931
TITLE: The Architecture of the American Indians
IN: Source Book in Anthropology, Revised edition, edited by A. L. Kroeber and T. T. Waterman (Harcourt, Brace: New York), 512-524
[Originally in *American Anthropologist* 29 (1927): 210-230, here slightly revised]

Pages 523-524: "Certain authorities" profess Old World inspiration for American Indian buildings. "The one architecture in all the world which to me looks like that of Middle America is not the Chinese anyway, nor yet the Egyptian, but the architecture of extreme southeastern Asia." While he would like to discuss the point, here he only cautions that a few voyagers landing could not have had significant effect. The Norse had no effect on the Indians. Only "business relations" could have transmitted cultural features of moment, in either direction, but there is no evidence for that.

W-059

AUTHOR: Waters, Frank
DATE: 1971
TITLE: The Book of the Hopi
IMPRINT: Ballantine Books: New York

Page 31: "The Hopis came to America from the west, crossing the sea on boats or rafts from one 'stepping stone' or island to the next." A similar interpretation can apply to the Quiché Maya origin myth where the tribes are said to have crossed where the waters parted, stepping on stones in a row. [Wuthenau: Further, their migration myth gives a detailed description of the hollow papyrus used to make their rafts.]

W-059B

AUTHOR: Waters, Frank
DATE: 1975
TITLE: Mexico Mystique. The Coming Sixth World of Consciousness
IMPRINT: Swallow Press: Chicago

Pages 73-78: In a New Age-toned book, the author refers to "in-flowing streams" of cultural influence on Mexico. Acknowledges Mertz, Gordon (Paraiba), Covarrubias, Heine-Geldern, and a few others. Sees himself in a position between isolationists and extreme diffusionists.

W-060

AUTHOR: Watson, Douglas S.
DATE: 1935
TITLE: Did the Chinese Discover America? A Critical Examination of the Buddhist Priest Hui Shên's Account of Fu Sang, and the Apocryphal Voyage of the Chinese Navigator Hui-Li
IN: California Historical Society Quarterly 14:47-58

Summarizes the older, fundamental literature in English, and presents a one-page translation of a descriptive document on Fu Sang from the Great Chinese Encyclopedia. Adds, and plumps for, data on one Hee-Li, 217 B.C., who traveled to and from Fu Sang, according to an otherwise unknown document cited by a Christian missionary who claimed to have found and copied it in an interior town's archive in the 19th century.

W-061

AUTHOR: Wauchope, Robert
DATE: 1962
TITLE: Lost Tribes and Sunken Continents
IMPRINT: University of Chicago Press: Chicago

The author's statement that he presents his material on unorthodox theories of the origin of American Indians and cultures with "deliberately unemotional restraint" is belied by his tone, and the juxtapositioning of topics in his presentation. Heine-Geldern, Ekholm, and Meggers are indiscriminantly mixed in with Le Plongeon, Churchward, Lord Kingsborough, Wiener, the Verrills, Gladwin, Heyerdahl, and Elliot Smith. Wauchope makes it clear that to him and other serious scholars none of these materials deserves serious consideration, only amusement.

[C. E. Joel provides a lengthy, trenchant critique of Wauchope's handling of diffusionism in a review article "Lost Sages and Their Sunken Oracles," *The New Diffusionist* 2/9:165-177.]

W-062

AUTHOR: Wauchope, Robert
DATE: 1970
TITLE: Introduction
IN: The Indian Background of Latin American History; the Maya, Aztec, Inca, and Their Predecessors, edited by Robert Wauchope (Knopf: New York), 13

Native identification of Quetzalcoatl with Venus strengthened early Spaniards' belief that the Mexican Morning Star ceremony, in which a sacrificial victim was spread-eagled on an X-shaped scaffold and shot in the side with an arrow, was actually a New World version of Jesus' crucifixion. ("Jesus had said, 'I am . . . the bright and morning star.' ")

W-064

AUTHOR: Weatherwax, Paul
DATE: 1954
TITLE: Indian Corn in Old America
IMPRINT: Macmillan: New York

Chapter 12 ("Corn from Asia?" pages 132-138): Bonafous (1836) proposed a pre-Columbian presence of maize in Asia, whence it came to Europe, but "his evidences . . . have been so completely discredited and are now so seldom encountered that there is no need to waste further time with them." He laments Stonor and Anderson's revival of the idea as irresponsible. Such indirect indications of its pre-Columbian presence in Asia are open to the uncertain evaluation of all circumstantial evidence. Despite "numerous tantalizing suggestions that the American continents had other visitors from the Old World, and occasional small groups might have crossed the Pacific, no plausible route or means has been suggested as to how maize could have crossed the ocean; the Pacific islands yield no evidence of maize agriculture, although the sweet potato evidently did make that crossing.

W-067

AUTHOR: Webber, Bert
DATE: 1984
TITLE: Wrecked Japanese Junks Adrift in the North Pacific Ocean
IMPRINT: Ye Galleon Press: Fairfield, Washington

Builds on Brooks' compilation and assesses his theory of an infusion of Japanese genes and culture among Northwest Coast Indians via wrecks.

W-068

AUTHOR: Weber, Gertrude
DATE: 1978
TITLE: Das Thema von Leben und Tod in Bezug auf die Petroglyphen von Las Palmas/Chiapas, Mexiko [The Theme of Life and Death in Relation to the Petroglyphs of Las Palmas/Chiapas, Mexico]
IN: Tribus 27:143-157

Cross-cultural comparison of skeletal imagery in rock art from Chiapas with that in other parts of the world. Emphasis on duality of life and death rather than diffusion.

W-070

AUTHOR: Weberbauer, A.
DATE: 1945
TITLE: El mundo vegetal de los Andes peruanos [The Vegetal World of the Peruvian Andes]
IMPRINT: Estación Experimental Agrícola de la Molina, Dirección de Agricultura, Ministerio de Agricultura: Lima [New edition, translation, revision, and amplification of *Die Pflanzenwelt der peruanischen Anden* (Wilhelm Engelmann: Leipzig, 1911)]

Page 619: Regarding Amaranthus caudatus, he notes that it is probably of American origin because of the many native names, but some botanists maintain that it was imported from Asia or Africa.

Page 620: Gives three local names for Ipomoea batatas: camote, cumara and apichu. [Compare, of course, Polynesian kumara, etc.]

W-071

AUTHOR: Weckler, Joe
DATE: 1939
TITLE: Review of *Excavations at Snaketown, Volume 2, Comparisons and Theories,* by Harold S. Gladwin
IN: American Antiquity 5/2:180-189

A paragon of reviews. Good-humored and courteous but also very well informed and incisive. Weckler picks apart much of Gladwin's early version of interhemispheric racial history, teaching lessons in data, method, and epistemology that HSG seems never to have learned.

W-074

AUTHORS: Wei-Chiao Huang, and Donald L. Cyr

DATE: 1989

TITLE: Feng Shui in Modern Taiwan

IN: Dragon Treasures, edited by Donald L. Cyr (Stonehenge Viewpoint: Santa Barbara, California), 77-87

Geomancy, only indirectly worth a look from a comparative New World point of view. [Compare C-059.]

W-075

AUTHOR: Wei Chu-Hsien

DATE: 1970-1971

TITLE: China and America: A Study of Ancient Communication between the Two Lands, vol. 1: The Discovery of Chinese Inscriptions in America; vol. 2: Chinese Decorative Motifs Found in America [in Chinese with English summaries]

IMPRINT: Privately printed: Hong Kong [The copy of this volume seen by Sorenson is owned by an Asian specialist at Brigham Young University. It has folded in a four-page statement in English by Wei with an attached Chinese circular; the English piece is headed, "Chinese Inscriptions Discovered in America—A Generalization," and contains minor additional information. Another copy, seen by Raish in another library, is dated March, 1982. It contains the (same?) four-page introduction, but no English summaries]

Vol. 1: "The Discovery of Chinese Inscriptions in America," by Wei Chu-hsien, pages 15-21. This is the author's brief introduction in English. The author began his career as an archaeologist in China. After encountering a challenging passage in the Chinese classics, he spent 10 years going through a thousand classical documents and compiled his findings in 81 essays. Fragments of his work have been published, notably a (proposed) table of contents plus summary plus an essay on tobacco, by Current Publications Co. of Hong Kong, 1969, under the title "The Chinese Discovered America!"

He now plans to publish his work in 12 volumes of which this is the first (double) volume. The others will be

(3) Chinese cultural relics in America;

(4) Customs common to the two lands;

(5-7) American animals, plants and minerals known to the Chinese;

(8) Pacific islands near America known to the Chinese;

(9) Geography of America according to the Chinese;

(10) Pre-Ch'in and Ch'in knowledge of America;

(11) Han, Wei and later knowledge;

(12) America already known to other peoples than the Chinese (Japan, Korea, India, Russia, Africa, Europe).

[There is no bibliographical indication that the last 10 of these reached print. The introduction to Raish's 1982 copy states that the author's plan was to divide the work into ten parts and to publish it in three volumes. The titles of the parts are not the same as those given above.]

Coming into contact in Hong Kong with Prof. Liu Tun-li, known in the U.S. as Dr. Dennis Lou [in the present bibliography see Lou Wing-Sou, Dennis (Liu Tun-Li), especially L-326 which is an introduction to Wei's volume 1], they found a community of interests in this topic. Here (pages 19-21) the author comments briefly on three photographs of pottery excavated in America on which Chinese script occurs, furnished him by Lou. One from Peru is a nude female, an Indian agricultural goddess seated on a tortoise with coiling snakes at her feet and corresponding to the Chinese deity called Chen-wu who presides over the North Quarter in Chinese cosmology [compare L-274]. In each hand the figure holds a metal plate inscribed with characters referring to a major temple in Hupei province; calligraphy is of the Wei dynasty, early 6th century A.D. He supposes that the Chinese deity reached China from the north via Bering Strait. One of the characters on the Peruvian piece stands for "corn." [Would it have done so prior to A.D. 1500?]

Pages 23-24: A summary in English entitled "Chinese Script Discovered in Mexico." So far 20 characters have been found in America. Although the native American script is of the same ideographic type as Chinese, it developed in different ways. The 20 characters identified in Mexico stand for, e.g.: bright door, rain, water, axe, moon, eye, fur, dance. He also has a chapter entitled "Chinese Script of the Eskimos." Illustrations in the Chinese portion compare Chinese and American motifs.

W-076

AUTHOR: Weilbauer, Eugen
DATE: 1979
TITLE: Kannte das alte Amerika das Rad? [Did Ancient America Have the Wheel?]
IN: Amerikanistische Studien: Festschrift für Hermann Trimborn anlasslich seines 75. Geburtstages / Estudios americanistas: Libro jubilar en homenaje a Hermann Trimborn con motivo de su septuagesimoquinto aniversario, edited by Roswith Hartmann and Udo Oberem (Haus Volker und Kulturen, Anthropos-Institut, St. Augustin, Austria), 2:278-288

Distinguishing "vertical wheel" from "horizontal wheel," he concentrates on the latter, discussing particularly the kabal and other versions of quasi-potters' wheels.

W-077

AUTHOR: Weitlaner, Robert J.
DATE: 1940
TITLE: Notes on Chinantec Ethnography
IN: El México antiguo 5/6:161-175

Pages 161-168: The Chinantec musical bow. Describes this instrument and provides a review of the literature on New World occurrences, many being plotted on a hemispheric map on page 165. A superior bibliography on the bow is given on pages 116-168. It "may well be an old culture element."

Pages 170-172, 174: Fish poisoning. Again he gives local Chinantec material, then summarizes the literature on distribution. Cites Beals in support of this practice being "part of a very old culture stratum in the Americas." Whereas it has usually been treated as South American, here he cites Mexican and Guatemalan data also.

W-078

AUTHOR: Weitzberg, Fritz
DATE: 1922
TITLE: Contribución a la historia del descubrimiento precolombiano de América [Contribution to the History of the Pre-Columbian Discovery of America]
IN: Memorias de la Sociedad Científica "Antonio Alzate" 40:97-107 (México)

On the basis of maps, he supposes there was 15th century knowledge of land to the west, although Brandan, the Zeno brothers, and other sources are only fantastic tales. Others came from the Pacific, as per Humboldt. A warlike black population was already reported to Columbus by people in Haiti on his second voyage as living to the south or southeast of the big island. P. Martir reported that among the Caribs were indications of a foreign, imported culture, namely, a piece of white marble and an individual who could read. Z-005 purports to tell us how to explain these facts—two fleets of hundreds of ships sent by Mohamed Gao from Guinea into the Atlantic. Some of those must have arrived in America.

W-079

AUTHOR: Welch, John W., editor
DATE: 1981
TITLE: Chiasmus in Antiquity: Structures, Analyses, Exegesis
IMPRINT: Gerstenberg: Hildesheim, West Germany

Articles by Welch, Smith, Radday, Watson, Porten, and Fraenkel demonstrate the use of the chiasmus stylistic form in Sumero-Akkadian, Ugaritic, Old Testament, Aramaic, Talmudic, New Testament, Greek, Latin, and Book of Mormon writings. [Compare C-234 for Mesoamerica.]

W-080B

AUTHOR: Wellmann, Klaus F.
DATE: 1978
TITLE: Über Felsbilder in Ecuador [On Rock Art in Ecuador]
IN: Almogaren 8:225-235

Sees evidence of a connection with European megaliths.

W-080C

AUTHOR: Wellmann, Klaus F.
DATE: 1981
TITLE: The Algonkin "Stemmed Form" and the Camunian "Paddle": A Cross-cultural Analysis of Similarities and Differences
IN: Tribus 30:231-239

Rock art motifs from Camonica Valley, Italy, and Peterborough, Ontario, are compared. Though morphologically similar he concludes that distinct iconographic connotations apply.

W-081

AUTHOR: Wells, Peter S.
DATE: 1989
TITLE: Cross-cultural Interaction and Change in Recent Old World Research
IN: American Antiquity 54:66-83

Page 66: Characterizes the studies of "epigraphy" in the New World in the manner of Fell as without value.

W-081B

AUTHORS: Welsch, Robert L., John Terrell, and John A. Nadolski
DATE: 1992
TITLE: Language and Culture on the North Coast of New Guinea
IN: American Anthropologist 94:568-600

Methodology. Statistical analysis of material culture assemblages obtained at villages on the north coast of New Guinea reveals similarities and differences most strongly associated with geographic propinquity, irrespective of linguistic affinities. Show that similarity in material culture can mask marked heterogeneity in language. Since language is frequently used to index peoples on the assumption that it is a useful key to their other characteristics, this analysis implies the need for reconsideration of how prehistoric cultural complexes in Melanesia [and presumably elsewhere] are defined and interpreted "ethnolinguistically." [Compare such persistent anomalies in the literature as "the Maya area" and "Melanesia."]

W-082

AUTHORS: Welsch, RobeWen Ch'ung-I
DATE: 1961
TITLE: Bird-ancestor Legends of Northeast Asia, Northwest America, and the Pacific

IN: Bulletin of the Institute of Ethnology, Academia Sinica 12:102-106 [Taipei]

From the English summary. Certain parallels are pointed out in legends concerning ancestors or totemism. An example is the belief shared by Hawaiians and Chinook Indians that mankind was formed from a bird's egg. But we have no way to determine the relations among the three areas based on these legends.

W-082B

AUTHORS: Wendel, Jonathan F., Andrew Schnabel, and Tosak Seelanan
DATE: 1995
TITLE: An Unusual Ribosomal DNA Sequence from Gossypium gossypioides Reveals Ancient, Cryptic, Intergenomic Introgression
IN: Molecular Phylogenetics and Evolution 4/3 (September): 298-313

The "African" clade or descent group of species of cotton is found in terms of genetic sequence markers, surprisingly, to include a single Mexican diploid, G. gossypioides, from the Isthmus of Tehuantepec (Oaxaca). The nature of the evidence for this link "reflects something important about the evolutionary history of the species." Their favored explanatory hypothesis for the relationships shown involves hybridization, that is introduction of "African" genetic characteristics on the scene in Mexico to join in the formation of G. gossypioides. This may have happened "as recently as during the last several thousand years, subsequent to the origin of domesticated G. hirsutum and its spread to Oaxaca." [An event speculatively relatable to movements from Africa to Oaxaca suggested by Foster and Jairazbhoy.]

Incidentally the genetic tree (page 306) shows Hawaiian cotton (G. tomentosum) to be derived from the same root as G. hirsutum of the New World tropics, and Galapagos cotton (G. davidsonii) to be even more recently linked with the cotton of Baja California. [Perhaps compare K-044, K-051C?]

W-083

AUTHOR: Wensinck, Arent Jan
DATE: 1916
TITLE: The Ideas of the Western Semites Concerning the Navel of the Earth
IMPRINT: Koninklijke Akademie van Wetenschappen, Verhandelingen 17/4 (J. Muller: Amsterdam)

[For potential comparison with navel of the earth beliefs in America, Asia, and Oceania.]

W-084

AUTHOR: Werner, R.
DATE: 1973
TITLE: Nose Flute Blowers of the Malayan Aborigines (Orang Asli)
IN: Anthropos 68:181-191

"There is . . . no historical unity or similarity in the development of the nose flute in different continents." The only areas where nose customs are preserved are among natives of Oceania, India, and the Americas. [On the distribution of these and of nose flutes, see W-223]. The biting or cutting off of the nose was punishment for adultery in North America, Samoa, and Micronesia and in tales in India in connection with jealousy. In New Guinea the coloring of the nose was done to show sadness after someone died, and the same significance held for a colored nose in the Americas. In New Guinea, blowing a flute was done to increase the fertility of fields, while "at rituals a nose flute was blown in India, Bali, Sulawesi, Tahiti and the Matto-Grosso."

W-085

AUTHOR: Werner, Sabine
DATE: 1982
TITLE: Zur frühen chinesischen Seefahrt [On Early Chinese Sea Travel]
IN: Zur geschichtlichen Bedeutung der frühen Seefahrt, edited by Hermann

Müller-Karpe, Kolloquien zur Allgemeinen und Vergleichenden Archäologie, Band 2 (C. H. Beck: München), 87-95

Specifically limited to the Ch'in Dynasty, a cogent review of the material.

W-086

AUTHOR: Wernhart, Karl R.
DATE: 1983
TITLE: L'école d'ethnologie de Vienne et la situation actuelle de l'ethnohistoire [The School of Ethnology of Vienna and the Current Status of Ethnohistory]
IN: L'Ethnographie 79/90-91:61-68

The Viennese School of Ethnology was long dominated by culture-historical theory initiated by Graebner and Ankermann and the concept of kulturkreis from Frobenius, but critical revision has taken place since 1931. Today the school's position opens itself toward other European and American tendencies, trying to integrate them in a new synthesis.

W-087

AUTHOR: Werth, E.
DATE: 1957
TITLE: Die erste Besiedlung Amerikas und die Herkunft der amerikanischen Urkulturen
[The Initial Settlement of America and the Origin of Ancestral American Cultures]
IN: Naturwissenschaftlicher Verein für Schwaben, Abhandlungen 12:5-21

Considers the Indians descended from Polynesians who traveled the equatorial counter current east to the Panama region. Polynesian-Amerindian parallels in artifacts support the thesis.

W-087B

AUTHOR: Wescott, Roger Williams
DATE: 1977
TITLE: Ancient Transatlantic Contacts? A Review of Fell, Van Sertima, and Von Wuthenau
IN: Kronos 3:84-89

Finds positive and negative things about each. Finally, "if Fell, Van Sertima, and Von Wuthenau are right and Old World mariners from the time of the Minoans to that of the Vikings did indeed visit America, a major question remains to be answered: Why is the record of their traffic not more abundant?" Furthermore, an ethical and social issue confronts us as much as do historical and scientific problems: "if diffusionist logic is followed consistently, it obliges [?] us to conclude that the American aborigines had not only urbanism but horticulture introduced to them by more sophisticated people from the Eastern Hemisphere and that, without such external stimulus, they would never [?] have developed a way of life more advanced than that of nomadic hunting and food-gathering." Are Indians now to be "intellectually denigrated" in the way in which sub-Saharan Blacks used to be?

W-087C

AUTHOR: Wescott, Roger Williams
DATE: 1995
TITLE: Early Eurasian Linguistic Links with North America
IN: NEARA [New England antiquities research Association] Journal 29/1-2:40-43

Contrasts two positions in historical linguistics, phyleticism and isolationism. The former holds that language groupings can usually be included in still large groups (phyla), on the model of biology. Isolationists are generally reluctant to construct interlanguage relationships. Uses sample materials from Callaghan [C-003], Sadovszky [S-008 to S-017], and Stubbs [S-502]. His conclusion is that "much of the early North American vocabulary is Eurasian in origin," but he cannot say how much of that was inherited and how much borrowed. Whatever the detailed stratigraphy of linguistic influences, "there is little likelihood . . . that North America ever experienced a prolonged period of complete linguistic isolation."

W-087D

AUTHOR: Wescott, Roger Williams
DATE: 1995
TITLE: Types of Cultural Diffusion
IN: NEARA [New England antiquities research Association] Journal 29/1-2:35-39

Examines the history of the concepts diffusionism and inventionism and related concepts, such as borrowing and imitation. One observation: "When diffused, each invention has to be, to some extent, re-invented in the minds of the receivers." Decries the dualistic thinking and terminology in Western thought which tends to put diffusion and invention at false odds instead of facilitating understanding of their connectedness.

W-087E

AUTHOR: West, Robert C.
DATE: 1950
TITLE: The Floating-Garden Agriculture of Kashmir and Mexico. A Case of Diffusion or Independent Invention? (Abstract only)
IN: Annals, Association of American Geographers 40/2:143-144

Use of mud-covered mats floating on water occurs only in Kashmir and the Valley of Mexico. They constitute "a remarkable example of parallelism," which at first glance suggests diffusion. Moreover, recent evidence that some cultivated plants were shared between Old and New Worlds "indicates the strong possibility of (either) chance or deliberate trans-Pacific voyages on which man may have transported not only plants but other culture traits." But distance, lack of intermediate examples, and "certain differences in techniques of garden construction and cultivation" point rather to independent invention since there is no historical evidence to indicate the technique was introduced to either place from anywhere else.

W-088

AUTHOR: West, Robert C.
DATE: 1961
TITLE: Aboriginal Sea Navigation between Middle and South America
IN: American Anthropologist 63:133-135

He quotes from a 1525 Spanish document from the west coast of Mexico (mouth of the Balsas River) which has the local Indians aware of people from the south arriving in large canoes who brought trade goods, staying for a number of months at times when the weather was not favorable for their return.

West suggests two candidate groups: Cueva Indians (Coclé culture of Panama) and the Manteo of Ecuador, both of whom were reported by Oviedo y Valdés in Spanish Colonial times as sailing large boats. The Pearl Islands off Panama are suggested as stopping or staging points.

Polynesia is also a possible point of origin for these voyagers, but reasons are given from the language used in this account to describe them that weaken this possibility.

W-092

AUTHOR: Wheatley, Paul
DATE: 1971
TITLE: The Pivot of the Four Quarters
IMPRINT: Aldine: Chicago

Analyzes the urbanization process in seven ancient world regions including China and Mesoamerica. Holds that urban centers develop through a three- stage process, and emphasizes developmental similarities in the geomantic essence of Chinese and Mesoamerican centers (without referring to or implying diffusion).

W-092B

AUTHOR: Wheeler, Jim
DATE: 1982
TITLE: Comment on Ben Finney's Review
IN: Archaeoastronomy 5/3:8

"A member of Dr. (George W.) Gill's 1981 expedition" to Easter Island challenges Finney's indication that there is no evidence of South American interaction with Polynesians. He cites three: the Rapa Nui legend about the arrival of a party of strange men from the east; physical anthropologist Gill's excavation and analysis of human remains from ancient tombs on the island "some of (which) were found to be of American Indians"; and the carved stone wall at Vinapu which "is almost identical with the stone structures at Pisac and Machu Picchu in Peru." Interprets legends as reporting settlement by a group "from the West (apparently from the Marquesas Islands)" between A.D. 500 and 1000. These exiles were ("it appears") descendents of Andeans who were attempting a voyage back to South America when they landed on Easter Island. A few hundred years later, the small group of men arrived from "the East."

While he was on the island in 1981 a Dutch couple were there who had just sailed "across the currents but with the winds" (from South America) in April in a 40-foot catamaran with a crab-claw sail and no motor. "I am now convinced that it is possible to sail from any part of the South American west coast to any part of Polynesia, but I doubt that the reverse is true."

W-093

AUTHOR: Whitaker, Ian
DATE: 1954
TITLE: The Scottish Kayaks and the "Finn-men"
IN: Antiquity 28:99-104

Summarizes the literature reporting men in kayaks who have arrived in the British Isles. After considering alternatives, he concludes that they must be Greenland Eskimos driven by storm or inexplicably voyaging by intention via Iceland and the Faeroes. Two Eskimo artifacts found on shore are described. One of the vessels, unquestionably an Eskimo kayak, is preserved in Aberdeen Museum.

W-094

AUTHOR: Whitaker, Ian
DATE: 1977
TITLE: The Scottish Kayaks Reconsidered
IN: Antiquity 51:41-45

He supposes that the kayaks and their Greenland Eskimo sailors were taken captive by European voyagers and carried to near Scotland (and, it is now known, Holland) where some probably tried to escape, resulting in landfalls of their vessels. It is uncertain, therefore, whether any derive from genuine native crossings, although the suggested view does not account for Eskimo harpoon heads found on the shores of the British Isles.

W-095

AUTHOR: Whitaker, Thomas W.
DATE: 1948
TITLE: Lagenaria: A Pre-Columbian Cultivated Plant in the Americas
IN: Southwestern Journal of Anthropology 4:49-68

Lists archaeological occurrences of this cucurbit that was common to the Old and New Worlds in pre-Columbian times, and briefly sketches Old World occurrences. He concludes that, (1) several types in both hemispheres were not shared, but, by and large, judging from sizes and shapes, Lagenaria materials from both hemispheres are rather closely comparable; (2) the plant occurred in North America at least several centuries before European discovery and in Peru at least 1000 years earlier; (3) the burden of proof is on those who believe that Europeans introduced the plant after the conquest.

W-096

AUTHOR: Whitaker, Thomas W.
DATE: 1971
TITLE: Endemism and Pre-Columbian Migration of the Bottle Gourd, Lagenaria siceraria (Mol.) Standl.
IN: Man across the Sea: Problems of Pre-Columbian Contacts, edited by Carroll L. Riley, et al. (University of Texas Press: Austin), 87-95

Lagenaria siceraria originated in tropical Africa. How it reached Mesoamerica (by 5000 B.C.) and South America (by 3000 B.C.) cannot be determined, but it may have been by human carriage.

W-098

AUTHORS: Whitaker, Thomas W., and Junius B. Bird
DATE: 1949
TITLE: Identification and Significance of the Cucurbit Materials from Huaca Prieta, Peru
IMPRINT: American Museum Novitates no. 1426 (American Museum of Natural History: New York)

Discussion of the archaeological dating and cultural uses of the gourd fragments from Huaca Prieta, by Bird, and identification of them by Whitaker. He finds Lagenaria siceraria, Cucurbita ficifolia, and C. moschata all present from the preceramic period on. C. ficifolia has never been reported before from a South American archaeological collection. [Compare M-190.]

W-099

AUTHORS: Whitaker, Thomas W., and George F. Carter
DATE: 1954
TITLE: Oceanic Drift of Gourds: Experimental Observations
IN: American Journal of Botany 41:697-700

Their experiments show Lagenaria gourds will float up to seven months in marine water with survival of viable seed. From what is known of winds and ocean currents, this length of time would be sufficient for gourds to drift from tropical Africa to the coast of Brazil. [Compare C-010.]

W-100

AUTHORS: Whitaker, Thomas W., and Junius B. Bird
DATE: 1961
TITLE: Note on the Longevity of Seed of Lagenaria siceraria (Mol.) Standl. after Floating in Water
IN: Torrey Botanical Club Bulletin 88:104-106

Results of experiment support the possibility of dispersion of bottle gourd seeds by natural means.

W-101

AUTHORS: Whitaker, Thomas W., and Glen N. Davis
DATE: 1962
TITLE: Cucurbits: Botany, Cultivation, and Uses
IMPRINT: L. Hill: London; and Interscience: New York

Pages 3-4: Cucumis anguria (West India Gherkin) was a botanical puzzle for a long time, but definitive work by Meeuse has established that it had an African origin, reaching the New World over 300 years ago probably through the early slave trade, then it became almost endemic in the New World.

Pages 5-7: Lagenaria siceraria is reviewed in detail. Archaeology demonstrates its cultivation in North and South America for thousands of years; it dates in Egypt to the 5th dynasty and has a name in Sanskrit. Experiment by Whitaker shows that it could possibly have been distributed to the shores of the New World without the aid of man but there is no proof that this happened.

W-102

AUTHOR: White, Barbara McNutt
DATE: 1962
TITLE: A Demonstration of the Validity of Parallel-like Development between the European Mesolithic and the New World Archaic
IMPRINT: Unpublished; M.A. thesis, Ohio State University

Thesis not seen but the abstract reads: "Certain similarities have been observed in the European Mesolithic cultural development and the Archaic stage of prehistory in the New World. The purpose of the thesis is to demonstrate a parallel-like development of cultural complexity and technology in both the Old and New Worlds."

W-102B

AUTHOR: White, K. D.
DATE: 1984
TITLE: Greek and Roman Technology
IMPRINT: Cornell University Press: Ithaca, New York

Methodology.

Pages 10-12: Four mechanisms for diffusion of technology: migration of an inventor or craftsman, trade (ideas stimulated by goods), war and conquest, publication.

Pages 56ff.: Difficulties of innovation in dislodging old devices or solutions to problems.

Pages 127-140: Advantages of human over animal transport and practical problems with the use of wheeled vehicles including road difficulties.

Pages 158-161: A history of qanats.

W-103

AUTHOR: White, Leslie
DATE: 1945
TITLE: Diffusion vs. Evolution: An Anti-Evolutionary Fallacy
IN: American Anthropologist 47:339-356

See W-104.

W-104

AUTHOR: White, Leslie
DATE: 1957
TITLE: Evolution and Diffusion
IN: Antiquity 31:214-218

A brief, simplified historical sketch of anthropological thought on evolution and historicism (including both independent development and diffusionism). Extravagances and errors have been committed on all sides. It is now clear that both evolution and diffusion are universal and fundamental processes.

Regarding the question of cultural relationship between New World and Old World cultures, the prevailing view is for independence, however in recent years, especially since Heine-Geldern and Ekholm have marshalled evidence in support of Asiatic influence, "one is not nearly so sure."

W-104B

AUTHORS: White, John J., III, and Beverly H. Moseley, Jr.
DATE: 1993
TITLE: Burrows Cave: Fraud or Find of the Century?
IN: The Ancient American 1/2:4-15 (Colfax, Wisconsin)

A display of and comments on photographs of eight artifacts "allegedly removed by Mr. Russell Burrows of Olney, Illinois, from a cave near his home state between 1982 and 1988. Taking these items at face value as genuine ancient artifacts [as the authors enthusiastically do], observers may conclude that Phoenicians from the great city-state of Tyre were likely participants in prehistoric events surrounding what has become known as Burrows Cave. Some of the finds include portraits of Semitic-looking people,

Egyptian-like art, a Judaic-like icon, Bel symbols, the Chief Ras symbol, coins, Phoenician writing and Ogam writing."

W-104C

AUTHOR: White, Peter
DATE: 1974
TITLE: The Past Is Human
IMPRINT: Angus and Robertson: London

Accepts possible occasional voyages from Asia to America but sees no evidence that they had any effects if they occurred.

W-104D

AUTHOR: Whitehead, R. A.
DATE: 1976
TITLE: Coconut
IN: Evolution of Crop Plants, edited by N. W. Simmonds (Longman: London and New York), 221-225

Coconuts probably reached the New World from Polynesian islands, although the distance is considerable. "Spread might have been by drifting or it might have been assisted by man."

W-105

AUTHOR: Whiting, Alfred F.
DATE: 1944
TITLE: The Origin of Corn: An Evaluation of Fact and Theory
IN: American Anthropologist 46:500-515

Both the original analysis of the problem of the origin of corn by botanists and subsequent reinterpretations are difficult for non-specialists to follow, hence men like Spinden, Kroeber, Lowie, and Thompson failed to understand the matter. There continues to be a view among anthropologists that the problem is subject to a conclusive botanical analysis, which is not true. Any solution must rest on a series of generalizations of a very high order of abstraction. No satisfactory solution is likely, given present information. Summarizes past theories and current hypotheses. Can we eliminate the possibility that corn originated in the Old World? One is tempted to say "Yes, definitely," but if it should be shown that the gourd [or any other early crop plant] was brought to America by cultural rather than natural means thus showing that American agriculture was not wholly indigenous, the certainty with which we now state that corn is of New World origin might have to be modified. Nevertheless, as things stand today, the chances of corn having originated in the Old World are virtually nonexistent.

W-106

AUTHOR: Whitley, Glenn R.
DATE: 1974a
TITLE: The Fulvous Tree Duck as a Cultural Tracer
IN: Anthropological Journal of Canada 12/1:10-17

An Asian watercraft (the jangada raft) and an Asian waterbird (the fulvous tree duck) are both found on the coast of Brazil, and the names of both raft and fowl are very similar to those names in use in south Asia. Lack of occurrences between East Africa and South America of this tame duck is puzzling unless it traveled with humans. This could have been from Madagascar around the Cape of Good Hope to Brazil thence to Mexico.

W-107

AUTHOR: Whitley, Glenn R.
DATE: 1974b
TITLE: Tame Curassow Birds as Indicators of Cultural Diffusion
IN: Anthropological Journal of Canada 12/2:10-15

Uses names to support the idea that the tame curassow originated in Tupí- Arawak country in northern South America and spread northward to include Mexico at an early date, along with the spread of root crops as hypothesized by Sauer.

Also tentatively concludes that New World bird domestication represented a diffusion from southeast Asia by way of Africa, as indicated by bio-linguistic analysis, cultural traits associated with the birds, types of birds used, and correlation with other traits such as blowguns and fishing techniques.

W-109

AUTHOR: Whittaker, Gordon
DATE: 1984
TITLE: Calendar and Script in Protohistorical China and Mesoamerica
IMPRINT: Unpublished; Habilitationsschrift, Fakultät für Kulturwissenschaften, Universität Tübingen

Fluent in Chinese, he analyzes the day names and their signs in China and Preclassic Mexico.

W-109B

AUTHOR: Whittaker, John
DATE: 1992
TITLE: The Curse of the Runestone: Deathless Hoaxes
IN: The Skeptical Inquirer 17/1:57-63

Assuming that the Kensington Stone has been shown a fraud, he proceeds to give a quasi-anthropological interpretation of why "the hoax" persists.

W-110

AUTHOR: Whittall, James P., Jr.
DATE: 1971
TITLE: The Spirit Pond Runestones
IN: NEARA [New England Antiquities Research Association] Journal 6/6:42

Discusses the Spirit Pond map stone, Inscription Stone, and Norse Folk Stone.

W-111

AUTHOR: Whittall, James P., Jr.
DATE: 1975a
TITLE: The Inscribed Stone from Comassakumkanit
IN: Epigraphic Society Occasional Publications 2/44, Part 1: 1-3

The inscribed Bourne stone was apparently known in the 17th century, having been recovered in the area of Great Herring Pond, two miles from Cape Cod Bay. [See F-032 immediately following for a proposed translation.] Whittall reports that a Prof. O. Strandwold in the 1940s felt that the characters were runic and of Norse origin and provided a very loose translation on that basis. [Also see S-498.]

W-112

AUTHOR: Whittall, James P., Jr.
DATE: 1975b
TITLE: Precolumbian Parallels between Mediterranean and New England Archaeology
IN: Epigraphic Society Occasional Publications 3/52:1-5

The first penetration of the North Atlantic was probably by Bell Beaker (Neolithic) folk from Iberia. A fishing site on Mohegan Island 10 miles off the coast of Maine yielded a carbon-14 date of 1800 B.C., associated with "a 'bronze' projectile point." At North Salem is a megalithic complex which is apparently a temple inspired from the Western Mediterranean; the site was constructed around 2000 B.C. by people from Malta (he gives eight [rather generalized] traits from Malta seen at the North Salem site) and was again occupied around 400 B.C. by people from Iberia. Other traits are mentioned shared with Iberia (e.g., "walls," "niches," triangular "drill marks").

Also, further evidence of Mediterranean parallels are scattered through all New England states, including "numerous bronze artifacts."

W-113

AUTHOR: Whittall, James P., Jr.
DATE: 1977
TITLE: Anforetas Recovered in Maine
IN: New England Early Sites Research Society Bulletin 5:1-5

Discovery by a diver on the Maine coast in 1971 of two ceramic storage vessels similar to those recovered off Lagos, Portugal, and considered Roman there.

W-113B

AUTHOR: Whittall, James P., Jr.
DATE: 1978
TITLE: Parallels between Inscribed Stones in Vermont and the British Isles
IN: Early Sites Research Society Bulletin 6/1:21-27

See W-113C.

W-113C

AUTHOR: Whittall, James P., Jr.
DATE: 1989
TITLE: Architecture and Epigraphic Evidence for Christian Celts in Connecticut, circa 500-700 A.D.
IN: Atlantic Visions (Proceedings of the First International Conference of the Society of Saint Brendan, September 1985, Dublin and Kerry), edited by John de Courcy Ireland and David C. Sheehy (Boole Press, Dún Laoghaire, Co.: Dublin, Ireland), 133-142

Reports archival and field studies over the past ten years at six sites or site complexes near the Thames River in eastern Connecticut which support the thesis that the area was occupied by Christian Celts sometime between A.D. 500 and 700. Related forms of structures, (apparently defensive) walls and placed stones, are on a scale that imply either a sizeable population or a fairly long occupation by an intrusive group, for the architecture is completely foreign to that of colonial settlements and farmsteads or of Amerindians in this drainage. The most prominent feature is stone chambers of drywall corbelled construction. These chambers have counterparts in Ireland and Scotland in medieval times. A radiocarbon date on a sample from one such chamber area falls between A.D. 1100 and 1390. A souterrain (trench dug into a hillside with a long passage and inner chamber within, all covered with earth) at one site is the first known example in New England; parallels in Ireland and the Hebrides are of the Late Iron Age. Several inscriptions are also illustrated and discussed.

W-114

AUTHOR: Whittall, James P., Jr., ed.
DATE: 1990
TITLE: Myth Makers: Epigraphic Illusion in America
IMPRINT: Early Sites Research Society: Rowley, Massachusetts

An initial try at a critique (both positive and negative) of "American epigraphy" covering part of the ground of but later superseded by M-206D.

W-116

AUTHOR: Whittlesey, Charles
DATE: n.d. [c. 1880]
TITLE: Inscribed Stones, Purporting to Be in Hebrew from Licking County, Ohio
IN: Proceedings of the 3rd International Congress of Americanists (Brussels, 1879), 2:399-404

Resumes earlier publications by him on the Newark and Grave Creek stones and purportedly related materials which he had published with the Western Reserve Historical Society. He has tried to contact, by correspondence or in person, as many as possible of the persons reportedly present at these discoveries, but he finds them reluctant to talk. Presents some facts about D. Wyrick and the Newark Stones and emphasizes that American archaeologists, but, unfortunately, not all European ones, believe these are frauds.

W-117

AUTHOR: Wicke, Charles
DATE: 1966
TITLE: Olmec: An Early Art Style in Pre-Columbian Mexico
IMPRINT: Unpublished; Ph.D. dissertation, University of Arizona [University Microfilms International Order No. 6505521. Published, revised, 1971 as W-118]

Cites sources that claim Negroid origin for the Olmec giant heads.

W-118

AUTHOR: Wicke, Charles
DATE: 1971
TITLE: Olmec: An Early Art Style of Pre-Columbian Mexico
IMPRINT: University of Arizona Press: Tucson

Pages 145-146: Brief mention of Ekholm regarding possible derivation of the feline motif from China. This is quickly dismissed.

W-119

AUTHOR: Wicke, Charles R.
DATE: 1982
TITLE: The Sylvilagus Satellite, or the Mesoamerican Hare on the Moon (Abstract only)
IN: Abstracts of Papers, 44th International Congress of Americanists (Manchester, 1982), (School of Geography, Manchester University: Manchester, England), 141

Beliefs about a rabbit appearing on the visible face of the moon occur in India, China, Japan, and Mesoamerica. In Egypt the rabbit was associated with the moon-god, Un-nefer.

W-120

AUTHOR: Wicke, Charles R.
DATE: 1984
TITLE: The Mesoamerican Rabbit in the Moon: An Influence from Han China?
IN: Archaeoastronomy 7/1-4:46-55 [Translated and adapted with permission of the author, 1990, as "Le lapin mésoaméricain sur la lune: une influence de la Chine des Han?," *KADATH* 74 (1990): 40-48]

Identifies a complex—moon associated with the rabbit, a goddess, and a hallucinogenic substance. Expectable variations in stylistic detail aside, these themes appear together in Han Chinese art and myth and in Classic and Postclassic Mesoamerica.

W-121

AUTHOR: Wickersham, James
DATE: 1894a
TITLE: Japanese Art on Puget Sound
IN: American Antiquarian and Oriental Journal 16:47-49

Three Japanese from an 1833 shipwreck were enslaved by the Makah. In 1805 a dozen Japanese on a junk landed at Sitka. There were a dozen known wrecks in the Aleutians, two on Queen Charlotte's Island and many south of there. Over the centuries the numbers must have been large. [Compare Q-012 and K-026C.]

W-122

AUTHOR: Wickersham, James
DATE: 1894b
TITLE: Origin of the Indians: The Polynesian Route
IN: American Antiquarian and Oriental Journal 16:323-335

Responding to Cyrus Thomas, the author argues that evidence does not favor settlement of America via Polynesia but the reverse, based upon sailing conditions. "The North Pacific current is the migration route over which that grandest of races, the Mongolian, sent out, either by accident or design, its people to occupy the continents of America" as well as the Pacific Islands.

W-122B

AUTHOR: Wickersham, James
DATE: 1895
TITLE: An Aboriginal War Club
IN: American Antiquarian and Oriental Journal 17:72-76

A cast of a club was exhibited in Tacoma in 1894 said to have been dug from a mound in Colorado and "believed to have come from New Zealand." Wickersham counters that this form of club was "quite common throughout the vast stretch of country between Alaska and Peru, including Puget Sound, Columbia River, Great Salt Lake, Pueblo villages, Mexico, Central America and thence to the land of the Incas where it was reproduced in bronze." [Compare K-059.]

W-124

AUTHOR: Wickersham, James
DATE: 1897a
TITLE: The Mongol-Mayan Constitution
IN: American Antiquarian and Oriental Journal 19:169-176

Concerns the quadripartite organization of world space in the thought of peoples in China and North, Central, and South America. The scheme connects directions, seasons, colors, elements, activities, visceral organs, navel of the world concept, astrology, and governmental forms. He refers to this scheme as forming a "quadriform constitution" especially clear in the Chinese and the "Aztec-Mayan" civilizations.

W-125

AUTHOR: Wickersham, James
DATE: 1897b
TITLE: The Religion of China and Mexico Compared
IN: American Antiquarian and Oriental Journal 19:319-329

Compares some religious symbols, rituals, deities (both Chinese-Mexican and Japanese-Mexican comparisons), and the concept of divine kingship.

W-127

AUTHOR: Wiener, Leo
DATE: 1920-1922
TITLE: Africa and the Discovery of America, 3 vols.
IMPRINT: Innes and Sons: Philad, New York [Reviewed by Elise Richter, *Anthropos* 23 (1928): 436-447, and in D-135]

Vol. 1: Discussion of the spread of tobacco, the sweet potato, and the yam, as reconstructed from interpretations of words and historical inferences.

Vol. 3: Negroes with their trading masters were in America before Columbus. They reached the West Indies first, from which they entered eastern South America. Again from the Antilles, they went into North America, their presence marked by mound construction. Their chief cultural influence, however, was through the Negro colony in Mexico (involving Teotihuacan), from where they influenced neighboring tribes, at least indirectly, all the way to Peru. Evidences are chiefly word comparisons [the quality of which was attacked by many reviewers].

W-128

AUTHOR: Wiener, Leo
DATE: 1921
TITLE: Africa and the Discovery of America
IN: American Anthropologist 23:83-94

A vigorous response to Dixon's [D-135] review of W-127. Dixon follows with a vitriolic rejoinder (pages 94-97).

W-129

AUTHOR: Wiener, Leo

DATE: 1925

TITLE: The Philological History of "Tobacco" in America

IN: Proceedings of the 21st International Congress of Americanists (Part 2, Gothenburg, Sweden, 1924), pages 305-314

A short version of his three volumes: e.g., forms of the word tubaq for incense are in Semitic and Sanskrit; the Nahuatl and Tarascan words for tobacco and pipe are from Arabic. American tobacco words all start at the Atlantic coast and work into the interior, hence tobacco was imported from the Old World.

W-130

AUTHOR: Wiener, Leo

DATE: 1926

TITLE: Mayan and Mexican Origins

IMPRINT: Privately printed: Cambridge, Massachusetts

A lavishly illustrated but barely documented volume of self-indulgent speculation. Essence: "The major part of the religious concepts of the Mandingos [who reached America from West Africa], hence of the Mayas and Mexicans, arises from linguistic speculations bequeathed by the Arabs in their astrology and astronomy, as derived from a Hindu source, hence it is now possible to maintain that the American civilizations were derived from Africa after the ninth century [A.D.]" "Unquestionably, the archaeological dogs will continue to bay at the moon and will pursue the same vociferous methods as in the past, in order to suppress the [i.e., Wiener's] search for the truth."

W-132

AUTHOR: Wiercínski, Andrzej

DATE: 1969

TITLE: Ricerca Antropológica sugli Olmechi [Anthropological Research on the Olmecs]

IN: Terra Ameriga 18-19:17ff. [Associazione Italiana Studi Americanistici, Génova]

Tlatilco and Cerro de las Mesas skeletal materials show negroid features among other characteristics.

W-132B

AUTHOR: Wiercínski, Andrzej

DATE: 1971

TITLE: Racial Affinities of Some Ancient Populations in Mexico

IN: Anthropological Congress Dedicated to A. Hrdlicka, pages 485-499, Prague

Sketches elements of the alochthonist-autocthonist controversy over the origin of civilization in America.

W-133

AUTHOR: Wiercínski, Andrzej

DATE: 1972a

TITLE: Interpopulational Differentiation of the Living Amerindian Tribes in Mexico

IN: Proceedings of the 39th International Congress of Americanists (Lima, 1970), 1:213-229

Neologisms and difficulties in use of English make this paper difficult to follow.

He sees the need for more and improved taxonomic analysis on Amerindians because of the poor descriptive and analytic quality of much that has been published hitherto. Among the correlations in characteristics which he notes as minor elements: the "Olmecs" were of very mixed origin including "some strange admixtures of Armenoids together with African Negroids from the Western Mediterranean" of megalithic culture; some Nahuas show "extremely high similarities to the Pacific race" which may suggest a migratory influx from North China in Shang or Chou period landing on the Guerrero coast then expanding to Morelos and Vera Cruz to participate in the formation of the Olmec civilization.

W-134

AUTHOR: Wiercínski, Andrzej
DATE: 1972b
TITLE: Inter- and Intrapopulational Racial Differentiation of Tlatilco, Cerro de las Mesas, Teotihuacan, Monte Alban and Yucatan Maya
IN: Proceedings of the 39th International Congress of Americanists (Lima, 1970), 1:231-248
[Also 1972 in *Swiatowit* 33:175-197 (Warsaw)]

He undertook a new examination of all available Mexican series of prehispanic skulls (N-193), involving multivariate analysis of metric and cranionometic traits established by use of standardized techniques. Among his observations: ancient Mexico may have been inhabited by a chain of interrelated populations which cannot be regarded as typical Mongoloids; one source for visible Negroid traits (Tlatilco) is transatlantic migrants from the Afro-Iberian Megalithic area; also there seem to have been sporadic immigrants from the Western Mediterranean area; possible elements represent (Shang) China; an Armenoid constellation of traits could be from the Mediterranean or by convergence. All these are, of course, in addition to basic Laponoid, Ainoid, and Mongoloid elements which formed the core of Mexico's Preclassic populations.

W-135

AUTHOR: Wiercínski, Andrzej
DATE: 1972c
TITLE: An Anthropological Study on the Origin of "Olmecs"
IN: Swiatowit 33:143-174 (Warsaw)

Presents the results of a comparative analysis of racial structure of two series of crania from Tlatilco and Cerro de la Mesas. He concludes, admitting that he might "take a heavy risk of a possible severe discussion," that "a strange transatlantic, more or less, sporadic migration did occur," and that " 'Olmec' or La Venta civilisation arose as a consequence of inter-mingling process of civilisatory impulses of Shang China and megalithic ideas of 'Prospectores' from Mediterranean Basin which have been superimposed in early phases of Preclassic Amerindian Agriculturalists" [*sic*].

W-137

AUTHOR: Wiercínski, Andrzej
DATE: 1975a
TITLE: Some Problems of the Taxonomy of Living and Past Populations of Amerindians
IN: Proceedings of the 41st International Congress of Americanists (Mexico, 1974), 1:116-126

Inventories the confusing literature on racial taxonomy of New World Indians. Frequencies of polymorphic genetic traits and morphological traits are contrasted for large numbers of Amerindian populations. Finds that genetic data are not superior to morphological for establishing racial typologies.

W-138

AUTHOR: Wiercínski, Andrzej
DATE: 1975b
TITLE: Afinidades raciales de algunas poblaciones antiguas de México [Racial Affinities of Some Ancient Peoples of Mexico]
IN: Anales, Instituto de Antropología e Historia 1972-73:123-144 (México)

Identifies evidence for several Old World racial groups in Mexico. [See W-134.]

W-139

AUTHOR: Wiercínski, Andrzej
DATE: 1976
TITLE: Pyramids and Ziggurats as the Architectonic Representations of the Archetype of the Cosmic Mountain
IN: Almogaren 7 (Graz, Austria) [Reprinted 1977, *Katunob* 10:69-111 (Greeley, Colorado)]

The cosmic scheme common among central civilizations in the Old World as represented at Teotihuacan. [See W-140.]

W-140

AUTHOR: Wiercínski, Andrzej
DATE: 1977
TITLE: Time and Space in the Sun Pyramid from Teotihuacan
IN: Polish Contributions in New World Archaeology 1:87-103 (Kraków)

Socio-cultural activities of the people in all ancient centers of civilizations, with Mexico an extreme example, were ideologically regulated by astro-biological religions. The nucleus of these religions was everywhere the same, built into the frame of the oldest megalithic cultures somewhere in the western Mediterranean or Near East and from which came stimulus to construct monumental architecture that served both for cultic and astronomical purposes. This architectonic inspiration, together with the lineal unit equal to 0.829 meters (the "megalithic yard") was brought to Mexico (Teotihuacan) by sporadic transatlantic migration in the 3rd and/or 2nd millennium B.C. It came from the western (Mediterranean) wing of megalithic cultures (following Dominik J. Wölfel, "Die Religionen des vorindogermanischen Europa," in the volume *Christus und die Religionen der Erde* 1:161-537 [Thomas Morus: Vienna, 1951]). This paper demonstrates that the form and dimensions of the Sun Pyramid at Teotihuacan reflect the astronomical calendric cycles so important in the astro- biological religion of ancient Mesoamerica. The model central to this religion is summarized. It is visualized in the iconic-numerical code of concentrically organized Mandalas (the richest example being the famous Aztec "Calendar Stone") as a Cosmic Tree, or in the form of a grave or temple-pyramid as a Cosmic Mountain (citing Eliade and Schwabe). It was also dynamically represented in the system of rituals of cyclic public feasts and ceremonies. His working hypothesis is that Olmec civilization resulted from infusion of megalithic ideas (noting papers by Alcina Franch on transatlantic movements) into an Amerindian background, intermingled with transpacific impulses from China dating between Shang and Chou periods.

W-141

AUTHOR: Wiercínski, Andrzej
DATE: 1980
TITLE: Canon of the Human Body, Mexican Measures of Length and the Pyramid of Quetzalcoatl from Teotihuacan
IN: Polish Contributions in New World Archaeology 2:103-123 (Kraków)

Civilized societies in both Old and New Worlds were ideologically regulated by astrobiological religion in which sacral buildings were coded, iconically and numerically, involving astrologically-significant measurements from or of the human body. He previously showed this for the Pyramids of the Sun and Moon at Teotihuacan and here he does the same for the Temple of Quetzalcoatl. (Stencel et al. showed it for Angkor Vat, *Science* 193:281-287.) Both the architectonic dimension units and the calendric cycles which they represent relate to the length measures in Nahuatl which are body-based; these are typical for ancient Mexico since Marshack found them also in the Olmec mosaic from Las Bocas.

W-142

AUTHOR: Wikander, Stig
DATE: 1967
TITLE: Maya and Altaic—Is the Maya Group of Languages Related to the Altaic Family?
IN: Ethnos 32:141-149

Even with a superficial acquaintence with the Maya languages, one is struck by the number of apparent similarities in both vocabulary and structure with the Altaic language family. These must be considered accidental. But he here gives 12 words which show "astonishing similarity in meaning as with form." From these he offers a working hypothesis that Maya dialects have kept the Ur-Altaic initial labial.

W-143

AUTHOR: Wikander, Stig
DATE: 1970
TITLE: Maya and Altaic II
IN: Ethnos 35:80-88

Revises the list offered in W-142 and presents further parallels which he considers linguistically significant. Believes he demonstrates, on the basis of three pairs each, that the two voiceless velars of Maya, traditionally written *k* and *c,* were represented in Modern Turkish by *k* and *g*.

W-144

AUTHOR: Wikander, Stig
DATE: 1972a
TITLE: Maya and Altaic III
IN: Orientalia Suecana 19-20:186-204 (Uppsala)

See W-143.

W-145

AUTHOR: Wikander, Stig
DATE: 1972b
TITLE: Chichenitzá - an Altaic Name
IN: Studia Linguistica 25/2:129-130

Following on W-142 and W-143 he reports three instances of palatalized velars followed by the vowels *e* or *i,* so that now he "can reckon with a well established Maya-Altaic soundlaw."

W-146

AUTHOR: Wilbert, Johannes
DATE: 1974
TITLE: The Thread of Life: Symbolism of Miniature Art from Ecuador
IN: Dumbarton Oaks Studies in Pre-Columbian Art and Archaeology, No. 12 (Dumbarton Oaks: Washington, D.C.)

After studying many thousands of spindle whorls from Ecuador, the author here distills some interesting observations and representations, supposing that a general cult of fertility is often represented on the whorls.

Pages 20-21: Discusses E-109 and E-108 on the Bahia culture. After listing the eight traits noted by Estrada and Meggers as likely of Asiatic origin, he notes two spindle whorls that agree. One strikingly shows contrasting side-by-side figures carrying burdens, by tumpline and by Asiatic "coolie yoke." The other shows a funeral procession in which a cadaver is borne on a litter. Less striking but interesting is another whorl showing a bird-man figure "almost identical" to rock carvings on Easter Island, while granting that this might be coincidental. He believes that Heyerdahl and Jett have convincingly argued the feasibility of transpacific contacts by voyaging. Later in the monograph he gives naturalistic explanations for other Old World parallels for his whorl designs: the serpent as a phallic symbol, and the hocker figure as related to birth and sex.

W-147

AUTHOR: Wilbert, Johannes
DATE: 1977
TITLE: Navigators of the Winter Sun
IN: The Sea in the Pre-Columbian World: A Conference at Dumbarton Oaks, October 26th and 27th, 1974,

edited by Elizabeth P. Benson, (Dumbarton Oaks: Washington, D.C.), 17-46

Canoe-connected technology, concepts, sociology, and mythology of the Warao, notable voyagers of the Orinoco area.

W-148

AUTHOR: Wilhelm, O. E.

DATE: 1957

TITLE: Las gallinas de la Isla de Pascua [Chickens of Easter Island]

IN: Boletín de la Sociedad biología de Concepción 32:133-137 (Chile)

Early statements about these chickens are cited along with his own observations. They were and are very extensively used in most ritual [there is no hint that a new type arrived with Europeans, let alone became important in diet or ritual]. The earliest description says that they resembled, broadly at least, European chickens.

W-149

AUTHORS: Wilhelm, O. E., and L. Sandoval

DATE: 1955

TITLE: Genealogías y seroantropología de los Pascuenses [Genealogies and Seroanthropology of the Easter Islanders]

IN: Boletín de la Sociedad biología de Concepción 31:119ff. (Chile)

Wilhelm began blood group studies on Easter Island in 1934 and has continued. With the help of local informants he has identified the (only) 128 persons with exclusively native ancestries as well as subgroups of the reputed descendants of the long ear element and of other tribes. Among the whole set of unmixed-with-Europeans, blood types A and O are found. Those descended from the long ears are exclusively of blood group O. Other subgroups or tribes have both O and A. The presence of blood features other than the major groups is mentioned. They anxiously await the results of the Norwegian tests; these two helped draw that sample.

W-151

AUTHOR: Wilkinson, Richard G.

DATE: 1975

TITLE: Techniques of Ancient Skull Surgery

IN: Natural History 84/8:94-101

Evidence of trephination at Monte Alban dating 500 B.C. to A.D. 700. Ten skulls are described.

W-152

AUTHORS: Wilkinson, Richard G., and Marcus C. Winter

DATE: 1975

TITLE: New Evidence of Trephination from Monte Alban

IN: Proceedings of the 41st International Congress of Americanists (Mexico, 1974), 1:127-130

They add to the distribution and typology of this operation which is found in both Old and New Worlds. Five more examples, from the IIIb period at Monte Alban (c. A.D. 650), are reported. The site should be considered "a major center of experimental surgery."

W-154

AUTHOR: Willard, Theodore A.

DATE: 1933

TITLE: The Lost Empires of the Itzaes and Mayas; An American Civilization, Contemporary with Christ, Which Rivaled the Culture of Egypt

IMPRINT: Arthur H. Clark: Glendale, California

He is non-committal on origin, only throwing out a possibility here and there of diffusion/migration. For example, on page 152, "Could the Chanes or Itzaes have brought this jade from their native country, where people wore turbans, sat cross-legged on cushions, and had Mongolian features?"

W-154B

AUTHOR: Willcox, R. R.
DATE: 1972
TITLE: The Treponemal Evolution
IN: Transactions, St. John's Dermatological Society 58:21-37

Considers that endemic syphilis was common in pre-Columbian Europe.

W-155

AUTHOR: Willett, F.
DATE: 1962
TITLE: The Introduction of Maize into West Africa: An Assessment of Recent Evidence
IN: Africa 32:1-13

Two routes from America are indicated, West Indies-Venice-East Mediterranean-NileChad-west coast of Africa (initially via Spanish vessels), and Guianas/Brazil-west coast of Africa via Portuguese and Dutch vessels. These routes correspond to the two subspecies of maize found in West Africa: hard- and soft-grained. Considering the dates, the two varieties would appear to have arrived in West Africa together about 1530-1540. [This complex history and hurried chronology is denied by Jeffreys. See also S-409.]

W-156

AUTHOR: Willetts, William
DATE: 1958
TITLE: Chinese Art
IMPRINT: Penguin: Harmondsworth

Plate 4, page 87: Turquoise mosaic is shown on a dagger handle dating Shang through Han China. [Compare J-075 for Mesoamerica.]

W-158

AUTHOR: Willey, Gordon R.
DATE: 1955
TITLE: The Prehistoric Civilizations of Nuclear America
IN: American Anthropologist 57:571-593

On Old World-New World contacts, he is unconvinced by arguments (e.g., by Heine-Geldern and Ekholm) of linkages in style, art and architecture, but certain technical features do argue for pre-Columbian contact. Possibilities include patolli (though it might be ancient and have come via Northeast Asia) and rocker stamped pottery, but he retains doubts.

W-159

AUTHOR: Willey, Gordon R.
DATE: 1962
TITLE: The Early Great Styles and the Rise of Pre-Columbian Civilization
IN: American Anthropologist 64:1-14

Notes similarities between Chavin and Chinese feline representations in art but does not accept a direct connection between the two areas.

W-160

AUTHOR: Willey, Gordon R.
DATE: 1964
TITLE: Review *of Aboriginal Cultural Development in Latin America*, edited by Betty J. Meggers and Clifford Evans
IN: American Anthropologist 66:442-446

As to transpacific diffusion, he says "I am as yet undecided," although the similarities to Asia are "notable." And "from what I have seen of Jomon (Japanese) and Valdivia pottery, there is, indeed, a case for a connection at circa 3000 B.C. Such a contact would have brought pottery to the Americas, presumably for the first time." And he disagrees with Meggers, who suggests that such contacts would have had unimportant consequences for the development of native New World cultures. He thinks pottery had profound importance to their development.

Also, diffused religious belief and forms of worship he does not think of as inconsequential embellishments of a culture. If transpacific contacts to western South America did occur, they were probably of signal importance to the culture history of the New World.

W-161

AUTHOR: Willey, Gordon R.
DATE: 1966, 1971
TITLE: An Introduction to American Archaeology, 2 vols.
IMPRINT: Prentice-Hall: Englewood Cliffs, New Jersey

Vol. 1, pages 19-24: A critique of diffusionism.

Vol. 2, page 16: Sees the derivation of most New World pottery from the Valdivia complex, of transpacific origin.

W-162

AUTHOR: Willey, Gordon R.
DATE: 1985
TITLE: Some Continuing Problems in New World Culture History
IN: American Antiquity 50:351-363

No other subject in American archaeology has brought about such heated discussions as the role of Old World contacts. No Old World manufactured object has yet been found in an indisputable, undisturbed New World context. If nothing concrete can be shown in the next 50 years, proponents should stop talking about it. [Compare M-109 re. Madagascar; or has any Near Eastern object ever been found in Greece?]

W-163

AUTHORS: Willey, Gordon R., and Jeremy A. Sabloff
DATE: 1974
TITLE: A History of American Archaeology
IMPRINT: W. H. Freeman: San Francisco; and Thames and Hudson: London

Pages 172, 174: Claims for transpacific diffusion are "dubious and debatable." Regarding Heine-Geldern's views "it is still fair to say that these questions have not been finally resolved," while Valdivia-Jomon relationships have not been accepted by a majority of Americanists.

W-164

AUTHORS: Williams, Brad, and Choral Pepper
DATE: 1967
TITLE: The Mysterious West
IMPRINT: World: Cleveland

Includes journalistic-level information on the Los Lunas "Phoenician" inscription of New Mexico.

W-165

AUTHOR: Williams, David
DATE: 1949
TITLE: John Evans' Strange Journey
IN: American Historical Review 54:277-295, 508-529

Reports on Evans' visit to the Mandan in search of evidence of their Welsh ancestry, which led to his disillusionment with the notion.

W-166

AUTHOR: Williams, David
DATE: 1963
TITLE: John Evans and the Legend of Madoc, 1770-1799
IMPRINT: University of Wales Press: Cardiff

A reduced version of W-165 printed as a separate item with parallel pages in Welsh and English.

W-167

AUTHOR: Williams, Gwyn A.
DATE: 1979
TITLE: Madoc: The Making of a Myth
IMPRINT: Eyre Methuen: London

A history in American life from the 16th to the 20th centuries of the widespread Madoc myth and of the idea of Irish and Scandinavian voyages. The documentation is in a three-page bibliographical discussion.

W-168

AUTHOR: Williams, Gwyn A.
DATE: 1980
TITLE: Frontier of Illusion: The Welsh and the Atlantic Revolution
IN: History Today 30:39-45

Includes discussion of Thomas Jefferson, John Evans, and other advocates that certain Indian groups displayed characteristics derived from Madoc, the legendary Welsh voyager.

W-172

AUTHOR: Williams, James
DATE: 1930
TITLE: Christopher Columbus and Aboriginal Indian Words
IN: Proceedings of the 23rd International Congress of Americanists (New York, 1928), pages 816-850

A long, critical, generally successful review and rebuttal of Leo Wiener's handling of statements by Columbus, Las Casas, and others in his three-volume work on Africa and America.

W-173

AUTHOR: Williams, Mary Wilhelmine
DATE: 1923
TITLE: The Vinland Sagas and the Historians
IN: American Scandinavian Review 11:42-45

"An examination of the attitude of historical writers towards the story of the discovery of America by Icelanders and Norwegians." Early in the 19th century skepticism was general, but a steady trend toward acceptance culminated in the most recent edition of the *Encyclopedia Britannica* which accepts Norse discovery as fact. Suggests that due to Holand's efforts, the same result may eventually ensue for the Kensington Stone.

W-174

AUTHOR: Williams, O.
DATE: 1953
TITLE: Plant Evidence for Early Contacts with America: A Review
IN: Ceiba 3:220-221 (Tegucigalpa, Honduras)

Critical of Carter on plant evidence for transpacific voyaging [C-077].

W-174B

AUTHORS: Williams, Robert C., Arthur G. Steinberg, Henry Gershowitz, Peter H. Bennett, William C. Knowler, David J. Pettitt, William Butler, Robert Baird, Laider Dowch-Rea, Thomas A. Burch, Harold G. Morse, and Charline G. Smith
DATE: 1985
TITLE: GM Allotypes in Native Americans: Evidence for Three Distinct Migrations across the Bering Land Bridge
IN: American Journal of Physical Anthropology 66:1-19

Typings for immunoglobulin G allotypes of 5392 Native (North) Americans from ten samples, done over the last 20 years, are reported. Groups represented are Pimans, Puebloans, Pai, and Athabascans. Genetic similarity is demonstrated at two loci, while the heterogeneity that exists is consistent with "what is known about the prehistory of Native Americans and traditional cultural categories" [whatever that means]. The Pimans, Puebloans, and Pai are descendents of the Paleo-Indians, while the Apache and Navajo are related to the Na-Dene. Typings done on South American Indians can be explained in terms of their Paleo-Indian ancestry. Siberia appears to be a good candidate for the ancestral homeland "of contemporary Native Americans."

W-175

AUTHOR: Williams, Samuel Wells

DATE: 1881

TITLE: Notices of Fu-sang, and other Countries Lying East of China, in the Pacific Ocean

IMPRINT: Tuttle, Morehouse and Taylor: New Haven
[First published in *Journal of the American Oriental Society* 11 (1881); reprinted in V-057, pages 230-248]

Does not believe Fu-sang was in America but in the Loo-choo (Ryukyu) Islands, south of Japan.

W-175B

AUTHOR: Williams, Stephen

DATE: 1991

TITLE: Fantastic Archaeology: The Wild Side of North American Prehistory

IMPRINT: University of Pennsylvania Press: Philadelphia

A book developed as a text for the author's class of the same title at Harvard. His material consists mainly of lively but at some points inadequately informed or heavily biased jibes at the easiest targets among diffusionists and other unconventional archaeological writers.

W-175C

AUTHOR: Williams, Stephen

DATE: 1992

TITLE: Who Got to America First? A Very Old Question

IN: Anthro Notes, National Museum of Natural History Bulletin for Teachers 14:1-4, 13

A précis of W-175B.

W-177

AUTHOR: Williamson, A. W.

DATE: 1881

TITLE: Is the Dakota Related to the Indo-European Languages?

IN: Minnesota Academy of Natural Sciences, Bulletin 2:110-142

Dakota may be related to Indo-European, he claims.

W-178

AUTHOR: Williamson, A. W.

DATE: 1882

TITLE: The Dakotan Languages and Their Relations to Other Languages

IN: American Antiquarian and Oriental Journal 4:110-128

Page 111: Light hair and blue eyes among the Minnetares and Mandans cannot be attributed to Caucasian admixture. The language is compared to Indo-European, being more like Icelandic and Gothic than like anything else.

W-179

AUTHOR: Williamson, George

DATE: 1877

TITLE: Antiquities in Guatemala

IN: Annual Report of the Board of Regents of the Smithsonian Institution . . . [for] 1876, pages 418-421

Site of Naranjo near Guatemala City has rows of standing stones [as in the Near East]. [See S-238.]

W-180B

AUTHOR: Williamson, J. A.

DATE: 1962

TITLE: The Cabot Voyages and Bristol Discovery under Henry VII

IMPRINT: Hakluyt Society: Cambridge
[A new edition, with updated notes,

of his 1929 *The Voyage of the Cabots and the Discovery of North America* (London)]

In 1480 the most noted navigator in England sailed from Bristol to look for an island called "Brasylle" west of Ireland. That year also the English king authorized an official and three merchants of Bristol "to seek for and discover a certain island called the island of Brasil" by sending three ships out, which, however, returned two months later unsuccessful. Clearly there was knowledge being bruited about, presumably from a successful voyage earlier, of such a place to westward.

W-181

AUTHOR: Willis, William
DATE: 1955
TITLE: The Gods Were Kind: An Epic 6700 Mile Voyage Alone across the Pacific
IMPRINT: Dutton: New York [French edition Livre Contemporain: Paris, 1959]

An adventurer rafts alone from Peru to Samoa in 115 days with no theory in mind.

W-182

AUTHOR: Willis, William
DATE: 1965
TITLE: Alone against the Sea
IN: Saturday Evening Post (September 25): 38-42ff.

See W-181. Further epic rafting in the Pacific.

W-183

AUTHOR: Wilson, Daniel
DATE: 1877
TITLE: Prehistoric Man: Researches into the Origin of Civilization in the Old and New World, 3rd edition, revised and enlarged
IMPRINT: Macmillan: London

Polynesians arrived in South America then moved northward.

W-185

AUTHOR: Wilson, David M.
DATE: 1980
TITLE: The Vikings and Their Origins
IMPRINT: Thames and Hudson: London

An introduction based on archaeology. Chapter 3 includes an account of the Greenland and North American voyages between A.D. 870 and 985.

W-186

AUTHOR: Wilson, Edward F.
DATE: 1890
TITLE: Indians and Japanese
IN: Our Forest Children 3/12 (=n.s. 10): 153-154 (Sault Ste. Marie, Ontario)

Resemblances between Japanese and Ojibwa languages.

W-187

AUTHOR: Wilson, Michael
DATE: 1978
TITLE: Cyclones, Coconuts, and Chickens across the Sea: Dispersal Theory and Cultural Diffusion
IN: Diffusion and Migration: Their Roles in Cultural Development, edited by P. G. Duke, et al. (University of Calgary Archaeological Association: Calgary), 65-105

An unfocused broadside that asserts that diffusion of seeds by "tramp birds," claimed to be demonstrated (along with the effects of wind-blown seeds) in the revegetation of denuded volcanic islands, may explain the presence of plants distant from an indigenous area. Thus man need not have been involved in (crop) plant spreads.

He also claims that classification of biological specimens by older botanical workers was superficial and unreliable. So he does not believe that sweet potatoes were accurately identified in much of Oceania by early European explorers.

He criticizes Carter's publications that claim the presence of Asiatic chickens in South America before European contact, claiming that the evidence is either not sufficient or can be explained other than as showing diffusion.

W-188

AUTHOR: Wilson, Thomas
DATE: 1890
TITLE: A Study of Prehistoric Anthropology
IN: Report of the United States National Museum for the Year Ending June 30, 1888, Part 3, Number 6, pages 597-671

See L-089 re. grooved axes in China and North America, which depends on this source.

W-189

AUTHOR: Wilson, Thomas
DATE: 1896
TITLE: The Swastika, the Earliest Known Symbol, and Its Migrations; with Observations on the Migration of Certain Industries in Prehistoric Times
IN: Report of the United States National Museum for the Year Ending June 30, 1894, Part 2, Number 6, pages 757-1011

Its origin was in the Old World, from which it diffused to the New.

W-191

AUTHOR: Winchell, N. H.
DATE: 1907
TITLE: Precolumbian Elephant Medals Found in Minnesota
IN: American Anthropologist 9:358-361

A volume by J. Brower illustrates a bronze medal bearing the date 1446 found near Hastings, Minnesota. Two identical medals have since been found in North Dakota and Minnesota. The author shows that these were Italian devotional medals and that one of La Salle's exploring companions was an Italian chevalier. They brought large amounts of trade goods ("trinkets") with their expedition. Presumably this was the source from which these medals dispersed among the Ojibwa.

W-193

AUTHOR: Winning, Hasso von
DATE: 1958
TITLE: Figurines with Movable Limbs from Ancient Mexico
IN: Ethnos 23:1-60

Presents a classification of over 300 jointed figurines, mainly from the Valley of Mexico (Azcapotzalco) but including specimens from Veracruz, Tampico, and Jaina. The figurines from the Mexican highlands fall into two major groups, those having the head attached with strings, and those where the head and torso are molded in one piece. Various subtypes, based on patterns of headdresses, are established. The great majority are confined to Classic Teotihuacan. Similarities of design with pottery decorations and some Teotihuacan symbols are interpreted. The concept of producing jointed figurines was first invented in the Preclassic of the Guatemala highlands and again roughly 500 years later in Mexico, probably in central Veracruz. [Compare E-050.]

W-195

AUTHOR: Winning, Hasso von
DATE: 1960
TITLE: Further Examples of Figurines on Wheels from Mexico
IN: Ethnos 25:65-72

The four specimens described include a jaguar and a dog. A figurine of a monkey [skin?] draped on a platform has tubular axle housings and is Late Classic from central Veracruz (Remojadas). This joins a figure of a human male sitting on a four-legged platform (the legs perforated for wheels) from Nayarit as perhaps the first evidence for the concept of "vehicle" in Mesoamerica. [However, von Winning in a personal communication to Sorenson in 1989 reported that the human figurine on the Nayarit specimen has proved to be a fake, though not the wheeled platform, which is evidently pre-Columbian. The Paul Cheesman collection of artifacts, in Provo, Utah, contains a ceramic specimen conceptually related, consisting of a human figure seated in a sort of chair on wheels.] In any case it is apparent that these pieces would not have been toys.

W-196

AUTHOR: Winning, Hasso von
DATE: 1962
TITLE: Figurillas de barro sobre ruedas procedentes de México y el viejo mundo
[Clay Figurines on Wheels from Mexico and the Old World]
IN: Amerindia 1:11-39 (Montevideo)

Wheeled figurines from Mexico represent mainly animals; those from Europe, the Near East, and the Indus Valley include animals, chariots, and complex assemblages which had ritual associations. They occur first in Mesopotamia (2000-3000 B.C.) and were made to the end of the Roman empire. Identical methods of attaching the wheels occur in the Old World and in Mexico. [See F-139 for much fuller documentation on the Old World.] He is vaguely disfavorable to a diffusion origin.

W-197

AUTHOR: Winning, Hasso von
DATE: 1969
TITLE: Ceramic House Models and Figurine Groups from Nayarit
IN: Proceedings of the 38th International Congress of Americanists (Stuttgart-Munich, 1968), 1:129-132

He summarizes a study of 36 ceramic models of houses with clay figurines representing occupants. All are reportedly from tombs in southern Nayarit. He distinguishes five types, one of which is a four-shed roof bearing a tall crest with lateral projections at the ends of the slightly curved roof which is higher in the center. This is a detail that differentiates the Nayarit roof from the Asiatic saddle roof seen on house models from Ecuador and China. A particular painted motif on the models closely resemble the god's eye [thread cross] motif from Cora and Huichol Indians; they attribute supernatural powers to it. One of the models shows nine figurines bearing a human figure on their shoulders, presumably a person of higher rank. The models are estimated to date between the 1st and 7th centuries A.D.

Page 132: These models, appearing in such a limited area, deserve external comparison as to source. The concept of making house models of clay appears to have been introduced from Asia to South America in the 2nd century B.C. together with other traits. We do not know that the concept passed from Ecuador to Mexico, although Ecuador at one time maintained maritime contacts with western Mexico. Ecuadorian models from Manabí are quite different from those of Nayarit. There remains the probability that the concept could have been introduced directly from China, where clay imitations of houses, carts, horses, etc., were made for grave offerings, and chronological parallels are known. But any comparison between Chinese and Nayarit house groups must be confined to the general concept of placing miniature ritual and village-life scenes as grave offerings. [Compare P-147.]

W-199

AUTHOR: Winning, Hasso von

DATE: 1971

TITLE: Keramische Hausmodelle aus Nayarit, Mexiko [Ceramic House Models from Nayarit, Mexico]

IN: Baessler-Archiv 19:343-377 [In Spanish as, "Las maquetas cerámicas de Nayarit," in *Las representaciones de arquitectura en la arqueología de América*, I, coordinador Daniel Schávelzon (Universidad Nacional Autónoma de México: México, 1982), 55-85]

Forty-four clay house models and several village scenes from Nayarit are described in detail.

Nayarit house models may have originated in Ecuador. The *ojo de diós* (thread cross) design on Nayarit maquetas is almost identical to and contemporaneous with designs in Tierradentro (southwest Colombia) chamber tombs. Following Marschall [M-109] he lists 10 characteristics shared by model houses in Nayarit and China. A Chinese origin "cannot be discarded," although neither can it be documented archaeologically.

W-200

AUTHOR: Winning, Hasso von

DATE: 1973

TITLE: Mexican Figurines Attached to Pallets and Cradles

IN: Proceedings of the 40th International Congress of Americanists (Rome and Genoa, 1972), 1:123-131

Figurines in Mesoamerica showing adults lying on slabs or couches are limited to Western Mexico and south-central Veracruz. They represent a ritually inebriated person in a trance-like condition intended to facilitate contact with the gods. [For Chinese parallels see W-204, though not necessarily with the meaning he suggests].

W-201

AUTHOR: Winning, Hasso von

DATE: 1974

TITLE: The Shaft Tomb Figures of West Mexico

IMPRINT: Southwest Museum Papers 24 (Southwest Museum: Los Angeles)

Pages 34,64, 82, 98, 104: Evidence of syphilis is clear in figurines as illustrated and discussed.

Pages 81-82: This figurine complex is noteworthy for "the accurate portrayal of pathological symptoms, suggesting the predominance of such diseases as tuberculosis, syphilis and ascites."

W-202

AUTHOR: Winning, Hasso von

DATE: 1975

TITLE: Die mythologische Bedeutung einer olmekischen Jaguarskulptur [Mythological Meaning of an Olmec Jaguar Sculpture]

IN: Zeitschrift für Ethnologie 100:224-237

An Olmec jaguar head sculpture with 18 small human figures in back, attached symmetrically in 3 rows, suggests a representation of the Olmec origin myth, an expression of a fertility theme. Significant parallels with Chinese and circumpacific art motifs are noted, evident in (1) the jaguar (=tiger) motif; (2) the vertical arrangement of similar motifs, in this case figures standing on top of each other; (3) their squatting posture (hocker motif); and (4) their back-to-back placement. These specific Southeast Asian-derived parallels suggest the expansion of traits of Heine-Geldern's "Old Pacific Style" into the Olmec core area by the end of the first millennium B.C.

W-203

AUTHOR: Winning, Hasso von

DATE: 1989

TITLE: Trans-Pacific Contacts with Mexico—A Review of Recent Research
IN: Reprint Proceedings, Circum-Pacific Prehistory Conference, Seattle, August 1-6, 1989, part VIII, Prehistoric Trans-Pacific Contacts (Washington State University Press: Pullman), articles separately paginated

Summarizes studies at Tübingen by Barthel and his students (see B-085 and G-089). Their structural studies have revealed Hindu syncretistic manifestions in religion and astronomy/astrology (along lines initiated by Kirchoff and Kelley) and their encoded transformations and adaptations to Mexican pictorial conventions in the codices of the Borgia Group. Under strict methodological guidelines, this approach goes far beyond the visual comparisons of Heine- Geldern. Other investigations are summarized on Hindu-Maya syncretisms in inscriptions and iconography at Palenque.

W-204

AUTHORS: Winning, Hasso von, and Olga Hammer
DATE: 1972
TITLE: Anecdotal Sculpture of Ancient West Mexico; Ceramic House Models and Figurine Groups Mounted on Slabs
IMPRINT: Los Angeles County Natural History Museum: Los Angeles

Survey of figural groups in West Mexican mortuary ceramics. Particular attention is paid to house models, figure groups, and ritual bed figures that have Chinese parallels. [Compare M-109.]

W-205

AUTHOR: Winsor, Justin, editor
DATE: 1889
TITLE: Aboriginal America, volume 1 of Narrative and Critical History of America
IN: Houghton-Mifflin: Boston

Pages 59-117: Pre-Columbian Explorations. The Norse.

Page 72, note 2: Guignes described a manuscript that made him believe Arabs reached America, and he is followed by Munoz, but others (cited) dispute this.

Pages 74-75: Basque voyaging and language connections to America are assessed (many citations; most not in the present bibliography); accidental voyages would have been possible, as witness the sternpost of a European vessel which Columbus saw at Guadalupe.

Page 76: References [not herein] concerning "Skolno" and Cousin as discoverers before the Spanish.

Pages 76-82: An extensive survey of the literature, chiefly of the early 19th century [much not included herein], is given on migrations or contacts from Asia to America, including Fu-sang.

Pages 87-111: Detailed review of the old literature [much not here] and opinions on the Vinland voyages and the fate of the Greenland colonies.

Page 97: A report of the discovery of runes on the Potomac was printed in a Washington newspaper in 1867, which was accepted as true by Gaffarel and Gravier, although it was promptly exposed as a hoax (in *Historical Magazine*, March and August, 1869).

Pages 116-117: Possible migrations from Africa are briefly discussed, with references to obscure sources.

W-206

AUTHOR: Wintemberg, W. J.
DATE: 1942
TITLE: The Geographical Distribution of Aboriginal Pottery in Canada
IN: American Antiquity 8/2:129-141

He maps what is now known of the subject. "Speculations as to the implications of the distribution so far as intercontinental movements are concerned are useless because our knowledge of pottery distribution is still very incomplete." As to McKern's [M-214] postulated movement from Asia via the Yukon to the Great Lakes area, there is still a gap of approximately two thousand miles unfilled by pottery.

W-208

AUTHOR: Winzerling, E. O.
DATE: 1956
TITLE: Aspects of the Maya Culture
IMPRINT: North River: New York

Page 13: "Even in their isolation trans-Pacific or trans-Atlantic influences did reach them or their forbears, for certain similarities cannot be attributed to mere chance." The most likely source was Buddhist missionaries from Asia. A few comments along this line are scattered throughout the short book, with more in the last chapter.

Page 99: "It has not yet been established with finality that the Middle-American and Peruvian cultures are free from extra-American influences." Indonesian and Polynesian "influences" are mentioned.

W-210

AUTHOR: Wirth, Diane E.
DATE: 1978
TITLE: Discoveries of the Truth
IMPRINT: Privately printed: Danville, California

In connection with a Book of Mormon orientation, the author briefly discusses or mentions some Old-New World parallels along the lines of D'Alviella, Cyrus Gordon, Irwin and Wuthenau.

W-211

AUTHOR: Wirth, Diane E.
DATE: 1981
TITLE: The Tree of Life Offers Evidence of Precolumbian Contact
IN: Pursuit 14:168-171 (Little Silver, New Jersey)

The Assyrian tree of life symbol/scene is compared with Mesoamerican art, and some comparative information is presented for other Old and New World cultures. Follows W-230 closely on major points. The clear similarities must be evidence of transoceanic voyages.

W-212

AUTHOR: Wirth, Diane E.
DATE: 1986
TITLE: A Challenge to the Critics: Scholarly Evidence of the Book of Mormon
IMPRINT: Horizon: Bountiful, Utah

Review of a range of evidences of transoceanic contacts, discussed here in relation to the Book of Mormon, referring to such matters as wheeled figurines, tree of life motif, Wuthenau's figurine heads, and the Tlatilco roller stamp, with citations to the literature.

W-213B

AUTHOR: Wirth, Diane R.
DATE: 1994
TITLE: An Ancient Wall at Chatata, Bradley County, Tennessee
IN: The Ancient American 7:20-25

Reopens investigation of the wall and characters initially reported in R-033 and R-034. After examinining published and private communications in the matter, Wirth went to the site with relatives of the discoverer and found one fragment of the "characters" described. Geologists tell her that the marks were produced by mollusks in mud which fossilized as sandstone with the appearance of man-made markings. She thinks the feature deserves more investigation.

W-214

AUTHOR: Wirth, Hermann

DATE: 1934

TITLE: Der Aufgang des Menschheit; Untersuchungen zur Geschichte der Religion, Symbolik und Schrift der atlantisch-nordischen Rasse, 2. Auflage [The Rise of Mankind; Researches on the History of Religion, Symbolism and Writing of the Atlantic-Nordic Race, 2nd ed]

IMPRINT: Eugen Diederichs: Jena

Humans originated in the circumpolar region; he points to parallels between Germans and North American Indians.

W-215

AUTHOR: Wise, Jennings C., edited, revised, and with an introduction by Vine Deloria, Jr.

DATE: 1971

TITLE: The Red Man in the New World Drama: A Politico-Legal Study with a Pageantry of American Indian History

IMPRINT: Macmillan: New York; and Collier-Macmillan: London

The first two chapters cover "four and a half centuries" of Norse, Welsh, etc., impact on eastern North America. The romantic sweep of this account fits with its lack of serious documentation. We are told that Leif and successors built a network of trading villages from Newfoundland to Florida which, however, were eventually ravaged by native warfare and finally (c. 1350) by the Black Death [apparently this had little effect on the Indians]. Later visits by Sinclair and N. Zeno found much evidence of these former riches but no survivors. Meanwhile the Norse who settled "Westland" (Ontario) via the St. Lawrence Valley became deeply involved in establishing the Huron confederacy (the political ideas were theirs), only to be destroyed (except for subsequently absorbed remnants) by "swarms" of Iroquois invading from the south.

W-216

AUTHOR: Wissler, Clark

DATE: 1917

TITLE: The American Indian; An Introduction to the Anthropology of the New World

IMPRINT: Oxford University Press: New York [Second edition 1922]

Page 47: "The cotton complex of the entire world is essentially one . . . and it was . . . diffused from a single center."

Pages 69-70: He proposes a possibly separate, Asiatic origin (via Bering Strait) for the pottery of the Mandan-Hidatsa of the northern Plains.

Chapter 21, "New World Origins," page 390: Repeated efforts to see the origination of the higher culture complexes of the New World in the Old World have been based mainly on speculation, "but some of the facts we have cited for correspondences to Pacific Island culture have not been satisfactorily explained." He follows Dixon that certain features like those in the Pacific Islands appear to mass upon the Pacific side of the New World, giving a semblance of continuous distribution with "the Island culture." There is no great a priori improbability that some of these traits did reach the New World from the Pacific Islands, but these could not have been very important in the already developed American cultures.

Page 393: A few mythical conceptions seem to have carried from the Old World to the New (see pages 208-209).

Pages 375-386: A brief characterization of the role of diffusion in culture history.

W-217

AUTHOR: Wissler, Clark

DATE: 1933

TITLE: Ethnological Diversity in America and Its Significance

IN: The American Aborigines: Their Origin and Antiquity. A Collection of Papers by Ten Authors, Assembled and Edited by Diamond Jenness. Published for Presentation at the Fifth Pacific Science Congress (Canada, 1933), (University of Toronto Press: Toronto), 167-216 [Reprinted Russell and Russell: New York, 1972]

In several pages on the history of thought on the origin of American Indians, he notes that from the beginning (18th Century), trans-Siberian migrations were the favorite theory.

Page 179: Lists only 12 "specific traits" that he is able to identify that are common to all American Indian groups. He then admits that these are "after all, . . . not specific": e.g., "the family group," "practise of magic," "a belief in spirits," "dance forms," "songs," "a varying body of mythology," and "knowledge of twisting string," and these would hold for "the primitive Old World as well." He then discusses such cultural categories as weaving, clothing, warfare, metals, etc. The New World presents about the same range of variations as the Old. After general treatments of geographic regions and "the development of cultures," he concludes that such variety would have taken considerable time to develop.

Page 215: The strongest claims for Old World influences (via diffusion) are based on continuous geographical distribution, e.g., slat armor from northern Asia. But finally, the great variety of cultures and traits in the New World has obscured whatever may have been transferred directly from the Old World.

W-217B

AUTHOR: Wistrand-Robinson, Lila

DATE: 1991

TITLE: Uto-Aztecan Affinities with Panoan of Peru, I: Correspondences

IN: Comparative Studies in South American Indian Languages, edited by Mary Ritchie Key (University of Pennsylvania Press: Philadelphia), 243-276

Methodological. The author has worked with Cashibo and Comanche languages and here compares them in detailed ways. She takes the former as a representative of Panoan languages (in the Peruvian rain forest) and the latter (in Oklahoma) as a representative of Uto-Aztecan. Phonological and grammatical correspondences are striking. Using the Swadesh method of glottochronology she derives a figure of 1650 years for separation of the two languages. She finds that "grammatical correspondences and processes . . . are equally as important as the phonological ones." Comparison of proto-languages or reference to other languages in each family actually tends to obscure the clear relation between the two specific, living languages. However, no extended historical or geographical interpretation of the relationship is offered in this paper. [It is notable that this relationship became apparent only when the two distant target languages happened to have been studied by one linguist, a coincidence rarely to be encountered.]

W-218

AUTHOR: Witthoft, John

DATE: 1964

TITLE: Alleged Phoenician Inscriptions from York County, Pennsylvania

IN: Pennsylvania Archaeologist 34/2:93-94

Laboratory studies by the Pennsylvania Geological Survey and National Bureau of Standards were made on inscribed stones collected by W. W. Strong of Mechanicsburg, Pennsylvania, and selected by him for this study. Some marks proved to be the result of natural weathering of olivine veins (shown this, Strong decided to reject those "inscriptions"). Others were unweathered but contained fresh steel dust "throughout their extent." The author believes that the frauds "were foisted upon [the late] Dr.

Strong by some of his associates who searched for Phoenician inscriptions with him."

W-219

AUTHOR: Wittkower, R.
DATE: 1938-1939
TITLE: Eagle and Serpent: A Study in the Migration of Symbols
IN: Journal of the Warburg and Courtauld Institutes 2:293-325

Examines the wide distribution of the eagle-seizing-serpent motif. The motif represented originally, in the Mediterranean area, antagonism between good and evil with the triumph of good. The Graeco-Roman idea spread to India then to China with Buddhism but also via Southeast Asia into the Pacific. He accepts its diffusion to the New World from the Old on chronological grounds and considers two possible routes, from India to Polynesia to America or Scythia to eastern Siberia to America.

W-220

AUTHOR: Wittmack, Ludwig
DATE: 1890
TITLE: Die Nutzpflanzen der alten Peruaner [Useful Plants of the Ancient Peruvians]
IN: Proceedings of the 7th International Congress of Americanists (Berlin, 1888), pages 325-349

The banana was pre-Columbian in Peru.

W-221 See now W-233B.

W-223

AUTHOR: Wolf, S.
DATE: 1941
TITLE: Zum Problem der Nasenflöte [On the Problem of Nose Flutes]
IMPRINT: Harrassowitz: Leipzig

Distribution of the nose flute around the world, including the New World.

W-223B

AUTHOR: Wölfel, Dominik Josef
DATE: 1925
TITLE: Die Trepanation. Studien über Ursprung, Zusammenhänge und kulturclle Zugehörigkeit der Trepanation [Trepanation. Studies on the Origin, Connections, and Cultural Affiliation of Trepanation. First Study: The Cultural Affiliation and the Unified Origin of Trepanation in Melanesia and America]
IN: Anthropos 20:1-50

A comprehensive examination of the literature on trepanation and club forms throughout Oceania and America. He concludes that trepanation in Oceania and the New World is essentially identical in cultural terms. He believes that trepanation and war clubs of wood and of stone with wooden handles form a complex shared by both areas.

W-223C

AUTHOR: Wölfel, Dominik Josef
DATE: 1955
TITLE: Eine Felsgravierung eines neolithisch-bronzezeitlichen Schiffstypus und anderes aus der Archäologie der Kanarischen Inseln [A Rock Engraving of a Neolithic-Bronze Age Type of Ship, and Other Matters on the Archaeology of the Canary Islands]
IN: Afrikanische Studien, no. 26: 183-197
[The program of the IV Congrés International des Sciences Anthropologiques et Ethnologiques (Vienna, 1952) listed this author as giving a paper entitled "Transatlantic Relations of Ancient American High Cultures." The proceedings subsequently stated, in a list of "conférences publiés ailleurs," that Wölfel's paper could

be found in "Afrikanistische Studien, Westermann-Festschrift, Berlin, 1955." W-223C appears therein as listed here. Presumably this was, or was part of, the conference paper, reshaped and retitled more modestly by the author]

Believes all of coastal western and Mediterranean Europe, Morocco, and some of the east Atlantic islands might have been reached by relatively primitive navigation techniques, that is, large dugout canoes propelled by many oarsmen. Such are known archaeologically in Holland and Scotland in the Mesolithic. [Also compare W-140.]

W-224

AUTHOR: Wolff, Werner
DATE: 1937a
TITLE: Le déchiffrement des hiéroglyphes Mayas et la traduction de quelques tableaux de hiéroglyphes [The Decipherment of Maya Hieroglyphs and the Translation of Several Hieroglyphic Pictures]
IN: L'Ethnographie 33-34:111-115

An Asian connection is claimed in general terms.

W-225

AUTHOR: Wolff, Werner
DATE: 1937b
TITLE: Déchiffrement de l'écriture de l'île de Pâques [Decipherment of the Writing from Easter Island]
IN: Bulletin de la société des oceanistes 1:98-142

The characters on the rongorongo tablets are related to Egyptian. [Compare W-227.]

W-226

AUTHOR: Wolff, Werner
DATE: 1938
TITLE: Déchiffrement de l'écriture maya et traduction des codices [Decipherment of Maya Writing and Translation of the Codices]
IMPRINT: Librairie Orientaliste Paul Geuthner: Paris

Chapter 5, "Parallélisme entre l'Orient ancien et l'Amérique ancienne," presents his thinking and evidence on these points: the Mayans knew the Phoenician alphabet; their day names follow the order of that alphabet, in general [compare Kelley in K-042]; the characters and their names relate to the zodiac which is known in Eurasia; the ages of the world demonstrate a similar link; the greatest symbol of the unity of Orient and America is the pyramid with many shared symbolic meanings [compare W-140]. A second volume [which seems never to have appeared] is promised to present the Oriental-American connections in detail.

W-227

AUTHOR: Wolff, Werner
DATE: 1948
TITLE: Island of Death: A New Key to Easter Island's Culture through an Ethno-psychological Study
IMPRINT: J. J. Augustin: New York

Pages 108-126: Theories about the origin of Easter Island culture, including similarities between Easter Island and the Americas. Includes fragments of Heyerdahl, Rivet, etc. [Compare B-111.]

W-228

AUTHOR: Wood, Corinne Shear
DATE: 1975
TITLE: New Evidence for a Late Introduction of Malaria into the New World
IN: Current Anthropology 16:93-104

Absence of malaria is an argument for pre-Columbian separation of the populations of the two hemispheres. Lightly reviews the literature on malaria in pre-Columbian America vs. post-Columbian introduction, strongly favoring the latter. Her experiments suggest (or at least lead to the hypothesis) that the prevalence of O blood group in America correlates with (causes?) resistance to bites from mosquitoes (however, she used only an African species). Commentators raise many problems about the experiment, and some are more accepting than she of possible pre-Columbian presence of the disease.

W-229

AUTHORS: Woodbury, Richard B., and James A. Neely
DATE: 1972
TITLE: Water Control Systems of the Tehuacan Valley
IN: Chronology and Irrigation, edited by Frederick Johnson, volume 4 of the multi-volume set, The Prehistory of the Tehuacan Valley (University of Texas Press: Austin), 81-153

Pages 139-149 ("Chain Well Systems"): Gives preliminary information on an irrigation technique in use in Mexico and South America essentially similar to the qanat system of the Middle East and Spain. Usually thought to have been introduced from Spain (as these authors hold for this area), chain wells were also known, apparently, in prehistoric America as indicated by sources here cited.

W-230

AUTHOR: Woodford, Irene Briggs
DATE: 1953
TITLE: The "Tree of Life" in Ancient America, Its Representations and Significance
IN: University Archaeological Society Bulletin 4:1-18 (Brigham Young University: Provo, Utah)

Summary of her master's thesis [B-366] detailing a complex of stylistic and conceptual parallels in scenes representing the "Tree of Life" in the Near East and Mesoamerica.

W-231

AUTHOR: Woodward, A.
DATE: 1930
TITLE: Shell Fish Hooks of the Chumash
IN: Bulletin, Southern California Academy of Sciences 28:41-45

Similarity of these hooks from the Santa Barbara area to some used in Polynesia.

W-232

AUTHOR: Woodward, John
DATE: 1977
TITLE: An Early Ceramic Tradition on the Pacific Coast
IN: Masterkey 51/2:66-72

Reports ceramics from Lake River, Washington, [which Stenger, S-430, finds related to Japan or Korea].

Page 71: Woodward sees a Jomon-like similarity and possible B.C. date.

W-233

AUTHOR: Woolley, Leonard
DATE: 1934
TITLE: Ur Excavations, vol. II, The Royal Cemetery
IMPRINT: Published for the Trustees of the British Museum and the University of Pennsylvania by Oxford University Press: London

Pages 262-283: Use of semi-precious minerals in mosaics is one of the most characteristic traits of Sumerian civilization. [Also common in China and Mesoamerica.]

W-234

AUTHOR: Woolley, Leonard
DATE: 1937
TITLE: Digging Up the Past
IMPRINT: Penguin: Harmondsworth, England

Page 76: The cylinder seal is a peculiar type of artifact not likely to be invented independently in two different countries. Paper-using people would never invent the cylinder seal, hence Mesopotamia is the obvious origin point. [Re. their appearance in America, compare A-047, A-053, and B-272.]

W-235

AUTHOR: Worcester, G. R. G.
DATE: 1966
TITLE: Sail and Sweep in China: The History and Development of the Chinese Junk as Illustrated by the Collection of Junk Models in the Science Museum.
IMPRINT: Her Majesty's Stationery Office: London

Historical background material given is limited, but the descriptions of construction and operation of various forms of junks is unusually detailed. The author served for many years in the River Inspectorate of Chinese Maritime Customs and travelled widely in China until imprisoned in World War II. No dugouts are known from China. Implies that if they existed long ago, the tradition was overwhelmed by the raft tradition. "It is quite reasonable to suppose that China's development of her built-up craft came straight from the raft," although he says nothing specific describing such rafts.

W-236

AUTHOR: Wright, A. C. A.
DATE: 1949
TITLE: Maize Names as Indicators of Economic Contacts
IN: Uganda Journal 13:61-81 (Kampala)

A valuable compendium of sources and preliminary analysis foreshadowing Jeffreys' work on maize names in Africa. Tentatively notes the anomaly of the East Africans crediting India as the source for their maize. The received view that the Portuguese brought it to the coast and it spread from there seems an unlikely simplification. Also concludes that the plant had been introduced into Ethiopia from a Turkish source as well as from the Portuguese in the 16th century. Notes that among the Hausa in West Africa the source they credit is Egypt.

W-236B

AUTHORS: Wright, E. V., and D. M. Churchill
DATE: 1965
TITLE: The Boats from North Ferriby, Yorkshire, England, with a Review of the Origins of the Sewn Boats of the Bronze Age
IN: Proceedings of the Prehistoric Society 31:1-24

Nautical capacity of early northwestern Europeans to voyage in the Atlantic.

W-237

AUTHOR: Wright, G. Ernest
DATE: 1938
TITLE: Lachish—Frontier Fortress of Judah
IN: Biblical Archaeologist 1:28-29

"Though operations on the skull seem to have been well known to the ancients, only the Incas of Peru are at present known to have used the same method as the surgeons at Lachish," ca. 600 B.C.

W-238

AUTHOR: Wright, G. Ernest
DATE: 1943
TITLE: How Did Early Israel Differ from Her Neighbors?
IN: Biblical Archaeologist 6:1-20

Page 3: The names Canaan and Phoenicia both appear to derive from the purple dye industry, indicating the age and importance of the pattern in the eastern Mediterranean. [Compare G-076.]

W-239

AUTHORS: Wright, Louis B., and Elaine W. Fowler
DATE: 1971
TITLE: West and by North: North America Seen through the Eyes of Its Seafaring Discoverers
IMPRINT: Delacorte: New York

Pages 29-38: Section on pre-Columbian voyages across the Atlantic, mainly by Erik, with a touch of Brendan and Madoc.

W-239B

AUTHOR: Wright, Ronald
DATE: 1992
TITLE: Stolen Continents: The Americas through Indian Eyes since 1492
IMPRINT: Houghton Mifflin: Boston

Diffusionist "crackpot ideas" are "subtly racist" implying that Amerindians could not have done what they did without help. There may have been odd contacts between the hemispheres but they were neither culturally nor genetically significant.

W-239C

AUTHOR: Wright, R. R.
DATE: 1902
TITLE: Negro Companions of the Spanish Explorers
IN: American Anthropologist 4:217-228

There is evidence to suspect the presence of pre-Columbian Negroes. Cites a letter from Justin Winsor [see W-205] which notes the possibility of the equatorial current carrying Guanche and African canoes to America, recalling that skulls had been found in caves in the Bahamas which seemed to resemble those from ancient tombs in the Canaries, and noting that some ancient American ceramics represent Negro physiognomic features.

W-240

AUTHOR: Wuthenau, Alexander von
DATE: 1965
TITLE: Altamerikanische Tonplastik: Das Menschenbild der Neuen Welt [Ancient American Pottery: Depictions of Man of the New World]
IMPRINT: Holle: Baden-Baden [French translation *Terres cuites précolumbiennes*, (Albin Michel: Paris; and Crown: New York, 1969)]

The first of this author's works, exhibiting the extensive collection of chiefly Mesoamerican figurines which he sees as showing Asiatic, Semitic, European and African faces. While his ethnic identifications may seem to some to overreach, others of his comparisons are unmistakable, striking, and unexplained by orthodox archaeologists.

W-241

AUTHOR: Wuthenau, Alexander von
DATE: 1966
TITLE: Representations of White and Negro People in Precolumbian Art
IN: Proceedings of the 36th International Congress of Americanists (Barcelona and Seville, 1964), 1:109-110

A short version of W-240 presented at the ICA as a slide show.

W-242

AUTHOR: Wuthenau, Alexander von
DATE: 1975
TITLE: Unexpected Faces in Ancient America, 1500 B.C.–A.D. 1500; the Historical Testimony of Pre-Columbian Artists
IMPRINT: Crown: New York

Page 27: Dr. A. de Garay, a Mexican scientist, found sickle cell anemia, an indicator of Negro admixture, among Lacandon Indians [but centuries after African slaves were introduced into Mexico by the Spaniards].

Page 28: Clearly Negroid representations in America can be identified as early as 1200-650 B.C. in terracotta and other materials.

Pages 31-32, 34-37: The half-god, half-devil, Humbaba, opponent of Gilgamesh in Babylonian lore, is said (citations) to represent viscera/labyrinth/volcanoes (the labyrinthine look of lava?), and he shows up in parallels from Babylon, Carthage, Sparta, and Ur as well as in faces from Veracruz, Tlatilco, Chiapas, Colombia, and Ecuador. This figure is the remote ancestor of the fire god (Huehueteotl) in America.

Pages 32-43: The god Bes, of Nordic and Mediterranean occurrence, is paralleled by a split-bearded figurine from Guerrero published and discussed in V-001B and shown here in Appendix 2d. "On all Phoenician expeditions this mascot was carried along in the form of small terracotta effigies." He shows what he considers another (Maya) example. Four Mesoamerican examples of what he sees as the Star of David are shown. Contrary to claims by some, this design is old (at least 7th century B.C.) in the Near East.

Pages 43-46: Also discussed are the phylactery representation on the Tepatlaxco stela and incense burner parallels in Israel and Guatemala. In Jerusalem he has seen a museum specimen of a Jewish three-prong brazier, the prongs consisting of three bearded heads. Here (pages 44-45) he illustrates an incense burner of Las Charcas phase (before 500 B.C.) in the Guatemalan Museum, which includes on its side a very Semitic face. [See also S-361.]

Plate 18b is a gold specimen from the Quimbaya region of Colombia, c. A.D. 600, which shows a stick stuck across the human figure's mouth which "might be related to an ancient ceremony still performed in Zaire." Plates 24-28 show faces with what he considers sure Asiatic and Negroid features.

A very recently found clay fragment from Tlatilco represents a bearded head only 4 cm. high which is incredibly similar to Greek and Phoenician items, a counterpart to the face on the magnificent Guatemalan incense-burner in the Musee de l'Homme. Also reputedly from Tlatilco is a Negroid Silenus mask (page 181). The small head excavated by García Payón in 1933 from the Calixtlahuaca pyramid, according to Prof. Boehringer from Germany fits typologically with Roman figures of about A.D. 200. Where did all these people come from?

Page 51, 53: Summary of Book of Mormon migrations supplied him by N. Steede while a student under the author in Mexico. Jakeman and Ferguson are briefly mentioned. This Mormon material Wuthenau considers appropriate background information about the problems involved in his book, without entering into religious matters.

Pages 52, 54: The split-bearded head from the Balsas region is "quite obviously . . . the god Bes, who was well known in Egypt [and] . . . Phoenician excavation sites." (Prof. Hintze of Darmstadt confirms the Bes character of the mentioned head; he also reports that similar representations have been found in the Altai mountains). Four strange-looking heads from Guerrero (shown) compare with figures from Baluchistan.

Page 56: The possibility that some Vikings or half-Vikings found their way south to Mesoamerica should not be summarily dismissed, inasmuch as our never-failing pre-Columbian artists have bequeathed evidences of this.

Page 58-59: Archaeological pieces representing Negro or Negroid people have been found, especially in Archaic or Preclassic sites, in all parts of Mexico and in Panama, Colombia, Ecuador, and Peru. Asiatic types are frequently represented very clearly in art. And white types, chiefly with Semitic characteristics, were probably numerous. Six faces are "Semitic types," five of them judged by him Preclassic, ranging from Nayarit to Chiapas and the Maya area.

He is particularly struck by the Xochipala figures from Guerrero, which show a chiefly white people who seem to have dropped out of the sky on the American continent over three thousand years ago. He concludes that a connection to the Old World is not improbable; there is a close affinity of these figures and ancient Egyptian (3rd-5th dynasties) art, including absolute identity of their coiffures. But there was probably an earlier Archaic Oriental (Japanese) immigration to the same Guerrero area. These foreigners he calls "Contra-Olmecs."

Page 61-62: It is unfortunate that Coe (and others) writing about the Olmec fail to account for the clear negroid features in the giant stone heads. "Enigmatic heads of men of different races" from Guerrero include putative caucasoid examples and others recalling "archaic Japanese" figurines.

Pages 69-70: One of the "Contra-Olmecs" appears as the Semitic-faced figure on La Venta Stela 3, conventionally called by the name "Uncle Sam," which hides its significance. He has prepared a collection of photos of figurines showing Chinese features, particularly pigtails (which, he is told by Dennis Lou, occurred in China since the sixth century B.C.) All Wuthenau's specimens (three are pictured in Appendix A5) are from Preclassic sites, about 500 B.C.

Page 73: There are those who dodge the issue of beards on such figures by considering them "false beards." But the so-called false beards often look astonishingly like those on Greek and Etruscan sculptures.

Pages 75-76: "Chiefly in Guerrero, archaeological discoveries emerge from time to time which have no connection or very little in common with those of other pre-Columbian cultures. Famous in this respect is the small double-bearded terracotta head which was found in the Balsas River district, and which we now recognize without any doubt as a representation of the Phoenician and Egyptian deity, Bes." [Compare V-001B.] Wuthenau considers some of these finds "Urweisse" (early whites) because they belong more to the white species of mankind than to any other; they are also often old, on the order of 2000 B.C. in part. For example, one of these on his page 61 "looks like a Hittite or a Persian" (found north of Acapulco 4 m. below the surface).

Pages 77-81: Several similar heads are shown which he puts at ca. 500 B.C. "I personally have not been able to discover among these distinguished personages a single 'real Indian.' " Another group ("goggle-eye type") first appeared on the Pacific Coast of Guerrero and Oaxaca in very remote times. Some look pre-Hellenic Mediterranean. Japanese reminiscences appear in others, which leads to mention of Evans and Meggers, whom he believes, although they should consider a possible landing of Jomon folks in Guerrero from whence they later reached Ecuador. Heads from Esmeraldas, Manabí, Tumaco, and the Chibcha area, though later, resemble his "Japanese" heads from Guerrero.

Pages 83-87: Very marked Negroid and "Semitic-Hebrew" features are shown and discussed. The latter are probably priests, with high hats, and without exception they are shown weeping. More "white" examples are given, some very Greek-like, and mainly from Tlapacoya.

Page 94: He considers Tlapacoya the place of first arrival of the "semi-Asiatic" Olmecs, who came among an established, very different population.

Page 96: Based on figurines and also ceramics, he claims that a few hundred years before the Christian era (evidently in the Ticoman/Cuicuilco period) a fundamental shift in population can be seen in central Mexico.

Page 101: Jointed dolls from Teotihuacan are mentioned, which he judges were individual portraits retouched after being made in molds.

Page 130: "The two leading races" in Mesoamerica" are Negroid (a la Olmec stone heads) and Semitic-looking (La Venta Stela 3);

these two types are also consistently shown in the gold collection of the Bank of Colombia.

Pages 147, 171: A Chinesco type figure has an old man with a pointed beard seated in an Oriental position of meditation. Plate 127 shows from Jalisco, "a beautiful white woman in pre-Columbian times," clearly of the Mediterranean.

Plates 164 and 165: A Jewish face on an incense burner from Iximche, Guatemala (probably Classic): "I doubt whether any art historian in the world, if he viewed its almost biblical features without knowing its origin, would assign this piece to pre-Columbian America."

Page 175: Illustrates a Phoenician clay mask from Carthage. If it had been found in Mexico, it would have been classified as showing Huehueteotl (the fire god). "In reality, this mask is connected with the cult of Humbaba, a Phoenician deity, guardian of the forest of Lebanon, the most ancient prototype of which originated in Ur."

[Unless critics assume that Wuthenau's collection consists of all modern fakes or colonial pieces, they constitute a corpus that demands detailed examination, but it has been carefully ignored by conventional archaeologists. Compare B-477.]

W-242B

AUTHOR: Wuthenau, Alexander von
DATE: 1981
TITLE: Visages inattendus en Amérique ancienne
[Unexpected Faces in Ancient America]
IN: Kadath: Chroniques des civilisations disparues, no. 42: 43-46 (Brussels)

Jade plaques from La Venta Offering 4 are discussed and sketches reproduced. Clyde-Ahmad Winters takes the inscriptions on the plaques to be written in Malinké-Bambara of the Mande group of languages of West Africa, though originally from Nubia, and his reading for the inscription on plaque no. 2 is shown, labelled as "olmèque-mande." Wuthenau then discusses the "consanguinity" of Kushites and Olmecs, illustrated with five of the Olmec stone heads and a quite similar head of "Taharka, King of Kush and Upper Egypt." Mexican authorities who have pointed out the presence of blacks in ancient America are Alfonso Medellin Zenil, Melgarejo Vivanco, and Gonzalez Calderon. The chronology for the Olmec fits the Black dynasts in Egypt and Nubia. Also points out figures on three of the Izapa stelae which seem to him to show Blacks.

W-243

AUTHOR: Wuthenau, Alexander von
DATE: 1987
TITLE: Unexpected African Faces in Pre-Columbian America
IN: African Presence in Early America, edited by Ivan van Sertima, (n.p.: n.p.), 56-75
["Incorporating Journal of African Civilizations, Dec. 1986, vol. 8, no. 2." "All inquiries should be addressed to Transaction Books, Rutgers—the State University, New Brunswick, New Jersey"]

Discussion and illustration of figurine and sculptural faces from Mesoamerica (plus two from Ecuador and Peru) with African characteristics which he assumes to be pre-Columbian. Some appeared in his other publications; some are new.

W-244

AUTHOR: Wycoff, Don G.
DATE: 1973
TITLE: No Stones Unturned: Differing Views of Oklahoma's Runestones
IN: Popular Archaeology 2/12:16-31

An unusually comprehensive and balanced treatment by a professional archaeologist of alleged rune-marked stones in Oklahoma [see the writings of Gloria Farley]. Raises critical issues and concludes that claims that they were made by Vikings are unsupported. Sees them as either natural cracks caused by weathering, Indian carvings, or the products of 19th-century Americans.

X-001

AUTHOR: Xu, H. Mike
DATE: 1996
TITLE: Origin of the Olmec Civilization
IN: University of Central Oklahoma Press: Edmond, Oklahoma

In a short but heavily-illustrated monograph, the author, a teacher of Chinese language, identifies Chinese writing characters on Mesoamerican Olmec artifacts at Chalcatzingo, La Venta, Tres Zapotes, etc. The characters include those meaning sun, rain, water, worship, sacrifice, wealth, land, mountain, and plants. In particular, jade celts in Offering No. 4 at La Venta are reproduced in line drawings to show characters. Two celts lack legible inscriptions, but the other four name kings and ancestors of the Shang people; his readings are given (revised from Shuang, see S-241B). Supposes that Shang Chinese refugees carried knowledge of their culture to southern Mexico at the end of their dynasty in 1122 B.C. Some symbols (eagle, dragon/serpent, tiger/jaguar, cleft head motif) are shared, along with archaeoastronomical orientation of sites.

Y-001

AUTHORS: Yacovleff, E., and F. L. Herrera
DATE: 1934-1935
TITLE: El mundo vegetal de los antiguos peruanos
[The Vegetal World of the Ancient Peruvians]
IN: Revista del Museo Nacional 3/3-4/1:243-322 (Lima)

Vol. 3, page 283: Reports the presence of Pachyrrhizus (yam bean) in Paracas and Nazca times.

Y-002

AUTHOR: Yamanouchi, Sugao
DATE: n.d.
TITLE: The Arrowshaft Smoother in World Prehistory and Its Bearing on the Chronology of Jomon Pottery
IN: 8th International Congress of Anthropological and Ethnological Sciences, (Tokyo and Kyoto, 1968), Abstracts: Sectional Meetings, (Science Council of Japan: n.p.), 246

Arrowshaft smoothers appear first in Europe and Asia around 2500 B.C., and reached Japan not earlier than this, "at the beginning of Jomon pottery." Identical artifacts appear in tool kits and grave goods in North American Indian sites, from which he supposes transmission from Asia after the indicated date.

Y-002B

AUTHOR: Yarmolinsky, Avraham
DATE: 1937
TITLE: Early Polish Americana: A Bibliographical Study. With an Appendix: A Legendary Predecessor of Columbus
IMPRINT: New York Public Library: New York

The appendix is about Johannes Scolvus, reputed precursor of Columbus.

Y-003

AUTHOR: Yarnell, Richard A.
DATE: 1970
TITLE: Palaeo-ethnobotany in America
IN: Science in Archaeology: A Survey of Progress and Research, Second edition, revised and enlarged, edited by Don Brothwell and Eric Higgs (Praeger: New York), 215-228

Table C on page 225 shows the age of the earliest dated remains of 20 common pre-Columbian American plants (e.g., sweet potato, 2700 years old in Peru). Table C on page 225 shows the age of the earliest dated remains of 20 common pre-Columbian American plants (e.g., sweet potato of the Mochica era in Peru dates to 2800 years ago.)

Y-004

AUTHOR: Yawata, Ichiro
DATE: 1958
TITLE: The Affinity of Japanese and North American Prehistoric Pottery
IN: Miscellanea Paul Rivet, Octogenario Dicata, Universidad Nacional Autónoma de México, Publicaciones del Instituto de Historia 1/50 [Proceedings of the 31st International Congress of Americanists (São Paulo, 1954)], 2:867-869

Does not believe the indications of similarities in Jomon and Ecuadorian pottery are due to voyaging.

Y-007

AUTHOR: Yde, J.
DATE: 1948
TITLE: The Regional Distribution of South American Blowgun Types
IN: Journal de la société des américanistes de Paris 37:275-317

Page 312: Inventive creativity of native Americans is a sufficient explanation for cultural parallels with the Old World, in this case the blowgun, without involving diffusion.

Y-008

AUTHOR: Yen, Douglas E.
DATE: 1960
TITLE: The Sweet Potato in the Pacific: The Propagation of the Plant in Relation to Its Distribution
IN: Journal of the Polynesian Society 69:368-375

He discusses evidence for reproduction of the plant by seed. Spread of the plant and development of varieties conceivably could have been much faster if seeded than by vegetative reproduction. The possibility that birds could have carried seed into Polynesia is mentioned but is not, at this time, offered as a serious hypothesis.

Y-011

AUTHOR: Yen, Douglas E.
DATE: 1963
TITLE: Sweet-Potato Variation and Its Relation to Human Migration in the Pacific
IN: Plants and the Migrations of Pacific Peoples, A Symposium Held at the Tenth Pacific Sciences Congress (Honolulu, 1961), edited by Jacques Barrau (Bernice P. Bishop Museum Press: Honolulu), 93-117

Noting the need for serious studies of variability of the sweet potato as a contribution to unraveling the disputed issues of origin and spread of the plant, he discusses that variability in all areas of Oceania and proposes secondary centers of variability in Hawaii, Easter Island, New Zealand, New Guinea, and the Philippines. However he draws no culture-historical inferences from this.

Y-013

AUTHOR: Yen, Douglas E.
DATE: 1971
TITLE: Construction of the Hypothesis for Distribution of the Sweet Potato
IN: Man across the Sea: Problems of Pre-Columbian Contacts, edited by Carroll L. Riley, et al. (University of Texas Press: Austin), 328-342

Careful, nearly exhaustive consideration of the evidence convinces him that the sweet potato was widely distributed in Polynesia no later than the 11th century, thus human carriage from South America at an earlier date than that is unavoidable. Both methodological and factual issues are discussed.

Y-014

AUTHOR: Yen, Douglas E.
DATE: 1974
TITLE: The Sweet Potato and Oceania: An Essay in Ethnobotany
IN: Bernice P. Bishop Museum, Bulletin 236 (Honolulu)

Tests a tripartite hypothesis for the distribution of the sweet potato in the Pacific. Its transfer from South America to Polynesia he supposes to have occurred between A.D. 400 and A.D. 700.

Pages 2-4: Summarizes eight hypotheses previously presented in the literature.

Appendix 1 gives extensive lists of vernacular names for sweet potato from America and throughout the Pacific basin. This is the most comprehensive treatment of names in the literature.

Y-014B

AUTHOR: Yen, Douglas E.
DATE: 1976
TITLE: Sweet Potato
IN: Evolution of Crop Plants, edited by N. W. Simmonds (Longman: London and New York), 42-45

There is general agreement that cross-disciplinary evidence indicates an American origin. Archaeological remains of tubers extend back in a Peruvian cave to a C-14 date of 8-10,000 B.C. It is uncertain whether these indicate cultivation. On the history issue, he refers the question to Y-014.

Y-016

AUTHOR: Yetts, W. Perceval
DATE: 1939
TITLE: The Cull Chinese Bronzes
IMPRINT: University of London, Courtauld Institute of Art: London

Page 75: Northwest Coast style comparisons.

Y-017

AUTHOR: Young, L. M.
DATE: 1966
TITLE: The Parahyba Inscription
IN: New World Antiquity 13/11-12:109-119

A useful resume of the literature reporting the original piece and various copyings and translations since that time. E. Sykes adds further observations on the complicated literature [which nobody seems to have examined in toto].

Y-017B

AUTHOR: Young, L. M.
DATE: 1974
TITLE: Phoenician Inscriptions in British Guiana
IN: New World Antiquity 21:109-111

George Dennis, who had written on Etruscan antiquities, found Phoenician-like inscriptions near Essequibo while a colonial official. He made copies and sent them to the British Museum where a curator confirmed that they looked rather like Phoenician characters. Nothing was said of them later.

Y-018

AUTHOR: Young, Ulysses
DATE: 1940
TITLE: Distribution of Watercraft in Africa
IMPRINT: Unpublished; M.A. thesis, University of Pennsylvania

A compilation, at a low level of scholarship, of materials from ethnographic sources on papyrus rafts, bark boats, dugouts, plank boats, and outriggers which is of some descriptive interest.

Y-019

AUTHOR: Ypsilanti de Moldavia, Georges
DATE: 1951

TITLE: Les Nègres dans l'Amérique précolombienne [Blacks in Pre-Columbian America]
IN: Revue de la société haitienne d'histoire, géographie et géologie 22/82:44-45 (Port-au-Prince)

It has been clearly established that Negroes had relations with the American continent before the Christian era and played an active part in the development of the great empires and pre-Columbian kingdoms. They formed part of the population from Mexico to Patagonia. They were directly involved in music, the making of instruments, and dance. Various authors (Orosco y Berra, Rafinesque, Humboldt, Quatrefages, etc.) speak of their presence. The Popol Vuh mentions them.

Y-020

AUTHOR: Ypsilanti de Moldavia, Georges
DATE: 1962
TITLE: Los Israelitas en América precolombiana [Israelites in Pre-Columbian America]
IMPRINT: Talleres Nacionales: Managua, Nicaragua

The first 154 pages try to show that America was visited by Israelites, Egyptians, Greeks, Sumerians, Chinese, and others of the Mediterranean area and Asia. Many tribes of Indians descend from them. For evidence he depends on traditions and word and name comparisons, weaving a detailed and fantastic narrative (e.g., the Tupi were descended from the Carians and came on Phoenician ships in the 10th century B.C.; they, taught by Egyptian engineers, constructed great public works on the Island of Marajo). Cites and quotes people like the Verrills, Brasseur, and Charencey. Dr. Ludwig Schwennhagen in a letter of 1926 claimed that in Northeast Brazil the Phoenicians and Hebrews had colonized and exploited mines and he had copied many inscriptions related to such mines. This book reproduces a dozen or more "inscriptions." For example, on page 63 are drawings of glyphic-looking "archaic China" characters from Piedras Funerarias, Colombia, "Greek characters" from Bandi, Colombia, and "Hebrew-aegean characters" from Ceará, Brazil.

Page 139-140: F. D. Waldeck ("Descriptión du bas-relief de la croiz dessin aux ruines de Palenque") affirms that in excavations at Acapulco in 1832 he found a Japanese statue at a depth of 20 feet. Le Page du Pratz in "Historia de Luisiane," about the trip of the Indian Moncacht-Ape across North America [when?], says that arriving on the Pacific coast he was told that every year bearded white men came to that land who bore arms that "shot thunder." Those men came not only for commerce but took by force wood and also slaves (the author assumes that these were not Spaniards). P. Fournier in his book "Hidrographie" says that Vikings and Bretons had discovered Brazil before Cabral.

Z-001A

AUTHOR: Zaki, Andrzej
DATE: 1981
TITLE: Uwagi o archeologii wyspy wielkanocnej [Notes on the Archaeology of Easter Island]
IN: Symposiones, I: 231-253 [Paper delivered at the First Symposium of the Polish University in Exile (PUNO) in London, on 15 October 1978]

The author "went on archaeological expeditions to Polynesia" in 1977-1978, including Easter Island. Much that Heyerdahl proposed as evidence for his theory of American connection is no longer valid today. His specialized claims should still be examined by appropriate experts—of particular significance, whether serological features tie the islanders to the mainland and occurrence of the sweet potato, which "may have been conveyed on the current of the sea." The absence of [certain] South American features, and also of Polynesian features, needs consideration. He doubts the stone monuments connect to the Andean area; they could just as well relate to northern Peru, Colombia, Mexico, China, or Indonesia. He does not rule out "sporadic landings by American visitors . . . both here and on other Polynesian islands."

"Mountain archaeology and ethnographic research in the culture of contemporaneous mountain peoples reveal amazing coincidences of form in farming, building, objects of daily use, religious practice, etc. among tribes living sometimes thousands of miles apart." In the absence of intermediate links, these must be explained by convergence. "The endless search for imitations [parallels due to diffusion] smacks of hypercriticism, and is an unwarranted negation of man's creative inventiveness." Failure to conserve Easter Island archaeological areas has resulted in damage to some, including three ruin groups where obsidian artifacts and waste "show a strong resemblance to South American types."

Z-001B

AUTHOR: Zechlin, Egmont
DATE: 1935
TITLE: Das Problem der vorkolumbischen Entdeckung Amerikas und die Kolumbusforschung
[The Problem of the Pre-Columbian Discovery of America and Research on Columbus]
IN: Historische Zeitschrift 152:1-47

What do we mean by "discovery? Critically handles the Norse and then the purported ante-Columbians (Pining, Scolvus, Cousin, etc.).

Pages 43-47: On pre-Columbian contacts properly speaking, mentions various theories (Egypt-Middle America, China-America, Oceania-America).

Z-003

AUTHOR: Zeidler, James A.
DATE: 1977-1978
TITLE: Primitive Exchange, Prehistoric Trade and the Problem of a Mesoamerican-South American Connection
IN: Journal of the Steward Anthropological Society 9/1-2:7-39

An important methodological piece which asks not whether maritime contacts took place, but rather how. Transoceanic contacts literature remains largely at the stage of making lists of shared traits, which the author believes can now be transcended in the Ecuador-Mesoamerica case, and he tries here to do that.

No later than 3400 B.C., the start of Valdivia, remains show that deep-sea voyaging capabilities were present.

Z-005

AUTHOR: Zéki Pacha, Ahmed
DATE: 1919-1920
TITLE: Une seconde tentative des Musulmans pour découvrir l'Amérique
[A Second Attempt by Moslems to Discover America]
IN: Bulletin de l'Institut d'Egypte 2:57-59 (Cairo)

Around 1300 A.D. a sultan of Guinea, Mahommed Gao, built a fleet to search for land across the Atlantic, but the expedition never returned. One hundred fifty years earlier eight Arabs sailed from Lisbon on a similar mission, without known result.

Z-007

AUTHOR: Zerries, Otto
DATE: 1942
TITLE: Das Schwirrholz
[The Bull-Roarer]
IMPRINT: Strecker und Schröder: Stuttgart

Types and distribution of the bull-roarer throughout the world, kulturkreis interpretation.

Z-008

AUTHOR: Zerries, Otto
DATE: 1953
TITLE: The Bull-roarer among South American Indians
IN: Revista do Museu Paulista 7:275-309 (São Paulo)

Amplification of material on this area in Z-007. Distribution and uses of the bull-roarer.

Z-011

AUTHOR: Zevallos Menéndez, Carlos
DATE: 1965-1966
TITLE: Estudio regional de la orfebrería precolombina de Ecuador y su posible relación con las areas vecinas [Regional Study of Pre-Columbian Metal Working of Ecuador and Its Possible Relation with Neighboring Areas]
IN: Revista del Museo Nacional del Historia 34:68-81 (Lima)

Discussion of metallurgical techniques employed on the Ecuadorian coast, especially the Milagro culture of Guayas basin. Supports a transpacific introduction for many basic techniques.

Z-011B

AUTHOR: Zhongpu, Fang
DATE: 1980
TITLE: Did Chinese Buddhists Reach America 1,000 Years before Columbus?
IN: China Reconstructs 29/8:65-66

A brief positive summary of the Fusang notion.

Z-012

AUTHOR: Ziderman, I. Irving
DATE: 1986
TITLE: Biblical Dyes of Animal Origin
IN: Chemistry in Britain (May): 451-454

Spells out the precise chemistry of the two purples (tekhelet and argaman) and of scarlet (tola'at-shani, "worm of scarlet" or crimson). Purple dye from shellfish was first used on Crete in the Bronze Age. Over time this was a closely guarded industrial secret, so details of techniques are poorly known. Several species of scale-insects or wood-lice grow on oaks and yield scarlet dye, kermes; only some have been identified. Cochineal, imported from Mexico by the Spaniards, quickly replaced kermes from the 16th century onward. Species and chemistry are detailed.

Z-014

AUTHOR: Zimmerman, Mark E.
DATE: 1928
TITLE: Circular Shrines in Quivira, and the Jehovah of the Ohio Mound Builder
IN: Kansas State Historical Society Collections 17:547-558

Comparison of remains in Rice County, Kansas, with alleged symbolical remains in Ohio attempting to show that builders of the mounds used a certain triangle as a symbol of Jehovah. He concludes that they were Celtic-Israelites from Wales.

Z-016

AUTHOR: Zinsser, Hans
DATE: 1960
TITLE: Rats, Lice, and History
IMPRINT: Bantam Books: New York

Pages 254-261: Was typhus in humans in America before the Spaniards? We cannot tell, but perhaps. Reasons are given at some length for his conclusion. Mooser thinks so (based on Tarascan and Aztec words, for example). For the Aztecs, he considers it "more than likely." And much historical evidence involving lice found on mummies suggests that typhus was present in South America.

Z-016B

AUTHOR: Zuckerman, Lord
DATE: 1990
TITLE: Phony Ancestor
IN: The New York Review of Books 37/17:12, 14-16

Pages 12, 15: Speaks of Sir Grafton Elliot Smith as "the foremost neuroanatomist of [his] day" who was "at the top of his profession." He was "firm in his opinions and unafraid of controversy, yet also ready to have his own views overturned whenever he was convinced either by new evidence or a new interpretation that he had been wrong."

Z-017

AUTHOR: Zuno, José Guadalupe
DATE: 1952
TITLE: Las llamadas lacas michoacanas de Uruapan, no proceden de las orientales
[The So-Called Michoacan Lacquers of Uruapan Did not Come from the Orientals]
IN: Cuadernos americanos 11/3:145-165

Chao and "Doctor Atl" in a 1921 newspaper article in Mexico proposed that about A.D. 600 Chinese navigators reached west Mexico and brought laca ("lacquer"). He here describes the technologies in West Mexico and China and believes they are different. The Mexican craft peaked only in the 18th century under European stimulation; it may not be ancient at all. [Compare J-060 and J-075.]

Index

See Introduction to the Second Edition (volume 1, page x).